The Nature and Purpose of Accounting

edited by

Don E. Garner
Illinois Institute of Technology

Dennis M. Murphy
California State University/Los Angeles

Wadsworth Publishing Company, Inc.
Belmont, California

ISBN: 0-534-00411-3

L. C. Cat. Card No.: 75-3957

Printed in the United States of America

1 2 3 4 5 6 7 8 9 10/80 79 78 77 76 75

44,041

Preface

Articles in this collection were selected and organized to add meaning and life to the study of financial and managerial accounting. They were taken from business literature to enhance the understanding of the serious reader by illustrating that accounting is not an exercise unto itself but is "the economic cement that holds the modern economy together."[1]

Accounting changes continually. A readings collection is an excellent way of bringing current and continuing topics into focus. Accordingly, we have included articles on numerous topics of interest: the Financial Accounting Standards Board, The Cost Accounting Standards Board, the Certificate in Management Accounting, the Certified Internal Auditor, human resource accounting, social responsibilities, SEC regulations, numerous accounting standards and reporting problems, financial analysis, international standards, managerial accounting, career opportunities and requirements, computers, auditing, and many other issues with which the profession is concerned.

There are several threads, in addition to public accounting, which are increasingly important to accounting. As business becomes more international, accounting must respond with a world-wide perspective. Not-for-profit and governmental aspects of accounting are of greater concern as larger amounts of economic resources are managed in these areas. The interdependence with all of the other disciplines in the business, economic and related fields is crucial to the relevancy of accounting. Managerial accounting is continuing its growth. Articles highlighting these threads are found throughout.

The collection, containing 116 articles, represents a wide range of thought on accounting from many countries. Original publication dates are primarily from the past three years, but dated articles of historical and continuing value are included. Most of the leading business, financial, and accounting periodicals have made contributions. Many outstanding scholars are included among the authors. Articles by experts, who are close to their subject material, were especially sought out for inclusion.

---

[1]*Lybrand Journal*, Fall, 1972, p. 52

Chapter 1, covering the nature and purpose of accounting, and chapter 2, on the accounting environment, provide a broad and substantial introduction to the subject. The sequence of articles in chapters 3 through 7 follows that traditionally taken in the study of financial and managerial accounting.

The recommendations contained in *A New Introduction to Accounting*[2] were closely considered in preparation of many of the topics to be covered. The table of contents clearly discloses this influence. Of course, we also used our own ideas. But we believe that this collection is in consonance with the Price Waterhouse sponsored study.

A good balance has been achieved between traditional topics and new areas. The articles presented should add significant depth and breadth to accounting courses as they have been traditionally taught as well as to courses which follow the recommendation of the Price Waterhouse sponsored study. Of the nine chapters included, five are designed to be used with the course outlines commonly found in the study of accounting. These sections contain 75 articles which can readily be used to add to student understanding and appreciation of the traditional accounting course. Chapter 8 contains articles on career opportunities in accounting, a subject of vital interest to all students. Chapter 9 is a practical section in which three important areas are discussed: professional issues in public accounting, computers, and writing ability.

Although emphasis in some parts is placed on the newcomer's needs, the collection will lend itself to other uses. Studies in contemporary problems of accounting and in the development of accounting principles are such areas. Professors whose courses are in related fields of business will find this collection a welcome addition to aid the student's understanding of accounting. Persons seeking renewal in their appreciation and perspective of accounting and general readers wishing to become more familiar with the subject will find that this book fills many of their needs.

We thank the authors and copyright holders whose individual names appear with their contributions. Their work, appearing here, will again benefit readers.

Many people gave us inspiration, suggestions, and help during our work, which we gratefully acknowledge. We want to especially thank James Morton, University of Alabama; Ron Burrows, Northern Illinois University; Larry Dean, Illinois Institute of Technology; Edwin Bartenstein, Michael Diamond, Robert Zahary, California State University, Los Angeles. Emily Chang's direction of the accounting library collection and Judy Levin's and Ben White's assistance at California State University's library were of enormous help to us. Throughout our project, Felicia Murphy provided us with indispensable aid.

Don E. Garner

Dennis M. Murphy

---

[2]Mueller, Gerhard G. (ed.), *A New Introduction to Accounting* (Seattle: The Price Waterhouse Foundation, July, 1971).

Contents

vii   Contents

x Contents

xi Contents

1

The Nature and Purpose of Accounting

Several questions are pertinent to the understanding of the nature and purpose of accounting. What is accounting? Why does a society need accounting and accountants? What does an accountant do? What are the contributions of accounting? The articles in the first part of this collection help answer these questions and in so doing, present a cogent, realistic picture of the nature and purpose of accounting.

The leading article by Arthur Litke (page 2) sets the tone for the book: accounting information is relevant in an integrated, changing environment. The main theme in this article is that the accountant must continue to provide information which is relevant in a changing society. The assumption in these articles is that managers of resources require information to make a variety of decisions.

The second article, "The 'Useless' Accountant," (page 5) first appeared in the *Journal of Accountancy* in 1915 and demonstrates that accounting's products are required by society, even though the content must change to meet changing information needs. It also demonstrates that decision makers outside an organization must be continually provided with relevant information to make decisions for the best allocation of society's resources.

The process by which relevant information is provided to society's decision makers is described well in Sig Dembowski's article "The Management Accountant" (page 6). The article establishes that accounting is an indispensable tool for many types of decisions, including custodial and performance-evaluation. The author also aptly describes what an accountant does to process and report information, the attributes needed by accountants, and the way in which accounting fits into the total management information system.

Frank Broaker (page 14) and Walter F. Stuhldreher (page 16) address the question of whether accounting is an art or a science. Neither writer gives a clear answer, but each one discusses the nature and purpose of accounting at length. As noted by Litke, the increasing size and complexity of society places changing demands for performance on managers of resources: as the society and its material needs change, information provided for decisions must also change.

Chapter 1 emphasizes that accounting is not a discipline by itself, but it is a tool used for and interrelated with many other areas of thought, usefulness, and productivity.

1

_____

_____

1　　　　　　　　THE KALEIDOSCOPE

Arthur L. Litke

(Reprinted by permission from *The Federal Accountant*, vol. 22, no. 2 (June, 1973): 1-3.)

(Arthur L. Litke was National President of the Federal Government Accountants Association.)

The rapidly changing scenes in which a financial manager operates might be compared to a kaleidoscope. In carrying out his activities and responsibilities, he tries to focus on many disciplines and considerations, but before conclusions are reached, the scene becomes an intermingling of many considerations. This is particularly disturbing to many of those who have been trained and disciplined in systematic and orderly approaches to the solutions of problems in a given field. Many problems faced by financial managers are a many-faceted affair requiring a social conscience and contributions from many fields.

Historians will probably characterize the 1970s as a socially sensitive decade. Social consciousness is affecting most activities through influences expressed in many different ways. The environment, ecology, pollution, energy crisis, quality of life, and consumerism are words and ideas that only a few years ago were limited in use, but today are part of everyone's language and convey different meanings to different people. Financial managers in federal, state, and local governments are at the focal points for administering the social action programs of the country. They must find new methods and techniques to compile, analyze, and report information relating to social actions which managers of government need to make better decisions.

Quantification has always been the key element in reporting systems. But more and more, qualitative inputs are a necessary ingredient for internal and external decision making. There is a need to identify more of the qualitative control areas and to devise ways of reducing them to quantifiable form in order to create more precise and objective methods of reporting, evaluating, and planning future social programs. As the public becomes more conscious of social involvement and demands more information and evaluations, the accountants are in the ideal position to make their mark on social advancements.

Human resources accounting is one area which should be of vital concern to financial managers in government. The methodology of "employee accounting" is receiving some attention in commercial circles. One would think that government organizations in particular would be interested in this type of accounting because people are one of the most valuable assets in many government organizations. Personal service costs comprise a major portion of many agencies' budgets. Human resources accounting can go far beyond the mere question of expensing or capitalizing hiring and training costs. Ideas have been advanced that it should include other considerations such as whether the decision-making process has improved or deteriorated, whether performance goals

are higher, and whether employee morale has improved. While problems
are attendant to the quantification of relevant data in these areas,
such considerations have significant effects on productivity and financial performance.

Being an expert in a particular area of financial management does
not imply freedom from the need for knowledge in other fields. Quite to
the contrary, retaining status as an expert in any field requires general awareness of the development in other fields. Many of the measurement techniques used by financial managers are taken from other fields,
particularly those of the mathematician, the statistician, the engineer,
the economist, and others. In this age of involvement, the work of
others, such as the ecologist, sociologists, environmentalists, psychol-
ogists, and others, must be considered.

During a period of rapid change, boundaries between the various
professions and disciplines become less distinct and might even clash.
This should not disturb those who are involved in the change. Each
should look toward the end result and seek to capitalize upon the innovations and new discoveries in fields other than his own.

ACCOUNTING—AND ACCOUNTANTS—MUST CHANGE

The present philosophy and methodology of accounting will hardly
serve the needs of a rapidly changing society. As one example, one
might point to the cost principle in accounting. It is often said that
accounting is the language of business. But as a matter of fact, decision makers have a small vocabulary in accounting because its use is
limited and often irrelevant. The gauge of yesteryear's dollars to
measure stewardship and evaluate performance is questionable. Present
day managers should not only be held accountable for the historical
dollars entrusted to their care, but more importantly, they should be
held accountable for the preservation of the current and future economic
values of their organization. The cost concept as used in current accounting is predicated on the assumption that the purchasing power of
the dollar, the unit of measurement, is relatively stable and therefore,
that variations in purchasing power of the dollar may be disregarded.
Inflation has been a way of life for a long time, and it is expected
that, even though it may be controlled, it is going to continue into the
future. A more meaningful gauge than historical cost appears necessary.

RESEARCH CAPABILITY ESSENTIAL

The development of responsive reports, including the formulation of
social indicators is not an easy task. Neither can it be done without
considerable research capabilities. The question presents itself then
as to how necessary research might be accomplished. It would seem that
a concerted and coordinated effort at the federal level would be desirable. Because of fund and manpower limitations, the research capability
of the Federal Government Accountants Association for a major project is
impracticable. A coordinated effort by one or more of the central control agencies in the federal government, perhaps working through the

Joint Financial Management Improvement Program (1)*, may be the most desirable. In any event, a fragmented approach by individuals or individual agencies does not appear to be the most effective and efficient way
to accomplish the task. The establishment of social indicators has not
been a major concern of government in the past, but there is a crying
need for action.

INDICATORS—NOT JUST INFORMATION

When the Comptroller General issued the "Standards for Audit of
Governmental Organizations, Programs, Activities and Functions" last
fall, he pointed to the need for cooperation among federal, state and
local governments in solving public problems. This need becomes more
critical with each passing day because of the overwhelming demands being
made by the many fragmented social programs draining the economy. The
advent of the revenue-sharing program increased the need for indicators
to control and evaluate the effectiveness of social programs. Just as
the old type financial information will not serve current and future
needs, neither will the old type financial audit be responsible to those
needs. Changes in audit concepts will have limited value unless new
types of indicators to serve the new ends are devised. The phony pre-
ciseness of current reporting must yield to the recognizable inexactness
of more comprehensive reporting.

THE KEY: RELEVANCY

As the populace becomes more social conscious, greater demands will
be made not only for more information but for more *relevant* information.
These demands cannot be met under the current way of doing things. Although the computer will be of great assistance in providing more information, it will be of limited use from the standpoint of providing
relevant information. To meet this end, innovations are needed in the
financial management area. This will come about only if those on the
firing lines have an inordinate amount of initiative and perception.

FOOTNOTE

1. Leadership of the Joint Financial Management Improvement
    Program is provided jointly by the Comptroller General
    of the United States, the Secretary of the Treasury, the
    Director of the Office of Management and Budget, and the
    Chairman of the Civil Service Commission.

---

*Numbers in parentheses refer to footnotes which appear at the end of
each article.

QUESTIONS

1. In what ways does accounting aid the decision maker?
2. Can accounting provide qualitative as well as quantitative information?
3. What are some of the problems in providing qualitative information?

---

2   THE "USELESS" ACCOUNTANT

(Reprinted by permission from *The Journal of Accountancy*, vol. 20, no. 1 (July, 1915): 41-42. Copyright 1915 by the American Institute of Certified Public Accountants, Inc.)

A western correspondent has drawn our attention to an article appearing in *Moody's Magazine*, entitled "The New York, New Haven and Hartford Railroad Company." In that article the following sentence occurs:

> *To the investor, two of the most useless creatures in the world are an engineer with his appraisals and an expert accountant with his certified statements; for the more the investor reads of both, the more certain he is to buy securities at inflated values and lose his money.*

Upon what then is the investor to rely? Analysis by those who attempt to guide investors, perhaps. Possibly our readers are familiar with *The Manual of Railroads and Corporation Securities*, which, like the magazine, bears the name of "Moody," and in which the securities of various railroad companies are discussed and analyzed. Reference to this manual discloses the following analysis in the 1913 volume:

> *The bonds I consider to be absolutely safe and suitable investment for banks, trustees, and the most careful private investors.*
> *The stock can also be considered at the present time as an investment of the most conservative class. The table suggests that present dividend is barely being earned, but a study of the other columns and especially the "train-load" column shows the real latent power existing in this system. Moreover, the new stock issues have been largely for refunding purposes, and thus increased dividend requirements are to a large extent offset by decreased interest charges. . . . Of course, to trustees and other investors of Massachusetts, Connecticut and certain other states where this stock is a non-taxable investment, it should at times be an especially good purchase, although at the same price American Telephone and Telegraph stock is worthy of consideration.*

Of course, when dividends on New Haven stock were discontinued later in 1913, the commentator's views were somewhat modified in subsequent volumes.

Incidentally, examination of a file of annual reports of the New Haven road shows that the annual balance sheets were certified by auditors for some years prior to 1908, but not thereafter until after the change in administration.

In such circumstances the question will arise in one's mind as to whether or not the investor is wise in dispensing with those useless creatures, the accountant and the engineer. Certainly the answer to the question upon what the investor can safely rely as a substitute is not altogether clear.

QUESTIONS

1. The article in *Moody's Magazine* says that accountants are useless. If they are useless, who is in a better position to provide people or institutions with the needed financial information?

2. Why would the following people or institutions be interested in presentable and accurate statements: 1) stockholders, 2) creditors or banks, 3) labor unions, 4) consumer groups, 5) the U.S. Government, 6) local and county governments, 7) management of the corporation?

3. When you, as an individual, are presenting financial statements to a bank or other lending institution is it necessary for *you* to have clear and accurate financial information? Who would be a judge of such information? Would you be a better judge than an independant accountant?

---

3   THE MANAGEMENT ACCOUNTANT

Sig Dembowski

(Reprinted by permission from *Management Accounting*, vol. 54, no. 10 (April, 1973): 9-12.)

(Sig Dembowski is Chief Accountant, Ecom Corporation, Irvine, California.)

Accounting is generally defined as the process of analyzing business transactions and recording them to show the results of operations. Responsible for this activity is the management accountant, who must oversee the day-to-day input and output of the company's financial and statistical records. He is equivalent to a manager in a shop, who must meet production schedules with the equipment, supplies, and personnel

available. He must have the technical knowledge to understand the function of his department or section, the ability to delegate assignments,
and the ability to communicate.

TECHNICAL KNOWLEDGE

An important prerequisite to classifying business transactions is
the understanding of company policies and the capability of applying
them to normal recurring transactions, as well as to unusual or unexpected items. A major benefit in having a good knowledge of line activity is reduced guesswork. Of course, a good "account manual" is a must
in areas of coding assignments. All items included in the budget or
forecast will then present little difficulty and can be classified at
the source. Unusual items that were not considered in the budget must
be classified individually. For this reason, it is important that instructions on coding procedures should originate with the management
accountant.

A review and understanding of the budget by the management accountant will help him develop areas of income or expense that he can delegate to specific individuals for classification and control. The budget, however, should not be used to control reports, but to alert him to
items that may have either been omitted or recorded in error. Items of
this nature include professional services performed, delayed billings,
prepayments belonging to future periods, payroll or time card adjustments, and freight charges on large capital additions.

With the aid of a good budget and proper adjustments, management
can be supplied with up-to-date information beyond the scope of what is
normally described as historical reporting.

The management accountant should review the reports for possible
misstatements, vital omissions, or errors which should then be discussed
with the person responsible for the preparation of the report. A procedure should be set up for immediately handling items that may have an
effect on a current decision. Quite often vital information that could
have an effect on an important decision is lost because it does not
reach the proper person in time.

ABILITY TO DELEGATE

The ability to delegate is the mark of a successful management
accountant. Failure to utilize available personnel during critical
periods may delay the completion of management reports and financial
statements. Too often, when monthly trial balances are needed, the
management accountant has many small tasks to be carried out. In attempting to perform rather than control these tasks, he creates an
unnecessary bottleneck. All supervisory and daily routine duties are
shelved while he gets himself totally engrossed.

How does the management accountant go about assigning the many specific tasks? One solution is to prepare a Financial Statement Control
Chart and a Financial Statement Task Assignment List. (See Figure 1 and
Table 1.) Many functions can be performed simultaneously, while others
are delayed until the needed information is available. An important
fact to remember is that when there are delays in receiving information,

the management accountant must initiate action to obtain the missing information. These incidents should be properly documented so that corrective action can be accomplished in the future.

FIGURE 1

FINANCIAL STATEMENT CONTROL CHART

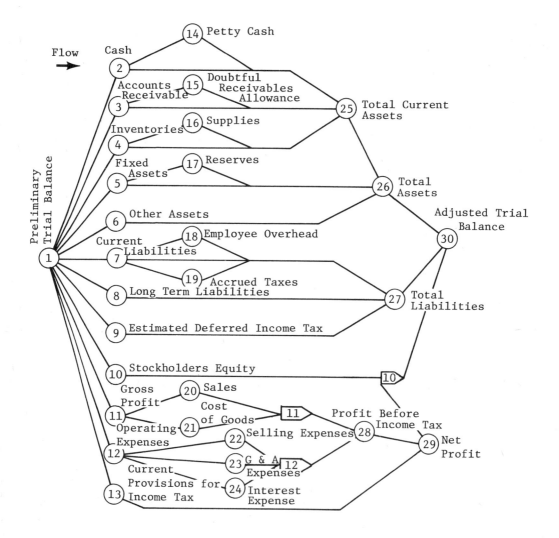

Each month the expansion of the control chart will allow the accountant to delegate more assignments, keeping control over the work.

TABLE 1

FINANCIAL STATEMENT TASK ASSIGNMENT LIST

Assigned to employee	Assignment
A	1. Preliminary trial balance or general ledger cards Major break by major controls (2-13) 30. Adjusted and final trial balance Consolidate assignments 26, 27, 10.
B	2. *Cash* Confirm balance to cash book. Verify bank reconcilliations. Prepare cash flow analysis when required. 14. *Petty Cash* Insure that imprest balances are correct. Verify any audits during period. 25. *Current assets* Consolidate assignments 2, 3, 4.
C	3. *Accounts receivable* Review subsidiary ledger including control balance. Receive from "K" copy of any entry for un-billed sales. 15. *Allowance for doubtful receivables* Prepare aging statement. Recommend any write-offs. Compute required balance and make entry.
D	4. *Inventories* Confirm balance with subsidiary ledgers. Receive from "K" cost of goods entry. Verify if any unprocessed receivers or shippers are on hand. Review open on order items. 16. *Supplies* Prepare any standard overhead entries.
E	5. *Fixed assets* Confirm balance to subsidiary ledgers. Verify any new acquisitions. Investigate any abandonments or sales and prepare appropriate entries. Appraise any installation or shipping charges. 17. Reserves Evaluate depreciation expense charges for period.

F   6. *Other assets*
            Investigate any unprocessed items.
            Inspect prepayment registers for write-offs.
        26. *Total assets*
            Consolidate assignments 25, 5, 6.

G   7. *Current liabilities*
            Verify balance to subsidiary ledger.
            Confirm any payments made for notes due.
            Receive from "L" entry for accrued interest
            expense.
            Identify balance in accrued liability ac-
            counts.
        18. Employee overhead (benefit) accounts
            Evaluate all balances and charges for
            reasonableness.
            Confirm overhead factor being utilized.
        19. *Accrued taxes*
            Evaluate all accrued tax accounts for sales,
            payroll, and income—state and federal.
            Receive entry for current tax accrual from
            "M."

H   8. *Long-term liabilities*
            Confirm balance to notes payable register.
            Look for any balances that should be trans-
            ferred to current.
            Verify balances in deferred compensation
            accounts.

I   9. *Estimated deferred income tax*
            Confirm balance with tax department.
        27. *Total liabilities*
            Consolidate assignments 7, 8, 9.

J   10. Stockholders equity
            Check all changes during period.
            Receive from "M" current profit entry.
            Survey for any stock options taken.
            Check for any entries for stock dividends.
            Verify dates of payment for cash dividends.

K   11. Gross profit
        20. Sales
            Investigate any unbilled items and give copy of
            entry to "C."
        21. Cost of goods
            Compute cost of goods sold and give copy of
            entry to "D."

L   12. Operating expenses
        22. Selling expenses
            Compute any commissions due salesmen
            and prepare journal entry.

Send commission due reports to sales manager
for approval and payment.
23. General and administrative expenses
Confirm to budget areas and investigate
large variances or unusual balances.
24. Interest expense
Compute any accruals and submit copy of
entry to "G."
28. Profit before income tax
Consolidate assignments 11, 12.
Remit amount to "M" (no entry).

M   13. Current provision for income tax
Compute income tax on estimated basis from
profit received from "L."
Prepare journal for profit and tax provision, copies given to "G" and "J."
29. Net profit
Consolidated assignments 13, 28, remit to
10.

The flow chart identifies the functions; however, the important
thing is assigning the specific persons to perform the required tasks.
Assignments are given to individuals who are responsible to the management accountant for their normal routine duties. Each month as the flow
chart unfolds, he works with management to obtain the required manpower.
The management accountant is in the same position as a coach on a foot-
ball team or the manager of a baseball team. The rules are set by someone else, and he is limited by the talent and the number of players.
Proper use of the team members and their development is vital for flexibility to meet unforeseen circumstances. The name of the game is "teamwork," and the rules must be preplanned before the game, and very often
changed during the game. The key to teamwork is sharing and passing on
information that might be of dollar or idea value.

The members of the team are persons who process documents or data
of many types. Each member must know the product he is producing and
must be informed of its ultimate use and importance. More often than not
there is more talent than appears evident and it is the management accountant's responsibility to fully develop this talent. The management
accountant must also be able to accept new members, and he must effectively develop and train them for promotions to higher positions.

The actual training and development of new members by the management accountant is accomplished by having them assist him in performing
his duties. In delegating assignments, the development of team members
must be considered as critical. The flow chart and its supporting docu-
mentation must be fully utilized as a training tool. Each member should
be required to perform all functions of the accounting department on a
rotating basis, and should be permitted to propose changes to the flow
chart. Suggestions for better use of available personnel and equipment
should be encouraged from all members of the team, including trainees.
Whenever the management accountant moves up to a higher position, he

must be prepared to release some of his authority to a trained member of the group.

The authority that the management accountant has in delegating tasks makes him responsible for the proper assignment of the work. He must communicate what is desired without confusion, and see to it that feedback and review is established. There are usually three basic errors committed in assigning work. They are:

1. Assignments are given to the first person available.
2. Assignments are allowed to become permanently fixed in personnel and make-up.
3. Suggestions and comments from personnel are minimized or ignored.

ABILITY TO COMMUNICATE

How often is a new system or concept implemented with enthusiasm and hard work, only to fail some time later? A review often finds that although personnel changes occur, job assignments become static. The management accountant must document (if only for a check upon himself) his specific plan for reviewing assignments, and for discussions with those involved. During the discussions, the management accountant should ask questions, and then be a good listener.

Accountants have been accused of speaking a language all their own. The statement is true, but so does every profession have a language of its own.

The accountant has the language of words and numbers at his disposal to impart information. He uses it in the communication of financial data to others. This data should be readily and accurately understood by the accountant's staff and those for whom it is prepared. A financial statement would then communicate information about a company more readily than if it was written in prose. A good start in communicating with and training an individual is with an explanation of the account manual covering its application to specific receipts, disbursements, or entries. It should be explained that all items of a specific type are coded under a specific number for summarization into reports. However, the explanation should be minimal since a good account manual would include a brief introduction explaining its use. It would also include account numbers and a full description of what is, and at times what is not, represented by the balance recorded under each specific valid number.

The management accountant, in the space of a few hours, often deals with all levels of management, staff, line supervision, and line personnel. The usual method of communication by the management accountant is through reports. They are the means of communicating meaningful information to management and others.

Prior to preparing any report, the basic questions of "who" and "what" must be answered. The "who" are the individuals who are to receive the report, and the "what" is the information the report must convey. Many reports serve more than one purpose and some receive wide distribution. It is important to know what is the basic reason for the report and what are the supplementary uses for the report. As changes occur, we often find the report not serving its primary purpose.

Communication involves both understanding and being understood; therefore, skill in giving and receiving communication is necessary. Written reports are designed to furnish data to: management, supervision, stockholders, government agencies, external auditors, and internal departments (e.g., tax department). The reports can take the form of work sheets, schedules, or letters; each report takes the format that would best transmit the data that is desired and/or required. We must keep in mind that our reports convey what the reader not the writer needs. Feedback from readers could eliminate misunderstandings, and help improve the skill of the writer.

Keeping in mind who will receive the variety of reports that have to be prepared, the "what" that should be reported includes the following: financial, statistical, and budget information. The reports should be prepared on a periodic basis (weekly, monthly, quarterly, semi-annually) and should be on a comparative basis (with prior years, industry, or budgets), whenever any of these periods or comparisons are required for sound management decisions.

The purpose of reports is to aid management in the control of business operations. Each level of management must determine the information it desires to execute its responsibilities, keeping in mind the decision-making value of the information requested. The reports should convey:

1. reliability   meet standards
2. inclusiveness   serve purpose of report
3. clarity   use language the reader will understand
4. timeliness   received in time to assist in decisions
5. materiality   relative judgment, not rules
6. comparability   valid comparisons
7. availability   proper number of copies
8. readability   easily understood by the reader

Supplying information to management cannot be a hit and miss affair. It must be preplanned to attain maximum value. Reports must have a predetermined schedule as to their preparation and priority. Some reports are necessary for the completion of other reports and statements. Attached to monthly financial statements should be the management accountant's statement which includes: 1) date of preparation, 2) distribution, 3) an explanation of unusual variances in the report, and 4) any information pertinent in using the report for decision making.

Graduates in accounting upon entering industry soon forget what they have learned about proper reporting. There is, therefore, a need for continuing education within the firm to strengthen this communication technique. To respond to management's needs, accountants should attach a letter which explains in laymen's terms what benefits the report will have to its reader. Effective communication means expressing yourself in a way that is understood by the reader or listener. Communication is a waste of time if the person receiving the report does not understand it.

The accountant's letter should be based on observations made by the management accountant and should contain opinions based on this knowledge. Management should encourage rather than discourage this type of explanatory reporting. The letter should be a maximum of one page, typed, double-spaced, and should include any illustrations considered necessary. Feedback on this type of reporting would, of course, assist the management accountant and his staff.

It is at this point that the management accountant may influence management changes and company policies by his suggestions, fulfilling his role as part of the management team. It is not so much the setting of policies, but a chance to express his ideas that is of importance. The expression of ideas of many people will be more beneficial to the company than if only a few participate.

CONCLUSION

The dramatic advancement in electronic data processing has made it possible to supply management with almost any type of information it needs. The credibility of this information, however, rests upon the management accountant. He must insure that the input into the records is properly classified and processed on a timely basis. He must also confirm the reliability of information presented to management and help to make and improve policy decisions.

Each company varies in its policies, types of employees, and equipment available; therefore, the management accountant must adapt to fit into his current environment. In an ever changing environment, methods of operation should be constantly reviewed and improved whenever they will result in benefits to the company. Being a good management accountant is like being a good coach or manager—results obtained with the material available rates the team and its individual members.

QUESTIONS

1. How is accounting defined?
2. What are the major functions of the management accountant?
3. Is the management accountant's job unchanging? Why or why not?

---

4   ACCOUNTING AN EXACT SCIENCE

Frank Broaker

(Reprinted by permission from *The Journal of Accountancy*, vol. 1, no. 4 (February, 1906): 328-330. Copyright 1906 by the American Institute of Certified Public Accountants, Inc.)

In the last century, accounts were kept on sticks of wood, and a depositor received as a receipt, the split half of a stick of wood, upon which had been nicked or cut by the clerk of the pike, in Roman numerals, the amount of the deposit. The other half was retained and repre-

sented the depositor's account. At the making up of accounts chaos
reigned, and to put an end to this novel but complex system, which cost
more to adjust at the close of a fiscal period than all of the current
mechanical wood-chopping bookkeeping, these crude accounts were loaded
in a wood wagon, carted to the English Parliament, inadvertently placed
upon a stone, some unknown person started a fire and the wooden accounts
as well as the Houses of Parliament were destroyed. While ancient works
on bookkeeping are valued for their antiquity, it is yet to be recorded
that any person has a single wooden account in memoriam.

Bookkeeping in the last century was mechanical. An entry of each
transaction was made in a blotter, a day-book, then journalized and
posted to a ledger. A trial balance was then taken of the total debits
and credits of each account, after which another trial balance was deduced and headed "Balance Sheet" which latter comprehended the net or
resultant balance of each account. The sequential arrangement of the
accounts displayed capital properties, expense, receivable, payable and
drawing accounts mixed together. In 1812, Oliver P. Gould published a
work advocating an improvement whereby only net balances, debit or
credit of each account should be stated in a balance sheet; the first
two columns to be headed trial balance, the second two columns, resources and liabilities, the third two columns, losses and gains, and
the fourth two columns the capital account, and by these mechanical
methods to submit the results of a business to the proprietor.

Accounting comprehends the science of giving exact technical expression to the results of a business in such form that fixed assets,
such as plant, visionary equity in real estate, machinery, furniture and
fixtures, which represent capital expenditures not available for payment
of current liabilities except in a winding up of affairs are not merged
with floating assets, i.e., cash, goods, bills receivable, etc., which
latter only are available for the payment of debts. Liabilities should
be ranked in the order of their liquidation. A banker does not loan on
a surplus consisting of plant, visionary equity in real estate, machinery, etc., for the reason that unless these properties were sold, the
loan would continue forever.

Investigations may be classed as a branch of accounting and the
business public may well be aghast at the fortunes made by high finance
methods. To restore public confidence, certified public accountants of
recognized ability and integrity are called upon to investigate, account
and report upon the financial and business condition of affairs, not
only of a proprietor, firm, bank, railroad or insurance corporation,
but universities, that hitherto had not seriously considered the benefits of the teaching of accounting, are brought to a stern realization
that keen business sagacity, criminally developed, unless the accounts
are systematically kept, is no respector of college learning or abnormal
intelligence, and that reading of poetry, fiction, or historical remi-
niscence does not add to the wealth of the country.

One of the greatest railroad corporations in this country has by
skilled accounting and clever engineering merited the confidence of its
stockholders to such an extent that when any amount of cash is required
it increases and sells its capital stock to its stockholders in preference to bonding the shareholders' interests.

The President of the United States publicly endorses the public necessity of an audit, and when respectable men of standing in financial
and political circles are detected in the nefarious practice of swind-

ling confiding investors, and the state departments of banking and insurance blindly and stupidly permit wholesale frauds to continue until the finances of the people have disappeared, then and then only is proper accounting appreciated to its full extent.　The time has passed when the public will accept in explanation of extravagant disbursements for president's salaries, abnormal commissions, and transfer of year's profits out of reach of policy holders, the plain statement, "not earned, but it was voted."

QUESTION

1.　In what ways is accounting an exact science?

5　　　　　　　　　ACCOUNTING: ART OR SCIENCE?

Walter F. Stuhldreher

(Reprinted by permission from *The Federal Accountant*, vol. 22, no. 2 (June, 1973): 74-76.)

(Walter F. Stuhldreher is Financial Services Manager of IBM's Electronics System Center at Huntsville, Alabama and a lecturer at the University of Alabama at Huntsville.)

It would appear that this question is being discussed more now than ever before in business publications, informal sessions, etc. For example: *Forbes*, October 1, 1970 issue: "CPA's like to say that accounting is an art, not a science."　On the following page of the same issue: "In financial reporting today, what the balance sheet giveth, the footnote frequently taketh away. . . . What, another horror story about accounting?"　Also, *Fortune*, December, 1970: "Accountants like to point out that accounting is a social science, not an exact science."　Even the stately *Conference Board Record* recently (April, 1971) contained an article "The Credibility of Accounting Principles."

The question became more than academic to me personally when my second semester freshman accounting class at the University of Alabama in Huntsville disputed my position on this question.　We then decided to send a questionnaire to the heads of the departments of accounting at one hundred colleges picked somewhat randomly from a standard reference. (We did attempt to obtain a geographic dispersal—otherwise they were randomly selected.)

The returns were astonishing.　An incredible 69 percent responded, and even more incredible 79 percent took the time to add additional comments.　Surely positive proof that the question is being actively debated within the accounting profession.

As Table 2 indicates, 50 percent of the respondents favored art, a clear-cut plurality. Some interesting geographic differences are apparent in Table 3, however. The SE and MW answers closely correspond to the overall average, and the SW and W categories also favor art, but to a lesser degree. The NE differs markedly in that science is a clear winner.

Which category felt strongly enough to support their answer with comments? Table 4 indicates not much difference existed between the vast majority (94 percent) of the respondents. Geographically (see Table 5) very little difference existed either.

A few comments:

Accounting is a science because of its basic foundation on laws of operation.

Accounting should *be a science. Many confuse the art of accounting presentation with the science of determining the amounts.*

Accounting is a social, empirical science organized around a (tantological) logical mathematical model.

Ultimately it is an art, but it has all the trappings of a science.

An art in that judgmental evaluations are involved and a science in that we are using more techniques from the hard sciences.

SEARCH NO FURTHER!!!!! I HAVE THE SOLUTION TO YOUR PROBLEM. There are accountants (Eh) and then again there are accounts (O Boy). When the detailed scientific expressions are presented in such a fashion that they are clear, concise and to the point—enlightening all those concerned and leaving those exposed in a richer position than before the information had been presented, the MATHEMATICAL-SCIENTIFIC SUBJECT becomes an ARTFUL FORM OF SCIENCE.

There is ample support for art over science if you study the evolution of accounting literature 1494-1970.

For many years it was hard for me to accept the definition using "art." But after much reading on the subject, I now conclude that accounting is an art. It cannot be a science. There are no scientific laws involved.

Accounting is a social phenomenon and as such has no natural laws to which it can turn as the physical sciences can.

Historically, it is an art because of its devotion to form and technique.

Accounting is an art because it seeks to accomplish certain ends. If it were a science it would be merely seeking basic knowledge.

Unfortunately, after 475 years of double entry we've found no scientific underpinnings for the practices and rituals performed by the practitioners.

Since Accounting Terminology Bulletin *No. 1 states: "Accounting is the art of recording, classifying, and summarizing. . . ." I hesitate to classify it any other way.*

You have got to be kidding, how many immutable laws of accounting can you enumerate?

SUMMARY

Obviously, this article has not attempted to settle this issue, but only to report the results of a study. Also obvious is the fact that the accounting fraternity, as represented by the respondents, is not in total agreement with the trade journals' opinion that all accountants consider accounting an art.

Perhaps the well known Robert N. Anthony, Professor of Management Controls, The Harvard Business School, and former Controller of DoD, summed it up best in his response to the questionnaire:

Every discipline has some aspects of both (even music and painting): the question is, does accounting have a sufficient body of principles to constitute a science?

Professor Anthony then answered his own question affirmatively.

I personally would answer his question negatively. How would you answer?

TABLE 2

Classification	Percent of Total Answers
Neither	3%
No Opinion	3%
Science	22%
Both	22%
Art	50%
	100%

TABLE 3

GEOGRAPHIC ANSWERS

	Neither	No Opinion	Science	Both	Art	Total
NE	0%	9%	37%	27%	27%	100%
SE	5%	0%	20%	15%	60%	100%
MW	0%	0%	27%	13%	60%	100%
SW	12%	12%	13%	13%	50%	100%
W	0%	0%	16%	42%	42%	100%

TABLE 4

Percent of respondents with written comments

Neither	No Opinion	Science	Both	Art	Average
50%	50%	80%	87%	79%	79%

(As indicated by Table 2, 94 percent of respondents chose science, art, or both.)

TABLE 5

Percent of respondents adding additional comments

NE	82%
SE	75%
MW	80%
SW	76%
W	88%
Average	79%

QUESTIONS

1. In what ways is accounting an art?
2. In what ways is accounting a science?

2

Accounting Environment

The following critical aspects of the environment in which accounting must operate and has operated have been singled out for study in Chapter 2: the interactions with economics, society, and the individual; the legal and political environment; historical development of accounting; and the role of accounting under differing socioeconomic systems. Each of these separate factors has had effects upon accounting. At the same time, they have been affected, in turn, by accounting. The study of the factors discloses how and why accounting came to be what it is today and will give insights into what accounting is likely to be in the future.

Eustace Le Master's article (page 22) written in 1922, discusses the interrelationships and interdependence of economics and accounting. It discloses that society's social and economic goals are well served and dependent upon accounting information. Equally, the form and content of accounting records and reports are dependent upon the economic and social environment in which the information provided will be used.

As the needs of society have changed, the public sector has become more important in the use of resources. Socioeconomic programs have grown up largely in the public sector but have also grown within the framework of profit-seeking organizations. The problems encountered in attempting to gauge and report on performance in this area are discussed by Allan L. Reynolds (page 26). Lack of measurement procedures and techniques for benefits produced by not-for-profit organizations and in socioeconomic programs lies at the center of these problems. Where the profit motive is absent, the job of the accountant becomes much more difficult. In a profit-seeking organization, profit is the ultimate gauge of performance. The lack of such a gauge in the public sector is aptly described by Reynolds as "the criteria-gap."

Clark E. Chastain (page 31) adds the important aspect of the interrelationship between the behavior of people and accounting. He explores the progress made in relating the behavioral science discipline to accounting problems. Understanding individual behavior is fundamental to the understanding of social, economic, and accounting problems of society.

The articles by Michael M. Boone (page 40) and the *Financial World* (page 49) provide insight into the legal and political parameters surrounding accounting. The Securities Act of 1933 and the Securities Exchange Act of 1934 together with court decisions over the years clearly require that accounting reports to the public be prepared with full and fair disclosure of all material facts. Boone elaborates on the specific requirements under the law which apply to both public accountants who issue audit reports on financial statements and corporate accountants who prepare financial statements. The *Financial World* article reviews the important role that the Securities & Exchange Commission (SEC) plays in the legal environment in which accounting operates. This article also aptly discloses that, of necessity, decisions of the SEC are at least partly political in nature.

The five articles in the historical development portion of this part of the collection give a perspective of how and why accounting has developed as it is today. John P. Young (page 52) argues persuasively that commercial development of an advanced type could not have been possible without accounting systems which had been brought to a high degree of perfection, even in antiquity. He cites many historical situations which support his proposition. This same theme pervades the other articles in this section.

The articles by J. Edward Masters (page 61) and Byron Defenbach (page 65) provide background on the history of accounting developments in the United States prior to 1915. As commerce and other organizations became larger and national in scope, the accounting profession met its needs for information by organizing professional associations for the advancement of accounting, by seeking recognition under the laws of the various states, and by encouraging education in accounting at the university level. The Defenbach article emphasizes, again, that accounting's environment has been greatly affected by political considerations.

Robert J. West (page 67) provides historical perspective from 1932 to the present enabling us to better understand the developments of the Committee on Accounting Procedure, the Accounting Principles Board, and the Financial Accounting Standards Board. These authoritative groups were charged with the responsibility of clarifying and establishing accounting principles or standards. West reviews the ways in which the Committee on Accounting Procedure and the Accounting Principles Board were able to meet this charge and the ways in which they failed. Based on this review, West looks to the future of the Financial Accounting Standards Board with mixed expectations.

The final section of this chapter contains articles which explore the ways in which accounting has responded and must respond to differing socioeconomic systems. As long as economic activity remains substantially within the borders of one country, nationalistic practices and institutions can more or less govern and standardize the conduct of accounting. Since the needs for information may differ from country to country, accounting practices and reports published in the various countries would be expected to differ. Such circumstances are discussed in the articles by David F. A. Davidson (page 76) on the European Economic Community and Robert H. Mills and Abbott L. Brown (page 82) on the Soviet Union.

6   ECONOMICS AND THE ACCOUNTANT

Eustace Le Master

(Reprinted by permission from *The Journal of Accountancy*, vol. 34, no. 2 (August, 1922): 100-105. Copyright 1922 by the American Institute of Certified Public Accountants, Inc.)

To the average man, it may seem to be a far cry from the theories of Mills and Taussig to the theories he holds concerning the duties of the accountant. Even the average business man may see only the remotest connection between "the science of wealth and its relation to human welfare" and the man who compiles his yearly financial statement. But the experienced accountant is in constant contact with the phenomena of business. He deals daily with the terms and results of utility, value, prices, money, credit, wages, rents, interest, profits, and so on. To him, a knowledge of economics occupies a position of prime importance in his equipment.

The accounting profession owes its existence to the greatest economic revolution in the recorded history of man. The almost total abolition of the domestic system and the tremendous growth of the industrial system of production in the white world have made our people a race of specialists. Modern inventions and the resultant increase in the capital goods of the world, the concentration of capital, the increase of production, the formation of huge credit machinery, the creation of hordes of dependent wage earners and other factors have given rise to many problems of determining the rewards due the various classes of producers and distributors. Competition, which had heretofore been either a beneficial stimulant to individual effort or the death struggle between individuals, brought the menace of great suffering to many in the failure of enterprises. Cost statistics became a necessity. The specialist who compiled the systems for the collection of masses of recorded figures and miscellaneous data on production and reduced voluminous detail to statements of fact came into being. He is the cost accountant. The specialist who supervised the complex system of recording the figures and kept the accounting machinery in running order became the executive accountant. The growth of credit facilities, the creation of industrial banks, armies of bondholders and stockholders have created a need for the public accountant. He is needed by the executive who desires accurate data to answer the questions: Am I making money? How? Where? How much? The accountant is a prime factor in the conservation of wealth and the prevention of waste. His very existence is inseparably connected with the most complex economic organization of the ages. A knowledge of the economic history of this era and a knowledge of the laws that produce its phenomena should induce in him the appreciation of his importance and the faith in his own usefulness to society to inspire him and spur him on to higher ideals and greater achievements.

The accountant without the knowledge of economic theory is comparable to the chauffeur without a working knowledge of gas engines and automobile construction. The chauffeur may be a capable driver. All may go well until some unusual occurrence disturbs the smooth-running machine. The chauffeur's ignorance may be the cause of the employer's weary tramp to other means of transportation. So the accountant may

compile data from a smoothly running accounting machine until one of the
many disturbing phenomena of our era interrupts the smooth course of
business. A strike, a deflation of credit, a new competitor, over-
production, a new invention, a flurry in prices, a war—these or many
more may wreck a business and compel the executive to seek new fields of
endeavor. The accountant's lack of knowledge concerning these economic
manifestations, their precursors and reactions may mean failure and ruin
to those dependent upon him.

The routine and elementary duties of the junior and semisenior are
constantly affected by economic theory. The analysis of accounts and
the classification of income, costs, and expenses are determined by the
application of tests and rules derived from the knowledge of the rewards
of capital, labor and enterprise. Even such an elementary task as the
classification of items composing manufacturing and trading statements
is simplified by and based on the theories of economics. The accepted
practice of treating cash discounts on purchases as income from capital
rather than as a reduction of costs is based on reasoning fostered by
the study of economic theory. In fine, a knowledge of economics is a
fundamental factor in accounting education and is necessary even in its
most elementary stages.

The accountant's report is the real measure of his ability. Nor
is the report to be judged good or bad by the number of its schedules of
figures and percentages, by its fancy covers or by the imposing degrees
following the signature on the certificate. Voluminous remarks are not
always necessary. A brief paragraph setting forth facts showing that
the law of diminishing returns is already in force may be far more effective in certain instances and may save an executive clamoring for
capital from disaster. A change in the expression of a certified balance sheet may reveal the working of an economic law in a business and
prevent a banker from sending good money after bad. Well reasoned comments on facts gleaned from masses of figures are worth far more to the
executive than the figures themselves. How is the accountant to comment
intelligently on his work, if he does not know the economic laws governing business? How is he to know for what facts and conditions to look
in his examination of records, if he does not know the economic causes
producing certain known conditions? How is he to know the relative
value of the various sets of statistics he has compiled? The accountant's work must not only be the result of a careful application of the
technical knowledge of his profession, but it must also be the result of
a careful application of knowledge gained from a thorough study of the
natural laws governing our complex business world. Important facts derived from figures, not schedules of figures, should be the meat of his
report. Comments on causes, not a recitation of known effects, should
be his report.

Recently the eastern creditor of a western dealer came hurrying
west. A large account was considerably past due and the dealer was
calling for more credit. The claim for additional credit was based on
figures showing a steady increase in the volume of sales in a period of
depression. The conclusion was that increased capital would insure success and future prosperity. After a conference, the dealer and the
creditor went to a firm of reputable attorneys. Amended articles of
incorporation were framed and provision was made for the flotation of
preferred stock. Times were hard and investors cautious. The creditor
conceived the idea of getting a certified balance sheet to gain the

confidence of prospective investors. In due time the balance sheet was rendered. It revealed a condition of weakness bordering on insolvency. Appreciated fixed assets had been cut down to cost and depreciation reserves set up. Inventories were shown to be over 90 percent of total current assets. Current liabilities were shown to be in excess of current assets.

The accountant invited the creditor and the dealer to his office to discuss the situation. He told them that additional capital was not the solution of the problem, but that on the contrary increased capital without a change of policy would mean a greater loss. The creditor was interested but the dealer was inclined to be indignant at such presumption on the part of a "figure-maker." The accountant then laid before the dealer a statement of sales and margins for the preceding three years together with an analysis of selling and administrative expenses. Sales showed an average increase of 25 percent a year. The margin percentage had declined from 25 percent to 20 percent of sales. Selling expense percentages had remained constant, but administrative expense percentages had risen from 10 percent of sales to 17 percent.

The dealer was selling semiluxuries in a field of limited competition. Being a salesman, he had one idea: that increased volume of business meant increased profits. He was not acquainted with the fact that in his business price governed demand. Nor was he acquainted with the fact that the factors that governed profits were percentage of margin, volume of sales, and cost of selling and administration. In his business, the greatest volume of profit was to be had by fixing the volume of sales by the margin percentage at the point where the volume of margins was greatest and the percentage of cost of selling and administration was the least.

The accountant recommended that the dealer raise his prices so that the margins would be 25 percent on staple competitive articles, 30 percent on semiluxuries and 35 percent or more on luxuries. He also told the dealer what cuts would be necessary in his office force in the near future.

The creditor was converted but it required pressure to convince the dealer. Within three months the dealer's losses changed to profits and in six months a normal profit of eight percent of sales was the yield of the business. The prediction of the accountant had come true.

The accountant's responsibilities do not cease with the performance of his professional duties. Like every other professional man, he is responsible to the community for his station in life, his education, and the application of his specialized knowledge to public affairs. The accountant is particularly well fitted to render service to the community by his close and intimate association with many businesses. If he is not well grounded in the theory of economics he is likely to prove a menace rather than a help.

Loose thinking in economics is responsible for much of the popular discontent of our day. The year 1920 witnessed a nation-wide campaign against so-called profiteers. Government checkers, pseudo-accountants, combed the books of large and prosperous retailers for sensational data. Reputable concerns were haled before grand juries and the data secured by the government agents were placed before them. Indictments were issued and some of the concerns were tried—and acquitted. Cases were dismissed wholesale. But irreparable injury to the reputations and businesses of respectable and law-abiding concerns was done by the

activities of ignorant and irresponsible government officers. Had the
government accountants known the principles of economics, the masses of
figures turned out by them would never have reached the grand juries.
They would have been able to get convincing evidence against the true
profiteer and would never have attacked the men who were not taking advantage of an economic phenomenon to gouge the public.

In many cities, broad-minded and educated accountants made their
influence felt by intelligent criticism of the governmental policies.
In some cities, civic bodies gave them the privilege of their platforms.
Much was done by the accountant trained in economic theory to restore
confidence in the popularly discredited retailer.

In the year 1912, the Pacific northwestern pine belt witnessed the
failure of many lumber manufacturers and a general depression of the
lumber industry, due in a large measure to unintelligent competition.
The pine manufacturers then combined in an association for the exchange
of cost data and production records. Intelligent competition restored
the industry to normal conditions. The small manufacturer enjoyed prosperity until the recent general depression. And yet this same association was attacked recently by an important government commission.

It is for the accountant with his assembled figures and his sound
economic reasoning to help protect our industries from the attacks of
probably conscientious but mistaken officers of government bureaus and
commissions. It is also his duty to aid the government by the same
means to discover unfair methods of competition, profiteering, monopo-
listic combinations, and kindred evils. This he can do only by being
thoroughly familiar with the laws governing the phenomena of business.

A knowledge of business economics is essential to the successful
performance of nearly every accounting task from the most elementary to
the most complex. The great schools of the country, notably the universities of California and of Pennsylvania, have recognized this fact.
Economics is a subject each student of accounting must study. The man
who is dependent upon the correspondence school for his education should
not confine himself to technical subjects, but should supplement his
work with a thorough study of economics. He should be so familiar with
its principles that he is able to read the financial page of the morning
paper with as much interest, and understanding as he reads the sporting
page. It is only by the combination of the technical knowledge of his
profession and a knowledge of economics that he can render his greatest
service to industry and the nation.

QUESTIONS

1. Why is accounting essential to productive economic activ-
    ity?
2. Why does the accountant need to know economic theory?
3. What happens when the business man ignores economic
    theory?
4. The author talks about the concept of profit. How do you,
    as an employee, profit, working in the marketplace? What
    is your profit? How is it measured?

7

EXAMINING PERFORMANCE OF SOCIOECONOMIC
PROGRAMS—THE CRITERIA-GAP

Allan L. Reynolds

(Reprinted by permission from *Footnote*, winter (1971-1972): 64-69.)

(Allan L. Reynolds is deputy director of the HEW Audit Agency.)

Given sufficient time and reasonable cooperation, an individual trained in data gathering and analysis should be able to establish a factual account of the operations of a public or business entity. He can present this unevaluated picture to management for appropriate consideration and action.

However, if he is a trained evaluator with the added responsibilities of evaluating operational control systems, measuring the effectiveness of operational performance and suggesting appropriate means for improvement, he needs a standard rule or test by which judgment can be formed. He needs a measurement criterion. Further, when the evaluations extend to systems or programs outside the evaluator's field of expertise, he must rely on criteria provided by others who possess the requisite knowledge and experience.

Appraisals of operational effectiveness and efficiency may be facilitated by readily available and firm criteria, often quite specific and quantifiable. Measurements may be based on profits, share of market statistics, or economic indicators. They may be provided by preestablished norms, or targets, or by comparative performance of similar entities. Even contract terms or prescribed policies and procedures may provide pertinent criteria.

There is, however, some danger in accepting as absolute, standards which are actually general or vague. An example would be a contract term that required "prompt delivery."

The appropriateness and applicability of a standard must be clearly established, and even an applicable standard may be erroneous. In some instances, the deviation from the standard may be appropriate; it is the criteria that requires correction.

These and other considerations related to the selection and use of criteria are fairly evident and hopefully are understood and successfully applied by operating management, auditors, and others concerned with reviewing operational performance. Not so evident, however, are the practices which might be used where these more normal sources of criteria are unavailable.

THE CRITERIA-GAP

When auditors assume responsibility as trained evaluators to review the effectiveness and efficiency of socioeconomic programs, they often find at least a partial criteria-gap. How can they determine that:

1. medical services rendered to health care beneficiaries were
    necessary and represented quality care?
2. special elementary education projects provided a suitable
    educational gain for enrolled students?
3. the number of successful rehabilitations was commensurate
    with what should have been accomplished with the resources
    applied?
4. the appropriate level of financial and social assistance
    was provided within available resources to eligible public
    assistance clients?
5. best scientific effort was applied to health research
    projects?

These are not minor considerations. They go to the heart of the
objectives of much of the major social legislation adopted in recent
years. Possibly somewhat indicative of their complexity is the magnitude of the programs involved. The total fiscal year 1971 federal budget alone for the health, education, and welfare programs mentioned is
about $20 billion. Expenditures by state and local governments, uni-
versities, research centers, industries, and individuals add substantially to the total expenditures for these programs.

Nor are these questions for which the auditor is somehow uniquely
gifted with answers. In fact, the state-of-the-art of social accounting
currently precludes an answer validated by audit to many such questions.
Partial answers are sometimes available, and more complete answers
should gradually emerge as experts are able to expand the base for measurement of performance in socioeconomic programs.

Special circumstances often tend to intensify the criteria-gap.
For instance, a problem of measurement is created when program benefits
are identifiable only over an extended period. Review of such programs
in the organizational or early operational stages may preclude performance evaluation—particularly when the program has a fairly nebulous end
product such as "improved planning."

The partnership participation of federal, state and local governments in many of the socioeconomic programs can create multiple, sometimes conflicting procedures, requirements and expectations. This is
not unexpected because of the differing views which may be held by responsible officials at these various levels of government—views which
will probably reflect the varying makeup of the constituencies served by
these public administrators. Evaluation must be preceded by selection
of the correct criteria from conflicting ones, placing an added burden
on the evaluator.

There are even some conflicting views as to how this selection is
to be made. One view holds that the federal criteria prevails, since
state and local government must comply with these criteria. The alternatives to compliance are forfeiture of federal funds or refund of federal funds received but not expended in accordance with federal requirements. An opposite view holds that the ultimate responsibility and,
therefore, the pertinent criteria are those of state and local government, since they are closer to the problem, are more familiar with the
interests and demands of the constituents, have their own money invested
(often equally and in some cases substantially exceeding the federal
investment), and are able to better establish measures of success given
the specific conditions in their constituency.

THE AUDITOR'S ROLE

Further, it may be questioned whether it is the auditor's responsibility to audit performance or to audit the reliability and use made of operational control systems designed to evaluate management performance. Also, is it the auditor's role to attempt to establish performance criteria in the absence of management specifications of such standards?

It seems to me that one of the auditor's primary and certainly more comfortable roles is to evaluate the operational control systems. However, when such systems are nonexistent or weak, direct evaluation of performance will usually be necessary to report clearly to management the effect of these situations and to recommend needed system improvements where this effect is found.

The prescription or adoption of performance criteria is a function of management. This is a central theme of much of the literature related to the practice of management. However, when this role has been abrogated or when the state-of-the-art precludes establishing specific criteria, the auditor may still be able to identify criteria applicable to a specific situation. Provided the logic of the auditor's suggested criteria is demonstrated to management and found acceptable, the results obtained by application of these criteria should provide a valid measure of performance.

SOME SOLUTIONS

As a practical matter, many socioeconomic programs have not readily lent themselves to criteria prescription. Nonetheless, there are at least several means by which applicable criteria might be obtained, including the following, which I believe have been used with sufficient and successful frequency to demonstrate their usefulness.

Criteria of Extremes

If the quality of performance of a number of randomly-selected socioeconomic projects of like objectives were quantified and plotted, it would be reasonable to expect the plotting to produce a bell-shaped curve. Hopelessly inadequate and clearly outstanding performance would exist at the extremities of the curve. When no actual curve can be created because of the inability to quantify performance, the auditor may still be able to convincingly show others that the project under examination falls at one of the extremes of performance. For example, if the vast preponderance of funds made available for improving the educational attainment level of deprived children is continually spent primarily for noninstructional activities, it is reasonably certain that the project expenditures will contribute little to their intended purpose. Where available, this conclusion may be substantiated by student scores in standardized achievement tests. But even in the absence of such test results, the criteria of extremes should suffice.

Note, however, that as performance moves away from the extremes, how much more difficult the analysis becomes. In the cited example, it is evident that some noninstructional support, such as administration, supplies, food, and the like, will be necessary if instructional activities are to be fully effective. But should this be ten percent? Twenty percent? Fifty percent? Because of the variations in project design, possibly no set percentage can be specified. Only those obviously extreme cases of poor performance can be used to show the effect of inadequacies in the operational control system which permitted such extremes to exist undetected or which, although detected, were allowed to continue uncorrected.

Criteria of Comparables

Comparisons can be drawn between like projects. For example, if several rehabilitation projects are assisting the same types of clients in similar circumstances, valid comparisons may be possible of the relative rates of successful rehabilitation. The major danger in this approach occurs if there is a failure to assure that data are drawn from truly comparable projects, or at least adjusted as necessary to provide a basis for comparison. Also, cost/benefit studies of alternate or competing programs may encounter partial criteria gaps. Principles for establishing cost comparisons are available and, although difficult to apply in some cases, the task is not usually insurmountable. However, such cost comparisons would be useless in the absence of a means of measuring the relative benefits of each project.

Criteria of the Elements

Performance criteria may be expressed in such broad general terms for a program or project that no measures to evaluate program performance are possible. Such program objectives as "improve urban life," "limit pollution of the environment," "reduce dependency" and the like are highly desirable attainments, but performance of projects with such goals are not measurable against such broadly defined objectives. However, breaking the projects down on a functional, organizational or systems basis will often produce elements which can be measured.

The effectiveness of design of a delivery system or of only the input and processing elements of the system may be subject to evaluation and thereby an inference drawn as to the probable performance of the system. To illustrate, in an education project, criteria may be readily available against which such system's input as teacher qualifications, student eligibility, class size, curriculum, teaching media, and other factors may be measured. In this instance, while educational attainment may not be directly measurable, the effectiveness of the system designed to provide educational attainment can be measured and its potential inferred, based on expert criteria.

In other cases, dissecting an organization or program on a functional or other segmented basis may produce needed information. For example, the effectiveness of performance of the Medicare system (where effectiveness is defined as providing necessary services to eligible individuals at a reasonable cost) is accomplished by separate audits of providers, fiscal intermediaries, state agencies and federal agencies. The audits of each of these entities is further broken down into the examination and measurement of performance of special elements, functions, or systems. For example, audits of fiscal intermediaries paying beneficiary claims under the supplemental medical benefits portion of the program would place major stress on the intermediaries' systems related to payment controls, price controls and utilization controls. Not only do performance criteria exist for each of these control systems, but even significant details of system design have been specified. An illustration of the latter are edit criteria specified by the Social Security Administration for use by its fiscal intermediaries in claims processing to detect duplicate billings. The results of the audits of each segment or function of each organization audited can be summarized to draw a conclusion as to that organization's performance. Further, by summarizing the performance of a selected sample of all organizational elements participating in the program, valid conclusions on overall performance can also be drawn. In other words, a major program with its broadly stated objective can be progressively subdivided until a level is reached where performance evaluations are feasible. The results of these detailed examinations can then be progressively summarized to arrive at a composite picture of program performance.

Criteria of Expertise

Possibly the outstanding problem when using expert opinion as a criteria source is the frequency with which experts disagree. If not careful in selecting expert support, the auditor could easily become involved in a situation of "my expert versus your expert." One solution is to reach agreement beforehand with the responsible program managers as to the acceptability of a particular expert. Also, the problem can sometimes be resolved by the use of expert pronouncements in the form of principles, standards or position papers of recognized professional groups such as the National Education Association and the American Medical Association. While all experts may not be in agreement, pronouncements of recognized organizations in their field of expertise nonetheless should predominate and be the more acceptable evidence to management.

Another source of expert advice often is found within the organization being audited. Care must be exercised that the advice obtained from qualified experts, employed by the organization under audit, is not unduly influenced by organizational management. This does not usually seem to be a problem when the advice is sought for the review of individual transactions, cases or other detailed examinations. For example, objective medical advice is usually obtainable within an organization when determining if medical services claimed represent covered services or utilization of medical services is reasonable, given the medical condition of a specific claimant. Inhouse advice on matters of broad policies, procedures, and practices is more likely to be suspect.

CONCLUSION

Audits of governmental units, like management of these units, must place primary emphasis on the quality and effectiveness of service, and the efficiency with which this service is provided. However, the traditional motivations (and measures) of business, such as loss of customers because of poor service or profit reductions or losses because of inefficiencies, do not apply—at least not in the same form. But elected and appointed representatives, and those who elect or appoint them, badly need measures of performance of their governmental units. In fact, I suggest that a public accounting of the actual performance of these units would be the single most important stimulus for improving public administration.

Yet to advance performance stewardship reporting, criteria are needed and the reliability of reported performance needs to be verified. In the absence of formulated criteria, several ways have been suggested in this article whereby criteria may be constructed and the results made available to management for initiating corrective action on specific deviations, working toward further formulation of criteria, and further refining and utilizing performance reporting.

QUESTIONS

1. What is the major problem in establishing and reviewing socioeconomic systems?
2. Can the criteria problem be overcome? If so, how?

8   ACCOUNTING AND BEHAVIORAL SCIENCE:
              SOME INTERRELATIONSHIPS

Clark E. Chastain

(Reprinted by permission from *The Michigan CPA*, vol. 24, no. 3 (November–December, 1972): 10-17.)

(Clark E. Chastain is a member of the faculty of the University of Michigan at Flint.)

The practice of accounting can probably be traced at least to 5,000 B.C. when merchants of the various Biblical lands determined their profits from simple merchandising and barter transactions. Although it is likely that humans have wondered about their behavior since their early existence on earth over one million years ago, recorded study and observation may be carried back to the writing of Herodotus around 5,000 B.C.

The parallel in the development of the two disciplines—accounting and behavioral science—may be continued. Accounting, as it is known in our century, unfolded in its development in the 19th century along with the industrial revolution. The behavioral sciences of greatest importance to accounting emerged as scientific disciplines in the same century. Prominent founders include Wilhelm Wundt (1832-1920) of modern psychology, William James (1840-1920) of American psychology, Sir Edward Tyler (1832-1917) of anthropology, and Auguste Comte (1798-1857) and Herbert Spencer (1820-1903) rendered the first systematic treatments of sociology.

Accounting made rapid strides in its development in the early 20th century, especially in participating strongly in the managerial process of guiding corporations—by this time managed to a large extent by professionals separate from the stockholder-owners—toward their goals. The philosophy of the corporate accountant was similar to the manager in the period 1905-1920. After all, the accountant was partially a staff man serving management and in varying degrees an active participant in the management function.

The guiding philosophy of what information to account for, what information to communicate, and the format used was essentially economic. The goal of the corporation was economic gain, the individual was motivated and controlled by economic incentives, and decision-making was economically oriented. The engineer's point of view played a strong role in organization theory; hence, man was to some extent regarded as an adjunct to a machine, and the major consideration in the management of him was to seek maximum productivity. Principles of management centered around "a departmental approach, grouping activities according to their specialty for their more efficient performance, placing strong emphasis on span of control, precise delegation of authority, accountability, and clearly fixed responsibility." (1)

Professor Caplan, in his recent book, has summarized the behavioral assumptions underlying the "classical school of management" under these headings: organizational goals, individual participants, management, and management accounting. (2) The emphasis on these assumptions is economic, largely to the exclusion of social, emotional, and human factors.

The interrelationships between accounting and behavioral science continued to remain largely undeveloped until after World War II, but both fields continued rapid growth in their own domain over the first half of this century. (3) Developments in the philosophy of business management and its concern for the human factor were progressing, however. The first development was the well-known pioneer study of Elton Mayo of the Hawthorne plant of Western Electric in Illinois in 1927-1932. He found that the social relationships between workers and between them and their supervisors were more important in increasing productivity than changing the physical working conditions. Post World War II saw increased emphasis on human relations, or added consideration for the behavioral needs of employees in business.

The 1950s witnessed the first major criticism that accounting as a major control in business failed to elicit the positive element in human behavior.

DEVELOPMENTS OF THE RELATIONSHIP BETWEEN ACCOUNTING AND BEHAVIORAL SCIENCE

Chris Argyris found in a study of the effects of budgets on people in 1952 that the factory supervisors viewed budgets and accounting personnel as imposing external demands on them and pressuring them to achieve budgeted performance without working out an agreed-upon goal through joint participation. (4)

In 1959, two studies important for accounting and business curricula recommended training business students in the behavioral sciences. These studies were *Higher Education for Business* by Robert A. Gordon and James E. Howell, and *The Education of American Businessmen* by Frank C.

Pierson. Shortly after, in the early part of the decade, various accounting scholars called attention to behavioral implications within
accounting and emphasized the need for study of these.

A little later researchers, some of them accountants by training,
reported upon behavioral aspects of audits and budgets; the first dealt
with the effects of audit anticipation upon individual behavior, and the
second with theoretical models of budget control. (5) In 1966, Robert
H. Roy and James H. MacNeill published *Horizons for a Profession: The
Common Body of Knowledge for Certified Public Accountants*, a widely discussed publication. (6) This study urged training and research in organization and group behavior. They recommended "that the common body
of knowledge for beginning CPA's include fundamental training both in
psychology and sociology, with emphasis upon those parts of both subjects focused upon the behavior of formal organizations." (7)

Articles on behavioral science aspects of accounting, both theoretical and reporting empirical research, are being published in an increasing number. Some conferences and symposia sponsored by accountants
are being devoted entirely to this area. The American Accounting Association has begun a training program in behavioral accounting. Professional development courses are offered in this area for practitioners
and educators. In 1969, a readings in *Accounting and Its Behavioral Implications* was published. (8) A committee of The National Association
of Accountants studied the behavioral aspects of managerial accounting.
In 1971 the first supplementary textbook for classroom use—*Managerial
Accounting and Behavioral Science* by Caplan—was published. References
to behavior are now appearing in conventional accounting books. And the
American Institute of Certified Public Accountants is strongly considering testing candidates for the CPA examination on accounting and behavioral science topics.

ACCOUNTING, SCIENCES, SOCIAL SCIENCES, AND THE BEHAVIORAL SCIENCES

As an aid in understanding the relationship between accounting and
behavioral science, let us briefly examine each of the topics: sciences,
social sciences, behavioral sciences, and accounting. Our examination
is in the order that the topics are mentioned because they go from the
more general to the specific.

Sciences has been described in many ways but the briefest definition is as a body of systematic knowledge. Kolasa has characterized
science more broadly as:

1. systematic and
2. empirical so that the information obtained this way can be
3. ordered and
4. analyzed for the results to be
5. communicable
6. cumulative

In effect he has described the scientific process, its purpose being to understand what is happening, to learn why events occurred, often
explained by a theory or hypothesis, to predict what will happen in
other similar situations, and, finally to be able to control events.

The social sciences include the application of the scientific process to studies of the activities of man in contrast to the physical sciences that concentrate on the physical environment. The disciplines included are large in number—anthropology, sociology, psychology, history, political science, business administration, accounting (at least partially), ecology, economics, geography, linguistics—and some authors include others. The fields included are many in number because of the many viewpoints from which man and his social activities are approached.

The behavioral sciences—and the definitions vary greatly—are social sciences, but the number of fields included is usually smaller than those labeled as social sciences. The critical test is whether the field inquires into the behavior of humans. Thus, history may describe the events of man, but where it does not inquire into his behavior it is a social science, but not a behavioral science. Only some areas of many disciplines, for example political science, may be labeled as behavioral. The behavioral sciences question how people behave, why they behave as they do, and what is the relationship between man's behavior and the overall environment. For accounting, it is important that we define behavioral science broadly enough to include the individual, small, formal, and informal groups that he participates in, the organization, the business environment that the organization relates and communicates to, and the broader social or cultural level.

The behavioral scientists usually consider the core behavioral disciplines as anthropology, psychology, and sociology. Accountants and investigators of organizational behavior, however, seldom use the findings and knowledge of anthropology and substitute social psychology because of its importance for linking individual to group behavior.

Accounting is being confronted most directly with the behavioral sciences through its importance in the managerial process, although the implications are much broader. Management—as the administration of organization resources—has been said to be behavioral because it deals with human behavior in the business context. (9) But, other writers point out that business administration goes beyond planning and controlling human behavior; to performing these functions for money, materials, structures and equipment, and for product processing. (10) Maneck S. Wadia believes, however, that some aspects of management "come close to becoming a behavioral science." (11)

The changing views of accountants toward considering behavior may be inferred from a contrast in definitions. An older and often-quoted definition of accounting is the one by the American Institute of Certified Public Accountants: "Accounting is the art of recording, classifying, and summarizing in a significant manner and in terms of money, transactions, and events which are, in part at least, of a financial character, and interpreting the results thereof."

A more recent definition is one by an American Accounting Association committee in 1966 which defined accounting as "the process of identifying, measuring, and communicating economic information to permit informed judgments and decisions by users of the information." (12) The critical change in definitions is the inclusion of nonfinancial transaction data, and some authorities are suggesting that in the future it may include social data. Also of importance, the new definition is more externally oriented toward the needs of the users than the older one. In discussing the future of accounting theory, the committee refers to it as "an information system." These broader contexts of accounting are important for discussion of accounting and the behavioral sciences, for they point up the broader role accounting is assuming for communicating information regarding individual, group, and organizational behavior and the effects of this process.

Whether accounting is an art or a science, and more specifically a social science, has been debated for decades. The AICPA has defined accounting as an art, apparently largely because personal judgment and evaluation play a great part in classifying financial data and in the matching of various expenses such as depreciation accruals against revenues. George O. May, a pioneering giant in the development of accounting practice in the United States, contended that accounting was an art. He wrote, late in his career in 1950, that income "is not capable of scientific ascertainment," but is a:

> *matter of estimate and opinion to be determined by mutual agreement. It is essential to determine what are the fruits of the year's activities and this can be done only on the basis of estimates and on fundamental conventions which must find their warrant not in "truth" but in usefulness and practicability. (13)*

However, for decades a group of accountants have argued that conventional accounting dealing with the financial transactions has been a social science and that the scientific method should be applied in major tasks such as income determination where the problem is to apply the applicable basis of revenue and then match related costs against revenues. (14)

Although the development of accounting may have been largely as an art, and accounting, unlike some other disciplines, developed largely in response to the practical needs of industry, much of its work in industry and academic studies today meets the requirements for a science. The accountant often uses rigorous and precise means to collect empirical data in a systematic manner. These means include natural observation, field studies, clinical settings of individual's and groups' overtime, surveys, and experiments. Analyses of the data are being made by statistical procedures, operations research techniques, mathematical models, computer simulations, laboratory experiments, field studies, and analyses of empirical data. In summary, many facets of accounting are becoming more scientific.

The increased emphasis on the scientific method in accounting is important in accounting research and in solving business problems. The developing awareness of many accountants of the personal, group, and organizational behavioral implications of accounting, is pressing the extension of the methods of science. Just as many political scientists have observed that their field is more truly a science when they use the social science methods of analysis to study human behavior, the same observation appears to be applicable in accounting.

SOME RELATIONSHIPS BETWEEN ACCOUNTING AND THE BEHAVIORAL SCIENCES

Reference has been made to the American Accounting Association committee to prepare *A Statement of Basic Accounting Theory* in 1966 which stated that accounting is an information system and should communicate, in addition to financial transactions, data on socioeconomic activities. They stated that the behavioral sciences should be used in performing the accounting function whose purpose is "to improve control methods and decision-making at all levels of socioeconomic activities." Three concepts of accounting were stated: motivation, measurement, and communication; and that the motivation concept required that "the cause of socioeconomic activities must be related to individual wants and organizational goals such as the desire for income (short- and long-term), prestige, power, and mixed and conflicting objectives." For future accounting theory, the authors suggested research into:

1. the nature of social, organizational, and individual wants
2. the impact of measurements on human actions
3. the nature of information and measurement.

Obviously, the behavioral sciences and individual, social, and organizational needs and goals were very important in the minds of committee members.

Mention has already been made of the AICPA's study, *Horizons for a Profession: The Common Body of Knowledge for Certified Public Accountants*, in 1966 which recommended that training for beginning CPA's include "psychology and sociology, with emphasis upon those parts of both subjects focused upon the behavior of formal organizations." (15) This study has inferred an important relationship between accounting and behavior.

Let us briefly review some reasons why accounting should consider behavioral implications and broaden its scope beyond that of measuring financial transactions. First, all fields in the social and physical sciences are beginning to research how their discipline affects man and his behavior, how it meets his needs, and why. Fields are becoming much more interdisciplinary and are combining their knowledge and skills with others. The converging point of this effort is around the behavior of individuals. Probably the growth of disciplines, often somewhat in isolation from others, was in part because of needs of individual professionals at that time to be somewhat isolated. Today, however, as individuals including professionals in the specialized areas recognize and accept greater interdependency of personal needs, there is a tendency to tear down old boundaries and to work mutually with other scientific specialties. Similarly, in order for accounting to progress, it must work with the behavioral science discipline to find out how it affects individuals and what they want and need from it.

Second, conventional accounting records financial transaction data which are the results of negotiations between individuals or groups of individuals. In effect, accounting has been recording, measuring, and communicating data about human behavior for decades and even centuries.

Third, accounting measures the performance of an organization or for a group of individuals. Net income, a major tool of accountants, is the most widely reported and used measure of an organization's performance. Because accountants are measuring an important aspect of behavior, they will probably want to know something about organizations in addition to the dollar recognition of revenues and expenses.

Fourth, accounting is a major device for communicating information throughout an organization. (16) It has been suggested that the

accounting information system could and should communicate other socioeconomic data in the firm that has not been included in financial transaction data. In order to follow this suggestion, it will be necessary
that accountants study the areas of communication and information. They
may wish to inquire what it is that members of an organization wish to
have communicated to them and what effect various messages have upon
them. Much of the breakdown, it has been suggested, lies in the accountant failing to be in tune with the coding and receiving processes
of the user of accounting information.

Fifth, many of the accounting functions in an organization are for
the economic control of costs, assets, expenditures, liabilities, etc.
But these controls also have vast important social effects on the individuals involved. For example, a budget may serve to motivate personnel
or in some cases it may restrict their performance because of failure to
recognize some of their individual emotional needs. An example of this
may occur where the concerned members of a department are not invited to
participate in determining the budget. Standards for the costs of producing items may do the same thing. In order to assure the meeting of
social needs which are important for individual performance and ultimately for the economic success of a unit, accountants must know how
their controls interact with the social aspects of individuals.

Some of the strongest criticisms of accounting, the major control
system in an organization, by behavioral scientists have been that it
does not positively motivate participants, that it is often punitive,
and that it provides low diffusion of information which is often inaccurate. For example, the accounting system affects behavior through
setting levels of aspiration, reinforcing attitudes, reporting success
and failure of individuals, and in providing events that allow for
participation. But according to T. W. McRae "designers of accounting
control systems know little, if anything, about recent research findings
on human behavior." (17)

Caplan maintains that accountants do not ignore human behavior but
they base their control systems on obsolete assumptions. He outlines
the classical management assumption that employees are lazy, inefficient, motivated only by economic factors, and need external controls.
Brummet alleges that accounting fails to account for its investment in
human resources, one of its most important assets. Likert argues that
there is a tendency to exploit human resources in order to maximize
profits in the short run at the expense of later periods. This practice
is destructive to the social and psychological bonds of the organization
—the attitudes, expectations, perceptions, habits, motivations, and be-
liefs of the individual participants.

Expenditures on training and developing management personnel are
also erroneously expressed, according to Likert, because much of the
outlay results in an asset that benefits the future, i.e., managerial
training in large part is a long-run investment. Accounting control
systems tend to be punitive rather than supporting, and detrimental to
self-esteem, self-acceptance, self-direction, and psychological success,
state a number of organizational behavioralists. They state that the
controls are imposed from above, are much of the time unfair, place emphasis on failure to accomplish them, and often do not explain the participants' reasons for failure. Because such controls are policing in
nature, the upward flow of information is filtered, distorted, and re-
tarded.

The punitive nature of accounting controls may build up strong hostility toward accountants. Agyris quotes some comments of this nature from employees: "Most of them (accountants) are warped and they have narrow ideas. Most of our accountants are narrow and short-sighted— they are what I call shiny pout bookkeepers. They are technicians. They don't know how to handle people. One of the worst human problems we have is the poor job of selling that is done with cost records and budgeting control." (18)

Agyris explains the negative feelings toward accountants as follows: "Success for the budget supervisor means failure for the factory supervisor! The finance man cannot take the shortest possible route between the foreman and himself . . . the finance man achieves his success when his boss knows he is finding errors." (19)

Behavioral scientists criticize the caution, stewardship, secrecy, and security with which accountants treat financial and economic information, for they feel that this is not supportive to the employees, detracts from their sense of responsibility and self-worth, and may lead to lowered morale and efficiency. The behavioral scientists believe that much of the accounting data should be available to employees to aid them in making their work contribution according to their self-need for performance. It should not be withheld from them and used as a lever by top management in imposing external control over them, they assert.

The tendency for accountants, say organizational theorists, is to make the business system a closed one that is relatively unresponsive to its environment, and lags in external communication. This may result in lowered efficiency and rigidity to change that is necessary for the survival of the organization. This is partially a vested interest, for accountants substitute their controls for monitoring the progress and achievement of the company in the place of the controls that would be provided by the external environment. The results may be undue emphasis on lowering costs at the expense of more aggressive movement toward more profitable areas. It may be contended that variances from the cost standards are errors that should be avoided instead of accepting them as environmental forces that should be studied, perhaps allowed for, in setting company goals and might even signal profitable opportunities to exploit.

In summary, accounting is probably one of the most influential and controlling elements of the individual, the small group, the mass of humans who constitute the organization, and the relating of the business to and its functioning in the environment. It seems desirable that as a first step, accountants examine their relationship to people and become familiar with their expected behavior under alternative variables. Some changes may result in our accounting systems once we process specific knowledge of how and why individuals behave as they do, in contrast to basing it on assumptions, some of which are probably erroneous. Accounting is also probably an instrumental factor in the progress of an organization. Accountants must study environmental factors and promote the diffusion of this information throughout the firm, rather than imposing or aiding a closed communication system within the organization.

FOOTNOTES

1. Arthur B. Toan, Jr., "Does Accountancy's Views of Human Behavior Meet Today's Needs?" *Price Waterhouse Journal* (September, 1971), p. 14.
2. Edwin H. Caplan, *Management Accounting and Behavioral Science* (Reading, Mass.: Addison-Wesley, 1971), pp. 17, 30-31.
3. See James D. Edwards, *History of the Public Accounting Profession*, AICPA, 1960, for accounting; Maneck S. Wadia, *Management and the Behavioral Sciences* (Boston: Allyn and Bacon, 1968), for the behavioral sciences.
4. *The Impact of Budgets on People*, The Controllership Foundation, 1952.
5. N. C. Churchill, et al., "Laboratory and Field Studies of the Behavioral Effects of Audits," in C. P. Bonini, ed., *Management Controls* (New York: McGraw-Hill, 1964). For budget analysis, see A. C. Stedry, *Budget Control and Cost Behavior* (Englewood Cliffs, N.J.: Prentice-Hall, 1960).
6. AICPA, 1966.
7. Op. cit., p. 234.
8. N. J. Bruns, Jr., and D. T. DeCoster, *Accounting and Its Behavioral Implications* (New York: McGraw-Hill, 1969).
9. James L. Latham, *Human Relations in Business* (Columbus, Ohio: Charles E. Merrill Books, 1964), p. 3.
10. Rollin H. Simonds, Richard E. Ball, and Eugene J. Kelley, *Business Administration: Problems and Functions* (Boston: Allyn and Bacon, Inc., 1962), p. 9.
11. *Management and the Behavioral Sciences: Text and Readings* (Boston: Allyn and Bacon, Inc., 1968), p. 30.
12. Committee to Prepare a Statement of Basic Accounting Theory, American Accounting Association, 1966, p. 1.
13. George O. May, "The Choice Before Us," *Journal of Accountancy* (March, 1950): 206-207.
14. Arthur C. Kelley, "Can Corporate Incomes be Scientifically Ascertained? " *The Accounting Review* (July, 1951): 289-298. Also see H. R. Hatfield, J. H. Sanders and N. L. Burton, *Accounting Principles and Practices* (Boston: Ginn and Company), p. 3.
15. Roy and MacNeill, op. cit., p. 234.
16. T. W. McRae, "The Behavioral Critique of Accounting," *Accounting and Research* (Spring, 1971): p. 84.
17. T. W. McRae, op. cit., p. 84.
18. *Harvard Business Review* (1953): pp. 103-106.
19. Ibid., p. 104.

QUESTIONS

1. Mr. Chastain says that the accountant will have to get
    involved in behavioral implications.
    a. Is an accountant qualified to judge and report on
        human behavior?
    b. How can behavioral implications affect what and how
        the accountant compiles and reports information?

---

9   MANAGEMENT ACCOUNTANTS AND THE SECURITIES LAWS

Michael M. Boone

(Reprinted by permission from *Management Accounting*, vol. 54,
no. 12 (June, 1973): 18-22.)

(Michael M. Boone is a practicing attorney with the law firm of
Haynes and Boone, Dallas, Texas.)

During the past decade, several landmark court decisions considerably broadened the responsibilities and liabilities of accountants.
Much has been said to remind public accountants of their legal liabilities and to educate them about the duty of proper financial disclosures
under the Federal Securities Laws as interpreted and applied by the
courts and the Securities & Exchange Commission (SEC), but it may be
that too little has been done to adequately advise the management accountant of the impact of these recent legal decisions and SEC actions
on his personal liability. Many management accountants are not cognizant of the extent of their legal liabilities, civil as well as criminal, in the preparation of financial statements.

This article focuses generally on some of the basic responsibilities placed on the management accountant by the Federal Securities Laws
and briefly discusses their attendant liabilities. In that context, the
developing law of fair financial presentation will be analyzed. Also,
specific attention will be given to those antifraud provisions of the
securities laws which have the greatest impact on the accountant.

THE SECURITIES LAWS

The two primary pieces of federal legislation in this area, the
Securities Act of 1933 (Securities Act) and the Securities Exchange Act
of 1934 (Exchange Act), impose on companies a duty of disclosure of all
material information in order that public investors can make informed
investment decisions whether to buy, sell, or hold securities. Essentially, accountants bear the responsibility of making full disclosures
of adequate and meaningful financial information. The failure to properly adhere to this duty can amount to fraudulent conduct resulting in
substantial personal liability. Indeed, the onerous liability provi-

sions contained in the Federal Securities Acts are aimed at encouraging compliance with the law of full and fair disclosure.

Basically, the Securities Act and the Exchange Act deem the communication of information which is materially false or misleading or which omits a material fact to be fraudulent conduct when made in connection with a securities transaction. If the fraud is willfully and knowingly perpetrated, there is criminal liability. But in any event, the persons behind the fraud are civilly liable. To the accountant who acts without criminal intent, this liability means that if he is responsible for disseminating fraudulent information, financial or otherwise, he is liable to the defrauded investors for monetary damages. Furthermore, the SEC may file a civil injunctive suit or other legal action against him.

Unfortunately, many accountants labor under the false belief that they are safe from civil liability and SEC action so long as they do not knowingly make an improper financial disclosure. This belief can lead to personal ruin; unlike common law fraud, Federal Securities Law fraud is not limited to intentional misrepresentations or omissions. Under the securities laws, civil liability does not depend on the existence of an evil intent. A noble and pure heart will not serve as a defense, for recent judicial decisions have clearly held accountants civilly liable for deficient financial disclosures negligently made. The careless preparation of financial statements can be disastrous.

Often an accountant who is not in the forefront of a company's operations believes that he is shielded from liability by those members of management above him. Be that as it may, the argument of a management accountant that liability for fraudulent financial statements rests solely with the company and its principal officers and directors is likely to fall on deaf ears in a courtroom. Without doubt, a company has direct statutory liability for fraudulent disclosures which it disseminates. Such liability is also extended to officers, directors, and controlling shareholders of the company. But even when a management accountant does not fall within any of those classifications, he can still be found liable if he participated materially in the preparation or dissemination of fraudulent disclosures. Aiders, abettors, and coconspirators in a fraudulent disclosure are equally accountable at law with the persons primarily responsible for the fraud. In short, the management accountant's assistance in the preparation of false or misleading financial statements may be substantial enough to bring him within reach of damaged investors or some type of government action. A management accountant simply cannot take the duty of disclosure for granted.

FAIR FINANCIAL DISCLOSURE

The courts have translated the duty of disclosure, as it relates to financial statements, into what is commonly referred to as the duty of fair financial disclosure. In the context of fraud, this means that financial statements which are materially false or misleading or omit a material fact do not present fairly the financial position of the company and are thus fraudulent. The most critical question facing the accounting profession is: "By what standards will the courts test the legal sufficiency of financial disclosures? Will lay or professional standards of what is fair disclosure be applied?"

The case of *United States vs. Simon*, (1) commonly referred to as the Continental Vending case, has had considerable bearing on the question of proper financial disclosure. While the case involved the liability of public auditors, it has equal application to management accountants in the preparation of financial statements. In that case, two partners and an audit manager of a national accounting firm were convicted of criminal fraud in connection with the certification of certain financial statements of the Continental Vending Machine Corporation. The criminal charges are based on violations of the Exchange Act and mail fraud statutes. The crux of the government's case was that the certified financial statements of Continental Vending Machine did not adequately disclose that substantial loans made by the corporation to an affiliate were in turn loaned by the affiliate to the president and largest shareholder of the corporation.

At the trial, the defendant accountants had eight expert witnesses testify that in the contested balance sheet the disclosures about the loans to the affiliate were in accordance with generally accepted accounting principles. When the case was submitted to the jury, the defense requested the trial judge to instruct the jury that if they found the disclosures in the balance sheet were in accordance with generally accepted accounting principles, the defendants must be acquitted. The court refused to do so, stating:

> . . . *proof that the defendant did act in accordance with such generally accepted auditing standards and accounting principles is evidence which may be very persuasive but not necessarily conclusive that he acted in good faith, and the facts as certified were not materially false or misleading* . . .
>
> The critical test . . . is whether the financial statement here, *as a whole*, fairly presented the financial condition *of Continental* . . . (2) (emphasis added)

In short, the district court adopted the view that compliance with generally accepted accounting principles does not necessarily mean that there has been a full and fair disclosure. The critical test was whether the financial statements presented fairly the financial condition. However, the appellate court in that same case indicated that when the profession has adopted specific rules or prohibitions, those disclosure standards must be given considerable weight in deciding whether there has been a fair financial disclosure. Conversely, it would appear that when an accountant has alternatives and great latitude in choosing the manner of financial presentation, the layman's viewpoint of what is a fair disclosure may be the standard applied. In view of this judicial approach to the problem of financial disclosure, the accounting profession should hope that the new Financial Accounting Standards Board will move swiftly to eliminate the many alternatives in present-day accounting disclosure standards. Such action should aid in reducing the risk of liability to the management accountant.

In considering whether proper financial disclosures have been made, the accountant must always bear in mind that the primary purpose of the Federal Securities Laws is to protect the public investor. Financial disclosures contained in a periodic report filed with the SEC, a proxy

statement, a prospectus, a press release, etc., must be presented so
that an average prudent investor—not an average prudent accountant—
can make an informed investment decision. The management accountant
must, to some degree, place himself in the shoes of the reader of the
financial statements to see if the disclosure is adequate and meaningful.

DISCLOSURE IN CORPORATE FINANCE

An area of corporate life in which the management accountant plays
an essential role is corporate finance. Equity and debt securities
financings are commonplace occurrences for businesses of all sizes.
Such financings may range from the issuance of a promissory note in a
simple bank loan to a public offering of millions of dollars of securities. Regardless of their form, such corporate financings fall within the purview of the Federal Securities Laws. As a result, it is
mandatory that disclosures of material financial data along with other
corporate information be made to prospective purchasers of a company's
securities. For this reason, the management accountant is often called
upon to prepare financial information for dissemination to prospective
investors. Among company personnel, he is the one primarily responsible
for the full and fair disclosure of the financial condition of his company. Anything short of that mark may easily fall within the ambit of
securities law fraud.

Fraudulent Registration Statements

The Federal Securities Acts contain several antifraud provisions
which apply to transactions involving a company's issuance and sale of
securities. However, particular attention needs to be given to Section
11 of the Securities Act which deals specifically with liability for
fraudulent registration statements. A registration statement is the
disclosure document filed with the SEC when a company makes a public
offering of its securities. The prospectus, which composes the greater
part of the registration statement, is the primary selling tool. Section 11 imposes civil liability on each person who signs a registration
statement that contains, at the time it becomes effective with the SEC,
materially false or misleading statements, financial or otherwise. Each
principal executive officer, a majority of the board of directors, and
the principal financial or accounting officer are required to sign the
registration statement.

The requirement that the chief accountant must sign the registration statement clearly mirrors the congressional desire to place a heavy
burden of responsibility on the management accountant. The accountant
will want to be extremely careful in making sure that there has been
full and fair disclosure in the registration statement before he at-
taches his signature. Because, by signing a registration statement, he
personally assumes the potential civil liability of Section 11 which is
the total dollar amount of the securities being registered. Needless to
say, when the accountant is not sufficiently aware of the accuracy of
the content of a registration statement, the financial disclosures in

particular, he would be well advised not to sign it.   Ignorance will not excuse him from Section 11 liability.

Due Diligence

A false and misleading registration statement, however, is not necessarily fatal to the accountant who signs it; several defenses from liability are written into Section 11. The most important defense to the accountant is commonly referred to as the "due diligence" defense. As to any false or misleading parts of the registration statement prepared by someone other than an expert, an accountant will not be liable under Section 11 if reasonable investigation caused him to believe that when the registration became effective the statements in it were materially true and did not omit any material fact.

This defense is premised on the necessity of a personal verification that there has been a complete and fair disclosure of all material information about the registrant in the registration statement. Accepting statements at their face value is not enough; there must be a reasonable investigation. In judging what is a reasonable investigation by an accountant and what is reasonable ground to believe, the standard of reasonableness "required by a prudent man in the management of his own property" is applied.

The noteworthy case of *Escott vs. Barchris Construction Corporation* (3) was decided in late 1968. There the company's financial statements were found to contain deficient disclosures resulting in liability to several defendants, including the company's chief accountant. The court in that case gave the first judicial interpretation of what is a proper "due diligence" defense.

Every management accountant who is an officer or director or who participates in the filing of registration statements should read the Barchris case because it is comprehensive in its discussion of the responsibilities imposed on management, the underwriters, and public auditors in the preparation of a registration statement, and it outlines their liabilities under Section 11. The court was very clear in holding the officers of the Barchris Construction Corp., including its chief accountant, to a high standard of care in fulfilling the duty of full disclosure and satisfying the defense of "due diligence." Certainly, the case emphasizes that the management accountant must be cautious in his work.

Special Knowledge. The management accountant has a special relationship to his company because he has intimate knowledge of its financial condition and business operations. He is in a position to verify corporate information. And above all, the management accountant is expected to be more knowledgeable of his company's accounting matters than anyone else in the company. For these reasons, the amount of effort required of an accountant to exercise "due diligence" with regard to proper financial disclosures in a registration statement or any other type of financial disclosure is much greater than that placed on anyone else connected with a registration. If financial statements are false or misleading, it will be extremely difficult for the management accountant to prevail on the basis of a "due diligence" defense. This rule applies to audited as well as unaudited statements. The financial statements belong to the company, not to the independent accountant. Most assuredly, the certification of financial statements by a public auditing firm does not relieve the management accountant of his responsibilities under Section 11.

Materiality. Section 11, like other fraud provisions of the securities laws, creates liability only for material misstatements, not insignificant ones. While the matter of "materiality" will be discussed again below, consider here what the Barchris court defined as material facts; that is, those matters which an average prudent investor needs to know before he can make an intelligent, informed decision whether or not to buy a security. (4)

Prudence dictates that the accountant should exercise the greatest care and place the most emphasis on disclosing financial facts that would have the most significance to an investor. Disclosures concerning the problem areas and vital points of the company should be concentrated upon since they are likely to be the subject of a challenge if the company runs into difficulty.

Effective Date. The accuracy of the registration statement is measured at its effective date. Usually it takes a few months from the time a registration statement is first filed until it is declared effective by the SEC. During this interim period, changes may occur in the company which affect the accuracy or completeness of the information contained in the original filing. Thus, prior to its effectiveness, the registration statement will be amended to properly update and correct the information in the original filing. In fulfilling this aim, the accountant should take particular note of any changes in earning trends, liquidity, collectibility of receivables, contingent liabilities, and other financial changes. An exercise of "due diligence" demands that all accounting information be properly updated to a date as close as possible to the effective date. Like the auditor, the management accountant should make a subsequent examination of the financial disclosures to determine if there are any material changes since their original preparation.

FINANCIAL DISCLOSURE REQUIREMENTS

Another important area in which the management accountant is constantly involved concerns corporate disclosures to the public and the SEC when the shares of his company are publicly traded. According to congressional philosophy, investors are not adequately protected when trading securities unless they have available current information on which to base investment decisions. In implementing this view, several provisions of the Exchange Act impose a specific duty of continuous public disclosure of corporate information on publicly held companies.

Reporting to the SEC

Public companies are required to file periodic reports with the SEC; such reports are available for public inspection. An annual report on Form 10-K, which includes factual business information and financial statements certified by an independent accountant, is required. A Form 10-Q consisting primarily of interim unaudited financial statements must be filed quarterly. Finally, a Form 8-K report has to be filed after the end of any month in which any of certain specified events occur or, more generally, when any material corporate event occurs, such as a major acquisition or bank financing. The management accountant is involved in preparing the 10-K and 10-Q forms due to the financial statements included therein. He may also participate in a Form 8-K filing. As is the case when his company sells securities under a registration statement, the management accountant is exposed to personal liability if these filings are materially defective.

One problem of particular concern to the management accountant should be mentioned. The Form 10-Q is a relatively new disclosure device adopted by the SEC. The unaudited interim financial statements included in a Form 10-Q must reflect all adjustments which are, in the opinion of management, necessary for a fair statement of the results for the interim period. In preparing a Form 10-Q, the proper adjustments and allocations are often a matter of judgment, and therefore, can sometimes be a delicate problem. The same is true of the accounting treatment that may be given to unusual transactions occurring during such interim period. It is often advisable for the management accountant to consult with the company's auditors for their comments in advance of filing Form 10-Q. This procedure will reduce possible mistakes and eliminate the possibility of the auditors determining at year end that some treatment was improper.

One other point of interest to the management accountant should be briefly discussed. Form 8-K specifically requires that a company disclose the engagement of a new independent accountant. In doing so, a company must state in a letter to the SEC, supplemental to the Form 8-K, whether there were any material disagreements with its former independent accountant during the 18-month period preceding the engagement of the new auditor. In addition, the company's letter must be accompanied by a letter from the former auditor stating whether he agrees with the company's letter. This disclosure requirement should deter the practice of shopping for auditors who will agree with management's position on a particular accounting matter. It obviously takes some pressure off the public auditor who disagrees with management. But more important, if there have been disagreements between the auditors and the company, it waves a red flag to the SEC and the public that there is some question about the financial disclosures being made by the company. Consequently, a company will want to think twice before it places itself in such a position.

Informing the Public

Federal Securities Laws also make it incumbent upon each publicly traded company to disseminate material information informally to the public. In addition, the national stock exchanges require listed

companies to make similar disclosures.   Such informal disclosures generally take the form of a public press release.   As to what information
should be disclosed and when it should be disclosed by management, the
well known *SEC vs. Texas Gulf Sulphur* case has spelled out some guidelines which state that only material facts must be disclosed.   Material
facts were also defined by the Texas Gulf Sulphur court as those which
"affect the probable future of the company and those which may affect
the desire of investors to buy, sell or hold the company's securities."
(5)
     However, the definition of materiality is easier to state than to
apply.   A great deal of judgment is involved in determining what is
material.   Furthermore, it is perhaps more difficult to know when
information becomes material.   These decisions simply depend on the
facts of each situation; there are no clearly delineated rules that can
be followed.   And unfortunately, a decision of materiality is usually
judged by the 20-20 hindsight of a judge or jury.
     Whenever a material event, favorable or unfavorable, occurs, prompt
disclosure should be made to the public unless there are valid corporate
reasons for not doing so.   In the context of accounting, the types of
information most likely to be deemed material would include such matters
as significant changes in earnings from prior years or from those publicly projected or announced, change in dividend rate, significant
financings or acquisitions, any occurrence which will materially affect
earnings, and major problems of liquidity.   A press release of such information must be complete, accurate, and not misleading.   The information to be disclosed should be definite.   In that regard, a company has
a duty to keep prior disclosures current and a duty to correct prior
statements that become inaccurate.   It is incumbent upon the management
accountant to make sure that there is a follow-up on any material
changes in prior financial disclosures.

Deficient Disclosures

     With regard to the periodic reports made to the SEC and informal
disclosures made to the public, the management accountant may face civil
and criminal liability under the Federal Securities Laws if such disclosures are deficient.   Consequently, these types of disclosures of
financial information should be approached by the management accountant
with the same care that one would use in satisfying "due diligence"
defense of Section 11.

INSIDER TRADING

     One other area of liability under the Federal Securities Laws can
affect the management accountant.   This liability involves a person's
trading in securities on the basis of material inside information that
is undisclosed and not equally available to the general public.   This
problem of securities trading relates directly to the affirmative duty
of disclosure.   Rule 10b-5 promulgated under the Exchange Act by the
SEC prohibits the use of fraud in connection with the purchase or sale
of securities.   It condemns unfairness in a securities transaction.
Stated differently, this means that an accountant with undisclosed

material information cannot utilize such knowledge to his advantage over other investors.

Under this antifraud rule, a management accountant can literally expose himself to millions of dollars of liability if he trades in the public market with undisclosed material information or on the basis of material misrepresentations. For instance, the 11 defendants in the Texas Gulf Sulphur case faced private lawsuits aggregating claims of $77 million. Because a management accountant is often aware of material undisclosed facts about his company, the best advice that can be given him is simply this: He must forego trading in the market until such information has been publicly disclosed. Furthermore, he must not advise anyone else of such undisclosed information until it has been publicly disclosed.

Timing

This advice presents several questions of importance. First, when is information publicly disclosed so that an accountant can freely trade? The court in the Texas Gulf Sulphur case held that public disclosure has been effected when there has been publication over the "media of widest circulation." The Dow Jones tape would probably be such a medium; however, releasing information to the news media or to Dow Jones may not be entirely sufficient. The SEC maintains that information is not disclosed until the public has absorbed the news. How long it takes to absorb the news is a factual question as far as the SEC is concerned. The New York Stock Exchange advises that insiders should not trade until the information has appeared in the press. In any event, a person should probably allow some time for the public dissemination of the information through normal news channels. Some period of waiting after disclosure of results of operations should be maintained before the accountant can trade safely.

Tips

Another important facet of rule 10b-5 is that a person is liable if he communicates (i.e., tips) undisclosed information to someone who trades on such information. Therefore, to prevent undesired leaks of information, undisclosed corporate information should be confined to a limited number of individuals in the company. The management accountant may sometimes encounter the tippee problem when he is interviewed by a broker or security analyst about the financial condition of his company. In fact, several lawsuits have been brought against tippers of undisclosed information to such types of persons. Material facts must be disclosed publicly without any favoritism to a particular person. During such an interview, the accountant of a company often finds himself in a precarious position at a time when he has possession of material undisclosed information. In this case, it is sometimes advisable for the accountant to avoid interviews with investment advisers, brokers, newsmen, and the like. Attempts to circumvent untimely disclosure may likely result in the accountant making misleading statements which are equally reprehensible.

CONCLUSION

Without question, the management accountant must recognize that the present clamor over extensions of accountants' liability involves him as much as it does the public auditor. In view of the hazards of his occupation under the Federal Securities Laws, the accountant must approach his duties with utmost care. He must be alert for changes and developments in accountants' liability and accounting disclosure standards from future court decisions, SEC actions, and pronouncements of the recently formed Financial Accounting Standards Board. The management accountant must not succumb to pressures which adversely affect his objectiveness in making financial disclosures. In every case, his primary goal should be to make sure that financial disclosures are adequate and meaningful to their users.

FOOTNOTES

1. 425 F. 2d 796 (2nd Cir., 1969).
2. United States District Court S.D.N.Y. No. 66 Cr. 831, Sept. 17, 1968.
3. 283 F. Supp 643 (S.D.N.Y., 1968).
4. Ibid., p. 681.
5. 401 F. 2d 849 (2d Cir., 1968).

QUESTIONS

1. What is required of accounting reports by the Securities Act of 1933 and the Securities Exchange Act of 1934?
2. Why is full and fair disclosure so important to the economic well-being of the country?
3. Today, approximately 30 million people in the United States own shares of corporations. What purpose do these 30 million people serve to you, assuming you are working for either private industry, government, or some private nonprofit organization?

10   SEC: CASEY AT THE BAT

(Reprinted by permission from *Financial World*, vol. 139, no. 3 (January 17, 1973): 30.)

The mills of the gods grind slowly but no more slowly, it seems, than the administrative machinery of many federal agencies, including the Securities & Exchange Commission.

Under the aggressive and often bold leadership of its outgoing chairman, William J. Casey, the SEC has moved in many specific areas during the past year to correct some of the more obvious abuses and inequities that exist in the securities industry. But owing to the cumbersome method of proposing new rules, holding public hearings, inviting comment and finally promulgating the rules, it is difficult to assess the progress made to date.

Some of the most important issues remain to be resolved, such as the question of institutional membership on the stock exchanges, fuller disclosures in prospectuses and annual financial reports to stockholders, better accounting methods, and the privileged nature of information available to insiders only.

But if there is one thread that runs through the numerous speeches Casey has made since he became chairman of the SEC in April, 1971, it is the strong belief that the individual investor is entitled to the fullest possible disclosure of information concerning assets, liabilities, capitalization, revenues, earnings etc. of publicly held companies, whether they are traded on the exchanges or in the over-the-counter market. Casey has pushed hard for improvements in prospectuses and annual financial reports, better accounting methods, and a minimum of secrecy.

Speaking before the Practicing Law Institute in New York November 27, Casey said: "Sadly, we have seen in the past that changes in disclosure philosophy have often produced new prospectuses that are every bit as larded with boiler plate and as useless for imparting information as the 'old' prospectuses they replaced. The Commission's intent in this regard remains the same as it was last year when I addressed the Corporate Secretaries in Los Angeles; that is, to produce meaningful disclosure, understandable to all investors, so that capital values can be determined on a fair, competitive basis and not by sleight-of-hand."

Unfortunately, the SEC, which derives its basic authority from the Securities and Exchange Act of 1934, has a multitude of responsibilities in other areas governed by the Public Utility Holding Company Act of 1935, the Investment Company Act of 1940, the Internal Revenue Code, the Bretton Woods Agreements Act of 1945, the Trust Indentures Act of 1939, and the Investment Advisers Act of 1940. It carries out its responsibilities through a set of rules about as complex as any administered by any agency of the federal government, rules that are often misunderstood or misinterpreted, so that even lawyers who specialize in dealing with Commission regulations are sometimes confused. It has a relatively small staff of 1,560 persons to carry out its responsibilities.

Casey, a former Wall Street lawyer himself, recognized some of these difficulties. Late last year he appointed a Corporate Finance Forms Advisory Committee of persons familiar with Commission filings and, based on a report by that committee, the SEC is considering new rules designed to provide the public with clearer standards.

Sen. Harrison A. Williams (D.-N.J.) and Rep. John E. Moss (D.-Calif.), chairmen of the key Senate and House subcommittees that deal with legislation affecting securities have for many months been working on a draft of a proposed new Securities Act of 1973. It will include a number of harsh proposals, such as a provision that prohibits institutions that manage investments of insurers, mutual funds, and pension funds from holding membership on any stock exchange.

On January 4, in what was probably his valedictory as SEC chairman —he has been nominated by President Nixon as Under Secretary of State for Economic Affairs—Casey addressed a luncheon session of the board of directors of the New York Stock Exchange. In that speech, Casey outlined what he regards as the main requirements of the securities industry today. First and foremost among these is financial solidity. A new SEC rule requires that customers' funds cannot be used by brokerage houses in the business except in secured lending to customers. Another requires that all statements filed by brokers must undergo an examination by outside accountants.

Other reforms urged by Casey are what he calls an "even start" for investors so that insiders do not have any unfair advantage over the general public, and an "honest count," by which he means that the tendency of accounting practices to exaggerate earnings and growth and obscure declining performances should be made impossible.

"The thing I want my tenure at the Commission to be remembered for is formulating the method and making the decision to cut through to the heart of this problem by requiring disclosure of accounting policies and of the significance of variations—changes in methods, use of methods other than those prevailing in the industry, differences between methods used for financial reporting and tax purposes."

"TERRIBLE SWIFT SWORD"

Other needs Casey stressed were an open system, in which all transactions could be brought out in the open by a comprehensive transaction and quotation system giving all qualified brokers access to the market, and what he described as "a terrible swift sword." By that he meant swifter, more timely enforcement procedures when manipulative practices are discovered.

"It doesn't do enough for the public investor when a year later somebody is slapped with an injunctive action and perhaps two years later indicted for criminal conduct," he declared.

There is no question but that Bill Casey will be missed at the Securities & Exchange Commission, which he has reorganized and redirected in less than two years as its chairman. Where it goes from here depends in no small measure on the philosophy of whoever succeeds him. For even though there are five members of the SEC, it is the chairman who usually has the most decisive voice in shaping its policies.

QUESTIONS

1. Why has Congress given the SEC the power to regulate accounting practices?
2. What are Casey's major criticisms of accounting? Are these justified?

11   ACCOUNTING IN ANTIQUITY

John P. Young

(Reprinted by permission from *The Journal of Accountancy*, vol. 12, no. 7 (November, 1911): 513-525. Copyright 1911 by the American Institute of Certified Public Accountants, Inc.)

(John P. Young was editor of the *San Francisco Chronicle*.)

A high stage of commercial development could not be attained by any community unless it were accompanied by a more or less elaborate system of accurate accounting, and that presupposes the use of some convenient means of recording transactions in a permanent form.

This assumption will scarcely be questioned by anyone familiar with the requirements of trustworthy bookkeeping. But it appears that there are many scholarly persons who assume that ancient peoples managed to evade this necessity and were able to carry on great and varied operations with a system, or rather lack of system, as crude as that of the barkeeper who chalked up the drinks obtained by his customers on trust on a board kept back of the bar.

About ten years ago the editor of *The Outlook* in an article on abbreviations, in which considerable learning was displayed, endeavored to demonstrate that the Roman propensity to avoid spelling out long words and sentences was induced by the fact that their principal medium for writing was the tablet covered with wax on which the writer scratched what he had to say with a stylus.

This suggested to your lecturer the desirability of demonstrating that the use of paper was general in antiquity, and that the tablet, despite the fact that it is frequently alluded to in classics in a manner calculated to confuse, was never employed in the time of Cicero except for temporary purposes, just as we now sometimes employ a slate or something else from which an erasure may easily be made.

The investigation proved very interesting and disclosed the fact that from the very earliest period of which we have knowledge, that can be considered historical, there must have been systems of accurate accounting, and that the ordinary medium for recording transactions was paper, and not, as is sometimes carelessly assumed, such durable materials as clay tablets or, as suggested by *The Outlook*, the tablet covered with destructive wax.

It is hardly necessary to describe to an assemblage of the sort I am addressing the limitations upon accuracy which adherence to the use of clay or wax would entail, and I feel assured that all my hearers will agree with me that no perfect system of accounting could be attained unless a medium as flexible and handy in every particular as paper existed.

It therefore seemed to me that if the evidence pointed to extended commercial intercourse in antiquity that fact in itself furnished conclusive evidence that paper was used thousands of years before our time in all ordinary transactions, and that the tablets with the wedge-shaped inscriptions, discovered in recent times in that region which was once ancient Babylon, were intended to serve as permanent records.

Among these tablets is found a large proportion of contracts and accounts. Some of the latter are what might be termed primary entries, and this fact has led to the assumption that the bookkeeping of the Sumerians was done on soft clay which was afterwards baked. It is perhaps presumptuous to place against the opinion of an archeologist that of a practical man, but it is only by viewing the subject from every standpoint that the truth can be ascertained.

The learned in such matters assert that the Babylonians, or the people who spoke the Sumerian language, and inhabited the plains of Mesopotamia, named the twelve signs of the zodiac and divided the equatorial into 360 degrees at least 2200 years before our era, and that they also determined the length of the sidereal year and were accustomed to reckon the latitude of the stars from the zenith of Elam just as we reckon longitude from the meridian of Greenwich.

Being deficient in astronomical knowledge, and weak in mathematics, I made inquiry concerning the nature of the calculations necessary to arrive at the above results and learned that the necessary calculations would fill many sheets of paper. The conclusion drawn was that if the assumption that the Sumerian astronomers employed clay they would have had to start a brickyard every time they wished to work out a result; and that bookkeepers, on occasion, might find it necessary to run several of them in order to prepare a satisfactory balance sheet.

Among the resurrected knowledge concerning this ancient people we have a codification of laws attributed to Khammurabi. A German Assyriologist ventures the opinion that the culture of the people for whom this code was made had attained its completed form some five or six thousand years before our era. It would be rash to challenge his assumption for from this code we are enabled to extract that the cities of that period maintained an octroi; that there were customs and ferry dues collected and highway tolls and water rates imposed, all of which implies the existence of a complexity which is the product of a slow and laborious evolution.

From the code we also learn that trade was practiced on an extended scale and that agents were far afield. The law strictly defined the relation of principal and agent and that of creditor and debtor. Claims could not be enforced unless they were properly entered, and a false entry on the part of an agent was penalized threefold, and if the principal was found guilty of a similar offense he paid a sixfold penalty. There were banks and the use of drafts or checks was common, and the resurrected tablets show that there were innumerable legal decisions concerning contracts, deeds of conveyance, bonds, receipts, inventories, and accounts of all kinds.

Although much is left to conjecture, and we have yet to learn of the methods of these ancient accountants, we may reasonably be sure that they were methodical for when courts of law are invoked to settle disputes between debtor and creditor care is taken to secure accuracy. And indeed that is indispensable to the conduct of affairs on a large scale. It is unthinkable that there should be a great commercial development without the accompanying feature of systematic accounting, and it is equally certain that the operations of a nation high in the scale of civilization, with revenues to collect and receipt for or disbursements to make, could be carried on without public accountants.

Coming down a little nearer to our time we find descriptions of the activities of a people whose name is almost a synonym for commercialism, and whose trading proclivities are frequently referred to in the Bible. The Phoenicians, whose bold navigators circumnavigated the continent of Africa, and whose merchants had dealings with all the peoples of antiquity must have developed some of the highest forms of accounting. They planted factories wherever the opportunity for trading offered, and these, being in the nature of permanent agencies, and operating on an extended scale, were necessarily required to make showings that would prove satisfactory to the parent establishment which was often a joint stock concern.

Of Sidon and Tyre we are told that they traded in fine linens from Egypt; blue and purple dyes from the isles of Elisha; silver, iron, tin, and lead from Tarshish, which they obtained from the Carthaginians; slaves and brazen vessels from Greece, Tubal and Mesech; emeralds, purple embroidery, fine linen, coral, and agates from Syria; corn, balsam, honey, and gums from the Israelites; fine wools from Damascus; polished ironware, precious oils and cinnamon from Dan, Javan (Greece) and Mezi; magnificent carpets from Dedan; sheep and goats for slaughter from the pastoral tribes of Arabia; costly spices from Arabia and India; precious stones and gold from Sheba and countries in the south of Arabia.

The operations of these great manufacturing cities of antiquity were by no means simple exchanges. They represented all the complicated forms peculiar to modern commerce and involved the use of the same machinery we now employ in the transaction of business. There is even ground for the assumption that they had brought their methods of accounting nearer to perfection than we have, and that they were enabled by a device resembling that of the clearing house to settle balances of all kinds with a minimum of metallic money.

The Greeks who borrowed much of their civilization from Asia, greatly improving upon it in many particulars, undoubtedly followed the business methods of the East. They admit their obligations in some particulars with a freedom which might impel the hasty reader of Grecian history to imagine that they were anxious to repudiate all claims of originality.

This is especially noticeable in the economics of Aristotle, who seems to find it necessary to furnish precedents for many of the practices of his countrymen in the customs of other nations. It is through this propensity we have learned of many things happening to other peoples than the Greeks of which we should have remained wholly ignorant had his works not survived.

It is to Aristotle that we are indebted for knowledge of the fact that most of the varied forms of credit we are now familiar with were well known to the ancients, and that in some respects their practices indicated a far better insight into the basic principles governing commercial intercourse than modern business communities possess.

Aristotle's definition of the functions of money is unassailable, and his descriptions of the various devices resorted to by active trading peoples to dispense with its direct use give us an insight into the business methods of numerous peoples. He tells us that notes as evidence of debt were in common use and he makes it clear by inference that the practice of discounting was prevalent. He speaks of loans made on the security of coming crops in order to provide the money for the payment of troops, and he lets us know that the funding plan was frequently resorted to in his time, all of which points to a mistake in the assumption that "a national debt is a national blessing" is a modern discovery.

We also learn from Aristotle and other Greek writers that the democracy of Athens was rather insistent that a full accounting of all transactions should be made by those who served them. It is evident from this that the system of public accounting was pretty well developed. That there were experts who made it their business to overhaul these accounts is abundantly testified to by the frequent accusations of "graft" brought against officials, some of whom appear to have been as vulnerable to improper influences in Greece a couple of thousand years ago as they are today in American cities.

The Greeks did not content themselves with well-ordered public affairs; those of the private citizen were evidently also looked after carefully. Xenophon in his book on economics gives a picture of the management of a household which indicates that the wife had responsibilities imposed upon her far greater than is commonly inferred from those fugitive allusions to the part she played among her women. He says: "Resources come into the house for the most part by the exertions of the husband, but the larger portion of them is expended under the management of the wife, and, if affairs be well-ordered, the estate is improved; but if they are conducted badly they are diminished." In another place he describes duties imposed upon the lady of the house, the performance of which must have required exact accounting as they involve the necessity of stock-taking with the view to the determination of whether the estate has been illy or profitably administered.

Transferring our attention from Greece to Rome we are not surprised to find that its citizens were appreciative of the value of exactitude which finds its expression in accounting, for has not Pliny the Elder told us that it was the custom of the Romans to imitate and make use of all the good things practiced by their neighbors or the people they conquered and assimilated?

If I had the same opinion of the Romans as that commonly entertained I should not quote them as an illustrious example; but I take the liberty of disagreeing with all those historians who have assumed that Rome was merely a conquering nation whose people were deficient in the manufacturing and commercial instinct, and assert broadly that no nation in antiquity surpassed it in all those practices which go to make up a great trading country.

The evidence is overwhelming that the conquests of Rome, like those achieved by its modern prototype, Great Britain, were the necessary outcome of a development which demanded expansion and that they were not inspired by a desire to despoil weaker peoples. It is not essential to the working out of my theme that I should furnish proof of this but in passing I may say that the wars with Carthage in their inception were trade conflicts pure and simple, an assertion borne out by the fact that they were terminated by commercial treaties, which secured for Rome the right to trade with Carthage and her colonies.

Now closet historians may conceive the possibility of a nation going to war with another nation to compel it to sell goods to its subjects, but I am sure you will not. The Carthaginians were manufacturers and traders and it is unthinkable that they would interpose obstacles to anyone buying from them, but if we are to believe the most eminent writers of history Rome made war upon them to secure that privilege. The assumption is rank nonsense. The treaty which concluded the first Punic war by its provisions gave the Romans the right to trade in Carthaginian

territory and within Carthage's sphere of influence, and might serve as
an excellent model for a modern reciprocity treaty which we all know has
as its inspiration the desire of both signatories to sell—the buying
matter always takes care of itself.

The misunderstanding concerning the industrial condition and attitude of ancient Rome is as great as that which has produced the impression that the Roman provinces were administered solely for the purpose
of plundering their inhabitants. Evidence which ought to conclusively
demonstrate that misgovernment was the exception is easily accessible,
and much of it has a direct bearing on the subject I am treating as it
vividly portrays the fact that the people of Rome demanded a strict
accounting from those who served them in an official capacity. But my
time will not permit me to treat this phase in detail, and besides there
is other testimony more to my point in the orations of Cicero.

That eminent legal luminary and politician in a speech in which he
appeared for an actor named Roscius, gave an excellent sketch of private
Roman bookkeeping which would permit any of my hearers to reconstruct
the system. Roscius had engaged to teach a young slave who was articled
to him his art, that of the comic actor. The slave was killed and the
actor brought an action against the man who killed him and recovered
damages to the amount of 100,000 sesterces. The man who had articled
the slave had also recovered damages from the slayer, and suppressing
the fact sought to make Roscius pay over one-half of the amount received
by him. In his argument Cicero dwelt at length on the reputation of
Fannius, the man who tried to overreach the actor, but his strongest
point was that directed against the suspicious character of the bookkeeping of Fannius. Cicero said:

> He says that I am indignant and sent the accounts too
> soon; he confesses that he has not this sum entered in his
> book of money received and expended; but he asserts that it
> does occur in his memoranda. Are you then so fond of your-
> self, have you such a magnificent opinion of yourself as to
> ask for money from us on the strength, not of your account
> books, but on your memoranda. To read one's account books in-
> stead of producing witnesses is a piece of arrogance; but is
> it not insanity to produce mere notes of writings on scraps of
> paper? If memoranda have the same force and authority and are
> arranged with the same care as accounts where is the need of
> making an account book? Of making out careful lists? Of
> keeping a regular order? Of making permanent record of old
> writings? But if we have adopted the custom of making account
> books, because we put no trust in flying memoranda, shall that
> which, by all individuals is considered unimportant and not to
> be relied on to be considered important and holy before a
> judge? Why is it that we write down memoranda carelessly;
> that we make up account books carefully? For what reason?
> Because the one is to last a month, the other forever; these
> are immediately expunged, those are religiously preserved;
> these embrace the recollections of a short time, those pledge
> the honesty and good faith of a man forever; these are thrown
> away, those are arranged in order. Therefore, no one ever
> produced memoranda at a trial; men do produce accounts and
> read entries in books.

Few of my hearers would have any difficulty in reconstructing the main features of Roman bookkeeping from what I have quoted. The remarks of Cicero apparently show that the Romans kept a cash book and ledger, and that the latter was posted regularly every month. I ran across a criticism some years ago in a book on *Commerce in Antiquity*, which was written towards the close of the 18th century by a Scotchman named Mac-Pherson, in which the author ventured the opinion that no journal was used, but the absence of reference to such a book is untrustworthy evidence, for its use may have been so familiar that Cicero did not deem it necessary to mention it.

It is hardly probable that great care would have been exercised in writing up cash transactions, and that loose memoranda of credit transactions would have been deemed sufficient. Although there is no direct statement to that effect, we may reasonably be certain that there was a day book, and that the complexities of Roman commercial intercourse pointed the way to the use of devices which would check the work of accountants.

The critic I have spoken to assumes that the hastily written memoranda, "with alterations or blottings," were posted from directly, and that they were thrown away every month, but this hardly seems probable. If that was really the practice, and there was nothing intervening between the destroyed memoranda and the ledger, the experting of books would have been a difficult procedure, although Cicero's reference to the evidence of witnesses to a transaction being of more consequence than the accounts suggests something of the sort.

The Romans long before Cicero's time had recourse to the joint stock system; and they had developed the business of banking to such a high degree that the moneyed men of the capital practically financed the world of the period. Some of the names of men most familiar to us were engaged in money operations on a scale that justly entitled them to be regarded as the Morgans and Rockefellers of their time. Private individuals are on record as making loans to countries to prosecute wars and industrial enterprises. Mining operations were carried on in the provinces on a vast scale for men who lived in Rome and furnished the capital. Pliny tells us that in Spain hydraulicking was engaged in to such an extent that mountains were literally washed away. In all the large provincial cities agencies of various kinds existed whose headquarters were in Rome.

It is inconceivable that these great and varied occupations could have been pursued without carefully devised and elaborated methods of accounting suited to each class of business. It is not probable that the petty shopkeeper kept his books in the same manner that those of Croesus were kept. Croesus, as you know, was the richest man in Rome in the period when Caesar and Cicero were flourishing, and if we are to believe Ferrero, the most recent of Roman historians, he was the most extraordinary product of the times, for actually, if we are to accept the verdict of the historians, although the greatest money-lender in Rome, he was also the active friend and backer of Catiline who, they say, was advocating the abolition of all debt, and to accomplish his purpose was quite ready to burn down the city.

But it is not to point out the inconsistencies or dwell on the obscure conclusions of historical writers that I refer to Croesus, but to call attention to the fact that his method of keeping track of affairs must have been highly elaborated to permit him to do what Plutarch tells

us he did, and what no historian has seen fit to challenge despite its
inherent impossibility. Croesus, he says, had an organized corps which,
when a fire occurred in the city, hastened to the scene and at once made
overtures for the purchase of the burning property, and that in the
neighborhood which happened to be menaced by the flames. As the habit
of mortgaging property was quite common in Rome, these operators must
have been walking halls of records to be able to carry on a business of
the kind suggested.

They probably did nothing of the sort. The evidence is not clear,
but the story points to the existence of some method of insurance
against fire. Marine underwriting we know as quite common, for we have
recorded instances, and nothing is more likely than that precautions to
insure against disaster on the sea would be imitated by those interested
in property on terra firma. Croesus was probably largely interested in
fire insurance and the corps spoken of by Plutarch was a body of men
similar to our fire patrols, and their business was to extinguish fires
before they gained headway. The misconception may have arisen through
this corps refusing to exert itself when they knew Croesus had no interest in preserving a particular property from destruction.

It is to emphasize the belief that a people as advanced in commercial practices as the existence of marine and fire insurance imply that
the operations of Croesus are cited, and to suggest that primitive methods of bookkeeping would have been out of place in such a stage of development; and also that it is in the highest degree improbable that
accounts were kept on paper that was rolled on a stick as most commentators of ancient affairs assume was the case with manuscripts. Mac-
Pherson declares that "the books of the ancients which were not like
ours, which are bound together by the inner sides of the leaves, but
were long rolls containing divisions called 'poginae' which we call columns," and takes issue with Scoliger, who in touching upon the subject of
accounts in antiquity assumed that what was paid out was written on the
face of the paper and what was received on the back of it. MacPherson
observes that this would be a very inconvenient arrangement, and I think
you would all agree with him if you ever tried to keep the accounts of a
big business on rolls of paper.

As a matter of fact there is no good reason for believing that
manuscripts in rolls were the only form of books known to the people of
the time of Cicero. Pliny, who edited an encyclopedia which embraced a
good deal, if not all, of the knowledge of his times, makes statements
that contradict such an assumption. He tells us that the manufacturers
of Rome made several kinds of paper, many varieties of which he express-
ly names, and he describes one kind which he says had the defect that
"upon a single leaf being torn in the press more pages were apt to be
spoilt than before."

Differing again from the Scottish critic who expresses wonder that
the Romans never hit upon any device for multiplying copies of a manuscript, I feel reasonably certain that they did have such a device, and
that it accounts for the extraordinary cheapness of books in the first
century of our era. I was led to investigate this branch of the subject
by the perception of the fact that a facsimile process of some kind
seems an absolute essential when governmental operations are carried on
at a distance from the central authority as they were during many centuries by the Romans.

In another case in which Cicero was the prosecutor, that against
Verres, we find him saying, "For I knew it was the custom of the collec-
tors who kept the records, when they gave them up to the new collector
to retain copies of the documents themselves." Of course, it is possible that these copies may have been laboriously produced by scribes,
but when we consider the fact, which has often been overlooked, that the
Romans were familiar with the process of transferring elaborate designs
chased on silver vessels, and that they also were accustomed to repro-
ducing patterns on walls, it seems in the highest degree improbable that
they never hit upon a method of multiplying copies of documents.

These are interesting speculations, but the obscurities in such
accounts as we have, while they challenge investigation, are not near so
important as the many perfectly clear statements testifying to the prev-
alence of careful accounting, and to the fact that accountants were held
in high esteem in antiquity. In the oration just referred to, that
against Verres, who by the way was a wonderfully accomplished grafter,
Cicero refers to the scribes as an honorable body of men, "because to
their integrity are entrusted the public accounts and the safety of the
magistrates."

It is true that he also had something to say about those who be-
trayed the trust reposed in them, but he characterized them as men un-
worthy their calling and intimated pretty broadly that they effected
their entrance into the honorable guild to which they belonged by improper methods. From his remarks it has been inferred by commentators
that although there were rules which made it necessary for any one to
obtain a position as public accountant to be a member of the order of
scriveners, that political boosting at times succeeded in putting men
into place who lacked the necessary qualifications. These Cicero round-
ly denounced, while he declared his perfect willingness to accept as
arbitrators in the case he was trying the men who were indignant that
their order should be disgraced by the presence of black sheep who had
gained their positions by the improper use of influence and money.

The speeches against Verres by Cicero completely establish that
there was no looseness in governing the Roman provinces. Curiously
enough they have been drawn upon to support the contention that the
provincial system of Rome was hopelessly corrupt, and that the people
of the provinces were regularly stripped by their governors. It is true
that Verres was a great scamp and answered perfectly to the description
of the man who would steal everything but a red-hot stove, but over and
over Cicero declares directly and by implication that his methods were
exceptional. Speaking of the unsatisfactory condition of Verres' accounts, and alluding particularly to the meagreness of detail concerning
an expenditure of 2,235,417 sesterces, he asked: "Is this giving in accounts? Did either I, or you, O Hortensius, or any man even give in
his accounts in this manner? What precedent is there of any such in all
the number of accounts that have ever been received by public officers?"

It is certainly extraordinary to infer general malversation from a
speech in which the declaration is made that the accused had violated
all precedents, and whose withering scorn of the offenses charged was
applauded by the jurors and the people, and which resulted in the voluntary retirement into banishment of the man who had used his office to
enrich himself. It would be absurd to assume that Roman provincial
officials never abused their powers, but it is still more absurd to

assume, as is commonly done, that the people of Rome were steeped in corruption to such an extent that they approved the rascalities of their officials.

If it were not for the fact that the zeal of the middle ages for the complete extirpation of all traces of paganism resulted in the destruction of a vast quantity of ancient literature, we should be able to get a clearer and more comprehensive view of accounting in antiquity. Unfortunately the monks have left us little of the purely technical of the past. They were ruthless editors and relentlessly cut out what they imagined would interfere with the attainment of eternal happiness hereafter, and as a result they interfered greatly with their present, definitely arresting the world's progress for many centuries.

But what we have left suffices to make plain that during hundreds of years the systems of public and private accounting had been brought to a high degree of perfection in antiquity, especially among the Romans. And even though we have but meagre details of what was accomplished under the empire, we are well assured that its vast governmental operations were made easier of accomplishment by the skill of trained accountants whose business it was to keep track of the enormous receipts from all sources and the disbursement of the revenues. And even if there was a foundation for the assumption that the decadence of Rome was due to the extinction of patriotism, and the degenerization of the people, we may be sure that good accounting never contributed to that result. We should rather seek for it in another direction. When men began to center all their thoughts on a hereafter, and despised the things of Earth, accounting must have had its usefulness curtailed until by degrees it was shorn of all its virtues, the knowledge of which almost wholly disappeared in the gloom of the dark ages, and it was not restored until the aspiration for material things, after the arrestment of nearly a millennium, again started the world on the road to prosperity.

QUESTIONS

1.   Why was a more or less elaborate system of accounting needed throughout man's economic development?
2.   Do you agree that paper or similar substance must have been used even in ancient times for accounting purposes? Why?
3.   What evidence is available to indicate that auditor's were needed at the time of Aristotle?
4.   Is accounting always tied to "the aspiration for material things"? Explain.

12   THE ACCOUNTING PROFESSION IN THE UNITED STATES

J. Edward Masters

(Reprinted by permission from *The Journal of Accountancy*, vol. 20, no. 5 (November, 1915): 349-355. Copyright 1915 by the American Institute of Certified Public Acountants, Inc.)

It is obviously impossible to give a full and detailed history of the accounting profession in the brief time (thirty minutes) at my disposal this evening, and I shall therefore of necessity only attempt to touch upon the more important events and notable achievements which stand out as landmarks in the history of the profession in this country down to the present time.

In looking back over the development of the profession in the United States, particularly during the past twenty or twenty-five years, and trying to measure it by the familiar method of comparison, the question arises: Is there any other profession either in this or any other country in which there has been an equal progress in the same length of time? I doubt if there is.

Accounting as a profession in the United States was probably unknown prior to 1870, and from that time to 1885 there were only a few individual practitioners and small firms—and even these few were not really well-trained accountants, but were what were commonly known as "expert bookkeepers." The practice during this period consisted mainly of investigating embezzlements, opening and closing books, examination of accounts in dispute or litigation and adjusting incomplete or incorrect accounts. Little, if any, auditing was done and certainly the broader and more important duties and responsibilities of the accountant of today were not then performed or assumed.

The rapid growth of business during the past twenty-five or thirty years, especially the formation of large concerns whereby immense sums of capital were concentrated and employed in certain undertakings, very materially increased the demand for improved bookkeeping methods and systems and particularly the services of capable accountants. For the profession to keep pace with this demand was no small matter when we realize that properly qualified accountants cannot acquire the necessary education and training short of several years. The general development of accounting in the United States, say from 1885 down to the present time, is marked by three steps of special importance:

1. organization of accounting societies
2. legal recognition through the enactment of CPA laws by state legislatures
3. educational opportunities and growth

ORGANIZATION OF ACCOUNTING SOCIETIES

It was perhaps only natural that the universally accepted principle, "In union there is strength," should be adopted in this case. Hence, in 1887 organization of accountancy in the United States had its birth, largely as a result of the interest and activities of Mr. Edwin

Guthrie, who that year spent some time in the United States, together
with Mr. John Francis, of Philadelphia, and a few other accountants of
New York and Boston. It was on the 20th day of September, 1887, that
the American Association of Public Accountants was formally incorporated
under the laws of New York, and while this is still the name of our national body, the original form of the organization has been materially
changed. In the beginning it was a national body with direct, individual membership, whereas the membership now consists, primarily, of the
state societies.

Ten years after this first organization was formed (that is, in
1897), the first state society was started, due largely to local needs
requiring local societies to assist in the work of building up the profession. One of the important results of these early organizations was
their influence towards the second notable step in the march forward,
that being legal recognition in the form of state laws regulating the
profession and creating the title or degree of certified public accountant.

The development and progress of the profession is closely associated with our national organization, so let us for the moment follow its
history and some of its achievements. In July, 1902, at a meeting of
the Illinois Association of Public Accountants, Mr. George Wilkinson
read a paper in which he set forth the great need of establishing a definite relationship among the local state societies, which at that time
were isolated and powerless to act in affairs of a national character.
He suggested a plan for the coordination of all existing organizations
by the formation of a federation of societies of public accountants.

A committee was formed and a meeting arranged for at Washington,
D.C., in October, 1902, consisting of prominent accountants from different parts of the country, when the "Federation of Societies of Public
Accountants in the United States of America" was formally organized.
This awakened a much deeper interest in the profession and stimulated
its growth. As a result of the untiring efforts of certain members and
the support of many others the next important event was made possible.

In 1904 the first *international* congress of accountants was held in
St. Louis, and attended not only by delegates from the different state
societies but also by representatives from Canada, England, Scotland,
and Wales. At this congress a plan was evolved whereby the next year,
1905, the two national societies, the American Association of Public Accountants and the Federation of Societies of Public Accountants, were
united, the name and seal of the American Association being retained,
but a new constitution drawn up and adopted, having for its motives:

1. the bringing together in friendly contact the different
   state societies and members of the profession
2. the encouragement and unification of CPA legislation.
   In this organization the principle was adopted that the
   national organization should not interfere with the local
   interests of the different states, but at the same time
   should cooperate with the constituent societies in all
   practicable ways.

Since 1904 the American Association of Public Accountants has held
annual conventions in the fall of each year in different states. The
opportunity they have afforded for accountants from all parts of the

country to meet and become better acquainted and exchange ideas on the numerous accounting principles and conditions, some of which were new as applied to the situation in the United States, has been of immeasurable benefit in establishing standards and ideals, reconciling differences of opinion, cementing the professional bonds of state societies and individuals, and last, but not least, in bringing to the attention of the business world right methods and practices, not only in accounting matters but also in the organization and conduct of business, for it is with business that the accounting profession goes onward hand in hand.

One of the best indications of the progress of the profession to a higher level is that during, we will say, the last ten or twelve years the public has relied more and more on the accountant for advice and guidance in business matters, quite apart from those of a strictly accounting nature. The growth in numbers has been rapid considering the rather limited educational advantages and opportunities to obtain the necessary experience. We have no exact data as to the total number of practicing accountants, including those not certified, but the steady increase in the membership of the American Association of Public Accountants gives a good idea of the growth. At the time of its original incorporation in 1887 the membership was less than 100, and in 1905, when it combined with the federation, the total was 597, and now it is approximately 1,100, having almost doubled in the last ten years.

There are many accountants not members of our state or national societies and who are not CPA's, the number probably far exceeding those that have obtained the degree.

LEGAL RECOGNITION

The first CPA law was passed by the state of New York in April, 1896, second by Pennsylvania in 1899, third by Maryland in 1900, fourth by California in 1901, fifth by Washington in 1903, sixth by Illinois in 1903, seventh by New Jersey in 1904.

Since 1904 similar state laws have been passed in rapid succession, the year 1914 being a record in that six states enacted such laws, namely: Arkansas, Kansas, Indiana, Iowa, South Carolina, and Texas, making a total number of thirty-nine states which now have CPA laws, leaving only nine without: Alabama, Arizona, Idaho, Kentucky, Mississippi, New Hampshire, New Mexico, Oklahoma, and South Dakota.

Although the laws of the different states vary in some respects, they are uniform in regard to the following particulars:

1. the title of CPA
2. a board of examiners to pass upon applicants
3. the penalty—an unauthorized person using title or initials "CPA" is guilty of a misdemeanor—which is punishable by fine or imprisonment.

The fact that during the last nineteen years thirty-nine states have put CPA laws upon the statute books is another striking illustration of the steadily increasing activities of the profession and represents a great deal of time and effort by those individual accountants who have fathered the legislation in the respective states.

As might be expected, not all the laws enacted are ideal, and while much has been done toward uniformity there is still great need for improvement in the standards, qualifications, etc. In this connection a difficult problem confronts us owing to the limitations of state laws. An accountant's practice almost invariably extends beyond the particular state in which he resides and from which he obtains the CPA degree, and, therefore, the rather complicated question of state rights, or rather control, arises—hence the desirability, and we may say almost the necessity, in the near future, of some form of national registration or granting of the degree. The accomplishment of this will doubtless be the next important step in this direction.

In addition to legal recognition in the form of CPA laws a few states have passed acts requiring the audit of certain kinds of business. For instance, the legislature of Massachusetts in 1910 made it compulsory for all savings banks to be audited once a year by a certified public accountant. This requirement has since been modified to the extent that the bank commissioner can make the audit if so desired by the bank. The statutes of Massachusetts further require an auditor's certificate or report in the following cases:

1. to the financial statements of all concerns borrowing money from saving banks
2. to the annual report of all corporations doing business in the state, which must be filed with the secretary of the commonwealth. The auditor in these cases is not required by the laws to be a CPA, although there is a growing tendency to select the accountant with the degree.

There has been a marked tendency during the past few years on the part of the general public and government authorities to avail themselves of accountants' services in safeguarding the interests of investors and in regulating business, which is still another evidence of the growth of the profession and the important position it has attained. It is only in comparatively recent years that it has become the practice of bankers to require in many instances the accountant's certificate to financial statements in connection with the flotation of securities or the granting of credit, and also to see that the auditor's certificate is attached to published reports to stockholders and others.

EDUCATIONAL OPPORTUNITIES AND GROWTH

As every institution, in order to succeed, must be built on a sound foundation, so it is with our profession, the groundwork being education. Those members practicing in the earlier days had very limited opportunities in the United States to obtain the particular education to fit them for the work; there were no schools and very little literature.

About 1892 the American Association of Public Accountants started in New York a small school for the study of accountancy which, however, was not long continued.

In 1900 Mr. Charles Waldo Haskins organized classes for the study of accountancy subjects at the school of commerce, accounts, and finance of the New York University.

About this time certain members of the Pennsylvania Institute of Certified Public Accountants started evening classes for the study of accountancy and for the preparation of candidates for the CPA examinations.   These classes were afterwards turned over to the Wharton school of accounts and finance of the University of Pennsylvania.

Certain colleges and universities had previously started departments for the study of commerce and finance, the first being that of the University of Pennsylvania established in 1881.   To these departments have been added in many instances accountancy courses, until now nineteen of our colleges and universities are teaching the subject, besides numerous private schools, and there are in the neighborhood of from 10,000 to 15,000 students enrolled.   In the development of these schools many of our members have devoted much of their time at considerable self-sacrifice, and to these able and faithful pioneers the profession is greatly indebted.   As a result we have not only a profession but a learned one.

Along with the development of the profession and the educational progress came the official publication, *The Journal of Accountancy*, which was first started in 1905.   It is issued monthly and the present circulation is about four thousand.

To bring the subject down to the present moment, this occasion marks the first joint meeting of the national bodies of accountancy in the Dominion of Canada and the United States of America.   May it be the beginning of a closer affiliation of the profession in the two countries, thus assisting to fulfill even better in the future that which is required of us, and to make our profession of still greater importance and usefulness to the business world.

QUESTIONS

1.   What gave impetus to the beginning of the public accounting profession in the United States?
2.   What are the benefits derived from professional organizations in an economic sense?
3.   Why were CPA laws adopted?

---

13   ACCOUNTANCY IN IDAHO

Byron Defenbach

(Reprinted by permission from *The Journal of Accountancy*, vol. 21, no. 1 (January, 1916): 50-51.   Copyright 1916 by the American Institute of Certified Public Accountants, Inc.)

A paragraph in the interesting report of President Joplin indicates that there remain only nine of the United States whose laws do not recognize the profession of accountancy. Idaho is one of these states, and it might be of interest to the readers of *The Journal of Accountancy* to hear some of the arguments put forth in that state on the two sides of the question of legislative enactment.

House bill No. 194 was introduced in our last session of the state legislature. It was based on existing laws of similar import in Washington and Oregon. It provided for its own financial support without expense to the state and was intended for the "examination of, and issuance of certificates to, qualified applicants, with the designation of certified public accountant."

It was argued in support of the measure that Idaho was bordered by Washington, Oregon, Utah, Montana, and British Columbia in all of which the CPA degree was provided for by law; that the peculiar shape of Idaho made every part of it comparatively near to some important business center in a neighboring state such as Spokane, Portland, Salt Lake, and Butte; and that Idaho men practicing accountancy were thrown into competition with nonresidents bearing credentials which no amount of professional efficiency would enable the home men to obtain. It was also shown that the by-laws of corporations were more and more frequently written to require periodical audits by certified public accountants, and that Idaho citizens were absolutely estopped from doing such work.

Outside the question of foreign competition, it was said that the Idaho accountant was in the position of a doctor under such a system as would necessitate his proving his educational qualifications to each individual patient who might be in need of professional services.

The measure as written had the support of most of the accountants of the state, and was not opposed by any of them.

In fact, no opposition of any kind developed in either branch of the legislature, and the bill passed both houses by substantial majorities.

It was vetoed by Governor M. Alexander in the following language:

> *House bill No. 194 has failed to receive my approval.*
> *This act seeks to create another board for special protection*
> *to a single class of individuals engaged in business within*
> *this state . . . I do not believe that it is wise to permit*
> *professions to organize themselves under protection of the*
> *law appointing certain of their own numbers to prescribe*
> *qualifications and rules whereby others who may desire to*
> *engage in such professions may be debarred from doing so.*

This veto is dated March 11, 1915, after the adjournment of the legislature. Had the action been taken at an earlier date it is believed that the bill could have been passed by the necessary two-thirds vote over the governor's disapproval. Due credit should be given to the author of the bill, F. S. Randall, member of the Idaho house from Lewiston. An effort will be made in the next session to pass this or a similar measure.

QUESTIONS

1. Do the CPA laws create a monopoly? Is this good or bad?
   Explain.
2. Why do you think Idaho eventually passed the CPA law?
3. Can certain regulated monopolies be in the best interests
   of society?

---

14 FINANCIAL ACCOUNTING STANDARDS
BOARD: A THIRD GENERATION IN THE
DEVELOPMENT OF ACCOUNTING PRINCIPLES

Robert J. West

(Reprinted by permission from *The Florida Certified Public Account-ant*, vol. 12, no. 2 (January, 1973): 5-13.)

(Robert J. West is a member of the faculty at the University of
South Florida in Tampa.)

The Financial Accounting Standards Board (FASB)—an outgrowth of
the now well-known Wheat Committee Report and the successor to the Accounting Principles Board (APB) of the American Institute of Certified
Public Accountants (AICPA)—is expected to be in operation around the
beginning of 1973. The FASB will assume formally the responsibilities
of its immediate predecessor, the APB, and the predecessor to the APB,
the Committee on Accounting Procedure of the AICPA. Since in many respects the FASB represents a third generation organizational structure
within which accounting principles may be developed, it seems appropriate to reflect for a moment on the accomplishments (as well as the lack
thereof) on the part of the previous organizations that held the primary responsibility for the development of accounting principles during
the late 1930s until the present.

Quite often a look at the historical events which lead to the current structure of an organization provides the insight necessary for
relevant evaluation and analysis as to whether or not the new organizational structure (the FASB) will enable the accounting profession to
attain its objectives; objectives that under the previous organizational
structures in the eyes of supporters proved to be only partially attained, or in the minds of critics, not attained at all. In this paper
the writer presents first a brief historical perspective of significant
events which led to the structuring of the FASB and secondly, analysis
and prediction as to whether or not the accounting profession with the
FASB will be able to attain the goals that eluded its predecessors.

HISTORICAL PERSPECTIVE: 1932-1959

The birth of the Securities & Exchange Commission (SEC) through the Securities Acts of 1933 and 1934 provided incentive for the private sector to become deeply concerned and involved with the development and clarification of accounting principles. Incentive for deeper involvement in this critical area of financial accountability stemmed in part from the fact that the Securities Act of 1933 gave to the public sector via the SEC and other regulatory agencies the authority to:

> . . . *make, amend, and rescind such rules and regulations governing registration statements and prospectuses for various classes of securities, and defining accounting, technical, and trade terms used in this title. . . . prescribe the form or forms in which required information shall be set forth, the items in which required information shall be set forth, the items or details to be shown in the balance sheet and earnings statement, and the methods to be followed in the preparation of accounts, . . .(1)*

Since its inception, the AICPA demonstrated keen interest and leadership in the private sector for the structuring and development of the financial reporting practices and procedures commonly referred to as generally accepted accounting principles. Formal progress in this endeavor began in 1932 when the AICPA's committee on cooperation with stock exchanges recommended five rules (2) to the New York Stock Exchange for consideration. These five rules plus an additional statement concerning donated stock were adopted by the AICPA membership in 1934 and represented the beginning of a long and often frustrating attempt by public sector institutions to clarify acceptable accounting principles and procedures.

As a result of the early cooperative effort between the AICPA and the New York Stock Exchange, the Committee on Accounting Procedure of the AICPA was formed in 1938. The objective of the AICPA and the Committee was to develop a program of accounting research and the publication of opinions. These opinions should ". . . narrow areas of difference and inconsistency in accounting principles, . . ." (3) During the twenty years of its existence the Committee issued 51 Accounting Research Bulletins (ARBs), many of which still constitute expressions of generally accepted accounting principles in their respective areas. While the ARBs did serve as a media through which generally accepted accounting principles could be clarified, the ARBs did little to eliminate the sometimes multitude of ways in which a business transaction could be reported within the framework of generally accepted accounting principles.

Illustrative of the flexibility in acceptable accounting practice and the lack of disclosure condoned by the Committee is the position taken in October, 1954 when ARB 44 was issued. In ARB 44 the Committee expressed the opinion that accelerated depreciation methods were "systematic and rational" and therefore constituted acceptable accounting methodology. However, a requirement that the depreciation method followed in the preparation of the financial report must be disclosed was not forthcoming until much later when APB Opinion No. 12 was issued in December, 1967. Thus flexibility in measurement methodology was ac-

ceptable but disclosure of the specific method followed was not required
by the Committee on Accounting Procedure.

For the valuation of inventories, the Committee in ARB 43 permitted
the use of FIFO cost, average cost, and LIFO cost. Criteria for the selection of an inventory pricing method was to be ". . . the one which,
under the circumstances, most clearly reflects net income." (4) However, the Committee never considered the definition of the accounting
concept of periodic net income, although it did recommend disclosure of
the inventory pricing methodology.

Perhaps due mainly to the lack of disclosure and the numerous acceptable ways in which a transaction or event could be quantified and
reported to statement users, the profession of accountancy endured a
turbulent period during the mid and late 1950s. Criticism was abundant,
both from within the profession as well as from outsiders. Widely publicized were examples of two companies, identical in every respect with
the exception of the accounting practices followed. (5) Large variances
were disclosed in reported earnings per share figures, caused not by
managerial effectiveness in the use of resources, but instead caused by
managerial effectiveness in the selection of accounting reporting policies. Perhaps it was this flexibility that caused Leonard Spacek, then
senior partner at Arthur Andersen & Company, to declare: "My profession
appears to regard a set of financial statements as a roulette wheel for
investors—and it's their tough luck if they don't understand the risk
that's involved in interpreting any accounting report." (6)

Additional criticism was directed towards the Committee for its approach to the problem of accounting principle development. It was often
argued that too much time was spent in a "putting out brush fires" approach to accounting problems rather than devoting attention and resources to the researching of fundamental issues and the development of
a consistent theoretical structure. Inconsistency in logic is quite
frequently found in the ARBs simply because of the pragmatic problem
solving approach that was the *modus operandi* of the Committee on Accounting Procedure. And as one might suspect, when an ad hoc problem
solving approach was utilized the Committee often found itself expressing opinions to the effect that several alternative practices were
equally acceptable without spelling out the conditions that must exist
in order for each alternative to be acceptable.

In spite of the many criticisms that were leveled at the Committee
and the ARB program, the Committee did serve as a vehicle by which prevailing contemporary views and practices concerning a problem could be
synthesized and publicized in the format of a quasi-official pronouncement, namely an ARB. Authoritativeness of the ARBs, however, rested
with their general acceptability by the generators and the users of the
accounting reports. Effective enforcement of the ARBs, however, rested
with the SEC.

HISTORICAL PERSPECTIVE: 1959-1973

In September of 1959 the "second generation" organizational structure (the Accounting Principles Board) was created by the Council of the
AICPA with the hopes that it would:

*. . . free the world of the blight of alternatives in account-
ing principles. (7)   The APB was to represent a fresh and new
approach to the development of accounting principles.   Its
familiar sounding objectives were . . . to narrow areas of
difference and inconsistency in accounting practices, and to
further the development and recognition of generally accepted
accounting principles, through the issuance of opinions and
recommendations . . . (8)*

One of the prime goals of the new organizational structure was to
emphasize research.   An accounting research division was established
within the AICPA.   While independent of the APB, the research division
functioned to provide the members of the APB with in-depth research
studies and informative treatises dealing with accounting problems.
The APB was to consider the studies, but was not bound by them, in
rendering its formal opinions.

During the Board's tenure, it has been active; the APB has issued
(as of December, 1972) 25 APB Opinions and currently has plans to issue several more before it is succeeded by the FASB in January, 1973.
In addition to the APB Opinions, the Board has issued four APB Statements, three of which are concerned directly with accounting principles
and reporting disclosure.

Depending upon the individual questioned some conclude that the
APB has been fairly successful in its endeavors, while others feel that
it has been a complete failure.   Those who would defend the APB point to
the decisive positions that it took in the narrowing of accounting alternatives.   Specifically the following could be included in a list of
its accomplishments:

Opinion No. 3 recommended (but did not require) that an all financial resources version of the funds flow statement be an integral part
of financial reports.   When the persuasive nature of Opinion No. 3 did
not achieve the desired objective, Opinion No. 19 was issued in which
the all financial resources version of the funds flow is required whenever an income report accompanies a statement of financial position in
a financial report.

Opinion No. 9 resolved to a great extent the "all-inclusive;
current-operating" argument over the determinants of periodic net income.

Opinion No. 11 settled much of the interperiod income tax allocation controversy in that it required comprehensive tax allocation be
implemented when there exist timing differences between financial and
taxable net income.

Opinion No. 22 requires that in those reporting situations in
which there exist alternative accounting measurement techniques, the
measurement principle followed must be disclosed clearly.

Another frequently mentioned "plus" which should be included in any
listing of APB accomplishments occurred in 1964 when the Council of the
AICPA recommended to the membership ". . . that departures from Opinions
of the Accounting Principles Board (as well as effective Accounting Research Bulletins issued by the former Committee on Accounting Procedure)
are disclosed . . ." (9)   Prior to the issuance of this recommendation
by the Council, a statement user was not always certain whether or not
the APB Opinions which pertained to the situation were being followed,

or whether "substantial authoritative support" might justify an alternative procedure.

Critics of the APB argue that the APB has been "too little, too late." Quite often, the general feeling has been that the APB, in order to gain the necessary majority of its eighteen members for the publication of an Opinion, sometimes "waters down" its original position. And, in some situations, it has been known to reverse completely a previously held position. Such a view appeared recently in the financial press: "The accounting profession's rule-making body, already typecast as Casper Milquetoast for repeatedly watering down stiff accounting proposals in recent years, appears ready to play the same role in a new drama." (10)

Perhaps the "Casper Milquetoast" image of the APB was nourished by the series of events which took place within the APB during the development and issuance of Opinions No. 16 and 17, Opinions concerned with the accounting for business combinations. Many of the early proposals (for example, the relative size criteria which began at a ratio of nine to one and was toned down until it was eliminated completely in the final version of APB 16) were modified significantly in order to gain the two-thirds majority of the Board necessary for the issuance of an APB Opinion. In fact, if it were not for splitting the Opinion on business combinations into two separate Opinions, APB 16 on purchase versus pooling of interests and APB 17 on goodwill accounting (the Board had planned originally to treat these issues in a single Opinion), the new rules would not have been adopted by the APB. A brief description of the Board's strategy follows:

> *Three members were against the total package; however, only three others opposed the business combination rules. By splitting them, Opinion No. 16 passed. Two other members dissented to the intangible assets Opinion bringing the total Opinion No. 17 nays to only five, a passing mark. If it had been issued as a single document, these would have been eight dissents and the 'bloody battle' would have continued. (11)*

The first reversal of a previously held position came in 1964 with the issuance of Opinion No. 4. In Opinion No. 2 the APB favored the deferral method in the accounting for the investment tax credit. In Opinion No. 4, the Board reversed its position. It is well-known the Board was reacting to a statement (Accounting Series Release No. 96) from the SEC to the effect that the Commission would not uphold APB Opinion No. 2, and without the support of the SEC, the APB Opinion had little meaning.

In 1971, the APB attempted to eliminate the duality in accounting methods prevalent in the accounting for the income effects of the investment tax credit when it circulated an Exposure Draft of a Proposed APB Opinion on the subject. In the Exposure Draft the Board again expressed a preference for the deferral method, the position taken originally in 1962 with Opinion No. 2. The APB withdrew its support of the deferral method when the United States Congress passed legislation which provided that "no taxpayer shall be required, without his consent to use . . . any particular method of accounting for the credit." Thus in the light of an exposure draft recommending the deferral method, congress legislated the acceptance of either deferral or flow-through when reporting to federal agencies.   In effect, the congressional act legislated an accounting principle.

Many critics of the APB charge that the Board moves too slowly and that repeatedly major problems are not studied and Opinions publicized until years after the accounting problem began to appear.   The following statement typifies the thinking of those who hold this view:

> . . . the APB did not face up to requiring a corporation to consider the potential impact of convertible debentures on earnings per share until 1969, years after James J. Ling, an imaginative pioneer in financial strategy started using them at at Ling-Timco-Vought to acquire companies.   And only late last year did it start probing the off-the-balance sheet financing of jet aircraft and other kinds of leasing devices. (12)

Much of the progress made by the APB during the twelve years of its existence is in the area of publicizing accounting practices and, where alternative practices and/or principles exist, requiring disclosure of the specific accounting methodology used in the financial report.   This progress has been achieved largely through the issuance of APB Opinions and Statements.

Much of the lack of progress on the part of the APB may be attributed to the "quasi-independent" nature of the Board and reliance upon others for implementation of its opinions.   Each member of the Board is part-time, and as such carries a dual responsibility as a member of his own firm or organization as well as a member of the APB.   Pressures might arise in which the Board member's responsibility for the public interest conflicts with the Board member's firm and client responsibilities.   Quite often perhaps, the part-time Board member with dual responsibilities causes a lack of timeliness and/or tends to promote compromise of position—the end result of which is described by Mr. Philip K. Defliese, Chairman of the APB, in testimony before the Wheat Committee, as a ". . . 'damned if you do and damned if you don't attitude.' . . ." (13) by persons to whom the APB is responsible.

Perhaps the demise of the APB and the creation of the FASB were accelerated in the late 1960s when the basic question of "fairness" and "generally accepted accounting principles" was cited in the *Continental Vending* decision. (14)   In *Continental Vending*, Judge Henry J. Friendly took the position that the first responsibility of the independent accountant was to be "fair" and that this meant much more than merely "fair within generally accepted accounting principles."   A very stimulating part of Judge Friendly's benchmark decision, the full impact of which is yet to be known, reads:

> The first law for accountants was not compliance with generally accepted accounting principles but, rather, full and fair disclosure, fair presentation and, if principles did not produce this brand of disclosure, accountants could not hide behind the principles but had to go behind them and make whatever disclosures were necessary for full disclosure.   In a word, 'present fairly' was a concept separate from 'generally accepted accounting principles,' and the latter did not necessarily result in the former.

If compliance with accounting principles must result in a fair presentation to all of the various segments of society, then, there exists an urgent need to incorporate the views of as many of the various segments of society as is possible in their development. It is this notion that gave weight to the voices of those who desired to establish the Wheat Committee.

STRUCTURE OF THE FINANCIAL ACCOUNTING STANDARDS BOARD

Out of the Wheat Committee Report (15) came the FASB, the third generation structure for private sector leadership in the development of generally accepted accounting principles. Membership on the Board consists of seven full-time members, of which four shall be accounting practitioners and three shall be chosen from among academicians, lawyers, financial analysts, financial executives, etc. Board members are appointed by the Board of Trustees of the Financial Accounting Foundation (FAF), a group of nine individuals (four CPAs from public practice, two financial executives, one financial analyst, one academician, and the President of the AICPA) whose primary responsibilities are to raise funds to finance the operations of the FASB as well as to appoint Board members. They shall serve staggered appointments of five years and are required to sever their business affiliations.

An advisory council consisting of twenty nonpaid members selected so that not more than five members represent a single sphere of activity shall be established by the Board of Trustees of the FAF. Its responsibilities shall consist of assisting the Board in setting its priorities, advising on the establishment of task forces, and expressing views on Board proposals.

WILL THE FASB BE SUCCESSFUL?

The major criticisms that are directed towards the APB center around the Board's ineptness in its ability to discharge its responsibilities in a timely manner. The functioning of the Board has been hampered because of:

1. part-time membership of CPAs who have dual responsibilities,
2. reliance on "voluntary acceptance" of its pronouncements rather than required implementation of its pronouncements, and
3. an inability and/or unwillingness to issue an opinion that deviates far from the position that government regulatory agencies are willing to accept.

Many of these obstacles faced by the predecessor APB will be alleviated —but not eliminated—by the structure of the FASB.

Part-time Membership and Dual Responsibilities

Perhaps the most significant structural change is the provision for full-time members of the Board who have severed all relationships with their former organizations. This provision should allow the Board to concentrate on the development of general accounting standards, as opposed to the "brush fire" problem solving approach. In addition, the appearance of independence (if not independence in fact) should be enhanced by full-time Board members. Awareness of the profession's obligation to represent the public interest should be greater because three of the seven members are selected from fields outside of the public accounting profession. A full-time Board without business affiliation ought to be able to operate at a faster speed than its part-time predecessors.

By accepting the structure of the FASB and the FAF the accounting profession is lessening its influence on the development of accounting principles. Membership on both the predecessor organizations to the FASB consisted of a vast majority of accounting practitioners all of whom were CPAs. Under the new FASB structure, only four members of the seven member Board are CPAs and an affirmative vote of five members is necessary to approve a standard. Likewise, a two-thirds majority is necessary for action on the nine member FAF (except for structural changes in which case eight affirmative votes are necessary) and only five CPAs can be appointed. Thus, one can expect a much broader representation of views in the pronouncements of the FASB than was ever possible under its predecessors. Hopefully, this will be translated into inquiry and pronouncements which are concerned with fundamental questions and broad principles rather than techniques for handling specific problem situations.

Acceptance of FASB Pronouncements

Acceptance of a FASB pronouncement has two separate but related aspects: acceptance by accounting practitioners and acceptance by government regulatory agencies, mainly the SEC. Acceptance of pronouncements by members of the AICPA at present is not mandatory if the practitioner can find elsewhere "substantial authoritative support" for a principle that differs with an APB opinion. An attempt was made in the direction of mandatory compliance in 1969 but the AICPA membership defeated a Council proposal that in effect would have required compliance with APB opinions by AICPA members. This issue is to be voted on again in late 1972 and if adopted should provide the compliance "stimuli" that should enhance the potential for success on the part of the FASB.

Acceptance of FASB pronouncements by the SEC and other regulatory agencies represents another major obstacle for the Board. In the final analysis the SEC has the legal authority to govern the accounting practices of a majority of the reporting entities in the United States. More recently, congress has deemed it necessary to "don the hat of accounting theorist" and legislate accounting procedures for the investment tax credit. Although in the past the SEC and the AICPA have worked together more or less in harmony, a structure that separates the role of developer from that of enforcer becomes untenable when the enforcer disagrees with the developer. In the future when important and controversial issues that affect a large segment of the economy arise, the writer foresees an increasing amount of involvement by government in the development of accounting principles. In those situations where government action runs counter to FASB pronouncements (assuming, of course, that the FASB is willing to issue such a pronouncement) CPAs must stand ready to issue qualifications in their audit reports. A look at the past record gives one little hope for the future in this regard, unless, of course, compliance with FASB pronouncements becomes mandatory on the part of accounting practitioners.

FOOTNOTES

1. 48 Stat. 85 (1933), as amended, 15 U.S. Code 77s (1958 edition).
2. The five rules are concerned with unrealized profit, capital surplus, earned surplus of a subsidiary created prior to acquisition, treasury stock, and receivables from officers and employees.
3. American Institute of Certified Public Accountants, *Accounting Research and Terminology Bulletins*, Final Edition (New York: The Institute, 1961), p. 8.
4. Ibid., p. 29.
5. Perhaps one of the best examples of this phenomenon is the Company A—Company B profit and loss comparison developed by Leonard Spacek and presented as part of a speech to the Financial Accounting Class at Harvard University September 25, 1959. In the illustration Company A uses liberal, but acceptable, accounting principles and had earnings per share in the amount of $1.79 while Company B uses conservative, but acceptable accounting principles and reports earnings per share in the amount of $.80. For a complete comparison see Selected Addresses of Leonard Spacek, *A Search for Fairness In Financial Reporting* (Chicago: Arthur Andersen & Co., 1969).
6. Frederick C. Klein, "Accounting Reform" *Wall Street Journal*, May 16, 1966.
7. Earnest L. Hicks, "APB: The First 3600 Days" *The Journal of Accountancy*, September, 1967, p. 56.
8. *APB Accounting Principles: Current Text As Of February 1, 1971*, Volume One (New York: Commerce Clearing House, 1971), p. 32.
9. Council of the American Institute of Certified Public Accountants, "Disclosure of Departures from Opinions of the Accounting Principles Board" (Special Bulletin, Effective December 31, 1965).
10. *Wall Street Journal*, February 16, 1972.
11. Edmund R. Noonan and James M. Quibley, "Impact of New Rules on Accounting for Business Combinations," *World* (Published by Peat, Marwick, and Mitchell & Co., Spring, 1972), p. 7.
12. "Accounting: A Crisis over Fuller Disclosure," *Business Week*, April 22, 1972, p. 56.

13. Gordon M. Johns, "Reflections on the Wheat Committee Recommendations," *The CPA Journal*, July, 1972, p. 534.
14. CCA Fed. Sec. L. Rep. (2nd Cir. Nov. 12, 1969).
15. Report of the Study on Establishment of Accounting Principles, *Establishing Financial Accounting Standards* (New York: American Institute of Certified Public Accountants, March, 1972).

QUESTIONS

1. What caused the Congress to enact The Securities Act of 1933?
2. What caused the Congress to enact The Securities Exchange Act of 1934?
3. What was the condition of financial reports before 1930?
4. Where did the phrase "in accordance with accepted accounting principles" originate?
5. What arrangements were instituted between the American Institute and the SEC to develop accounting principles?

15   ACCOUNTING IN THE EUROPEAN ECONOMIC COMMUNITY

David F. A. Davidson

(Reprinted by permission from *The International Accountant*, vol. 42, no. 248 (September, 1972): 84-86.)

(David F. A. Davidson is a partner, Arthur Anderson & Co., an international firm of accountants.)

It is now clear that those of us concerned with accounting in this country are going to have to broaden our horizons and think much more in European terms rather than purely nationally. Harmonization will take place with Europe in accounting just as it will in many other fields and it would be foolish to assume, as many people appear to, that this will be a one way process. It behooves us all to familiarize ourselves with accounting practices in existing EEC countries so that we understand the influences which will be felt.

Certain basic differences between this country and EEC relevant to accounting and the accountancy profession are well known:

1. The first is that share ownership is much more widespread
    in this country, e.g., there are 3,300 quoted companies in
    the U.K. compared with 2,500 in all EEC countries. We
    have four times as many as the runner-up, France, with
    830. The market capitalization of our quoted companies
    (£50 billion) is nearly 4 times that of Germany, the next
    largest, at £13 billion. Thus, accountancy serves a
    smaller and different market on the Continent.
2. In the U.K. there is a statutory obligation for all com-
    panies of whatever size to have their accounts audited by
    independent professionally qualified auditors. In no
    present EEC country does the obligation for audit go so
    far.
3. The Companies Act 1967 (2nd Schedule) lays down various
    disclosure and accounting requirements and also lays down
    the form of the audit report which requires not only com-
    pliance with the Act but disclosure of "a true and fair
    view" of results. Thus the responsibility given to audi-
    tors is much greater than in EEC countries.
4. The number of accountants in the U.K. engaged in public
    practice, about 25,000, is much higher than in any of
    the EEC countries.
5. As a result of its strength in the U.K. the accountancy
    profession has largely formulated accounting principles
    whereas on the Continent they have been based much on
    the law, with a heavy emphasis on taxation.

Having made these overall comparisons, I must point out that it can
be highly misleading to think in terms of Continental practice because
in reality there is no such thing. Variations from one country to another are great and for this reason I propose examining each of the EEC
countries in turn, starting with the one which has a system closest to
our own, that is The Netherlands.

THE NETHERLANDS

In fact there are very many likenesses between The Netherlands and
the U.K. as far as accountancy is concerned. The profession there is as
long established as it is in this country and the standards maintained
are very high. Qualifying requirements for The Netherlands Institute
are stiff and involve training for eight years. Ethical standards are
also very similar to our own. There are approximately 3,000 members of
the Institute, about half of whom are in practice. Of the latter about
60 percent work in six large firms, of which the largest employs 1,500
people.

All public companies are required to have an independent audit.
There are about 400 quoted companies in Holland, some of which are well
known international firms. The Act on Financial Statements of 1971 has
established disclosure and presentation requirements and it is interesting to note that this Act requires the accounts to reflect the results "fairly and systematically." This is the closest any of the Continental countries come to the U.K. concept of "true and fair view," as
distinct from mere compliance with the law.

One difference is that private companies with total assets below about £1m and share capital less than £650,000 do not have to publish accounts or appoint auditors.   Another point of interest is that replacement accounting is quite commonly used, an indication of the fact that The Netherlands is in the forefront of accounting theory.

GERMANY

Germany, as one might expect, has a well developed, but highly legalistic, approach to accounting.   The central consideration in financial reporting in Germany is compliance with the requirements of the law.   The statutes of the Federal Republic and the decisions of the courts have prescribed in considerable detail the procedures to be followed by companies in reporting financial information to the owners and the public and the accounting practices to be followed.   These practices are strongly influenced, usually on the side of conservatism, by tax laws since tax incentives, including those resulting from accelerated depreciation, can be realized only if amounts deducted for tax purposes are charged to expense for financial accounting purposes.

It is significant to note that about 70 percent of the equity of German public companies is controlled by banks and this is the main reason why accounting is influenced by tax and creditor considerations rather than the demands of a wide investing public.

There are about 550 quoted companies in Germany with market capitalization around 13 billion.   Public companies must be audited by qualified auditors known as Wirtschaftsprufer.   Since 1971, this requirement also applies to very large private companies (GmbH's).   The Institute of Wirtschaftsprufer was formed in 1931 and now has about 2,800 members practicing through about 300 firms or companies, some of which are owned by banks and the largest of which (1,500 employees) is owned by the state.

There is a long training period to qualify as a Wirtschaftsprufer involving firstly a degree, at least six years' practical experience plus several examinations.   In practice, it is rare to qualify before the age of 35.   Many start by qualifying as Steuerberater, which is basically a tax adviser, for which the tests are somewhat less onerous.

Accounting firms carry out all the same functions as U.K. firms, tax consultancy, etc., but it is interesting to note they do not have quite the same relationship with the tax authorities who actually come in and carry out their own audit of taxpayers' records instead of relying on reports from the accountants as in this country.   It is also interesting to note that fee scales for statutory audits are based on size of the company as well as time spent.   Indemnity insurance is compulsory.

The wording of the standard auditor's report reveals an important difference from this country.   Under the Corporation Act of 1965, the opinion is directed solely to conformity with the books, articles of association and the legal requirements and the auditor does not address himself to the more philosophical question of "true and fair view."   The government has been endeavoring to build up the capital market and as this develops there will undoubtedly be more attention paid to accounting principles as such.

LUXEMBOURG

There is an accounting profession consisting of 24 Experts Comptables, all of whom are in practice (three partnerships and 12 sole practitioners).

All Luxembourg companies require auditors. These do not have to be Experts Comptables although this may change soon. The professional firms provide all the usual services in addition to auditing and they have been in much demand as a result of the increased use of tax-exempt Luxembourg holding companies.

BELGIUM

Turning now to Belgium, we begin to see greater divergences from U.K. practice. There are several professional bodies but basically the profession is in two sections:

1. Reviseurs d'Enterprises—concerned solely with auditing and numbering about 300.
2. Expert Comptables—concerned with general accountancy work as well as auditing—about 1,600 members.

In order to become a member of the Institut de Reviseurs d'Enterprises, a person must be aged between 25 and 65 years, he must have completed a three-year training period, taken a university diploma in economics or business administration, or have passed equivalent examinations set by the Institute. Membership of the College National des Experts Comptables is somewhat similar although possibly less restricted. Candidates must pass examinations in accounting, law, administration, economics, mathematics, statistics, and ethics. Exemption from these examinations may be obtained by economics and business graduates. A five-year training period must then be served with a member, at the end of which professional examinations are taken.

Whilst the Belgian Commercial Code has stipulated the appointment, in certain circumstances, of a statutory auditor, nevertheless it has, with one exception, failed to define who is empowered to undertake a statutory audit. Thus, in theory, he need not be trained or qualified in accounting or auditing. Since 1953, however, Belgian company law has required companies which have solicited funds from the public to engage at least one statutory auditor from the Institut de Reviseurs d'Enterprises.

There are 580 quoted companies in Belgium, some very large. All public companies must publicize their accounts but neither the Belgian profession nor the company laws have defined on a comprehensive basis the principles underlying accounting and financial reporting, and Belgian companies follow a variety of practices. Since an accounting practice which has been applied in the preparation of the annual financial statements which is acceptable for tax purposes must be followed in the determination of taxable income, the tax law and regulations have a significant influence on financial reporting practices. The scope of an examination made by a statutory auditor, whether or not he is a member of the Institute, is generally less extensive than the scope of examinations made by U.K. auditors and there is no specified form of report.

FRANCE

Turning to France, we find a fast-developing, although in some respects a still immature, state of accounting practice and the accounting
profession—a state in which old and questionable practices continue to
exist side by side with new and improved ones. The more important developments which are changing the face of French accounting are Le Plan
Comptable and the Commission des Operations de Bourse (COB).

Le Plan Comptable was developed in 1947 by a government-established
commission, and revised in 1957, as a standard system of reporting. Although initially imposed by law only on nationalized industries and on
state-controlled or subsidized business entities, subsequent pronouncements point toward ultimate application, by type of industry, to all
commercial and industrial enterprises. This is now in the process of
being implemented. Unfortunately, however, although the plan gives published financial statements of French companies an appearance of uniformity, in many respects this still does not go beyond the depth of
form. For the majority of accounting and valuation questions, alternative approaches are available: and the results are strongly influenced
by the general requirement that companies must follow the same principles in their financial reporting that they adopt for tax purposes. In
practice, disclosures of the accounting methods and practices used in
the preparation of financial statements is not common.

Hopefully, the COB will have a more fundamental and positive influence. The COB, which is sometimes likened to the U.S. Securities & Exchange Commission, was established in 1968 to control all information
made available to shareholders or published by quoted companies (of
which there are 830), and to monitor and enforce their compliance with
legal financial reporting requirements. Its performance to date offers
a sound basis for hope that the inadequacies that still plague French
financial reporting will be eliminated in due course. It is unfortunate
that the efforts of the COB cannot yet be effectively supported by a
strong auditing profession. Strangely, although every French company
must appoint one or more Commissaires aux Comptes (statutory auditors),
only 60 percent of those on the list of officially approved statutory
auditors are qualified as Experts Comptables, and despite serious legal
and professional attempts to upgrade auditing standards, statutory
audits still may consist of little more than inquiries directed to company personnel.

The standards of qualification as a Commissaire aux Comptes who are
concerned solely with auditing and who number about 6,000, are not high.
This does not apply to Expert Comptables, who have at least a three-year
training period, do several examinations as well as a thesis on accounting. Not many qualify before the age of 30.

Statutory auditors work for fixed fees and are prohibited from
doing other work for their clients. This is one reason why the more
highly skilled Experts Comptables prefer doing other work such as consultancy. The COB has recommended that these rules be changed and they
are also insisting on higher auditing standards for quoted companies.

It, therefore, appears that we shall see considerable improvements
taking place within the near future.

ITALY

In Italy, accounting practices are governed firstly by the Civil Code which lays down certain rules as to content and the basis of valuation but only in very general terms, and secondly the tax laws.

Every company must have between three and five auditors (known collectively as the Sindaci), two of whom must be qualified. However, the duties of the Sindaci are ill-defined and in practice the work they carry out would not be sufficient for them to express an opinion such as contained in the U.K. auditors' report. They attend board meetings and inspect cash and securities every quarter.

The profession is basically in two sections. Firstly there are Doctors of Commerce (Dottori Commercialsti), numbering about 15,000 with roughly half in public practice. Then there are Accountants and Commerical Experts, who number about 7,000, mostly in practice. The main difference between the two is that the former are orientated towards the academic aspects of professional practice whereas the latter places emphasis on the practical side. Most carry on business as sole practitioners although partnerships are beginning to come in. The full range of services is usually provided with statutory audit work representing only a small fraction.

One of the major problems in Italy is that accounts are not relied on in the determination of taxable incomes. The inductive method is used—this is based on sales and various factors relative to the type of business, etc. Appeal procedures are very costly and in practice it is necessary to negotiate a settlement with the tax inspector. Accounts are therefore designed to produce the best tax advantage and it is not at all uncommon to omit sales, understate assets (especially inventories), introduce fictitious liabilities and so on. Secret bank accounts are an essential part of the system. Presumably changes will take place, but it is very hard to imagine that they will be as rapid as elsewhere.

CONCLUSION

Thus, we have a very "mixed bag" of European accounting and although there are various forces at work it has to be admitted that harmonization will be a very slow process. Wider share ownership in Europe will undoubtedly have an important effect although there is something of a chicken and egg problem in that the public will not invest until they have greater faith in accounts. The stock exchanges and similar bodies will exert a strong influence but here also the direct effect will be limited to quoted companies.

Properly directed, the accountancy profession should be able to play a major role even though it has been said, not entirely in jest, that accounting is far too important to leave to accountants. It certainly has to be admitted that experience in this country and the U.S.A. has revealed certain dangers in leaving accounting questions wholly to the profession. It is to be hoped, however, that in the harmonized system which eventually emerges in Europe, the role of the accountancy profession as such will be enhanced.

An unduly legalistic view of accounting, such as we have noted earlier in some countries, must be avoided and the draft EEC directive recently issued on the "Annual Accounts of Limited Companies" seems to be doing this. Although to us it may appear preoccupied with form rather than substance, it does leave most matters of principle to the accounting profession. It was also encouraging to hear recently that in response to criticisms from the U.K., the draft directive is being amended so that much more emphasis is given to presenting a true and fair view.

Professional bodies from the EEC country have formed an advisory body to the Commission called the Groupe d'Etudes, and, thus, the first step towards professional cooperation and harmonization has been taken. Progress will be slow because of the wide divergences in political, financial and social environments, but the essential point is that the European profession as a whole accepts the common challenge and tackles the problems in a spirit of unity.

QUESTIONS

1. What are the major differences of accounting between the United Kingdom and the European Economic Community?
2. What are the major differences of accounting between the United States and the European Economic Community?
3. Do you believe that the differences noted above need to be or can be resolved? Why?
4. Why is readily available accounting information necessary to the wide-spread share ownership in any country? Why is wide-spread share ownership desirable?

---

16   SOVIET ECONOMIC DEVELOPMENTS AND ACCOUNTING

Robert H. Mills
Abbott L. Brown

(Reprinted by permission from *The Journal of Accountancy*, vol. 121 (June, 1966): 40-46. Copyright 1966 by the American Institute of Certified Public Accountants, Inc.)

(Robert H. Mills is a member of the faculty in the College of Business Administration, Lehigh University. Abbott L. Brown is a member of the firm of Price Waterhouse & Co.)

Accounting and control—this is the main thing that is required for the proper functioning of the first phase of communist society. . . . Be able if necessary to learn from the capitalists. Adopt whatever they have that is sensible and advantageous. Lenin

Professor E. Liberman, a leading Soviet economist, wrote a stimulating article on a more important role for "profits" in *Pravda* on September 9, 1962. His remarks touched off one of the most controversial, continuing debates in Soviet economic thought since the great intellectual debates of the 1920s which preceded the Soviet decision to industrialize. His principal suggestions are aimed at motivating Soviet enterprises and firms to seek higher output targets for themselves, encourage the introduction of new technology and new products, and improve the quality of production. In order to achieve the above goals, Liberman's plan calls for less reliance on planned targets and greater use of profit incentives in allowing more freedom for the enterprise manager to more intelligently use resources and achieve greater efficiency.

At the present time, with only a very few exceptions which will be discussed later, planned targets for Soviet firms are handed down from higher administrative units. The manager of the individual firm generally seeks to have target goals set as low as possible since the firm and its personnel are compensated according to the degree of plan fulfillment. Firm managers are reluctant to encourage new technology, new products, and better materials and to improve quality standards, because such changes represent uncertainty. These changes are possible barriers to goal fulfillment in physical terms as well as exerting a direct effect on important cost of production figures.

Liberman's plan calls for the elimination of all centrally planned goals except targets of quantitative production, product assortment, and destination and date of delivery. He feels the factory manager's principal task is the efficient production of quality goods with the elimination of as many predetermined constraints that impede this goal as possible. In order to achieve this goal, Liberman suggests a new measuring tool, the "profitability rate." This is defined as the total profit of the firm in relation to its stock of fixed and working capital. (1) The profitability rate would be important to the plant manager and his subordinates since it would be the sole measuring stick of the size of the bonus fund which the firm and its employees will receive. The plant manager could improve the profitability rate by either increasing the numerator, profits, or decreasing the denominator, fixed capital, and working capital, or some combination of the two.

"Profitability norms" would be established for different industries and firms for a period of two, three, or five years into the future. These norms would serve as a guidepost against which to match the achieved profitability rate in determining bonuses to be awarded to firms. An attempt would also be made to make comparisons of performance between comparable firms. Firms which develop new products or new processes would have lower profitability norms to help offset initial costs and unforeseen problems. Norms would be raised for those firms not innovating. These actions would supposedly induce firms to experiment with new products and new technological methods.

While profits have been calculated for Soviet firms in the past, the measurement of income has been only one of several yardsticks used in determining plant efficiency. More emphasis has been placed on goal fulfillment in terms of meeting or bettering predetermined targets of physical quantities of output and unit costs of production. If Professor Liberman's proposals are widely adopted, the role of income measurement will be much more important to plant managers and higher echelons of state administration than it ever has been before.

Before examining what progress has been made in using profits as an increasingly important incentive device, a brief review of current Soviet accounting practice is in order, noting in particular those areas differing from general American methodology and procedure.

CURRENT SOVIET ACCOUNTING PRACTICE

In the Soviet economic system, accounting alone plays the major role in the whole system of prices and costs with only token assistance from market processes in a few isolated consumer goods industries. The determination of periodic income for the Soviet firm is of secondary importance. This is true because the Soviet firm is not fully independent from a financial standpoint, and few decisions to date have turned on whether the reported earnings are positive or negative. The results of operations are only a vague constraint on the firm's access to resources since resource allocation is basically the domain of the master planners attached to central administrative units.

The Soviet firm maintains one set of documentary records. The record-keeping is called *uchet* and consists of accounting, statistics, and technical records. Accounting is separate from the other two types of records. Accounts are kept under the double-entry system. In general, according to Professor Robert Campbell, "Soviet accounting is virtually identical with traditional capitalist accounting." (2) One very important difference is that accounting rules and procedures are fixed and highly formalized by centralized control over accounting practices. Central administrative units gather monthly reports from all firms based upon standard forms from each industry with the information on these reports drawn from a standardized set of accounts for that industry. As a result, there exists comparatively little controversy in most areas as to the proper way of handling business transactions.

The purpose of such rigidly constructed reports is to facilitate better centralized control and planning. The reports are used in the evaluation of the administrative organizations and resource allocation process and are an integral tool in developing regional and national economic plans.

One area of considerable interest and importance, for several reasons, is cost accounting. The virtual absence of the influence of the market mechanism on prices, except for a few consumer goods to be discussed later, necessitates the determination and fixing of prices primarily on the basis of cost accounting reports. These reports are valid only to the extent that they have been properly prepared and reflect accurate cost data. The unit cost of production has been cited as "probably the most emphasized indicator of success or failure of an enterprise in the U.S.S.R. . . ." (3)

Professor Campbell has summarized the main deficiencies of Soviet cost accounting, upon which unit cost of production figures depends, as resulting primarily from poor estimates of the costs of capital consumption (depreciation), improper allocation of current expenditures among individual kinds of output, failure to charge certain outlays to cost of product, and the use of broad aggregative accounts with the result that expense flows through the plant are poorly traced, costs of individual products or of separate processes are often not ascertainable, and so on. (4)

Problems of rapidly changing technology and the factor of obsolescence, as well as changing price levels for capital goods, plague the Soviet firm as well as its American counterpart in measuring capital consumption (depreciation) costs. The problem of depreciation measurement in the Soviet Union is complicated by the fact that an attempt is made to allocate the estimated cost of major repairs, as well as the original cost of the asset, over the life of the asset. Thus, the depreciation charge consists of two parts. One part is the amortization of original asset cost and the other is an allocation for estimated major repair costs.

The major repairs are called capital repairs; theoretically, these capital repairs are not supposed to extend the life of the asset or increase its productivity over what was anticipated at time of original acquisition. Moreover, to be classified as a capital repair, the repair preferably should occur less than once a year. An example of a capital repair is the rebuilding of an entire engine which does not increase the machine's former productivity or presumably prolong the entire machine's life beyond the original estimate. In actual practice, even though broad guidelines are highly formalized, the distinguishing between capital repairs and ordinary repairs is not clear-cut with resulting differences in the handling of borderline cases.

The apparent rationale for including estimated long-run capital repair charges as part of the depreciation charge is that actual capital repairs would tend to be bunched in time. While this reasoning might hold true for individual assets, it is hard to believe it would apply to broad aggregates of assets held by Soviet firms where a fairly uniform pattern of capital repair charges might be anticipated each period. With heavy emphasis on unit costs of production as a major criterion in evaluation of the operating efficiency of a Soviet firm, the inclusion of estimated capital repair charges as part of the depreciation charge is a device for smoothing out the impact on the cost of production over long periods of time.

All the Soviet depreciation rates are established according to the following formula: The depreciation rate (r) equals $[(V + R - S)/LV]$ 100, where V equals the original value, R equals estimated total expenditure for capital repairs, L equals the expected life of the asset, and S is the estimated salvage value, if any. For example, an asset with an original cost of 5,000 rubles and estimated total capital repairs of 5,000 rubles over a ten-year life with zero salvage value would have a rate of depreciation of 20 percent with 10 percent for capital consumption and 10 percent for capital repairs.

While this method may smooth long-run unit costs, it may not give the best measure of periodic income depending on assumptions as to the pattern of service flows from depreciable assets. It is basically consistent with the straight-line method of depreciation as applied to original asset cost. The method may result in over- (under-) depreciating assets if actual capital repairs are less (more) than estimated capital repairs. It does add an additional complication and subjective element in the estimating of the cost of future repairs including the frequency, quantity, and changes in future prices of such repairs. In addition, a decision must be reached about how much of the depreciation charge applies to capital repairs and how much to original cost expiration since the two portions of the depreciation charge are handled differently.

The portion applicable to the original cost of the asset is recognized as an expense by the Soviet firm but is remitted in cash to the central economic center.   The cash remittances of all firms are pooled at the central location where decisions are made about the distribution of funds for replacement and for new investment.   The portion of the depreciation charge for capital repairs is recognized as an expense, but a reserve fund is established at a state bank which is at the disposal of the Soviet firm making the deposit.

The following example is offered to clarify how the Soviet system operates in regard to capital consumption recognition.   Throughout the example we will refer to the account State Equity Fund.   Actually there is more than one such account.   These accounts are of the proprietorship or the long-term obligation nature.   We will refer to the Central Bank, meaning one of the central banks where funds are kept and distributed according to decisions made by higher administrative units.   The account titles in our example will not necessarily agree with Soviet terminology but are used for clarification of concepts and similarity to American usage.

For this example, assume that a firm has fixed assets of 5,000 rubles for an opening debit balance and an opening credit balance to the State Equity Fund of 5,000 rubles.   Furthermore, assume the fixed assets have an estimated life of 10 years with zero scrap value and that estimated future capital repairs are 5,000 rubles.   This results in a

$$\left(\frac{5,000 + 5,000}{10 \times 5,000} \right) 100 = 20 \text{ percent depreciation rate, with one-half of the}$$

charge for capital repairs and the other half to be sent to the central pool as a result of capital consumption.   The Soviet firm records 1,000 rubles (20 percent × 5,000) as an expense, debiting Cost of Production and crediting Allowance for Depreciation as follows:

Cost of Production	1,000	
Allowance for Depreciation		1,000

Next, the firm debits the State Equity Fund for the full 1,000 rubles and credits 500 rubles to a Reserve for Repairs Fund and credits the other 500 rubles to a Liability to Central Bank account:

State Equity Fund	1,000	
Reserve for Repairs Fund		500
Liability to Central Bank		500

At periodic intervals, cash is remitted to the Central Bank for eventual reallocation by central authorities for replacement and new assets with the following entry being made:

Liability to Central Bank	500	
Cash		500

Assuming capital repairs of 500 rubles are made this period, the firm makes the following two entries:

Capital Repairs	500	
Cash		500
Reserve for Capital Repairs	500	
State Equity Fund		500

To complete the record-keeping, the Allowance for Depreciation account is debited and Capital Repairs is credited with the interpretation being as having made good some of the depreciation on the asset:

Allowance for Depreciation	500	
Capital Repairs		500

How accurate have capital consumption charges been under the above system? According to Professor Campbell, ". . . the charges for depreciation entered in Soviet cost calculations have always been far too low as estimates of capital consumption." (5) In connection with the revaluation of fixed assets in the U.S.S.R. in 1960, the depreciation shown on the books for all assets was only half the actual depreciation.

A strong theoretical argument can be made for the Soviet method of including estimated capital repairs cost in attempting to allocate total capital costs over estimated service lives of fixed assets. The difficulty lies in correct implementation of the concept with the additional uncertainties of forecasting both volume and price levels of capital repairs anticipated.

Another problem with Soviet capital consumption recognition is that depreciation rates are not established by individual firms but are established by higher administrative units. Since firm managers have quotas and standards to meet, physical output and cost reduction are important goals. Managers may tend to be wasteful of capital assets in order to keep both physical output high and unit cost of production low. In addition, managers are not penalized for failing to make assets serve out the estimated service lives envisaged at the time they were acquired. When assets are sold or disposed of, any retirement gain or loss is transferred directly to the State Equity Fund and does not even enter into Profit and Loss computations. (6)

In summary, the Soviet system for the recognition of depreciation is geared to an attempt to provide the best long-run average unit cost data possible. This is important since prices, in turn, are often based on reported costs. It would appear that depreciation charges in general have been understated in the past primarily because of the difficulties of estimating capital repair costs as part of the depreciation base and the failure to adequately recognize obsolescence in the establishment of depreciation rates by central authorities. All depreciation rates are calculated by one basic formula in the Soviet Union in contrast to numerous formulas available to American firms. The Soviet firm does attempt to spread capital repair costs over the entire life of the asset, whereas American firms would basically adjust depreciation to be recognized in the future only after capital repair expenditures have been made. Retirement gains or losses do not enter into profit and loss computations for Soviet firms in contrast to general American practice.

All the above factors would contribute to significant differences in income measurement between Soviet and American firms where capital consumption costs were an important item. The procedure of remitting to a central bank for reassignment that portion of the depreciation charge pertaining to the original value of the asset while retaining local control of funds for capital repairs is a unique evolutionary device which the Soviets have found useful in a planned economy. Prior to 1938, funds for capital repairs were also remitted to the central bank for reassignment.

In addition to the problem of recognition of capital consumption costs, another major concern of Soviet accounting is the allocation of costs to production. The allocation of direct material and direct labor costs provides no special problem since they can be directly attributed to specific outputs. This is usually done but there are some exceptions to direct assignment of these costs. (7) For the Soviet manufacturing firm, overheads are generally accumulated in four broad accounts called shop expenses, general plant expenses, auxiliary shops (factory service centers), and nonproduction expenses including selling, maintenance of finished goods warehouses, research, etc. Shop expenses and general plant expenses are almost always distributed to output in proportion to wages of production workers. This tends to introduce errors where there is a high ratio of shop expenses to production wages, and substantial portions of the overhead are more related to machine operations than to direct labor. The expenses of auxiliary shops (factory service centers) were previously included in general plant expenses but recently there has been a tendency to keep them in a separate category and assign them to the production shops benefited. The nonproduction expenses are generally distributed among outputs in proportion to total factory costs being treated as some type of general overhead. General plant and shop expenses are usually assigned to unfinished production only in planned amounts with the remainder charged off to finished production. It is felt desirable to do this for control purposes to avoid accumulation of excess expenditures in unfinished production accounts. These procedures can result in distortions in cost reports, balance sheet valuations for unfinished and finished product, and income measurement.

Attempts to allocate overhead of Soviet firms are generally fairly crude. It also must be recognized that traditional period expenses such as selling, general administration, and research are allocated in some fashion to the cost of product's becoming part of the inventory accounts. Most of the expenses of the numerous higher administrative control units are not allocated to the Soviet firm but are absorbed by the national budget. Furthermore, much research that is done on behalf of firms and industries is financed out of the national budget and is not charged to the individual firms on the theory that they are of benefit to the economy in general. There are certain outlays that are not included in the cost of production but are charged directly to profit and loss, such as losses on canceled orders, inventory shortages and losses, expenditures on fruitless experiments, fines, penalties, forfeits, losses from production risks not envisaged in the plan, losses of subsidiary enterprises, and losses from stoppages. Many of the practices described above would of necessity produce income and valuation measurements significantly different from American practice.

There are some additional weaknesses in the Soviet system of accounting if profits are to play an ever more important role and maximum efficiency is desired. Reports to higher administrative units are geared toward emphasizing the operation of the plant as a whole as well as placing too much emphasis on unit costs of production. Too little attention has been focused on looking at the internal operations of the enterprise in terms of the cost of individual processes, operations and responsibility units. The concept of flexible budgeting is apparently not employed or employed only in rare cases. Fixed budgets, drawn up in great detail by central control authorities, are alleged to be infrequently employed as a control device by plant managers. (8)

One reason for the lack of better internal accounting information is that the chief accountant of the Soviet enterprise has traditionally been the servant of higher administrative agencies and not of the enterprise manager. In addition, the low level of mechanization available for clerical functions has necessitated the accumulation of quantitative data in broad aggregates. There apparently has been some slight improvement in internal reporting recently, however. (9) The caliber of people attracted to accounting in the Soviet Union has not been very high because of low pay, long hours, excessive bureaucratic rules, controls, and volume of detailed work.

Having examined in some detail differences in accounting practice and income measurement between Soviet and American firms, let us now examine those areas where "profits" are playing a more important role.

SOVIET EXPERIMENTATION WITH PROFITS AS AN INCENTIVE AND THE "MARKET" MECHANISM

In the summer of 1964 the reformers who advocate less centralized planning and more reliance on the market mechanism and the measurement tool of profits as a primary incentive device were finally given an opportunity to test their theories. The factory managers apparently had even more freedom and flexibility than originally advocated by Liberman. (10) Two large clothing factories were permitted to negotiate prices and sell suits and dresses directly to 22 retail stores. The stores placed orders directly with the factories for the kinds of goods consumers wanted. The factories were to be judged by the profits made on goods actually sold by their retail stores. Factories had a free hand in setting their production schedules and deciding on their work force.

Within six months inventories were sharply reduced and both profits and quality had improved substantially. One of the factory managers reported that the profit margin had risen to 7 percent, that the average pay per employee had increased from $94 a month to $110 and that the factory was making better suits at a cheaper price. (11) So successful was this experiment that Premier Kosygin, shortly after assuming office late in 1964, announced that the new system would be spread in gradual stages throughout the consumer goods industry. He further asserted that eventually the reforms would be extended to all Soviet industry. In January of 1965 the first 400 clothing and shoe firms which were spread across Russia, together with 78 of their raw material suppliers, were authorized for the changeover.

IMPLICATIONS FOR THE FUTURE

It would appear that if the results of these larger field trials basically confirm the remarkable results achieved by the initial two clothing factories, the Soviet economy is taking its initial baby steps down the road to a more market-oriented system where prices and the profit motive are powerful tools in regulating economic behavior and resource allocation. Assuming the initial steps are successful, it would be fair to estimate that the role of centralized economic planning and control will gradually diminish in relative importance in the Soviet system.

Lenin, if he were alive, would probably approve of this change since he has been quoted as having said, "Vital work we do is sinking in a dead sea of paperwork. We get sucked in by a foul bureaucratic swamp." The problem of the growing bureaucracy in the U.S.S.R. was sharply stated by Professor Glushkov, a leading Soviet cybernetician, who estimated recently that the planning bureaucracy would increase 36-

fold by 1980, requiring the services of the entire population unless
there were radical reforms in planning methods. (12)

Assuming that the role of profits does attain a higher status in
the Soviet economic system, what changes, if any, might be anticipated
in their accounting practice? For purposes of preparing external reports that will still need to be submitted to central administrative
units, accounting rules and procedures will continue to be fixed and
highly formalized by means of centralized control over accounting practices. There will be little, if any, opportunity to influence reported
profits by the adoption of alternative procedures other than those
rigidly prescribed by the state. For example, it is not conceivable at
the present time that in the same industry Soviet firms could choose one
of several different valuation or amortization methods relating to depreciation, inventory, research, development costs, etc. Rigidity in
terms of when and how revenues are to be recognized as well as cost
classifications and valuations are to be expected. This is true because
the Soviet state is the owner of Soviet enterprises. It quite properly
will continue to insist on centralized review of operating reports and
statements of financial condition in order to make comparisons with
other firms.

Allocations of resources for new investments will probably continue
to be made by central authorities. However, profit performance and
demonstrated demand-supply relationships may continue to be more important in making these allocations than they have been in the past. It
would seem that major improvements might be expected in the areas of
budgeting, internal reporting and overhead allocations. If plant managers are to be given more freedom to operate in response to market demands, it would make sense that operating budgets might be prepared
first at the local level and then reviewed by higher authorities. Both
fixed and flexible budgets should become more important control tools in
local management's hands than they have been.

In order to maximize profits, better internal reports are also a
necessity. The reporting of costs by processes, cost centers, and responsibility units as well as the principle of "exception" reporting to
higher management should increase. More effort needs to be devoted to
estimating as carefully as possible at the local level the probable
costs of new products before they are introduced. Better methods of allocating overhead must also be developed.

Greater emphasis on profits with greater local autonomy might be
accompanied by less emphasis on the broad unit cost of production than
heretofore. In other words, it is assumed prices might be more flexible
in general in response to market conditions and much less emphasis
placed on broad, stable, long-run unit cost of production figures on
which to base the overall price structure. This might result in the
treatment of general administrative, selling and research expenses as
period costs with no attempt made to allocate them to cost of production
through broad overhead accounts.

If profits do assume a role of primary importance in Soviet reckoning, it seems imperative that better financial control systems be developed. This means that higher caliber people must be attracted to the
Soviet accounting profession and that the responsibility of the accounting staff of the Soviet enterprise be given primarily to the local firm
managers. Furthermore, the need for mechanization of the handling of
quantitative data is great.

There still would be a need for good external auditors to render reports to higher administrative units.   These auditors would probably function in basically the same role as independent accountants in this country.   The internal audit function would become recognized as an important tool of control by the Soviet enterprise managers to see that the firm's policies and procedures are being carried out.

In summary, a more prominent role for profits and reliance on the marketplace should lead to greater flexibility in the hands of Soviet firm managers.   These managers, in turn, will look increasingly to sound financial reporting and control systems to assist them in their responsibilities.   Lenin's advice "to learn from the capitalists" applies not only to the role of profits and the market mechanism but also to the proper accumulation and use of accounting data.

FOOTNOTES

1. Marshall I. Goldman, "Economic Controversy in the Soviet Union: Liberman's Goals for Economic Reform," *Foreign Affairs*, April, 1963, pp. 498-512.

2. Robert W. Campbell, *Accounting in Soviet Planning and Management* (Cambridge, Mass.: Harvard University Press, 1963), p. 11.

3. E. Joe DeMaris and Richard B. Purdue, "Accounting in the U.S.S.R.," *The Journal of Accountancy*, July, 1959, p. 48.

4. Robert W. Campbell, "Soviet Accounting and Economic Decisions," *Studies in Accounting Theory*, W. T. Baxter and Sidney Davidson, Editors (Homewood, Ill.: Richard D. Irwin, Inc., 1962), pp. 357-358.

5. Campbell, *Accounting in Soviet Planning and Management*, p. 75.

6. For American firms following the "current operating" concept of net income reporting, material gains and losses on disposition of depreciable assets would be direct additions or deductions from cumulative retained earnings.

7. Campbell, *Accounting in Soviet Planning and Management*, p. 105.   Apparently it is fairly common practice to distribute not only overheads but also direct expenses on a very arbitrary basis.   This may be particularly true in those cases where there is a wide range of outputs where all costs may be distributed among products in accordance with some predetermined formulas.   Costs may be accumulated in plant-wide accounts, such as materials, wages, shop expenses, etc., and then distributed to products for the period in accordance with superior administrative unit's norms.   Any excess above norms would then be distributed according to the planned norms.   As a result, there is no real ex post accounting by product line.

8. Leon Smolinski, "What Next in Soviet Planning," *Foreign Affairs*, July, 1964, p. 605.

9. Campbell, *Accounting in Soviet Planning and Management*, p. 186.

10. Liberman's original proposal called for the continuance of planned targets of quantitative production, product

assortment and destination and date of delivery. It may
be that Liberman felt it was necessary, from a practical
political standpoint, to retain the above constraints on
the evolutionary road to a more market-oriented economy.
11.   Condensed from *Time* magazine, "Russia Tests the Profit
System," *Reader's Digest*, May, 1965, pp. 107-111.
12.   Smolinski, op. cit., p. 602.

QUESTIONS

1.   What major economic difference can you cite between the
United States and Soviet systems which make accounting
in the Soviet Union less objective than in the United
States?
2.   Can you see any disadvantages to complete central control
of accounting principles? Explain.
3.   Can you see any disadvantage to complete central control of
economic activity? Explain.
4.   What problems can arise from basing the transfer price of
goods and services on cost?
5.   Why is the Soviet depreciation system less economically
viable than the U.S. system? Does the Soviet system have
any theoretical advantages? Explain.
6.   List the differences between the U.S. system and the Soviet
system of accounting.
7.   Do you believe the Soviets can ever have economic freedom
without political freedom? Or vice versa?

3

The Contemporary Financial Accounting Model Under "Generally Accepted Accounting Principles"

To understand the specific ways in which accounting does its job, the very practical reasons for specific accounting procedures and practices as they are generally carried out need to be evaluated. Chapter 3 allows such an evaluation. Its organization follows the outline of study generally taken in financial accounting. Practical examples have been included for each major topic. Reading of these pieces in conjunction with study of accounting procedures and practices should greatly enhance the understanding of both procedural details and conceptual bases.

The accounting cycle consists of the recording, classifying, summarizing, and reporting of transactions. It is primarily procedural, and yet theory does underlie the procedures used. The theoretical issues of single versus double entry and cash versus accrual basis are fundamental to how the accounting cycle is operated. Joseph Hardcastle (page 98) and Ellis M. Williams (page 99) discuss these issues. The accounting cycle can be viewed as a system of accounting. Jay R. Owens (page 108) illustrates how the computer can be used to perform the necessary steps in the accounting cycle in a systematic, efficient manner. Basic to any accounting system are source documents, books of account, and various other records. E. Read (page 94) and the *Book-Keepers Journal* (page 97) present information on these essential records which add practical reality to our study of the accounting cycle.

The next seventeen articles in this chapter are organized by topics in the order in which they are typically covered in financial accounting. Some of the examples are procedurally oriented. Paul Hoffmeyer's article (page 116) on the use of the data stamps on personal checks and James Carberry's article (page 137) on the number of days per year to use in interest calculations are procedurally oriented. Other examples are to help the reader understand the importance of the accounting item to decision makers: The William Wurts article (page 118) on money market investing, the *Cleveland Plain Dealer*'s piece (page 122) on Addressograph-Multigraph Corporation's accounting changes, and Lindley B. Richert's discussion (page 143) of AT&T's change in credit rating. Still other examples are included to aid understanding of the theoretical bases for the accounting of various topics: *Business Week*'s discussion (page 146) of bond repurchase gains and losses, *Wall Street Journal*'s (page 164) reporting of Memorex's change in accounting procedures, and Don J. Summa's (page 173) piece on tax versus financial accounting.

17   ACCOUNTING FORM DESIGN

E. Read

(Reprinted by permission from *Book-Keepers Journal*, vol. 26,
no. 203 (Autumn, 1970): 68-71.)

(E. Read is a public relations officer of Kalamazoo Ltd.)

Bookkeeping changes in the last century have seen a jump from bound
books to computers. Whilst mechanization is often necessary, there can
be considerable drawbacks, and there may be better alternatives—it is
not known whether mechanization pays unless one also knows the cost of
the most efficient hand method. Disadvantages include the facts that:

1. Machinery can be increased only in large units.
2. Breakdowns can happen at inconvenient times where there is
   a deadline to be met, e.g., when wages are being prepared.
3. Work is often mechanized simply because machine capacity
   is available.
4. Jobs are often organized to suit the machine instead of
   the business.

When mechanization is being considered the following points should
be borne in mind:

1. The cost of mechanization should be compared with that of
   the best manual method available, which may not be the
   method currently being used.
2. Sufficient spare time must be allowed on the machines to
   cover peak periods, breakdowns, maintenance and service.
3. Sufficient trained operators must be available to cover
   holidays and sickness.

The basic considerations in form designing should take the following into account:

1. A minimum of writing and a minimum of copying. The latter
   is undesirable because of wasting time and of the possibility of errors, which necessitates checks and rechecks.
   Multicopying documents are ideal in that they require a
   minimum of copying. The carbons are already loaded, which
   is time saving, and there is no chance of their being put
   in the wrong way up. Perfect copies are obtained because
   the carbon is new each time, and less expensive carbon can
   thus be used. Perforations are torn off and sheets and
   carbons detached. A typical specimen consists of a)
   invoice b) statement (where customers are dealt with only
   infrequently) c) sales ledger copy (which can be filed and,
   when the account is cleared, payment matched with copy invoice so that no ledger is required) d) delivery advice
   (without £ s. d. which is blocked out by shading) e) con-
   signment slip (for use by stores) f) statistics copy.

Another form requiring a minimum of writing and copying is designed for use by multiple concerns to satisfy
the requirements of branches. This form is completed,
usually in duplicate, by the branch shop placing the order.
There are four columns providing for different times of
delivery and quantities required, and to indicate whether
quantities received are more or less than ordered. From
these forms the total production required is obtained,
goods are invoiced to the branch shop and a reconciliation is made of goods ordered and received. The original
document is used throughout to arrive at a production summary, analysis of sales of each item and £ s. d.

2. Information must be available quickly when it is called
    for.

3. The ever-increasing demand for figures and statistics
    should enable them to be available with a minimum, if any,
    increase in staff or cost of purchase of elaborate ma-
    chinery.

4. A form should be as simple as possible—complications
    should be avoided.

5. A form should be logically laid out in a planned sequence.
    As an example, a specimen plant and machinery register
    sheet, designed from the financial aspect, has been
    planned in such a way that what is required can be picked
    out easily and all the necessary information shown in the
    correct sequence. Provision has been made for details of
    machine supplier, location, cost, tax allowances, depre-
    ciation, maintenance, and repairs.

6. A form should be easy to complete and interpret. The de-
    signer of a form should consider who is going to fill it
    up and who is going to use the information provided—
    quite often in different places and involving different
    grades of labor. All too often, a designer thinks of a
    form only from the point of view of what he requires from
    it and not as to how it appears to the person who is going
    to complete it; e.g., the form may have to be completed
    out of doors by vanmen or commercial travelers.

7. Another essential point in form design is to consider
    whether the form can or should perform more than one func-
    tion. For example, in a particular printer's order form
    all information required is detailed giving variations
    available, e.g., size, quality, manner of punching. No
    copying is necessary, requirements being filled in or
    ringed round. To serve more than one function, order
    forms are perforated at the bottom, the detachable slip
    being used for costing purposes. The order form follows
    the job round the factory, the costing information being
    detached to serve its own function, and the two being re-
    lated by their reference number.

8. An important factor is the size of the form, particularly
    if it is to be stored, bound or housed for reference. In
    general, and also for convenience, the size should never
    be larger than is absolutely necessary. Over the last
    thirty years, forms have been getting smaller.

9.   Another important factor is the weight or thickness of
      paper. The presumption that "thick paper is good and thin
      paper is not good" is wrong, and quality and weight do not
      necessarily go together. In deciding as to weight or
      thickness of paper the number of copies required and bulk
      if to be stored have to be considered. If several copies
      are required paper is needed which will allow good impres-
      sions, e.g., in the case of multiple forms top copies
      should be as thin as possible and thicker copies should
      be at the bottom. As to quality, the life of invoices
      and statements etc. is of short duration whereas company
      minutes, share registers etc. may have to last for 50 to
      100 years, so the quality is varied according to the use
      and expected life. Also to be considered is the amount
      of physical handling to which the form will be subjected.

10.   Color can be of enormous value if intelligently used,
      e.g., printing or shading in different colors, or differ-
      ent tints of paper. Shading can be helpful if rightly
      and wisely used, e.g., a sheet with nine analysis columns
      can have alternate columns shaded blue. Where there are
      a number of columns it is easy to confuse them and put
      an entry in the wrong one, so shading helps to break up
      the form and guide the eye to the right place. Another
      help is for every fifth horizontal line to be a heavy
      one. In column headings it is best to number rather than
      attempt to title them as they usually get quickly out of
      date. To save having to keep copying out descriptions
      the bottom sheet can be full size containing typed or
      handwritten column headings, with the sheets on top having
      their description headings cut off.

11.   Line spacing is important, e.g., in the case of a check
      if it is to be typed.

12.   Another important point is the question of registration.
      Many forms are used and prepared two or more at a time
      so that it is necessary that the information contained in
      them is reproduced exactly in the correct position on all
      the forms. Examples include a) multicopying forms, such
      as invoice, statement etc. where space for the name of
      the customer and columns for details of goods must be in
      the same position on each document b) wages sheet, payee's
      slip, etc., where columns for details of wages, deduc-
      tions, etc., must be in the same position on each sheet
      c) sheets for use with a pegboard.

13.   Perforation is important and consideration must be given
      to the type and use of the form, how long it is to re-
      main intact and how quickly it is to be separated.

14.   Also to be considered is the method of disposal of any
      accounting or statistical document after it has served
      its immediate purpose. It may require some period of
      storage, in which case the manner in which it is to be
      housed must be considered. The type of punching required
      depends on whether the forms can be fastened together
      permanently or whether they may be required to be brought
      back temporarily into use. If the form is to be typed

punching is required in such a way that the form will not catch in the typewriter and tear. Plant and machinery sheets, for example, can have holes punched so that they can be stored in a visible container, salient facts being shown up by the use of signals.

15. Another type of form is the check list. The preprinted list of requirements ensures that information is in the order required by production operations and that no item is forgotten.

16. An accounting form is the working tool of a routine which itself must be soundly conceived; furthermore, the main cost of a form is not the cost of paper and printing but the clerical time involved in handling it.

Form designing is a complicated job needing a specialist, since well-designed forms save time and money—particularly executive time, which is the time which it is most important to save.

QUESTIONS

1. Why are details so important in accounting?
2. Where repetitive actions need to be taken, how can standardization help?

---

18   KEEPING TRACK OF LEDGER CARDS

(Reprinted by permission from *Book-Keepers Journal*, vol. 26, no. 204 (Winter, 1970): 87.)

In any busy office where there are perhaps 5,000 or 10,000 ledger accounts, it will be found that at any given time a number of ledger cards have been removed from the ledger trays for various reasons. This can cause much delay to the bookkeepers when they are offsetting the posting media in the ledger trays. In one office, it used to be a regular daily occurrence for the bookkeepers to spend a lot of time inquiring from the other members of staff and from other office departments whether they had "such-and-such" a ledger card, as they wanted to post an item to it.

This problem was solved by having a printer print a quantity of OUT cards, similar in size to the ledger cards. About a dozen OUT cards were placed at the front of each ledger tray. Any clerk who wished to extract a ledger card for any purpose, replaced it with one of these OUT cards, on which she marked the date the card was taken out, the name and address on the ledger card and her own name. When she had finished with the ledger card, she filled in the date on which she returned it, replaced the card with the ledger card, and put the card at the front of the tray with the others.

This effected a considerable saving of time in the tracing of missing ledger cards, particularly at month's end when extracting the monthly trial balance to agree the control accounts.

QUESTIONS

1. What do you think the author means by ledger cards?
2. If you were doing accounting work for Bankamericard, Master
    Charge, or any other major credit card, what type of in-
    formation would you want to keep on each individual who has
    a card and on the sum of the monies owed to you in total?
3. In keeping track of this information is it important to
    have each cardholder's account correct? Why?

---

19   SINGLE ENTRY

                          Joseph Hardcastle

(Reprinted by permission from *The Journal of Accountancy*, vol. 2,
no. 3 (July, 1916): 202-203. Copyright 1916 by the American Institute
of Certified Public Accountants, Inc.)

"Single entry," the much despised "Single Entry!" I can scarcely
muster up the courage to stand up in defense of it. I do not remember
an author who has had much to say in its favor. The very name is a mis-
nomer, and to use it shows our ignorance of its import. It should be
called, as we shall see later on, simple entry. And yet, in spite of
this disparagement of it, it must have considerable merit, especially in
certain businesses, or it would have gone out of existence long ago. It
is generally used by the small retailer, and very often by business carried on, on a most extensive scale. So much for those businesses called
"undertakings," that is, businesses run for the purpose of making money.
But when it comes to those businesses whose function is to collect revenue and pay incidental expenses in order to accomplish under the direction of trustees some purpose other than that of making money, then the
accounts are very often kept by simple entry, although they may be kept
by double entry; and in the accounting in the courts the presentation of
these accounts is by simple entry.
    The Treasury accounts at Washington, the Bank of England accounts,
municipal accounts, such as those of the City of New York, etc., etc.,
are said to be kept by simple entry. The presentation to the courts of
the accounts of executors and of testamentary trustees, of assignees,
of receivers in bankruptcy, and receivers in general, are by simple
entry.
    Double entry is the bookkeeping adapted to those businesses called
"undertakings," for its power of analysis is great, and thus it gives

a help in the study of economy as connected with these businesses, in its "profit and loss" or other equivalent account, while it provides safety to its capital by providing economic funds to meet wear and tear, to meet losses on sundry debtor accounts, etc., in its reserve funds. In undertakings, the ruling idea is economy, *economy*, ECONOMY.

QUESTIONS

1. Differentiate between single entry and double entry bookkeeping.
2. What kinds of businesses might use single entry?
3. Are profits and losses still computed under single entry? How? Would you say that this turns the single entry into double entry? Explain.
4. What are the benefits of double entry that make its use superior to single entry?
5. Do you think, contrary to Mr. Hardcastle, that government accounts might benefit by the use of double entry? How?

---

20   THE USE OF CASH AND MODIFIED CASH
                     BASIS FINANCIAL STATEMENTS

Ellis M. Williams

(Reprinted by permisson from *The Florida Certified Public Accountant*, vol. 12, no. 2 (January, 1973): 17-24.)

This commentary is an outgrowth from observations of common reporting abuses in the use of cash basis and modified cash basis financial statements. These comments are directed to profit oriented businesses. There is no attempt to include a discussion of reporting in connection with nonprofit organizations even though many of the concepts discussed in this article do apply to these organizations.

The cash and modified cash basis reporting methods can be found in use in organizations where there is particular emphasis on certain reporting requirements such as reporting in accordance with a particular agreement or with federal income tax laws. Such organizations may be proprietorships, partnerships, joint ventures, or closely-held corporations.

RELATION TO GENERALLY ACCEPTED ACCOUNTING PRINCIPLES

Cash or modified cash basis reports do not ordinarily purport to present the financial position or the results of operations of an enterprise in accordance with GAAP and are usually considered to be of limited usefulness. The statement of assets and liabilities presented on a cash basis usually reflects only assets and liabilities resulting directly from cash transactions. The statement of revenues collected and expenses paid is only by coincidence the equivalent of a statement of income. The omission of various accrued assets and liabilities prevent cash or modified cash basis statements from being anything more than statements of certain recognized assets and liabilities and statements of certain recognized revenues and expenses.

Accrual basis accounting addresses itself to proper matching of revenues with their related costs. Under accrual basis accounting, revenues are generally recognized when the earning process is complete or virtually complete and an exchange has taken place. Expenses must be related and coordinated within the policies and circumstances controlling revenue recognition. Under the cash basis method, income is recognized as cash is received, expenses recognized as cash is disbursed, and assets and liabilities recognized and expire as cash is exchanged. Modified-cash basis statements vary as to their income and expense recognition depending on the basic assumptions. Material differences can and generally do arise when comparing cash and modified cash basis reporting with accrual basis reporting. Therefore, the cash and modified cash basis methods should be used only in special circumstances and cannot be considered as acceptable reporting substitutes for accrual basis reporting.

"TELL IT LIKE IT IS"

Clarity is extremely important in the cash and modified cash basis statements. A reader can be easily misled if a statement is not obvious in its meaning. Titles such as "balance sheet" and "income statement" are not appropriate terms when used in connection with these types of statements. "Balance sheet" is a term considered to mean a statement of financial position prepared in accordance with generally accepted accounting principles, just as an income statement and statement of retained earnings, together, represent the results of operations. Therefore, it is misleading to associate such terms with a statement presentation that is not intended to present the financial position or results of operations.

Statement on Auditing Procedures No. 33 reiterates this point in stating that the first standard of reporting does not apply to statements that do not purport to present financial position and results of operations. (1) The cash and modified cash basis statements generally do not purport to present the financial position and results of operations; therefore, when using these incomplete reporting methods, the statements must make clear what information is presented and how it is presented.

No standard wording has been devised to cover all the possible circumstances in titling cash and modified cash basis statements. However, the wording used must be descriptive. Statement titles such as the following might be appropriate:

1.   Statement of Certain Assets and Liabilities
2.   Statement of Recognized Revenues and Expenses

3. Statement of Assets and Liabilities Arising from Cash Transactions
4. Statement of Cash Receipts and Disbursements
5. Statement of Assets and Liabilities (Cash Basis)
6. Statement of Revenues Collected and Expenses Paid

The wording used in these statements for captions and disclosures require considerable care to assure clarity of meaning. The statement reader can easily be misled by careless wording or inferences. For instance, in a modified cash basis statement where receivables and payables are material and are not recognized in the statement presentation, the use of the term "current assets" and "current liabilities" is meaningless and misleading. In most cases, the object of showing the classifications of "current assets" and "current liabilities" is to give the statement reader an idea of the company's "current" financial position. If material omissions are made in presenting what is implied to be a "current position," a reader may be misled. To avoid misleading inferences in this situation, the terms "current assets" and "current liabilities" should be avoided in the statement presentation.

It may be appropriate and desirable in cash and modified cash basis statements to disclose information concerning maturity dates on certain receivables and payables; however, there should be no implication that what is shown is the "total current assets" or "total current liabilities" unless, in fact, that is what is shown. Disclosures of the desired "maturity" information can be made through parenthetical treatment on the face of the statements or in notes to the statements.

"Retained earnings" is another term that should not be used in connection with cash and modified cash basis statements. Retained earnings is more than just a residual amount and, generally, has meaning only in accrual basis statements prepared in accordance with generally accepted accounting principles. Further, the term "net income" is generally not appropriate for the cash or modified cash basis statement. The term that should be used is something such as "excess of revenues received over expenses paid" or "excess of revenues recognized over expenses recognized." Be descriptive —"tell it like it is."

PRESENTATION

When presenting cash and modified cash basis statements, it is important the reader be reminded that all assets and liabilities of the company are not disclosed. For this reason, major captions such as "assets recognized" and "liabilities recognized" should be used. The method or manner in which these assets and liabilities are recognized is dependent on certain basic assumptions which should be fully described in a note to the financial statements. No hard and fast rules can exist concerning such recognition or statement format.

The main emphasis in the cash basis statements is in providing meaningful summaries of cash transactions. An example of such statements is shown in Table 6. In the example, the statement of cash receipts and disbursements represents a summary of cash transactions occurring during the reporting period. In the statement of assets and liabilities arising from cash transactions, the assets recognized consist of the unexpired tangible assets, exclusive of inventories, acquired for cash or through the assumption of a note payable. The liabilities recognized in this example are those unpaid liabilities arising from the receipt of cash or the effective receipt of cash.

The order in which the recognized assets should be reported on the statement of assets and liabilities arising from cash transactions is one which begins with cash and generally corresponds to asset liquidity. The list should be an informative summary of the "assets" but without reference made to "current assets." Contra accounts such as "accumulated depreciation" should not be shown since the account does not result from a cash transaction. However, in modified cash basis statements, accumulated depreciation is generally included in the statement presentation.

Liabilities arising from cash transactions should be reported in the order which generally corresponds to the chronological order of the maturity dates without making the distinction between "current" and "long-term" debt. Debt maturity information and other relevant data can be provided in the following manner:

Six percent note payable in quarterly installments of $500,
plus interest; final payment due October 31, 1972, $2,500

The "capital" section of a cash basis report offers something of a reporting problem. As previously stated the term "retained earnings" should be avoided due to its possible misleading inference. Further, the reference to this section as "equity" could be misleading due to the omission from the statements of various accrued assets and liabilities. Therefore, the best approach in handling the capital section is again "tell it like it is." Treat the section as a residual amount and refer to it as "excess of assets recognized over liabilities recognized." Disclosure concerning the capital stock could be provided in a note to the statements, or if the statement preparer desires to have the capital stock information on the face of the statement, the residual balance could then be referred to as "excess of assets recognized over capital stock and liabilities recognized."

Modified cash basis statements should generally follow the guidelines described for cash basis statements except that the modified cash basis method of recognizing assets, liabilities, revenues, and expenses will usually more nearly approximate accrual basis accounting. The modified cash basis reporting method by its very nature will vary in its recognition principles and will require different types of formats for different types of situations. However, the basic guide in Table 7 should be adequate under most circumstances.

DISCLOSURE

Disclosure of the principles of accounting and basis of presentation is a most important disclosure in cash or modified cash basis reporting. Such disclosure is made through proper selection of statement titles, use of informative captions, descriptive information on the face of the statements and, last but not least, explanatory notes to the statements. Generally, the notes should disclose the basis on which income and expenses and assets and liabilities are recognized. It is usually advisable to remind the reader of the significant items omitted from the statements such as material receivables, payables, or inventories.

When federal income tax requirements differ from generally accepted accounting principles, financial statements are sometimes presented using the same basis as that used for federal income tax reporting. In such a case, the statements are considered to be special presentations and should be treated in the same manner as modified cash basis statements. The alternative note in Table 7 is an example of appropriate disclosure for such financial statements.

CONCLUSION

The cash and modified cash basis statements are special purpose statements that are not intended to present financial position and results of operations in accordance with generally accepted accounting principles. These statements are not usually suitable for general distribution. Under most circumstances, the accrual basis statement is the preferred presentation.

The cash or modified cash basis statement, if clear in meaning and if used in the right manner with adequate disclosures, can be beneficial in special circumstances. Extra care, however, should always be taken to avoid any misleading inferences when using this type of special presentation.

TABLE 6

CASH BASIS STATEMENTS

C B Corporation
Statement of Assets and Liabilities
Arising from Cash Transactions
December 31, 1971

Assets Recognized (Note A)	
Cash	$ 1,000
Marketable securities	3,000
Property, plant and equipment	
Land	10,000
Building	25,000
Equipment	9,000
Total	48,000
Liabilities Recognized (Note A)	
Taxes withheld from employees	500
$7\frac{1}{2}$ percent note payable in monthly installments of $1,000 plus interest (unsecured)	7,000
7 percent note payable to stockholder, due January 14, 197- (unsecured)	10,000
Total	17,500
Excess of Assets Recognized over Liabilities Recognized (Note B)	$ 30,500

C B Corporation
Statement of Cash Receipts and Disbursements
For the Year Ended December 31, 1971

Cash Receipts
Sale of merchandise	$150,500
Proceeds from stockholder loan	10,000
Proceeds from the sale of equipment	2,000
Other	1,500
	164,000

Cash Disbursements
Salaries	45,000
Purchase of merchandise	112,000
Taxes (other than federal income taxes)	2,500
Federal income taxes paid	1,500
Repairs and maintenance	1,000
Note payments—principal and interest	13,000
Telephone	500
Dues and meetings	900
Insurance	600
Office supplies	1,000
	178,000
Excess of Cash Disbursements over Cash Receipts	14,000
Cash Balance—January 1, 1971	15,000
Cash Balance—December 31, 1971	$ 1,000

C B Corporation
Notes to Cash Basis Statements
December 31, 1971

Note A   Method of Accounting and Presentation
The accounts of the Company are maintained, and these statements are presented, on the cash basis. Receivables, payables, accrued expenses, accumulated depreciation and inventories are not reflected in these statements. Accordingly,
the statements do not purport to present the financial position, changes in financial position and results of operations
of the Company in conformity with generally accepted accounting principles.
Note B   Common Stock
The Company has authorized 4,000 shares of $1 par value
stock with 2,000 shares issued and outstanding. Capital contributed in excess of par value of common stock is $10,000.

TABLE 7

MODIFIED CASH BASIS STATEMENTS

M C Corporation
Statement of Certain Assets and Liabilities
December 31, 1971

Assets Recognized (Note A)		
Cash		$ 10,000
Marketable securities, at cost, which		
approximates market		2,000
Inventory of merchandise—at the lower		
of cost (FIFO) or market		11,000
6 percent first mortgage receivable		
(6,000 receivable within 12 months)		20,000
Property, plant and equipment—at cost		
Land	$15,000	
Building	40,000	
Equipment	20,000	
Total	75,000	
Less accumulated depreciation	12,000	63,000
Total		106,000
Liabilities Recognized (Note A)		
Taxes withheld from employees' wages		1,500
Federal income taxes payable		3,300
8 percent unsecured note payable to bank		
(due within 12 months)		9,000
$7\frac{1}{2}$ percent first mortgage note payable		
in monthly installments of		
$2,000, plus interest; final		
payment due November 30, 197–		29,000
Total		42,800
Excess of Assets Recognized over		
Liabilities Recognized (Note B)		$63,200

M C Corporation
Statement of Recognized Revenues and Expenses
For the Year Ended December 31, 1971

Revenues Recognized (Note A)	
Sales of merchandise	$100,000
Gain on sale of fixed assets	2,000
Interest	500
Total	102,500

Expenses Recognized (Note A)

Cost of sales	$50,000	
Auto expense	500	
Depreciation	3,000	
Insurance	1,700	
Legal and accounting	400	
Miscellaneous	700	
Office supplies	500	
Repairs and maintenance	1,200	
Salaries	24,000	
Payroll taxes	1,600	
General taxes	2,000	
Federal income taxes	3,300	
Travel and entertainment	600	
Telephone	1,500	91,000
Excess or Recognized Revenues over Expenses		$ 11,500

M C Corporation
Statement of Changes in Excess of Assets Recognized
Over Liabilities Recognized
For the Year Ended December 31, 1971

Excess of Assets Recognized over Liabilities Recognized—January 1, 1971		$ 54,200
Increases		
Excess of recognized revenues over expenses for the year ended December 31, 1971	$11,500	
Proceeds from the sale of 100 shares of $1 par value common stock	5,000	16,500
		70,700
Decreases		
Dividends paid—$1 a share	3,000	
Purchase of 100 shares of Treasury stock at $45 a share	4,500	7,500
Excess of Assets Recognized Over Liabilities Recognized—December 31, 1971		$ 63,200

M C Corporation
Notes to Modified Cash Basis Statements
December 31, 1971

Note A   Method of Accounting and Presentation
The accounts of the Company are maintained, and these statements are presented, on a modified cash basis. Under this
method, a) income and expenses are recognized only at the
time cash is received and disbursed, b) depreciable fixed
assets are depreciated over the lives of the properties
using the straight line method, c) merchandise inventories
are recognized at the beginning and end of the year, and d)

federal income taxes are accrued. Since various receivables and payables and accrued and deferred income and expense items, which may be material in amount, are not reflected, the financial statements do not purport to present
the financial position, changes in financial position and
results of operations of the Company in conformity with generally accepted accounting principles.

Note B   Common Stock
The Company has authorized 4,000 shares of $1 par value
stock with 2,100 shares issued, of which 100 shares are held
in the Treasury. Capital that has been contributed in excess of par value of common stock amounts to $25,000 and the
cost of the Treasury stock held is $4,500. (Alternative
note presentation for a modified cash basis statement when
the method used follows the federal tax method.)

Note A   Method of Accounting and Presentation
The accounts of the Company are maintained, and these statements are presented, in accordance with the method of accounting followed for federal income tax reporting purposes.
Under this method, a) income and expenses are generally recognized only at the time cash is received and disbursed, b)
depreciable fixed assets are depreciated over the lives of
the properties using the straight-line method, c) merchandise inventories are recognized at the beginning and end of
the year, and d) federal income taxes are accrued. Since
various receivables and payables and accrued and deferred
income and expense items, which may be material, are not reflected, the financial statements do not purport to present
the financial position, changes in financial position and
results of operations of the Company in conformity with generally accepted accounting principles.

FOOTNOTES

1.   Committee on Auditing Procedures, "Statement on Auditing
     Procedures No. 33," *Auditing Standards and Procedures*
     (New York: American Institute of Certified Public Account-
     ants), p. 88.

QUESTIONS

1.   What is the difference between the cash method and the ac-
     crual method? Define each.
2.   Why is the accrual method used as the generally accepted
     method for preparation of financial reports for investors?
3.   Is a cash receipts and disbursements statement of use to
     anyone? Whom? Why?

3. Would the public have a better understanding of expenditures of the U.S. government under the accrual method?
Explain.
4. Could Congress do a better job of appropriating funds if
the U.S. government accounts were on an accrual basis?
Explain.

_____

_____

21　　　　　　　FIN-PAC: FINANCIAL PLANNING AND
　　　　　　　　　CONTROL GENERAL ACCOUNTING SYSTEM

Jay R. Owens

(Reprinted by permission. Copyright 1973, *The Arthur Andersen
Chronicle* (March, 1973): 30-35.)

The FIN-PAC General Accounting System, a series of generalized
computer programs developed by the Firm, is an installation aid used by
our personnel to assist clients in developing and installing general
accounting and responsibility reporting systems. FIN-PAC performs the
three basic functions which are common to general accounting and reporting systems—validates and controls transaction data, posts transactions to ledgers, and prepares accounting and financial management
reports.

GENERALIZED DESIGN CONCEPT

One of two approaches is usually followed in implementing computer
systems:

1. Custom design a system to meet the unique requirements of
one user.
2. Compromise the user's requirements to take advantage of
the savings in system development costs offered by a
standard software package.

A third approach, generalizing the design of computer systems, in
many cases, represents a better alternative to the automation process
than either of the first two. Using a generalized design approach, a
computer system is designed so that those procedures that are most
likely to vary among users or to change after the system is installed
can be tailored according to the user's specifications at some future
time.
　　The FIN-PAC General Accounting System was developed by the Firm
using a generalized design concept. Those aspects of general accounting
that are common to most users have been identified and precoded for generalized application. Procedures which are subject to change because
of the individual policies and preferences of each company have been
isolated so that the user can select, without doing programming, from
among a variety of processing options. This approach means it is

easier to change the system after installation to accommodate new or
revised source documents and reports, and for revisions to the company's
organizational structure.

The FIN-PAC system can be tailored to accept almost any input format and coding structure and to prepare reports in a variety of formats
to meet the general accounting requirements of most users without imposing a fixed set of reports. Instead, each user specifies the content, sequence, level of detail, and format of the reports needed to
meet its general accounting reporting requirements. The system imposes
no practical restrictions on the size or number of data elements,
classifications of data, or their arrangement on the source documents.
This flexibility makes it possible to use a company's existing chart of
accounts, department numbers, coding structure, and source documents.

REDUCED SYSTEM INSTALLATION TIME AND COST

FIN-PAC has been installed in both large and small organizations in
many industries. These experiences have shown that FIN-PAC does assist
clients in implementing general accounting and responsibility reporting
systems in less time and with less cost than required to design and program comparable custom systems. This is possible because the availability of FIN-PAC programs reduces the detailed system design requirements
and eliminates or reduces computer programming.

Because the FIN-PAC programs are already tested, the requirement
for system testing is reduced. Only the user's added specifications
need to be tested. Costs are further reduced because the shorter time
required for implementing the system also reduces such time-dependent
activities as supervision, administration, progress reporting, and meetings. Cost and time estimates are improved because the volatile areas
of programming and system testing are reduced and fewer steps need to
be estimated.

USER SPECIFIES PROCESSING AND REPORTS

The operation of the FIN-PAC system is illustrated in Figure 2.
The FIN-PAC system performs the following three basic functions which
are common to all general accounting and reporting systems:

1. validates and controls accounting and statistical trans-
    action data
2. posts transactions to ledgers
3. prepares accounting and financial management reports

The processing performed and the reports prepared by the FIN-PAC
system are controlled through user specificiations which are stored in
the following system reference files:

1. cycle parameter file: allows a user to supply dates for
    reports and to specify special processing options such
    as suppressing the printing of certain reports and indi-
    cating whether the processing is for a preliminary or
    final closing.

FIGURE 2

OVERVIEW OF FIN-PAC GENERAL ACCOUNTING SYSTEM

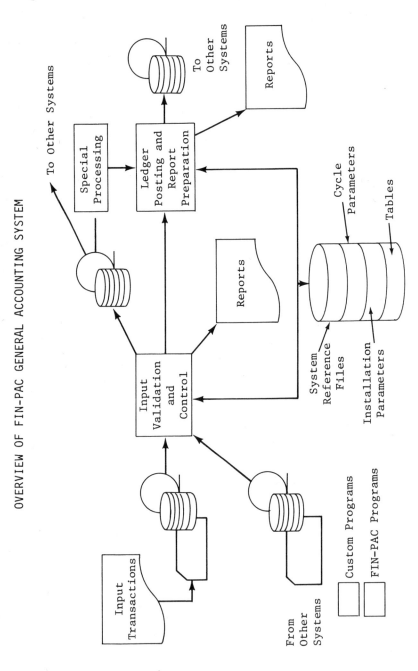

2. installation parameter file: defines the format and vali-
    dation rules for input transactions, the ledgers to be
    posted, the reports to be prepared, the content and format
    of reports, and other processing specifications
3. table file: allows the user to specify valid account num-
    bers, department numbers, responsibility area numbers, and
    other code tables

The capabilities of the FIN-PAC General Accounting System are discussed in the remainder of this article.

USER DEFINES REPORTS, CODING STRUCTURES AND LEDGERS

Through user specifications, the FIN-PAC system can be instructed
to produce reports which meet many of the client's specific needs. The
user has the ability to control the sequence of data, the format of report titles and column headings and the arrangement of data in each
detail and summary line on a report. Reports such as the following can
be prepared: summary level balance sheets, income and expense ledgers,
responsibility reports, detail ledgers, and supporting transaction
lists.

The FIN-PAC General Accounting System also allows the user extensive flexibility in defining the coding structure dictated by his information needs. Examples of coding structures which can be used with
FIN-PAC General Accounting Systems are illustrated in Figure 3.

FIN-PAC classifies and accumulates data in ledgers which are the
source from which reports are prepared. The user can define the classifications of data (specific accounts) to be included in each ledger, the
sequence of data within the ledger and the level of detail at which data
is maintained. For example, one ledger is typically established for asset and liability accounts and another for revenue and expense accounts.
These ledgers become the source for the balance sheet and the income
statement. Additional ledgers (departmental expense or sales analysis)
may be established to accumulate data for other reports.

Up to nine categories of data can be included in each account or
statistical classification appearing within any ledger. The following
suggest the wide range of data that the user might specify for each
ledger account: actual income or expense, original budget, revised budget, labor hours, machine hours, material cost, labor cost, and non-labor
expenditures. Furthermore, FIN-PAC reports may be developed for a wide
range of time periods:

Month (or other specified period)
   Current
   Previous
   Corresponding last year
Primary Fiscal Year
   Year-to-date—current year
   Year-to-date—last year
   Total for the year—current year
   Total for the year—last year

Alternate Fiscal Year (see below)
   Year-to-date—current year
   Year-to-date—last year
   Total for the year—current year
   Total for the year—last year
Inception to Date
   Total from inception to current date
   Total from inception to end of last year

The ability to accommodate two fiscal years (for example, January to December and July to June) enables FIN-PAC to prepare reports for governmental or regulatory bodies, trade associations, or other organizations on a fiscal-year basis other than that used for internal reports.

DATA VALIDATION AND CONTROL

FIN-PAC verification of the accuracy of data entering the system includes:

1. code audit: All account numbers, department numbers, project numbers, and any other codes are validated against corresponding tables of valid numbers.
2. format audit: All source data may be checked to determine that the format is correct. For example, checks can be made to verify that numeric fields contain only numbers or to determine specified fields are not blank.
3. batch balancing: Both accounting entries and statistical data may be grouped into batches and balanced to predetermined control totals. The system reports any discrepancies between the total of the transactions and the batch control total. The user has the option to accept or reject the data in out-of-balance batches.
4. entry balancing: The equality of debits and credits in each entry (including, but not limited to: voucher, journal entry, or sales invoices) can be verified by the system. Out-of-balance entries can be rejected or a balancing entry can be generated by the system and posted to a suspense account for subsequent correction.

FIN-PAC accepts data from punched cards, magnetic tape, or disks. Transactions may be entered at any time during the reporting period. Errors are rejected as soon as they are detected in the processing, and valid transactions are retained until the end of the period when they are posted to the various ledgers. The user can specify any reporting period—daily, weekly, monthly, or other.

FIN-PAC prepares a set of six control reports that establish audit trails, control the data in the system and help the user correct errors and reenter data that was rejected by the system. These control reports are: batch control, out-of-balance vouchers or entries, input transaction listing (optional), coding error suspense entries, rejected transactions, and program-to-program controls. These and other computer-generated controls are coordinated with appropriate external controls to enable the user to verify processing accuracy.

FIGURE 3

EXAMPLES OF CODING STRUCTURES WHICH CAN BE USED WITH FIN-PAC

Major
Medical
Center

Account	Dept.	Pro- gram	Fund
x x x x x	x x x	x x x	x x x

Diversified
Corporation

Co.	Account	Job	Cost Center	Detail
x x	x x x x x	x x x	x x x	x x x x x x

Oil and Gas
Corporation

Co.	Account	Property	Detail	
x x	x x x x x	x x x x x x x	x x x x x	x

⤒ Billing Class

Food
Manufacturer

Div.	Loc.	Account	Cost Center	Project
x x x	x x x	x x x x x x x x x	x x x x x	x x x x

⤒ Plant

Governmental
Unit

Dept.	Div.	Loc.	Unit	Account	Ob- ject	Pro- gram	Project
x x x	x x x	x x x	x x x	x x x x x x x	x x	x x	x x x

FIN-PAC ACCOMMODATES CUSTOM PROGRAMS

The user can include special ledger posting and report editing programs as part of the FIN-PAC system. Users may also write separate programs to perform other specialized processing. The FIN-PAC system can
direct data to and receive data from these programs.

SYSTEMS ANALYSIS A PREREQUISITE

Preliminary systems analysis and design work is required to define
the user's general accounting and reporting requirements. This work is
a prerequisite to determining the extent that FIN-PAC can be used to
satisfy these requirements. Of course, there are situations where the
use of FIN-PAC may not meet all of the user's requirements and additional custom programs may be needed to perform special processing. In some

situations, the user's special requirements may be such that the use of FIN-PAC may not be appropriate.

SUMMARY

The FIN-PAC system produces general accounting and responsibility reports. In many cases it can be installed without additional computer programming. The user defines and specifies the processing and report requirements; he does not have to conform to fixed input formats, charts of accounts, or reports. Specific benefits that FIN-PAC provides are:

1. reduced installation time and cost
2. flexible input
3. input validation and control
4. flexible reporting

When using FIN-PAC, the user has a flexible system that can be modified and expanded to meet changing requirements. New source documents, reports, companies, and locations can be added by the user without programming.

QUESTIONS

1. What functions can the FIN-PAC system perform?
2. What are some of the advantages of a computerized accounting system over manual accounting systems?
3. Why is coding necessary in a computer system?

22   SEC SEEKS FULLER DISCLOSURE OF LIQUIDITY,
          CREDIT COSTS BY FIRMS AS AID TO INVESTORS

(Reprinted by permission from the *Wall Street Journal* (April 13, 1973). © Dow Jones & Company, Inc., 1973.)

The Securities & Exchange Commission proposed accounting rule changes that would require corporations to disclose more fully their liquidity and borrowing costs.

The proposals would require a company to provide in its financial reports:

1. detailed disclosure of compensating balances, or cash that the company must leave on deposit in banks under borrowing agreements
2. unused lines of credit available to the company from banks or insurance companies

3. the cost of short-term borrowings, expressed in terms of
    annual rates of interest

The new proposals are part of the SEC's efforts aimed at requiring
corporations to provide more financial information to investors.

"RESTRICTED FUNDS"

Last year the SEC decided to require companies to provide some information on their compensating balances and other "restricted funds,"
such as commitments to pay for future contracts. That rule was to take
effect on June 30. But the latest proposals, which call for a more detailed presentation of such balances, are designed to replace the earlier rule.
The SEC asked for comments on the new proposals by June 15 and said
it plans to make them applicable to financial statements for periods
ending after August 31.
An SEC official said the new information would give investors a
better picture of how much of a company's cash is readily available and
how much is tied up in compensating balances or subject to other restrictions.
In connection with disclosing short-term borrowing costs, the proposals would force a company to detail how much commercial paper it had
issued. Commerical paper is short-term, unsecured notes issued for
cash.

"INCREASING IMPORTANCE"

"The separate statement of commercial paper outstanding is a recognition of the increasing importance of this form of short-term borrowing
in corporate financial management," the SEC said.
An agency official said the decision to require disclosure of borrowing through the use of commercial paper was prompted in part by the
1970 financial collapse of Penn Central Transportation Company. The
railroad subsidiary of Penn Central Company, currently in Bankruptcy Act
reorganization proceedings, borrowed extensively by issuing commercial
paper.

QUESTIONS

1. What is a compensatory balance?
2. What does "an unused line of credit" mean?
3. What is commercial paper?
4. Why does the SEC want the additional information described
    in the article disclosed?
5. Explain the difference between commercial paper and U.S.
    government paper.
6. Would there be an interest rate difference between commer-
    cial paper and U.S. government paper? Why or why not?

23

USE COMBINED DATA STAMP FOR CONTROL ON PERSONAL CHECKS

Paul Hoffmeyer

(Reprinted by permission from *Hospital Financial Management* (June, 1973): 46. Copyright 1973, Hospital Financial Management Association.)

Economists tell us that cash flow is vital to the success of any enterprise. The successful organization is the one that has cash in the bank and minimum receivables and is current in the payment of its creditors. Money is expensive, particularly during periods of inflation, and great emphasis must be centered upon timely cash collection and loss control.

Many commercial enterprises, grocery and variety discount store chains in particular, have concentrated for some time upon cash collection at the time of purchase. They have required customers who pay for products and services with personal checks to present adequate identification and, in some instances, to be photographed. The practice of vouching for the validity of an individual's personal check is an accepted business practice. Rubber stamps have been designed to record validating data on the back of the check. The following is an example of the data stamp.

FIGURE 4

Name . . . .

Address . . . .

City . . . . Tel. . . . .

I.D. . . . . No. . . . .

Sales Check . . . .

Approval . . . .

Some organizations record driver's license numbers, credit card numbers and Social Security numbers and compare signatures. The sales clerk or cashier generally enters the data that does not appear on the face of the check. The type of identification and serial numbers are recorded along with the sales ticket's numerical control number. Approval is generally made by a supervisor who examines and matches the identification and compares signatures.

Checks are generally endorsed for deposit to the organization's bank account at a later time and by a different individual. These steps are fine to insure the receipt of a negotiable check, but I believe they can be improved by combining the personal data and bank endorsement stamp. Thus, one stamp both restricts payment and assists in verifying the negotiability of the check. The stamp for a particular organization might appear as follows:

FIGURE 5

Name . . . .

Address . . . .

Phone . . . .

I.D. . . . . No. . . . .

Control No. . . . .

Pay to the order of
THE FIRST TRUST CO.
For deposit only
THE ABC COMPANY
11-119800

The concept of combining the data in one stamp has been presented to our local banks, which have accepted it.

In most instances, it is not necessary to complete all the data items on the combined stamp. Normally, the name and address is imprinted on the face of the check. If the check is payment for services rendered to an individual other than the check maker (for example, medical services), it may be helpful to enter the first and last name of the patient. A medical record number or patient identification number may also be entered on the stamp for later identification and relating the payment to a specific time and point of service.

The stamp, designed primarily to vouch and restrict payments made to cashiers or sales clerks, also helps greatly in controlling payments by mail. The following procedures might be used. The individual opening the mail stamps the check. The individual who records payments may enter data to designate that the payment be applied against a particular open account in situations where the maker was responsible for several open accounts. When a particular account has not been designated by the maker, and several unpaid accounts exist, the payee may elect to apply the payment against the oldest outstanding balance. Should a question arise regarding the unpaid balances, where several accounts exist, the cancelled check can be requested to substantiate the account application of the check.

In summary, the combined stamp was developed to:

1. provide data to confirm the negotiability of the check before acceptance

2. restrict payment at time of receipt
3. provide data to designate payment to a particular open
    account when more than one account exists
4. provide data to secure negotiable payment should the
    initial check be returned by the bank for nonpayment

QUESTIONS

1. Why are checks and cash an asset area that must be con-
    trolled very tightly?
2. In what ways are the suggested internal control pro-
    cedures useful?

24 MONEY MARKET INVESTING: THE BASIC FUNDAMENTALS

William W. Wurts

(Reprinted by permission from *Newspaper Controller*, vol. 26, no. 4
(January, 1973): 4.)

(William Wurts is Senior Account Executive, Merrill Lynch, Pierce,
Fenner & Smith, Inc., Seattle.)

Certain criteria are essential when considering the question of excess corporate cash. If you find you have as much as $100,000 available
as a so-called "free credit balance," and if these funds are available
for a minimum of one week—preferably even longer—then you are a candidate for short-term money market investment. The $100,000 figure can be
lowered to $50,000 or even $25,000 if the time horizon, i.e., the date
the funds must be called back, is lengthened considerably.

If invested at six percent for six months, $50,000 earns $1,500.
That is $1,500 more than it would earn sitting idle in a checking ac-
count, and $500 more than in a regular bank savings account. Whether
your company is an active prospect for money market investments is a
factor of both the amount of money involved and the length of time it
can be invested.

"LITTLE KNOWLEDGE" NO RISK

When it comes to such investments, I don't buy the idea that a little knowledge is dangerous. So long as liquidity and safety are carefully considered, any error in judgment on the investor's part normally
reduces itself to a lower rate of return, rather than dramatic loss of
principal.

Yield and degree of safety vary inversely. The higher the quality
of the investment, the lower its yield is apt to be. Safety of principal and yield considerations must always be balanced against one another
when making money market investment decisions. Here is a run-down of
the instruments, in order of safety:

Treasury bills. A dollar bill with a time lag. While riskless in
terms of principal, they tend to be the most volatile of all money instruments, because the Federal Reserve Open Market Committee adjusts the
nation's money supply by buying and selling huge amounts in the dealer
market.

Government agency securities. The various short-term obligations
of the several corporate instrumentalities of the federal government.
While mostly not guaranteed by the Treasury, they are so close to riskless that the spread between them and Treasury bills is usually unwarranted, on a quality basis.

Municipal bonds and notes. An interest-bearing promise to pay,
with a specific maturity, generally over one year in the case of bonds.
A note has a maturity of one year or less.

ACCEPTANCE SAFER THAN CD

Banker's acceptances. A draft drawn on a bank by a borrower under
a prearranged line of credit, usually in letter-of-credit form. The
borrower is liable for payment, and so is the bank on which the acceptance is drawn. An acceptance is a stronger instrument than the same
bank's certificates of deposit, because two parties are liable to the
investor for payment.

Negotiable certificates of deposit. A time deposit in amount of
$100,000 or more with a specific maturity date and a specified coupon
rate of interest. While any commercial bank can issue such certificates, only CDs of the largest banks are marketable. The CDs of the
first 20 or so in the country can easily be traded in amounts of several million dollars; CD trades of $25 million and more have often
been consummated.

Repurchase agreement. The sale of a money instrument (by a dealer
or a bank to an investor), and the simultaneous repurchase of the same
security at the same price. While the trades occur simultaneously the
settlement dates, when money changes hands and interest begins, are

different. The period in between gives the investor a hedged-up, very
short-term (one to ten days or two weeks), investment at an attractive
rate of return.

Commercial paper. Negotiable short-term promissory notes issued
by well-known corporate borrowers for a term up to 270 days; sold by
dealers who may operate as principal or agent, or directly—chiefly
through banks. Dealers tend to offer higher rates in longer maturities
(over 30 days), than direct issuers, while "directs" tend to be most
favorable in the shorter areas, i.e., one to three weeks.

A word about normal, nonnegotiable bank CDs is in order. When investing around $100,000 or more you should consider the rate available
from your local banker on such instruments. However, since the contract
is not marketable, you will have trouble collecting if you suddenly wish
to recall your funds. Some banks will make you a loan for the balance
of the period before the CD matures, but at an interest rate considerably above what the bank is paying.

As to commercial paper, there are basically two types—direct finance company paper and so-called dealer paper. Examples of the former
include GMAC, Ford Credit, CIT, Allstate Credit, J. C. Penney Credit
Corp., etc. Typically, this type of paper is issued through banks and,
occasionally, direct to ultimate buyers by the finance company itself.
As a rule, this paper has no secondary market, although under certain
conditions some companies will repurchase their own paper prior to maturity. It is normally issued either at par or on a discounted basis
and can be written in odd amounts to the nearest thousand, say $82,000.
The minimum is usually $25,000, but with some companies it is $100,000.
Your bank may not have a service charge for handling your purchase
order. This is worth looking into because, as the illustration shows,
a $20 fee can wipe out almost a full 1 percent on a $25,000 purchase to
mature in 30 days.

Generally speaking, direct finance paper is competitive with dealer
paper in maturities up to 30 days. Beyond that, dealer paper is generally more attractive. Dealer paper enjoys a good secondary market: it
can be sold back to the dealer before maturity, normally at the going
interest rates. In effect, dealer paper is underwritten or inventoried
by the dealer firm from the corporate issuer. It is then sold directly
to investors. While minimum size is normally $100,000, our firm within
the past year started selling pieces as small as $25,000. In effect, we
have succeeded in bringing commercial paper down to the level of the
small investor or the medium-size corporate buyer.

GUIDELINES FOR BUYERS

If you are going to invest in commercial paper, or any other money
market securities, set down on paper some guidelines and minimum quality
requirements to be followed in your purchases. Here are some examples:

1. If NCO/Moody's or S&P rating is available, minimum
    rating must be P-3 and A-3 respectively.

TABLE 8

REDUCTIONS IN YIELD CREATED BY A FLAT
$20 COMMISSION OR SERVICE CHARGE

Days	30	60	90	180	360
Amount					
1M	24.00%	12.00%	8.00%	4.00%	2.00%
2M	12.00	6.00	4.00	2.00	1.00
3M	8.00	4.00	2.67	1.33	0.67
4M	6.00	3.00	2.00	1.00	0.50
5M	4.80	2.40	1.60	0.80	0.40
6M	4.00	2.00	1.33	0.67	0.33
7M	3.43	1.71	1.14	0.57	0.29
8M	3.00	1.50	1.00	0.50	0.25
9M	2.67	1.33	0.89	0.44	0.22
10M	2.40	1.20	0.80	0.40	0.20
15M	1.60	0.80	0.53	0.27	0.13
20M	1.20	0.60	0.40	0.20	0.10
25M	0.96	0.48	0.32	0.16	0.08
50M	0.48	0.24	0.16	0.08	0.04
100M	0.24	0.12	0.08	0.04	0.02

2. If commercial paper ratings are not available, minimum
    bond ratings should be "A" by Moody's, S&P, or Fitch's
    for industrials and finance companies and BAA (BBB) for
    utilities.
3. Maximum position in any one corporation should not be more
    than 25 percent of invested funds (assuming total invest-
    ment of $1 million or more). Diversify!

One quick note should be made here of the difference in discount
interest and so-called par equivalent interest. In the first instance,
such as a U.S. Treasury bill or piece of commercial paper, you are putting up only the discounted amount, whereas in the second instance, such
as a commercial paper or government agency issue, you are putting up the
full face value of the instrument. What might be of interest, however,
is that a rough rule of thumb states that on a 90-day maturity there is
a 1/8 percent difference between a rate quoted on a discounted basis and
one quoted at par. Hence, a price of dealer commercial paper yielding
$5\frac{1}{2}$ percent is the equivalent of a bank CD yielding $5\frac{5}{8}$ percent on a par
equivalent basis, assuming the maturity is 90 days. This is important
to keep in mind when comparing various money market instruments.

Normally, on the settlement date, you must have "good funds"—a
cleared balance or "fed funds"—in your account. This necessitates depositing check drawn on a local bank the day before, or wiring—through
your local bank and the Federal Reserve System—the funds on the morning
of the settlement date. In this latter case, the settlement and actual

trade date can be one and the same. This is the most common way of handling settlement for transactions.

When you're purchasing money market securities, deal with experts whenever you can. If it's Merrill Lynch or any other competent firm, and you're not in a major metropolis, ask the office manager to recommend the account executive who specializes in this area. In short, deal with a pro.

On the question of the proper settlement of transactions, a few words are in order. Normally you must have "good funds," meaning a clear balance, or "Fed funds" in your account on the settlement date. This necessitates depositing a check drawn on a local bank the day before, or wiring—through your local bank and the Federal Reserve System—the funds on the morning of the settlement date. In the latter case, the settlement and actual trade date can be the same. We call this a "cash trade" or "same-day settlement." It is the commonest way to handle transactions.

QUESTION

1. What are some ways in which temporarily excess cash can be profitably and safely invested?

---

25   A-M CHANGES ITS ACCOUNTING

(Reprinted by permission from the *Cleveland Plain Dealer* (April 26, 1973).)

Addressograph-Multigraph Corporation increased its allowance yesterday for doubtful and uncollectible accounts by $6.5 million, resulting in a $3.25 million, or 40 cent a share, charge against fiscal 1973 earnings.

The company said analysis of accounts receivable showed an additional provision should be made for doubtful items, bringing the reserve to $12 million. A-M said it has expanded its staff and tightened its procedures to collect as many of the doubtful accounts as possible.

For the first six months of its fiscal year, which ends July 31, 1973, Addressograph reported net income of $5.6 million, or 69 cents a share.

QUESTIONS

1. Does every company expect to collect every dollar of credit it grants? Explain.

2. From an economic standpoint, when and where is the break-even point for writing off bad accounts?
3. Should credit granting be the salesman's job or someone else's responsibility? Explain.
4. As an outside auditor or accountant auditing someone's books, how do you determine if an account receivable is good or bad? What type of information do you rely on? Where do you find the information?

---

26   SPEEDING ACCOUNT COLLECTION

(Reprinted by permission from *Book-Keepers Journal*, vol. 26, no. 205 (Spring, 1971): 94-95.)

This is an example of how a jobbing printer employing about 100 people used training to solve one of the problems isolated when the analysis of training needs was carried out. The firm had a small office under the control of a chief clerk covering sales, estimating, purchasing, wages, and costing.

THE PROBLEM

When the company considered problems, one in particular stood out. The collection of accounts was very slow and credit to the extent of 90-100 days was being given to the company's debtors. A speedier collection would bring much-needed cash in to the company.

First, the manager responsible for the analysis looked at the method used for costing to see whether the system was wrong or needed improvement. He did this *before* considering any training aspects of the problem.

WAS THE SYSTEM RIGHT?

Two men in the office were responsible for collating information on:

1. time worked on the job from work tickets
2. materials used
3. outwork and special purchases related to the job

These two clerks were experienced and had the knowledge needed to do the job, but were inclined to be a little unsystematic in their way of working.

Two girls in the office were responsible for:

1. applying cost rates to time worked and calculating the labor cost

2.   working out cost of materials
3.   adding up total costs of the job
4.   transferring the costs to a control summary
5.   passing the summarized costs to the chief clerk for
     pricing

The girls had tables to help them make their calculations and a
small desk machine to help them add up the total costs. The chief
clerk, who had other duties as well as pricing, passed the priced dockets to the invoice typist without delay and it was clear that he was
not causing the bottleneck.
It was decided that the method was sound and that with one or two
minor changes it should stay as it was.

THE TRAINING REMEDY

The jobs of all four cost clerks were then examined in more detail.
Some simple training helped the two men become more systematic in their
way of working. This improved the rate at which they passed dockets
through.
When the jobs of the two girls were examined more closely and the
knowledge and skill of the two girls compared with the requirements of
the job it became clear that:

1.   They were not good at arithmetic.
2.   They did not understand how to use the calculating tables
     because they were unsure they cross-checked all figures
     by manual calculation.
3.   They did not understand the importance of the job or how
     it fitted into the system.

Simple training programs for the girls were devised, organized, and
controlled by the chief clerk. As a result, the summarizing of the cost
sheets was speeded up and this meant that invoices were sent sooner to
customers. The period for collection of accounts was reduced approximately by 20 days because the collating of costing information inside
the company had been speeded up.

QUESTION

1.   Why is it desirable to collect accounts receivable in the
     shortest possible time?

---

27   TWO CONVICTED IN PANAMA COPPER CABLE PLOT
        TO SWINDLE BANK OF AMERICA OF $5.8 MILLION

(Reprinted by permission from the *Wall Street Journal*, (April 2, 1973). © Dow Jones & Company, Inc., 1973.)

A federal jury convicted two men of swindling $5.8 million from the Bank of America in a Panama copper caper. U.S. attorney William D. Keller said Kenneth N. Dellamater, a 60-year-old attorney, and Robert D. Pollock, 45, will be sentenced April 16 by Judge Charles H. Carr. Maximum sentences could range up to 15 years of imprisonment and $20,000 in fines.

A former Bank of America official, Edward Snead, previously pleaded guilty to two counts of issuing bank funds without authority, in connection with the scheme to defraud the bank. According to Mr. Keller, Snead caused the bank to disburse about $5.8 million to a Panamanian company, Oceantech Panama Incorporated, from February to August, 1971.

Oceantech, a company set up by Dellamater and Pollock, obtained a $5 million revolving line of credit from the Bank of America through a parent company, Oceanographic Geophysical Corporation, Long Beach, California, also formed by the two men. Supposedly, the loan was to finance the salvage of thousands of miles of copper cable reputedly sunken in the coastal waters of Panama.

Dellamater and Pollock obtained the credit by submitting projections to the bank's general loan committee showing that the project could produce profits of $250 million. The loan committee agreed to give the credit if the two men would secure guarantees from the Chase Manhattan Bank in New York, insuring Bank of America against any losses.

However, Snead disbursed the money without receiving any guarantees and delayed sending letters of credit to the bank department, which would check on them, thereby concealing the fraud from other officials. Meanwhile, the U.S. attorney said, Pollock and Dellamater were supplying Snead with copious, but fraudulent, international commercial invoices of fictitious copper cable to keep the bank's record in apparent order.

Mr. Keller said the two men never did find any salvageable cable, although they told Snead they were "reeling in the cable like the dickens."

Dellamater and Pollock were convicted on one count of conspiring to violate federal laws against unlawful disbursement of bank funds and two counts of aiding and abetting Snead in violating those laws. Each count carries a maximum sentence of five years.

Snead will be sentenced for his part in the copper caper by federal judge Lawrence T. Lydick on April 24. He could receive up to ten years in jail and $15,000 in fines, Mr. Keller said.

The U.S. Attorney's office said the fate of the more than $3 million as yet unrecovered isn't completely known, but Dellamater and Pollock did spend much of it on a Panamanian shipyard and on the fruitless search for the copper cable.

"Any loss which the bank may incur will be very substantially less than the ($5.8 million) figure mentioned (by the U.S. attorney)," a Bank of America spokesman said. He declined to estimate the size of the loss.

QUESTIONS

1. As a result of the situation described in the article, Bank of America has an accounts receivable that cannot be collected. What will happen to the bank's income in 1973 as a consequence of this bad debt?
2. How might it have been possible for Bank of America to guard against this loss? Would it have been worth the cost?

---

28   KEEPING TABS ON INVENTORIES IS A HEADACHE
            FOR COMPANIES DESPITE MODERN TECHNIQUES

Harry B. Anderson

(Reprinted by permission from the *Wall Street Journal* (April 25, 1973). © Dow Jones & Company, Inc., 1973.)

Things were finally starting to look a little rosier at Paterson Parchment Paper Company, a big office supply and paper concern.

At the end of the first nine months of 1972, Paterson Parchment showed a small operating profit, compared with a year-earlier loss. An official predicted that the company would also have an operating profit for all 1972, after several years of big losses. True, the company was facing a large write-down from the sale of its copying machine division, but the division had been a loser, and in the long run Paterson Parchment stood to gain by disposing of it.

However, things didn't turn out as well as expected. Last month Paterson Parchment announced that the company had another big loss in 1972 despite the encouraging gains of the first nine months. The reason? A chagrined management explained that accountants at a key division, in effect, had been counting the same inventory more than once. The blunder made it necessary to write down earnings in the three years since 1970 by a whopping $1.3 million.

Paterson Parchment's woes may be extreme, but inventory problems are hardly uncommon. Despite the advent of computerized accounting and sophisticated management techniques, keeping tabs on inventories is still full of pitfalls—as increasing numbers of companies seem to have discovered lately. One dramatic example: Whittaker Corporation, a big Los Angeles conglomerate, was recently forced to buy back two subsidiaries it had sold to another company when a $6.3 million inventory shortage in the subsidiaries' accounts was uncovered.

FROM OVERBUYING TO THEFT

Inventory problems that have been reported recently range from simple overbuying of goods to outright theft. For example, Wichita

Industries Incorporated, based in New York, said that write-downs of
slow-moving inventory in its mechanical controls division accounted for
as much as $20,000 of the company's 1972 net loss of $91,767. Drug Fair
Incorporated, a Washington-based drug retailer, said a recent downturn
in earnings can be attributed partly to what is euphemistically known as
inventory "shrinkage"—warehouse pilferage and shoplifting—as well as
overbuying of goods that later had to be sold at discounts.

Paterson Parchment's problems were apparently the result of inexperience. A company spokesman says that in 1970 and 1971, it made
"major changes" in accounting personnel at its Kee Lox Manufacturing
Company division, leaving the unit "without top-level people" to look
after the books.

One of the worst mistakes occurred when the division, which makes
inked ribbons and carbon paper, reworked a substantial amount of finished goods to improve the inking. The accountants failed to remove the
original value of the reworked inventory from the books. Instead, they
made duplicate entries. The error was eventually discovered through a
physical inventory, but in the meantime the company had been seriously
underestimating the division's cost of goods sold. This is a key figure that many companies arrive at by subtracting the value of year-end
inventories from the year-earlier figure. Consequently, profits were
being overstated.

Nobody knows how many companies have inventory problems. There has
been a spate of news stories on the subject in recent months, and some
management experts say that as the economy heats up—and inventories increase—the problems may intensify. According to the Commerce Department, inventories have been rising rapidly in recent months, climbing
$1.8 billion in February to $197 billion. It was the seventh consecu-
tive monthly rise of more than $1 billion.

SURPRISES AHEAD

"You're going to see much more activity in the inventory area,"
predicts Emanual Weintraub, a member of the Institute of Management
Consultants in New York. "Inventory management is better when things
are bad and worse when business is good. I'd be willing to bet that
nearly every time you find a major surprise in earnings, you'll find
a major surprise in inventories."

Such surprises aren't new, of course. Retailers long have made
systematic provision for inventory losses as a result of shoplifting
or light-fingered employees. Every now and then, a major scandal
points up the seemingly endless possibilities for inventory frauds.
Such a case was the salad-oil swindle of the early 1960s, in which vast
sums of money were lent against nonexistent stores of vegetable oil.
The back office problems that put a number of brokerage houses out of
business in the late 1960s were in reality inventory problems—keeping
track of the millions of pieces of paper that are the raw materials of
the securities industry.

Great strides have been made in inventory control in recent years,
management experts say. "Inventory control is a highly refined science
dealing with measurable variables," says David Boodman, vice president
of Arthur D. Little Incorporated, the Boston management consulting firm.
Successful control techniques "have become commonplace in a lot of

industries," he says, "and they're in all the textbooks." But, he is quick to add, "the surprise is that there are still lots of companies" that aren't using them.

Inventory control takes more than fancy management techniques. According to Jack Brier, chairman of Kleinert's Incorporated, an apparel and shoe concern, inventory control systems are only as good as the people who use them.

Mr. Brier should know. For the year ended last October 7, Kleinert's reported a net loss of $67,000, in contrast to a year-earlier operating profit of $689,000, or 80 cents a share. In a letter to shareholders last December, Mr. Brier said that one reason for the deficit was a breakdown in a new inventory control system at the company's newly acquired Danoca division. "We had a standard cost accounting system, but it wasn't applied," Mr. Brier asserts. "The people didn't have the capability to understand it or follow through." Some have since been fired.

TRACING THE PROBLEM

Sometimes, inventory problems can be hard to pin down. RPS Products Incorporated, a Baltimore-based auto-parts distributor, had been expecting earnings for the year ended last June 30 to top 95 cents a share. But the company discovered a huge inventory shortage and wound up reporting a new loss of $449,000, in contrast to a year-earlier profit of $1.1 million, or 89 cents a share. Now it is believed that about 25 percent of the inventory that the company should have had on hand wasn't there. How it was lost—or whether indeed it was ever present— isn't known. The company hadn't taken a general physical inventory for over a year.

Physical inventories, which are conducted about once a year by most firms, generally catch any discrepancies between recorded inventories and actual stocks. But interim financial reports, usually based on estimates of inventories, can often be misleading. RPS Products, for example, reported earnings of nearly $1 million in the first nine months of 1972, before it discovered its shortages.

Knowing the exact amount of inventories is important because it is used to calculate the cost of goods sold; this, in turn, is subtracted from sales receipts to arrive at a gross profit figure. The cost of goods sold is calculated by subtracting the amount of inventories on hand from the amount of inventories at the beginning of the reporting period, plus inventories acquired during the period. Between physical inventories, these figures are often rough calculations at best.

Physical inventories don't necessarily prevent errors. In the case of Whittaker, the Los Angeles conglomerate that had to buy back two subsidiaries when shortages were found, professional investigators found that the discrepancies had developed over four years. The shortages were "concealed by the alteration of accounting records, including physical inventory quantities," according to Whittaker.

Just who was tampering with Whittaker's books wasn't disclosed. The company's outside accounting firm, Arthur Andersen & Company, recently took the unusual step of paying Whittaker $875,000, but the firm denied any legal liability in the matter.

QUESTIONS

1. Is it humanly possible to keep track of an inventory valued at more than $100 million which includes hundreds of thousands of items? Explain.
2. For most businesses, why is it important to have accounting control over inventory at any point in time? Give three reasons.

---

29   PATERSON PARCHMENT INCREASES WRITE-OFFS,
                          WIDENING '70-'72 LOSSES

(Reprinted by permission from the *Wall Street Journal* (March 26, 1973). © Dow Jones & Company, Inc., 1973.)

Paterson Parchment Paper Company substantially increased its write-off of inventories at its Kee Lox Manufacturing Company subsidiary, widening net losses for 1970, 1971, and 1972.

Paterson said it expects the write-offs to affect 1972 results by about $200,000, instead of the $140,000 estimated last November 30. The company hasn't yet reported 1972 figures, but for the nine months Paterson reported operating income of $128,652, or 12 cents a share. An unrelated special charge of $1.5 million produced a nine-month net loss of $1.4 million.

The company also said the write-offs will increase 1971 losses by about $982,000, instead of the previously estimated $770,000. Before discovery of the inventory error, the company reported an operating loss for 1971 of $452,809, which was reduced to $275,186 by a special credit of $177,623.

In addition, Paterson said, the 1970 net loss will be increased by about $110,000. The company previously reported one of $885,348.

Kee Lox makes inked ribbons and carbon paper. A spokesman said the inventory problem arose mainly from an overstatement of values in 1971 caused primarily by "major changes in accounting personnel" at the division, which left Kee Lox "without top level people" to do the inventory accounting.

The spokesman said one of the problems arose when Kee Lox reworked finished goods to improve the inking. He said the subsidiary's accounts didn't remove the value of the reworked inventory from the books, but made another entry once the reworking was completed. Thus, what was in effect the same inventory was valued more than once.

The spokesman said Paterson has installed top accounting personnel at Kee Lox following discovery of the errors.

QUESTIONS

1. What is meant by the term "write off"?
2. Does the explanation of the inventory value decrease seem plausible? Could internal control techniques have prevented this accounting error? How?

---

30   DATA TRENDS CHARGED WITH FRAUD VIOLATIONS IN BOOKKEEPING PROCESS

(Reprinted by permission from the *Wall Street Journal* (June 27, 1973). © Dow Jones & Company, Inc., 1973.)

The Securities & Exchange Commission charged Data Trends Incorporated with fraud violations of federal securities law.

At the same time, the agency said the Parsippany, N.J., computer equipment maker consented to a court order permanently enjoining it from future fraud violations in connection with registration statements and financial reports filed with the SEC or issued publicly. The company consented to the injunction without admitting or denying the charges, the agency said.

According to the SEC's complaint, filed in federal district court in New York, Data Trends in 1970 and 1971 entered into agreements designed to give the company "a bookkeeping device or technique" to allow it to treat certain research and development costs as assets, rather than as charges against its current income, which would have created an operating loss.

The bookkeeping method, which the company used in its financial statements for the fiscal year ended June 30, 1970, was inconsistent with Data Trends' publicly disclosed accounting policy of listing its research costs as expenses in the period they were incurred, the SEC said.

In addition, the complaint said, Data Trends filed with the SEC registration statements that failed to disclose these accounting techniques.

The stock of Data Trends is traded over the counter.

In New York, Robert Hughes, chairman and president of Data Trends, said his company had believed its accounting procedures to be "totally accurate." Following the SEC charges, he said, it "adapted its accounting treatment to avoid any further question."

QUESTIONS

1. When a company spends money, it can charge the amount as an expense or capitalize the amount as an asset. Explain when an expenditure is an asset and when it is an expense.
2. Accepting the SEC's view, was a CPA wrong in certifying Data Trends financial statements? Explain.

31   IS NATIONAL LIBERTY A FALLOUT VICTIM?

(Reprinted by permission from *Business Week* (June 9, 1973): 32.)

National Liberty Corporation, the Pennsylvania-based insurance
holding company, has long been at odds with regulators over its hard-
sell advertisements for mail order health care policies. But now, one
insurance commissioner has stirred a new controversy by declaring insolvent National Liberty's subsidiary, National Home Life Assurance
Company. In 1972, it provided $85 million in revenues toward the six-
company group's total revenues of $117.9 million.

What caused Virginia Commissioner Everette S. Francis to reach his
drastic conclusion, which sent National Liberty's stock plummeting on
May 25 to $2\frac{3}{4}$ from 7, was his interpretation of National Home's 1972
financial statement. Ironically, even National Liberty's archest foes
in other state insurance departments find themselves backing the company and opposing the Virginia conclusion.

This week, the issue was being debated in the hallways at the annual meeting of the National Assn. of Insurance Commissioners at the
Washington Hilton. On hand to present the company's case were its
founder and chief executive, Arthur S. DeMoss, and its chairman, Robert
E. Slater.

THE TECHNIQUE

It all came about because of the way National Home writes off its
immense underwriting (advertising and policy acquisition) costs. They
are shifted to National Liberty and to National Marketing, Incorporated,
and paid off by National Home only after underwriting profits reach $1
million. This allowed National Home a profit of $1.1 million in 1972.

But Francis would have none of this. He demanded that $12.1 mil-
lion still owed to the parent and its marketing arm be listed as a
liability in 1972. By his figuring, National Home was insolvent by
about $600,000 ($11.5 million net worth against the $12.1 million).

What was confusing was the timing of Francis' declaration. In
April, 1972, National Liberty changed National Home's accounting after
complaints by insurance commissioners about a $17 million statutory loss
in 1971 caused by the advertising outlay. The new contractual arrangement actually took the risk of underwriting loss away from National
Home. No states complained, including Virginia—or even Missouri, where
National Home is incorporated.

Then on April 20 of this year, Francis told National Liberty that
he had reservations about the new financial statement. In retrospect,
it appears that in its rush to placate the commissioner, National Liberty reacted too quickly. By not fighting, National Liberty gave the appearance that National Home was, in fact, insolvent.

Francis followed up his April 20th letter by declaring that he
would not renew National Home's license until National Home appealed to
his superiors, the State Corporate Commission. At meetings with Francis

and the commission, National Liberty immediately offered to give National Home a $6 million infusion of capital, increase its deposit with the state treasury from the statutory $200,000 to $1 million, and file a revised 1972 financial report with Virginia, including a footnote explaining the new contractual arrangement.

Before the commission announced its findings, National Liberty fulfilled its offer. Thus, on May 24, the commission ordered National Liberty to do what it already had done. But, significantly, the order said nothing about National Home's accounting or about insolvency. The commission merely fined the company $1,000 for not originally including the footnote.

ANOTHER LETTER

The same day that the Corporate Commission announced its decision, Francis wrote to commissioners in the 47 states where National Home sells policies. Francis wrote that

> . . . we come to the conclusion that the company is insolvent and is in such condition that its further transaction of business in the state is hazardous to policyholders and creditors in this state, and to the public.

At midweek, National Home's license was still suspended. The parent was considering a suit because of the costly suspension and publicity.

Virtually no commissioners saw it Francis' way, including Pennsylvania's voluble Herbert S. Denenberg, who was the first to criticize National Liberty's past use of loosely worded advertising featuring Art Linkletter.

Among some financial analysts, there is concern over the projections against which National Liberty is amortizing its immense insurance advertising expenditures. Since the company's marketing approach and product are relatively new, it is still too early to predict with confidence the long-range loss ratio and renewal experience. Meantime, to help feed its omnivorous ad budget, it has borrowed $19.7 million from a First National City Bank syndicate and has drawn an additional $20 million of a $47 million line of credit (collateralized with stock) from a Girard Bank syndicate.

In the National Home controversy, some observers blamed post-Equity Funding jitters. After all, Richmond-based Fidelity Corporation of Virginia held $23 million worth of Equity Funding. With this scandal so close to home, Commissioner Francis may have over-reacted to what he viewed as unorthodox bookkeeping. As for National Liberty, it already has had more than its share of bad publicity (*Consumer Reports* just slammed its health insurance plan), and it, too, was thinking of Equity Funding.

QUESTIONS

1. What was the accounting problem that the Virginia Commissioner was concerned about?

2. Explain the accounting concepts of periodicity and matching. Why are these conventions of value to users of financial reports?

---

32   WHY COMPUTER LEASING IS DEEP IN RED INK

(Reprinted by permission from *Business Week* (May 26, 1973): 34.)

"There are two types of computer leasing companies," says D. P. Boothe, Jr., chairman of Boothe Computer Corporation, of San Francisco, "those that have taken a bath and those about to take one." In the case of his own company, the bath has already occurred.

Latest to go down the drain was Boothe President Paul W. Williams, Jr., who resigned last week. He has been replaced by John L. Farley, Jr., president of Farley Investment Corporation. Earlier this month, Boothe reported a 1972 operating loss of $37.7 million, or $17.70 a share. The chairman placed the blame on "deteriorating conditions in the computer leasing marketplace."

The main problem facing computer leasing companies is that they are at the mercy of the manufacturer who is also in the leasing business. The manufacturer leases equipment that costs him 20 percent to 40 percent of the list price he charges a company like Boothe. The maker can show a handsome profit on his leasing operations by depreciating his equipment over four to five years. But because of the added cost of equipment, the leasing company can show a profit and be competitive with the manufacturer's leasing operations only by offering computers at a lower rent over a longer period—eight to ten years.

SMALL EXPECTATIONS

The snag in this is that the manufacturers are constantly bringing out new equipment such as the IBM System/370, which makes the old equipment less attractive. And data processors, laments Boothe, "want a Cadillac even if they only need to go at Volkswagen speeds."

Boothe expects computer leasing revenues to drop from $36 million in 1972 to $31 million this year, with $27 million of this going to service debt. Last year Boothe projected a deficit between direct costs and rental revenues through 1978 of $34.3 million. It depreciated its IBM System/360 equipment from $125 million to $88.6 million. This reduced the company's net worth from $38.5 million at the end of 1971 to less than $1.5 million now.

Many of Boothe's competitors have fared as badly. This spring Rockwood Computer Corporation announced a $47.6 million write-down of System/360 computers, resulting in a net loss of $35 million in fiscal 1973. Late last year Randolph Computer Company, a subsidiary of Travelers Corporation, sold its leasing assets in IBM System 360s to First National Boston Corporation for some $61 million. Another computer leasing firm, DPF, Incorporated, took a $42.7 million write-down in 1972.

UNSOUND

David R. Caplan, senior computer analyst for Auerbach, Pollak & Richardson, claims that computer leasing "is not a fundamentally sound business in the first place." And he adds that the IBM System/370, with its higher purchase price, longer payback terms, and built-in peripheral equipment, "precludes success in the computer leasing business."

Boothe concedes that leasing companies are now "effectively blocked" from buying the latest generation of IBM mainframes. His company is intent on "enhancing" its computer portfolio, signing long-term contracts to lock in its customers, and branching out. Special attention is being paid to three subsidiaries: Courier Terminal Systems, Incorporated, which produces computer terminal devices; Boothe Airside Systems, which produces airport passenger loading equipment, and Producers Service Corporation, a manufacturer of precision optical printing equipment.

Asked whether he would reenter leasing if he could return to 1967 when his company was founded, Boothe said, "I rather doubt it."

QUESTIONS

1. How can one company depreciate their computers over four to five years while another firm depreciates the same type computer over eight to ten years? What happened to the leasing firms that were depreciating their computers over eight to ten years? Why did this happen? Does this situation prove that depreciation rates should be uniform across all firms? Why or why not?

---

33   THE ACHILLES HEEL OF RETAILING: ACCOUNTS PAYABLE

E. A. Weinstein

(Reprinted by permission from *The Journal of Accountancy*, vol. 127 (July, 1969): 48–49. Copyright 1969 by the American Institute of Certified Public Accountants, Inc.)

(Edward A. Weinstein is a member of the firm of Touche & Co.)

On November 1, 1968, a shipment of 50 dozen bathing suits was discovered in the "trouble line" of a large northern specialty store.

In the spring of 1968, a major manufacturer of menswear decided not to do business with a leading discount house. One hundred thousand dollars in receivables were consistently five months old over a four-year period. There were excessive unproved returns and unauthorized advertising allowances.

In the winter of 1967, shortage in a major western department store increased to 4 percent from 1.5 percent the preceding July.

In 1967, a large southern department store counted "locker stock" (consigned merchandise) in the hosiery department, and stumbled onto a $500,000 inventory shortage.

All of these problems were the result of weaknesses in the accounts payable department. Why do these problems occur? Must they continue? What can be the cost of not correcting such shortcomings?

Difficulties in the accounts payable department of retail stores are not new. Disputes over returns, advertising charged to the vendor, incorrect invoices, short or damaged shipments, etc., have existed almost from the inception of the first retail store. What is new is the complexity and volume of paperwork which must be processed in the accounts payable department of a modern store. This vast increase in paperwork flow is related to two facets of modern retailing:

1. the increase in stock keeping units, types of items sold by style, color, and size, and
2. the increase in branch stores.

In order to pay a vendor invoice, a store accounts payable department must match it to a purchase order and a receiving report, each containing the same information about style, color, number of items, cost, and point of receipt. This matching process, and with it the recording and payment process, is completely different today due to the increase of paperwork.

The increasing number and variety of items in a store, and the increase in receiving locations also multiply the possibilities of error by the many people involved in a merchandise transaction including the buyer, the salesman, and the many clerks employed by the vendor and the store.

Most store systems and personnel have not kept pace with this torrent of paperwork. The buying cycle of most stores is not computerized with the exception of check writing. Many store managements, rather than recognize the need to cope with the increasing complexities and volume of paperwork have looked at the accounts payable department as a prime area for cost cutting. Many retail accounts payable problems can be traced to:

1. cost cutting
2. failure to pay employees adequately
3. inadequate working conditions
4. lack of management attention
5. failure to hire competent people and keep them interested

CALCULATED RISKS

A manager of a receiving and marking department commented recently that management's goal should be to "maximize profit rather than minimize costs." Minimizing costs can result in increased profits when the cost reduction does not cause losses or result in greater costs than those displaced. All too often, however, management takes calculated risks which focus only on the cost element which, in general, can be determined. The risks vary and may be classified as follows:

1. In the best of calculated risks, the amount of loss in terms of dollars can be estimated; only the intangible cost of not policing employees cannot.
2. In other decisions on cost cutting, the amount of loss in terms of dollars cannot be estimated. Management feels that other controls partially reduce exposure to loss.
3. Finally, "gut" decisions are made. The amount of loss in terms of dollars cannot be estimated, or is not estimated, and the store has no real additional controls. Management merely "guesses" the possible consequences.

At store X, a calculated risk decision was made and the staff in the accounts payable department was reduced 10 percent. After a period of time, controls were neglected or reduced to a point which permitted practices as follows:

1. Unmatched receiving reports and invoices were not accrued.
2. The accounts payable manager hid invoices from internal auditors who were checking the department as a result of numerous vendor complaints.
3. Unauthorized "settlements" at 50 percent of the claimed amount were being made by the accounts payable manager.
4. Payments were made without proof of delivery. No check was made to the numerical control of receiving aprons to determine that the store was not making duplicate payments.
5. Buyers were allowed access to invoices before posting.
6. The accounts payable manager had a supply of receiving reports which he used to facilitate payments to vendors who complained of nonpayment.
7. There was no policy for writing off uncollectible balances from vendors. These accounts, which arose from returns, cooperative advertising and payment errors, were written off at the discretion of the accounts payable manager.

At store X, a buyer in a major appliance department was authorizing payment for merchandise never received. His fraud was not detected because he had access to invoices prior to posting which enabled him to falsify the purchase journal and, as a consequence, his departmental shortage. The fraud occurred because he was able to authorize payment without receiving report.

For two years, a special controller and an eight-man staff labored at store X to properly record and pay the backlog of unentered "prior season" invoices and receiving reports.

MAGNITUDE OF EXPOSURE

The size of transactions in the accounts payable department in a retail store makes it a prime area of management concern. Herbert A. Tripp, Jr., vice president of Federated Department Stores, has stated: "I think it is pretty well conceded that accounts payable is the area in which business generally has its greatest exposure to embezzlement of catastrophic proportions, because it is less difficult to commit large fraudulent disbursements than to misappropriate cash receipts in large amounts. Large individual transactions are, of course, more characteristic of accounts payable than of accounts receivable." He adds that "department stores have added materially to this general vulnerability by the way in which controls have been discarded to streamline and accelerate the movement of merchandise and the disposition of paperwork."

An accounts payable problem has many ramifications. It affects:

1. shortage statistics
2. inventory levels
3. vendor relations
4. ability to sell
5. store profitability
6. store financial condition. . .

QUESTIONS

1. Discuss the problems which can arise in the management of accounts payable. How could these problems be resolved?
2. Why is the accounts payable area a more sensitive one than accounts receivable?

34　　　365 DAYS MAY HAVE BEEN GOOD ENOUGH FOR CAESAR, BUT LENDERS FIND THAT 360 PROVIDE MORE PROFIT

James F. Carberry

In 46 B.C., Julius Caesar proclaimed that a year would be pegged at 365 days, with an extra day added every fourth year. What was good enough for Caesar has been good enough for the rest of us ever since except for the nation's bankers.

A lot of bankers are using a 360-day year to compute the interest they charge to borrowers on commercial and corporate loans. This means, in effect, that they are collecting a smidgin more interest on these loans than their stated "annual" interest rates would indicate.

Though the practice has been going on for many, many years, it is only recently that borrowers have gotten angry enough about it to fight back. Lawsuits have been filed in Chicago, Philadelphia, Portland, Ore., and elsewhere, alleging that because the banks calculate on the basis of a bobtailed year they are charging an effective interest rate higher than that stated on loan agreements. Sometimes, it is alleged, these charges violate state usury laws.

$145 MILLION A YEAR

Though only small amounts of money are involved in the difference between 365- and 360-day charges on any one loan, the nickels and dimes add up to an impressive pile.

Wright Patman, chairman of the House Banking and Currency Committee and the principal burr under the bankers' saddle, estimates that use of the bobtailed year results in overcharges to borrowers of at least $145 million a year. "This practice," he grumbled in a speech to Congress, "comes down to just plain old-fashioned greed. It is the kind of thing that saps the confidence of the American people in the banking system."

Use of the short year is sweeping. In a 1971 study, the Federal Reserve System found that most of the 232 banks responding based at least some commercial and corporate loan charges on it. More recent inquiries by this newspaper disclose that the practice is still widespread; for example, 15 of the nation's biggest banks admit to employing it.

According to the bankers, use of the bobtailed year began before the widespread use of adding machines; clerks who had to do the computations with pencil and paper found it a lot easier to multiply and divide by 360 rather than 365 or 366. Since nobody seemed to care much, the 360-day base continued in use through the age of calculators and now is imbedded in the banks' computer programs. "Converting our computers to a 365-day year would be a massive job," says one officer of a major bank.

BORROWERS AREN'T SYMPATHETIC

The argument that the 360-day year is custom and would be too much trouble to change meets with absolutely no sympathy among borrowers. They point out that some banks use the short year to figure the interest they charge borrowers, while using Caesar's year (despite the difficulty in multiplying and dividing) to figure their payout to savings account depositors. And the bankers' own bank, the Federal Reserve System, itself uses the 365-day year in calculating what it will charge member banks borrowing from it.

The 1971 study by the Fed indicates there is no pattern to use of the short year. The same bank, it found, may use the short year in calculating interest on one loan but not on another. ("Little guy" borrowers aren't affected, since their loans are usually repaid in monthly installments that cover a whole 365-day year.)

Harold L. Perlman, a Chicago businessman and lawyer, got angry enough about the whole thing to file a class-action lawsuit in 1970 against First National Bank of Chicago, a unit of First Chicago Corporation. The suit alleges that the bank overcharged Mr. Perlman about $5,000 by using the bobtailed year to calculate interest on two five-year loans totaling $1.7 million.

The suit also says that Mr. Perlman, who claims he learned of the short-year calculation only when he couldn't reconcile a bank interest charge with his own figures, wasn't told that his loans were based on a 360-day year. It asks that the bank refund the alleged overcharges to him and to every other customer who might be affected.

BENDING A LITTLE

First National replies that the 360-day year is traditional and
that Mr. Perlman, a longtime customer of the bank, was aware of this.
The bank moved to dismiss the lawsuit as a class action, but the Cook
County circuit court denied the petition; the bank has appealed to the
Illinois Appellate Court.

Banks have already lost a round in Oregon, where a federal district
court has ruled that actual interest charges on several loans made by
First National Bank of Oregon, a Portland-based unit of Western Bancor-
poration, were in excess of permissible state maximums. The reason: The
bank was using the 360-day year. First National has appealed. In the
meantime, another class action is pending in Philadelphia, where a lawyer has accused 20 banks of violating state usury ceilings through use
of the bobtailed year.

As the result of a New Jersey state supreme court decision, 38
savings and loan associations in that state were required to rebate to
borrowers about $2.4 million in overcharges resulting from their com-
puting mortgage interest rates on the 360-day year. The court had declared use of the bobtailed year illegal in mortgage contracts of more
than one year.

The banks are bending a little under the pressure. For one thing,
corporate financial officers now are a lot more aware of the bankers'
year. "We have many more corporate borrowers who've been insisting on
a 365-day clause in their loan agreements. They're getting it, because
we don't want them to go elsewhere," says an executive of a major California bank. In other cases, borrowers report that their bankers have
quietly abandoned the practice without being asked, or at least have
begun disclosing their use of the 360-day year in their loan agreements.

QUESTIONS

1. What are the reasons that the 360-day year is commonly
    used to compute interest?
2. What changes are taking place in relation to using the
    360-day year for computing interest?

---

35   BANKERS CONSIDERATIONS IN LOANING
                TO SMALL CLOSELY HELD BUSINESSES

Donald F. Kanoff

(Reprinted by permission of the Educational and Research Foundation
of the Connecticut Society of Certified Public Accountants, publishers
of *The Connecticut CPA*, vol. 36, no. 2 (December, 1972): 30-32.)

(Donald F. Kanoff is assistant vice president of The First New
Haven National Bank.)

Small businesses amount to approximately 90 percent of the business
units in our country. Some of the small businessmen who have received
financial counsel and assistance from their banks have grown strong and
important in their industries and to the nation as well. Many others,
whose future at one time may have appeared bright, have failed. There
is a high mortality rate among small businesses, particularly new ones,
and the small concern is much more vulnerable, primarily due to lack of
capital, than the larger one. Difficulties in securing trade and bank
credit, lack of experience in meeting the day-to-day decisions of business operations, uncertainty with respect to employees and suppliers,
and the absence of an established clientele, are all particularly acute
problems during the first and most critical year of a firm's existence.

It is important to note that small businesses represent a key part
of total banking customers. Almost all of these concerns need and deserve bank credit assistance. Every day bankers are faced with requests
for loans, both from previous small business borrowers and from new applicants.

Like the businessman, the banker can meet his responsibilities only
if his decisions are based on adequate and reliable information. The
bankers problem is to determine the degree of risk involved in each proposed loan. He must satisfy himself that every loan he makes will be
repaid according to the terms after profitable use by the borrower. He
does this by giving due consideration to many factors, not the least of
which is the analysis of the financial history of the business over a
period of years. This requires certain basic information as contained
in the balance sheet and profit and loss statements. It is not necessary that these figures be audited, however, an opinion by the CPA as
to the manner in which the statement has been prepared is of value.

To obtain complete financial information with respect to the financial factors often is a laborious, exacting task, not because of
unwillingness on the part of the applicant to provide the bank with
adequate information, but rather because many small businesses do not
maintain adequate records. The lender needs to obtain complete information regarding the company's assets, liabilities and net worth.
Similar information on the principals of the business, such as their
outside assets and liabilities, is needed as well. It is important to
know the company's sales, its expenses and its net profit or loss over
a period of three years. Few businesses can succeed if they keep no
record of their financial affairs, and the bank encourages that management set up adequate records for reporting purposes.

When the financial data have been obtained, the banker must study
them to determine whether sufficient credit strength is shown to warrant the advance requested. In the analysis of these figures, ratios
as such assume relatively little importance. The banker must endeavor
to determine whether the capital of the owners afford sufficient cushion, in light of all the circumstances, to justify the advance. Many
small businesses need equity capital rather than loans. Consequently,
it is generally necessary, when loans are arranged, to set up these
advances on a somewhat long term basis and to look to future earnings
for retirement of the loan. The margin of profit, therefore, becomes
an important consideration and it should be definitely established by
past performance and possibly even meaningful projections.

In all small business loans it is essential for the bank to obtain collateral wherever it is available and to require the personal endorsements of the principals. Frequently, the endorsements of the wives of the principals also will be required. The collateral and the endorsements often have much less financial value as strengthening factors then would appear at first glance, although they are very valuable from a psychological point of view.

Basic credit factors are similar in all loans; hence these considerations apply when appraising the loan application of a small business concern. The personal factor—the character and capacity of the management—is probably the most important single consideration. In addition, of course, the financial and economic factors must not be overlooked.

The starting point of a loan application is usually an interview between the principal of the business and the loan officer. The applicant will usually state the amount of the loan requested and its maturity. During the interview and investigation, the loan officer will need to obtain the answers to four basic questions:

1. What is the quality of the management?
2. What is to be the specific use of the proceeds?
3. What is the specific repayment source?
4. In the event that the loan is not paid from the intended source what is the alternate source of repayment?

The loan officer has at his disposal the applicant's credit file and in most cases he should have had an opportunity to review it before the initial interview. The review of the credit file will probably raise some questions with regard to the loan request. The customer should bring with him a current balance sheet and profit and loss statement. These statements should be studied with care and compared with the financial condition of previous periods.

Of importance to the banker is the quality of the business's management. Management is sometimes referred to as being the personal credit factor. As stated previously, the personal credit factor is the cornerstone of credit and is given the utmost consideration in the granting of a loan. It is well to remember that people, not financial statements, repay loans. Management personalities must be well understood before the figures on the financial statement are analyzed. Being intangible, the quality of management does not permit accurate measurement. The integrity and ability of management must be considered. Integrity is a component of character and is of concern whenever trust is put in an individual as that individual is expected to perform in an absolutely upright manner without any reference to outward circumstances. While integrity is an intangible quality and difficult to determine or measure the banker must determine in his own mind that his customer possesses the required integrity. The banker through necessity must largely rely on the borrower's reputation but he must realize that reputation does not necessarily reveal the true character of his customer. Integrity alone is not sufficient to repay the loan but must be coupled with financial ability to repay if the loan officer is to be satisfied. Business management must have the ability to carry out programs in all phases of business including sales, production, personnel, purchasing, and financial management.

The real test of management ability is how it handles adversity. Only a few of the banker's customers have been through the test of adversity and it is therefore difficult for the officer to find real evidence of high integrity and management ability among his borrowers.

The financial statements when properly analyzed can reveal much information about management ability. The figures, in the last analysis, are the results of either capable management planning or show the results of a lack of planning. It is imperative that the loan officer satisfy himself that the borrower has sufficient ability and experience in his line of business so that he can have some assurance that the financial condition of the business will remain satisfactory and the business will be profitable during the term of the loan.

In the granting of bank credit the banker must determine, based on the purpose of the loan, a suggested repayment schedule. Various names have been given to types of loans which reflect the purpose or repayment method of the loan. These names would include "self liquidating loan" which is used for the temporary increase of accounts receivable and inventory or both with repayment to come from the cash which is released as these same current assets are decreased in the normal course of business. A "bank partnership loan" is one in which borrowings fluctuate up and down on a seasonal basis and the business continues to owe the bank at its low points because of its inadequate working capital. Another term, "capital loan" describes the situation where current liabilities exceed current assets, in which case the bank is furnishing risk or venture capital.

In order to intelligently make unsecured business loans the banker must try to "see into the future." Since the repayment of the loan is an event which is to occur in the future, he must use all his abilities in order to determine whether or not a planned repayment will actually take place as intended. In order that a bank loan be successfully made it must, in addition to its specific source of repayment, have an alternate source of repayment in order to be a sound risk. The adequate existence of real working capital and real net worth throughout the loan is the real test of an alternate repayment source. The alternate sources could be profits retained in cash, shifting the loan to a secured loan or to another lender, or addition of permanent capital on the part of the owners. One of the vital reasons for looking at the alternative method of repayment is the fact that the banker cannot overlook the effect which economic conditions have upon the success or failure of a business. This, as previously pointed out, is particularly significant in every small business operation.

The banker needs to know as much about the borrower's business as is possible to arrive at an intelligent decision. By providing the banker with adequate statements that anticipate most of his questions the customer gains the banker's confidence and achieves prompt and understanding service. Thus, it is advisable for the banker, businessman and CPA to confer regarding the information needed in each specific loan request. It is also appropriate to recommend that after the necessary information has been assembled the three parties meet to review all aspects of the loan. The businessman will be able to explain his position with the assurance provided by adequate information. He will also be able to call on his CPA for professional support. The banker's confidence will be fostered by the ready availability of the necessary facts and the businessman should justifiably expect this confidence to translate into prompt credit service.

QUESTIONS

1. Discuss the considerations banks look for in businesses before loaning them money.
2. What is a self-liquidating loan?

---

36   AT&T'S PACIFIC TELEPHONE UNIT IS PARED
TO DOUBLE-A CREDIT CLASSIFICATION BY S&P

Lindley B. Richert

(Reprinted by permission from the *Wall Street Journal* (May 18, 1973). © Dow Jones & Company, Inc., 1973.)

In a landmark credit decision, the senior securities of giant Pacific Telephone & Telegraph Company lost their prime triple-A classification by a major rating service, Standard & Poor's.

The San Francisco utility is the largest member of the Bell System, which collectively accounts for more than 17 percent of all the new bonds issued by U.S. corporations. A weaker credit status will make it more expensive for the telephone system to raise between $4 billion and $4.5 billion in public funds needed for this year's record $9.5 billion construction program.

From a market standpoint, the downgrading of Pacific Telephone by one credit level to a double-A ranking further diminishes the illustrious reputation for investment safety long enjoyed by Bell System obligations. About a year ago, New England Telephone & Telegraph Company became the first majority-owned American Telephone & Telegraph Company subsidiary to be reduced to double-A from triple-A, also by Standard & Poor's.

(Moody's, the other major credit rating service, said it is maintaining its triple-A classification on Pacific Telephone's senior securities.)

"For many years, the Bell System issues were the standard by which the quality of most other bond borrowers were measured, but its enviable prestige is fading fast," commented one specialist. Given the continuing enormous clip at which the Bell companies are pouring out new debt offerings, it's only a matter of time before some of the other system members also are deprived of their premium rating, he added.

MAY 31 AUCTION

The new double-A classification applies to Pacific Telephone's pending auction May 31 of $200 million of 36-year debentures and $100 million of seven-year notes.

Furthermore, the lowered rating applies to the units' $2.4 billion
principal amount of notes and debentures already outstanding as well as
the company's 6 percent cumulative preferred stock. That total includes
about $2.27 billion of debentures, $75 million of notes and $82 million
of the preferred shares.

Standard & Poor's said its move reflected a "deteriorated" earnings
projection for Pacific Telephone bondholders since 1969. Income after
taxes that year exceeded the company's fixed-rate expenses by 3.46
times. But the important debt coverage had fallen to 2.43 times at
year-end 1972, according to the rating service. A triple-A rated telephone company should be able to exhibit a "three-times coverage," an
S&P spokesman said.

The agency added that Pacific Telephone's present depressed level
of fixed-charge coverage and uncertain prospects for adequate and timely
rate relief is a direct result of the California Supreme Court decision
in June, 1972. It annulled a year-earlier rate order directed by the
California Public Utilities Commission for Pacific Telephone to increase
intrastate rates effective July, 1971. These were designed to increase
company revenue $143 million annually.

"This, combined with the present rate of inflation, level of interest rates, and the massive expenditures required to maintain a satisfactory level of service to the consumer has made it necessary for
Standard & Poor's to take this action," said H. Russell Fraser, vice
president, corporate finance, and chief of S&P's corporate rating section.

A spokesman for Pacific Telephone, which is about 90 percent owned
by AT&T, said it knew last year there "would be a grave risk of having
our bond ratings downgraded" because of court-ordered refunds amounting
to $175 million. The order was part of the action by the California
high court last June when it overturned the utility's rate increase.

It said the downgrading "will increase our interest cost for new
debt by many millions of dollars," beginning with the debt financing
scheduled for the end of May. It said the only remedy is to "achieve
and maintain rates which will restore our earnings to the level necessary to regain the confidence of the investing community." Pacific Telephone has a $291 million proposed rate increase pending before the
state utilities commission—an increase which it has reduced twice from
the original $328 million.

One market analyst said, however, the cost impact on Pacific Telephone, as a result of the downgrading, will be substantially muffled
for right now by the unusually narrow rate spread between rating categories, caused by extremely light financing volume. It may result in
a cost increase of only about 0.02 to 0.03 percentage point on its pending $300 million sale, he said. However, the long-run effect will be
enormous after the market corrects the rate differential to a normal
range of about 0.15 percentage point over an extended period, he added.

In partial confirmation of that, the unit's $7\frac{1}{4}$ percent debentures
of 2008 fell a minimal 1/8 point, or $1.25 for every $1,000 of bonds,
in New York Stock Exchange trading yesterday.

BIGGEST BORROWER

Pacific Telephone's voracious appetite for capital has made it the
biggest borrower among AT&T's various operating units, accounting for

about $990 million in financings since 1968, an analyst notes.   The $300 million in new notes and debentures ranks to be raised at the end of May ranks among the largest amounts ever sought by a Bell unit.   The only bigger one involved $350 million of 7⅞ percent debentures by Southern Bell Telephone & Telegraph Company last March 20.

In addition to the new debt, Pacific Telephone also is seeking about $265.4 million through a rights offering to stockholders of record May 25.   The company has set a subscription price of $15.25 apiece on the 17,444,830 additional common shares in its rights offering.   The offering will be made on a basis of one share for each nine common shares held and seven common shares for each nine preferred held.   The offering will expire June 29.

QUESTIONS

1. What does the change in rating mean to a telephone bill of a California resident?
2. Why did Standard & Poor's change the rating of Pacific Telephone?
3. Why would outside individuals such as private investors, insurance companies, banks, or anyone else who happens to desire to buy a bond in Pacific Telephone be interested in a rating by someone who has no connection with Pacific Telephone? Is a rating system necessary?

---

37   BENEFICIAL CORP. DEBT GETS OFF TO SLOW START

(Reprinted by permission from the *Wall Street Journal* (May 16, 1973). © Dow Jones & Company, Inc., 1973.)

Beneficial Corporation's $75 million of 7½ percent debentures got off to a slow start at a price of 100.25 to yield 7.48 percent in 25 years, dealers said.

Blyth Eastman Dillon & Company, syndicate manager, wouldn't give a sales estimate late yesterday.   Some institutional investors had withdrawn their purchase orders when the terms were released.   Prior to that, the offering had been oversubscribed, a spokesman said, presumably at more attractive tenative price terms.

Rated double-A by Standard & Poor's, the debentures provide ten years protection against lower-interest cost refunding.   After 1983 they may be redeemed at various prices beginning with $1,026 for each $1,000 bond, and at declining levels thereafter.

The Wilmington, Delaware-based financial holding company will use proceeds to reduce outstanding short-term bank loans and commercial paper used mainly to provide subsidiaries with working capital.

QUESTIONS

1. What determines the price of a bond issue?
2. How do premiums and discounts occur when bonds are issued?
3. How will Beneficial record the debentures on their books
    of account?

---

38   INTERNATIONAL BANKNOTE OFFERS TO SWAP STOCK
                         FOR $10.6 MILLION OF DEBT

(Reprinted by permission from the *Wall Street Journal* (June 27,
1973). © Dow Jones & Company, Inc., 1973.)

International Banknote Company offered to exchange shares of its
common for its outstanding 6 percent subordinated convertible notes and
debentures due February 11, 1984. The company presently has outstanding
nearly $10.6 million in principal amount of its 6 percent subordinated
convertible notes and debentures.

International Banknote said the offer was made to reduce its outstanding indebtedness by converting it to equity, thus paring interest
expense, which presently amounts to about $634,500 a year over the 11-
year period to maturity. Moreover, the company said, the offer would
also increase the per-share book value, with an accompanying improvement
in the company's balance sheet ratios.

International Banknote said that acceptance of the offer by all
debenture or note holders would result in issuance of about 4.7 million
shares, or one share for each $2.25 principal amount of such notes and
debentures. The stock closed yesterday at 75 cents a share, unchanged,
on the American Stock Exchange. Acceptance by holders of 75 percent in
principal amount of the notes and debentures outstanding would require
issuance of about 3.5 million shares. The offer is due to expire July
19 unless extended.

The offer was made a day after holders at the annual meeting approved an increase in the company's authorized common shares to 25 million from 20 million. International Banknote is a holding company,
whose principal operating subsidiary, American Bank Note Company, is a
printer of engraved stock and bond certificates, currency notes and
travelers' checks.

QUESTIONS

1. Why would a company want to exchange stock for a bond?
2. How would this transaction be recorded in the books of
    account?
3. How would this transaction change the debt/equity ratio?

39   A FOOTNOTE TO WATCH

(Reprinted by permission from *Business Week* (June 9, 1973): 78.)

Accountants-can't-win department: When companies repurchase their
bonds, through sinking fund programs and the like, the difference between what they pay for the bonds and the bonds' face value must be
figured in earnings. In the past, companies often bought bonds back at
premiums above face value—which reduced profits. So they tried to
stretch the charge over as many years as possible. Some investors complained that that practice artificially inflated profit figures. What
companies should do, they argued, was take their lumps and charge earnings the full amount in the year that the bonds are repurchased.

So accountants changed the game. This year, for the first time,
companies must charge earnings all at once. But with yields high,
scores of companies are now buying bonds back not at premiums but at
discounts—a plus for profits, and sometimes a substantial one. So
naturally, some investors are complaining that the new accounting practice artificially inflates earnings.

Certainly, it's a footnote to watch for in 1973 earnings reports.
And it's likely to be in pretty small print in some statements.

QUESTIONS

1. Why does a $1,000 bond change value in the market place
    after it has been issued?
2. If an outstanding bond is paid off with the proceeds of
    a newly issued bond, is an economic gain likely to occur?
    Why or why not?

40   SHAREHOLDERS DECLINED LAST YEAR FOR
                        FIRST TIME, BIG BOARD STUDY FINDS

(Reprinted by permission from the *Wall Street Journal* (March 26,
1973). © Dow Jones & Company, Inc., 1973.)

Owners of stocks and mutual fund shares declined in number last
year for the first time since the New York Stock Exchange began keeping
such records in 1952, the Big Board said.

Expressing concern about the flight of the small investor from the
securities markets, the exchange estimated that the shareowner figure
dropped $2\frac{1}{2}$ percent last year to 31.7 million from 32.5 million at the
end of 1971.

"The exchange, as well as the entire securities industry, has been aware for some time that the small investor has been out of the market," James J. Needham, Big Board chairman, said in announcing the findings.

"The securities markets need the individual investor, both small and large, to provide liquidity and contribute to a smooth and efficient functioning of the auction market process," he added.

Discussing the 800,000-shareowner drop in 1972, Mr. Needham said the number of mutual fund holders fell 300,000 and that odd-lot trading continued to produce net sales by investors. Odd lots, which often are traded by small investors, generally are orders of fewer than 100 shares.

The exchange's holder estimates are based on a complex formula, with components including gross national product, national population, personal income, the number of member-firm offices and salesmen, odd-lot purchases and sales, total trading volume and mutual fund accounts, sales, and redemptions.

In addition, the Big Board periodically conducts a census based largely on corporations' shareholder rosters. The most recent census was taken in 1970 and showed 30.9 million holders.

Previous censuses produced the following results: In 1965 there were 20.1 million holders; 1962, 17 million; 1959, 12.5 million; 1956, 8.6 million, and 1952, 6.5 million.

QUESTIONS

1. Why would each of the following like to see the number of shareholders in this country increase?
    a. New York Stock Exchange
    b. companies listed on the NY stock exchange
    c. current holders of outstanding common stock
    d. the general public
2. What economic function do stockholders perform?
3. What economic function do stock exchanges perform?

---

41   SLOW DIVIDEND GROWTH WEAKENS STOCK PRICES,
SOME ANALYSTS THINK

Charles J. Elia

(Reprinted by permission from the *Wall Street Journal* (June 27, 1973). © Dow Jones & Company, Inc., 1973.)

The boys down at Growth Unlimited Ltd. used to snicker like crazy when the little old lady asked if the stocks they were pushing paid a good, safe dividend. After all, even a little old lady should have known that you bought stock for all those nifty earnings increases and resultant capital gains, not for the sake of a paltry dividend.

Well, although she isn't hanging around the office saying "I told you so" because she and many other small investors are out of the market altogether, it looks as if the little old lady may have been right. At least, the view that dividends do count for a lot is gaining ground in the investment business. And an increasing number of analysts and advisers are concluding that what has been happening to dividends in recent years explains more about the stock market's current malaise than inflation, the plight of the dollar abroad or Watergate.

That theory got a boost last week when the government loosened its restrictions on corporate dividend increases to permit companies to raise payouts by more than the 4 percent to which they had previously been limited. Stock prices immediately shot up by nearly 20 points, as measured by the Dow Jones industrial average, though much of the gain has been lost since. Still, the prospect of larger dividend increases has been one of the market's few bullish influences in recent weeks.

SLOW RISE IN PAYOUTS

The total amount paid out in dividends has been increasing. Last year, businesses paid out $26.4 billion, nearly half their after-tax profits of $53 billion. In the first quarter this year, dividends increased to a yearly rate of $27.3 billion, around 43 percent of yearly profits at the yearly rate of $63.7 billion.

The rate of increase has been declining for years, however, especially for industrial companies whose shares usually are considered blue-chip investments. Since 1966, according to Francis H. M. Kelly, an analyst for the securities firm of James H. Oliphant & Company, payments have risen only 4.4 percent a year, in contrast to the 10 percent yearly growth rate from 1961 through 1965. In manufacturing, dividends since 1966 have increased only 3.5 percent a year.

"Dividend-paying potential," says Mr. Kelly, "is the foundation of stock values." Although few analysts would dispute this, over the years it has been overshadowed by per-share earnings. Analysts came to take it for granted that corporate per-share earnings increases over the long run would almost automatically translate into dividend increases. And, they assumed, per-share earnings increases would also translate into higher stock prices.

It hasn't worked out that way lately. The price investors are willing to pay for earnings, as measured by the per-share price-earnings ratio, or P-E, has dropped sharply. So the share prices for many companies are stagnating even while their earnings continue to climb. The explanation, many analysts now believe, is that dividends aren't keeping up with earnings increases. "In my view," Mr. Kelly says, "the diminution of dividend growth has been the principal reason for a reduction in P-E multiples throughout the basic industries."

YIELDING TO INFLATION

In 1961, the average P-E of shares listed in the Dow Jones industrial average was 21, meaning that the average share of those companies sold at a price equal to 21 times per-share earnings. By last year, the ratio had dropped to 14, and at times this year it has fallen nearly as

low as 12. The price of a share in a hypothetical company with per-
share earnings of $1 in 1961 would have been $21 that year; had its
earnings risen 100 percent to $2 a share by 1972, the price would have
risen only 33 percent to $28.

Investors simply appear to be demanding higher yields—in dividends
or interest—on the securities they buy. And this means, some analysts
say, that investors are coming to terms with the hard realities of inflation; the price of money, like most everything else, has gone up.
"Yield will explain this whole P-E correction," says William M. B. Ber-
ger, a partner in the Denver-based investment management firm of
Fleming, Berger-Kent & Company. "We've seen bond yields go up and bond
prices go down, utility yields up and their stock prices down, so why
on earth shouldn't industrials do the same? Capital is worth more today, so why shouldn't industrials make their adjustment, too?"

The demand for yield is breathing new life into an old investment
idea—that investment gain, or total return, is the sum of dividends
plus price appreciation. As simple minded as this idea may seem, it
had been largely overlooked in recent years.

FUTILE STRIVING FOR GROWTH

For most of the 1960s, investors considered potential per-share
earnings increases the key measure of a security's attractiveness.
Indeed, in those days the securities that seemed most attractive often
paid nominal dividends, or no dividends at all. Because of the emphasis
on per-share earnings, investors and corporate managers preferred to see
earnings plowed back into expansion or diversification that would produce more per-share earnings increases. Though they expected that in
time dividends would rise, too, dividends weren't a key factor in many
investment decisions.

"Virtually 100 percent of the thinking in the 1960s went into earn-
ings-per-share growth, and little or no weight was given to the yield
factor," says M. Rollin Pelton, research director of Laird Incorporated.
But now, he says, "There's greater emphasis on having a larger part of
total return come from dividends."

The failure of many investment managers in striving for consistent
gains of 12 percent to 15 percent in stocks also partly explains the renewed interest in dividends. The professional money managers are redis-
covering the historical fact that a very large part of stock-market return always has consisted of dividends. A study in the late 1960s by
the University of Chicago, for example, deduced that from 1926 to 1965
an investor could have achieved an average 9.3 percent yearly return,
based on market averages; more than half this return, however, would
have come from dividends rather than stock-price appreciation.

Similar studies underscore the importance of dividends and show
that over shorter periods it's even more unreasonable to expect anything
like 12 percent or 15 percent market gains. Such studies have helped
bring about what Robert Colin, executive vice president of Faulkner,
Dawkins & Sullivan, calls "a return to realism" in the securities industry. "People tended to forget that yield was part of the total return
equation," he says. "Managers are starting again to look at the basis
and theory of investment. It's no longer a game."

Over the long run, many analysts believe, corporate managements—
if they can't boost their stock prices by increasing their earnings—
will have to boost them by increasing their dividends. The pressure is
especially compelling because yields on relatively safe bonds have risen
sharply in recent years to match or often exceed dividend rates on
"safe" stocks; bonds of many blue-chip companies today yield more than
do the common stocks of the same companies. As recently as 1957, however, the situation was the reverse; common stocks then yielded, on the
average, more than bonds—sometimes, as in 1950, nearly three times as
much as bonds.

"The fact is that there is an interest-rate cycle, and it does affect common-stock prices over time," says Mr. Pelton of Laird, Inc. He
believes that common-stock prices now are depressed partly because of
high bond yields. He believes that when the cycle is complete, dividend
yields once again could equal or exceed the return on bond investments.

Until last week, the prospect of fresh big dividend increases was
clouded by government price controls that held dividend boosts down.
Controls have "substantially hampered" the ability of corporations to
reward their shareholders, says Morris Offit, research chief at Salomon
Brothers. "We sense," he said before easing of controls, "that investors may come to feel they are sacrificing current return for appreciation that may never materialize."

QUESTIONS

1. If a company never intends to pay a cash dividend what is
    the worth of the stock?
2. Why is a company interested in seeing its stock price
    rise? Give five reasons.

---

42   STOCK REPURCHASES ON THE RISE

(Reprinted by permission from *Financial World*, vol. 139, no. 2
(January 10, 1973): 4.)

When a company decides to repurchase its own stock, it can accomplish its objective in several different ways. The most obvious way is
to place orders for a specific number of shares to be purchased on one
of the major stock exchanges. Purchases also may be made in off-board
transactions with holders of large blocks of stock. And of course,
there is the tender offer approach, in which a firm gives public notice
that it is willing to buy a certain number of its shares at a fixed
price.

There are advantages and disadvantages in each of these methods.
Regular stock exchange purchases, for instance, are subject to SEC
guidelines limiting these transactions to 15 percent of daily trading

volume. (The purpose is to prevent a company from manipulating the price of its stock by excessive buying on its own behalf.) Purchases from institutional investors are an effective way for a company to get its hands on a sizable quantity of stock but it may also have the effect of lessening what corporations often spend years in trying to accomplish —furthering institutional interest in their stock.

As for tender offers, they invariably require the payment of a fairly hefty premium over the prevailing market price of an issue in order to encourage holders to turn in their shares; thus, this method isn't likely to be employed in run-of-the-mill stock repurchase programs.

Why do companies want to buy in their own shares? The reasons most frequently cited are these: to accumulate shares for acquisition purposes; to have shares on hand for stock options; and to be ready for conversions of senior securities. Obviously, these are sound and conventional corporate objectives. But sometimes a company will announce with a good deal of fanfare that it plans to repurchase its shares because "it is the best investment we can find." Such an opinion may indicate that a relatively limited search has been conducted or it may suggest frustration with the market performance of the issue in question —in any case the opinion is scarcely an objective one.

Nevertheless, a stock repurchase program clearly can be a constructive influence on the price of a stock—even a relatively small number of reacquired shares will help a company's showing because the number of shares on which earnings are to be calculated is reduced.

The fact that a company is able to make a significant investment in its own stock is indicative of financial strength. Many companies now undertaking these programs wouldn't have been able to do so a few years ago when managements were more concerned about the liquidity of their balance sheets than about buying in their own stock.

Whether or not a stock repurchase program is a sound policy, therefore, depends upon the individual situation. When the purchases are made for conventional purposes such as future acquisitions or when a company simply has an excessive number of shares in relation to the size of its business, the program should be beneficial to the shareholders who retain their investment. On the other hand, a large-scale stock repurchase program may raise questions about the ability of management to invest capital in the business at a profit rate sufficient to make the company's shares interesting from a long-range investment standpoint.

The accompanying table lists 15 companies which have been adding to their holdings of treasury shares in recent months, according to their reports to the New York Stock Exchange. This alone doesn't justify investment purchase. But in addition, these firms have compiled favorable investment records and appear reasonably priced in today's market, qualifying them for investment consideration.

TABLE 9

COMPANIES BUYING THEIR OWN SHARES

Company	*Shares Held	Total Shares Listed	Percent Held
Aetna Life & Casualty	634,639	27,080,208	2.3
Borg-Warner Corp.	742,698	19,484,822	3.8
Brown Shoe	305,905	7,873,456	3.9
Campbell Soup	521,906	33,905,669	1.5
Carlisle Corp.	67,820	2,458,164	2.8
Crocker National	250,000	10,471,180	2.4
Dana Corp.	843,717	14,324,846	5.9
Gulf & Western Industries	2,797,150	18,958,347	14.7
Intertake Inc.	377,142	4,257,128	8.9
Johns-Manville Corp.	875,506	19,193,964	4.6
Marcor, Inc.	675,756	28,124,542	2.4
Scot Lad Foods	77,709	2,201,259	3.5
Stride-Rite Corp.	268,232	3,256,544	8.2
Texas Eastern Transmission	1,198,757	24,155,435	5.0
U.S. Industries	294,913	29,544,306	1.0

*Latest figures (through Dec. 22, 1972) as reported to N.Y.S.E.

QUESTIONS

1. Define treasury stock. How do you account for treasury stock?
2. Can treasury stock be an asset? Why or why not?
3. Why would a company be interested in buying back its own stock? What are some of the economic reasons for this?

43   MATTEL NAMES SPEAR PRESIDENT AND OMITS
                    ITS QUARTERLY DIVIDEND

(Reprinted by permission from the *Wall Street Journal* (March 21, 1973). © Dow Jones & Company, Inc., 1973.)

Mattel Incorporated, a financially troubled toy maker, announced appointment of a new president and the omission of its quarterly dividend.

Arthur S. Spear was named president in addition to being chief operating officer, and Raymond P. Wagner was named president of the Mattel Toys division. They succeed Ruth Handler, who formerly held both the corporate and the divisional presidencies.

Mrs. Handler was named cochairman, to share that office with Elliot Handler, who remains chief executive officer.

The Handlers founded Mattel in 1945. Mr. Handler served as president until 1967, when he was elected chairman and chief executive officer and Mrs. Handler was named president.

The company also said that directors voted to omit the dividend for the current quarter. The company paid $2\frac{1}{2}$ cents in previous quarters; the latest dividend was paid January 19.

Mattel declined comment on the reason for the management changes and the omission of the quarterly. The company recently announced that it expects to report a "substantial" operating loss for the fiscal year ended February 3, 1973.

For the nine months ended October 28, Mattel reported net income of $6.4 million, or 39 cents a share, compared with a year-earlier loss of $4 million, including a $1.1 million loss from discontinued operations. For fiscal 1972, the company posted a net loss of $29.9 million, including a $2.9 million special charge.

Mr. Spear, 52 years old, joined Mattel in 1964 after eight years with Revlon Incorporated. He has been a director since 1944 and was named executive vice president and chief operating officer earlier this year.

Mr. Wagner, 41, came to Mattel in 1967 after 14 years as a merchandising executive at Sears, Roebuck & Company. Last July he was named executive vice president, marketing, of Mattel Toys and senior vice president of the parent company.

QUESTIONS

1. What is the probable result in the market price of a firm's stock after a dividend has been omitted when one was expected to be paid? Why?
2. What apparently caused Mattel to omit the dividend?

---

44   SUSQUEHANNA TOLD TO PAY $2.8 MILLION
IN CONTRACT DISPUTE

Al Delugach

(Reprinted by permission from the *Los Angeles Times* (July 3, 1973): 8. Copyright 1973 Los Angeles Times.)

A San Diego court Monday awarded $2.8 million damages in a breach-of-contract civil lawsuit against Susquehanna Corporation, Los Angeles-based conglomerate.

Superior Court Judge Eli Levenson made the judgment in favor of Andrew O'Sullivan, former president and majority stockholder of a San Diego computer firm, Digital Development Corporation.

Digital Development presently is a subsidiary of National General Corporation, Los Angeles.

Susquehanna confirmed that it has indemnified from loss in the case of its codefendants, National General and Xebec Corporation, a National General subsidiary acquired from Susquehanna along with Digital Development.

ADEQUATE RESERVES

Susquehanna said its reserves for litigation were adequate to cover the award and that the court decision would therefore have no effect on its earnings.

Earlier Monday Susquehanna, which had a $5 million net loss last year, announced that it has completed a new bank loan agreement providing revolving and long-term credit of $20 million.

Susquehanna said the agreement with Bank of America enabled it to retire existing bank debt of $12.6 million.

In the San Diego lawsuit, O'Sullivan claimed that he had not received additional shares of Digital Development stock according to a profit ratio set out in his contract to sell the firm in 1967 to Xebec, then headquartered in Kansas City.

Judge Levenson said he was satisfied the defendants had tried to "frustrate" the terms of the purchase agreement. The court granted recision of the contract and awarded O'Sullivan $2,799,962 based on evaluation of his interest as of January, 1970.

Xebec was merged into Susquehanna in 1968. Susquehanna later formed a new corporation of the same name and sold it along with Digital Development, to National General in 1969 and 1970.

ACQUISITION UNDER WAY

National General is in the process of being acquired by American Financial Corporation, Cincinnati.

A controlling interest in Susquehanna is owned by Studebaker-Worthington Incorporated, New York.

Herbert Korholz, former president of Susquehanna, and the company were suspended last March by the Securities & Exchange Commission from association with any registered investment company. Each had consented in the order without admitting or denying charges that they violated SEC rules in the purchase and sales of securities involving Susquehanna.

The SEC case involved sale of Susquehanna's holdings in Pam American Sulphur Company in 1971 to Studebaker-Worthington.

Susquehanna's stock closed Monday on the American Stock Exchange at $3.50 per share, unchanged prior to news of the San Diego damage award.

QUESTIONS

1.   In accounting terms, what is a reserve? Is it an asset, a
     liability, an owner's equity, or some other type of account?
     Explain your answer.
2.   What entries might have been made by Susquehanna to set up
     the reserves for litigation? What entry should have been
     made?

---

45   PARKER CO. FINDS THAT THE SLEEPING BAG
                  IS MIGHTIER THAN THE PEN IN THE SUMMER

David M. Elsner

(Reprinted by permission from the *Wall Street Journal* (July 30,
1973). © Dow Jones & Company, Inc., 1973.)

What do sleeping bags and fountain pens have in common?
Not much. But it is one particular way that they differ that in-
trigues the Parker Pen Company and has spurred it into a diversification
program that so far includes not only sleeping bags but also outdoor
furniture and motorcycle jackets.
The difference is in seasonalness. Leisure products are big sellers in the spring and summer months. Pens, on the other hand, are most
in demand around back-to-school time and Christmas.
Parker was finding itself with a lot of idle cash on its hands during the spring and summer, explains George Parker, the company's 47-
year-old president and a grandson of one of the founders. In scouting
around for a way to make use of the money, Parker hit upon the booming
recreational-products business.
The two seemed to mesh perfectly: Pens supplied the money for
recreational products, which in turn returned the investment in plenty
of time for the big pen season. Leisure products now account for about
14 percent of Parker's annual sales.
That is only one of Parker's black-ink-producing strategies. At
the same time, Parker has chosen to ignore the mania for cheap ball-
point and soft-tip pens, putting out more expensive ball points and
soft-tips and emphasizing a line of fountain pens starting at about
$5 and ending at $150. In addition, the company is busy seeking new
outlets for its old products.
So far things have worked out exceedingly well. For the first
fiscal quarter ended May 31, Parker reported a 51 percent jump in earnings to $1.3 million, or 44 cents a share, from $861,000, or 29 cents a
share, in the year-earlier period. Sales rose 27 percent to $25 million
from $19.7 million. Mr. Parker says the second quarter won't match the
percentage gains of the first quarter but will be "excellent" nonetheless.
Indeed, since fiscal 1970, Parker's profits have grown at an annual
rate of 15 percent while sales have risen an average of 20 percent. "I

see no reason why we can't continue to do something in that area for the
foreseeable future," Mr. Parker says. For the fiscal year ended February 28, the company earned a record $4.8 million, or $1.61 a share, on
sales of $86.5 million. Analysts have predicted earnings for fiscal
1974 of $1.90 to $1.95 a share.

A FIRST STEP

Mr. Parker sees much bigger things for the future, however. "We're
trying to transfer Parker from a medium-sized manufacturer of writing
instruments to a large, world-wide manufacturer and distributor of consumer goods," he says. The leisure-time diversifications are a first
step.
   The leisure products will open up new markets for writing instruments, Mr. Parker adds. Earlier this year Parker bought Norm Thompson
Outfitters Incorporated of Portland, Oregon, a catalog mail-order house
specializing in recreational clothing and equipment. "There is no reason why we can't sell pens through the mail," Mr. Parker says.
   Similarly, Parker plans to get double-duty from the Garrick Company
of Dallas, a maker and distributor of glassware. Parker purchased Garrick last year. Garrick's products are sold through retail outlets that
stock only a sample or two. The orders are then sent to Dallas, where
the customer's initials are imprinted on the glassware, which is sent
directly to him. Again, Mr. Parker says, desk-pen sets can be sold in
the same way.
   Another recent acquisition is Wheels of Man Incorporated of New
Berlin, Wisconsin, a designer and distributor of clothing and accesso-
ries for motorcycles. Imperial Industries Incorporated, Montreal, a
maker of tents, camp cots and other camping gear, was purchased in 1969,
and Midwest Outerwear Incorporated, Port Washington, Wisconsin, a maker
of clothes for boating and winter sportwear, was acquired in 1971.

ROOM AT THE TOP

Another move has been to concentrate on selling smaller numbers of
middle- and high-priced pens instead of lots of cheap ones. In the late
1960s, when the cheap-pen market was booming, Parker decided to go to
the other way and beefed up its advertising on $10 and $15 gift models.
"The top of the line was relatively empty, and we had plenty of room up
there as it turned out," Mr. Parker says. This year Parker plans to
boost advertising by 25 percent.
   There is no doubt Parker was slow in hopping on the ball-point pen
and soft-tip pen bandwagons. "We could have come out with those pens at
the beginning, but they wouldn't have been better than anyone else's,"
Mr. Parker says. "We couldn't charge $5 to $10 for a piece of junk. It
would have given us a black eye." Today Parker sells a wide line of
ball-point pens and a soft-tip pen known as Big Red, a $5 replica of the
50-year-old, stocky Duofold model.
   Another of Parker's big pluses over the years has been its overseas
business. "We've always thought of our foreign operations as good protection against bad times in the U.S." Mr. Parker says. More than 55
percent of Parker's sales last year were foreign. The company set up
its first foreign distributorship in 1903 and opened plants in Canada

and England by 1924. Parker now has subsidiaries in 17 countries outside the U.S. as well as a number of foreign licensees and affiliates.

According to market surveys, Parker is one of the best-known American brand names abroad. Stockbrokers add that its highly visible name
and good earnings record have put it among the best-selling American
issues in Europe. Recently, Parker's foreign markets have done more
than just protect the company's American position. Devaluation of the
dollar has spurred foreign sales and was a major reason for Parker's
51 percent first-quarter earnings increase.

QUESTIONS

1. Why would a company like Parker have a seasonal sales pat-
    tern?
2. Why would a company want to be in business selling sleep-
    ing bags and pens when production and sales of these items
    are so different?

---

46   GREAT WESTERN UNITED TO RESTATE EARNINGS

(Reprinted by permission from the *Wall Street Journal* (March 23,
1973). © Dow Jones & Company, Inc., 1973.)

Great Western United Corporation said new accounting rules for
retail land sales companies will "materially reduce" the company's
retained earnings and its previously reported operating results. It
declined to estimate the amounts involved.

Through a subsidiary, Great Western Cities Incorporated, the company sells and develops real estate.

The parent company said new rules approved in January by the
Accounting Principles Board will require "extensive changes in the
corporation's accounting methods" for recording land sales and profit
for fiscal 1973 ending May 31. It also talked of restating "some" prior
years' financial statements.

Great Western United added that because of the accounting change,
reporting of its results for the third quarter ended February 28 will be
delayed. It added that it didn't know if required restatement of prior
years' results will delay report of its 1973 results.

The company said that although it's "still evaluating" the effect
of the new accounting rules on its Cities unit, it will change its land-
sales reporting from the accrual method to the installment method of accounting. As a result of the change, Great Western United continued, a
"substantial amount" of previously recorded gross profit will be deferred and reported in future periods as collected.

In a note to its fiscal 1972 financial statement, the company said
that as a result of working capital restrictions, its retained earnings,

which are unavailable for payment of cash dividends, were $66.6 million on May 31, 1972. In fiscal 1972 it earned $5.9 million, or 62 cents a share.

Under its current method of accounting, Great Western Cities reports up to 20 percent of land-sales prices on the installment basis, with gross profit recognized in proportion to the amount received. When 20 percent or more of the selling price is received, the entire balance of the sale and its expenses are recognized.

Generally, under the installment method, profit from these sales are reported as they are actually received. For federal income tax purposes, both Great Western United and its Cities unit have, in the past, reported a substantial part of land sales on the installment method in order to deter federal income tax payments on the sale.

QUESTIONS

1. When is revenue recognized from regular sales transactions? Why?
2. What is an installment sale? How does accounting for installment sales differ from that for regular sales? Why?

---

47   HEARD ON THE STREET

Bill Paul

(Reprinted by permission from the *Wall Street Journal* (August 27, 1973). © Dow Jones & Company, Inc., 1973.)

Has Levitz Furniture Corporation, at long last, finally brought operating expenses under control?

More than past allegations of securities laws violations by certain Levitz officials, it has been the furniture retailer's continuing inability to control costs that has caused earnings to cease their rapid growth. In turn, this has resulted in the price of Levitz stock plunging from the $40 range to as low as $5\frac{1}{4}$ over the last 12 months or so. (It closed Friday at $6\frac{5}{8}$.)

A year ago this month, Ralph Levitz, chairman and chief executive, conceded his company was "fat, dumb, and happy," and consequently, derelict in controlling expenses. Mr. Levitz initiated a cost-cutting program featuring payroll paring and management restructuring. Advertising was brought under control and a restructured commissions schedule was instituted to stop salesmen from pushing mostly low-cost, low-profit merchandise.

Last November, Levitz said operating results were improving. In March the company said the fiscal year ended January 31 had "ended on a

strong note, with operating profits at the highest level of the year in
both dollars and as a percentage of sales."

But then in May, the concern conceded that first quarter results
would be flat. (In fact, they wound up lower.) And later that same
month, Mr. Levitz told disgruntled stockholders that his program had, in
fact, been a failure. The problem, he said, continued to be excessive
advertising costs and overstaffing in nonselling departments.

Now Mr. Levitz is back professing the success of his program, and
this time he may be right if his figures are correct. In a telephone
interview from his Miami headquarters, Mr. Levitz says that since June
the company has been saving $500,000 a month by contracting its tele-
vision advertising to an outside concern rather than doing it in-house.
In addition, a crackdown on Levitz's new national operations manager on
inefficient operations has generated savings of some $250,000 a month,
about half the savings expected when Mr. Levitz's 90-day shakedown
program ends in October, the chief executive says.

So sure of his success is Mr. Levitz this time that last week the
company announced it was cutting prices across-the-board because, as
full-page newspaper ads boasted, "We have eliminated the fancy and expensive frills which do nothing but raise costs."

Mr. Levitz says the recent return of his brother, Leon, and Leon's
son, Gary, to the company's board indicates "a great deal more unanimity
within our family on how this business should be run."

Last year, both men were exiled from top management after the Securities & Exchange Commission charged the company with violations of
securities laws in connection with a registered 600,000 common share offering. Levitz settled the case, conceding certain findings of fact by
the commission. But before the settlement, the concern disavowed a
statement made to the Teamsters union by Gary Levitz that the company
wouldn't oppose a union organization drive if it was delayed until after
the offering.

"Originally," Ralph Levitz says:

*our concept was to sell a large volume of furniture at very
low prices. But then we had outsiders come in and tell us we
were selling too cheap. That helped our profits but hurt our
image. Now those outsiders either are gone or have been converted to the original principle.*

All this isn't to say that Levitz earnings are suddenly going to
resume their upward surge. Levitz says for the second quarter, ended
July 31, earnings likely were about the same "or a little bit better"
than last year's net of $2.7 million, or 16 cents a share, on sales of
$77 million. (Second quarter results are due out this week, Mr. Levitz
indicated.)

At the annual meeting in May, Mr. Levitz termed unrealistic his
earlier forecast that earnings in fiscal 1974, ending next January 31,
would be about 50 percent higher than fiscal 1973s $12.2 million, or
72 cents a share, on sales of $326.8 million. He declines to make a
new forecast, terming the action premature.

Moreover, Mr. Levitz says sales so far in August, are running only
about the same as a year ago, when the company hit record sales of more
than $1 million a day. While maintaining that level isn't bad, he
agrees "we need a big increase in volume" to see significant earnings
growth again.

And that will be easier said than done. Furniture manufacturing is starting to slow down, according to June figures of the Southern Furniture Manufacturers Association, which show that orders booked in June rose only 1.9 percent from a year ago, compared with a 24.3 percent increase for the first six months. Merrill Lynch, Pierce, Fenner & Smith, in a recent appraisal, said that while the long-term demand for furniture seems good, the near-to-medium-term outlook forces the brokerage firm to be cautious about stocks of furniture manufacturers.

Because of Levitz's past performance, some analysts give the impression of wanting to sit on the fence awhile, waiting to see how things develop. "The outlook is very unclear," says one analyst who has followed the company closely for a long time. "I think their cost cutting represents good sound competitive strategy. But I don't think any of their recent moves is great enough to change an opinion one way or the other."

QUESTIONS

1. Describe Levitz Furniture's operating problems.
2. Why would people, in August, 1972, be willing to pay $40.00 a share for Levitz Furniture? And only $6.00 a share in August, 1973?
3. When people or institutions buy a stock are they buying on a past record or a future expected performance?

48   LEVITZ FURNITURE (N)

TABLE 10

(Reprinted by permission for the *Wall Street Journal* (August 28, 1973). © Dow Jones & Company, Inc., 1973.)

Quarter July 31:	1973	1972
Share Earns	$.15	$.16
Sales	93,620,000	77,039,000
Net Income	2,565,000	2,699,000
6 Month Share	.27	.30
Sales	186,236,000	141,586,000
Net Income	4,608,000	5,052,000

QUESTIONS

1. Does it appear from this report that Levitz Furniture is
    having a continuing surge in profits?
2. What would you expect to be the effect upon the price of
    Levitz Furniture stock?

---

49   YALE EXPRESS MAKES IT OUT OF BANKRUPTCY

(Reprinted by permission from *Business Week* (April 7, 1973): 62.)

When Yale Express System, Incorporated, entered bankruptcy eight
years ago, practically everyone in the transportation business thought
it was finished. It had obligations of $36 million and assets of only
$12 million.

Yale was primarily a trucking business, and truckers are not eligible for the kind of Section 77 relief under the Bankruptcy Act that permits railroads to skip most tax and interest payments in order to keep
operating. To reorganize successfully, a bankrupt trucking company must
persuade its creditors to hold off liquidation with the promise of a
better return when the company becomes solvent again. Yale made it.

The company was discharged from bankruptcy on December 31, 1972,
and its creditors are being paid in full. And the company foresees a
profitable future. It has unloaded its money-losing freight-forwarding
operations. And Yale Transport Corporation, its trucking operation, has
moved into the black.

THE PROBLEM

Yale Transport is a medium-sized carrier of general commodities.
With current annual revenues of about $12 million, it is less than half
the size it was before the bankruptcy. Its routes cover the Boston-
New York-Washington corridor, an area of notoriously high operating
costs.

Before bankruptcy, Yale was a large carrier of department store
traffic. It also carried a lot of clothing, and transported such miscellaneous shipments as circus elephants—commodities that require premium service. Yale's chief problem was that it was not collecting premium rates for its service.

In 1965, the year it entered bankruptcy, Yale's operating ratio—
a percentage figure derived by dividing operating expenses by operating
revenues—was 137.6 percent. For December, 1965, the operating ratio
was 168 percent.

Complicating the situation was lax bookkeeping. For the first nine
months of 1964, Yale had reported a profit of $900,000. Then early in
1965, it suddenly announced for the whole year a preliminary loss of
$3.3 million, later after audit by Peat, Marwick, Mitchell & Company
reduced to $2.85 million. At the same time, 1963 figures were restated
to show a loss of $1.2 million rather than a profit of $1.1 million.

Stockholders were understandably irate, and both the company and its auditors were on the receiving end of mismanagement suits. Peat, Marwick blamed the incorrect 1963 figure on omission by the company's accounting personnel of significant information about liabilities and assets. Peat, Marwick eventually settled out of court stockholders' suits brought against it.

F. Ralph Nogg, a midwestern trucking and warehousing executive was named trustee in reorganization. Nogg decided that there was a need for the kind of overnight service between major eastern cities that Yale was providing and that the company could be reorganized if costs could be brought under control. In the meantime, he had to convince Yale's customers that a bankrupt company could provide dependable service.

In 1965, Yale salesmen made their calls armed with a personal letter from Nogg. The letter promised that if the company were to go under, the shipment would be delivered anyway. Back at headquarters, Nogg was casting a jaundiced eye on such expensive frills as computers and sophisticated terminal handling equipment.

"We had some conveyors," says Nogg, "that required an extra man to act as a picker. I found that the pickers weren't working more than a few minutes every hour. The contract said we had to use pickers on those conveyors, but it didn't say we had to use those conveyors. So we got rid of the conveyors and the pickers too." The extensive reliance on computers went also. "The officers use notebooks and pencils to do their figuring now," says Nogg "but they can tell you at 9:30 every morning the day's figure for profit or loss."

TRIMMING DOWN

According to Nogg, Yale also had far too many employees. It now has 220 drivers compared with about 800 in 1965. Total employment is about 500.

Yale also began to seek out the kind of business it could do best and most profitably. Probably the most important change, though, was that Yale began charging customers the full cost of the service. "When we haul an elephant now," says Yale Shapiro, senior vice-president for operations, "we don't do it for free tickets at the circus."

Says James Crosby, new president and chief executive officer: "Much of the business Yale formerly handled was at a loss rate. The decision was made to try to keep the business but to charge rates that reflected the extra service Yale was giving."

Whenever it can, Yale is persuading customers to operate through a centralized receiving and delivery point. It has instituted a program of spot checking shipments to see that they are correctly classified and properly weighed. A shipper who describes a shipment as a low-rated commodity when it is actually a high-rated one can cost a trucking company a considerable amount of revenue. Yale's spot checks have largely eliminated deliberate errors of this sort. The company also uses such techniques as unmarked security cars to reduce loss and damage payments, most of which involve theft. Such payments are now running at about 1 percent of revenues, an extraordinarily low figure. The rate ran as high as 5 percent just a few years back.

GOOD ADVICE

The first few years of the reorganization were touch and go. But by the end of 1969, a solid turnaround had been achieved. For 1970, revenues were $9.2 million, and the operating ratio was 98.4 percent. Estimates for 1972 are for revenues of $12 million and a very good operating ratio of about 94 percent.

Nogg, his job as trustee finished, has resigned and moved to Associated Transport, Incorporated, in New York, another firm with earning problems.

Reviewing the turnaround, Crosby says: "It's a matter of service. Yale is no longer trying to be all things to all people. We've found our place and we think we're going to continue to grow."

QUESTIONS

1. How did Yale Express make it out of bankruptcy? Do you think accounting control of expenses contributed to this turn around? How?

---

50   MEMOREX WRITE-OFF OF $35 MILLION SEEN
                        IN ACCOUNTING SWITCH

(Reprinted by permission from the *Wall Street Journal* (August 27, 1973). © Dow Jones & Company, Inc., 1973.)

Memorex Corporation said its board has decided to abandon deferred-accounting practices for research and development and lease-acquisition costs, and instead will charge such costs against income as incurred. Such a move would require the financially troubled company to take an immediate write-off of about $35 million.

The write-off figure, which had been included in a company announcement last month, is in addition to other previously reported anticipated write-offs. The other anticipated write-offs consist of $40 million from a decision to end mainframe and computer production and $10 million to $15 million from revaluation of certain other leasing assets, "assuming that the company's financial problems are resolved in a way which preserves the ongoing operations of its leasing business," Memorex said.

A spokesman confirmed that the write-offs would result in a negative net worth for the company. According to the balance sheet for 1972, Memorex had a net worth of $32.2 million.

Memorex said that the exact amount of the write-offs will be determined by an audit of the company's books as of last June 30, and that the decision to end deferral accounting for the aforementioned costs is subject to "discussion" with the Securities & Exchange Commission. The Memorex spokesman said he didn't know whether the SEC discussions are related to an appeal last week of the SEC's denial of a Memorex request for a filing extension on its second quarter 10Q earnings report.

The spokesman said talks between the company and Control Data Corporation, Minneapolis, a major computer concern, are continuing. He declined to elaborate. Control Data disclosed in mid-August it was holding discussions with Memorex about possible take-over of certain Memorex operations. Earlier this month, discussions aimed at Singer Company's acquiring voting control of Memorex for $15 million were broken off.

QUESTIONS

1. What effect will this accounting change have on the intangible assets of the company? On net income for 1973?
2. What does "negative net worth" mean?

---

51   SCHLITZ TAKES A CHARGE OF $8.3 MILLION
                        FOR 1972 TO COVER PLANT CLOSING

(Reprinted by permission from the *Wall Street Journal* (April 2, 1973). © Dow Jones & Company, Inc., 1973.)

Joseph Schlitz Brewing Company said the March 16 closing of its Brooklyn, New York, plant has resulted in an $8.3 million extraordinary charge against previously reported 1972 earnings.

The company had said earlier that it intended to write down its $6.2 million investment in the facility to its estimated realizable value and charge it against 1972 earnings.

The charge provided for a $5.2 million write-down of plant and equipment, $7.2 million of payments to employees and $3.6 million of other costs related to the closedown and disposal of the property. This amount, less the applicable income tax benefit of $7.7 million, resulted in the $8.3 million charge, the company said.

Schlitz previously reported 1972 operating earnings of $45.8 million, or $1.58 a share, on sales of $779.4 million, compared with net of $35.2 million, or $1.22 a share, on sales of $669.2 million in 1971. Net income for 1972 was reduced to $37.5 million, or $1.29 a share, by the extraordinary charge. There weren't any special charges in 1971.

QUESTIONS

1. Why did Schlitz write its plant down to net realizable value in 1972? Was this in accordance with generally

accepted accounting principles? In accordance with conservatism? In accordance with the going-concern concept?

---

52   PIGS, PURSES, AND PROJECT REDEPLOYMENT

(Reprinted by permission from *Forbes* (March 1, 1973): 38-39.)

At 60, Robert W. Reneker, president of Chicago's venerable and
conservative Swift & Company, may seem like the last person you'd
expect to find taking on the conglomerator's mantle á la Dallas' James
J. Ling. But he has. With 38 years at Swift behind him, in purchasing
and in sales, Reneker has decided the time has come to take the cleaver
to Swift itself, Ling-style; convert it into a holding company called
Esmark (S-Mark, get it?); break that into four Esmark-controlled companies—Estech (fertilizer and chemicals), GSI (insurance and data processing), Vickers Energy (oil) and Swift (food)—possibly have each offer
stock and let the market decide what the whole thing is worth. The
whole, Reneker clearly believes, will turn out to be worth more than the
sum of the parts.

Project Redeployment was what Jim Ling called the procedure when he
divided Wilson & Company into three parts; and as Ling proved, the procedure is by no means without its benefits. But the hard truth is that
the scheme probably signals that Reneker's five-year effort to upgrade
and diversify the U.S.' biggest meatpacker has fallen on hard times.

WIDEN THAT MARGIN!

When he took over in 1967, Swift was earning only $30 million, for
a meager 1 percent return on its $2.9 billion in sales. Outsiders had
for years shown what happened to Swift's earnings when its profit margin
was suddenly widened by one percentage point. But Swift had never
really cared about margins: Its true love was volume. "We'd wring our
hands," says Donald P. Kelly, Swift's financial vice president, "if we
lost a percentage point in national meat statistics. We'd ship East a
hundred cars of surplus beef a day just hoping we'd find buyers. No
one worried if we lost money."

Bob Reneker did. He set a minimum target of 12 percent return on
mature assets, double Swift's previous average, and if managers failed
to produce, Reneker promptly closed the facility. In five years he
eliminated over 13,000 jobs, almost a third of Swift's payroll, and
closed 330 of Swift's 700 plants, warehouses and offices. More positively, he sorted out Swift's higgledy-piggledy pile of meats, grocer-
ies, and agricultural products into clearly defined divisions, refined
their marketing strategies to emphasize higher margined branded products
like Pro-Ten beef, Brown 'N Serve sausages and Butterball turkeys, and
then backed them with a 60 percent increase in the advertising budget
to $30 million.

In all, Reneker's changes freed $170 million in cash, revived
Swift's plans for diversification that had been dormant since it bought

a small life underwriter, Globe Insurance, in 1958.   The money thus freed he redeployed as follows: $36.5 million for 600 Vickers gas stations in Kansas and Missouri, plus a small refinery in Ardmore, Oklahoma; $83 million for a 51 percent interest in TransOcean Oil, an exploration company with offshore Louisiana crude reserves; and $40 million for Mobil Oil's money-losing fertilizer business, an area where Swift was already established.

By 1972, Reneker could claim to be making some progress. After a sickening dip from $30 million to $15.8 million in fiscal 1968, his first full year at the helm, earnings recovered steadily to $34 million in 1971, as operating profit margins widened from 2.3 percent to 3.6 percent.   Reneker, talking cheerfully about Swift's being at its "fighting weight," confidently predicted that in fiscal 1973 the company would be earning at the rate of $50 million, or $4 a share, vs. $2.66 in 1971.

It was only a dream.   Livestock prices spurted.   But because of price ceilings, Swift was unable to translate the increase into higher product prices; and by August Reneker's financial men were warning that Swift's prospective profit increase could turn into a 20 percent decline.   Reneker turned to his accountants for help.

Swift had for 30 years been using the LIFO (last-in-first-out) method of inventory accounting, which has the virtue of preventing inventory profits from popping up as a kind of spurious net during periods of rising prices.   But prices last year were rising so fast that if Swift had charged the latest livestock prices against the full year's sales, LIFO would have taken a $15 million toll on Swift's pretax earnings.

Reneker quickly converted to first-in-first-out accounting, which raised the value of the company's inventory to reflect current prices. It also, in effect, lowered Swift's cost of sales and boosted profits, making Swift responsible for an extra $26.8 million in taxes over the next 20 years.   While he was about it, Reneker decided to make a few other accounting changes, the largest of which was a $2.6 million (21 cents a share after taxes) savings in payments to the company's pension plan, a side effect of Reneker's earlier payroll reductions.

Thanks to these accounting changes, for fiscal 1972 (ended October 31), Swift reported $2.90 a share vs. $2.66 a share reported (and $2 restated) in fiscal 1971.   A far cry from the $3.15 a share many analysts once had expected, but far better than the $2.14 Swift would otherwise have reported.

BRING ON THE S-MARK!

So far, the stock market has not been impressed. For all Reneker's efforts, Swift is still selling around 11 times earnings, just about at its low for the past five years. And why should it sell any higher? About 80 percent of sales and 75 percent of net still come from meat and grocery products business—and last year showed the chronic risks in that business. And prospects of changing that proportion significantly by internal growth are small.

Which is where Esmark comes in—"a gimmicky thing," Swift's Kelly concedes, "thought up by our advertising and PR people." Esmark's food subsidiary hopefully would command about the same multiple it does now. But what about Estech? A chemical company somewhat like it, International Minerals & Chemical, commands 14 times earnings. As for GSI, a good life insurance company with an aroma of EDP about it might bring 20 or 24 times. An oil company? Maybe 15. If Swift's stockholders approve the scheme later this month, those are the kinds of multiples Reneker hopes Esmark's new subsidiaries will show if they go public. With multiples like that, Swift would finally have the currency to diversify—to make acquisitions for stock or even raise money if need be by selling stock—and reduce its undependable food business to manageable proportions.

    Still to be answered: Will investors buy last year's gimmicks this year?

QUESTIONS

1. Is it right for one man to have the power to make 13,000 people lose their jobs? Explain.
2. What accounting change did Esmark make in 1972 to increase profits for that year? Explain how this must have been done.
3. Why was gross margin the important factor in Swift's conversion to profitability?

---

53   PROFITS RISE

FIGURE 6

(Reprinted by permission from the *Wall Street Journal* (May 4, 1973). © Dow Jones & Company, Inc., 1973.)

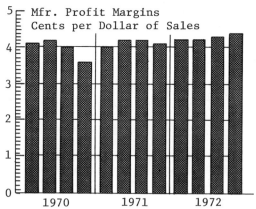

Profit margin of U.S. manufacturers after taxes rose to 4.4 cents per dollar of sales in the 1972 fourth quarter from 4.3 cents in the third quarter.

QUESTION

1. According to this chart, if sales are $100 what are
    expenses for a normal manufacturing firm?

---

54   AMERADA HESS EARNINGS ROSE 66 PERCENT IN
            SECOND PERIOD AND 42 PERCENT IN SIX MONTHS

(Reprinted by permission from the *Wall Street Journal* (July 24,
1973). © Dow Jones & Company, Inc., 1973.)

Despite some uncertainties involving its Libyan crude oil production, Amerada Hess Corporation had gains in earnings of 66 percent for
the second quarter and nearly 42 percent for the six months.

The company had June quarter net income of $33.3 million, or 89
cents a share, up from $20 million, or 54 cents a share, a year earlier.
Revenue rose more than 26 percent to $393.7 million from $311 million a
year earlier.

For the first half, Amerada Hess earned $70 million, or $1.88 a
share, up from $49.4 million, or $1.33 a share, a year earlier. Revenue
increased 17 percent to $799 million from $680.2 million a year earlier.

Net income for 1972s first half has been restated to reflect a
change in the company's method of accounting for costs of undeveloped
oil and gas leases made in 1972s fourth quarter. As a result of the
change, the company said, 1972 second quarter net income was decreased
nearly $1.5 million, or three cents a share, and 1972 first half net was
decreased $3.1 million, or eight cents a share.

In reporting earnings, Amerada Hess cited "uncertainties in realiz-
ations from Libyan crude oil production" sold to Royal Dutch-Shell Group
under long-term contract "as well as uncertainties in regard to the current Libyan negotiations on participation." Because of these uncertainties, Amerada Hess said it has recorded its Libyan profit based on its
estimate of the amount it will ultimately receive for the six months
ended June 30.

The company is a member of the Oasis group, one of three Libyan oil
producing groups negotiating with the Libyan government about new petro-
leum-producing arrangements demanded by the government.

Amerada Hess said plans have been completed to increase the crude
oil capacity at its St. Croix refinery an additional 150,000 barrels a
day. The new units, expected to begin operations during late 1974 and
early 1975, would boost total capacity of the St. Croix facility to
590,000 barrels a day.

QUESTION

1. The percentage increase figures for 1972 earnings look
    very high. Why might this be misleading?

_____

_____

55   JOHNSON & JOHNSON, SCHERING-PLOUGH
                        POST SECOND QUARTER SURGES

(Reprinted by permission from the *Wall Street Journal* (July 24,
1973). © Dow Jones & Company, Inc., 1973.)

Johnson & Johnson and Schering-Plough Corporation, both major drug
concerns, reported considerably higher second quarter profits. Johnson
& Johnson's earnings rose about 16 percent from the year-earlier period
and Schering-Plough's shot up 43 percent.
Johnson & Johnson said its net income for the period was $36.2 mil-
lion, or 65 cents a share, up from $31.3 million, or 56 cents a share,
the year before. Sales rose to $391.7 million from $338.7 million.
In the first half, Johnson & Johnson earned $71.4 million, or $1.27
a share, up from $61.8 million, or $1.10 a share, in the 1972 period.
Sales rose to $763.9 million from $663.2 million.
Schering-Plough said its net income in the second quarter was a
record $27.8 million, or 52 cents a share, up from $19.4 million, or 37
cents a share, the year before. Sales rose to a record $163.7 million
from $132.9 million.
The company's said its first half earnings rose to a record $55.3
million, or $1.03 a share, from $37.3 million, or 70 cents a share, the
year before. Sales rose to a record $318.7 million from $260.3 million.
Schering-Plough said that of the $18 million increase in first half
profit, about $4 million resulted from currency adjustments following
the devaluation of the dollar in February, and about $5.4 million re-
sulted from a reduction in the effective tax rate in Puerto Rico.
The company explained that under Puerto Rico's tax laws, earnings
on production in the Commonwealth aren't taxable for the first 14 years
of business. Schering-Plough had operations in Puerto Rico for only
part of 1972, and 1973 is the first full year.

_____

QUESTION

1. How reliable are quarterly earnings reports? Explain.

_____

_____

56   SEC TO NIP RISING USE OF CASH-FLOW DATA
                       MOVE WOULD MAINLY HIT REAL ESTATE FIRMS

Frederick Andrews

(Reprinted by permission from the *Wall Street Journal* (March 7, 1973). © Dow Jones & Company, Inc., 1973.)

The Securities & Exchange Commission is moving to nip the growing practice of reporting per-share cash flow figures.

A preliminary SEC draft in limited circulation rejects such figures as confusing and possibly misleading. The draft, prepared by the SEC chief accountant's office and other SEC staff members, would bar per-share cash-flow data from SEC filings, severely restrict them in annual reports, and generally discourage use of cash flow as a better measure of corporate results from the customary earnings figure.

"Cash flow" is usually defined as net income, plus certain noncash charges, principally depreciation. The SEC draft questioned whether this relatively simple formulation had any real use "in theory or in practice."

The proposal would mainly thwart real estate companies and real-estate investment trusts. Analysts say it could also affect numerous other industries where, for various reasons, noncash items are a large portion of charges against revenue. These include depletion allowances for oil companies, deferred taxes for leasing companies, and certain depreciation policies in cable television.

The proposal wouldn't affect the detailed "sources and uses of funds" statement currently required in corporate reports and certified by auditors. In addition, outside the real estate field, reporting of per-share cash flow remains infrequent.

Replying to an inquiry, John C. Burton, SEC chief accountant, said the draft differed somewhat from the latest version, but "its basic thrust" remains unchanged. Mr. Burton said he couldn't discuss the current version, which shortly will be submitted to the commissioners.

The SEC has rejected per-share cash flow figures in at least two recent proposed prospectuses. The measure is increasingly common in press releases on real estate results.

The real estate industry contends that because properties typically grow in value, the usual depreciation charges grossly understate true economic income. The depreciation yields substantial tax losses, however. But even using slower depreciation rates in reports to shareholders, realty companies report operating losses.

Some analysts contend this handicap has forced publicly traded real-estate concerns to seek reported earnings by selling investment properties, often against stockholders' long-term interests. They say the need has spawned intricate tax-shelter arrangements, designed to attract well-off investors and, at times, to allow the "seller" a continued stake in the property.

These deals, in turn, are blamed for another accounting controversy —over recognizing profits from the transactions. Currently, accounting authorities are questioning whether, in some instances, the "sales" are really sales.

The SEC draft described companies as using inconsistent definitions of cash flow and possibly violating Accounting Principles Board rules. It said the cash figures mistakenly implied that such funds were always free of other claims and immediately available for distribution to shareholders. Further, the draft contended investors have become accustomed to earnings per share, which in fact is closely linked to a stockholder's claim on equity.

The draft document urged an industry, if its accounting wasn't realistic, to take its problem to the new Financial Accounting Standards Board. In the meantime, it should treat new measures "with extreme caution."

As Mr. Burton has in the past, the draft prodded auditors to take more initiative in individual cases. It noted that an auditor may depart from the profession's authoritative pronouncements if following them would yield misleading figures. The SEC would take a close look at such departures, it warned, but "give great weight" to the auditor's and management's judgment.

In SEC filings the draft would allow, in addition to the usual figures, a careful explanation of why conventional accounting wasn't adequate, together with "supplemental data tables," but no per-share cash figures.

The same data might appear in annual reports. In addition, the reports might contain very limited use of per-share cash-flow data.

Last fall, a group of security analysts specializing in real estate urged a cash-flow measure as the industry's main "earnings" figure. They defined the measure as including maintenance and current taxes, but omitting depreciation and mortgage principal repayments. They also asked much greater disclosure of lease conditions, operating figures and mortgage financing for specific properties, together with independent annual appraisals of their value.

The analyst group argued that for years, sophisticated investors, such as insurance companies, have rooted real-estate investment values in cash flow. In addition, banks and other lenders tie credit conditions to the cash figure, rather than to reported earnings.

"Our net profits, by intent, will always be zero. No accounting period will ever look different from another—ever!" Ira M. Kroger, president of Kroger Properties Incorporated, Jacksonville, Florida, wrote in a recent letter to this newspaper.

QUESTIONS

1. In simple terms try to explain what is meant by cash flow.
2. How does cash flow differ from accrual accounting?
3. Why doesn't the SEC want per share cash flow data reported?

---

57   CONFORMITY OF TAX TO FINANCIAL ACCOUNTING

Don J. Summa

(Excerpted by permission from an article originally published in
The Arthur Young Journal (Spring/Summer, 1972). Copyright © 1972
by Arthur Young & Company.)

(Don J. Summa is a partner of the firm of Arthur Young & Co.)

Income as determined for federal income tax purposes and income as
determined for financial reporting purposes are based upon the same information about the transactions of a business enterprise. As a result,
most accounting methods used as the basis of determining taxable income
agree with the accounting methods used in determining income for
general-purpose financial statements. Both taxpayers and taxing authorities benefit to the extent that taxable income conforms to financial
accounting income, because such conformity seems important to the essential fairness of the taxing system and reduces the effort and cost of
tax law compliance and administration. Nevertheless, the extent to
which tax and financial accounting should conform is a matter with which
the Congress, the Treasury Department, and the accounting profession
have been concerned since the enactment of the first Revenue Act in
1913.
      It appeared at first that close conformity between tax accounting
and financial accounting would be pursued by both the Treasury and the
accounting profession, even though the Revenue Act of 1913 contained no
reference to accrual accounting. Income was to be determined solely on
the basis of receipts and disbursements. It soon became apparent, however, that the complexities of business could not be adequately reflected on a cash basis; and, at the urging of the accounting profession, regulations were adopted by the Treasury Department permitting
taxpayers to use the accrual basis of accounting even though it was
contrary to the express language of the law. The principles underlying
these regulations were subsequently codified in the Revenue Acts of 1916
and 1918.
      This direction, however, was short-lived. A widening gap between
tax and financial accounting emerged as the scope of successive revenue
acts broadened to include social, economic, and political objectives in
addition to the basic purpose of raising revenues. Judicial decisions
further widened the gap. However, except for differences created by
various administrations in their attempts to further certain economic,
social, or political objectives, it may be fairly stated that it is
only accidental that tax and financial accounting differ.

RECORD OF CONGRESSIONAL MODIFICATIONS

Although the ultimate objective of the federal income tax law is
the determination of business net income on an annual basis, various
social and economic theories have been incorporated therein since the
enactment of the Revenue Act of 1913. The federal tax law has been
used to promote such nonrevenue matters as stabilization of the economy,
encouragement of economic growth, and preservation of the competitive

position of small and new enterprises. It has been further modified to accommodate certain concepts based on the ability to pay. Nonrevenue-raising theories have been responsible for such concepts as the installment method of reporting, the completed-contract method, accelerated depreciation, and the investment credit. Use of the federal tax law as a vehicle to accomplish social and other ends was certain to create significant deviations between taxable income and financial income. However, these differences resulted because nonrevenue considerations were added to the tax law, rather than from disagreement as to the proper principles of accounting to be applied.

Many feel strongly that social, political, and economic matters should be dealt with otherwise than through taxation, but Congress continues to see fit to use the federal income tax law. This should not, however, prevent the achievement of reasonable conformity between tax and financial accounting where the differences are not so caused but are the result of misapplications of accounting theory over the years.

PRIOR JUDICIAL MODIFICATIONS

Judicial modifications have contributed significantly to the divergencies between tax and financial accounting.

A review of reported cases indicates that many controversies have involved different views of the proper method to be applied. Typically, taxpayers attempted to defer income or accelerate deductions, while the government, understandably, usually took the opposite view. It is apparent that, over the years, the courts generally severed any strong bond between tax and financial accounting.

The courts, however, have not been solely responsible for the deterioration of sound accounting reflected in their decisions. It appears that in many cases taxpayers failed to carry the requisite burden of proof by failing to show that the methods employed by them represented sound accounting practice. See, for example, *American Automobile Association*, 367 U.S. 687, and *Schlude*, 372 U.S. 128.

The recent case of *Van Pickerill and Sons, Inc.*, CA-7 (July 16, 1971), represents a view taken from time to time by the courts which demonstrates recognition that close conformity between tax and financial accounting is desirable. In this case, the Court held that state taxes, insurance premiums, and storage costs incurred by a wholesale distributor of liquor who purchased unaged whisky and stored it for either four or five years were proper annual deductions. The Court said that it did not believe that Congress intended the federal judiciary to decide, as a matter of law, accounting disputes in which there was a wide diversity of expert opinion. Since the taxpayer employed the "best accounting practice in the particular trade or business," his method clearly reflected income.

DIFFERENCES BETWEEN TAX AND FINANCIAL ACCOUNTING

Historically, the quest for close conformity of tax to financial accounting for a business enterprise has been concerned largely with resolution of the divergencies between tax and financial accounting for the following:

1. unearned receipts (prepaid income)
2. accrued expenses (estimated expenses)
3. inventory cost determination
4. intercompany pricing . . .

QUESTIONS

1. How does income for income tax purposes differ from income for financial reporting purposes?
2. Why do these differences arise?
3. Which is the better estimate of true earnings? Why?

---

58   ON THE COAST-TO-COAST TRAIL OF EQUITY FUNDING

(Reprinted by permission from *Business Week* (April 21, 1973): 68-72.)

More than $60 million in counterfeit corporate bonds were allegedly counted among the assets of Equity Funding Corporation of America. That was just one of a series of startling disclosures this week as the examiners of California Insurance Commissioner Gleeson L. Payne, along with their counterparts from Illinois, and federal agencies, raked over the remains of the $2 billion financial empire. While initial reports were shocking, there now emerges a far more detailed picture of fantastic, often surprisingly simple fraud, and of how Wall Street's most sophisticated money managers were drawn in by it.

In Los Angeles, rumors were rampant that Equity Funding's ousted chairman, Stanley Goldblum and executive vice-president, Fred Levin, had left for Israel. But in a conversation with *Business Week*, Levin said: "Neither Mr. Goldblum nor I have the resources to leave the country." Then he took off for a visit to Disneyland—leaving the insurance investigators to wend their way through a maze of Mickey Mouse accounting methods.

While the investigators sifted through the ruins of Equity Funding, a highly regarded mutual fund industry figure, Robert M. Loeffler, assumed control of the scandal-rocked financial services company as its freshly-appointed trustee in reorganization. Loeffler, 49, former senior vice-president and chief legal officer of Investors Diversified Services, Incorporated, in Minneapolis, feels his responsibility is the company's future while investigating agencies probe its past. "I have not talked to any of the former officers, nor do I desire to do so," he says. "It is really irrelevant to my job now."

But for most observers, the past still fascinates. On March 8, after the New York Insurance Department had passed along Equity Funding exemployee Ronald Secrist's allegations of scandal at the financial company, the California Department began a discreet investigation.

Illinois joined in the next day. "We weren't uncovering much," says
Payne, until March 30. "Then, one of our examiners went to Equity's
computer room and found a guy messing with the tapes." When challenged,
he said: "I'm erasing tapes. We do it every week because it saves
money." The examiner immediately informed Payne, who called the computer operator and told him to stop it. "Incidentally," says Payne,
"our examiner used a pay phone because he figured the phones in the
company might be tapped. And, in fact, about half of them were." Other
sources added that the phone taps were installed to keep tabs on the investigators.

That same afternoon, after checking with the California attorney
general, Payne ordered the company into conservatorship, a legal mechanism to preserve an insurance company's assets. "It was a risky decision," says Payne, who had never come up against anything like this in
his 25 years as an insurance executive. "If I had been wrong, there
wouldn't have been a hole big enough to bury both me and Ronald Reagan."

DIGGING IN

The immediate task was to secure all remaining assets. After
learning that there was $5.5 million in certificates of deposit and
Israeli bonds in a safe deposit box at a Wells Fargo Bank branch, the
inspectors began a frantic search for the key. One of them opened Levin's secretary's desk and there it was, attached to a tag labeled simply "safe deposit box." As for its contents, Payne says: "Well, we
think the bonds are good, but we'll just have to cash the CD's to find
out."

As for the $60 million-plus in counterfeit bonds, investigators are
still searching them out. Reportedly, they are stashed in a variety of
safe deposit boxes.

Illinois investigators were not so lucky. On March 30, they went
to Chicago's American National Bank to get information on more than $20
million in corporate bonds, whose presence had been certified at year-
end. The safe-keeping account was empty, and the records showed that it
had been for a year. On April 3, the Illinois Insurance Department
filed in state court for conservatorship over Equity Funding Life Insurance Company, which is incorporated in that state.

As the first week in April wore on, new and startling evidence
emerged. The investigators found an office with 10 employees whose job
it was to forge documents. It now appears that the ratio of phony to
good insurance was drastically underestimated, and of 97,000 policies
issued by Equity Funding, 63,000 were bogus and 34,000 were legitimate,
said the insurance authorities—sad news to the 30-odd reinsurers whose
total reinsurance in force for Equity Life is now pegged at $1.757 bil-
lion.

FRAUD BY COMPUTER

The scandal is one of the first major cases of fraud by computer.
Many of the employees either were kept in the dark or pressured into
silence.

In August, 1970, systems analyst Brian Tickler was hired to help put together a system for handling reinsured policies. He says he stayed with Equity Funding for 20 months designing the reinsurance system "four or five times, and it was rejected that many times."
Tickler claims:

My design would have enabled you to find out how much went where. We would have coordinated the policies, really made everything in the records available at your fingertips. Ultimately, we were told that the reinsurance department was not on our contract any more.

Donald Goff came to Equity Funding in 1970 as systems manager in the research and development section of the company's data processing division. Like Tickler, he was supposed to help modify the basic programs on the company's IBM 360/40 machine to suit the company's needs.
Says Goff:

We had to nail down the requirements of the company, and we kept coming across terms like "special class business," "Department 99," and "mass marketing." I was the project administrator, but I never got a straight answer on what all of that was. I was told, "You don't want to know about that."

P. J. Ronchetti, another systems specialist, says he was told that he would lose his job if he tried to pursue such questions. He, too, ran into Department 99—at that point a list of 11,000 names of "policyholders," but with none of the normal billing information.
What particularly startled Goff was what happened after material left his hands for the company's actuaries. They were situated three floors above the computer room, but with a smaller, IBM System 3 computer of their own. Goff and the other data processing people were kept away from the computer the actuaries used. Says Goff: "The actuary people ran several maintenance runs on the master. When they were done, the normal policy count was inflated tremendously over that which we submitted."

QUESTIONS AND ANSWERS

In the initial stages of the investigation, before the damning evidence was turned up, Levin apparently tried to forestall a full-fledged audit. On March 15, he sought the aid of a former Illinois insurance director, John Bolton, now a Chicago lawyer. At Levin's behest, Bolton asked the present director, Fred A. Mauck, if what was going on was a triennial examination and, if so, couldn't it wait until Equity Funding completed its planned merger with Executive National Life Insurance Company of California. Bolton was told that it was not just another audit. And in California, Richards Barger, a former California insurance commissioner, approached Payne's office. The message there was the same as in Illinois.
Early on March 31, the day after the state took over, Payne made his first visit to Equity Funding's executive suite. A man approached and asked what he was doing there. "I told him I was from the insurance

department and I was looking for some of my people," says Payne. "He asked who I was, and I told him I was the commissioner. I asked who he was, and he said he was Stanley Goldblum."

Payne says he asked if Goldblum had been served the take-over papers, to which the executive replied that the commissioner was making a "horrible mistake." Then, according to Payne, "Goldblum said he would ask only one thing of me. 'I want my men to continue selling insurance. You shouldn't deprive them of the right to feed their families.'"

WHAT NOW?

In Equity Funding's wake, Commissioner Payne called for the life insurance industry to assume the liabilities of any troubled life or disability company in the state. In past years, commissioners have not been able to find sponsors for such a bill. But, on April 5, a bill was introduced in the assembly by three of its leading Republicans. Illinois also has one in the works.

For the commissioners, however, the immediate task is fighting creditors to preserve Equity Funding's remains.

The appointment of Loeffler as trustee apparently had nothing to do with an arrangement under which IDS has agreed to manage Equity Funding's relatively small funds. Federal judge Harold Pregerson conducted his own exhaustive search for names of qualified candidates, and Loeffler's name is believed to have been suggested by staff members of the SEC. Rotund, informal, and described as having "a casual approach with a high-powered brain behind it," Oklahoma-born Loeffler joined the New York law firm of Donovan, Leisure, Newton & Irvine in 1948 after graduation from the Harvard Law School.

Loeffler represented Donovan, Leisure client Allan P. Kirby in his prolonged struggle with the Murchison brothers of Dallas over Alleghany Corporation, which controls IDS.

After Kirby ousted the Murchisons from Alleghany with Loeffler's help, Loeffler joined IDS to look after Alleghany's interests, and worked there with Ralph Saul, the former American Stock Exchange president now at First Boston Corporation. Saul says of Loeffler: "This is a man who could turn anything into a reasonable proposition. If anybody can do this job, he can."

The toughest legal struggle is likely to be over Seattle-based Northern Life Insurance Company. It was acquired by Equity Funding in 1972 for $39 million. Now the group of four banks, led by First National City Bank, which had loans of $52 million secured by most of Northern's stock, are laying claim to the Seattle company. But the commissioners counter that, as a subsidiary, it belongs to the parent.

Even as this clash of interests develops, a buyer for Northern is watching in the wings. SAFECO, a Seattle insurance holding company that had been outbid for Northern by Equity Funding, has discussed a takeover with a newly appointed group of Northern officers. But as Bruce Robb, SAFECO vice-president, puts it: "The thing is in such a mess now . . . it probably can't be sold. We're not making any kind of deal until we find out who owns it."

WHO GOT STUCK?

If the banks have a chance of getting back some of their investment in Northern Life, the Equity Life bulls on Wall Street have virtually no chance of recouping their massive losses.

A *Business Week* survey reveals that few money managers questioned
the basic concept on which Stanley Goldblum built Equity Funding. Because of the curtain of secrecy behind which some institutions—notably
the banks—hide their holdings and trading patterns, only the courts can
piece together the complete list of those left holding the bag. Only
the courts, too, can piece together the complete list of those who, on
intuition, inside information, or sheer inspiration, dumped it.

Among those left with the stock, the largest holders were Loews
Corporation, Fidelity Corporation, the Dreyfus Fund, the Ford Foundation, the Ohio State Teachers' Retirement System, and a big bunch of
foreign bankers whose confidence in the U.S. market, shaken by the second devaluation, can scarcely be restored by such a scandal.

Among those that sold were Chemical Bank and Bankers Trust. Somewhere—nobody quite knew where—was Morgan Guaranty: The biggest bank
trust in the world, with trust assets equal to half the holdings of
America's entire mutual fund industry, refused to confirm or deny whether it had bought, sold, or held Equity Funding.

ON BEING SAVED

Fidelity might derive some comfort from its chairman's opinion
that being left with the largest block of Equity Funding saved them from
a still more fearful fate. Harold J. Richards explains: "Had we sold
our Equity Funding stock, we would have had to give buyers a prospectus.
Any Equity Funding prospectus would have been phony, so people would now
be suing us. The Good Lord saved us."

Not everyone would agree that Fidelity stockholders, with a paper
loss of some $23 million, had been fortunate. Indeed, in just about
everything even remotely related to Equity Funding, they seem to have
flipped unerringly from frying pan to fire. Fidelity acquired its
579,000 shares in exchange for a 36 percent holding in Bankers National
Life—a holding, according to Richards, not worth all that much either.
He says: "We found ourselves stuck, after trying unsuccessfully to acquire the rest, with 36 percent of a company that wasn't doing well,
and which we couldn't turn into a really good company because we weren't
truly in control." When Equity Funding offered Fidelity the equivalent
of around $36 for Bankers Life shares trading at only $11, Fidelity
leaped. "We checked around," Richards recalls, "and Equity Funding was
endorsed by some good people."

Indeed it was. "All the big U.S. brokers have been pushing this
stock," grumbles a Geneva money manager. James Sublett, executive director of the Ohio State fund, says his fund started buying the stock
last July and continued until this February, when its position totaled
271,000 shares. The average price paid was a little over $34. The
total investment: $9.3 million. He adds that the fund had "no warning"
about the stock except the unusual activity. "Nobody called us to say
the stock was in trouble," he says.

DEFINING TERMS

Left with 170,000 shares, the Ford Foundation suffered a similar experience. "We bought the stock on the recommendation of three brokers," says Roger Kennedy, vice-president for financial affairs. "Only one got around to suggesting we bail out."

Dreyfus is equally frank about the $2 billion fund's purchase of its 140,000 shares, all bought since the beginning of this year. Attorney Lawrence Greens says; "Having been as high as $80, it was now around $28—and it looked like a very good buy."

Among the institutions that took large positions, but were lucky enough—or smart enough—to bail out were: Boston Company's two affiliates, Institutional Investors, Incorporated, and John W. Bristol, which together accumulated 865,000 shares, and sold them between March 15 and March 26; Chemical Bank, which, according to its executive vice-president, W. Perry Neff, had been "selling for several months" from a position estimated at 74,000 shares; and Bankers Trust, which confirms that it held 100,000 shares, and reportedly sold 98,800 on March 19.

For the losers, perhaps the best summary came from Dreyfus' Greene: "Everybody is bright about the Equity Funding concept now. Everybody says we should have known it was fallacious. But this is hindsight. When we bought, the company looked good—and nobody suspected its executives were anything but honest."

QUESTIONS

1. If Equity Funding goes bankrupt, who will lose: creditors, stockholders, policyholders, employees, others?
2. Who is responsible for the fraud: CPA's, state examiners, directors of the corporation, officers of the corporation, employees, others? Why?
3. How could this large scale fraud have been detected by the auditors?
4. How could the fraud have been prevented?
5. What changes in auditing procedures are needed?
6. What happens to internal control as collusion between individuals increases?

---

59   HELPING PROGRAM MANAGERS

Stewart D. McElyea

(Reprinted by permission from *The GAO Review* (Summer, 1973): 85.)

In summary, it is my judgment that all of us need to expand our ideas of what we can and should be doing to help program managers manage.

Of course, we need to help managers safeguard the resources given unto their control; but even more important, we need to help managers accomplish the tasks given them. Of course, we need to help managers avoid using their resources for illegal or otherwise unauthorized purposes; but even more important, we need to help them use the resources to do the things which will cause their efforts to be successful. Of course, we need to help managers be more economical in their operations; but more important, we need to help them be more effective in doing the things which are the reasons for their operations.

---

60   THE ROUND TABLE

Harold J. Mintern (editor)

(Reprinted by permission from *The Internal Auditor*, vol. 30, no. 2 (March/April, 1973): 66-70.)

(Harold J. Mintern is an accountant with Sunbeam Corporation.)

BACKLOGGED REPAIR SHOP = $250,000 UNNECESSARY PURCHASES

A routine audit of a telephone utility Apparatus Repair Shop confirmed the fact, known to management, that for over one year the shop had not been able to keep up with increased volumes of instruments returned for reconditioning. For "economic reasons" management had not authorized an increase in force or necessary overtime to bring the job under control.

The auditor-in-charge reasoned that if the backlog had not been permitted to accumulate, the number of new instruments purchased could have been reduced. A comparison of the types of telephone instruments purchased over the previous 12-month period with the types of telephone instruments backlogged, confirmed the auditor's suspicion that $250,000 in new instrument purchases could have been averted if the shop had been able to maintain a schedule of repairing and reconditioning on a reasonably current basis.

In addition, an in-depth appraisal of the Apparatus Repair Shop operation indicated that the cost of additional manpower and/or authorized overtime would more than have been offset by the savings in purchases of new instruments. Other areas where significant improvements could be made to increase shop productivity and contribute to the reduction of instrument backlog buildup in the future were also cost-justified (through reduced or deferred purchasing of new equipment) by the auditor in his final report to management. *Hawaii Chapter*

90 DEGREE TURN = $67,000
IN ADDITIONAL BILLING REVENUE

The auditor's review of billing to a gas utility customer engaged in the meat packing business disclosed discrepancies between the revenue and load consumption sheet that had been initially prepared by an industrial sales engineer.

The auditor called the Operations Department who requested a field inspection of the metering equipment at the customer's plant. The results of this inspection were negative. However, this did not satisfy the auditor. He personally visited the plant where he found the metering instrument turned at a 90 degree angle away from the equipment indicators. This setting registered only one-half of the $134,000 gas consumption during the previous 29 months in which the equipment was in use. *Indianapolis Chapter*

GASOLINE LEAK DETECTED
= SAVINGS $400,000

During a recent audit at a Midwest oil refinery, the auditors made a series of comparisons between supply storage tank measurements and truck loading rack shipment meter volumes. A consistent 2 percent loss trend, equal to a product value of $400,000 per year, was established.

The refinery operating superintendent was advised of this and ordered the underground pipelines and valves to be pressure tested. The lines failed to hold pressure and were dug up for further inspection. Several line holes and a faulty valve seal were discovered and repaired immediately, thus eliminating the $400,000 annual loss. Subsequent tank and meter comparisons by the internal auditors verified the correction of this product loss situation.

The lack of accurate measurement equipment and adequate control procedures, together with the large total processing volume, made it unlikely that refinery personnel would be able to detect these losses during their normal operations.

To prevent such losses in the future, the auditors recommended that tank gauges be installed to enable frequent comparisons of refinery deliveries with the truck terminal shipment volumes. *Chicago Chapter*

$10,000 SAVINGS
IN POSTAL CHARGES

In a large oil company, dunning notices commenced at 45 days delinquency, and automatic "duns" were forwarded at 15 day intervals up to 105 days at which time an agency analysis was forwarded to the credit department for review. Three form letters of increasing strength were forwarded at prescribed intervals. The last form letter, prior to credit card cancellation, was forwarded via "Certified Mail, Return Receipt." The form letters were prepared by the typing pool after having received a consolidated analysis from the Credit Department. The typing pool would insert the name, address, and delinquent balance. Approximately 150 such letters would be forwarded each day via "Certified, Return Receipt" at a charge of 53 cents.

An auditor's review of the system disclosed that about 60 percent of the account balances were less than $100 and some were as low as 50 cents, but continued to be mailed "Certified."

A recommendation was made to establish a limit cut-off point for "Certified" at $100 which resulted in a savings of over $10,000 per year in postal charges. *Philadelphia Chapter*

DEFECTIVE WATER METER = $20,000 SAVINGS

One of our liquid products is stored in 15,000 gallon tanks in concentrated form and diluted with water to the proper strength when loaded into tank trucks for customer delivery. Recurring large inventory shortages of this material prompted an audit investigation of loading procedures. The practice was to meter the appropriate amount of water into the tank truck, then to add the concentrated product until the total liquid in the tank reached the proper level, by measurement, for the quantity sold.

The auditor determined that the water meter was registering *about 6 percent more water* than was actually flowing into the truck. Thus, it took more concentrate to bring the tank to the proper level. An additional control was established by use of a calibrated *gauge* stick for measuring the water in the truck. The sales value of the shortage amounted to approximately $20,000 per year. *Tulsa Chapter*

$50,000 SALES AND USE TAX REFUND

Research into sales and use tax requirements as related to an audit of the company's procurement system resulted in tax recoveries in both the procurement phase and retail phase of the business. Recovery in the first instance was due to the application of one state's sales and use tax on purchased services where the company had furnished the component parts on which the services were performed. Recoveries amounted to $40,000 and continuing savings are estimated to amount to $12,000 annually.

Recovery in the second instance resulted from the auditor noting that recovery is allowed by certain states on the sales tax portion of the bad debt write off. Follow-up revealed that the company was not taking advantage of the recovery provision. Immediate recovery for allowable years amounted to $10,000. Continuing recovery will amount to approximately $3,000 annually. *Pittsburgh Chapter*

TAKE A PICTURE AND GET RESULTS!

Our initial audit report of scrap and salvage operations recommended alternative scrap disposal methods to realize greater financial return. Scrap was being disposed of through a local scrap processor who stored the scrap on his premises until volume and market conditions warranted sale on the open market. The scrap material consisted of aluminum chips and clips, stainless steel, magnesium, scrap iron, and other metals. Under the storage agreement the processor was required to segregate the material and to identify it with proper ownership labels.

Our audit included a visit to the storage site to observe house-keeping and storage practices. The absence of ownership identification of scrap and other undesirable conditions were highlighted in the audit report. Management expressed concern with the conditions reported but took no action.

Several months later we took a company photographer to the scrap site and made a "pictorial" audit, consisting of 14 photos of the stored scrap and scrap processing operations. We published a supplemental report, with accompanying photographs to document the previously reported conditions which still existed.

Results! Immediate management attention and assignment of responsibilities to put our original recommendations into effect. Truly, a picture is worth 10,000 words. *San Diego Chapter*

$20,000 INTEREST INCOME FROM ADVERTISING AGENCY AUDIT

The company's advertising agency billed the company on an estimated basis for radio and television commercials which were to be broadcast during the month. A review of several of these estimates indicated that the agency did not pay the media immediately after the broadcast of the commercial. The agency withheld the payments because of discrepancies in invoices. In the meantime, however, the company had already paid the agency. As a result, the agency had substantial amounts of the company's funds for their own use. At the recommendation of the auditor, the agency agreed to submit only those invoices covering media payments that would be paid during the current month. A subsequent review of this new billing procedure revealed that the company's cash flow was increased by approximately $400,000 during the last six-month period. The increased cash flow invested at a prime rate of 5 percent would realize a return of $20,000 on an annualized basis. *New York Chapter*

PREVENTING $200,000 LOSS THROUGH CONTROL OF VOIDED CASH TRANSACTIONS

The auditor's investigations of sizeable losses in the cash collections area disclosed that for a considerable period of time the head cashier had been processing fictitious voids and pocketing the proceeds. By processing the fictitious voids, the cashier was able to reduce recorded cash collections and make the funds available to herself. Additional factors contributing to the defalcation were:

1.   lack of adequate post-audit review of voids
2.   control of the cashiering personnel function (hiring, work-scheduling, firing, etc.) by the head cashier

Although the exact amount of the loss from this source could not be determined, it may have exceeded $200,000.

Major procedural changes have been made in the areas of void approval and review in order to strengthen internal control. Voids must now be explained, signed and approved, without exception. In addition, ongoing management scrutiny has been provided for, the Personnel Department has become involved in the cashiering personnel function, and a much-needed cashiering manual has now been prepared. *Los Angeles Chapter*

ANNUALIZED PURCHASING OF
DUPLICATING PAPER = $1,500 SAVINGS

An operational audit of the Reproduction, Stationery, and Mail Room Department revealed that consumption of duplicating machine paper amounted to approximately 560 cases per year. Monthly purchase orders were placed with low bidders for monthly needs. Further investigation revealed that one paper supplier offered greater discounts if an annual guarantee of 480 cases could be made. Monthly partial shipments would be provided as needed by the company. Savings in excess of $1,500 a year will result from negotiating a contract for annual requirements. *Salt Lake Chapter*

$5,000 RECOVERY ON
ADVERTISING AGENCY TALENT TAXES

One of the costs of television advertising is payroll taxes for talent used in the commercials. A review of these payments revealed that each of our agencies was charging a differing payroll tax percentage. All but one of the percentages being charged exceeded the total of the actual rates for the taxes involved. In addition, we were being charged throughout the year without considering whether or not individuals had reached the maximums for the various taxes.

Management's discussions with the agencies based on a report of these findings resulted in agreements to have each agency charge a percentage very close to the actual tax rate total. The agencies also agreed to observe the cut-off points for each type of tax. These agreements resulting in an annual savings of approximately $5,000. *North Jersey Chapter*

4

Reporting Problems

Preparing financial statements for issuance to the public is a difficult job. All of the myriad types of transactions entered into by a firm must first be expressed in terms of a common denominator, the dollar. The form and content of the financial reports must be decided upon. The amount and types of detailed data included in the reports must be such that the statements present fairly the overall results of the transactions.

The business literature is replete with suggestions for improvements in financial reporting. *Business Week* (page 187) noted in reporting on a survey of annual reports that there is a trend to include more and better detailed financial information in annual reports of corporations. There have been significant improvements in financial reporting, particularly over the past ten years. Yet much remains to be done. Articles in this chapter discuss a number of the criticisms of current financial reporting together with suggestions for improvements.

Financial statements are a report of one period of a firm's complete history. All of the statements issued periodically taken together over the entire life of a firm would tell the complete financial story. It would be fortunate, indeed, if financial statements could be issued only at the conclusion of a firm's operation. Because periodic reports are needed by decision makers, the reports are subject to misstatement. Estimates, assumptions, allocations, etc., made at the statement date often subsequently prove to be less than 100 percent accurate. Yet, in order to prepare reports as close to economic truth as possible, accountants must estimate, assume, and allocate. In taking these actions, accountants predict with a probability of one that subsequent events will bear out the data as presented. Herman W. Bevis (page 194) suggests that accountants are responsible for the appearance of precision in financial statements which is not actually present. He believes that the uncertainty which cannot be measured should be disclosed when issuing financial reports.

Forbes (page 191) reviews financial statements contained in annual reports to shareholders for a number of firms. They find some commendable. Their critical comments center mainly around inadequate footnotes to the statements and the lack of reporting by lines of business, sometimes called segmental reporting. The second *Forbes* article (page 203) takes a close look at the types of information that can be gleaned from careful reading of the footnotes which accompany financial statements.

186

While their analysis raises many questions about a firm's operations, it is apparent that footnotes contain information of high value for decision makers.

Robert A. Kleckner (page 200) is in general agreement with *Forbes* except that he centers his discussion around the lack of disclosure of essential facts in financial reports: facts essential to making valid comparisons with other firms and discovering what is actually happening in a firm. He presents an interesting list of items which he thinks should be disclosed in more detail. Most of these could probably be presented in footnote form. He also believes that more segmental reporting detail is needed.

Financial reports are not always issued annually; some firms issue them quarterly. The problems encountered in preparing and using annual reports are greatly compounded when quarterly reports are prepared. Financial reports issued between annual reports are often referred to as interim reports.

The *Business Week* article (page 207) on Mattel highlights the damage that incorrect interim reports can do. William F. Crum (page 210) presents the results of a survey of 75 firms' interim reports, comparing them with the recommended goals and standards for interim reports issued by the Committee on Management Accounting Practices of the National Association of Accountants. He concludes that most interim reports can be greatly improved in a number of ways.

William E. Langdon (page 216) raises the question of why financial reports need to be prepared on a segmental basis by lines of business. His discussion centers on the so-called conglomerate firms which have increased in number and size as a result of corporate diversification. Because these firms operate in more than one line of business, the problems of segmental reporting become acute. Accounting information from different lines of business is usually, under current rules, summarized and reported in total, making analysis extremely difficult, if not impossible. Langdon presents recommendations for implementing segmental reporting so that data would appear separately for separate lines of business.

---

61 THE ANNUAL REPORT BECOMES A CONFESSION

(Reprinted by permission from *Business Week* (April 21, 1973): 44–45.)

The push by the Securities & Exchange Commission to get corporations to tell more in their annual reports is starting to pay dividends. This spring's crop of annual reports shows more companies breaking out more details on their operations than ever before—and in more languages and glossier formats.

Further, a survey by the Financial Executives Institute indicates that most large companies are now in favor of giving shareholders more detailed financial data—though the survey also turned up a hard core of corporate managers who still are dead-set against fuller disclosure.

Of course, one reason so many companies are willing to talk now is that their profits were so impressive in 1972. When sales and earnings jump, management is usually eager to broadcast the news. But a more fundamental reason is that a growing number of shareholders now know about the existence of the 10-K report, the document that every publicly held company must file each year with the SEC. Since January 1, 1971, each company with more than $50 million in sales and with more than one major line of business has had to submit its 10-K, breaking down sales and pretax earnings for each product line that accounted for more than 10 percent of sales and pretax profits.

Companies are not required to give those sales and profit details in their annual reports. But the SEC, when William J. Casey was chairman, insisted that it makes little sense for a company to omit from an annual report information that is available in a 10-K in the SEC's public files.

MAKING HEADWAY

While there are still a surprising number of holdouts, a *Business Week* survey of 100 annual reports indicates that companies increasingly are heeding the SEC's jawboning on fuller disclosure. For 1972, 57 of those 100 companies broke down sales and earnings by product line, compared with 51 who did in 1971. In 1970 annual reports, which came out in the spring of 1971, only 32 managements put in 10-K profit figures. And the willingness to put 10-K profit figures in annual reports may be more widespread than the *Business Week* sampling reveals, since the sample includes a number of companies classified as single-line businesses.

Among the companies that broke out profit figures for individual lines of business for the first time are Combustion Engineering, Magnavox, Ogden, and Uniroyal. Ogden drew criticism last year for failing to do this. The company not only left profit figures for its individual operations out of its shareholder report, but it also broke the company down differently in its 10-K. In its 1972 annual report, Ogden provides shareholders with a five-year sales and profit rundown for its six lines of businesses.

The SEC is now considering a requirement that may force managements to present 10-K data in their annual reports. While the proposal stops short of requiring the step, it would require that a company disclose in either the 10-K or the annual report any items that are not reported in both. Perhaps even more persuasive to corporate managers is the danger that a shareholder might claim, and a court might sustain him, that 10-K profit information not included in the annual report was material information. In a climate where corporations are facing more and more court suits on liability, the reticence to divulge 10-K data takes on an increasing element of risk.

THE RIGHT TO KNOW

The research arm of the FEI surveyed 65 large companies on financial reporting last year and found that 75 percent endorsed the concept that investors have a right to product line or business segment profit figures. Those companies that opposed fuller disclosure based their

arguments on everything from anxiety over competitive implications to
concern about governmental interference.

In its publication, *The Businessman's View of the Purposes of Financial Reporting*, the FEI said several executives contended that,
since shareholders own a piece of the total company, their right to an
accounting is only for the total. They also feared that revealing exceptional profit areas might attract new competitors. Another concern
cited was that consumer and social activists would distort the information.

In contrast to such reservations, a small number of companies are
actually sending copies of their 10-K to shareholders along with the annual report. Browning-Ferris Industries, a Houston waste-systems company, did that this year. Several other companies, including Celanese
Corporation, which breaks out 10-K profit information in its annual report, now alert shareholders that additional 10-K information is available from the company.

One bit of 10-K information that many companies are still holding
out of their annual reports is the money spent on research and development. The reason frequently given is that disclosing the figure would
be competitively damaging. But the pressure for more disclosure is
having an effect here, too. In 1970, only 17 of the companies listed
the figure. In the 1972 survey, 35 included R&D expenses.

PREDICTED EARNINGS

The issue of profit forecasting in annual reports, which had executives in an uproar last year, seems settled at least for the near term.
The SEC is considering whether to permit companies "with a substantial
history of operation and experience in forecasting" to make profit forecasts in documents such as a prospectus. But it is unlikely that such
forecasts will be required as part of annual reports.

Of the reports in so far, only Atlanta-based Fuqua Industries Incorporated, includes earnings forecasts in its 1972 annual report. Says
J. B. Fuqua, the conglomerate's outspoken chairman: "If this is the
music we will have to march to, we are willing to lead the band." Thus,
Fuqua's 1972 annual report includes 1973 sales and earnings forecasts
for each of its eight lines of business.

SOCIAL ISSUES

The subject of corporate responsibility continues to get top billing in annual reports. Almost two-thirds of the reports in this
spring's sampling contain sections about pollution control, minority
hiring practices, and general corporate citizenship. In the First Pennsylvania Corporation report, Chairman John R. Bunting, for example, interviewed a cross section of people ranging from Ralph Nader to John D.
Rockefeller III on the role of business in society.

Scovill Manufacturing Company's annual report contains a "Social
Action Report" in the form of a balance sheet. Under the employment
opportunities section, for example, Scovill cites as an asset an increase in minority employment from 6 percent in 1963 to 19 percent last
year. Balancing this in the liabilities column is the statement that

the company needs "more upgrading of minority employees into higher
labor grade jobs."

This type of candor gives more credibility to pronouncements about
corporate responsibility. It is also indicative, says Richard Lewis,
president of Corporate Annual Reports, Incorporated, of a trend by managements to devote more annual report space to factual information.
"The shrinking research effort on Wall Street—fewer analysts doing
fewer reports—is probably the reason for this new emphasis," says
Lewis.

The 1972 report of International Foodservice Systems, Incorporated,
is cited by Lewis as an example of detail not usually included in an
annual report. Details of each IFS acquisition since the company's
founding in 1968 are given, as well as backgrounds of its 18 division
managers. Combustion Engineering doubled the number of pages in its
1972 annual report from that of 1971 to print an updated version of a
presentation to security analysts that the company made last fall.

Getting the attention of investors and shareholders has, of course,
been a traditional function of the annual report. One of the more intriguing efforts to accomplish this is the 1972 annual report from Bliss
& Laughlin Industries, Incorporated, a Chicago-based steel fabricator
that has diversified into construction and land development. The Bliss
& Laughlin report has five covers that fold out to form a picture of a
tree. In explanation, the company says its accomplishments in 1972 "are
best compared to the growth of a tree . . . distinctively and solidly
growing to meet the future."

FOREIGN APPEAL

The global spread of U.S. business also shows in more and more annual reports. An increasing number of companies are printing their
annual reports in foreign languages. Litton Industries and ITT have
been distributing foreign-language versions of their annual reports
since the mid-1960s, but Burroughs, Carrier, Cutler-Hammer, International Utilities, and Avis, have all just started doing it. Various annual
reports this year appear in German, French, Japanese, Spanish, Italian,
Dutch, and Swedish.

"The foreign-language editions are used as marketing tools as well
as devices to attract investors," says Dr. Edward M. Burke, executive
director of All-Language Services, Incorporated, a New York business
that translates annual reports.

ITT, for example, started a Russian version of its annual report in
1966 to help its European affiliates to promote the company at Soviet
telecommunications trade shows. The company now distributes 6,000 Russian versions of its report. And it augments its 450,000 English-
language versions with 50,000 reports in French, German, Italian, Spanish, and Portuguese.

QUESTIONS

1. What are the reasons that more companies are disclosing
    more financial information in annual reports?
2. Should the Securities & Exchange Commission require 10-K
    data to be presented in annual reports? Why or why not?
3. Do you think that earnings forecasts should be included
    in annual reports? Why or why not?

---

62   THE NUMBERS GAME: A FEW (FAIRLY) KIND WORDS

(Reprinted by permission from *Forbes*, vol. 111, no. 9 (May 1,
1973): 34-36.)

T. S. Eliot was right about April. April is the cruelest month.
Income taxes. Record rainfall. Meatless lunches with gloomy stock-
brokers. Scandal at Equity Funding. Astounding auditing oversight at
Whittaker.

Ah, but May was at hand. The merry month. Whistling mailmen bearing bundles of shiny new annual reports each day. Our desk hopelessly
buried under the latest published works of American industry.

What kind of crop of reports will May bring? For a preview, we began perusing the early-blooming ones.

Aha! Here was an interesting report. Little Anixter Brothers, Incorporated, out in Skokie, Illinois had cracked the full-disclosure
problem and saved a bundle in the process. They had simply slapped a
blue-and-white cover on their annual SEC Form 10-K and fired it off to
shareholders. Not as attractive, perhaps, as their 1971 effort, which
had been full of charts. But a good deal more informative.

Looking at Anixter's dismal earnings record (an 88 percent decline
from 1969 to 1971 followed by a loss in fiscal 1972), it wasn't hard to
see what had prompted this daring break with tradition.

Whatever the motivation, it was a good move, although we preferred
the solution of one company, Winnebago Industries, which last year
mailed its 10-K along with its annual report. Of 2,000 shareholders responding to the move, 90 percent said they were in favor of it.

To Anixter, then, the Making-a-Virtue-of-Necessity Award for 1972!
Next annual report in the stack: Bell & Howell. The company whose
1971 report had been sharply criticized for inadequate "lines of business" breakdowns by New York University's astute accounting professor
Lee J. Seidler. Let's see if B&H had mended their ways this year:

Well, what do you know! Divisional breakdowns of sales and earnings had been expanded from three to seven, with special mention of the

important Bell & Howell Schools operation—a specific Seidler criticism.
The result gave a far more meaningful picture of operations.

All that pressure from SEC Chairman William Casey was having its
effect. Casey had asked for disclosure of accounting policies, and for
details on management assumptions on long-term contracts—a frequent
source of write-offs. This year Bell & Howell showed a reasonable reserve for cancellations and bad debts on contracts in the Schools division—the lack of which in its 1971 report had also worried Seidler.

For Bell & Howell the coveted Reformed-Sinner Trophy.

Now what about the annual reports of the large multicompanies?
Those were the sinners that *really* needed reforming in terms of specific
divisional breakdowns by sales and earnings. We rummaged through the
piles on our desk and pulled out a few.

A curious reverse principle seemed to be at work. The more pain-
ful the multicompany's credibility gap, the better its 1972 line of business disclosure. Gulf & Western had about the most specific and most
comprehensible breakdown of divisional sales and earnings of any multicompany we looked at. G&W 1972 sales of $1.7 billion and operating in-
come of $146.5 million were broken down eight ways on a four-year basis
with additional breakdowns on depreciation, capital expenditures, and
subunit sales volume in each of the eight areas.

In contrast, a venerable blue chip like Westinghouse could only
bring itself to break down its 1972 sales of $5.1 billion and earnings
of $199 million four ways on a two-year basis. Westinghouse used too
much space, we thought, for large color photos; not enough for divisional breakdowns. The breakdowns used were just too big to be meaningful.
We were told, for example, that the Westinghouse Industry & Defense subsidiary consisted of 50 divisions in such diverse fields as elevators,
airborne radars, industrial controls, and real estate development. This
"subsidiary" had earned $64 million on $2.2 billion in sales. After
all, that one Westinghouse subsidiary was larger than and just as diverse as all of Gulf & Western put together. *That* is a breakdown?

But no blue ribbon for Gulf & Western's 1972 report, we decided.
Not only were G&W's footnotes to its financial statements tantalizingly
brief for a company that complex, but we were unable to find any summary of significant accounting policies—an Accounting Principles Board
requirement for all 1972 annual reports.

Who would get the Great Golden Eyeshade for Best Footnotes of 1972?
Monsanto had always had the best annual reports in the chemical industry, we thought. General Electric? Not to be ignored. But we finally
settled on International Minerals & Chemicals for a first in footnotes.

A few years back, the aftermath of the 1969 price collapse in
fertilizer left the company with a credibility-shattering $20.6 million
loss. In those days, IMC's footnotes were noted for their microscopic
size and mind-boggling complexity. Nobody could *read* the footnotes,
much less understand them.

Okay. IMC President Dick Lenon addressed himself to that little
problem in the 1972 report. Nine full pages of footnotes now precede
IMC's financial statements. Mammoth tabloid headlines scream out EX-
TRAORDINARY ITEMS or ESTIMATED LOSSES ON PLANT CLOSINGS AND INVEST-
MENTS. Descriptions of accounting policy are set off from other explanatory material in blue type. BIG blue type. Acres of white space
surround the verbiage, providing rest for the weary eye and rendering
the discussion less formidable in appearance. The footnotes themselves

are even reasonably comprehensible, if not altogether reassuring in content.

It was a handsome annual report all right. About the best we'd seen in terms of layout and style. No pretty pictures of fertilizer plants. No rhapsodic prose about feeding the world's hungry millions. Just brisk, lucid, well-organized summary comment.

But far *too* brisk, we thought. Two of IMC's four lines of business were in the red, and a third—having suffered a steep decline—was barely marginal. But we could find no explanation for that unhappy performance—in nine pages of commentary. Most of the space was devoted to forecasting and new developments—and to agriculture, which had accounted for all of IMC's handsome earnings gain (from $13.5 million in 1971 to $21.3 million last year). A clear case of accentuating the positive. Too much so, we thought.

Three last awards before getting down to work.

To tiny North American Publishing of Philadelphia, the Eyecatcher-of-the-Year Citation for its three-foot-long (suitable for framing), poster-size Semi-Annual Report featuring letters eight inches tall and six inches wide that spell out: "We Had a BIG IMPROVEMENT For the First Six Months" (from $16,000 to an unaudited $90,000).

Then, the *Forbes* Prize in Children's Literature goes to Macmillan, for an imaginative "young people's" version of their regular annual report. (For potential capitalists over the age of 11.)

And finally, the annual Barbie Doll Award for cuteness.

We had to concede that the celebrated International Multifoods publication ran away with that prize. We mean this report was wild, wild. In format it copies *Business Week*, with folksy, quote-filled copy. It contains 13 company advertisements. Articles by its favorite security analyst and its favorite trade book editor. Chatty explanation for those recurring tribulations which have kept the company's return on equity down to a decidedly mediocre 8.8 percent in recent years (below average even for food wholesalers).

Finally, this was the only annual report we have ever seen that contains a short quiz for shareholders. Sample question: "Who wants to be more to its customers than 'just a crown on our package'?" If you care, the answer is: the King Foods subsidiary. We know because we peeked at the answers on page 38.

QUESTIONS

1. What, as *Forbes* sees them, were the problems with annual reports reviewed? What was right with the reports reviewed?

63   CONTINGENCIES AND PROBABILITIES
                              IN FINANCIAL STATEMENTS

                              Herman W. Bevis

(Reprinted by permission from *The Journal of Accountancy*, vol. 126
(October, 1968): 37-40. Copyright 1968 by the American Institute of
Certified Public Accountants, Inc.)

(Herman W. Bevis is Senior Partner of Price Waterhouse & Co.)

What I wish to explore is one of the most interesting, most elusive
—but often extremely important—aspects of business operations, and of
the accounting which reflects these operations in financial statements:
contingencies, which are faced by just about every business under the
sun.
Some of these contingencies arise out of the risks which businessmen consciously take. Risk means that there is some degree of uncertainty as to outcome. The uncertainty may pertain to particular projects, or it may even extend to the future of the entire business. Risk,
then, denotes the presence of a contingency. Other contingencies derive
from external forces beyond effective control of the businessman, like
economic recessions, or an unexpected lawsuit, or changes in laws affecting business, or the development of a better product by a competitor.
Any businessman could add extensively to the foregoing general list
in enumerating the specific uncertainties, or risks, or contingencies,
which he faces. Moreover, most investors and creditors, when they stop
to think about it, also fully appreciate these imponderables. Yet many
of these same people, looking at a financial statement, see in it precision, penny accuracy, the "moment of truth" of the business. Somehow,
they do not appreciate that, as George O. May said, ". . . accounts
. . . cannot rise higher in the scale of certainty than the events which
they reflect. . . ." (1)
It is probable that accountants are more responsible than anyone
else for the glaring inconsistency between the appearance of precision
in financial statements and the known uncertainties which underlie them.
They have no doubt created an illusion of certainty in a number of ways.
Figures in financial statements, if not expressed to the penny, are often stated to the nearest dollar. Balance sheets always balance. Income and retained earnings statements tie in neatly with the balance
sheets. Earnings per share is expressed to the penny, and accountants
watch silently as they see the financial community impute significance
to a change from, say $4.27 to $4.34. Not much is said about uncertainties either in the financial statements themselves or in the educational literature which accountants issue to the general public. Everything suggests precision.
At the same time, accountants' own professional literature abounds
with words specifically denying such finality in financial statements.
They use words like "expectation," "judgment," "estimate," "assumption,"
"contingency," and "probability." But here they are mostly talking to
themselves, not to the lay users of financial statements.
It is the purpose of this article first to illustrate a bit more
some of the uncertainties which companies typically face. Then I wish

to go into the philosophy and technique which the profession has developed over the years for dealing with uncertainties in financial statements. Finally, I would like to examine a very important present-day
problem—accounting for income taxes—and contrast the prescribed method
of handling this item with the profession's consistent approach to other
uncertainties of the future; i.e., other contingencies.

SOME OF THE CONTINGENCIES
WHICH COMPANIES FACE

Most businesses sell on credit. At any given time, receivables
from a number of debtors are outstanding. Experience dictates that some
debtors ultimately will not pay. Which ones? How much will be uncollectible? This is a contingency which only the future can resolve without doubt. Both the accounts receivable figure (net of allowances for
doubtful accounts) in the balance sheet and the net income figure for
the year depend upon how much is set aside for what will ultimately
prove to be bad debts. The uncertainty can assume major proportions if
the company's business consists entirely of, say, financing on a 20-year
installment basis with a small down payment. What is going to happen in
the next 20 years to affect collections on these receivables?
Contingencies exist in inventories. Will selling prices or customer demand drop to the point that existing inventories cannot be sold for
as much as they have cost? If such is likely, this contingency of the
future should be met by a writedown now of the overpriced, or slow-
moving, or obsolete items. Such questions are critical if much of the
inventory consists of fashion merchandise, or toys, or is related to a
fad. How does one foresee the distinction between a passing fancy and
a new and permanent consumer interest? Remember hoola hoops? If the
inventory consists of accumulated costs on partially completed long-term
construction contracts, will these, when added to the costs to complete
the projects, exceed the contract selling prices? Those future costs
may not be susceptible of precise calculation, so here is another contingency which only the future can resolve for sure.
Plant, equipment, and intangible assets all are involved with uncertainties about the future. Unamortized amounts for these items
should not be carried in the balance sheet as assets unless they will
benefit the operations of future periods. But how long will they be
useful? If physical life continues, will they nonetheless be made obsolete by a competitor's action, or by general economic conditions?
Renegotiation, income taxes, lawsuits, pensions, and many other
matters present the businessman with questions of accounting *now* for
transactions or events the precise financial effect of which will be
known only as the future unfolds. This will become clearer as I recite
some of the philosophy and instructions which are contained in accounting literature regarding the uncertainties which underlie financial
statements. The quotations are exclusively from pronouncements by the
committee on accounting procedure and the Accounting Principles Board
of the American Institute of Certified Public Acountants. It will be
seen that there emerge from this literature

1. a candid recognition of the fact that uncertainties exist,
    and exist in varying degrees

2.   a philosophy for handling uncertainties in the preparation of financial statements.

GENERAL RECOGNITION OF THE
EXISTENCE OF CONTINGENCIES

*". . . the accounts for one period are but an installment
of what is essentially a continuous history," says the
Institute. (2)*

As history unfolds, it often sheds new and different light on past
installments; so it is in accounting. Chapter 8, Paragraph 3, of ARB
No. 43 says:

*. . . Allocations to fiscal periods of both charges and credits
affecting the determination of net income are, in part, estimated and conventional and based on assumptions as to future
events which may be invalidated by experience.*

The same theme appears in Chapter 10B, Paragraph 4:

*Financial statements are based on allocations of receipts,
payments, accruals, and various other items. Many of the allocations are necessarily based on assumptions, but no one
suggests that allocations based on imperfect criteria should
be abandoned. . . .*

Financial accounting, then, takes realistic recognition of the fact
that unknowns have to be dealt with in preparing financial statements.
   As has been said, the literature also faces the fact that there are
degrees of uncertainty—that some contingencies can be dealt with on the
basis of probabilities while with others there is not enough to go on to
arrive at a reasonable figure. (The statistical term "probability" is
actually not used much in Institute pronouncements. More often, forms
of such words as "estimate," "assumption," "expectation," "approximation," and "prediction" are used. However, often it will be evident
from the context that an assessment of probabilities is a part of the
judgmental process.)
   A philosophy for dealing with varying degrees of uncertainty is
outlined in the following citations:

*In the preparation of financial statements presenting
financial position or operating results, or both, it is necessary to give consideration to contingencies. In accounting a
contingency is an existing condition, situation or set of circumstances, involving a considerable degree of uncertainty,
which may, through a related future event, result in the acquisition or loss of an asset, or the incurrence or avoidance
of a liability, usually with the concurrence of a gain or
loss. . . .*

The contingencies with which this bulletin is primarily concerned are those in which the outcome is not sufficiently predictable to permit recording in the accounts, but in which there is a reasonable possibility of an outcome which might materially affect financial position or results of operations. . . .

. . . Contingencies may exist where the outcome is reasonably foreseeable, such as probable tax assessments which will not be contested, or anticipated losses from uncollectible receivables. Contingencies of this type which are expected to result in losses should be reflected in the accounts. . . . (3)

In keeping with the established accounting principle that provision should be made in financial statements for all liabilities, including reasonable estimates for liabilities not accurately determinable, provision should be made for probable renegotiation refunds wherever the amount of such refunds can be reasonably estimated. . . . In cases in which a reasonable estimate cannot be made, as where the effect of a new or amended renegotiation act cannot be foretold within reasonable limits or where a company is facing renegotiation for the first time and no reliable precedent is available, disclosure of the inability, because of these circumstances, to determine renegotiation effects and of the consequent uncertainties in the financial statements is necessary. (4)

It has been argued with respect to inventories that losses which will have to be taken in periods of receding price levels have their origins in periods of rising prices, and that therefore reserves to provide for future price declines should be created in periods of rising prices by charges against the operations of those periods. Reserves of this kind involve assumptions as to what future price levels will be, what inventory quantities will be on hand if and when a major price decline takes place, and finally whether loss to the business will be measured by the amount of the decline in prices. The bases for such assumptions are so uncertain that any conclusions drawn from them would generally seem to be speculative guesses rather than informed judgments. When estimates of this character are included in current costs, amounts representing mere conjecture are combined with others representing reasonable approximations.

The committee is therefore of the opinion that reserves such as those created . . . in amounts not determined on the basis of any reasonable estimates of costs and losses are of such a nature that charges or credits relating to such reserves should not enter into the determination of net income. (5)

Practical application of the accrual principle to the accounting for terminated war and defense contracts rests upon the possibility of making a reasonable estimate of the amount of the termination claim before its final determination by settlement. . . .

. . . When a particular termination claim or part thereof is so uncertain in amount that it cannot be reasonably

> *estimated, it is preferable not to give effect to that part of the claim in the financial statements. . . . (6)*

There emerges from the foregoing quotations a clear emphasis on appraising degrees of uncertainty. The question always is whether the realization of an asset, or the incurrence of a cost or loss, is, on probabilities assessed from evidence and experience, a reasonable expectation. If so, can the amount by quantified? If not, the contingency is not dealt with in the financial statements themselves but, rather, in footnote disclosures. If a basis for quantification exists, then an estimate, approximation or judgment as to amounts is to be made in the circumstances of each case.

There are many more places in ARBs and Opinions of the Accounting Principles Board where the handling of uncertainties of the future is dealt with specifically or by implication. It would unduly burden the body of this article to quote them all, but reference is made to the source material for those who wish to explore the subject further.

BASIC OBJECTIVES WHICH ARE PERTINENT TO THE HANDLING OF CONTINGENCIES

One might conclude, from the discussion to this point, that the handling of each contingency is a matter by itself, unrelated to the other elements of financial statements. This is not necessarily so. The overall philosophy is one of fairness in presentation, as is illustrated by these quotations:

> *. . . The fairest possible presentation of periodic net income, with neither material overstatement nor understatement, is important, since the results of operations are significant not only to prospective buyers of an interest in the enterprise but also to prospective sellers. . . . (7)*
> *If a provision for a reserve, made against income, is not properly chargeable to current revenues, net income for the period is understated by the amount of the provision. . . .*
> *. . . it is deemed desirable to provide, by charges in the current income statement . . . for all foreseeable costs and losses applicable against current revenues, to the extent that they can be measured and allocated to fiscal periods with reasonable approximation. (8)*
> *It is impossible to lay down general rules which can be applied satisfactorily in all cases. Here [regarding renegotiation] as elsewhere in accounting, there must be an exercise of judgment which should be based on experience and on a clear understanding of the objective to be attained. That objective is to present the fairest possible financial statements, and at the same time, make clear any uncertainties that limit the significance of such statements. (9)*

Thus, a basic objective in financial statements is neither overstatement nor understatement of periodic net income. It is recognized that sellers—as well as buyers—of an interest in an enterprise are affected by reported results of operations. There should be quantification of the financial consequences of transactions and events where this is possible and, if not, disclosure of the uncertainty which is not measurable.

It will be noted that throughout the preceding discussion the AICPA's concern has been with accounting problems oriented to the resources of the business. Does the business have a resource justifiable to be reported as an asset, or has it been diminished, or is it so conjectural as to be without demonstrable substance? Does the business have a claim on its resources justifiable to be reported as a liability, or is it so conjectural as to be without demonstrable substance? Most of these questions have their counterpart in the income statement: Has the business earned revenue or gain, or has it not? Has the business sustained a cost or loss, or has it not? This preoccupation of accountants with the resources of a business is fundamental. It is what makes businessmen and accountants talk the same language, for businessmen by their nature are also concerned with the acquisition, preservation, accretion, and exhaustion of resources.

FOOTNOTES

1. *Dickinson Lectures in Accounting* (Cambridge, Mass.: Harvard University Press, 1943), p. 47.
2. Accounting Research Bulletin No. 43, American Institute of CPAs, New York City, 1953, Chapter 2A, Paragraph 1. ARB No. 43 is a compilation of all prior bulletins issued by the committee on accounting procedure of the AICPA.
3. ARB No. 50, AICPA, 1958, Paragraphs 1, 2, and 3.
4. ARB No. 43, op. cit., Chapter 11B, Paragraph 4.
5. ARB No. 43, op. cit., Chapter 6, Paragraphs 6 and 7.
6. ARB No. 43, op. cit., Chapter 11C, Paragraphs 14 and 19.
7. *Accounting Research and Terminology Bulletin, Final Edition*, American Institute of Certified Public Accountants, New York City, 1961, page 7.
8. ARB No. 43, op. cit., Chapter 6, Paragraphs 3 and 4.

9. ARB No. 43, op. cit., Chapter 11B, Paragraph 3.

QUESTIONS

1. Explain why earnings reported on the income statement may or may not be correct for the period of time which the statement covers.
2. If net income does not represent an exactly correct statement of earnings for a period of time, what does the net income figure represent?
3. Why, if the financial statements are not exactly correct, do people use them?

---

64   DISCLOSURE IS THE WEAK SPOT IN AUDITS

Robert A. Kleckner

(Reprinted by permission from *Business Week* (June 30, 1973): 12.)

(Robert A. Kleckner is a member of the firm of Alexander Grant
& Co.)

To many accountants, the new Financial Accounting Standards Board
is the profession's last chance to clean itself up and avoid heavy-
handed government regulation and interference. The abuses of the conglomerate merger era and such well-publicized accounting failures as
Penn Central, the land development companies, and Equity Funding Corporation have brought the profession's problems to the crisis point. But
the FASB is doomed to failure if it believes the answer lies in the development of new accounting theory or the codification of accounting
principles—useful though such activities might be. The great problem
facing the accounting profession today is not theory or rules. It is
disclosure.

By disclosure, I do not mean making the complex financial statements of a giant corporation understandable to Aunt Jane. There is no
way to do that, and there is no simple number like earnings per share
that can summarize the convoluted, intertwined operations of a modern
corporation.

I mean revealing the essential facts about a company's activities
and its financial status in such a way that a trained user of financial
statements can determine what actually is happening and can make valid
comparisons with what is happening elsewhere in the economy. Today's
financial statements do not make full disclosure in this sense.

Too often, even a managing partner like myself, who must view financial statements prepared by partners of the firm who report to me,
cannot fully understand one or more transactions until the partner in
charge has explained the assumptions that lie behind the numbers. These
assumptions are not always reported publicly. But they are essential
information to the user of the statements. Without them, there is no
way to compare one company's performance with that of another in the
same industry or line of business.

MORE RULES WON'T DO

Some people have expressed the opinion that accounting statements
of similar corporations will themselves be similar only if the FASB
imposes a codified rulebook of accounting principles on everyone. I
can't see how this will work.

First, a rulebook tends to breed "loophole"-oriented mentality. If
the rulebook says that a deal structured one way produces a result and
that reduces earnings per share, the management will say, "Let's structure the deal another way to produce a different result under the rule-

book." Second, no rulebook can possibly cover all the present accounting issues or anticipate the issues of the future. Finally, I fear that
transactions which are the same in substance will be accounted for differently because the rules won't quite fit.

I believe the financial statements can be made more useful to the
business-oriented reader if careful reporting is required in these new
areas of disclosure:

1. Break down inventories according to the way in which they
    are expected to be sold, such as under requirements con-
    tracts, government contracts, subcontracts, retail, whole-
    sale.
2. Summarize fixed-asset acquisitions by year and depreciation
    method so that a competent financial analyst, comparing
    two or more enterprises, can adjust depreciation expense
    to comparable price levels.
3. Disclose management's justification for the capitalization
    of major intangibles, such as research and development ex-
    pense. Explain the basis for the realization period se-
    lected.
4. Provide a summary of the aging of accounts receivable at
    each balance sheet date.
5. Disclose certain nonaccounting information that could have
    drastic effects on future operations, such as the expira-
    tion date of union contracts and the dates on which such
    contracts can be reopened, marketing expectations and re-
    lated market budgets for the next fiscal year, and informa-
    tion about new products.
6. Present comparative industry statistics and management's
    commentary on them.
7. Present information on business segments. I suggest, as
    a partial solution to the present controversy surrounding
    the definitional aspects of this disclosure, that consid-
    eration be given to presenting the information according
    to the managerial units in which the enterprise conducts
    its business. For example, for a manufacturing enter-
    prise, the information could be presented according to
    major factory locations. For a national retail operation,
    the information might be summarized according to major
    geographical units.

Some of these disclosures either cannot or should not be covered by
the auditor's attestation. However, this fact should not deter management and the accounting profession from including such information as
part of the general-purpose financial package.

IN PLAIN LANGUAGE

In addition, the accounting profession can make great strides in
improving the way we communicate. Accounting reports too often are
couched in technical jargon, understood only by the professional. To
cite one example, we talk about "current assets" when what we mean can

be expressed better like this: "These are things we expect to turn into cash or its equivalent during the coming fiscal year."

The goal of this new disclosure ought to be comparability, so that a knowledgeable person can compare points of likeness and points of difference. Comparability does not require absolute uniformity of accounting, nor does it permit unrestrained flexibility. It does require disclosure sufficient to tell the user which things are essentially alike and which are different.

QUESTIONS

1. What does Mr. Kleckner see as the purpose of financial statements? Do you agree? Why?
2. If a rulebook approach to financial statement comparability won't work, what will according to Mr. Kleckner?

65   GIANT STORES LOSES AUDITOR'S CERTIFICATION
OF 1972 REPORT BECAUSE OF 'IRREGULARITIES'

(Reprinted by permission from the *Wall Street Journal* (May 24, 1973). © Dow Jones & Company, Inc., 1973.)

Giant Stores Corporation's independent auditor withdrew its certification of Giant Stores' fiscal 1972 financial report because of indications of what the auditor termed "substantial irregularities."

These apparent irregularities of the discount and catalog store chain have "thrown doubt" on the fairness of the 1972 report, the auditor, Touche Ross & Company, said. The apparent irregularities, the auditor told Giant and the Securities & Exchange Commission, included understatement of costs and expenses and, thus, overstatement of net income; and also overstatement of accounts and notes receivable, merchandise inventories and retained earnings, coupled with an understatement of accounts payable.

The net effect of such inaccurate statements would be to artificially inflate Giant Stores' financial health, as portrayed in the financial report, for the fiscal year ended January 29, 1972. Touche Ross previously had given that report a clean bill of health, with the standard auditor's statement that the reports "present fairly" the company's financial position.

Touche Ross apparently turned up the alleged 1972 irregularities in the course of auditing Giant Stores' books for fiscal 1973, ended February 3.

Withdrawal of an auditor's certification can affect a company's relations with the SEC and could hamper trading in the company's stock, an auditing source said. The SEC previously suspended over-the-counter trading in Giant Stores' stock, and the American Stock Exchange has halted trading on the exchange.

Giant Stores wouldn't comment on details of the irregularities and said it can't yet estimate their impact, if any, on the fiscal 1972 report. A spokesman did say that if any revisions are necessary, the costs will be charged to fiscal 1973. Touche Ross is proceeding with an audit of Giant Stores' fiscal 1973 report and is expected to finish it within six weeks, the company said. However, it added, Touche Ross already has warned that it "will be unable to express an opinion with respect to these financial statements."

Giant Stores officials refused to clarify this remark, and a Touche Ross spokesman referred all questions to the company. Presumably, inability to get its fiscal 1973 report certified, even if corrections for past irregularities are made, could hamper resumption of trading in Giant Stores stock.

Giant Stores does plan to get a fully audited and certified consolidated balance sheet for the six-month period ending August 4, said Glenn Cochran, president. That's the date set for determining the price Tandy Industries Incorporated will pay to acquire control of Giant Stores. Under previous financing arrangements, Tandy has rights to buy up to 62 percent of Giant Stores stock, but the price won't be set until an audit as of August 4. Tandy, meantime, has assumed operating control of Giant Stores.

QUESTIONS

1. What does an independent auditor's certification of financial statements consist of?
2. What is the value of the auditor's certification? Why does the SEC require it?

---

66   THE NUMBERS GAME: FIGURING OUT FOOTNOTES

(Reprinted by permission from *Forbes*, vol. 113, no. 9 (May 1, 1974): 38-40.)

"How do you read an annual report—intelligently, I mean?"

There was no ducking the question, difficult as it was, for it came from a promising young man who had just joined our staff.

"I've got an MBA, and I majored in economics at college, but I still don't get as much out of these things as I think I should. What's the secret?"

Well, as any serious investor knows, you read them backwards, we replied.

"Backwards?"

We reached across the desk and picked up a copy of Honeywell's 1973 annual report, which had just arrived with the morning's mail.

You start with the auditor's letter at the end of the financial statements to see if it's qualified, we explained. If the last sentence —the one that begins "In our opinion"—contains the words "subject to," you know right away that the outside accountants have serious misgivings about something in the financial statements. Lockheed's 1972 annual report had a "subject to" saying that about $1 billion of L-1011 aircraft inventory might never be sold. An important warning.

And sometimes you'll find an "except for" qualifier in that last sentence, we went on. You run into that when a company switches from one acceptable accounting method to another equally acceptable method— as when Kroger switched in 1973 from LIFO (last-in, first-out) to FIFO (first-in, first-out) inventory accounting. The auditor's letter alerted you to a footnote to the effect that the change boosted their earnings by over 50 percent.

Now let's see what Haskins & Sells has to say about Honeywell. Nothing. Honeywell got a "clean" opinion—which, of course, is what you'd expect. The great majority of companies do.

"What's next?" asked our young colleague. "The president's letter?"

No, no. You continue reading backwards. Next, you look at the footnotes. They'll often tell you things the president's letter carefully glosses over.

All right, now *here's* something interesting, we continued. Near the start of Honeywell's "Summary of Significant Accounting Policies"—a required disclosure—we see the company has an unconsolidated finance subsidiary.

"Excuse me, but why is that interesting?"

Well, because that tells you Honeywell is doing some "off-balance-sheet financing." Look, you have to bear in mind what type of company you're dealing with. Honeywell's traditional business is control systems, but the company now gets about half its revenues from computers. Now what do you suppose is the critical factor in a highly competitive field like computers—aside from technology?

"Well, let's see, it's a capital-intensive business. And lots of your revenues come from rentals or leases rather than sales. Your income gets spread out over several years. So I guess it would be capital."

Very good. Now back to this finance subsidiary. IBM has such a fat income stream from its base of heavily depreciated leased equipment that it is a net cash generator. But Honeywell probably isn't. So they have to get cash by borrowing against their leases. The finance subsidiary does that, and in the process it should generate a lot of debt that doesn't show up on the parent's balance sheet. Here it is in footnote 5.

Sure, look at that debt! Honeywell's finance subsidiary increased its long-term debt last year by $75 million, to $125 million.

We turned back to the parent company balance sheet.

See? If you had looked first at their consolidated balance sheet, you might have thought that long-term debt increased by only $28 million, to $386 million. But we know that's not right. In fact, Honeywell's long-term debt increased over $100 million last year if we include their finance subsidiary.

"But why do they bother to keep them separate?" asked our young friend, looking over our shoulder. "Even if they did consolidate that finance subsidiary, total equity of about $1.2 billion would still amount to 55 percent of capitalization. That's not much lower than the 62 percent they show now. And they probably don't earn as high a return in their finance subsidiary as they do in their main business, do they?"

You're right, they don't, we replied. They have, let's see, a 5 percent rate of return in that finance subsidiary compared with an 11 percent return in the basic business. But a finance company can operate with a high ratio of debt to equity. Honeywell's finance subsidiary, for example, has total debt that's 2.6 times its equity base.

"So it's a way of stretching your borrowing power."

Partly, but that's not the only advantage. The finance company can balance short-term commercial paper and long-term obligations and get better interest rates than Honeywell could negotiate directly.

"Smart move. But what did they do with that extra $75 million in long-term debt that the subsidiary borrowed?"

Okay, here it is. They had $113 million in short-term commercial paper borrowings in that subsidiary, and they used this long-term borrowing to roll over commercial paper into 25-year long-term debt. Prudent, given the sharp rise in the commercial paper rate last year.

Anyway, you see, by reading the footnotes first you can tell that Honeywell is playing a pretty sophisticated game. Look at note 3, for example, which shows when all borrowings come due. A nice steady stream of maturities there. No big "balloon" payments.

Now, let's see how they use that finance subsidiary. A little farther down in the accounting policies footnote, they tell us that they recognize earnings on leased computers as the money comes in over the life of the lease. That's conservative. Since they must need more cash than this actually produces, they sell some of the receivables from these leases to the subsidiary. Honeywell gets dollars it can use instead of lease commitments, and the subsidiary raises cash to buy the receivables by going into the money market and borrowing on the lease income.

"Well, but isn't that a chance for some fancy footwork? When they assign those leases to the subsidiary, do they then recognize the future income even though payment hasn't been made?"

Good question, we replied. There's potential for what's politely called "managing earnings." But the accountants won't allow it. They now have strict rules governing the recognition of lease income. By transferring those future leases, Honeywell gets the money borrowed against them for use as working capital. The summary of changes in financial position shows that this produced about $50 million last year. But that money doesn't get reported on the income statement. Instead, it appears on the balance sheet as a liability in the form of deferred rental income.

All right, now let's quick check through the rest of these notes here. Their inventories are on first-in, first-out. . . .

"Just like most companies."

Besides, the whole computer industry is on FIFO. Ideally, none of them should be—that's just one man's opinion.

Okay. They expense research and development costs as incurred, which is conservative. Oops! Wait a minute. They have a couple of exceptions here that could be important. Remember Memorex? Their

financial difficulties last year stemmed in part from $28 million in
capitalized research and development that had to be written off when
they couldn't sell the products.

Let's take a look at those exceptions. All right, they capitalize
R&D on cost-plus government contracts. No problem there since the future income to offset the expense is assured. But now in the second
exception they say they capitalize R&D expense on "hardware engineering
and product development expenses assigned to computer systems used internally, leased to customers or in the process of manufacture."

"That sounds like *all* computer R&D."

Not quite so fast, we warned. The note mentions only *hardware-
related* expenses which are capitalized; R&D for computer *software* is
expensed. Unfortunately, we don't know how much money is involved.

We flipped through the glossy pictures and text to see if Honeywell's annual report gave a figure for total R&D commitments. Here,
on page 21. They spent $269 million last year.

"But how much was capitalized?"

Who knows? You can see that reading the notes raised another good
question. Probably only a small portion of that amount, but they don't
tell us.

We proceeded. Depreciation . . . goodwill . . . nothing significant there. Computers are written off over a five-year period, which
seems reasonable. Goodwill—that's the premium over asset value that
Honeywell has paid for acquisitions—is less than 2 percent of total
assets. So we won't worry about what they bought. Foreign operations
. . . again no problem. The note says exchange adjustments weren't material.

Income taxes? According to Honeywell's income statement, the company is actually paying about $36 million less in taxes than it reports.
The difference shows up on the balance sheet as a deferred liability.
In other words, income for tax purposes is about $72 million lower than
the figure reported in the income statement.

"Is that possible?"

Oh, certainly, we said. Just about every company keeps two sets of
books. One for the tax collector; one for the stockholders. The note
here explains that the difference results from things like taking advantage of accelerated depreciation for tax purposes and writing off some
of that capitalized R&D we just discussed. That's normal enough.

But watch for big changes in the size of tax deferrals. They could
indicate that there has been an accounting switch somewhere that has
made a significant impact on the income statement. Honeywell's deferral
is about the same size as it was the previous year, so we won't worry.

There *is* an important tax item, though. A little further down in
footnote 7 we see that Honeywell has foreign tax-loss carryforwards of
$210 million. Now, let's see, this applies only to French income tax.
Okay, they're taking advantage of prior years' losses in a French computer company they got when they acquired the assets of GE's computer
business in 1970. And they're going to use that loss to offset tax on
future income earned in France.

Here, it shows up as an extraordinary item on the income statement
—34 cents a share out of a total of $5.46 earned last year. And they
go on to say that French law lets this loss carryforward stay on the
books indefinitely until it's used up, unlike our tax code which allows
similar carryforward only for a five-year period.

"So the tax loss is really sort of a long-term asset that doesn't show up on the balance sheet?"

Right, we said. Assuming, of course, that Honeywell eventually makes enough money in France to offset it. And assuming the French don't change their tax laws.

"I can see why they want to keep it off the balance sheet."

We took a quick look at the last note, contingencies and commitments. The important thing here was the listing of long-term leases and rental agreements. In a sense these represent a form of disguised borrowing. By leasing, they don't tie up as much of their own needed capital in real estate. But, like any other form of leverage, this entails greater risk. Payments on those leases—$31 million this year—are fixed costs just like interest on borrowed money.

And that's about it, we said, sliding Honeywell's annual report back across the desk to our young friend.

"To read an annual report the way you just did, you obviously have to know quite a bit about the company and its industry—not to mention accounting."

Well, sure. You have to do a little work, you know. If you're an investor and you're going to put your hard-earned money into this company, isn't it worth doing a little homework first?

"You've raised more questions than you've answered."

That's the whole point! For investors as well as for reporters.

QUESTIONS

1. After reading this article do you think accounting is an art or a science? Why?
2. Based on some of your past readings, who do you think created generally accepted accounting principles? Was it management or was it the CPA?
3. Do you think the CPA and/or management is making a fair representation of their financial data to their stockholders?
4. Who is the annual report written for? Is it the small stockholder, the large stockholder, the security analyst, or the public in general? Why is the annual report written in such a manner?

---

67   NEW BOSSES TACKLE MATTEL'S TROUBLES

(Reprinted by permission from *Business Week* (March 24, 1973): 23.)

An era is ending at Mattel, Incorporated, the troubled Hawthorne, California toy industry giant built from scratch by the entrepreneurial husband and wife team of Ruth and Elliot Handler. Long famous for its buxom Barbie dolls, the company is now beset by red ink, stockholder suits, and burdensome debt. This week Ruth Handler bowed out as president of both the parent company and its big Mattel Toys Division. She and Elliot, who own 30 percent of the stock, now share the chairmanship. He remains chief executive.

At the corporate level, Ruth Handler is succeeded as president by Arthur S. Spear, 52, an eight-year Mattel veteran and MIT graduate who spent another eight years at Revlon, Incorporated. Spear, who moves up from executive vice-president and chief operating officer, now has the title to match his recent role in the company. The change was made with the blessing, if not the urging, of Mattel's creditors, led by Bank of America. Ruth Handler's replacement as toy division president is Raymond P. Wagner, 41, who was a Sears, Roebuck & Company executive before joining Mattel and was most recently executive vice-president of the toy division.

Mattel this week also suspended its quarterly cash dividends. The company is expected to report a "substantial" loss for its fiscal year ended last February 5. A year earlier, it lost $29.9 million on sales of $272 million. Its toy sales had dropped 30 percent, and a heavy loser was its line of die-cast Hot Wheels toy cars. Mattel stock, which sold as high as 52¼ early in 1971, now languishes near 7. "We are in a tough spot, no question about it," says Robert S. Ehrlich, executive vice-president for finance.

ABOUT-FACE

Mattel appeared to be turning around when it reported a $6.4 million profit in fiscal 1973s first nine months. Toy sales rebounded and most of the acquisitions made by Ehrlich's predecessor, Seymour M. Rosenberg, an ex-Litton Industries' executive, did well. The acquisitions included playground equipment, magnetic tapes, and Ringling Bros. circus. The company's movie-making joint venture, Radnitz-Mattel Productions, Incorporation, has a winner in its first film, *Sounder*.

As recently as February 5, Elliot Handler was predicting that fiscal 1973 would be profitable. But 18 days later, Handler did an about-face and said his company would show a significant loss for the year.

The losses will come primarily from the company's electric music maker, Optigan, which was introduced in mid-1971 and failed in the marketplace, and from the acquired Metaframe Division, because it missed the trend to frameless home aquariums. Mattel is also drastically writing down toy inventories and substantially increasing reserves against its accounts receivable, which have tripled in the past three years.

Beyond those setbacks, Mattel's urgent problem is a restructuring of its debt. "Mattel concerned itself too long with pure growth, without a corresponding concern for profits and capital structure," says Spear. "It leveraged itself on short-term debt until it ran out of operating funds."

An $80 million line of revolving credit is up for renewal on May 31 and a $60 million term loan is due on July 1. Bank of America, which launched the Handlers with a $5,000 loan in 1945, leads the banking syndicate that made the term loan. Richard W. Manderbach, a Bank of America group vice-president, says Mattel "must get more equity in its financial structure," but he will not say when that will happen. Mattel wants to expand the term loan to $100 million, to be due in five years. Spencer Boise, Mattel's vice-president for public affairs, concedes that the bankers might force Mattel to consider other alternatives, "such as selling one of our subsidiaries."

SUITS

Adding to the company's woes, a stockholder suit filed last October accuses several Mattel executives, including Ruth Handler, of illegally using insider information when they sold 118,862 Mattel shares last summer and of reaping a profit of $900,000 to $1.5 million. The suit maintains the executives knew when they sold the stock that the company was suffering a sharp earnings drop for the quarter ended July 29, 1972, although the company was still issuing "bullish reports."

In another suit earlier this month, two Philadelphia stockholders filed a class action on behalf of those who bought Mattel stock between early 1972 and last month, when the stock fell from $34.75 to $5.50. The suit alleges that the Handlers and other executives misrepresented Mattel's financial position.

Mattel's relations with Wall Street are also seriously strained. Elliot Handler's sudden reversal in February of his company's prospects have left deep wounds at such brokerage houses as Drexel-Burnham, which had earlier promoted Mattel stock.

In the midst of its troubles, Mattel has trimmed its toy line from 425 items to 300 while adding preschool and riding toys. Nathan Greenman, executive vice-president of Greenman Brothers, Incorporated, a major toy wholesaler, rates Mattel's 1973 line as "very fine," although he adds it is too early to tell about its acceptance for the Christmas selling season. "Nothing's hot now," he says.

The Mattel 1973 line includes a Jonathan Livingston Seagull game that urges players to "find your way through self-limiting obstacles to the ultimate state of perfection." That is good advice for Mattel. But Spear concedes it will still take hard work before Mattel will soar like Jonathan—or even like the Mattel of the 1960s.

QUESTIONS

1. What is your estimate of the quality of interim reports which Mattel issued?
2. If interim reports were certified by CPA's do you think such reports would be more reliable? Explain. What are some problems of certifying statements for short periods of time?

---

68   INTERIM REPORTS: DO THEY MEET
                           MAP STANDARDS?

William F. Crum

(Reprinted by permission from *Management Accounting*, vol. 54, no. 11 (May, 1973): 26-28.)

(William F. Crum is a faculty member at The University of Southern California.)

Every three months, owners of common stocks of listed corporations in the United States receive reports from the corporate headquarters of their companies. Corporations listed on the New York Stock Exchange and the American Stock Exchange must, as a minimum, provide their shareholders with an announcement about earnings for the quarter completed, as well as the cumulative earnings for that part of the fiscal year to that point. Presumably such an interim report provides stockholders and financial markets with information that will inform them of the progress of the company since its last complete annual report.

However, a study of the quarterly reports of 75 companies does not indicate that any substantial amount of really valuable and useful information is being disclosed in most current interim reports. The sample studied consisted of quarterly reports received by the author between August 9, 1972, and September 25, 1972. It is a fairly random collection of industrial firms, but it does include two airlines and two utilities. It does not include any rails, banks, savings and loan associations, or insurance companies. This limitation in scope of the sample should be considered in any evaluation of the summary presented in this article.

ADHERENCE TO MAP GUIDELINES

The 75 reports were analyzed carefully to note how many meet the recommended "Guidelines for Interim Financial Reporting" set forth by the Committee on Management Accounting Practices (MAP) of the National Association of Accountants as published in the August, 1972 issue of *Management Accounting*. Succinctly and explicitly stated, the Guidelines contain 12 goals or standards of expected preparation that every interim report should meet.

How well do present interim financial reports measure up to these Guidelines? The analysis of the 75 reports surveyed would seem to indicate that interim corporate reports have quite a way to go if they are to come close to achieving the goals set forth in the preamble of the Guidelines. Let us go down the list item by item.

Timing of Reports

1. Companies that currently report publicly should present at
    least three quarterly reports a year; a report for the
    fourth quarter is encouraged.

Most, if not all, companies present three quarterly reports a year, and it is probable that most include a fourth quarterly report as well. Nothing was found to indicate any failure to observe Guideline 1.

Fiscal Period

2.   "The interim reporting period should be regarded as a portion of the annual fiscal period rather than as a fiscal period in itself."

Adherence to Guideline 2 could not be ascertained from study of the quarterly reports. It is tentatively assumed, however, that most, if not all, companies do regard the interim reporting period as a portion of the annual fiscal period rather than a fiscal period in itself.

Consistency With Annual Reports

3.   Accounting principles and practices of interim reports should be consistent with those accounting methods used in the annual financial statements.

As to Guideline 3, none of the interim reports studied contained any indications that the accounting principles and practices used were not consistent with those used in the annual financial statements. However, this finding must not necessarily be taken as proof that no difference existed; there was simply nothing stated either way on the subject.

Minimum Content

4.   As a minimum, the interim statement should show sales and revenue, income taxes, income before extraordinary items, extraordinary items, net income for the interim period as well as for the year to date, and a comparison with the same period of the previous year. A balance sheet or statement of changes in financial condition should be included when a material financial transaction has taken place which would lead the company to believe these reports are significant.

All reports appeared to meet the level of disclosure set by Guideline 4. However, only 11 interim reports provided a balance sheet, and only two provided statements of changes in financial condition. These latter statements were urged by the Guidelines, under certain conditions, and inclusion of both would be appreciably more informative to all present users of interim reports.

Changes in Practice

5. Changes in interim or annual accounting practice or policy
    should be disclosed. Dollar impact of change applicable
    to the interim period and effect on year-to-date amounts
    should be reported.

The disclosures sought in Guideline 5 were not found in any of the
interim reports studied. Perhaps none took place, but certainly nothing
was found to indicate any such changes had been made or were contemplated.

Restating Prior Periods

6. "No restatement of prior interim periods should be made
    for changes in estimates or assumptions used as a basis
    for reporting."

Guideline 6 also seemed to be included overtly in the reports
studied. If any restatement of a prior interim period took place because of any change in estimate or reporting assumption, nothing was
said about it. Again, it is possible no restatement occurred, but
there were no positive statements to prove it.

Extraordinary Items

7. "Interim reports should comment on important developments,
    extraordinary items and unusual transactions and disclose
    them in the period in which they occur."
8. Extraordinary items are defined as those that will be ex-
    pected to be set forth as such in the fiscal year state-
    ments. Unusual transactions are considered to be those
    that are material with respect to operating results of
    the interim period, but which are not expected to be shown
    as extraordinary items in the fiscal year statements.

In terms of adherence to Guidelines 7 and 8, the survey of the 75
statements revealed that:

    a. Forty-one reports contained information accounting at
        least in part for the increase or decrease in sales or
        revenue.
    b. Thirty-nine reports contained some explanation account-
        ing at least in part for the increase or decrease in
        earnings, aside from the increase or decrease in sales
        or revenue.
    c. Forty-six reports contained information about capital
        additions or dispositions, mergers, acquisitions, new
        plants or stores, and the like. Admittedly, some of
        the information here was very meager, but it at least
        was provided the reader so he could make his own con-
        clusion about its effect on earnings.

    d. Thirty reports provided information about new products, new growth areas for the business, or other factors which could conceivably affect earnings.

    e. Fifteen reports provided analysis or breakdown of the profitability or unprofitability of product lines or major subdivisions of the company. Again, the information was quite broad and general in most instances, and often merely mentioned increases in certain areas or declines in others. Specific percentages or figures were rarely given.

    f. Thirteen reports made reference to the current status or settlement of pertinent major court litigation, decisions of government regulatory bodies, or laws passed by Congress or the states which might affect them.

    g. Nine reports contained some reference to labor problems, settlement of strikes, or current problems arising from unsettled strikes.

Consolidation

9. Interim financial statements should be on a consolidated basis if annual reports are so presented.

It is believed all reports studied were prepared in accord with Guideline 9, though nothing specifically was stated except that most headings of statements included the word "consolidated."

Pooling

10. Combined results of pooled business for the current and all prior periods should be included in the report. Any material divestiture should be reported in the period when it takes place.

Guideline 10 refers to results of poolings or divestitures and their reflection in the reports. Nothing was noted to indicate this kind of event in any report; it may well have been observed, but not specifically described.

Attestation

11. Attestation by independent public accountants for interim financial statements is not required, but counsel with such public accountants is recommended relative to changes in accounting methods, extraordinary items, or other significant transactions that might arise in that interim period.

Conformity to Guideline 11 cannot be determined readily. Only one company presented an auditor's opinion with its interim six month report,

which also contained a balance sheet and a series of footnotes similar
to those found in the annual report. It might be presumed that the appropriate corporate financial and accounting management had been consulting frequently with independent public accountants as to extraordinary or questionable matters, but no report of any such fact was found
in the interim reports. It is, perhaps, something that one could hardly
expect to find mentioned very often.

Consistency With SEC Reports

12.   It is also required that all financial data should be
consistent with that provided the SEC covering the same
period.

Nothing was found in the reports to indicate methods inconsistent
with Guideline 12. It is again something one would not logically expect
to find overt reference to in an interim report unless some regulatory
body specifically requires that a statement to this effect be made.

ADDITIONAL OBSERVATIONS

A few other interesting aspects of presentation or nonpresentation
of helpful information in interim reports are worth mentioning. All 75
reports gave the earnings per share figure so widely devoured by the security markets. At the same time, only 10 reports gave any additional
ratios or financial statistics to indicate actual or relative changes in
level of production, operation, or activity. These 10 were mostly in
the petroleum industry but also included the two airlines surveyed.
Fourteen reports gave information about new management changes, new appointments to top positions, new titles, and background aspects on the
personnel involved. Six reports discussed major changes in management
responsibilities or reshuffling of work assignments, including any major
realignment of the entire organization.

Interim reports varied from some that provided almost no information except sales, earnings, and earnings per share to a few that provided quite a wealth of information. Most reports fell in between these
extremes, tending to provide very little substantive knowledge except
sales, earnings, earnings per share, and a few rather offhanded remarks
now and then to better explain some favorable or unfavorable change
since the previous report.

It would appear that most corporations have, at this time, a long
way to go to approach the level of disclosure implied by Guidelines 7
and 8. It is also possible that many more corporations should be providing a balance sheet or a statement of changes in financial condition
in their interim reports as suggested in Guideline 4. It seems that
very few firms are doing this at the present time.

Remarks made by William J. Casey, then Chairman of the Securities &
Exchange Commission, before the annual meeting of the American Institute
of Certified Public Accountants in Denver on October 2, 1972, should be
given careful consideration insofar as they may well indicate a philosophy and attitude to which corporate management should give careful attention. Mr. Casey stated the SEC had moved to require companies to

make more timely and detailed disclosure of financial information that
may adversely affect their profit picture. He also "urged accountants
to review interim reports of their clients before they are issued to
the public and to consult with clients on reporting problems as they
arise." The Chairman of the SEC continued by stating that "A once-a-
year appearance on the scene to bless an annual audit report doesn't
conform to public expectation of the auditor's role." (1)

Guideline 11 did not specifically recommend that interim reports be
attested to by the independent public accountant, though there exists a
considerable amount of feeling in many areas of our economy that this
attestation might be desirable and should be a longer-range objective of
both the SEC and the public accounting profession. Only one company
out of the 75 surveyed is now doing this; and thus it might seem to be
a considerable task to convince the others of the desirability of such
an added step.

Most of the other Guidelines, specifically numbers 1, 2, 3, 5, 6,
9, and 10, are of a type the observance of which is not provided in
present interim reports. The absence of any footnote or mention of the
practice referred to cannot be taken to imply either that the problem
did not exist or that it was handled either properly or improperly.

CONCLUSION

Interim financial reports serve a useful purpose. How well they
meet the needs of our economy is something else. Certainly the majority
of corporations could, and perhaps should, provide much more information
in their reports than is presently being supplied. It would cost them
very little, either, in more printing, postage, or editorial work. The
failure to do more may be a matter of inertia and apathy; it is easy to
keep on doing what has been accepted in the past. That hardly makes it
right in these days of active public interest in the financial institutions of our society. Surely it must be apparent that it would cost
very little more to provide stockholders with additional information of
the kind suggested. It is difficult to see how disclosure of such information could in any way affect the competitive strategy of the company or have any adverse effect once it is made known to the shareholders and the public generally.

FOOTNOTE

1. The *Wall Street Journal* (October 3, 1972): 3.

QUESTIONS

1. What is an interim report? Of what does the interim
    report consist?
2. Why are interim reports needed?
3. Are interim reports now certified by independent auditors?
    What would be the advantage(s) of such certification?

---

69   EXTENDED FINANCIAL REPORTING
                           BY DIVERSIFIED COMPANIES

William E. Langdon

(Reprinted by permission from *Cost and Management*, vol. 47, no. 1
(January-February, 1973): 50-53.)

The strong trend in recent years toward corporate diversification
has caused several areas of controversy to surface. One such issue is
segment reporting. Briefly, concern is being expressed by the financial
community (the suppliers of new capital) and the government sector (concerned with maintaining a competitive economic environment) that not
enough information is supplied by consolidated financial statements to
allow them to perform their functions adequately.

A number of recent studies done by the National Association of Accountants and the Financial Executives Institute have stressed the fact
that, although consolidated financial statements meet current accounting
standards of disclosure, they no longer provide sufficient data for the
growing number of external readers representing various interest groups.
These studies suggest that "knowledge of segment operating results is
essential to making sound investment and credit decisions with respect
to companies whose component activities differ significantly in rates of
growth, profitability and risk." (1)

This article will explain why these groups are requesting more
data, what form the data should take, and finally the guidelines for
preparing segmented reports as recommended by the Financial Executives
Institute.

GOVERNMENT

Conglomerate reporting has come under scrutiny by a number of government agencies (primarily in the U.S.) such as the Anti-Trust Division of the Department of Justice, the Federal Trade Commission, and the
Subcommittee on Anti-Trust and Monopoly of the Senate Committee on the
Judiciary.

These agencies require additional financial disclosure in order to
determine:

1. the degree of concentration a firm has in a particular
    industry (i.e., how extensive is IBM's share of the
    typewriter market?), and
2. the extent of "cross-subsidization" within a conglomerate
    group

The government is concerned that profits obtained in industries in which
a firm possesses a substantial monopoly are not used to subsidize sales
in competitive industries at a loss or at an abnormally low profit.

Such practices would make it almost impossible for the single line producer to remain in the industry even though he may be a more efficient producer than the larger conglomerate. In fact, even if cross-subsidization were nonexistent, competition could still be lessened by virtue of a single line producer's awareness that if he behaved more competitively he could be subject to retaliation by a conglomerate which in their industry could operate at a loss without materially affecting their overall profit position.

The point here is that unless these government agencies are supplied with sufficient information (i.e., segment reports) to evaluate whether, where and to what extent conglomerate firms are engaged in cross-subsidization, their knowledge of such practices will at best be fragmentary and competition lessened. (2)

FINANCIAL COMMUNITY

It is unlikely that present government involvement in the area of financial reporting could have caused such interest in segmented financial statements had it not been for the increasing pressure for more disclosure by members of the financial community. An NAA study, entitled *Financial Reporting for Security Investment and Credit Decisions*, found that 80 percent of the security analysts interviewed felt a significant shortcoming of corporate annual reports was the failure to provide sales and earnings breakdowns for major product and market segments.

Growing corporate concern for the information needs of the security analyst is the result of three factors:

1. Continuing shortages of capital on the part of most limited companies.
2. Growth in the absolute size and depth of the market for industrial capital (prominent in this growth is the increasing numbers of institutionalized investors).
3. Investors are being served by professional analysts and managers whose technical skill has advanced rapidly. (3)

The objective of a financial analyst is to select companies for his client that meet the client's desired standards of risk, profitability and return. To meet this objective, the analyst will make forecasts about the various levels of demand for company products, price outlooks and expected changes in operating costs. In single-product, single-location firms, calculations for profitability, risk and growth will be relatively simple; however, as a company gets larger and occupies several locations or gets involved in a variety of unrelated product lines, these key investment variables may differ for various locations and operations within the company. Thus it becomes critical that the security analyst have information concerning the product lines of a diversified company and the market share for each so that he can build up a *composite* profit picture for the conglomerate and the success or lack of success a company's management will have in meeting competition. If information about the industries or markets a company participates in and the extent of activity in each does not appear in the financial statements, the analyst can do little more than make a blind guess at a conglomerate's potential as an investment.

Let us now look at some of the concerns raised by management over
the use of segmented statements and how the FEI and NAA studies respond.

Allocation of Joint Cost

It has been argued that, as there are currently no auditing principles in this area, any allocation of joint or common costs will be
rather subjective, making comparisons between companies impossible.

The NAA study, *External Reporting for Segments of a Business* by
Backer and McFarland, agrees that it is *unlikely* any uniform classification of segments based on industry or product characteristics would be
feasible. The authors point out, however, that analysts do not expect
to make inter-company comparisons of segment performance (i.e., the intent is not to compare Company X's chemical division with that of Company Y). Rather, the analysts' objective is to try to build up an earnings forecast segment by segment and no comparison between companies
will be made until the complete consolidated outlook is finalized. Thus
there is no concern over the uniformity of the breakdown and it is
agreed that segmented financial statements should be tailored to the
company—all the analyst asks is for consistency from period to period.

This NAA study suggests that the contribution margin approach be
used for segment presentation, i.e., segments are charged with separable
costs and revenues only and any items which are incurred by the company
as a whole are left unassigned.

This approach is favored by the CICA Handbook, section 1700 "Financial Reporting for Diversified Companies" released in August, 1971, as
Table 11 indicates.

Fear of Competition

Many executives feel that further detailing of financial statements
could provide competitors with useful information such as profit margins, etc. This could produce a shifting in sales emphasis or result in
new competitors entering the industry, both of which could lead to long-
run damage to profits.

The NAA study previously cited does not accept this argument. It
concluded that a significant amount of information would *not* be revealed
in broadly based segment reports. (5)

Interviews conducted with several executives by the authors of this
study indicated that the executives already knew substantially more
about their competitors than the proposed segment reports would reveal
although the reports might confirm what were now only estimates of uncertain accuracy.

The authors conceded that, where disclosure could give away a major
change in corporate strategy or allow competitors to enjoy benefits from
innovations without participating in development costs, or where for any
other reason management feels disclosure would not be in the best interest of the shareholders, it might be best to indicate this in the notes
to the financial statements rather than make extended disclosure.

TABLE 11

EXAMPLE OF PRESENTATION OF SEGMENTED INCOME DATA (4)

(This example has been provided by the Institute's Research
staff.)

Segmented Income Data for the year ended December 31, 1973
(In thousands of dollars)

	1973		1972	
	Sales	Segment Margin	Sales	Segment Margin
Segment A (1)	$ 5,324	$ 648	$ 4,872	$ 585
Segment B	8,776	1,427	9,321	1,102
Segment C	2,776	640	1,827	466
	16,876	2,715	16,020	2,153
Elimination of inter-segment transactions (2)	1,736	183	1,872	411
	$15,140 (3)	$2,532	$14,148 (3)	$1,742
Common costs, net of common revenues		1,236		861
Net income for the year		$1,296 (3)	(3) $	881

1. The segments for which information is disclosed, as well as
    the basis of segmentation, would be clearly described.
2. A summary of the methods of pricing transfers within an
    enterprise may be appropriate in certain circumstances,
    e.g., "Inter-segment transactions are priced at close
    approximation of open market prices for similar products
    and services."
3. These figures would agree with sales and net income for the
    year as shown in the Income Statement (or Consolidated In-
    come Statement, as the case may be).

Before leaving this area, the following points should be kept in mind:

1. No company would have a net advantage if all were required to make similar disclosure.
2. The "availability of reliable information about a company's operations has been a major factor in expansion of capital markets. Management has often opposed increased disclosure, but in the long run the economy has benefited from the willingness of more individuals to invest in corporate securities. In countries where little information is available, relatively few individuals have been willing to invest in corporate securities." (6)

The Financial Executives Institute has issued the following set of guidelines which takes into account many of the concerns discussed above:

Recommendations (7)

1. Companies which are unitary in nature, that is, which operate almost completely within a single broadly-defined industry, or which are highly integrated, should not be expected to fractionalize themselves for reporting purposes.
    A. Unless a company has components which
        (1) operate in different industries, broadly-defined, and
        (2) experience rates of profitability, degrees of risk, or opportunities for growth independent of other components, and
        (3) meet the test of materiality (as stated in 2-b), the company should be considered unitary in nature
    B. Companies, or parts of companies, whose segments transfer substantial amounts of products to or receive substantial amounts of products from, or render substantial services to, other segments with which they are integrated in a product sense, should be considered unitary in nature rather than diversified.
2. Companies which to a material degree have activity in more than one broadly-defined industry should meet the extended disclosure requirements in item 3 following:
    A. Activity in more than one broadly-defined industry exists when a company either
        (1) receives gross revenue from,
        (2) derives income from, or
        (3) utilizes assets in industries subject to significantly different rates of profitability, diverse degrees of risk, or varying opportunities for growth.
        No present system of industry or product classification appears ideally suited to the identification of

broad industry groups for reporting purposes. If any of the existing systems (including the Standard Industrial Classification at the two-digit level) is applied without consideration of a company's historical development and the inter-related nature of its established activities, the disadvantages to shareholders may be substantial. Considerable discretion to management in defining broad industry groupings for the purpose of meeting the disclosure requirements in item 3 is essential.

B. Ordinarily, a "material degree," as the term is used here, means 15 percent or more of a company's gross revenue. If the amounts of gross revenue are significantly disproportionate to the amounts of income from, or the assets employed in, diversified components, as compared to other components of the company, a more representative test of the materiality of the diversification should be used.

3. Management, because of its familiarity with company structure, is in the most informed position to separate the company into realistic components for reporting purposes. Therefore, management should determine the number and scope of a diversified company's reporting components and report the activities of those components within the following guidelines:

A. Identify and describe the components which are subject to separate reporting.

B. Disclose any significant changes from the previous period in the composition of the reporting components.

C. For each reporting component:
(1) Disclose sales or other gross revenue.
(2) Disclose the relative contribution made by each component to the income of the enterprise. The contribution to income made by each component may be calculated before or after the allocation of common or corporate costs but in any case should be clearly described. In the event of a change in the method of computing or reporting either gross revenue or the relative contribution to income of the reporting components, the change should be clearly described.

D. If the method of pricing intra-company transfers or allocating common or corporate costs significantly affects the reported contribution to income of the reporting components, the method used should be disclosed in general terms similar to the following:
(1) "Corporate expenses were allocated to the reporting components on the basis of a formula giving approximately equal weight to assets employed, sales, and number of employees."
(2) "Intra-company transactions are priced at close approximations of open market prices for similar products and services."

4. Disclosures recommended under item 3 may be included in parts of the annual report other than the formal financial statements at the discretion of management. Whether in narrative or tabular form, they should be grouped and should carry a clear indication of the limitations of their usefulness. Words similar to the following may prove useful: "The data supplied in (specify pages, paragraphs, or schedules) present certain information relative to the nature, principal types, and results of the company's diversified activities. No assurance can be or is given that they have been prepared on a basis comparable with similar data for other companies."

5. Because of the innovative nature of these recommendations and the innate complexities of reporting diversified activities, the recommendations should be applied with judgment and flexibility by all concerned. In those cases where management sincerely believes the recommended disclosures, if followed, would have significantly adverse effect upon the interest of shareholders, a statement to this effect should be made in lieu of extended disclosures.

SUMMARY

Segmented financial statements have long been recognized as a valuable source of information for internal reporting purposes. An increasing number of external users of financial statements feel that this type of reporting should also accompany the annual reports of diversified companies as it will provide them with the type of information required to perform their tasks effectively. As a result, it would appear that in the not too distant future the accounting principle of disclosure will be amplified to accommodate this desired change in external reporting for conglomerates.

FOOTNOTES

1. *A Framework for Financial Reporting by Diversified Companies* by Rappaport and Lerner (New York: NAA, 1969), p. 9.
2. At present the Canada Corporation Act (section 121-1) permits the parent company to present to its shareholders consolidated statements only, i.e., they need not submit statements in unconsolidated form.
3. *External Reporting for Segments of a Business*, Backer and McFarland (New York: NAA, 1968), pp. 4-5.
4. *CICA Handbook*, Section 1700.
5. *External Reporting for Segments of a Business*, NAA, p. 82.
6. Ibid., p. 85.
7. *Financial Reporting by Diversified Companies*, R. K. Mautz (New York: FEI, 1968), pp. 157-158.

QUESTIONS

1. Define segment reporting.
2. For what types of corporations would segment reporting provide useful information?
3. Describe the additional data which would be useful, if provided, by segment reporting by corporations.
4. What are the arguments against segment reporting?

5

Some External Uses
of Accounting Information

Financial statements are a primary source of information for decision makers who are external to the firm. The analysis of a firm's worth
is based in large measure upon the data contained in the statements.
Many other sources of information are also used. But the financial statements are the centerpiece of the analysis. The articles is Chapter 5
present ways in which accounting reports are used to help assess the worth
of a firm. Most of the articles are written with the investor in mind.
The fact that accounting data is just one of many information inputs to
investors' decisions is clearly pointed out.

Fundamental analysis, long championed by Graham and Dodd, has comparisons of accounting data at its very heart. Richard J. Stinson (page
225) reviews the continuing usefulness of fundamental analysis. In the
process, he shows us that the basic worth of a stock depends upon ". . .
a company's assets, its earning power, its past record and future prospects." The gauging of the first three of these depends on the ways in
which the accountant does his job.

While accounting reports are central to the analysis of a firm's
worth, other types and sources of information cannot be ignored. *The
Wall Street Journal* article (page 229) lists additional details which
the SEC requires firms to disclose on stock registration statements and
in annual reports to the SEC. Most of these are not accounting-based
data but all are important to investors.

Of accounting data, the most intensively used are the earnings-per-
share figures. These are used to compute the price to earnings ratio
widely viewed by investors as a comparative gauge of stock market
prices. *Forbes* (page 232) indicates the importance that stock market
participants place on growth in earnings.

In order to illustrate more clearly how accounting data and other
information is used to establish the worth of a firm, two examples of
financial analysis have been included (pages 235 and 237). The analysis
centers on profitability in the future and on the prospects for dividends. Accounting information is treated as fundamental to the evaluation. It is, in essence, a scoreboard of past performance upon which to
base estimated performance in the future.

70   GRAHAM & DODD—ALIVE AND WELL

Richard J. Stinson

(Reprinted by permission from *Financial World*, vol. 130, no. 20 (May 9, 1973): 8, 9, 37.)

A fortnight ago, on TV's Wall Street Week, the analyst guest, a big-name money manager, waxed enthusiastic about investment opportunities: "There are some unbelievable bargains in the market today," he explained to his sophisticated studio colleagues. And, presumably, investors in the viewing audience were duly impressed.

Or were they? By now they've been barraged with so much similar advice they can't be blamed for being skeptical. "Bargain basement prices," "bare bones valuations," a stock market that is "one great big discount store." Yet prices continue to slide.

Indeed, the very day our Wall Street analyst-turned-TV-personality was speaking of "unbelievable bargains," the Dow Jones industrials had just slumped more than 15 points to a new low for '73, and the New York Stock Exchange's comprehensive composite index of all 1,500 issues had ended the week looking more ragged than at any time since 1939—the year the Big Board computer memory goes blank.

Investors, it seems, are far from convinced that today's prices represent value. Indeed, they're not too sure any more just what "value" is—at least as far as stocks are concerned. Many, disenchanted with the market, are more partial to bonds, savings accounts, real estate, antiques, art, coins, precious metals, commodities—even foreign currencies.

But stocks? Putting a fair price on General Motors or AT&T—not to mention IBM or Xerox—they've learned through bitter experience, isn't as easy as it was supposed to be back in the days of a rip-roaring bull market.

Even the "experts" are puzzled—notwithstanding all the talk about "bargains." Indeed, for today's typical money man, the concept of what constitutes value is probably as elusive as it was back in 1934, when Benjamin Graham and David L. Dodd came out with their first edition of *Security Analysis*.

Most of the current crop of security analysts, research directors and fund managers were brought up with "Graham & Dodd" as their bible. But that doesn't mean they agree with—much less follow—its preachings.

Graham, now nearly 80, came to Wall Street in 1914 and carved out a highly successful career, finding time also to put in teaching stints at UCLA and Columbia, where coauthor Dodd was professor of finance. His astuteness in making millions himself proved to hard-headed Wall Streeters that theory and practice weren't necessarily antithetical. And the book's unusual combination of erudition and down-to-earth common sense assured its acceptance as *the* standard text for investment courses in schools across the country.

Graham, as might be expected, has some very definite ideas about value in common stocks. Several generations of security analysts probably have his theory of "central value" indelibly imprinted on their minds, even if they remember little else.

In a nutshell, stocks fluctuate in a broad cycle from rich to cheap and back again, and there's a "normal" or "central" value that's defined by the extremes. The idea, if one wants to be successful in the market, is to buy when they are below this central value and to sell when they are above it.

This, of course, sounds suspiciously like Baron Rothschild's simple but pungent advice to "buy them when they're cheap and sell them when they're dear." It also sounds about as hard to implement.

But Graham doesn't stop there. He devotes chapter after chapter in his fourth edition (McGraw-Hill, 1962) to grappling with the problem of what the "intrinsic value" of a stock really is, based on a company's assets, its earning power, its past record and future prospects. After all, in the final analysis, he'd say, this is the basic worth of a stock around which market prices swing in their wide arc.

Clearly, everybody can't win at this game. Indeed, only a small minority are ever going to be smart enough—and patient enough—to ferret out true values. That, automatically, excludes most of the public. "Everyone knows," Graham says, "that most people who trade in the stock market lose money at it in the end."

No wonder such a dismal point of view became less and less popular as the 'fifties and 'sixties progressed. In the prevailing euphoria, everyone could make money. A common stock was a good buy regardless of price. Happiness was a stock that doubled in a year.

Even Graham himself began to have doubts as to just how relevant some of his theories about basic value were in the new era that had dawned after World War II. In 1961, looking back over the previous decade, he said: "Beginning sometime in 1955, our value standards and the actual market level parted company." If the 'fifties posed a dilemma for an analyst of his patently conservative bent, the "soaring 'sixties" must have seemed nothing less than absurd.

From his villa in Majorca, Graham doubtless watched the denouement in 1969-70 with grim satisfaction. In 1972, in his book *The Intelligent Investor* (Harper & Row, rev. ed.), it's clear that he finally feels at least partially vindicated.

The market's collapse, he says, "should have served to dispel an illusion that had been gaining ground during the past two decades. This was that leading common stocks could be bought at any time and at any price, with the assurance not only of ultimate profit but also that any intervening loss would soon be recouped by a renewed advance of the market to new high levels. That," he says, "was too good to be true."

In Graham's view, the great postwar bull market was a vast speculative bubble that finally burst. "At long last the stock market has 'returned to normal,' in the sense that both speculators and stock investors must again be prepared to experience significant and perhaps protracted falls as well as rises in the value of their holdings."

Investors, analysts, stockbrokers, and just about anybody else connected with the market would agree that the climate has indeed changed radically. "This isn't the same market we had a few years ago," is a familiar complaint. There are almost as many shareowners as in the late 'sixties, but they're not active. With nobody but institutions doing much trading, the market lacks liquidity. Stock offerings find few buyers and, as a result, prices erode.

This is reflected in a host of different ways. Some broad-based, unweighted averages show most stocks not only below their 1970 panic lows but below those of the mid-'sixties as well. Half the issues on the Big Board sell for ten times earnings or less. Hundreds of stocks are selling below book value.

The Dow, always deceptive, though at some times much more than at others, has been astonishingly so of late. Not only are most stocks down much more than the 11 percent the Dow is from its all-time peak, but even most of this average's components have behaved rather poorly, with a handful of issues like Eastman Kodak, duPont, Procter & Gamble, and Sears, Roebuck accounting for the bulk of the advance since the '70s lows.

None of this, moreover, provides even an inkling of the carnage that's occurred over-the-counter, particularly among what were once hot new issues.

By comparison, of course, investors in General Motors are a lot better off. But GM is down nearly 40 percent from its all-time high, despite record first quarter earnings which investors have chosen to ignore, as they have the almost uniformly sparkling reports of most other companies.

Does this mean that earnings are no longer important? Some argue that this is indeed the case. Disparaging Graham & Dodd's traditional emphasis on profits, some members of this fraternity glibly maintain that "record corporate profits ought to produce record stock prices." Most analysts know better. The market tends to discount future earnings in advance. Often, the market moves down while earnings are moving up.

But the Dow industrials, other analysts are quick to note, now sell for less than 14 times '72 profits and probably "only" about 12 times current results. They fail to consider that P/E's have been steadily declining since 1961, and that changes in multiples tend to be in the opposite direction from changes in earnings.

Present multiples may look "cheap" by recent standards. But they're probably what Graham would call "reasonable," at best. Graham, don't forget, looks to buy when stocks are *undervalued*, and it's doubtful if prices of most issues have declined to the point where they could be characterized that way, company managements and many analysts to the contrary notwithstanding

If stocks are not irresistibly attractive on fundamentals, why buy them? That's Graham's view. His approach entails lots of diligent digging into balance sheets and income statements. What is a company's financial strength? Is its debt-to-equity ratio within safe limits? How about interest coverage—the number of times fixed charges are earned? Does it have ample liquidity?

If the fundamentals are sound, and there's demonstrated earning power through thick and thin, then it's time to consider price. P/E's vary from one industry to another. Is the P/E appropriate for its industry? Is the dividend record consistent and does the yield offer sufficient appeal? Is the outlook such as to suggest that the P/E is low relative to future earnings? Do prospects indicate the payout could be raised?

Of course, some would say P/E's are far less useful than they used to be. They even belittle reported earnings as practically meaningless in determining value. "If you examine how these numbers come to be," says an accountant, "it's clear they just can't possibly play any role in security analysis." A Harvard professor insists "that we live in what may be a turning point in the history of investment analysis," with less attention paid to individual stocks and more emphasis on overall market swings.

Graham would be the first to agree that security analysis shouldn't stand still. And probably, more grudgingly, he would admit that the dark days of the 'thirties colored everybody's thinking, including his own. Then, corporations worried whether they'd ever emerge from the depression, and they piled up as much cash as they could. With investor confidence at such a low ebb, their stocks often sold for less than the liquidating value of their net current assets.

Times, obviously, have changed, almost beyond recognition. Inflation has taken its toll in many ways and distorted "book values" to the point where they often have little practical significance. Dividends, anathema to investors of the 'sixties who wanted "growth at any price," are being kept artificially low by government ceilings. Thus, yield, for the time being, has also lost much of its former usefulness as a gauge of a stock's worth.

Quality growth stocks, moreover, seem still to defy gravity, as well as Graham's "old fashioned" laws. Their high P/E's represent one of the strangest disparities of all in today's topsy-turvy investment structure. Graham's basic tests of value, strictly followed, would have kept investors out of IBM, Xerox, Polaroid, even Proctor & Gamble—not to mention innumerable other institutional favorites.

But even this act of levitation could come to an end. Lots of high-flyers have already fallen off their perches, and the precipitous plunges they've taken suggests what would happen if the funds and banks decided all at once it was time to sell. The remaining glamours, says one analyst, may be "mere vestiges of the old bull market which, in time, will degenerate in the same fashion as the latter."

At any rate, there's a clearly discernible trend back to "basics" on the part of many investors, large and small. Fast vanishing—if not already dead—are thoughts of making a quick killing. That, in Graham's view, is a first step in the process of taking an intelligent approach to investments.

Some money managers—a tiny minority, to be sure—are even beginning to question whether equities, with their inherent higher risks, are really preferable, after all, to bonds when these fixed-income securities are providing yields well above those on most stocks. That's coming full circle, literally. If inflation is licked, this trend could turn into a stampede, with seriously depressive effects on equity prices.

All signs suggest that the yen among most investors today is for more security, more safety, greater assurance of a future return commensurate with reduced risk. That's just plain old Graham & Dodd, no matter how you slice it. It is, in Graham's words, a "return to reality." Perhaps when it's all over, there really may be some "bargains" lying around.

QUESTIONS

1. What is a price/earnings ratio?
2. What does the price/earnings ratio mean?
3. What is meant by discounting future earnings?
4. Briefly describe Graham's "intrinsic value" and how this
    fundamental approach is used in an investment strategy.
    How does accounting help in establishing the "intrinsic
    value"?

---

71   SEC TELLS FIRMS TO DISCLOSE MORE ABOUT OPERATIONS

(Reprinted by permission from the *Wall Street Journal* (June 14,
1973). © Dow Jones & Company, Inc., 1973.)

Buyers of both hot issues and blue chips will soon have more information on which to base their investment decisions.
The Securities & Exchange Commission adopted a fat package of rules
requiring companies to disclose more data about their new products, competitors and management when registering securities with the agency for
public sale, as well as in their yearly reports to the SEC.
The rules, which were proposed last July, reflect the agency's determination to increase the amount of information all companies must
provide the investing public, as well as its efforts to cool down markets for hot issues, securities that experience sharp price run-ups
after being issued by young, frequently unseasoned companies.
The latest big hot-issues market, when young companies were scram-
bling to sell shares to investors looking for quick profits, occurred
several years ago, during the stock market's headier days. Investors
are more cautious now and the number of new companies going public has
declined sharply, SEC officials said, but the agency is continuing a
hot-issues investigation it began last year.
In issuing the new rules, which take effect August 1, the SEC also
warned underwriters of their obligations to avoid potential conflicts of
interest when selling issues of new companies to customers with discretionary accounts—those in which the broker has permission to make
transactions without consulting the customer.
Overall, the rules "are designed to result in disclosure of more
meaningful information concerning all registrants and to communicate
more effectively to the investing public the economic realities concerning new registrants," the SEC said.

CHANGES DETAILED

All companies will be required to include in their registration statements and annual reports filed with the SEC:

1. "More meaningful information concerning the methods of competition" in their industry or major product lines, with emphasis on such matters as price, service, warranties, and product performance.
2. Additional facts about the responsibilities, experience, and background of corporate executives and other key personnel, such as research scientists or sales and production managers. Any legal proceedings, such as bankruptcy or criminal convictions, involving directors or executives will have to be disclosed, as will family relationships between executives and directors.
3. "Specific disclosure" about publicly announced plans to introduce new products or enter new lines of business, with details on the amount of additional engineering or research necessary to bring the product to market.

The agency decided against adopting an earlier proposal that companies be required to disclose market studies about new products or business ventures. "There are unresolved questions about the reliability of market studies generally," the commission said. It added, however, that if companies are introducing a new product with such a study, they will have to disclose this fact.

OPPOSITION FROM COMPANIES

In general, the SEC received "a lot of resistance" from companies to its proposals, "particularly in the areas of product development and competition," an SEC official said.

In the new-issues area, the SEC said a company registering for the first time and without a three-year operating history must include in its filing a "plan of operation" describing the period of time the proceeds from the sale will satisfy its cash requirements and whether it anticipates a need to raise additional funds in the next six months to meet operating expenses.

The agency decided against a proposal that would have required a new company to include a cash budget in its registration statement, saying concerns "with limited track records may not have the experience, expertise, or resources to prepare reliable cash budgets." The agency said it may require such budgets later, however·

The SEC also scrapped a current rule that exempts companies in "the promotional or development stage" from filing quarterly financial reports. The aim is to make such information available on a more timely basis.

An important change for first-time issuers and their underwriters requires that the registration statement identify any principal underwriter that intends to put shares from the offering into discretionary accounts of its customers, along with an estimate of the amount of shares it plans to put into these accounts.

RULES FOR UNDERWRITERS

The SEC has concluded that underwriters sometimes contribute to sharp increases in the price of new issues by restricting the supply of the stock when they allocate securities to discretionary accounts. To prevent this, the agency warned underwriters that they must tell customers of any conflicts of interests that may arise when they both underwrite an offering and put the shares into discretionary accounts as a way of disposing of shares the underwriters contracted to sell. In such cases, the underwriter must generally tell the customer about the company and obtain his consent to purchase the shares, the SEC said.

First-time issuers must also provide underwriters with stock certificates representing the shares being sold, so the underwriter can quickly send them to purchasers. In the past, purchasers have had to wait for certificates, and this has restricted their ability to sell the shares they own.

New issuers will be required to disclose how they selected the price for their shares. Frequently prospectuses say only that "the initial public offering price has been arbitrarily determined by the company," and the SEC claims that the price of these shares often "bears little or no relationship to the issuer's assets, earnings, or other criteria of value."

"BOILERPLATE"

This change is in line with a new requirement that all companies avoid or explain "boilerplate" phrases, which are often financial jargon describing a company's prospects or the risk in the securities sold.

The agency also warned underwriters that they must "make reasonable investigations to assure that registration statements contain full and fair disclosure." In the past, inexperienced underwriters have tended to sell speculative issues and often they haven't made these inquiries, the SEC said.

These investigations are known as "due diligence inquiries." Last year the SEC told the National Association of Securities Dealers, the self-regulatory organization for the over-the-counter securities market, to establish standards for this generally private, little-understood process.

The NASD has proposed a tough set of 16 specific "due diligence" standards, which have been widely criticized by its members. NASD sources say some of the proposals may be relaxed, although the organization expects to promulgate a set of tight rules later this year.

QUESTIONS

1. Should the investor have access to all company information? What are the arguments for and against this?
2. List the nonfinancial information described in the article which the SEC now requires regulated firms to include in

their registration statements and annual reports. Why is
this information important to investors?

3. Can an intelligent analysis of the business prospects of a
   firm be made using only the firm's financial statements?
   Explain.

4. Can an intelligent analysis of the business prospects of a
   firm be made without using the firm's financial statements?
   Explain.

---

72   THE GREAT IMBALANCE

(Reprinted by permission from *Forbes*, vol. 111, no. 9 (May 1,
1973): 23.)

Question: When is $2 billion worth four times $2 billion?

Answer: When you are dealing with a stock market that worships
growth and sneers at solid earnings.

Here are figures on 20 great American corporations, household names
all. All are good companies, some superb.

Group I has combined earnings of nearly $2 billion. Combined sales
of $43 billion.

Group II has combined earnings of nearly $2 billion. Combined
sales of $16 billion.

Equal in earnings, the two groups are worlds apart in market value.
Group I sells for a combined $22 billion, 11 times earnings. Group II
sells for $92 billion, 46 times earnings.

How account for the $70 billion difference?

The $70 billion is the premium that the current investment bias
puts on so-called growth. Group I consists of profitable but slow-
growing companies. Group II is all growth and glamour.

Is $1 worth of *growth* earnings worth close to $4 in *cyclical* earnings? The stock market says so. But the stock market isn't always
right, not in the long run.

Our statisticians did a little more work. They went back five
years. They found that five years ago the Standard Ten had earned a
combined $1.6 billion. Their earnings grew 22 percent over the period.
The Growth Ten earned about $1.2 billion. Their earnings grew about
59 percent over the same period.

The difference is there, but how big? The gap in the earnings
growth between the two groups was only about $380 million. Assuming
that the growth differentials hold, five years from now the growth group
will be earning maybe $3.1 billion, the standard group maybe $2.6 billion. That $500 million differential is by no means in the bank, how-
ever; it could turn out to be less. Nevertheless, current prices say
that the prospective earnings differential is worth a premium of $70
billion to those who buy the stocks now.

Can a potential $500 million in earnings flow five years from now
be worth $70 billion in cash today? If the answer is no, then one of

three things must be true: Either the growth stocks are terribly over-priced, the standard stocks are terribly underpriced, or both.

TABLE 12

THE STANDARD GROUP

All numbers in millions	Sales	Net Income (before extraordinary items) item) 1972	item) 1968	Market Value 4/11/73
Alcoa	$ 1,753	$ 103	$ 105	$ 1,156
BankAmerica	1,651	192	133	3,128
Chrysler	9,759	220	291	1,885
General Foods	2,424	113	103	1,324
Goodyear	4,071	193	148	1,981
ITT	8,600	477	204	4,099
Southern Pacific	1,449	108	88	963
Union Carbide	3,261	207	157	2,582
U.S. Steel	5,402	157	254	1,842
Westinghouse	5,087	199	135	3,348
TOTAL	$43,457	$1,969	$1,618	$22,308

TABLE 13

THE GROWTH GROUP

	Sales	Net Income (before extraordinary items) item) 1972	item) 1968	Market Value 4/11/73
Amer Home Products	$ 1,587	$ 173	$ 112	$ 6,691
Avon	1,005	125	71	7,809
Coca-Cola	1,876	190	110	8,539
Eastman Kodak	3,478	546	375	22,940
Johnson & Johnson	1,318	121	50	6,979
Lilly	820	126	71	5,802
Merck	958	148	93	7,153
Minn Mining & Mfg	2,114	244	167	9,617
Polaroid	571	43	59	4,369
Xerox	2,419	250	129	12,059
TOTAL	$16,146	$1,966	$1,237	$91,958

QUESTIONS

1. Why did the Group I stocks sell for multiples (price/
    earnings ratios) substantially below the Group II stocks?
2. Can you answer the question in the last paragraph of the
    article with only the information given? If not, what
    additional information do you think might be helpful?

73   MEATY RESULTS AT MCDONALD'S

(Reprinted by permission from *Financial World*, vol. 139, no. 9
(May 2, 1973): 12.)

You may not think much of a chain of hamburger stands as an investment, but when a company has sold 11 billion hamburgers, owns over 600
units and licenses about 1700 more, operates a "university" to train
practitioners of its trade and spends over forty million dollars in advertising annually, then those hamburger stands start looking a lot more
glamorous.

Whoever thought of making those arches, McDonald's symbol, gold in
color, must have had a premonition of things to come. Now a major factor in the growing fast food restaurant field, second in total units
only to the Kentucky Colonel, McDonald's revenues have increased by
seven times since 1967, with share earnings up five-fold.

McDonald's is more than just a hamburger vendor. The company's
carefully developed menu also includes french fries, a fish sandwich,
hot apple pie, milk shakes and other beverages, as well as hamburger
variations. Currently undergoing testing as possible menu additions are
fried onion rings, cookies, and a breakfast of eggs, bacon and cheddar
cheese on an English muffin. Not all such seemingly promising products
make the grade. Past experiments with fish and chips and roast beef,
for example, just didn't catch on, at least not to a sufficiently profitable extent.

Over one fourth of the almost 2,300 McDonalds units in place at the
end of 1972 were company-owned, and sales by these units accounted for
79 percent of total revenues. McDonald's secondary source of revenue is
from rental income. The company leases property for many of its sites
and then subleases the location to its licensees at higher rentals.
While just 15 percent of total revenues, this source represents a far
more important slice of pretax income. Furthermore, these leases, which
generally extend over a 20-year period, provide a locked-in flow of future revenues (provided that the units and licensees don't fail, of
course).

So far in 1973, McDonald's has repurchased for common stock some 58
units from its licensees. Repurchase has been an ongoing process for
many years; the earnings of the acquired licensees, when added to those

of McDonald's, are then reflected in the market price of the stock, currently at some 67 times earnings, a price far in excess of that which the company paid for them. This is not exactly internal growth, but it has made for an interesting way of adding to earnings and financing expansion of company-owned units.

In 1972, total revenues advanced 31 percent from those of the prior year, aided by acquisitions and new store openings. Net income was up by 38 percent.

TABLE 14

MCDONALD'S CORPORATION

	Revenues (Millions)	Earned Per Share	Price Range
Years ended December 31:			
1972	$385.2	$0.94	a77 $\frac{3}{8}$-37 $\frac{1}{8}$
1971	290.6	0.68	39 -14 $\frac{3}{4}$
1970	200.3	0.49	15 $\frac{1}{2}$- 9 $\frac{1}{8}$
1969	143.3	0.39	14 $\frac{3}{4}$- 8 $\frac{1}{8}$
1968	97.8	0.29	11 $\frac{1}{8}$- 5 $\frac{5}{8}$
1967	53.7	0.20	8 $\frac{1}{8}$- 2 $\frac{3}{8}$
1966	42.7	0.15	2 $\frac{7}{8}$- 1 $\frac{1}{2}$
1965	35.4	0.13	2 $\frac{5}{8}$- 1 $\frac{1}{8}$
1964	25.9	0.08	.... - ....
1963	18.1	0.04	.... - ....

a-1972-73 to April 25. Note: Paid 2 percent in stock in 1967.

For 1973, the outlook is for further gains in both areas, with the numerous acquisitions also contributing significantly to earnings progress.

McDonald's fine record (compounded average annual revenue growth at 48 percent and share earnings growth of 36 percent over the last five years) cannot be disputed, and further progress is foreseen. However, whether McDonald's can continue to grow at or near the pace that it has in the past is open to some questions. Those who foresee its growth continuing at the present pace for many years hence, have brought the stock to its current high price-earnings multiple. Yet, there are some factors which could have moderating effects on future growth.

There is hardly a consumer who is not aware of the spiraling cost of meat. Having already felt the effect of these rising prices, McDonald's put through menu price increases at the end of last January. But the continuing ascent of meat costs may mean additional increases or company absorption of the added costs. Other costs, too, such as those for supplies and labor, may also outpace revenues. There is particular concern, if the minimum wage is raised substantially, that McDonald's, whose workers are mostly students paid at minimum levels, will painfully feel its effect.

Additionally, problems of market saturation, as prime locations and markets are filled by the company and competitors, and some leveling off in per-unit volume from the sharp rises in the company's earlier stages of growth, must be reckoned with.

The effects of these problems vary in intensity and McDonald's is not standing by waiting for them to take their toll (for example, new markets are being sought in Canada and overseas). However, the high valuation accorded the shares by investors at present is subject to re-examination should some of these problems intensify to the extent that they would have a significant impact upon earnings. As a result, investors should be cautioned about the speculative aspects involved with stocks such as this one, trading at levels which discount growth many years into the future. While the American public continues to delight in McDonald's hamburgers, shareholders may find some resistance to higher stock prices.

---

74   SEARLE GIVES BIRTH TO NEW PRODUCTS

(Reprinted by permission from *Financial World*, vol. 139, no. 26 (June 20, 1973): 12.)

In 1960, G. D. Searle & Company was first to come out with oral contraceptives—a major breakthrough in the pharmaceutical world. But by no means has Searle's research department packed up and gone home since that time. New and improved products are critical to a drug company's performance, and Searle, although smaller in size than the industry's leaders, has remained among those in the forefront with important developments because of outstanding research.

Searle's birth control pills approached record sales levels in 1972, but have been superseded (for the first time in a decade) as the leading contributor to revenues by another class of products: Aldactone and Aldactazide, two antihypertension drugs that, combined, have captured 18 percent of corporate revenues.

These and other pharmaceuticals are expected to continue to experience strong growth, but Searle is looking to broaden its horizons beyond drugs in the health care field. "While pharmaceuticals will continue to be the major thrust of Searle's activities . . . we believe that our diversified operations will contribute increasingly to our sales and earnings," said chief executive officer Daniel Searle recently. That will hopefully be the case.

Since the start of diversification activities about seven years ago, developing nonpharmaceutical activities have made very little contribution to earnings. But last year's profit turnaround in the medical instrumentation area was an encouraging sign that these nondrug interests will achieve further importance to Searle.

Searle's strong emphasis on research has provided the impetus for past growth and will be the source from which future growth will emanate. Aware of this, the company allocates large amounts of money to research and development; it boosted these expenditures 33 percent last year to where they accounted for 13.2 percent of net sales—a goodly-sized outlay even for a drug company.

Searle's dedication to research continues to pay off in new products. What may turn out to be an important contributor to profit, although probably not until 1975, is a low calorie sweetener first discovered by the company seven years ago. The product, which differs from others in that it is metabolized into amino acids, will first be used as a table-top sweetener, but its potentials for use in dry foods is now also being studied. Production is planned in conjunction with Ajinomoto, a Japanese company that can contribute the technology in the manufacture of amino acids. The companies are awaiting the sweetener's approval by the F.D.A. as a food additive. The possible hazards of cyclamates have resulted in its withdrawal from the market; and questions concerning the safety of saccharin may cause it to eventually follow the same path. If Searle's discovery can successfully fill the huge void of these products, it could prove the best sweetener of all to future profits.

TABLE 15

G. D. SEARLE & COMPANY

	Net Sales (Millions)	Earned Per Share	*Dividends	Price Range
Three months ended March 31:				
1973	$ 73.2	$0.26	a$0.46	b40$\frac{5}{8}$-33$\frac{1}{2}$
1972	62.3	0.22	....	....-....
Years ended December 31:				
1972	$271.9	$1.01	0.43\frac{1}{3}$	36$\frac{1}{2}$-24$\frac{1}{8}$
1971	226.9	0.87	0.43$\frac{1}{3}$	24$\frac{3}{4}$-17$\frac{1}{4}$
1970	201.5	0.77	0.43$\frac{1}{3}$	18$\frac{3}{8}$-11$\frac{1}{4}$
1969	163.9	0.69	0.43$\frac{1}{3}$	16$\frac{7}{8}$-11$\frac{3}{4}$
1968	147.7	0.65	0.43$\frac{1}{3}$	19$\frac{1}{2}$-12$\frac{3}{4}$
1967	136.0	0.64	0.43$\frac{1}{3}$	20$\frac{3}{8}$-12$\frac{1}{2}$
1966	113.5	0.54	0.43$\frac{1}{3}$	22 -10$\frac{7}{8}$
1965	108.3	0.57	0.43$\frac{1}{3}$	23$\frac{3}{8}$-16$\frac{3}{4}$
1964	86.5	0.61	0.33$\frac{1}{3}$	28$\frac{1}{8}$-18$\frac{3}{8}$
1963	71.4	0.47	0.24	21$\frac{3}{8}$-10$\frac{1}{8}$

*Paid in every year since 1935.   a-Indicated annual rate.
b-To June 13.   Note—Per share data adjusted for 3-for-1 split in May, 1973.

Other results of research and development efforts are also coming to fruition. For instance, a compound to treat irregular beating of the heart has been developed, and a new drug application has recently been filed with the F.D.A. Also related to the heart, Searle is doing research with prostaglandins. These hormore-like substances are said to have significant potentials in heart failure treatment.

While Searle sees continuing growth for oral contraceptives, it is not putting its eggs in one basket when it comes to birth control. An intrauterine device specifically for use immediately after birth has recently been introduced in the United States; and in England, a copper intrauterine contraceptive has been brought to market. Application has been filed for its use in the U.S.

In 1972, earnings advanced 16 percent on a 20 percent sales gain. However, pretax earnings were up by only 7.7 percent. The difference is attributable to additional tax savings from Puerto Rican operations, which pared the tax rate to 21.5 percent from the prior year's 27.4 percent. Exemptions for Puerto Rican taxes on certain products extend until 1979 and for others until 1981. But with its tax rate not expected to sink any lower, Searle's earnings this year will depend on operations per se to extend the gains. And so far, so good. Pretax earnings for the first quarter surged ahead 27 percent, year to year. With, in fact, a higher tax rate, net income was ahead 20 percent.

Searle's directors have indicated a higher dividend will soon be paid on the recently 3-for-1 split shares. It will be the first dividend increase in some eight years. Yet those investors seeking income would do best to look elsewhere. Searle's funds are best put to use in other areas, especially research. If its past research efforts are an indication of its future, the shares appear to have favorable potentials for continued growth.

6

Developing Accounting Principles for External Reporting

Chapter 2 discussed the historical development of the accounting profession's role in the economy of the United States. A very important part of this development was the movement toward better accounting practices and reports spearheaded by first the Committee on Accounting Procedure, then the Accounting Principles Board, and currently the Financial Accounting Standards Board. The *Business Week* discussion (page 275) of the Financial Accounting Standards Board prospects, and the George D. Cameron, Ralph Gudmensen, and Jack R. Bell article (page 279) on why accountants must conform to new pronouncements bring up-to-date the status of the profession's efforts to improve accounting practices and reports.

Over the years there is little doubt that dramatic improvements have taken place. Since accounting is the language of business and business is always changing, it would seem illogical to expect that accounting would not need to change. The changes usually are triggered by authoritative pronouncements, currently from the Financial Accounting Standards Board or the SEC. As would be expected, controversy attends the development of changes. This chapter presents first some overriding considerations which affect proposed changes. Then, a number of important unresolved individual issues are discussed by the contributors.

Allan W. Wright (page 241) noted in 1914 that as economic activities become more complex practice must have theory to guide its development. Without theory to base new decisions upon, practice would simply grope for correct solutions inefficiently. Theory must, of course, be measured against empirical evidence to test its validity. In establishing validity, the objectives of the theoretical model and the practical uses of it need to be kept in mind. The S. Kerry Cooper and Dan M. Guy article (page 243) reviews and analyzes the positions of eight large CPA firms on the question of what accounting objectives should be. These positions are close in many respects, differing primarily on the identification of the users of financial statements together with their information needs and on the valuation techniques which should be used in preparing accounting reports.

Alternatives available for the valuation of a firm's assets are aptly described by M. Edgar Barrett (page 252). The Herbert C. Knortz article (page 262) sets forth the arguments for departing from historical cost toward "economic realism." Robert K. Mautz (page 268) defends historical cost against changing to valuation methods which may not be objective enough for consistent, comparable reporting. The term "fair value accounting" is used by all three authors. This term has been defined as any method of accounting used that departs from historical cost toward economic values. The controversy centers on the questions of how far to go along this route and how to report the results of these new valuation methods.

Two important changes taking place economically are that the governmental sector has continued to control more of the economic resources of the country and that business has increasingly become international in scope transcending national borders. These changes have significant implications for the development of accounting standards and practices. Joseph F. Wojdak (page 284) compares accounting concepts and theory used for private enterprises to the concepts and theory applicable to governmental units. Reasons for these differences are well explained.

In earlier eras, commerce expanded to a national scope; economic activities have continued to expand to become global in nature. The multinational firm has come to dominate much of the world's economic activity. Accountants have had to report on these global activities. Differences among the various countries' accounting principles and practices have caused problems of inconsistency and lack of comparability in these reports. The problems, too, are now global in nature. Charles N. Stabler (page 296) discusses two avenues of approach to solution to these global problems. *The Wall Street Journal* report (page 301) highlights the increased international scope of business. They review attempts by accounting professionals world-wide to bring order and uniformity to accounting reports.

The remaining seven articles are concerned with specific problems of importance facing accountants as they attempt to keep their methods and reports abreast of the business world's needs. G. A. Anderson (page 304) takes up the task of trying to decide when figures are material in relation to the total picture presented by accounting reports. Michael L. Moore (page 313) presents the development of conservatism together with its relationships to other accounting concepts and its proper use. Robert Comerford (page 321) points out the reasons why so few firms have incorporated such procedures into their accounting systems. He clearly discloses why accountants need objective evidence for entries in accounting records. In 1918 Livingston Middleditch, Jr. (page 329) wrote about the need for accounting reports adjusted for general price level changes. His arguments are as real today as they were then. Solomon Fabricant (page 335) presents an economist's view of the price level change problem and in the process brings the reader up-to-date on the developments in this area. The *Wall Street Journal* chart (page 335) and the *Los Angeles Free Press* graphic presentations (page 346) disclose the impact and progress of inflation.

75   THEORY AND PRACTICE

Allan W. Wright

(Reprinted by permission from *The Journal of Accountancy*, vol. 17, no. 6 (June, 1914): 431-434. Copyright 1914 by the American Institute of Certified Public Accountants, Inc.)

> *The importance of principle is to be emphasized through-out. In simpler situations a shrewd empirical tact suffices; in complex ones sound practice is more and more dependent on sound theory. Knowledge of principles is necessary to offset the limitations of experience and the narrowness of interests; the corrective of application is needed to make principles real and vital. (1)*

In these words Professor Jastrow states a principle that may be followed with profit by every accountant who desires eminence and success.

The words theory and theater come from the same Greek root. A theater is "a place for seeing." In Greek theaters the spectators sat on the slope of a hill, where they could look down upon the play.

The word theory, which has been defined to be an organic development of the relations between the parts of any systematic whole, carries the same idea of things seen in the large, as from an elevated and detached viewpoint. If one could be suspended above a city, he would lose sight of small things, but would be able to form a perfect theory of its design. Its boundaries by field and water, its grand divisions, its dissevering streams and boulevards and arteries of traffic, its parks and monumental buildings would stand out in bold relief, and the relations of parts to parts would be clearly seen.

Similarly the decisive outlines and outstanding importances tend to emerge in the regions of knowledge as one rises to a superior and comprehensive vision. Fundamental laws and doctrines appear. Frameworks of principle, upon which practices are molded and by which they may be explained, are discerned, while details sink to the levels of their relative importance.

"Shrewd, empirical tact!" How blind to his chief means of progress is the accountant who depends upon shrewd tact! He feels his way as one in the dark. Finding an office poorly organized, he experiments here, adventures there, tries this device, that expedient and the other procedure, until by slow, laborious and costly experience an organization of more or less efficiency is developed. He confines himself to applying the results of his own observation, and gropes his way. It is such as he that would put cashiers in charge of customers' ledgers.

A wiser man realizes that sound practice is dependent upon sound theory. He avails himself of the deep insight which science gives. He applies the theory evolved from the experimentations of other men. To him theory is a torch that casts upon practice the illumination of principle.

The illustrious German strategist, von Moltke, recognized the dependence of sound practice upon sound theory. As early as 1857 he foresaw the Franco-Prussian war of 1870. In anticipation of it he constructed plan after plan; that is, he theorized upon the subject of war between France and Prussia. With the fundamental elements of the situation before his mind, the German armies, arms and equipment, transport facilities, means of subsistence, the geographical and climatic conditions, the rules of the art of war, and the resources and probable movements of the French, he continuously revised and perfected his theory for thirteen years.

In accounting, as the complexities of our civilization and commercial machinery increase, the importance of sound theory increases. The experimentation that may be permissible in the corner grocery will not do for the great company with many, far-flung offices. The issues are too grave to be left to the chance findings of empiricism.

Knowledge of principles, or theory, is necessary to offset the limitations of experience, or practice, and practice is necessary to vitalize, correct and confirm theory. This statement by Professor Jastrow has been expressed by another writer as follows: "Theory, without practice to test it, to verify it, to correct it, is idle speculation; but practice, without theory to animate it, is mere mechanism. In every art and business, theory is the soul and practice the body."

It is interesting to note that this interdependence and reaction between theory and phenomena, or practice, is to be observed in the progress of all knowledge and the growth of all science. First the slow and unconscious observation by primitive races of men of natural occurrences, such as the apparent movement of the heavenly bodies. Then when considerable progress had been made, questions about the meaning and causes of the phenomena and the connections between them. Next the establishment of an hypothesis to explain the phenomena. Then, from the hypothesis, as a new starting-point, another series of observations by which to test the correctness of the hypothesis. Then more of hypothesis, observation and inference, until by successive repetitions of the process we have arrived at the present state of knowledge.

From the accountant who is content to practice a method without knowing its theory, no progress is to be expected. His thoughts will never rise from the details to the principles of his work.

Progress comes to men of aspiring spirit; men who thirst after an ordered knowledge, and are not satisfied until phenomena are explained by, and resolved into, causes and reasons, principles and laws. But those who would accomplish this may not remain on the level of details, or below their level, submerged by them. They must rise above them, where a comprehensive survey is possible, where relationships can be rightly seen, and things assume their true proportions.

Captain A. T. Mahan, the well-known naval authority, has effectively expressed this idea in the following words:

> . . . *first, the diligent and close study of details, by which knowledge is perfected; and, second, a certain detachment of the mind from the prejudgments and passions engendered by immediate contact, a certain remoteness, corresponding to the idea of physical distance, in virtue of which confusion and distortion of impression disappear and one is enabled not only to distinguish the decisive outlines of a scheme, but also to relegate to their true place in the scheme subordinate details, which at the moment of occurrence had made an exaggerated impression from their very nearness.*

The pursuit of principles is important to the accountant because the discovery and formulation of them requires conscious effort to grasp the larger aspects of things, to take a bird's-eye view of a situation.   This will enlarge his horizon, expand his powers and sharpen the edge of his discrimination.

The accountant who strives to master the theory of his profession will do more than insure the soundness of his practice.   He will form a habit of mastery.   He will think his problems through, and comprehend clearly the philosophy of their solution.   He will strengthen his powers of analysis.   He will increase his self-confidence, initiative and resourcefulness.   And who does not know that these are powerful factors in the making of success?

FOOTNOTE

1.   Introduction by Joseph Jastrow, head of the department of psychology in the University of Wisconsin, to *Psychology in Daily Life*, by Carl Emil Seashore, professor of psychology in the State University of Iowa.

QUESTIONS

1.   How would you define theory?
2.   Why is theory important to accounting practice?
3.   Why is practice necessary for theory?

---

76   CPA FIRMS VIEW ACCOUNTING OBJECTIVES

S. Kerry Cooper and Dan M. Guy

(Reprinted by permission from *Financial Executive*, vol. 41, no. 6 (June, 1973): 42-58.)

(S. Kerry Cooper is a faculty member at Louisiana State University. Dan M. Guy is a faculty member at Texas Tech University.)

In March, 1971, the AICPA chartered two study groups.   One of these, the Wheat Committee, has seen its recommendations become reality. A Financial Accounting Foundation has been established and the Financial Accounting Standards Board has started operations.

The other group, chaired by Robert E. Trueblood, will present its findings later this year.   It was asked to "refine" the objectives of financial statements to facilitate the establishment of guidelines and criteria for improving accounting and financial reporting.

To do this, the Trueblood Committee solicited views from accounting firms and other interested groups. This article analyzes the views of one testifying group—large CPA firms. The analysis concentrates on

1. measurement bases and methods
2. identification of financial statement users

Each CPA firm presented its views on accounting measurement bases and methods. (1) The views ranged from a strong cost-based, transaction-oriented approach to avant-garde proposals for new directions in accounting measurement.

The testimony on identification of financial statement users was not as extensive as was the testimony on measurement. However, most of the firms proposed unique considerations.

ERNST & ERNST

Ernst & Ernst and Price Waterhouse & Company offered the most conservative views of any major firm presenting testimony to the Trueblood Committee. E&E endorses the stewardship concept of financial reporting as the basic objective of financial statements. The firm recommends disclosure of certain supplementary information (non-transactional in nature) if that information can be supported by "reasonably objective evidence." E&E strongly supports the cost-based, completed-transaction process of income determination and balance sheet valuation. Supplementary data would be offered only "in those relatively rare cases when their disclosure is deemed essential to fair presentation of financial condition or results of operations, and when they can be determined and measured on a satisfactorily objective basis." Such supplementary data might include price-level adjustments and current-value disclosure.

E&E apparently believes that existing accounting measurement bases and methods are adequate and that any revision may result in calamitous legal repercussions. They question the competence of accountants to determine current values and warn that:

> If independent accountants extend their professional activities beyond the bounds of their professional competence, the possibility of incurring serious legal and other responsibilities must be expected.
>
> "Economic value" . . . is such an ambiguous concept that any effort to determine and report it should be attempted only by those whose legal responsibilities are of a far different type than those now borne by accountants.

In discussing the needs and rights of users, E&E states that existing interests, rather than potential or possible interests, should get primary consideration. Potential shareholders or creditors are secondary users with secondary rights. Unfortunately, the legal ramifications of the primary-secondary user philosophy are unclear. Courts might treat a buyer or prospective buyer the same as a potential seller or holder of stock.

E&E states that it is not practicable to custom-design special-purpose financial statements for special needs of different users.

Therefore, the firm opts for a general purpose statement since ". . . it serves all effectively and favors none unduly."

PRICE WATERHOUSE & COMPANY

Price Waterhouse & Company recommends that the historical-cost measurement base and methods now used in accounting should be kept. PW asserts that financial statements are useful only if they are simple, definite, practical, general, universal, timely, selective (limited as to information reported), and oriented to an economy where management and ownership are largely divorced. PW argues that value-oriented accounting does not meet these criteria. Dollar-oriented, historical-cost-based accounting does. PW favors disclosure of large value increases in assets, but would not incorporate them into the accounting process. To do so would anticipate expected profits (a departure from the completed-transaction approach) and would be prospective reporting. A valuation approach would be a marked departure from objectivity and would reduce the credibility of accounting information.

PW would retain the current emphasis on the income statement as opposed to the balance sheet. They argue that no set of financial statements can be constructed that can summarize all the ways in which a firm differs from others. Yet,

> *Differences in employee morale, plant location, research creativity and market sense do cause differences in the success with which an enterprise achieves its goals (i.e., earnings). The purpose of financial reporting should be to measure how effective the organization has been in reaching these goals.*

PW also objects to a valuation approach because "it is essential that numerical expressions in financial statements avoid the rubber ruler aspect of mixing various kinds of fair values and costs." It is surprising, then, that they oppose price-level adjustments in the accounting process, since price-level changes make dollars highly elastic accounting measures. Even more surprising is their explanation for opposing price-level-adjusted statements—that the public is well aware of changes in the purchasing power of the dollar and can make their own adjustments. Since many view a little inflation as a good thing, who are accountants to report it (and perhaps dispel certain salutary illusions)?

The position of PW regarding the design of financial statements is summarized by the underlying thesis of their entire proposal: "General purpose financial statements are designed to report to *investors* [emphasis added] on the use of funds they have invested in their enterprise in such a way as to facilitate their investment decisions of the future." PW adds that accountants need not apologize to lenders, economists, or sociologists for not stating assets at liquidation value, for not adjusting financials to dollar equivalents, and for not recording human values. "These are matters outside general purpose financial statements." Moreover, such statements are meant for actual and potential investors, not employees, creditors, estates, or other secondary users.

In summary, PW's conservative philosophy is: "It remains true that he who departs from cash basis accounting has the burden of justifying his departure."

ARTHUR ANDERSEN & COMPANY

Arthur Andersen & Company, which has a reputation as something of a maverick in its approach to accounting principles, takes a considerably different and much more comprehensive approach than PW. AA recommends that valuation, not allocation and matching, should be the focus of the accounting process. Income or loss should be the difference between successive balance sheet measurements. The balance sheet should contain only severable economic resources and the claims to those resources. Historical cost would be used only when it offers a reasonable basis for valuation. AA argues that cost was originally employed in accounting simply as a convenient and conservative measure of value. Gradually, when coupled with the realization and matching concepts, cost became an objective of accounting rather than a method of valuation. AA states:

> *Thus, there exists a well-entrenched system of reverse measurement where the cost-matching process is directed principally at determining earnings. The balance sheet is "plugged" with debits and credits, which may or may not represent economic resources or liabilities and which may or may not portray value data. As a result balance sheets often include huge deferred charges that are difficult to support as elements of financial position. They are at best "soft" assets—fluffy dreams of the future that do not possess the hard characteristics of economic resources. Similarly, balance sheets often include as liabilities meaningless deferred credits that do not represent obligations.*

Earnings, under the AA scheme, are the increases in net economic resources of a firm. Economic resources are elements of wealth that possess economic value because they are useful, scarce, and exchangeable. Because they are separable from the firm and exchangeable in the market, they have intrinsic value that is separate from the fortunes of the firm. Cash, inventories, plant and equipment, land, natural resources, and accounts receivable (claims to the economic resources of others) are examples of economic resources. Intangible assets and deferred charges are not economic resources because they are not separable from the enterprise.

For an economic resource to be recorded as an asset, it must possess reasonable measurability. (This criterion would exclude such items as human resources.) Its value should approximate the price it commands in exchange; this may be cost, market price, or reproduction cost. For many assets, particularly inventories and plant equipment, cost is the best initial valuation. It is also a suitable continuing valuation basis, barring an obvious and significant divergence between historical cost and current value. Reporting at realization value is appropriate when obvious losses in economic value occur in this asset group. For obvious and significant increases in the economic value of, say, plant and equipment, the most useful value concept is likely to be current replacement cost less estimated depreciation.

AA has long been a proponent of price-level accounting, but in their statement they assert that "it may be more practicable to go directly to a value approach to accounting." The effect of changing price levels would be recognized by a "capital maintenance adjustment" to stockholders' equity. Thus, earnings, measured by an increase in economic resources, would not include the effects of general inflation or deflation.

What nonmanagerial groups need financial statements? AA indicates that any individual—creditor, investor, employee, etc.—who makes economic decisions about an enterprise needs financial statements. General purpose financial statements are the proper vehicles for communicating this information. However, AA offers one warning: User evaluations and interpretations of financial statements should not be allowed to affect, or to be introduced directly into, the financial presentation.

ARTHUR YOUNG & COMPANY

Arthur Young & Company, like PW and E&E, recommends that financial accounting should, with some exceptions, be based on historical cost and completed transactions. Unlike these firms, however, AY advocates price-level accounting.

AY rejects current-value accounting on the grounds that, in many businesses, this basis would not have the necessary degree of reliability, comparability, and verifiability. The firm does suggest consideration of "supplemental disclosure of estimated values of major asset holdings if such values can be determined by reasonably objective and generally accepted methods" and if there is a reasonable possibility of sale.

Two of AY's nine reporting guidelines pertain to nonmanagerial users and the types of financial statements they need. AY concludes it is impractical to design a single set of financial statements to satisfy all user groups. Consequently, only the needs of a primary user group should be considered in constructing these statements. Present and future equity security investors and creditors make up this primary user group. AY recommends that the needs of other users be met through special reports.

Should financial statements be designed to communicate with untrained users? According to AY, financial statements should be directed to the "reasonably informed" investor, not solely to skilled financial advisors. "Preparers of financial statements should assume a reasonable understanding on the part of the reader of the business reporting enterprise, the industry or industries in which it operates, conditions in the economy, and general business practices." Unfortunately, as AY mentions, no one knows who this hypothetical reasonably informed investor is.

COOPERS & LYBRAND

Philip Defliese (APB chairman), speaking as a representative of his firm and not the APB, urged attempts to "reflect current rather than historical values and to give more recognition to intangible and personnel resources." However, he said this was currently impractical and should be approached through a major, long-term research project. He sees the Trueblood Committee's greatest potential contribution as the "refinement of realization of income concepts" within the context of historical-cost accounting.

Defliese later elaborated this view in a written brief.   Again he urged a cautious, deliberate approach:

> *Evolving and implementing a grand design for change in the practice of a profession can hardly be done overnight—especially when the theoretical basis of the profession's discipline is a subject of disagreement.   It is not only a question of the research, an immense project in itself, but also of the logistical burden of maintaining consensus.   At every step, a new working agreement of compromise must be achieved between many disparate interests, otherwise the applicability of the final results will be limited.*

Defliese feels the study group should assign objectives to short-range, long-range, or intermediate-range categories, and indicate the problems associated with each objective.   Of particular interest are his views on a current valuation approach to accounting measurement (which he considers a long-range item):

> *Current values are fine to look at, but one must consider the question of when do the values actually inure to the benefit of the owner.   In short, when are these values realized? . . . Whatever framework we adopt, the concept of income realization cannot be entirely divorced from the concept of income determination.   Transaction-oriented accounting must remain as an underpinning to provide objectivity even if we move toward a current-value framework.   Implicit in this view is the need to examine all current values to distinguish those that are expected to be realized ultimately through sale or exchange and those that are destined to enter the earning process through utilization.*

In the short range, Defliese advises continued adherence to historical cost but suggests many changes in this traditional framework. These include the refining of income realization concepts on an industry-by-industry basis and the restructuring of the financial statements.

In the intermediate range, Defliese sees the need in supplementary price-level-adjusted statements.   Further,

> *. . . perspective can be achieved by requiring disclosures of current values alongside the historical costs of those resources whose values are soon expected to flow through the income stream.   The practice gained in this exercise should be useful in the ultimate shift to value accounting whenever that implementation becomes feasible in the future.*

Defliese notes a fundamental distinction between two groups of users—public investors and private creditors.   He proposes that the study group concentrate on public investors (a person or institution that purchases debt or equity securities).   Private creditors are banks, insurance companies, and vendors who can obtain special information because of contractual or jurisdictional relationships.   The needs of these private groups are purely secondary.

In answering the question: "Can financial data be simplified to the point where the man on the street can understand it?" Defliese answers definitely "No." Attempts to reduce financial statements to the lowest common denominator are unrealistic.

PEAT, MARWICK, MITCHELL & COMPANY

PMM contends that if their firm or any other group of accountants knew the answers, there would have been no need for the Trueblood Committee. They assert that specific inputs to the study group should come from users, not producers, of accounting information.

The firm urges the study group not to let its conclusions be restricted by the "traditional, historical-financial role of accounting." PMM generally endorses the views expressed in an article by a member of its professional practice department, "Accounting in the Technological Age," by Robert K. Elliott. The article is futuristic in thrust. Elliott recommends the use of current and liquidation values rather than historical or price-level-adjusted costs.

Concerning users, Elliott states:

> . . . *specific user groups generally have immediate interests narrower than the interests of society as a whole. Accountants therefore should not accommodate the interest of any user group, unless those interests coincide with the interest of society as a whole.*

J. K. LASSER & COMPANY

J. K. Lasser endorses the concept of multi-value reporting as recommended by the American Accounting Association's *A Statement of Basic Accounting Theory* (1966). The firm asserts that historical-cost-based financial statements are still useful from a stewardship approach and as a basis for financial records, but current value reporting would be at least as useful:

> *With realistic values on the balance sheet, the price-to-book-value ratio could conceivably become as significant in investor decisions as the price-to-earnings ratio. . . . Similarly, current values would provide the income statement with more realistic depreciation (and appreciation) among other costs and expenses, thus providing that statement with a more realistic economic portrayal and therefore a better basis of comparison between like businesses.*

To obtain these "realistic values," a number of current value approaches would be employed. Property, plant, and equipment would be valued at market, as determined by appraisal. Marketable securities and inventories would be valued at net realizable value (sales price less disposition cost). Work in process would be carried at a value between cost and selling price proportionate to the degree of completion. The valuation method to be used would be dictated by the likely disposition of the asset. Exit values (liquidation values) are appropriate only when the going concern assumption is not applicable. Price-level-adjusted values are impractical and have little use unless the rate of inflation exceeds six percent a year for a number of years. Since marketable securities and inventories are likely to be sold, they should be carried at realizable value. Property, plant, and equipment is ordinarily held for use and not for sale. Therefore, neither realizable value nor replacement cost is appropriate since there is "no intent to replace them in ordinary circumstances." Since resale of fixed assets is not ordinarily anticipated, the market value as determined by appraisal should not be reduced for any possible future costs of disposition.

Dual reporting is recommended. The balance sheet, income statement, retained earnings statement, and statement of changes in financial position would be prepared in two-column form: one on the cost basis and the other on the current value basis.

> *Such dual reporting would eliminate one complaint against a major change in statements such as this: that prior years are no longer comparable. Since the historical cost columns would compare with the past, users would have continuity until enough years have passed for all columns to be comparable.*
>
> *The solution is not a panacea, but it would be a workable start. Current values are a reasonable objective and they can be audited.*

J. K. Lasser's presentation contains the most extensive discussion of user needs. The firm maintains that financial reports directed solely toward the shareholder as the dominant user cannot achieve the objectives of accounting. Using APB Statement No. 4's list of direct and indirect users as a departure point, Lasser adds three additional user groups:

1. the general public
2. accountants
3. accounting educators

Can financial statements be made more understandable by either special purpose reports or a single multiple user report? J. K. Lasser opts for the single multiple user report, or general purpose statements. The reason given for this selection is that it is impossible to control the distribution of special purpose reports.

ALEXANDER GRANT & COMPANY

Alexander Grant recommends that "the accounting profession and management should move toward financial statements which present accounting information on the basis of fair values or price level indexes." As a first step, the firm proposes that selected valuation information be shown in supplementary statements labelled "not auditable." Apparently, Alexander Grant feels that the main problem in moving to current valuation bases and methods is the lack of established audit procedures for these approaches.

*The multiplicity of underlying facts and circumstances for
business enterprises suggests that there is a need for the
adoption of multiple valuation bases. Multiple valuation
bases will permit closer approximation of the recording of
economic events when they occur. This is a worthwhile goal.
However, the difficulty of auditing multiple valuation bases
should be carefully considered.*

Financial statements should be general purpose in nature, oriented
to the trained financial advisor (contrast with Arthur Young's reasonably informed investor). Attempts to communicate with untrained nonmanagerial users who spend no more than 15 minutes reading an annual
report are unrealistic.

*We can easily picture the confusion of a Maori tribesman
suddenly confronted with the population and hyper-activity of
cities like New York, Chicago, and Los Angeles. We believe
that the untrained user is faced with a similar "cultural
shock" when he attempts to read and understand financial
statements.*

SUMMARY

First, all but one firm favor continuation of some form of historical-cost-based accounting. That is, the firms either favor "what
is" or they encourage dual reporting, historical cost combined with
fair values or price level adjustments.

Second, price level accounting is recommended in a supplemental
reporting format by three firms. Three other firms feel that price
level accounting is not as desirable as some form of value accounting.
Two firms appear to oppose price level adjustments.

Third, concerning current or fair value accounting, five firms
propose that such values be disclosed along with historical costs or as
an eventual replacement for historical costs. On the other hand, three
firms seem to oppose introduction of current values into the financial
accounting process.

Obviously, the firms disagree most on how to identify nonmanagerial
users of financial statements. Three concepts emerge:

1. a narrower definition—users are those who have an existing
   investment interest in a firm
2. an intermediate definition—users are those who have an
   existing or a potential investment interest in a firm
3. a broad definition—users are any persons or institutions
   who use financial statements for decision-making purposes

The last summary observation, agreed upon by all eight firms, is
that general purpose financial statements are better communication vehicles than are special purpose reports. Of course, definition of what
constitutes a general purpose statement varies according to user identification. The two cannot be conceptually segregated.

In conclusion, it is apparent that virtually all major CPA firms are opposed to radical departures from extant accounting and most prefer to hew closely to the status quo. The reasons for this conservative position may be debated, but the nature of its likely impact on the future course of accounting principles is unmistakable.

FOOTNOTE

1. Although nine CPA firms presented written or oral testimony to the study group, only eight are considered in this article. Laventhol, Krekstein, Horwath & Horwath is omitted because its presentation was confined to projections and forecasts. Robert F. Richter of LKH & H and C. B. Hellerson of Hurdman and Cranstoun, Penny & Company, also presented testimony concerning their personal views.

QUESTIONS

1. Which of the views on accounting do you agree with? Explain.
2. What does valuation as a focus of the accounting process mean, as used in the Arthur Anderson statement?
3. Why does Arthur Young reject current-value accounting?
4. Do you think that the lack of a clear theoretical basis for accounting practice caused the wide disparity of views presented? Explain.
5. Do you think that the lack of a clear understanding of financial statement users needs contributed to the wide disparity of views presented? Explain.
6. Why do you think that all but one firm favored the continuation of historical-cost based accounting?

---

77 PROPOSED BASES FOR ASSET VALUATION

M. Edgar Barrett

(Reprinted by permission from *Financial Executive*, vol. 41, no. 1 (January, 1973): 12-17.)

(M. Edgar Barrett is a faculty member at Harvard University.)

The determination of a firm's net income figure might be seen as being fundamentally dependent upon the valuation of the firm's assets. More specifically, the change in the retained earnings of the firm—as expressed by the difference between the retained earnings accounts in the firm's opening and closing balance sheet for a given period—can be seen as the prime determinant of the firm's reported net income figure.

This approach to income determination does not provide a definition of the term "assets." Neither does it dictate how assets are to be valued. Rather, net income for the period is defined as consisting of the change in the retained earnings of the company between the opening and closing dates of the period. Thus, while we do not intend to focus upon such issues at this workshop, it should be noted that the resolution of many of the current specific issues of controversy in financial reporting would not render inapplicable this approach to income determination. For example, an agreed-upon method of valuing the non-purchased goodwill or the human resources of a company would not affect this approach.

Obviously, some adjustments are required in using this approach to income determination. For example, cash dividends declared have to be added back to the retained earnings at the end of the period, and adjustments are needed to compensate for capital transactions. However, the basic relationship between the valuation of a firm's assets and its net income figure remains. (This assumes, of course, that assets are not revalued with a direct adjustment to the retained earnings account.) It is because of this basic relationship that we have chosen to view alternative financial reporting frameworks in terms of asset valuation.

There are many possible bases for asset valuation. Five of the more prominently mentioned bases are the following:

1. historical cost or market, whichever is lower (the traditional financial reporting base)
2. historical cost or market, whichever is lower—adjusted for general price-level changes
3. economic value
4. market value
5. price-index replacement cost

A brief explanation of the concepts identified by these terms and an indication of some of the attributes of each concept follows:

HISTORICAL COST OR MARKET, WHICHEVER IS LOWER

Concept

This approach is possibly best known for its use in the valuation of inventory. Whenever it becomes evident that current value (as expressed by market price or replacement cost) is significantly less than the carrying value as determined on the basis of historical cost, the current value is adopted as the reported asset value. For example, if it becomes apparent that inventory acquired at a cost of $50,000 can be sold to net only $35,000 (after selling costs), the reported value is reduced to $35,000.

The concept of historical cost itself is probably best described by reference to Paton and Littleton:

*In ideal situations cost is gauged by the amount of cash which
is immediately expended to acquire the particular commodity or
service involved. For many transactions, however, the payment
of cash is delayed for some time and in these cases true cost
is measured by the amount of cash that would have to be expended if final settlement were effected at once . . . (1)*

Attributes

Historical costs represent the results of armslength transactions
between the independent parties. They are presumed to represent the
". . . best available evidence of fair market value at the moment of exchange. . . ." (2) However, the continued use of the historical cost
valuation results in a postponement of the recognition of increases in
value until such time as the increase in value is "realized." "Realization," in general, is assumed to occur at the time of sale of the asset
or product.

Decreases in the value of an asset are, as noted above, recognized
at the time that such decreases become apparent. This method, which
emanates from the accounting doctrine of conservatism, is generally required when the "utility" of an asset is no longer as great as its cost.
The drop in "utility" might emanate from ". . . physical deterioration,
obsolescence, changes in price level, or other causes. . . ." (3)

HISTORICAL COST OR MARKET, WHICHEVER IS LOWER—
ADJUSTED FOR GENERAL-PRICE LEVEL CHANGES

Concept

The U.S. dollar and other prominent currencies have not proven to
be stable yardsticks for economic measurement. With a moderate degree
of inflation as the general rule, the reported costs of assets on a
firm's balance sheet do not often represent dollar expenditures measured
in terms of equivalent purchasing power.

In order to adjust for the resultant anomaly in income measurement
and asset valuation, some authors have suggested that general price-
level indices such as the Gross National Product Implicit Price Deflator
prepared by the Office of Business Economics of U.S. Department of Labor
be employed.

The concept of financial reports adjusted for general price-level
changes should not be confused with proposals to adjust financial reports by the use of specific price indices in order to approximate current replacement cost. (The concept of price-index replacement costs is
discussed in a later section of this paper.) A committee of the American Accounting Association discussed the concept of general-price-level-
adjusted financial reports as follows:

*. . . the adjustment of historical dollar costs—the restate-
ment of these costs in current dollars of equivalent purchasing
power as measured by a general price index—is independent of
estimated replacement costs or replacement policy. It differs*

from the conventional original dollar cost concept only in that it recognizes changes in the value of the dollar and reflects these changes in the amortization of costs and in the determination of periodic income. Its application is independent of possible or probable future price changes, either upward or downward, since only past changes in the value of the dollar are reflected in the adjusted figures. (4)

Attributes

Financial reports adjusted for general price-level changes would have the objective of stating all accounts in terms of a common measuring unit. Another American Accounting Association publication dealt with the subject as follows:

The principal point to keep in mind is that the dollars of different years represent different amounts of commodities and services and that amounts expressed in dollars of various years should not be compared, added, or subtracted unless adjustments are made so that the dollar represents a uniform measure of business activity. . . . A useful analogy can be drawn between price-level adjustments and the conversion of foreign currencies. It would not occur to anyone to add amounts stated in pounds, pesos, francs, or even Canadian dollars to amounts stated in United States dollars without first converting the foreign currencies with the use of appropriate exchange rates. Yet we are in the habit of treating dollars of different years as identical even though, like the foreign currencies, they represent different amounts of goods and services and should be converted to a constant-dollar basis in order to make them comparable. (5)

It is not simply because of a desire to report all assets in terms of a common measuring unit—and thus maintain mathematical internal consistency in the financial reports—that general price-level adjustments have gained support. The resultant financial reports are also intended to produce more meaningful data for users of the reports.

. . . To assist the share owners and the public at large, who must make far-reaching decisions on the basis of accounting reports, public accountants should ask management to provide supplements disclosing the effects of changes in the general price-level or insist on doing so themselves. (6)

Adjustments for general price-level changes may be viewed as an attempt to have financial reporting continue to adhere to the notion of historical cost, with "historical cost" measured in terms of constant purchasing power. Alternatively, such adjustments may be viewed as one of the steps in accounting for changes both in the general price-level and in the prices of specific assets. In any event, supporters of such adjustments claim they are a necessary step in rationalizing financial reporting data.

> *. . . without adjustment of the figures the income statement*
> *suffers from price-level changes by the lack of comparability*
> *of the accounting figures, . . . and from the resulting*
> *diminished significance of reported net income. The balance*
> *sheet also suffers from lack of comparability of the various*
> *items. Cash and receivables and the unpaid liabilities are*
> *expressed in current dollars, but the inventories and espe-*
> *cially the plant and equipment are collections of noncompara-*
> *ble items since they are almost always a hodge-podge of vari-*
> *ous post-period dollars representing different amounts of*
> *purchasing power over commodities and services. (7)*

ECONOMIC VALUE

Concept

The economic value of an asset is the net present value of all future cash flows associated with that asset. Thus, all future cash flows
attributable to the possession and/or use of an asset—discounted at an
appropriate rate, measured in a constant monetary unit, and aggregated—
are a part of an asset's economic value.

A business enterprise may be viewed as engaging in a continuous
process of acquiring factors and converting them (over time) to cash.
The idea of valuing an asset at the present value of the future cash receipts into which that asset will be converted might thus be seen as an
attempt to measure explicitly what corporate management assesses implicitly each time it acquires an asset.

Attributes

The information requirements of this concept are such that widespread adoption of the concept is quite unlikely. The future cash flows
applicable to an asset, the timing of such cash flows, the applicable
discount rate (time value of money), and relevant price-level changes
are all necessary ingredients for the implementation of this concept.

With the exception of adjustments for price-level changes the method is widely employed in long-term contractual situations. The bulk of
these situations involve long-term receivables or payables. However, it
should be noted that long-term contractual situations probably constitute a minority of the total assets employed by most corporations.

MARKET VALUE

Concept

When an asset is initially acquired, it is recorded at cost because
that is the ". . . best available evidence of fair market value at the
moment of exchange." (8) Some feel that the "best available evidence of

fair market value" should continue to be the objective of asset valuation. "Market value," as used in this document, is not intended to imply "liquidation value" or "scrap value." At the theoretical extreme, "market value" is assumed to be equivalent to the contribution made by an asset toward the market value of the product or services which may be produced with it. However, the use of market value is often advocated only for those assets for which a "market" exists. Thus, the criterion of feasibility has been recognized by some of the supporters of this concept.

Attributes

The former Director for the then American Institute of Accountants, James L. Dohr, wrote:

> *The financial significance of property is manifestly to be determined largely from present facts and prospects rather than from past facts; the latter are ordinarily of importance only so far as they may be said to indicate what is likely to happen in the future. As a result the present value of property is, generally speaking, the factor of outstanding importance; it indicates, with varying degrees of accuracy, what the owner may expect to realize upon a sale; it determines his borrowing capacity insofar as the property is concerned; it fixes his liability for various forms of taxation; it reflects his earning capacity as owner; it may be said to measure his ability to make gifts; it is the basis upon which the property may be insured. (9)*

Dohr concluded:

> *. . . the significance of items of property at any given time is frequently determined by present or market value. Manifestly present value cannot be ignored entirely or even relegated to footnote comment if accounting is to be of maximum usefulness to the various interested parties. As a matter of fact as time goes on and business enterprises change hands or as businesses are reorganized under various statutes, there is a continuous process or restatement in terms of present values. (10)*

The use of market value as a basis for asset valuation has already gained a significant foothold in published financial statements. Marketable securities held by investment trusts, certain agricultural products, and certain basic metals, and other extractive products are commonly reported at market value.

The use of market value has significant implications for the determination of income. Management, presumably, continually considers the alternative advantages of continued use or disposal of those assets for which there is a market. It can be argued that the sacrifice of alternative proceeds is the relevant "cost" in the measurement of income. The failure to recognize market value distorts the measurement of income in this sense, as the financial statement user is unable to evaluate management's ability to analyze the alternatives and select those which are economically most advantageous.

PRICE-INDEX REPLACEMENT COST

Concept

The approximation of current replacement cost by the application of specific price indices is intended to allow for the inclusion of "holding gains or losses" in the determination of asset value, without allowing for the inclusion of any "operating profits." "Holding gains or losses" are those changes in value which (from the firm's point of view) are attributable to external market factors. Thus, a holding gain would result from a sudden increase in the cost of replacing a particular asset.

A distinction should be made between *replacement* cost and *reproduction* cost. Replacement cost refers to the cost of *equivalent* property, and reproduction cost refers to the cost of *identical* property. We refer to the former in this context. Paton and Paton discussed this issue as follows:

> *It should be understood that the significant replacement cost is the cost of providing the existing capacity to produce in terms of the most up-to-date methods available. Thus it's largely a waste of time to estimate the cost of replacing an obsolete or semiobsolete plant-unit literally in kind; such an estimate will neither afford a basis for sound appraisal of the property nor furnish a useful measure of current operating cost to replace the capacity represented in the existing asset with a machine of modern design. To put the point in another way, cost of replacing in kind is a significant basis on which to measure the economic importance of property in use only in the case of standard, up-to-date facilities. (11)*

Attributes

The rationale for the use of "price-index replacement cost" is the assumption that the resultant balance sheet figures would have greater economic significance than unadjusted historical cost information. A major emphasis is upon sharpening the measurement of income by distinguishing between operating profits and holding gains and losses. The former are presumably attributable to management and are believed to be more likely to be indicative of reasonable future expectations, while the latter tend to be less predictable and unrelated to dividend and growth potential.

"Price-index replacement costs" can be based on known and accepted published price indices and historical acquisition costs. Specific prices are available for a wide variety of commodities and materials. Generally they are provided by agencies such as the U.S. Department of Commerce. Thus, it may be argued that this method retains whatever objectivity advantage may properly be attributed to historical costs. Some additional cost is involved in the application of certain computational techniques, when compared to the use of unadjusted historical costs. However, given the ready availability of specific price indices, this additional cost should not be excessive.

Probably the best-known advocates of price-index replacement cost are Edgar O. Edwards and Philip W. Bell. In 1961 a text was published by the University of California Press in their names. This text, *The Theory and Measurement of Business Income*, is now in its fifth printing and continues to receive well-deserved attention. The authors describe the attributes of price-index replacement cost as follows:

> *The use of indexes . . . to adjust known historic costs in order to estimate current costs of purchase implies the necessity of individual judgment, of course. So, too, does the estimation of an asset life and the establishment of a pattern for depreciation charges over the life of the asset. But we believe that*
>
> *1. the derivation of current values for fixed assets can be accomplished on a consistent and objective basis with the information now available*
> *2. the quality of the information and the speed of reporting should improve if there is more extensive use of the data*
> *3. such estimates would be necessary only for some of the fixed assets held by the firm, i.e., only for those assets not currently marketed*
> *4. historic costs would be retained in the accounts*
> *5. . . . adjustment on the basis of . . . (certain) indexes would make a substantial difference in the information available to managers and outsiders on operating gains and holding gains—for the decade 1947-1949 to 1957-1959, prices in general rose by only 15-18 percent, but construction costs increased by 40 percent, and the price of machinery rose by 50-70 percent. (12)*

OTHER CONSIDERATIONS

Appraisal Value

Reference is often made to appraisal value as a possible basis for asset valuation in published financial reports. The Association of Appraisal Executives describes appraisal values as the result of a systematic professional analysis of "property facts, rights, investments, and values, based primarily on a personal inspection and inventory of the property." (13)

We did not list appraisal value as a concept worth serious consideration for one fundamental reason: the appraiser is generally acknowledged to use the five possible bases already listed in arriving at the appraisal value. In particular, economic value, market value, and price-index replacement cost bear heavily upon the appraisal value decision. Thus, to say that "appraisal value" is the best possible base for asset valuation is, to some degree, to beg the question of "how will appraisal value be determined?"

Legal Issues

The presentation of financial reports which meet all the requirements of "generally accepted accounting principles" does not necessarily mean that the courts will hold the financial reports "fairly
present the financial position." For example, Mr. Trienens cites the
following example:

> *Defendants had requested a charge to the jury permitting a*
> *guilty verdict only if the financial statements as a whole*
> *were found not to fairly present Continental's financial con-*
> *dition according to generally accepted accounting principles.*
> *The lower court, upheld on appeal, rejected this proposed*
> *instruction, and instead instructed the jury that the criti-*
> *cal test was whether the financial statements as a whole*
> *"fairly presented the financial position of . . ." . . . Thus,*
> *in a court of law, when liability hinges on the fairness of*
> *presentation in a financial statement, the role of generally*
> *accepted accounting principles may be purely advisory. (14)*

This example is merely one of a series which could be cited in support of the assertion that the courts have considerably broadened the
responsibilities of both management and the independent auditors in the
area of financial reporting.

Methods of Presentation

A determination of the method in which fair value reporting information would be presented is not crucial to a discussion of the merits
of fair value reporting. Nevertheless, some general indication of how
such information could be presented might be worthwhile. Three possible
methods of presenting fair value reporting information are as follows:

1.   The provision of *supplementary* "fair value" financial re-
     ports might become compulsory. This would entail the
     presentation of two complete sets of financial reports;
     one prepared under the current financial reporting stand-
     ards and one prepared under yet-to-be-devised "fair value"
     financial reporting standards.
2.   One set of "dual" financial reports might be employed.
     Under this method, two columns of figures would be shown
     for each year in each financial statement. The first
     column would contain figures emanating from the applica-
     tion of current financial reporting standards, while the
     second column would contain figures emanating from the ap-
     plication of "fair value" financial reporting standards.
3.   The "fair value" financial reports might become the pri-
     mary financial statements. This would mean that they
     would be the only financial reports required. Thus, the
     financial reports as currently prepared would be phased
     out completely.

It should be noted, however, that many people believe that the introduction of "fair value" reporting will continue to be done on a piecemeal basis. This implies that fair value reporting information will replace the current financial reporting information on a slowly evolving item-by-item basis.

FOOTNOTES

1. W. A. Paton and A. C. Littleton, *An Introduction to Corporate Accounting Standards,* American Accounting Association (1940), p. 26.
2. Ibid., p. 27.
3. American Institute of Certified Public Accountants (AICPA), Committee on Accounting Procedure, *Restatement and Revision of Accounting Research Bulletins*, Accounting Research Bulletin No. 43 (New York: AICPA, 1953), p. 30.
4. American Accounting Association, Committee on Concepts and Standards Underlying Corporate Financial Statements, "Price Level Changes and Financial Statements," Supplementary Statement Number 2, *The Accounting Review* (October, 1951), p. 471.
5. Perry Mason, *Price-Level Changes and Financial Statements, Basic Concepts and Methods*, American Accounting Association (1956), p. 10.
6. Solomon Fabricant, "Inflation and Current Accounting Practice: An Economist's View," *The Journal of Accountancy* (December, 1971), p. 39.
7. Perry Mason, op. cit., p. 11.
8. Paton and Littleton, op. cit., p. 27.
9. James L. Dohr, "Cost and Value," *Journal of Accountancy* (March, 1944), p. 193.
10. Ibid., pp. 195-196.
11. William A. Paton and William A. Paton, Jr., *Asset Accounting* (New York: Macmillan Company, 1952), p. 325.
12. Edgar O. Edwards and Philip W. Bell, *The Theory and Measurement of Business Income* (Berkeley, University of California Press, 1961), pp. 187-188.
13. Association of Appraisal Executives, *Basic Standards of Appraisal Practice and Procedure*, Washington, D.C., Association of Appraisal Executives (1936), p. 10.
14. Howard J. Trienens, *The Law and Current Value Accounting* (unpublished manuscript). Later published as "Legal Implications of Current Value Accounting," Trienens and Smith, *Financial Executive* (September, 1972), p. 60.

QUESTIONS

1. Briefly describe each of the five possible bases for asset valuation discussed in Mr. Barrett's article.

2.   What are the arguments for and against each basis?
3.   What solution would you propose to the accounting
     dilemma of asset valuation?
4.   Why is asset valuation critical to the income statement?

---

78   THE CHALLENGE OF ECONOMIC REALISM

Herbert C. Knortz

(Reprinted by permission from *Financial Executive*, vol. 41, no. 1 (January, 1973): 18-21.)

(Herbert C. Knortz is senior vice president and comptroller, International Telephone & Telegraph Corporation.)

The function of financial reporting to the public is to present effectively the financial condition of an enterprise and the changes in that condition from one day to another. Effective reporting of information can take place only under concepts which deal with the real world and it must reflect the understanding which the users of this information have concerning that reality. This distinction is important: it is not only the real fact that matters, but what people believe about real facts. Unless public reporting meets the challenge of economic realism, its credibility will remain in doubt.

Conventional reporting today fails miserably to meet the needs of an informed business community because of its compliant attitude toward two great evils of financial reporting:

1.   reliance on historic cost
2.   the principle of realized earnings

These evils, more than any other factors of accounting practices, have caused legislatures, courts, and the public to be suspicious of financial reports of reputable companies certified by reputable public practitioners.

It is encouraging to note that many people are working on the problem of increased realism. If we can find a solution to this problem, we will automatically resolve many of the accounting controversies which have plagued us for decades. But the problem is complex and its solution will require that we accept a new attitude about values reported by corporations. This new concept is described as "fair value accounting," but a better term is "economic realism." Realism is a fact, while fairness is at best a subjective judgment.

NATURE OF FAIR VALUE

Many writers have tried to isolate the essential characteristics of fair value, but there is still a considerable amount of confusion.

For instance, the Accounting Principles Board suggested that market quotations be used as an indicator of the fair value of equity securities. But market quotations are determined by emotions and represent only those people who chose to sell a security, not those who chose to retain it.

Others have emphasized that fair value is an appraisal value established by expert analysis assessing a market of free buyers and sellers. This type of value, of course, runs the difficulty of subjective measurements and great difficulties of definitive measurement.

Still others who have dealt with this subject have referred to price-level accounting, replacement costs, insurable values, tax basis valuations, etc., as various forms of fair value.

There seems to be general agreement that historic costs are not representative of current real values except in the case of businesses with extremely short cycle times, such as a retail operation or a trading venture.

Economic realism, in my sense of the term, is a representative expression of many of the economic values and opportunity costs involved in a going concern. These values may not be too far from fact as prices are generally interpreted by the general public. Furthermore, they must be currently updated so as to have immediate significance. They may be identified as the sum of all future cash flows, but these cash flows must be interpreted with due recognition of all current alternatives, including a perpetual holding of a physical asset.

Accountants have been accused by the *New York Times* of having a "predilection for arcane intellectual combat." In pursuing that tendency, they have been known to confuse not only themselves but the public and business community as well. Historic cost is a prime example of this confusion. It is supported not on the basis of its intellectual propriety, but on the grounds of its measurability. Yet no one in the business world uses historic cost as a fact in itself. There are some situations where it is used as one element of a relationship to determine taxable profit or the shares under a profit-sharing plan, but I know of none who rely on historic cost alone as the basis of a transaction.

ADVANTAGE TO MANAGEMENT

Almost every newspaper carries an item describing a court action, an analytic report, or a conceptual indictment that challenges the propriety of corporate reporting. No longer may business leaders assert their innocence by claiming adherence to generally accepted accounting principles. The courts do not accept such a defense, and they look with a jaundiced eye upon the use of official books of account which are at variance with more realistic valuations.

Establishing a technique which brings the books of account more closely in line with realistic valuations would restore credibility to financial reports. As long as accounting records are an accumulation of data from the past and have no pertinence to the "now" period, business will be on the defensive.

Management may make its private reassessments of valuations and take action based upon them, or it may choose to use less definite information and make the result of the use of such information available to the public. In the first case, there is the potential for a charge of insider awareness; in the second instance, there will be a suspicion that management has doctored the data to increase or decrease reportable income. In my opinion, if responsible methodologies are used, the latter course is less dangerous. The danger of a misstated approximation of real value is far less than the known imperfection of historic cost.

No system of financial reporting which refuses to recognize the changing values of corporate assets over the years can claim to represent responsible public information.

Obviously, an arm's length transaction between two parties is one representation of an existing value, but that value is seldom of a freely determined nature nor does it necessarily represent the ongoing economic worth of ownership. Rather, it represents a liquidation sale in which economic values are greatly depressed. In any event, it should not be necessary to dispose of a piece of property to identify its worth. Furthermore, holding costs are involved in retaining any property and opportunity costs are foregone in any transaction. An appropriate charge must then be levied against the increment in values which has taken place during the period of retention or opportunity. In the recent controversies over leasing and ownership problems of accounting, one sees that the costs of maintaining a lease are borne in one period while the benefits from the disposition of properties occur in a different period. In my opinion, there has not been a satisfactory reconciliation between the costs of using property and the benefits of owning it.

In the summer of 1970, the profession spent a considerable amount of time dealing with the subject of goodwill. It was determined in connection with that activity that the going price for companies was as much as 100 percent over current book values. Is this not a sufficient indictment of historic costs? The discrepancy arose in part because the accounting profession fails to measure the value of intangible assets such as distribution systems, company names, patents, etc.

However, another form of goodwill is derived because the profit contained in inventory and the current value of fixed assets are not reflected in the books of account. It is necessary, therefore, in arriving at a transfer price, for a corporate management to apply rather loose approaches to the determination of a sales price. Since the balance sheet is virtually worthless, it has become traditional in many situations to use a times/earnings multiple. But this inaccurate device is only a substitute for the imperfect condition of the accounting record. It is certainly presumptuous for corporate controllers to issue a statement of financial condition that really represents nothing more than a mechanical balancing of a series of debits and credits under a conventional processing mode. There is a great emphasis in the accounting world upon the operating margin of a company. Because of the short cycle time of most businesses, it is assumed that the difference between the sales price and the cost price is a useful measurement device. With the exception of depreciation transactions and certain reserve adjustments, this is probably true. However, the businessman does not need assistance in interpreting or pricing the effect of transactions which occur frequently and in relatively small size. He gets all he needs to know by repetition and experience. What he and the investor need is assistance in pricing those factors which are involved in the infrequent activities of business, those which pertain to long-term investment and to potential alternative use or disposition. It is not enough to price the nails in the house; we must determine the value of the real estate. The accounting discipline should not be satisfied with forcing investors to apply the times/earnings test in lieu of a more objective and definitive form of equity identification.

DISADVANTAGES OF FAIR VALUE

It is easy to claim that historic cost fails to yield perfect knowledge and that some form of economic realism would give a less imperfect value. Yet some consideration must be given to the complexities and difficulties inherent in a significant change in the basic discipline of accounting.

The first problem which comes to mind is the problem of measurement. It is important to remember that the business society needs a measure which is objective, which avoids delays in reporting, and which can be used relatively inexpensively. At the present time, it seems impossible to provide all of those characteristics for a broadly based segment of business, but it is important to make small steps forward while techniques are perfected and methodologies are devised. In the meantime, management must be scrupulous in adhering to the test of portraying a "reasonable image of reality."

If management eventually achieves a significant representation of fair value, it will find it necessary to record an unrealized form of appreciation. This appreciation will bring with it at least two issues. One of these—the stockholders' claim that the recorded surplus should be distributed appropriately in the form of dividends—will be relatively easy to deal with. Since cash realization will not have taken place for a portion of the values, this request for dividend disbursement may prove to be a subject of controversy.

The second issue associated with the reporting of unrealized income will be the taxing of significant values even though not yet realized. The international companies are already concerned with the suggestion made from time to time that they should pay taxes on earnings in foreign countries even when those earnings have not been made available to the parent company in the United States. If a full concept of fair value is introduced, the amount of surplus accumulated in the older corporations of America will represent a staggering addition to the undistributed surplus and a great gain in the deferred tax account.

Perhaps the most significant problem associated with the acceptance of a fair value concept will be that associated with the legal liabilities involved in corporate actions based upon the new statement of values. At the present time the accounting statements are so unrepresentative that the courts are often deluded in understanding that profitable transactions have taken place merely because historic cost is offset against current price. If, instead, current costs are associated with disposition prices, there may be some reason to question the wisdom of many corporate actions which take place regularly. But this questioning is in accordance with the objectives of accounting, and fair value should not be set aside simply because the legal liabilities have not yet been realistically identified.

APPROACHES TO FAIR VALUE

The literature often deals with "fair value" as though it were a separate and distinct subject from all other problems of accounting. Instead, fair value is the culmination of a great desire on the part of our society to reach a greater understanding. Most of the accounting movements of the past 20 years have been gradual approaches toward the new conceptual theory. Perhaps it would be well to list some of these for consideration:

Cost or Market. Many years ago we determined that the market would be acceptable for valuation in accounting if it was on the down side. This was a basically conservative consideration which asserted the propriety of market tests but was not brave enough to accept increments that might subsequently be revised.

LIFO Accounting. LIFO accounting rejected fair value practices but attempted to absorb fair value in the income statement. Unfortunately, in the process, the LIFO technique produced inventories which were completely out of phase with the realities of the market place.

Price-Level Accounting. In the years subsequent to 1945, price-level accounting received considerable attention in accounting literature. It was suggested that the index approach to maintaining the value of the monetary unit should be built into account practices. In due course the accounting profession invited companies to submit supplementary data dealing with this subject. However, since the corporate financial reports still had to be produced on a historic cost approach, most corporations saw nothing but added expense and nuisance in calculating alternative values.

Discounting of Long-Term Receivables and Payables. As a result of the activities in specific industries, it was discovered that corporations were recording as receivable values the proceeds of sales, when in fact those proceeds really included the costs of money resulting from a long-term contract. Since these costs were not invested until a later period, it was improper to use the face value of the receivable or payable as the basis for the accounting record. A discounting approach was eventually instituted. The discounted value is, of course, a closer approach to the financial reality.

Goodwill and Business Combinations. The ultimate compromise resolution of this controversy failed to dispose of the essential problems. However, the debate did determine that accounting records failed to show the market value of acquired companies and that subsequent income statements failed to represent an absorption of the cost paid by the latest managers in terms of their goodwill. Unfortunately, this controversy evaded the question of whether all accounting should be placed upon a goodwill approach; rather it dealt arbitrarily with those companies that had been involved in an acquisition. Nevertheless, an attempt was made to restate values according to current market tests.

Equity Accounting. Once again the profession attempted to move away from the historic cost of an investment by recognizing the retained surplus of a corporation even when that corporation could only be influenced but not controlled. Certainly, equity accounting is an imperfect approach to economic realism, but it is a step away from historic cost, just as in an earlier day the concept of the consolidation represented a movement away from the historical cost of investments in controlled subsidiaries.

Marketable Securities. The Accounting Principles Board finally indicated, in connection with its preliminary draft on the valuation of equity securities, that it accepted the search for fair value as an objective. Unfortunately, the APB saw market value as equivalent to "fair value" or economic realism. It ignored the concept of the going concern and built its castle upon the vascillating emotions of stock market listings. The APB did move from the historic cost base, and in the current versions of its tentative considerations, the Board suggests that unrealized earnings should be charged to surplus, while the realized earnings should be charged to the income statement with the balance sheet reflecting market values.

It would not be appropriate to suggest that all of the difficulties with the fair value technique have been resolved. However, we have determined conclusively that historic cost is a conceptual failure. Accounting evidence indicates that balance sheets are not representative of economic value. Even measurement and objectivity of conclusions will not justify or support erroneous answers. It may be difficult to measure values perfectly in the extractive industries, in oil fields, in woodland operations, etc., but much of the groundwork for fair value is already being done, and a value which is 75 percent accurate is considerably better than one which is known to be 50 percent wrong.

It is important to be certain that, as we move from historic cost to economic realism, we do not deprive companies of the economic worth that they have accumulated during years of operation. Piracy is not the privilege of accounting principles. Where change takes place, provision must be made for a transition of such a nature that income, whether realized or unrealized, shall in the fullness of time have passed into an income statement once—and once only. It will not be appropriate to have the values in some instances appear in the surplus statement, while in other cases they appear as credits to ordinary operations.

Although it is necessary to be receptive to various devices that might assist the transitional procedure, the objective should not be to present to the investing public a series of alternative values. The accounting profession should be strong enough to identify within its own principles the fundamental value to be used in the appraisal of corporate success. To evade this professional determination, thereby placing it in the hands of financial analysts, investors, or businessmen, would represent the spreading of doubt, a redundancy of costs, and an imperfect reliance on conceptual propriety.

PROGRESS TOWARD REALITY

Many difficulties will be associated with the implementation of a value concept based on economic realism. But relatively few defenses stand between present practices and concepts that would yield a more believable reality. In my opinion, accounting will succeed in maintaining its credibility and character only if it meets the challenge of economic realism.

QUESTIONS

1. Define fair value accounting.
2. Why does Mr. Knortz believe that conventional accounting fails to meet the information needs of the business community?
3. Can fair value accounting be practically implemented? How?

---

79   A FEW WORDS FOR HISTORICAL COST

Robert K. Mautz

(Reprinted by permission from *Financial Executive*, vol. 41, no. 1 (January, 1973): 18-21.)

(Robert K. Mautz is a member of the firm of Ernst & Ernst.)

Those who would do away with historical cost based accounting (including an income realization test based on transactions completed by the reporting company) tend to assert, either directly or indirectly, a number of propositions such as the following:

1. Conservative and cautious accountants are the only ones who have any interest in cost data.
2. Accountants opt for historical cost solely because it is objective and therefore provides them with a measure of protection.
3. No one who makes management or investment decisions reads or relies on traditional (historical cost based) financial statements.

4. Historical cost figures are so grossly out of date as to
    be worthless for decision-making purposes.
5. Substituting some form of current value for transaction
    prices will so improve financial reporting that it will
    then become useful to those who must make decisions of
    an investment or credit nature.
6. Current value data unquestionably and always provide more
    useful managerial and investment information than do
    historical cost data.
7. Accountants are competent to determine or at least "at-
    test" to current values.
8. If accountants do not provide current values in finan-
    cial reports, someone else will.
9. The use of current value in corporate financial statements
    is soundly based in income theory.
10. "It is better to be vaguely right than precisely wrong."

What an indictment of traditional accounting! And what a curious
blend of unsupported assumptions, outright error, and implied failure
of professional responsibility. Let us examine some of these.

USE OF HISTORICAL COST

A common approach by those who attack historical cost is to argue
that it has but one virtue and that one of value only to self-protective
accountants. Over time, the unsupported proposition has been asserted
that historical cost accounting was invented by accountants for accountants, and that no intelligent businessman, if he were not coerced by his
accountants, would have the least use for it. Can any reasonable person
hold such a view? One does not have to be a student of accounting history to know that accounting emerged, not from the inventions of accountants concerned with their possible liability, but from the practices and patterns of thought of businessmen intimately involved in
making operating decisions.
    Accounting is what it is today not so much because of the desires
of accountants as because of the influence of businessmen. If those who
make management and investment decisions had not found financial reports
based on historical cost useful over the years, changes in accounting
would long since have been made. Indeed, changes have been made. Our
practices for valuing receivables, marketable securities, and inventories all represent departures from strict transaction price accounting,
departures desired by businessmen, not accountants. (It is true that in
recent years accountants have become more active and more effective in
imposing accounting rules on management, but this is a recent development—and one we may someday regret.)

USEFULNESS OF TRADITIONAL ACCOUNTING

And here we find the response to another unfounded assertion—that
no one finds traditional financial statements useful. What kind of an
irresponsible claim is this? Can those who make it cite any valid evidence in support of their charge? Certainly my own experience on two

FERF research projects contradicts this charge emphatically. Nor is
there anything in Professor Morton Backer's extensive research, reported
in his *Financial Reporting for Security Investment and Credit Decisions*
(published by the National Association of Accountants, May, 1970), that
gives credence to such a contention. Who uses traditional accounting
data? Businessmen do; businessmen charged with managerial, credit, and
investment decisions use traditional accounting data, and they use them
quite effectively.

The basic concept of profit that guides the thinking of most practical businessmen is found in that telling little phrase, "buy cheap and
sell dear." The pursuit of profit requires that one add sufficient
utility of time, place, or form to the materials, product, or services
one buys, so that they can be sold above cost. The most common, the
best understood, the simplest, the most versatile concept of profit is
the excess of selling price over cost.

A decision to continue or discontinue a product, a division, a department, or a plant hangs to a considerable extent upon whether continuance of the operation is expected to show a favorable spread between
revenue and cost. Anyone can understand this most simple and most widespread notion of business success. It can be applied to few or many
transactions, to a simple or a complex operation, to the results of the
activities of the entire business or any part of it, to past activities
or to future expectations. No other income concept can make that statement. Traditional accounting is structured around this idea. In current jargon, it fits management's decision model.

Are there any feasible alternatives? Not really. Change in the
present value of future cash flows is recommended by some as a more useful concept of income. But can you imagine trying to segregate anticipated cash flows in order to determine economic values on a departmental, divisional, or product basis? Others would price assets at exit
values and compute net income as the increase or decrease of exit values
over time. Would you like to undertake the task of determining the exit
values of the assets of a major company in such a way that the success
of departments or products is shown clearly? One must question whether
determination of current values is either feasible or conceptually sound
for a total company. When one tries to apply the idea to segments,
chaos results.

Businessmen are not insensitive to the possibility that historical
costs may differ from current costs. Fluctuations in market values are
important and do not go unrecognized. At the same time, one must be
realistic. Is the difference between historical cost and current cost
likely to be a greater source of difficulty in the use of data for decision making than the use of current value data whose validity is unknown and whose meaning is perhaps in no way relevant to the planned
activities of the company? Here we must recognize a trade-off; historical costs that bear little resemblance to current costs may have little
managerial usefulness. But asserted current values whose validity is
subject to suspicion present an equally real problem. When that validity problem—at best an unknown quantity—is as great or greater than
the historical-current cost difference, historical cost is the more
reasonable choice for decision purposes.

"ERRORS" IN HISTORICAL COST

If historical costs are both substantially different from current costs and so important in the determination of profit that the difference is a material one, admittedly adjustment of some kind may be needed. How often does this happen? For companies whose inventories turn a number of times a year, the effect of using historical rather than current costs for inventories is unlikely to be significant except in the most extreme conditions. For companies whose depreciation on fixed assets is not an influential part of total cost, the impact of price level changes on fixed assets is unlikely to be of real importance to any one other than a purist.

CHANGES IN MARKET VALUE

The illustrations that come most readily to the hand of the historical cost critic are those of investments and land. Substantial increases in the market value of these assets go unrecorded under traditional accounting, and it is alleged that the failure to include such changes in income grossly misleads readers of financial statements to the great detriment of those who sell their shares in the company without knowledge of the change. A first point in rebuttal is that disclosure of such changes can be made readily without any need for shifting from a historical cost to a value basis of accounting. Parenthetical disclosure can alert readers to the fact of market value changes with no need to recognize the change as an element of current income.

And parenthetical disclosure is all that is warranted. Does anyone obtain more useful information if a company is forced to recognize as income changes in the market value of assets which the company has no intention of selling? If land is to be used in operations and the company has no intention of disposing of it in the foreseeable future, of what current income significance is a change in its value? If the securities are to be held as long-term investments regardless of current variations in market values, how significant are those variations? Once disclosure is provided, what additional useful information is revealed by including such value changes in income?

The current valuer responds that the land and the investments could have been sold, that management should be held accountable for changes in value which it could have realized. How far should we indulge in such "might-have-been" accounting? Assuming management had funds available, it could have purchased additional securities when the market was low and could have sold them when the market was high. Should these possible transactions be reported also? Is this accounting? Or only wishful thinking?

There is much concern on the part of some accountants that management has too much discretion in the "management of earnings" through the selection and timing of transactions. An alternative is to require management to report on the basis of the transactions that might have taken place. Does anyone want to accept that possibility? Who will decide just what the possibilities were? And on what basis? Historical cost accounting is soundly based on recognition of the effect of actual, not merely possible, transactions. Recognition of the latter would constitute such a change in the measure of successful business

operations that it would undoubtedly have significant effects upon the
way in which business is done. Change the score-keeping and change the
game. Change the game and where does one stop? Do we have any real
understanding of the impact on business activity of such a drastic
change in income determination?

Would data based on such changes provide more useful information
for managerial decisions, for investment and credit decisions? The contention is that it would, but what evidence is given? Is the fact that
a company now has its factory on very high-priced land, which it has no
intention of selling, a factor that should encourage shareowners to hold
their shares although other indications encourage sale? Should shareholders be encouraged to be critical of management because it did not
dispose of long-term investments during the current year whenever the
market price at the end of the year has declined? Is immediate profit
the only reason for holding assets?

ECONOMIC INCOME AND CORPORATE INCOME

But comes the response, "You are denying the very nature of economic income. Such increases in value are income and unless they are
recorded and reported by accounting, we are not presenting economic
reality." Come now, let's not play with high-sounding phrases. What
for goodness sake is "economic reality"? Better, what is not "economic
reality"? Are possible transactions economically more real than actual
transactions? Are might-have-been prices more real than actual transaction prices?

The claim that current value accounting is soundly based in economic theory and that it more truly reflects economic income is of
doubtful validity. Those who advance this dubious argument typically
begin by quoting Professor Hicks' famous definition of a person's income (*Value and Capital*, Clarendon Press, Oxford, 1957): ". . . it
would seem that we ought to define a man's income as the maximum value
which he can consume during a week, and still expect to be as well off
at the end of the week as he was at the beginning." Who can question
such a reasonable, common sense, down-to-earth definition?

Professor Hicks, for one. Those who read Professor Hicks, rather
than merely quote him, find in the very chapter in which this definition appears, that he examines it further and finds it sadly lacking.

But this is not all. Professor Hicks' definition is of a person's
income, and we are concerned with reporting the income of corporations.
Some accounting theorists find this of little consequence. They blithely equate the net worth of a corporation with the individual's ability
to consume, and proceed on the assumption that increases in net worth
are income. They really ought to read Professor Hicks more carefully.
There is so little similarity between the two, between a person's
ability to consume and a corporation's net worth, that Hicks' definition of income, if it ever was valid, fails to fit the corporate situation. A person, in Professor Hicks' terms, is a consumption unit; he
defines income as the amount one can consume. Corporations do not consume in the sense that a person does. Corporations are intended to be
production units, to produce so others can consume. Could a corporation that consumed its net worth continue to exist? Yet an individual
who consumed all his resources would still exist, indeed many of us do

so each month. How can we then identify two such disparate ideas: corporate net worth and personal ability to consume?

Yet our theoretical friends compound that error with another. To measure the corporation's net worth, they would value the individual assets and total them to get the value of the company. Is not the whole equal to the sum of its parts? Only if all the parts are included. The piecemeal valuation of individual assets can take no realistic account of the contribution to income made by good management, by organization, by high employee morale, or by any one of a number of other important intangibles. On whatever terms assets are valued and added, the total is unlikely to include all the income-contributing resources of the company.

Given such gross weaknesses in concept and computation, how can anyone seriously contend that current value accounting has a sound basis in economic theory?

So the critics return to the attack by pointing out that neither does historical cost accounting have a sound basis in economic theory. Nor does it so contend. Historical cost accounting is willing to rest its case on the common concept of profit—sales price less cost—and to argue that whatever lag there may be between historical cost and current cost, it is, except in extreme cases, less of a hazard to those who use accounting data than would be the hazard existing if values were introduced into income determination.

DETERMINATION OF CURRENT VALUES

Whom would you trust to value the assets of any major company you might wish to select as an example? Do you find accountants to have any superior talents in this direction? If not, on whom should they rely? What do you think would have happened to the balance sheets and income statements of some of the hy-flyers in the mid-1960s if historical costs had been abandoned in favor of current value? How would current values have been determined in the late 1960s when such companies were in trouble? Who would have measured those values? How would they have been measured? How would the independent CPA have determined that any given value was or was not a fair representation? How would independent CPAs have withstood the management's argument that other companies were overvaluing and they had to compete with those companies in the market for available funds? One financial vice president in discussing this topic with me stated, "We couldn't stand the pressure," and you could almost see the possibilities turning on in the back of his mind. If independent CPAs cannot exercise control over such a relatively simple matter as consistency in the application of depreciation methods, how would they control determinations of current value?

"OTHERS WILL DO IT"

To the expressed fear that if accountants do not present financial statements on a value basis, someone else will, one need only query "Who?" Who is blessed with the ability to forecast future cash flows and discount them to the present on a basis sufficiently valid that, recognizing the pressures and uncertainties of the real world, others

will accept them? Who can determine exit values for all assets so objectively that all will find them satisfactory? If there be such a
man, let him now step forward. Certainly, financial analysts attempt
to forecast the future success of corporations (or is it the probable
reaction of the market to the anticipated future success?). But do
analysts attempt this on an asset-by-asset valuation basis? I know
of none who do. Nor any who seek such information from others. Indeed,
financial analysts turn out to be some of the strongest proponents of
traditional, conservative accounting that one can find, and only because
they find such data so useful for their own investment decision purposes.

Now we come at last to that old and well-worn bromide: "It is better to be vaguely right than precisely wrong." Certainly the current
valuers are vague; they have that in their favor. But are they right?
Do they offer any solid evidence that the data they propose would in
any, some, or all cases be more useful than the data that accounting now
provides? Do they offer anything more than strong assertions and a
few horrible examples of how unuseful cost can be in extreme cases?

Rightness, as it applies to accounting, lies in the appropriateness
of the treatment to the circumstances. Certainly one can conceive of
circumstances in which historical cost ceases to be useful. But that
is not the question. What is proposed here—and comprehending the full
impact of value accounting is important—is that we should abandon a
proven concept of income, an established procedure that lends itself to
known controls, a quality of information that has served well and whose
limitations are well known, and accept in their place a vague prescription for current values whose usefulness is not established, for which
there is very little expressed demand from those who use accounting
data, and for which no known controls are available. And we are urged
to do all this on a broad scale.

Never mind the fact that parenthetical disclosures of values within a traditional framework would provide as much information with much
less risk. Never mind that there is little expressed demand for the
extent of change advocated, and that contracts, customs, and agreements
are based on that which is so blithely to be abandoned. The winds of
change blow strong and the Age of Aquarius has arrived so we must get
on with it. I find this a very unappealing prospect.

If I were a corporate executive, or a financial analyst, or a fund
manager, or a substantial shareholder, and if you were to offer me a
choice between

1. historical cost-based financial statements in the tradi-
    tional format with parenthetical and other supplementary
    disclosures of market values for those assets held during
    material price changes,
2. financial statements containing someone's notion of the
    current values of the company's several assets, whether
    determined on a basis of discounting anticipated future
    cash receipts, appraisals, market values, or whatever,
    with changes since the last such set of financial state-
    ments included in income.

My choice would be an easy one. Whatever the failings of historical
cost, mending these with supplementary disclosures is a far more

promising prospect than any significant shift to unknown, undefined, and uncontrollable values.

If at this point you have the impression that I am so irrevocably attached to historical cost that my mind is closed to other possibilities, let me enter a demurrer. Historical cost has served well in the great majority of cases in the past; it will continue to do so. From time to time in the future as well as in the past, modifications of historical cost accounting may become necessary. If these are made on a pragmatic basis and have obtained general acceptance, I will have little difficulty in accepting them.

I am strongly in agreement with the conclusions of a recently published research study sponsored by the Financial Executives Research Foundation which holds ". . . that there is no inherent rightness in any given accounting method apart from the circumstances in which it is to be applied." Time is much too short to expound on that conclusion, but a corollary seems clear. Under given circumstances or to meet the needs of specific conditions, departures from otherwise accepted principles may be necessary. We have already accepted some departures from the cost principle. In time we may need to accept some additional departures. But as I have tried to suggest here, there is far from adequate evidence to justify its general rejection at this time or in the foreseeable future.

QUESTIONS

1. Why does Mr. Mautz think that accountants are not totally responsible for what accounting is today?
2. State Mr. Mautz's major arguments for historical cost-based accounting?
3. Do you agree with Mr. Mautz's arguments, expressed as questions, against current values being used in accounting reports? Explain.
4. "What for goodness sake is 'economic reality'? Better, what is not 'economic reality'?"

---

80   THE ACCOUNTANTS' LAST CHANCE

(Reprinted by permission from *Business Week* (March 31, 1973): 91.)

This week, the seven members of the new Financial Accounting Standards Board went on display before 1,300 of their former colleagues and clients in accounting, industry, and government. Also on hand for the dinner at New York's Waldorf-Astoria were the 27 representatives from the academic, business, banking, legal, and Wall Street communities who will advise FASB.

The public display marks the beginning of the FASB's reign. It also marks the first time that the accounting rule-making process has been brought out from under the total domination of the nation's certified public accountants.

But privately, financial executives recognize that the FASB may be the last chance to avoid government control of accounting. The Securities & Exchange Commission has the ultimate authority for setting accounting standards. In the past, the SEC had delegated this task to the accounting profession. After well-publicized accounting failures of the late 1960s—the quarrels over real estate accounting, leasing, and accounting for investment tax credits—there is growing sentiment to take that authority away from the private sector. If the FASB flubs its job, accounting rules in the future almost certainly will be set by government edict.

Marshall S. Armstrong, the FASB's first chairman, is well aware of the threat hanging over him. These days he is running fast to get the board's initial organizational problems out of the way so that it can get down to wrestling with critical accounting issues. A major criticism of the Accounting Principles Board, the CPA group that until now has made the rules, was that it took far too long to reach a decision.

BROADER-BASED

To correct that, the FASB has been installed as a full-time, well-paid, and independent group of seven to replace 18 part-time participants who received their compensation from their parent CPA firms. Only four of the seven FASB members need be CPAs, and outsiders have a voice in their selection, as well as on the advisory 27-member council, the board's key sounding board.

"When we think about issues, there must be public thinking about issues," Armstrong insists. "Without public involvement, the FASB will not be successful," says Armstrong, 58, the former head of George S. Olive & Company, an Indianapolis-based accounting firm.

The FASB and the advisory council will meet at least quarterly. Among other things, the council will review any interpretations or clarifications of existing accounting rules that the FASB might make. Outsiders also will be asked to sit on special task forces that the FASB means to create to delve into specific accounting issues. And Armstrong intends to expand greatly the procedures that the APB adopted late in life. The board will hold public hearings on opinions that it is considering. It will see that drafts of proposed accounting rule changes are circulated for public comment before final vote.

Four of the FASB members, including Armstrong, already are on board at the FASB's offices in High Ridge, a sprawling, ultramodern industrial park outside Stamford, Connecticut. These include John W. Queenan, 67; Donald J. Kirk, 40; and Walter P. Schuetze, also 40, all of whom were partners in Big Eight CPA firms.

Arthur L. Litke, 50, now chief of the Federal Power Commission's Office of Accounting & Finance, and Robert T. Sprouse, 51, now professor of accounting at Stanford University's Graduate School of Business, will join the FASB early next week. The seventh member, Robert E. Mays, 61, controller of Exxon Corporation, is expected to begin his board duties by July 1. In exchange for annual salaries of $100,000 (Armstrong receives $125,000 as chairman), FASB members are required to sever all ties with their existing organizations. They are limited to two five-year terms.

Right now, Armstrong is doing a number of things to get the new organization off the ground:

1. He is working out the delicate transition of power from the APB, an arm of the American Institute of Certified Public Accountants, to the FASB, which is appointed by the Financial Accounting Foundation, a new and independent body that represents business, accounting, the academic world, and Wall Street.
2. He is assembling administrative, research, and technical staffs. The annual budget for FASB operations is projected at more than $3 million, providing a staff of 65 to 70 persons.
3. He is establishing working relationships with other bodies that influence accounting principles, including the SEC. He also has met with the head of the newly formed Cost Accounting Standards Board, set up by Congress last year to develop uniform standards for government contracts. Its rules will affect FASB positions.

The FASB will decide by mid-April just which of the myriad of pressing accounting issues it will tackle first. In Armstrong's words, the FASB has "a full pipeline" of topics to be considered.

HOT ISSUES

For instance, there is the matter of financial reporting by diversified companies. The SEC already requires that its annual 10-K reports from corporations with major unrelated product lines show the sales and earnings for each broad business activity. But accountants have not come up with rules in this area, so companies do not have to break down their figures in annual reports to shareholders.

The FASB also will have to come up with guidelines on how gains and losses from foreign currency translations are to be treated—a key issue for 1973 in light of the recent U.S. dollar devaluation and the present floating exchange rates.

A ruling on marketable securities is also long overdue. Many accounting observers have urged that such assets be carried at current market value rather than at acquisition cost, as many companies now list them on their balance sheets. APB attempts to deal with the issues were abandoned amid a storm of controversy.

One of the most emotion-laden issues involves accounting in the oil and gas industry. The debate centers on how to treat exploration expenses. The dominant international oil companies as a rule immediately write off the cost of unsuccessful drilling efforts. But more companies, including most of the smaller ones, use a "full-cost accounting" method to capitalize such costs and write them off over a number of years.

Earnings can be quite different from year to year, although perhaps not in the long run, depending on which method is chosen. And the recent batch of proposed disclosure rules by the SEC has added fuel to the imbroglio by suggesting that companies using full-costing should also show what their earnings would be under the alternative accounting method.

TREATMENT OF LEASES

The SEC also has asked the new board to take a look at the whole question of leases—and to decide if this popular kind of "off-the-balance-sheet" financing should be capitalized and carried on the balance sheet. The potential company liabilities on leases can be enormous, particularly among airlines and large retail chains that lease rather than own much of their equipment or facilities.

The FASB's timetable on this issue will hinge on what the APB does in the next few weeks on a leasing proposal it is considering. That proposal would require companies only to spell out lease obligations in much greater detail. But if it passes, Armstrong says that the disclosures would enable the FASB to gauge the effect of putting leases on the balance sheet before it tackles the technical issues. If the APB takes no action, however, the new board will be prodded to undertake its own research study at an early date.

PICKING UP SPEED

As a former APB member, Armstrong is sensitive but realistic about criticism that the FASB may be as slow moving as the APB—particularly in its first year. "Don't expect us to solve marketable securities and oil and gas accounting overnight," he cautions. But he is confident that, once the full-time FASB and its large research and technical staffs get rolling, "you can expect more speed from the effort."

Armstrong also is working on an early-warning system, perhaps using the advisory council and the FASB's technical staff, to keep the board apprised of immediate problem areas on a day-to-day basis. That way, he says, the FASB may be able to nip abuses in the bud before they blossom into full-grown controversies.

QUESTIONS

1. Do you think that the SEC will dictate accounting standards if the Financial Accounting Standards Board fails? Explain.
2. Why do you think that the SEC has delegated their ultimate authority over accounting standards to the AICPA since 1934?
3. What is the difference between accounting standards and accounting principles?
4. What advantages will the FASB have that the APB did not?

81   ACCOUNTING CHANGES: WHY CPAs MUST CONFORM

George D. Cameron, III
Ralph W. Gudmundsen, Jr.
Jack R. Ball

(Reprinted by permission from *Management Accounting*, vol. 54, no. 8
(February, 1973): 26-28.)

(G. D. Cameron, III is a faculty member at University of Michigan.
J. R. Ball is quality control supervisor for Bendix Aerospace Systems
Division, Ann Arbor, Michigan. R. W. Gudmundsen is a member of the firm
of Ernst & Ernst.)

Whenever the Accounting Principles Board of the AICPA issues an
opinion calling for changes in corporate financial statements, management prepares for a confrontation with the independent CPA. Management
knows he will insist on changes in the published financial statements to
make them conform with the new opinion. This concern over financial
statement is understandable, particularly if the changes would have an
unfavorable effect on the financial statements. Despite this urge to
resist change in financial statements, management should consider why
change is necessary and why the CPA must insist on it.

Accounting principles evolve to cope with changes in the ways business is conducted. This evolution appears clearly in the development of
such techniques as single proprietorship accounting, partnership accounting, joint venture accounting, corporate accounting, fiduciary accounting, and cost accounting. Yet it would be naively simplistic to
ascribe all changes in accounting principles to business evolution. The
CPA, primarily through professional associations, has effected deliberate changes in accounting principles. This area of change is the chief
concern of this article. Further, only those factors which might help
management better understand the reasons for deliberate change are of
concern here. Some of the principal factors that management could well
ponder include these traits of CPAs:

1. professional outlook
2. code of ethics
3. professional liability

PROFESSIONAL OUTLOOK

In the practice of professions, deliberate change born of research
and study guards against decadence. As experience with established
principles accumulates, changes are found to be needed in the applications of principles and in the principles themselves; new principles
emerge generating additional waves of change. In its interest in developing and refining principles, accounting conforms with the experience of other professions.

Management has much to lose by successfully opposing statement
changes borne on the tides created by the evolution of accounting principles. The usefulness of the CPA's opinion to management rests almost

entirely upon the confidence of the public in the public accounting profession. Without the public's confidence, the CPA's opinion of management's financial statements would become meaningless to third parties, and the statements would suffer substantial loss of credibility. To maintain the public's confidence in his opinion and thereby maintain the value of his opinion to management, the CPA must insist that the tides created by the evolution of accounting principles be allowed to run their course in the financial statements. Management should be assured that the evolution reflects changes in business practices or genuinely better understanding of business practices. The CPA's concern for deliberate change from study and research is no phony exercise or indulgence in professional snobbery; changes are needed and expected of the profession.

CODE OF ETHICS

CPAs are guided in their practice by a code of professional ethics, a voluntary assumption of self-discipline advising the public that the profession will protect (or attempt to protect) the public interest.

However, the code of ethics applicable to CPAs has a unique characteristic; it requires him in his historically primary service, the attest function, to place the public interest above the interest of his client. In attesting financial statements, the CPA is responsible primarily to third parties who may read his report. Thus, his professional ethics take on more than usual importance.

In view of the importance of the code of professional ethics to the CPA, management should consider that in discharging his responsibility to third parties, he must evaluate the fairness of management's financial statements in the light of generally accepted accounting principles. In connection with this rule, management should remember that whenever the APB speaks, "generally accepted accounting principles" are automatically generated. Thus, as a matter of professional ethics, the CPA must keep abreast of APB opinions. If management's statements are based on accounting principles that conflict with a new APB opinion, he may have to insist on changes in order to render an unqualified opinion or a report free of distracting disclosures.

PROFESSIONAL LIABILITY

While financial statements are basically the representations of management, the CPA has a professional liability for the information contained in the financial statements on which he reports. His primary responsibility (hence liability) for the statements is to third parties, not to management. To understand this position, management would benefit from a thorough review of the development and nature of the CPA'a liability.

Changes in Judicial Mood

While the body of law dealing specifically with "accountants" has been slow in developing, parallels may be drawn to the legal rules covering other professions and suppliers of services. The late 1950s and 1960s have seen a drastic shift in legal thinking insofar as the liability of suppliers of goods or services is concerned. The old rule of *caveat emptor* (let the buyer beware) has been repudiated, both legislatively (e.g., the Uniform Commercial Code) and judicially. The trend is distinctly in favor of extension of legal protection to the consumer, the customer, the client.

Another drastic shift in the "rules of the game" worth noting at this point concerns "privity." Briefly put, "privity" means "relationship" (based on a contract between plaintiff and defendant). It was used by manufacturers to deny warranty liability on their products where the product had passed through the hands of at least one independent middleman. But the concept of "privity" as a prerequisite to recovery against a manufacturer of defective goods has met all but unanimous judicial repudiation.

Thus far, however, relevant reported court cases indicate that privity of contract remains a key variable in the professional liability of the CPA. Whereas he is liable for fraud both to his client and to third parties on much the same basis, his liability for negligence and/or breach of contract will differ, depending on who is suing and on the nature of the action brought. It is difficult for a third party to mount a successful breach of contract action against a CPA unless the plaintiff can show a clearly intended "third party beneficiary" situation, i.e., unless the CPA's reports were clearly intended for the plaintiff's benefit. Even if such a plea is successful, its inherent limitation from the plaintiff's point of view is that recovery usually would be limited to the amount paid for the (defective) services rendered; the third party also would have to prove he suffered "special damages" which were within the contemplation of the parties to the contract when they made it. All in all, this would be a difficult case to prove.

Presently, a majority of jurisdictions continue to distinguish between the CPA's liability for negligence to his client and his liability for negligence causing harm to third parties. While he is clearly liable to his client for the consequences of his negligence,

> . . . as to third parties—even those who the accountant knew or should have known were relying on his audit—liability can be founded only upon fraudulent conduct, and proof of mere negligence will not suffice. (1)

In the case just cited, the court noted a "developing trend" of cases holding accountants liable to third parties (2) but indicated that the plaintiff had not proved that Colorado courts were ready to accept this new theory of liability. Nevertheless, the beginnings of a trend are surely there. In the light of developments in other areas of the law, it seems only a matter of time until the CPA's liability for "mere" negligence is extended to third parties, just as the liability of manufacturers has been.

Significance of the Changes

What meaning has all of this to the CPA? It means that he will be held more closely by the law to strict standards of quality performance. In cases of gross error or blatantly sloppy work, punitive damages are possible. Some different types of legal liability to which CPAs have been subjected are:

1. liability to employer or person in privity for damages which result from his failure to employ the degree of knowledge, skill, and judgment usually possessed by members of that profession
2. liability for false or inaccurate reflection of financial conditions presented by certified statements
3. liability for failure to discover defalcations or fraud because of lack of compliance with proper accounting procedure
4. liability for loss or damage due to erroneous advice or lack of due care of property
5. liability to third parties for false financial statements where the CPA has reason to believe that statements are incorrect and that said statement will be relied upon. (3)

Perhaps the key question from the individual CPA's point of view is: "How careful do I have to be to avoid legal liability?" Phrased another way, his problem is to gain advance knowledge of the standard by which he will be judged and then to hold to that standard. In this regard, the existence of the APB's standards may be considered as boon or bane, depending on one's point of view.

APB Pronouncements

In the pronouncements of the APB, the accounting profession has some generally accepted and generally known national standards of practice. The medical profession, for example, does not have any such national standards, and medical opinions of "good practice" vary even more widely than those of accountants. The CPA, therefore, has a more reliable gauge for his day-to-day practice than does the medical doctor. With some national standards as a guide, the CPA has less chance than a medical doctor of being subjected to liability simply because of "luck of the draw," i.e., due to the professional opinions of the experts who testify in his case.

On the other hand, the APB pronouncements may present a legal hazard for the individual CPA who does not abide by them. If observing APB opinions constitutes sound evidence of good practice, departing from them might in itself constitute a *prima facie* case of bad practice. No CPA would lightly assume the heavy burden of justifying the use of accounting principles that conflict with those supported by the APB. Hence, his insistence to management that their financial statements conform to the pronouncements of the APB stems to a large extent from the pressure of potential legal liability.

The Auditing Aspect

In addition to potential legal liability, there is also pressure from private and government regulatory agencies. Public accounting firms have been accused of failing to protect the "third party" public from distortion, misrepresentation, and fraud in the financial statements of their clients. In defense, independent auditors claim that their primary responsibilities are to assure that the statements are presented in accordance with "generally accepted accounting principles" and that the amounts presented are reasonable. The auditing firms do not guarantee that the client has accounted accurately for every penny earned and spent. Even if an audit of such scope as to justify such a guarantee were possible, the cost of such an audit would not be economically feasible to the client. Thus, a CPA must rely instead on sample tests of the data on which the client's statements and schedules are based. When his examination, based on such sample procedures, does indicate a need for change in the financial statements, he would be foolhardy not to insist on such changes as the condition for an unqualified opinion.

CONCLUSION

This article has emphasized three reasons why the CPA from time to time must insist on changes in financial statements. First, he is a professional practitioner and as such seeks to improve his service by deliberate changes in theory and practice born of research and study. Second is the need for him to respect the profession's ethics; the majority of CPAs are bound ethically in their attest function to treat the interests of statement readers as paramount. Finally, the need for him to consider his professional liability was discussed. The APB pronouncements were found to be a potential legal shield when statements conform with APB pronouncements but a strong potential legal hazard when they do not. Hence, he is motivated strongly to insist that the statements on which he reports conform with APB opinions.

FOOTNOTES

1. *Stephens Industries, Incorporated* v. *Haskins and Sells*, 438 F. 2d 357 (1971).
2. Ibid., p. 360.
3. *American Jurisprudence*, Second Edition, Vol. 1 (New York: The Lawyers Cooperative Publishing Co., 1962), p. 365.

QUESTIONS

1. Why do accounting principles change? Do you think that change is justified? Why or why not?
2. In economic terms, why must the CPA in performing the attest function, place the public interest above the interest of his client?

3. What is meant by third party liability? How can authoritative pronouncements help the CPA protect himself against this liability?

---

82   GOVERNMENTAL AND COMMERCIAL
              ACCOUNTING CONCEPTS

Joseph F. Wojdak

(Reprinted by permission from *The New York Certified Public Accountant*, now *The CPA Journal* (January, 1969): 29-37.)

(Joseph F. Wojdak is President of the American Cabinet Corporation. He was formerly a faculty member at Pennsylvania State University.)

The operations and programs carried on by state and local governmental units have been growing rapidly. Indeed, one writer has referred to local government as a major growth industry. (1) This growth has aroused in the public an increased interest in and awareness of the financial affairs of governmental units. As a consequence the public has called upon CPAs. In addition to serving on state and local advisory committees, CPAs are now being asked to audit and issue opinions on the accounting records and financial statements of governmental units. (2) It is reasonable to expect that governmental units will solicit the services of CPAs with increasing frequency in the future. It therefore behooves the CPA to have a very firm grasp and understanding of governmental accounting theory and concepts. With such an understanding the CPA will not be reluctant to become involved in the accounting aspects of local governments be that involvement in the form of "public service" without compensation or in the form of an official audit engagement.
Many accountants and CPAs have had a very limited exposure to governmental accounting theory and concepts. This article attempts to broaden that exposure. One often used method of communicating concepts is to identify or relate them to what is already known. In the following paragraphs some of the more important governmental accounting concepts are described by comparing and relating them to corresponding concepts used in private enterprise accounting.

PURPOSE OF ACCOUNTING INFORMATION

The purpose of governmental accounting is to "produce financial information in a form that is readily useful to all of the parties concerned." (3) The most important of these parties would include administrators and legislators of the governmental unit, the general public (taxpayers), political and social scientists. At the same time, private enterprise accounting has been defined as "the process of identifying, measuring, and communicating economic information to permit informed judgments and decisions by users of the information." (4) In a very broad sense the purposes of governmental and private enterprise accounting are the same. In other words, both essentially attempt to provide useful information to interested users. However, there are marked differences in the specific uses made of the information provided by the accounting systems of governmental units versus private enterprise units.

Private Enterprise Accounting

Private enterprise accounting is often dichotomized as financial accounting and managerial accounting. Financial accounting has as its primary objectives income determination and the measurement of financial position. Managerial accounting endeavors to provide information which will be useful in planning and controlling operations as well as measuring the performance of individuals and organizational units. The private enterprise has as its primary objective the generation of profits. Both financial and managerial accounting are designed to aid in the achievement of this profit objective.

Governmental Accounting

In contrast, the profit motive is lacking in governmental activities. The primary purpose of governmental units is to maintain a well-ordered and well-structured society as efficiently as possible (i.e., public service with a least cost combination of factors). Governmental units are creatures of the state and may only do what they are legally permitted to do. Legally they may be governed by state or municipal law, charter, constitution, statute, ordinance, or resolution. Thus, in comparing governmental and financial accounting it should be emphasized that in the past the accounting system of the governmental unit has been concerned primarily with adherence to legal provisions rather than with financial position and income determination. The internal purpose of accounting for private enterprises is to provide information for *planning, controlling,* and *measuring performance.* In contrast, the primary internal purpose of governmental accounting is to exercise *control* over the financial affairs of the governmental unit, i.e., seeing to it that legal provisions and formally adopted budgets are adhered to and have not been violated.

Compliance with the law is an all-pervading influence in governmental accounting. The law determines how revenues will be raised. Likewise, through legislative adoption of formal budgets, the law governs the manner in which revenues will be allocated to various funds and expended for various purposes. Accounting principles for private enterprises are not necessarily designed to reflect the legal aspects of transactions. This is the contrast to governmental accounting where legal requirements take precedence over generally accepted principles for governmental units.

TERMINOLOGY

The terminology of governmental accounting differs considerably
from that used in private enterprise accounting. However, many governmental terms do have a counterpart in commercial accounting. The more
important terms encountered in governmental accounting are defined below. These definitions have been adopted by the National Committee on
Governmental Accounting (NCGA). (5) In parentheses following each governmental term is the most nearly equivalent term in private enterprise
accounting.

Budget (Budget). A plan of financial operation embodying an estimate of proposed expenditures for a given period or purpose and the
proposed means of financing them.

Appropriation (Budgeted Expense). An authorization granted by the
legislative body to make expenditures and to incur obligations for specific purposes. Note: An appropriation is usually limited in amount and
as to the time when it may be expended.

Appropriation Expenditures (Actual Expenses). An expenditure
chargeable to an appropriation.

Revenue (Actual Revenue). For those revenues which are recorded on
the accrual basis, this term designates additions to assets which:

1. do not increase any liability
2. do not represent the recovery of an expenditure
3. do not represent the cancellation of certain
    liabilities without a corresponding increase in other
    liabilities or a decrease in assets; and
4. do not represent contributions of fund capital in
    Enterprise and Intragovernmental Service Funds

Estimated Revenue (Budgeted Revenue). If the accounts are kept on
the accrual basis this term designates the amount of revenue estimated
to accrue during a given period regardless of whether or not it is all
to be collected during the period.

Encumbrances. (This term has no equivalent in private enterprise
accounting since unperformed portions of executory contracts are not

recognized in the accounts. However, it might best be described in
conventional terms as an expense which is both contingent and estimated.) Obligations in the form of purchase orders, contracts, or
salary commitments which are chargeable to an appropriation and for
which a part of the appropriation is reserved. They cease to be encumbrances when paid or when the actual liability is set up.

Reserve for Encumbrances (Contingent Liability). A reserve representing the segregation of a portion of a fund balance to provide for
unliquidated encumbrances.

Fund Balance (6) (Retained Earnings). The excess of the assets of
a fund over its liabilities and reserves except in the case of funds
subject to budgetary accounting where, prior to the end of a fiscal
period, it represents the excess of the fund's assets and estimated
revenues for the period over its liabilities, reserves, and appropriations for the period.

Retained Earnings (6) (Retained Earnings). The accumulated earnings of an Enterprise of Intragovernmental Service Fund which have been
retained in the fund and which are not reserved for any specific purpose.
     The terms assets and liabilities have essentially the same meaning
in governmental accounting as they do in private enterprise accounting.

MAJOR CONCEPTS

Concepts such as objectivity, materiality, conservatism, consistency, disclosure and so forth, are equally applicable in governmental and
private enterprise accounting. However, several major concepts take on
a considerably different meaning when defined in terms of accounting for
a governmental unit versus accounting for a private business enterprise.
At least five major concepts should be examined in this respect:

1. accounting entity
2. budgeting
3. bases of accounting
4. matching
5. other

These concepts are discussed in that order in the following paragraphs.

Accounting Entity

Whereas the business enterprise is the accounting entity in private
enterprise accounting, the fund is the accounting entity in governmental

accounting. The NCGA has defined a fund as "an independent fiscal and accounting entity with a self-balancing set of accounts recording cash and/or other resources together with all related liabilities, obligations, reserves, and equities which are segregated for the purpose of carrying on specific activities or attaining certain objectives in accordance with special regulations, restrictions or limitations." (7)

The NCGA emphasizes that a fund is both a sum of money and other resources and an independent fiscal and accounting entity. Each fund constitutes a self-balancing group of accounts (i.e., a general ledger) which reflects assets obligations, the fund balance, revenues and expenditures, receipts and disbursements. Thus, the meaning of the term fund as defined above differs considerably from that term used in business enterprise accounting. In a business enterprise a fund is simply a *part* of the total assets of the business and is not a separate accounting entity.

In spite of its diverse activities, the business enterprise reports to the public as one unit or entity.

Government Fund Accounting

The governmental unit, on the other hand, reports as several entities or funds. The governmental unit must raise money from specific sources and expend it for specific purposes in accordance with restrictions and regulations imposed by law. Use of separate funds (entities) provides a convenient method for accounting for the specific revenue raised for specific purposes. In other words, the various functions of the governmental unit are separately financed and controlled by an individual set of legal provisions. Thus, complete segregation of cash and other assets as well as separate records of the operations of each function are necessary.

The number and kinds of funds established by a particular governmental unit are determined by the unit's activities, the methods of financing them and the underlying legal provisions imposed by law. The following types of funds will generally be found in most governmental units. This classification of funds is recommended by the NCGA. (8)

1.	general fund	5.	special revenue funds
2.	debt service funds	6.	trust and agency funds
3.	capital projects funds	7.	intragovernmental service funds
4.	enterprise funds	8.	special assessment funds

The NCGA recommends two other self-balancing groups of accounts be kept by governmental units. These are the general long-term debt group of accounts and the general fixed asset group of accounts. Although these accounts are self-balancing they are not technically funds. These two groups of accounts and the above eight funds have been adopted by most municipal units as an accounting and financial reporting structure.

BUDGETING

The budget is used by management in private enterprise accounting as a tool for planning, controlling, and measuring performance, but, it is not incorporated into the regular framework of accounts. In governmental accounting the budget has the same objectives as in private enterprise accounting except that a definite emphasis is placed on its control aspect.

Two other, more important differences in the governmental budget are:

1. the expenditure portion of the budget becomes law by passage of an appropriate act or ordinance and
2. large portions of budget revenues are based upon accurately determinable items such as assessed real estate values, number of licenses and permits to be issued, and so forth.

Thus, in the revenue and income estimates a high degree of certainty is present which permits greater accuracy in budgeting. These differences explain why budgeted revenues and expenses are recognized in the regular framework of governmental accounts. Accordingly, revenues are treated as realized and expenditures (expenses) are treated as accrued at the time the budget is passed and journalized. Further, the difference between budgeted revenues and budgeted expenses is debited or credited to the fund balance account.

When journalized, budgeted accounts assume opposite signs from their related actual accounts, i.e., budgeted revenues (equivalent to receivable) have debit balances and budgeted expenditures (equivalent to deferred charges) have credit balances. All funds *may* record budgeted revenues and expenditures for purposes of control. Usually only those funds established through a formal appropriation from the legislative body journalize budgeted amounts. Therefore, budgetary accounts will not typically be used in the general long-term debt and general fixed asset groups of accounts, the Intergovernmental Service Funds or the Enterprise Funds. At the end of the fiscal period of the governmental unit, both the budgeted amounts (in the budgetary accounts of the general ledger) and the actual amounts (in the proprietary accounts in the general ledger) are closed to the fund balance account.

Program Performance Budgeting

It appears that municipalities are beginning to develop a counterpart for managerial accounting in accounting for governmental units. Governmental budgets are often constructed on the fund basis and are the line-item type. They are utilized to prevent or control expenditures from exceeding the appropriations for a particular fund. In recent years it has become apparent that concepts of cost control cost minimization and performance measurement are needed in governmental accounting if the desired services are to be provided to taxpayers as efficiently as possible or with a least cost combination of factors. One of the most significant steps toward implementing these concepts in recent years has been the increased use of program performance budgeting.

Program performance budgeting "basically involves a definition of programs and organizational objectives and a budgeting of funds on a program basis that facilitates subsequent measurement of attainment of objectives." (9) Use of this kind of a budgeting concept signifies a

recognition, on the part of the governmental accountant, of an internal
or managerial reporting function which must be assumed.

BASES OF ACCOUNTING

While nearly all of private enterprise uses the accrual basis, in
governmental accounting several bases of accounting are currently in
use. These bases can be classified as the

1. accrual basis
2. modified accrual basis
3. cash basis
4. modified cash basis

The NCGA recommends use of only the first two of these methods.
The accrual basis of accounting, as used in governmental accounting, differs in several respects from the accrual basis as used in private enterprise accounting. As already mentioned, budgeted revenues and
budgeted expenditures are recognized in the accounts of governmental
units. Similarly, encumbrances are recorded in the accounts and closed
to the fund balance or retained earnings accounts at the end of the
budget period. Executory contracts, the equivalent of encumbrances in
private enterprise accounting, are not recognized in the accounts of
private accounting entities.
The accrual basis and, hence, the realization concept employed by
governmental units in accounting for *actual* revenues and *actual* expenditures is identical to that used in private enterprise accounting. For
example, property taxes would be recognized as revenue by the governmental unit when levied. Similarly, actual expenditures or expenses are
recorded in the accounts when the corresponding goods or services are
received (i.e., when the liability is recorded), regardless of when the
cash payments are made. When the cash basis of accounting is used,
actual revenues and actual expenditures are not recorded in the accounts
until cash is received or is paid out.

Use of Accrual Basis in Government Accounting

In governmental accounting as in private enterprise accounting the
accrual basis often is more desirable than the cash basis because:

1. the cash basis does not reflect the failure to make pay-
    ments for goods and services which have been used up
2. the accrual basis permits a more accurate comparison
    (i.e., matching) of revenues and expenditures or expenses
    by period

For these reasons, the NCGA has recommended that governmental units use
the accrual basis whenever practicable.
The accrual basis is not often used in practice and, when used, it
is frequently not strictly followed. Several factors are responsible
for such practices. Legal provisions may require the particular governmental unit to be on the cash basis for certain revenues and expendi-

tures. For example, governmental units often do not record accrued interest expense at year end. This is because legal provisions characteristically do not permit an expenditure to be made or incurred prior to making an appropriation for it. Since the accrued interest will be paid in the succeeding period it would be unlawful to record accrued interest expense in the current period. Correspondingly, revenues from license fees are not customarily billed by governmental units and thus, the revenue is not accrued. In addition, governmental units may feel it is unnecessary and too costly to accrue minor expenditures and minor sources of revenue. Because of these factors governmental units often use a modified accrual basis.

Under a modified accrual basis the accrual basis is used for *major* revenues and expenditures while the cash basis is used for minor revenues and expenditures. More precisely the NCGA has defined the modified accrual basis as "that method of accounting in which expenditures other than accrued interest on general long-term debt are recorded at the time liabilities are incurred and revenues are recorded when cash is received, except for material or available revenues which should be accrued to reflect properly the taxes levied and the revenues earned." (10) The modified accrual basis is suggested by NCGA for use in accounting for the General, Special Revenue, and Debt Service Funds while the full accrual basis is recommended for the other funds.

The fourth basis of accounting found among governmental units is the modified cash basis which is thought to be desirable because it is conservative. With this basis, accounting for revenues is on the cash basis and accounting for expenditures is on the accrual basis.

MATCHING CONCEPT

The matching concept takes on a different meaning in governmental accounting than it does in private enterprise accounting. In an earlier section, terms used in governmental accounting were equated with terms used in private enterprise accounting. Strictly speaking, this equating is probably valid for revenue, but not for expenses and expenditures.

In its most recent statement, *Governmental Accounting, Auditing and Financial Reporting*, the NCGA defined revenues as being essentially "Additions to assets . . ." This is in accordance with widely held concepts in financial accounting theory of revenue as an "inflow of assets . . ." (11)

Another important aspect of revenue in governmental accounting deserves mention. What may be revenue to a particular fund may not be revenue to the governmental unit as a whole. This case arises when a transaction increases the ownership equity of a particular fund but not of the governmental unit. Examples of such transactions would be

1. where one fund sells services to another
2. when the proceeds of a bond issue are treated as revenue of the Capital Projects Fund while the corresponding bond liability is carried in the general long-term debt group of accounts rather than the Capital Projects Fund

Contrast of Expenses and Expenditures

There are significant differences in the terms "expenses" and "expenditures" which alter the definition of the matching concept in governmental accounting. The following equations define the matching concept in private enterprise accounting (equation 1) and governmental accounting (equations 2 and 3).

1. revenues – expenses = income
2. revenues – expenditures = change in fund balance
3. revenues – expenditures – encumbrances = unencumbered
                                                fund balance

In private enterprise accounting, costs are incurred in the process of generating revenue signifying the existence of the profit motive. Expenditures are made or costs are incurred to acquire goods and services which will subsequently generate revenues.

For a private enterprise, total expenses of a period consist of that portion of total costs which have been used up in the process of generating revenue. Accordingly, only the expense portion of an expenditure is matched with revenue in private enterprises. The remaining portion of the expenditure is carried into the next period as an asset.

In governmental accounting, however, all expenditures, whether or not used up in the current period, are matched against revenues of the period. Governmental units match revenues and expenditures in order to determine the balance in the Fund Balance or Retained Earnings accounts rather than to determine income. This procedure is tantamount to matching revenues and expenditures by administrations. Therefore, the total expenditure made by the general fund for the purchase of a fixed asset is matched with revenue of the current period rather than being matched with revenues of both the current period and future periods. For this reason fixed assets are not carried in the general fund. Also, for this reason depreciation is not recorded in governmental accounts. In other words, the *total cost* of the asset purchased is deducted from the fund balance in the period it is purchased.

Another important difference in the matching concept as used in governmental accounting that should be clearly understood is that, theoretically, the expenses in equation 1 above, generated the corresponding revenue in the equation. In governmental equation 2, however, the *expenditures are not thought of as generating the revenue* in the equation. Expenditures are more the result of revenues than the cause of revenues. Revenues are thought of as making it possible for the governmental unit to carry on certain activities and services for its citizens. These activities and services are indicated by the expenditures made during the year.

As shown in equation 3 above, the application of the matching concept goes a bit further in governmental accounting and, in addition to expenditures, also matches executory contracts or contractual commitments (e.g., purchase orders, salary commitments) with revenues. The result of this matching process is an unencumbered balance in the Fund Balance account for the period. Encumbered balances are not available for appropriation in succeeding period because they have been earmarked, for contracts entered into in previous periods. In private enterprise accounting contractual commitments do not enter into the matching process.

OTHER CONCEPTS

A number of other concepts do not warrant extended discussion but are worthy of mention.

Depreciation

The NCGA takes the position that depreciation on general fixed assets should not be recorded in the accounts unless cash is actually set aside for their replacement. (12) If cash is set aside the depreciation qualifies as an expenditure for which an appropriation can be budgeted. In private enterprise accounting, depreciation is the process of allocating the cost of a fixed asset to the periods which benefited, in terms of revenues derived from the use of the asset. In contrast, general fixed assets of a governmental unit do not generate revenues.

In commercial accounting the primary purpose of the depreciation process is income determination. Since governmental units are not interested in determining income, by matching revenues and expenses or otherwise, the depreciation process serves no useful purpose. Depreciation may be computed to aid in making internal management decisions of the municipality, such as determining sales prices to recover all costs. However, the depreciation computations made for management purposes should not enter the accounts. (13)

Transactions

Private enterprise accounting is transactions-based. In contrast, governmental units record budgeted amounts in formal accounts prior to the occurrence of transactions with outside independent parties. Further, all the various aspects of a single transaction are not recorded in one place, but are scattered throughout the numerous funds or accounting entities which make up the government unit. For example, the proceeds of a bond issue may be deposited and accounted for in a Capital Projects Fund. The related periodic sinking fund payments may be drawn from the General Fund and deposited and accounted for in the Debt Service Fund. The general bonded debt and interest group of accounts will record the long-term bond liability as well as accrue the payments and earnings required in the Debt Service Fund to be able to discharge the bond obligation at maturity.

Tax Constraints

Governmental units are exempt from income and other taxes. As a result they are free to develop accounting systems and financial reporting principles without the constraint of simultaneously satisfying tax laws. Municipalities do not have to guard against the tendency to adopt reporting principles which minimize income taxes but, at the same time, distort financial reports.

Current Values

Governmental accountants need not be concerned with introducing current (market or replacement) values into their accounts and statements. Current value theorists want such values in the accounts so that measures of income may be improved. However, governmental units do not attempt to determine income and thus, historical cost remains the unchallenged valuation concept for most purposes.

Financial Reports

Most governmental units issue reports yearly. The contents can vary considerably. Generally, a balance sheet is prepared for all funds. In addition, four other statements can usually be prepared:

1. analysis of changes in fund balances or retained earnings
2. statement of expenditures and encumbrances compared with appropriations
3. statement of revenues—estimated and actual
4. statement of cash receipts and cash disbursements

A number of other special, less important statements are prepared for various funds and groups of accounts. In addition to these statements, a wide variety of statistical tables and summaries for items such as tax rates, tax collections, debt service charges, salaries of principal officials and the like will generally be included in a separate statistical section of the annual report.

SUMMARY

CPAs and other accountants are being called upon in increasing numbers to serve the public interest by participating in various aspects of governmental accounting. This trend is expected to continue. Governmental accounting principles have not been subjected to the rigorous theoretical study and examination as have accounting principles of private business enterprises. Nor is there an authoritative source of the stature of the AICPA and its Accounting Principles Board (or the newly formed FASB) to which the CPA may turn. However, in recent years the NCGA has made great strides to establish itself as the counterpart of the APB (FASB) in the field of governmental accounting.

Generally accepted accounting principles for private business enterprises are not always applicable to governmental accounting. Some of the more important differences in the application of basic accounting concepts and principles have been presented here. Given these circumstances and this introduction to governmental accounting theory, it is imperative that the CPA broaden his exposure even further if he is to serve local government and thus, the public interest, in the capacity of a professional.

FOOTNOTES

1. Bruce Joplin, "Local Government Accounting: It's Your Responsibility, Too," *The Journal of Accountancy* (August, 1967), p. 38.
2. Three examples of such activities can be found in the April, 1967 issue of *The Journal of Accountancy*:
    a. The Business Management Study Committee for Illinois in which some thirteen CPA firms and twenty individual CPAs participated without compensation ("Illinois Group Completes Management Study," pp. 10, 12).
    b. Three of the national CPA firms, without compensation and at the request of Governor Ronald Reagan, have devoted over 600 man hours studying California's General Fund finances. Because of the limited nature of the inquiry a disclaimer of opinion was issued on the fairness of the financial data presented ("CPAs Study California Finances," p. 12),
    c. A group of Michigan CPAs, known as the Governor's Task Force on Expenditure Management, was appointed by Governor Romney in 1962 and spent three years investigating ways to help the state government achieve an "adequate level of management efficiency" (John J. Fox, "Michigan's Task Force on Expenditure Management," pp. 37-42).
3. Irving Tenner and Edward S. Lynn, *Municipal and Governmental Accounting*, fourth edition (Englewood Cliffs, New Jersey: Prentice-Hall, Inc.), 1960, p. 2.
4. Committee to Prepare a Statement of Basic Accounting Theory, *A Statement of Basic Accounting Theory* (Evanston, Illinois: American Accounting Association), 1966, p. 1.
5. National Committee on Governmental Accounting (NCGA), *Governmental Accounting, Auditing and Financial Reporting* (Chicago: Municipal Finance Officers Association), 1968, pp. 151-172. An important task which the NCGA attempted in this statement was uniformity of terminology between governmental and private enterprise fields of accounting.
6. "Retained Earnings" is the appropriate equity account title to use in connection with funds of a commercial nature while "Fund Balance" is the appropriate equity title for other non-commercial type funds.
7. NCGA, op. cit., p. 161.
8. Ibid., p. 7-8.
9. John J. Fox, "Michigan's Task Force on Expenditure Management," *The Journal of Accountancy* (April, 1967), p. 38.
10. NCGA, op. cit., p. 11.
11. Eldon S. Hendrikson, *Accounting Theory* (Homewood, Illinois: Richard D. Irwin, Inc.), 1965, pp. 128-129.
12. NCGA, op. cit., p. 2.
13. There are some governmental operations, usually accounted for in the Enterprise or Intragovernmental Service Funds, which possess all the characteristics of a private enterprise (e.g., a municipally owned and operated power plant). To determine the costs and effectiveness of carrying on

such operations on a continuing basis it is often desirable to record depreciation in the accounts of the funds
involved.

QUESTIONS

1. What are the objectives of accounting for government?
2. Define fund as used in governmental accounting.
3. Why does governmental accounting require separate
   funds for various specific purposes?
4. Why are budgeted revenues and expenses recognized in
   the regular governmental accounts?
5. Describe program performance budgeting. How does the
   lack of the profit motive affect governmental efficiency?
6. How do the following differ under governmental accounting
   from accounting for profit-seeking units:
   a. bases of accounting
   b. matching concept
   c. depreciation
   d. financial reports

83　　　　　　　　MULTINATIONAL FIRMS NOW DOMINATE
　　　　　　　　　　　MUCH OF WORLD'S PRODUCTION

Charles N. Stabler

(Reprinted by permission from the *Wall Street Journal* (April 8,
1973). © Dow Jones & Company, Inc., 1973.)

A random selection of facts about world trade:

1. Of the 120 largest industrial corporations in Belgium, 48
   are controlled partly or wholly from abroad. And it is
   forecast that in a few years one of every five Belgian
   manufacturing workers will work for a foreign—and probably American—company.
2. German corporations now have more capital invested in
   South Carolina than anywhere else in the world except
   Germany. (The investment is in chemical and textile
   plants.)
3. Some 90 percent of Europe's production of microcircuits is
   controlled by American companies.
4. Switzerland's largest corporation, Nestle Alimentana S.A.,
   does 98 percent of its business outside Switzerland.
5. If a corporation's sales were to be equated with a nation's
   output of goods and services, then 51 of the world's 100

> biggest money powers would be international corporations and only 49 would be countries.
>
> 6. Large international companies currently do about $500 billion of annual business in each other's territories, or about one-sixth of the world's gross product. That's more than the entire gross national product of Japan.

The conclusion to be derived from these facts, analysts say, is inescapable: The era of the multinational corporation, the so-called super-company, is upon us—to the point that a few hundred concerns have in recent years grown beyond the size of all but the wealthiest nations and currently dominate much of the world's production, resources and financial affairs.

And they are still growing—growing, in fact, at a rate double that of purely domestic companies—and consequently are creating an economic and social movement that some observers compare in significance to the Industrial Revolution.

"TRULY REVOLUTIONARY"

"The multinational corporation is neither a new development in the world economy nor an unknown phenomenon in economic history, but its (current) effect on the international economic system is truly revolutionary," says a recent study by Lawrence B. Krause, a Brookings Institution economist. He explains: "The growth of international transactions of multinational corporations has already overwhelmed the more traditional forms of international trade and capital flows for some countries and has become much more important to the world economy in general."

If the importance of the multinational movement is undeniable, its effects have become a center of rising debate. Some welcome the trend, seeing the growth of the multinationals as promoting international cooperation and improving living standards throughout the world. But others fear the long-term results of the movement, citing in particular the threat to the sovereignty of nations.

Whatever the merits of the two sides' respective arguments, interviews with company executives and financiers, labor leaders and government officials in the U.S. and Europe demonstrate that multinational corporations, after two decades of spectacular growth, are currently under attack as never before. "There's no doubt the rapid development of this corporate beast has stirred up the natives," says Elliott Haynes, executive vice president of Business International Corporation in New York. The multinationals, he adds, "are seen as having enormous power—relatively uncontrolled."

The power of multinationals, in fact, has grown to the point that their role in the world's economy seems irreversible. "Both its adherents and opponents acknowledge that the multinational corporation is here to stay and will probably grow in the future," says a study by the U.S. Department of Commerce. "What is at issue at this juncture is the degree of freedom that should be allowed or the nature and extent of regulation that should be imposed on its present operations and future growth in order to make it better serve often divergent national interests."

HEART OF THE MATTER

Indeed, "divergent national interests" lie at the heart of the multinationals controversy. In theory, a multinational roams the world to acquire raw materials and capital where they are most abundant, manufactures products where wages and other costs are lowest and sells in the most profitable markets. This is the economic law of comparative advantage, which says in effect that everyone benefits most if each person does the kind of work he is best at. But in practice, pursuit of such comparative advantage sometimes appears to conflict with the national goals of governments or other powerful interest groups within a nation.

Take the case of Canada, where U.S. corporate ownership is a perennial political issue. U.S. interests currently own 45 percent of Canada's manufacturing operations, 56 percent of its mining and smelting and 60 percent of its petroleum and natural gas. As a result, the Trudeau government will this year seek broad legislative restrictions on foreign takeovers of Canadian companies. Its bill would require government scrutiny of foreign acquisitions of all but the smallest domestic concerns to ensure that a merger is "of significant benefit to Canada."

Across the Atlantic in the industrialized nations of Europe, which together encompass about one-third of U.S. foreign direct investment, the threat of new economic invasion by Japanese companies is stirring a burst of protectionist sentiment. "Foreign investment is broadly regarded as beneficial," says an economic adviser to the British government, "but there is a growing feeling that we're not getting as much benefit from it as we should. There's going to be a good deal more hard bargaining (on foreign acquisitions) in future years."

Already there are restraints, mostly informal but effective nonetheless, on the entry of foreign business into Common Market nations, especially if the foreigner plans a takeover of a domestic company in an industry considered to be vital. "Somewhere in a desk drawer of a top official of every capital there is a list of companies that they simply won't allow to be taken over," says an economist at the Brussels headquarters of the European Economic Community. "No more automobile companies are going to be taken over, for example, and no more computer companies."

The future of multinationals is even less secure in underdeveloped countries—the so-called Third World—where foreign corporations are often attacked as instruments of colonialism. Chile's Marxist government, of course, has simply expelled the unwanted companies, and in many other countries—Mexico, for one—the foreigners' operations are coming under tighter government controls.

"Today, among Third World Countries, only Brazil, some Central American republics and a few of the newer African countries give foreign investment a warm welcome," Harry Heltzer, chairman of Minnesota Mining & Manufacturing Company, recently said.

Most of the political fireworks touched off by multinationals, though, are in the U.S. The activities of International Telephone & Telegraph Company in connection with its operations in Chile have already had its executives on the griddle before a subcommittee of the Senate Foreign Relations Committee. Other major multinationals, in-

cluding Ford Motor Company, General Electric Company, and International
Business Machines, are slated to testify on a broad range of issues.

Concurrently, 86 Congressmen are cosponsoring the proposed Foreign
Trade and Investment Act of 1972, dubbed the Burke-Hartke bill for its
original sponsors, Rep. James Burke (D., Mass.) and Sen. Vance Hartke
(D., Ind.). The measure would raise taxes on the income of multinational corporations, curb capital flows, restrict transfer of patents and
technology to foreign affiliates and allow for curtailment of U.S. imports through quotas.

All the bill does, Sen. Hartke says, "Is ensure that our high
standard of living shall not be jeopardized by international piracy and
tax-loophole seeking and that less fortunate persons abroad shall not be
victimized by U.S. multinational corporations seeking advantage in sub-
standard economies at the expense of standard ones."

In a historic reversal of the traditional free-trade advocacy of
U.S. labor unions, the Burke-Hartke bill is strongly supported by the
AFL-CIO. Organized labor's researchers have estimated foreign operations of U.S.-based multinational corporations resulted in the "export"
of 500,000 jobs in the late 1960s—mostly to low-wage areas like Taiwan
and Hong Kong. And Elizabeth R. Jager, an AFL-CIO economist, contends
in a recent study that today's real world is "a far cry from the never-
never land of the (economic) textbooks."

As might be expected, however, business groups are mounting intense
opposition to the bill. Armed with data from the U.S. Department of
Commerce and from a blizzard of new studies by international trade
groups, businessmen are attempting to counter what they see as rising
protectionism. Referring to allegations that U.S. jobs are being lost
to other countries, for example, they cite a recent study of 125 major
multinational corporations showing that their employment in the U.S. in
recent years has risen two-and-a-half times as fast as employment in the
average domestic company. They also cite studies showing that only a
small portion, possibly 8 percent, of the output of foreign affiliates
of U.S. companies comes back as imports—with most of these imports
coming from Canada and other nations where wage rates are comparable to
those in the U.S.

Indeed, officials of multinational companies strongly maintain that
if they are forced to curtail overseas operations, the results will by
no means improve the lot of U.S. workers. "The Burke-Hartke bill assumes that if U.S. multinational corporations close down their manufacturing plants abroad, they will be forced to supply their markets from
plants built in the U.S. employing American labor. That is the key
fallacy of the bill," says an American Cyanamid Company analysis of the
situation.

The Department of Commerce corroborates this viewpoint. "If the
products in question weren't produced and supplied from abroad by U.S.
affiliates, they would likely be supplied by foreign competitors," the
department says. "The choice, therefore, is often not between U.S. or
foreign operations but between foreign operations and no operations at
all."

To further get their point across, many companies are taking the
issue straight to their employees and asking them to write their Congressmen and oppose protectionist measures. Typically, Monsanto Company has published in employee newsletters and posted on bulletin boards
a series of articles warning that 4,200 of its U.S. employees, or 10

percent of the company's work force, "are dependent on exports from our U.S. plants for their jobs."

Whether such opposition on the part of the multinationals will prove effective remains to be seen.   At the moment, observers feel that the fate of the Burke-Hartke bill is dubious, at least as a total package, largely because its provisions are so sweeping.   (President Nixon recently told Congress that "our income taxes aren't the cause of our trade problems and changes won't solve them," adding that the present system of taxing profits earned abroad "is fundamentally sound.")   But with Congressmen concerned about high unemployment in many districts and industries, some facets of the measure are expected to appear as riders on other legislation.

Along with political pressures, competition among themselves is making the going rougher for the multinational companies.   European and particularly Japanese multinationals have proliferated in recent years and are expected by most analysts to outpace the Americans in the years ahead.   "The thrust was from West to East, in the 1970s, but now it will be reversed," says Nicholas A. H. Stacy, managing director of Chesam Amalgamations & Investments Limited, a London merger consultant. Mr. Stacy recently visited the U.S. seeking merger candidates for his clients and returned to England, he says, "with the feeling that America is for sale.   I have several U.S. banks, insurance companies and some sizable industrial companies available for my clients."

Still, American multinationals are currently far and away the biggest and most numerous of all.   The Commerce Department lists some 3,000 companies as falling within regulations governing foreign investment.   (Most analysts, however, figure that no more than 200 account for the bulk of U.S. offshore operations.)   During the 1960s, U.S. companies more than doubled the overseas capital on their books, boosting direct investment to $86 billion in 1971.

And the operations of these and other nations' super-companies, despite the political and economic storms swirling about them, are expected to become increasingly multinational—and interrelated.   Fairly typically, Squibb Corporation, a New York-based pharmaceuticals and food company, invested $259 million overseas in the last five years and now projects foreign sales gains of 14 percent annually, against a 10 percent increase for domestic sales.   And, though the deal recently fell through, Squibb had planned to sell its Beech-Nut baby food business in the U.S. to a British company, Cavenham Limited, which in turn is an affiliate of a French company, Generale Occidentale S.A.

QUESTIONS

1. Explain the law of comparative advantage.
2. What implications do you see for accounting in the world-wide operations of businesses?
3. Presuming that you are living in the United States, of what interest is it to you that you can buy either a Datsun or a Ford automobile?
4. From an economic viewpoint, do you care who owns the stock of Datsun or Ford?   From a political point of view, do you

care who owns the stock of Datsun or Ford? From the
pricing of the auto point of view, do you care if the
Ford was built in the U.S. or if the Datsun was built
in Japan? Does this make a difference to you and if
so, how?

---

84   PANEL AIMS TO UNIFY ACCOUNTING METHODS
                ACROSS GLOBE, SEES STRONG EFFECT BY '83

Richard F. Janssen

(Reprinted by permission from the *Wall Street Journal* (July 2,
1973). © Dow Jones & Company, Inc., 1973.)

If the nuclear superpowers can't quite bring order to the world,
perhaps the timid bookkeepers can.

They're starting, at least, on a crusade to bring uniform standards
to the way businesses across the globe present their figures to the
public. Representatives of the accounting bodies of nine nations opened
the battle by forming an international accounting standards committee.

Practices vary so widely from one nation to another that there is
"a lot of suspicion and doubt about what comes from any other company,"
Sir Henry Alexander Benson, committee chairman and a senior partner in
Coopers & Lybrand here, told a news conference.

The panel hopes to have its first proposed international standard
circulating in about 18 months or so, Sir Henry said, with a "constant
stream" of proposals after that. Describing himself as an "enthusiast
and a bigot" in favor of uniformity, he predicted that "the effect will
be profound within the next ten years."

The problems also will be profound, participants at the initial
meeting agreed, because many sharply differing accounting practices are
entrenched in both law and custom. For instance, American corporations
typically present annual reports in which results of subsidiaries are
consolidated, while many European companies show them separately if at
all. "That way, if a subsidiary is losing money, a company can just
leave it out," one European accountant commented.

While accountants from the U.S. and other nations involved all report their own corporate clients to be eager for standardization, they
also tend to think their own national practices are the ones that
should be adopted. It's recognized that "there must be give and take,"
says Wallace E. Olson, executive vice president of the New York-based
American Institute of Certified Public Accountants. But he adds: "We
assume" that the results "won't be terribly inconsistent with the basic
standards that exist in the U.S."

TOWARD THE U.S. STYLE

There's already some movement abroad toward the U.S. style. But the movement also shows the magnitude of the differences. For instance, the West German chemical company, Badische Anilin & Soda-Fabrik AG, had started publishing figures on a basis that it says conforms to regulations of the U.S. Securities & Exchange Commission. On that basis, it had per-share earnings last year of 9.07 German marks.

But when the earnings "are adjusted according to the method of the German Association of Financial Analysts," Finance Director Rolf Magener explained earlier this year, "so-called extraordinary and noncurrent items are excluded," and earnings would show up as 12.47 marks. In reporting on the broader BASF group, the company uses German rules for German units, and SEC standards for foreign ones, in or out of the U.S. If the American rules applied to the whole group, the company says, stockholders equity would be increased the equivalent of almost $300 million.

By one accounting device or another, European companies tend to show as modest a profit and asset picture as they can, a trait that isn't often shared by American managements. "Don't believe me when I tell you how much difficulty we will have in maintaining earnings this year," confides one Continental executive.

To disclose their full dimensions, he explains, would only invite trouble from stockholders clamoring for higher dividends, from workers wanting higher wages, from customers complaining that prices could be reduced, from tax authorities wondering if they've been getting too little all along, and, perhaps most worrisomely, from left-wing politicians demanding crackdowns or nationalization.

Some Dutch companies treat themselves to a less lofty profit figure by adjusting for inflation; the effect is much the same as when government statisticians strip away price increases to show "real" wages or gross national product. The electronics company, NV Philips Gloeilampenfabrieken, reported net equal to $221.3 million last year, explaining that if it had followed U.S. principles the total would be $256.9 million.

Basically, Philips values assets such as buildings at the cost of replacing them, usually a much higher sum than the original cost. Depreciation is figured against these higher values, so a bigger sum is deducted in reaching net income. "We believe we are showing the truth," says P. C. Louwers, chief internal auditor. Asked if the company would give up this means of demonstrating the eroding effect of inflation on profit, he replies, it certainly wouldn't.

What Philips calls the "economical method" of adjusting earnings isn't accepted by the Dutch revenue men, Mr. Louwers adds. But it does let the company argue that if the government says it's taking profit at a 40 percent rate, the effect is really 50 percent of "real" earnings, he explains. Some such method of inflation adjustment is being considered by U.S. accountants, notes Mr. Olson of the American accounting institute.

"HIDDEN RESERVES"

Concealment of assets is a European practice that also will make standardization difficult. Some German executives more-or-less openly boast about the growth in "hidden reserves," and bank earnings reports contain such intriguing entries as "published reserves." Even with the reams of footnotes, concedes one candid bank aide, "we really might as well abstain from publishing any reserves figures because they aren't comparable" to those in the U.S.

Laws will have to be changed in many nations to yield more comparable reports, the accountants committee to be based here notes. Switzerland recently went through that process on bank accounting, with results that show the myriad possibilities. As the Basel-based Swiss Bank Corporation notes in its annual report, it has to show actual dividend and interest income on its own portfolio of securities. "Previous practice," it explains, "was to calculate a fixed interest on average security holdings which was then booked to interest received."

Aware of the pitfalls of getting into heavily specialized problems, the London committee will concentrate on fundamentals, Sir Henry says, such as a "crisp and clear" explanation of how assets are valued, the minimum amount of information to be made public, depreciation methods, and how currency conversions and associated companies are treated in consolidated accounts. They'll seek cooperation by governments and stock exchanges, to increase the prospects for "sanctions" to enforce standard rules, he adds.

The outgrowth of last year's Congress of Accountants in Australia, the new committee has members from the U.S., Britain, Australia, Canada, France, Germany, Japan, Mexico, and the Netherlands. But 40 to 50 more national accountancy groups are expected to become associate members soon. Standardization is "really imperative" as business becomes more international, Sir Henry says, "otherwise investors, and creditors and indeed the staff don't really know what they're dealing with."

QUESTIONS

1. Do you think that international standards of accounting are desirable and feasible for all aspects of accounting? For some aspects of accounting? Explain.
2. Describe the current state of world accounting principles.
3. When a firm changes the value of a depreciable asset, it can be said that they increase wealth and decrease current income. Discuss and explain the difference between wealth and income.

85   MATERIALITY IN ACCOUNTING

G. A. Anderson

(A paper commissioned by the Research and Publications Committee
of The Institute of Chartered Accountants of Scotland. First published
in *The Accountant's Magazine* (April, 1973), the official journal of that
Institute. It is reproduced here by permission of the Committee, the
editor, and the author.)

(G. A. Anderson is a member of the firm of Arthur Young McClelland
Moores & Co.)

EVOLUTION OF FINANCIAL STATEMENTS

When accounts were prepared on a cash basis there was no doubt as
to what should be included. All the information was factual and there
was no requirement to exercise judgment except in determining those figures which required to be separately disclosed and the general method of
disclosure. With the evolution of the accruals basis of accounting,
with the greater significance in accounting statements of items such as
stock and work-in-progress which depend on estimation or judgment, with
the increased scale of industrial and commercial undertakings and with
the greater speed with which financial statements now have to be completed, such statements of necessity became less precise.

In exercising judgment as to the value of an item of stock, as to
the possibility of a future sale or as to the recovery of a debt, it is
possible—indeed probable—that different individuals will arrive at
different results. One significant reason for this is that each will
attribute varying degrees of importance to the factors involved. In
short, they will have a different idea as to the materiality of factor A
in relation to factor B. In the same way, the degree of precision which
each assessor will use in arriving at his estimate or judgment will depend on how material he regards the result in relation to the context in
which it is to be used.

In determining the accuracy of the accrual for outstanding invoices
or of the provision required for bad debts or obsolete stock, the accountant has some regard to the size of the final figures in the statement—the profit, the total creditors, the sales ledger balances, and
the stock. His degree of precision is, or should be, affected by the
relationship of one figure to another. He is concerned with materiality
in accounting. It is a logical extension of materiality in accounting
to consider materiality in auditing, but that involves many additional
considerations and is outside the scope of the present study. The
thoughts which follow are based on the premise that the underlying
transactions are properly entered in the books of the undertaking, and
we consider solely the presentation of these transactions in various
financial statements.

THE MEANING OF MATERIALITY

The concept of materiality is vitally important in framing and understanding financial statements. A dictionary definition of the word "materiality" attributes to it such meanings as "substantial," "essential," or "important." In the various government and professional regulations, notably the Companies Acts 1948 and 1967, the pronouncements of the Accounting Standards Steering Committee and the regulations of the Securities & Exchange Commission in America, instructions are given as to what is to be done or disclosed with regard to material amounts, but in none of these regulations is "material" defined.

The Institute of Chartered Accountants in England and Wales issued a statement for the guidance of members, in July, 1968, entitled, "Interpretation of 'material' in relation to Accounts." In that statement there were the following words:

In an accounting sense, however, a matter is material if its nondisclosure, misstatement or omission would be likely to distort the view given by the accounts or other statement under consideration.

A United States definition was suggested by the legal counsel for the American Institute in 1933:

A material fact is a fact the untrue statement or omission of which would be likely to affect the conduct of a reasonable man with reference to the acquisition, holding or disposal of the security in question.

In the current text of the AICPA's Accounting Principles Board (soon to be wound up) the question of materiality is dealt with in the following terms in paragraph II:

The committee contemplates that its opinions will have application only to items material and significant in the relative circumstances. It considers that items of little or no consequence may be dealt with as expediency may suggest. However, freedom to deal expediently with immaterial items should not extend to a group of items whose cumulative effect in any one financial statement may be material and significant.

THE NEED FOR GUIDELINES OR A "STANDARD"

In many articles on the concept of materiality it has been claimed, rightly, that the assessment of how material an item is, is a matter of judgment. At a time when accounting conventions are under attack because the element of choice or judgment is applied in an arbitrary way, it is relevant to consider whether the free exercise of judgment does not require more precise guidelines than have been utilized in the past. The program of Statements of Standard Accounting Practice inaugurated in 1970 has as two of its objectives:

1. to narrow the areas of difference and variety in account-
    ing practice
2. to ensure the disclosure of accounting bases adopted in
    situations where accounts include significant items which
    depend substantially on judgments of value, or on the
    estimated outcome of future events or on uncompleted
    transactions

In view of the frequency with which the word "material" occurs in
Schedule 2 to the Companies Act 1967 and in Exposure Drafts and Statements of Standard Accounting Practice, it would seem impracticable to
achieve the foregoing objectives unless the areas of difference in assessing materiality are narrowed by disclosing the yardsticks against
which they are measured or setting down standard guidelines, departures
from which would require disclosure.
The proposals which follow are an attempt to:

1. propose suitable yardsticks against which to measure mate-
    riality
2. indicate guidelines appropriate in particular circum-
    stances, departure from which would require disclosure or
    comment

OTHER EXAMPLES

Standards or guidelines for assessing materiality are not a new
concept. The following examples are found in the United States of
America at present:

1. Regulations S-X, published by the U.S. Securities & Ex-
    change Commission, dealing with the Form and Content of
    Financial Statements contains, *inter alia*, the following
    requirements for disclosure of certain items if they
    exceed a certain limit:
    a. Rule 5—02 Balance Sheets
       . . . balance sheets filed . . . shall comply with the
       following provisions:
         7. Other current assets—(*a*) State separately . . .
            (3) any other amounts in excess of ten percent of
            total current assets . . .
         12. Other Investments—State separately, . . . any
             items in excess of ten percent of the amount of all
             assets other than fixed and tangible.
    b. Rule 5—03 Profit and Loss or Income Statements
       . . . the profit and loss or income statement shall
       comply with this rule . . .
       (*c*) If income is derived from both gross sales and op-
            erating revenues, the two classes may be combined
            in one amount if the lesser amount is not more than
            ten percent of the sum of the two items.
    c. Rule 5—04 what Schedules are to be Filed
       Schedule I Marketable Securities . . . —The schedule

> prescribed . . . shall be filed . . . (2) . . . if the
> amount at which other security investments is carried
> . . . constitutes 15 percent or more of total assets.
> Schedule II Amounts due from directors, officers, and
> principal holders of equity securities, . . . The sched-
> ule prescribed . . . shall be filed with respect to
> each person . . . from whom an aggregate indebtedness
> of more than $20,000 or one percent of total assets,
> whichever is less, is owed . . ."

2. Suggestions from accounting literature in U.S. of items
   to be considered material:
   a. Any account when it is the range of 10 to 20 percent of
      the average net income. (Carman G. Blough, "Some Sug-
      gested Criteria for Determining Materiality," *Journal
      of Accountancy*, vol. 89, pp. 353-354.)
   b. Any balance sheet account if it exceeds five percent of
      its balance sheet caption. (Delmer P. Hylton, "Some
      comments on Materiality," *Journal of Accountancy*, vol.
      112, pp. 61-64.)

ELEMENTS OF MATERIALITY

It is essential to recognize that there are two elements of an item
which are relevant to its materiality. The first and most obvious of
these is its quantum or amount and the second is its particular characteristic which, if significant to the proper understanding of a financial statement, might require it to be separately identified and disclosed. For example an item might be judged material if it represented,
say, five percent of the total assets, but it would be unnecessary to
subdivide each individual group of assets into its constituents until
each item were less than five percent of the total if the characteristics of two or more subdivisions were identical. There are obviously
items which require separate disclosure to comply with the statutes or
with Stock Exchange requirements, where the quantum is not material to
a proper understanding of the financial position (e.g., the remuneration
of the auditors). Conversely, there are items such as trade and other
debtors which in the context of a particular organization can be shown
as one item, irrespective of amount, but which in another context require separate subdivision by reason of a difference in security or
collectability.

A VALID COMPARISON?

If we follow the English Institute definition of materiality and
endeavor to assess whether a financial statement is distorted by the
nondisclosure, misstatement, or omission of a fact, we do so by means
of comparison. We compare the undisclosed, misstated, or omitted fact
with a suitable yardstick. Obviously the materiality which we are measuring is in the context of a particular statement (e.g., annual accounts) or set of statements (e.g., the last five years' accounts) so
that the yardstick must be chosen from *those statements*.

This fundamental principle is equally true for both the elements of materiality referred to above. The quantum element must have regard to the other figures within the statement or statements being considered. If it were to be suggested that the materiality in terms of size is affected by the figures in some other organization, then the yardstick is not the financial statement of one organization but the financial statements of a number of organizations. The characteristic element must be judged in relation to the purpose for which the statement is being examined. Is it significant to know that $£x$ of trade debtors' balances are due by export customers or that $£y$ of turnover is in respect to spare parts and not complete machines? If the answer is in the affirmative, then, given that the quantum is material also, there should be a subdivision and disclosure of separate figures.

The financial statements which give rise to questions of materiality in accounting are many and varied but the most common are—

1. the profit and loss account or income statement
2. the balance sheet
3. the statement of source and application of funds

In establishing guidelines to assess materiality it is not necessarily correct to regard one base as appropriate to each of these three financial statements. Nevertheless, the most common motive in examining a set of financial statements is to assess the earning power of the organization, and the most common yardstick is one based on earnings or profits. Accordingly that alternative is considered first.

A "PROFIT" YARDSTICK

The choice of a base for measuring materiality is considered in Appendix I of the paper "Materiality in Auditing" presented by the Canadian Institute of Chartered Accountants in 1965. In that Appendix the alternatives of

1. sales or revenue
2. actual net profit
3. "standard" net profit
4. actual gross profit

are reviewed. Sales, or revenue, is discarded since profitability is more important than volume, and actual net profit is discarded as being too unstable. The Canadian study prefers actual gross profits as being simple to use, objective and reasonably constant, but it suffers from the major drawback that the ratio of net profit to gross profit is higher for manufacturers than for wholesalers and higher for wholesalers than for retailers. The choice of such a base would be more restrictive in terms of net profit for manufacturers than for retailers and is not considered appropriate for the purposes of this paper.

It is therefore proposed that the base to be chosen for determining the quantum element of materiality in the Profit and Loss Account or Income Statement should be "standard" net profit. In this context the "standard net profit" would be the average net profit before taxation of the preceding five years. This standard would require to be adjusted

for any long-term trend or material change in size of the organization
during the five year period, but it should even out wide fluctuations
and avoid the need for additional disclosure of "material" amounts by
reason of a temporary drop in profits.

LOSSES OR LOW PROFITS

Where an organization is making losses or abnormally low profits
over a period of years the "standard net profit" base for measuring materiality is not appropriate. A break-even situation, where a profit
of, say, £5,000 is brought down from a turnover of, say, £5 million,
demonstrates the defects of a rigid arithmetical approach, and a fluctuating trend of profits and losses can produce the same result when
averaged over five years. Clearly these circumstances call for a reasonable alternative and sensible judgment, otherwise the statement would
become meaningless with a proliferation of figures. The English Institute statement of July, 1968 advises the consideration of the more normal dimensions of the business but is not more explicit than that.
There are two possible solutions to this problem, which are suggested as appropriate in the respective situations of

1. an organization making losses or low profits in an industry
    where normal profits are being earned by other concerns
2. an industry where profits generally are low in relation to
    volume of turnover (or total expense)

In the first case, of the exceptional company, it is suggested that
a notional "standard net profit" be computed by applying the appropriate
rate of return for that size of organization in that industry to the
actual capital employed. Such a calculation is obviously open to
criticism as being arbitrary or as involving further estimation, but
even with its defects it should provide an adequate guide as to an appropriate quantum of materiality in what is in any case an uncommon
situation.
In the second case, of the low-profit industry, it is relevant to
consider turnover (or perhaps total expenses) rather than "standard net
profit." In order to determine whether to base the materiality level on
such a "volume" yardstick, the ratio of profit to turnover (or total
expense) should first be ascertained. If this were, say, three percent
or less, the materiality yardstick should be related to the turnover
(or total expense). If the ratio exceeded three percent then the materiality should be based on the notional "standard net profit" as outlined above for the unprofitable concern in the profitable industry.

OTHER YARDSTICKS

We have regarded an item as being material if its nondisclosure,
misstatement, or omission would be likely to distort the view given by
the statement under consideration. Ignoring for the moment the nondisclosure of omission and dealing solely with misstatement in terms of
figures, let us consider a possible error in amount. Our yardstick is
required to assess the point at which an incorrect figure becomes

material or causes a material distortion. There are undoubtedly errors
in figures, which arise as between one balance sheet item and another,
but the most important errors in amount affect the profit and loss account or income statement either wholly or in part. If the quantum of
an error is measured against a yardstick based on the profit and loss
account it is likely to be regarded as distorting that statement before
it is regarded as causing a material distortion in the balance sheet.

In assessing the quantum element of materiality of a figure which
appears in both the balance sheet and the profit and loss account a
yardstick based on the latter statement would in normal circumstances be
more restrictive. For example, stock on hand at a year-end may be understated by an amount somewhere between £50,000 and £100,000. In determining the point at which this error could have a material effect on
the accounts as a whole it is likely that the error will fail to pass
the criteria set to judge materiality in the profit and loss account before it grows to a size where it fails to pass the materiality criteria
for the balance sheet. Therefore, the standard net profit yardstick
outlined above is appropriate for matters affecting both statements and
also the Sources and Uses of Funds Statement. In unusual circumstances
where the balance sheet figures are exceptional in relation to the other
statements a different base may be appropriate but the recognition of
such circumstances must be left to good judgment.

In questions of materiality which affect only one financial statement, i.e., only the Balance Sheet or only the Profit and Loss Account,
one is frequently concerned with the classification of items. That is
to say the nondisclosure, misstatement, or omission which we seek to
prevent could arise from an error in classification or grouping of
items, e.g., short- and long-term liabilities shown as one item, contingent liabilities omitted or abnormal profit on sale of assets netted
against depreciation. While the quantum is still very relevant, it is
essential that the characteristic of each item is recognized as being
significant enough to require separate treatment *in that context*.

In determining whether an item is material one must have regard to
the truth and fairness of the financial statement with or without the
item in question. In profit and loss accounts and income statements the
usual quantum yardstick must be the "standard net profit," but on questions of separate or omnibus presentation of revenue figures the omission or inclusion, disclosure or nondisclosure of an amount should be
related to the overall view and to the total of which it forms a part.
It may also be necessary to disclose the aggregate of a number of items,
such as exceptional credits in the profit and loss account, which individually fall well below the materiality level but which, in aggregate,
result in a significant increase in the disclosed profit. In every case
judgment will require to be exercised and statutory requirements observed, but some guidelines as to proportions may be of assistance. For
example, a figure may be considered material if it exceeds ten percent
of the "standard net profit" and may require separate disclosure in
terms of statute if it amounts to five percent of the total expenses
(e.g., hire of plant and machinery) or five percent of the total income (e.g., revenue from rents). In the interests of clarity in financ
financial statements any additional disclosure should only be made if
the difference in characteristics between two items is of sufficient
inportance to justify it.

For items that relate solely to the Balance Sheet, separate guidelines require to be established. Classification and disclosure of re-

serves, provisions, liabilities, and assets could be based on a materiality guideline of five percent of total assets or ten percent of the
balance sheet caption but again subject to separate identifiable characteristics which are material to a proper understanding of the Balance
Sheet and not merely additional analysis for analysis' sake.

The Source and Application of Funds Statements incorporates figures from both the Balance Sheet and Profit and Loss Account and it is
unlikely that any item not separately disclosed in the latter two statements will require disclosure in the former. It is more usual to find
figures grouped together for inclusion in the Source and Application of
Funds Statement and the guideline in this instance is solely one of
characteristic rather than quantum or amount.

RECOMMENDATIONS

It has already been stated in this paper that accounting conventions are criticized because judgment is being exercised in an arbitrary
way. Materiality will always remain a matter of opinion, but if accountants can agree upon a framework within which they will form that
opinion some at least of the criticism will have been met. It is recommended that there should, therefore, be established

1. a defined basis of assessing the profit of the organiza-
    tion against which to measure materiality, e.g., the
    "standard" net profit
2. a procedure for use when profits are low or losses are
    being incurred
3. specific percentage guidelines for judging the materiality
    of revenue items relative to
    a. the standard net profit
    b. other revenue items
    graded, if necessary, to take account of the size of the
    organization, i.e., lower materiality percentage for
    large organizations
4. specific percentage guidelines for judging the materiality
    of balance sheet items relative to
    a. the standard net profit
    b. the total assets
    c. other balance sheet items

Financial statements should be presented in conformity with these guidelines, subject always to the exercise of professional judgment in the
particular context. Where departure is made from the proposed guidelines, which results in omission or nondisclosure on the grounds of presenting a true and fair view of special circumstances, the reasons for
the departure should be disclosed.

Consideration should also be given to the possibility of requiring
financial statements to contain a note of the materiality limits adopted
in their preparation.

IMPLEMENTATION

There are three possible methods of securing widespread adoption of any proposals concerning materiality. These are

1. by statute
2. by making it a requirement of the Stock Exchange before granting or continuing a quotation
3. by the issue of an accounting standard

If the recommendations proposed above, or other ideas with a similar objective, were to be implemented by statute, it is considered that there would be insufficient opportunity to obtain the prior views of all parties interested—the professions, the city, the Stock Exchange, financial analysts, and others. Moreover, legislation is considered to be a much slower means of achieving results than the other possibilities and if the delay were reduced it would be at the expense of proper consultation. Finally, legislation would be more inflexible than an accounting standard.

It is considered that the guidelines and other proposals are as applicable to unquoted companies and other institutions as they are to quoted companies. Any requirement by the Stock Exchange for a quotation would not be mandatory for unquoted companies and would, therefore, be less effective and create an unnecessary double standard in financial statements.

The attempt to achieve a measure of uniformity in assessing materiality is extremely relevant to the aims and objectives of the Accounting Standards Steering Committee. A statement of standard accounting practice on the subject would be complementary to many of the statements already issued or proposed, and it is suggested that this is the most appropriate and quickest method of implementing these or similar proposals.

QUESTIONS

1. How would you define materiality?
2. In what ways would you determine whether or not an item was material?
3. How does the accounting treatment for a material item differ from that for an immaterial item?

86   CONSERVATISM

Michael L. Moore

(Reprinted by permission from *The Texas CPA*, vol. 45, no. 2 (October, 1972): 41-47.)

(Michael L. Moore is a member of the faculty at University of Texas at Austin.)

In recent years, the financial press has been increasingly critical of the flexibility of rules under which accountants operate. In 1970 and 1971, additional skepticism of accounting arose because of decisions evidenced in the financial statements of many companies (3) (26). These companies were referred to as "taking a bath," that is, their balance sheets were "cleaned up" by writing off or writing down selected assets. Conservatism was cited as the basic theoretical justification for these decisions.

Conservatism has never been adequately defined and its systematic application has not been operationalized. It is therefore understandable how the financial press could misconstrue the sudden widespread use of this modifying convention.

Most accountants merely have a "feeling" about conservatism and its application. There is great danger in relying upon this form of intuition. Since guidelines are seldom established and judgment of each accountant is the controlling criterion which determines application, excessive zeal can produce financial statement prejudicial to certain statement users.

It is not the purpose of this paper to propose guidelines, but to point out the forces which may influence the extent to which conservatism is applied and the possible consequences to users of financial statements if this application is overzealous.

CONSERVATISM

Definitions of Conservatism

Webster defined conservatism as being "the tendency to accept an existing fact, order, situation, or phenomenon and to be cautious toward or suspicious of change: extreme wariness and caution in outlook." (23, p. 483)

In other fields, for example political science, a similar definition of the term is offered. "In one of its aspects, conservatism is not so much a definable body of social thought as it is a temperamental predisposition in favor of caution. . . . In its more clearly political connotations, conservatism suggests a reverence for tradition. . . . (10, p. 416)

In accounting, a consensus concerning the meanings of conservatism is not apparent. For example, there is no reference to the word conservatism in *A Dictionary for Accountants*. (9) The AICPA has issued *Statement No. 4* in which conservatism is defined.

>*The uncertainties that surround the preparation of financial
>statements are reflected in a general tendency toward early
>recognition of unfavorable events and minimization of the
>amount of net assets and net income. (2, p. 15)*

Other writers in accounting have also offered definitions. Moonitz
defined conservatism as a "reaction to uncertainty and represents in essence a counsel of caution." (12, p. 47) Wilcox and Hassler stated that
conservatism means "literally preservation in safety. . . ." (25, p. 146)
Sorter, et al., defined conservatism as "a generic concept that embraces
many kinds of behavior including intolerance of ambiguity, solvency position, reluctance to change, minimization of book income, and risk
aversion." (19, p. 200) Additionally, conservatism has variously been
called a principle, (17) concept, (7) virtue, (11) philosophy or attitude, (4) doctrine or article of faith, (6) necessary condition, (13)
and fundamental principle of valuation. (21)
Conservatism in an operational context has meant that the lowest of
several possible values of assets and the highest of several possible
values of liabilities and expenses should be reported. The tenet "anticipate no profit and provide for all possible losses" implies that
revenues should be deferred and expenses should be accelerated. When
there is a choice among several alternative valuations of assets, liabilities, revenue, or expenses, the ones having the least favorable immediate effect on income should be chosen.
Not all accountants have agreed as to the proper role of conservatism in accounting. George O. May, on one hand, wrote:

>*to me, conservatism is still the first virtue of accounting,
>and I am wholly unable to agree with those who would bar it
>from the books of account and statements prepared therefrom
>and would relegate it to footnote. (11, p. 176)*

Paton on the other hand, disagreed.

>*The most objectionable and obstructive tradition of accounting
>is conservatism, so called. Accountants generally, without
>fully understanding what they are doing, kowtow to this tradi-
>tion. (14, p. 182)*

Ross writes of the "sins in the name of conservatism." (16, p. 84)
Sterling (4, p. 110) points out that in the popular Finney and Mil-
ler textbooks after four editions of referring to conservatism as a
"principle of accounting" in the fifth edition complain about the "fet-
ish of conservatism." Many writers do not acknowledge conservatism. (1)
(20) (21)

Development of Conservatism

Conservatism developed because it was felt that the tendency toward
caution was necessary to offset the optimism (often prematurely con-
trived) of business managers and owners. (8) Pressures from ultra-
cautious short-term creditors were influential in the accountants' selection of accounting methods. Creditors desire statements which re-

flect assets near liquidation values and liabilities reflecting even contingencies. This form of presentation provides a margin of safety.

Accountants also feel that understatement of asset values and income is a lesser danger to business managers and owners than overstatement. For example, the consequences of a loss, or possible bankruptcy, are assumed to be of greater consequence than a gain.

From a behavioral point of view, accountants probably prefer outcomes to be better than expected rather than worse. Conservatism at one point in time tends to produce the opposite effect in the future. For example, if an expenditure such as R&D is expensed rather than capitalized, current earnings will be lower. If in subsequent periods revenue attributable to R&D is generated, earnings will always be higher than the earnings that would be reported had the capitalized decision been made. Basing earnings projections on years in which conservatism is applied will likely result in projections lower than actual earnings. Reports with favorable variances are more desirable from a behavioral viewpoint than are reports depicting unfavorable variances.

For external reporting, conservatism is often related to the conservative bias that seems to influence applied statisticians in their attitude regarding Type I and Type II error (*alpha* and *beta* errors) in quality control. Devine (5) argues that the buyer's risk (*beta* risk) is of greater consequence than the seller's risk (*alpha* risk) and inasmuch as it is usually the buyer who inspects and has the power of acceptance or rejection, the rules of acceptance are expected to be tighter than the rules for rejection. Therefore, the support required for a decision to accept would be expected to be stronger than the support required for a decision to reject. Devine pointed out, as did Hendriksen, (8) that the consequences of an accountant rejecting a representation that was correct would not likely be as serious as accepting a representation that was incorrect. Rejecting a representation that was correct usually would lead to further checking and possible clarification of facts. Accepting a representation that was incorrect usually would not lead to further checking. The representation would then be reinforced by the reputation of the auditor.

When a certifying auditor attests to the fairness of financial statements, he becomes responsible to third party users for their fair representation. Liability suits against auditors for attesting that financial statements portray conditions which later prove to be an understatement appear to be unusual, while these suits against auditors for attesting that financial statements portray conditions which later prove to be an overstatement are numerous. (15)

Conservatism and Other Accounting Principles

Accounting practices which have evolved from conservatism have been accused of violating other principles and concepts in accounting, for example, consistency and disclosure, (12) objectivity, (16) comparability, (8) and going concern. (18) It has also been argued that conservatism is a more fundamental principle than the others. (21) An example of the alleged violations follow.

Consistency and disclosure. Two factors which may affect inter-period comparability are consistency and disclosure. The application of conservatism allegedly understates assets in earlier years and over-states income in later years. It is argued that this practice violates consistency in that periodic income statements are noncomparable. The understatement of assets creates "secret" reserves which if not disclosed violates disclosure principles.

Objectivity. The argument is made that conservatism is the opposite of objectivity. Ross (16) believes that conservatism suggests to accountants to use their judgments in deliberately understating values. Conservatism is a subjective construct, and the degree of its application depends on the risk preferences of the accountant.

Objectivity means to some writers that measurements are impersonal or exist outside the mind of the person making the measurement. There seems to be little agreement between these two constructs.

Going concern. Schrader, Malcom and Willingham (18) argue that since valuation of assets from conservative practices lean toward liquidation values, conservatism is in conflict with the "going concern" convention in accounting.

EXCESSIVE CONSERVATISM

Excessive conservatism or ultraconservatism as it is sometimes called is disapproved by even the staunchest supporters of a more moderate circumspectness. Excessive conservatism misrepresents the financial position of a company and is prejudicial to specified users. One problem that exists is defining what is excessive conservatism. Where is the line that separates a conservative practice from one that is ultraconservative? The answer appears to be in the mind of the individual auditor.

Pressures which would promote excessive conservatism are great; for the external auditor because of legal liability, for management because of pressures from taxing authorities.

Auditor Liability

Because of legal liability and the outcome of various liability cases, auditors are more sensitive to the consequences of *beta* errors, that is, attesting that something is correct when in fact it is not. As was mentioned above, recent suits have involved claims by injured third parties against auditors who attested that financial conditions were better than they actually proved to be. The threat of this liability has, in all likelihood, influenced auditors to be more conservative. Whether the imaginary line between conservatism and excessive conservatism is crossed with regularity is a matter of conjecture.

Tax Laws

Various tax laws may be instrumental in fostering conservatism in financial statements. Efforts have been made by the Treasury Department to stimulate national economic growth through incentives for investment. A few examples have been accelerated depreciation, guideline lives for asset depreciation, and the investment credit. These are tax minimization devices. Many companies have adopted the same financial accounting procedures as tax accounting procedures. Tax minimization may lead to ultraconservative financial statements when tax accounting procedures are used for financial accounting.

Closely held corporations which wish to minimize inheritance taxes would be inclined to use very conservative accounting procedures. Again it is not known whether the line between excessive conservatism and conservatism has been crossed.

SIGNIFICANCE OF CONSERVATISM TO USERS OF FINANCIAL INFORMATION

The financial information which reflect the application of conservative methods is of concern to the various users of this information. Credit grantors, potential investors, owners of stock, and management all have differing needs and therefore probably interpret financial statement information in a different—often unique—manner.

Credit Grantors

Credit grantors and potential investors need assurances that the financial position of a company is *at least as favorable* as it is represented to be. The margin of safety occasioned by the use of conservatism protects the credit grantor or potential investor from unfavorable consequences. With assets valued with the emphasis toward liquidation values, a cushion of protection against losses is provided.

Owners of Stock

The owners of stock require information enabling them to determine the proper valuation of stock. Conservatism may hinder acquisition of the necessary information for this purpose. Even if the owner of a stock knows that the company follows conservative accounting practices and understates income, the degree of conservatism and the relative effect on income are not disclosed. Ross (16) parallels this situation to setting an alarm clock fifteen minutes fast. This may be effective for a few days in getting up early, but the advance is soon subconsciously discounted. This analogy describes conservatism with full disclosure. The actual situation according to Ross is similar to someone setting the clock ahead each day by varying amounts undisclosed to the sleeper. The sleeper would be in much the same situation as someone reading a financial statement. The clock can be assumed to be fast (income understated) but there is no way to determine by how much.

Management

The effects of conservatism on management decisions are not readily apparent. Not a great deal is known about what information (with conservative coloration) is used or how this kind of information is used in the typical management decision. At least one writer, E. A. Whiting, (24) suggested that conservatism can affect certain types of decisions. He felt that the same attitudes that pervade in preparing published financial reports is carried through the accounts presented to management for use as a basis for policy decisions.

Whiting believes that it is of great importance that expenditures of continuing value are distinguished from expenditures applicable only to a certain period. In the accounts, however, many expenditures are capitalized or written off or written down rapidly by conservative depreciation methods. The period which bears a disproportionate share of the expenses because of this conservatism may look poor compared with other periods unless management makes a mental adjustment to the figures it received. If not, decisions are made on misleading information.

Whiting cites discounted cash flow analysis as an area where decisions on misleading information are possible. This is with respect to certain capitalize-expense decisions.

The worse sin is the treatment of expenditure of continuing value. Because it is written off in accounts, it is not regarded as capital expenditure and so escapes the net of DCF method of investment appraisal. Because there is no tangible asset, there is said to be no investment, although the amounts at stake may often be as large and as extensible over time as amounts "invested" in new plant or building. (24, p. 722)

The types of investments which Whiting referred to were, to name a few: new product development, computer system and programs, and advertising.

CONSERVATISM AND BIAS

It can be seen that conservatism biases information to the benefit to some and detriment to other users of financial information. The introduction of bias into financial statements has been rejected by some writers as being inconsistent with certain reporting objectives. The Study Group at the University of Illinois did not mention conservatism by name but stated as a basic postulate of accounting a statement with an anticonservatism accent:

Accounting data and reports have validity and usefulness for widely differing purposes. . . . This postulate is significant for accounting in that it carries a strong implication that accounting data should be free from bias favoring any particular user of the data. (22, p. 8)

The American Accounting Association held a similar view:

*The standard of freedom from bias is advocated because of the
many users accounting serves and the many uses to which it may
be put. The presence of bias which may serve the needs of one
set of users cannot be assumed to aid or even leave unharmed
the interests of others. It is conceivable that biased information could properly be introduced if it would aid one
group without injuring the position of any other, but this
conclusion cannot be reached with certainty in external reporting, where all potential users must be considered. Thus,
bias should be avoided in external general purpose reports.
(1, p. 11)*

CONCLUSION

It is difficult to draw conclusions about the existence of possible
abuses in financial reporting from the application of conservatism.   It
is likely that excessive conservatism is prejudicial to specified users.

Also, it is difficult to draw conclusions as to the role, if any,
that conservatism should have in financial reporting.   One group of individuals (principally theorists) contend that any use of conservatism
leads to bias.   The other group (mainly practitioners) argue that conservatism is a necessary element that reduces bias that would normally
be introduced into the statements by owners and managers.   These advocates of conservatism must then contend with the problem of guidelines
for application such that new biases toward any particular user are
not introduced.

Statement No. 4 explains the modifying convention of conservatism
in terms of a "means of substituting the collective judgment of the
profession for that of the individual accountant." (2, p. 66)   Stated
in another way, the judgment of the profession as a whole sets limits
on individual judgments.   Guidelines for some applications of conservatism are rather specific and well documented, for example, lower of cost
or market rule in respect to inventory valuation.   Guidelines for other
applications are unspecified.   It is this type of situation that appears
to cause the perceptions by the critics of financial reporting that the
rules under which accountants operate are loosely structured.

Conservatism appears to be a useful and practical mechanism for
tempering management optimism and justifying decisions made under significant uncertainty.   If, however, the practice appears to be abused
by applications which are interpreted as excessively conservative,
pressures toward greater regulation of accounting practice appears im-
minent.

FOOTNOTES

1.   AAA Committee to Prepare a Statement of Basic Accounting
     Theory. *A Statement of Basic Accounting Theory.* (Evanston,
     Ill.: American Accounting Association, 1966).
2.   Accounting Principles Board of the AICPA. *Statement of the
     Accounting Principles Board No. 4: Basic Concepts and Ac-
     counting Principles Underlying Financial Statements of Bus-
     iness Enterprises.* (New York: AICPA, 1970).

3. "The Big Bath," *Newsweek* (July 27, 1970).
4. Cattlet, George R. "Factors that Influence Accounting Principles," *The Journal of Accountancy*, 110, no. 4 (October, 1960).
5. Devine, Carl Thomas. "The Rule of Conservatism Reexamined," *Journal of Accounting Research*, 1 (Autumn, 1963).
6. Gilman, Stephan. *Accounting Concepts of Profit*. (New York: The Ronald Press Co., 1939).
7. Grady, Paul. "Inventory of Generally Accepted Accounting Principles for Business Enterprise," *Accounting Research Study No. 7*. (New York: AICPA, 1965).
8. Hendriksen, Eldon S. *Accounting Theory*. rev. ed. (Homewood, Ill.: Richard D. Irwin, Inc., 1970).
9. Kohler, Eric L. *A Dictionary for Accountants*. 3rd ed. (Englewood Cliffs, N.J.: Prentice-Hall, Inc., 1963).
10. McDonald, Lee Cameron. *Western Political Theory*. (New York: Harcourt, Brace & World, Inc., 1968).
11. May, George O. "Accounting Principles and Postulates," reprinted in Moonitz, Maurice and Littleton, A. C. (eds.) *Significant Accounting Essays*. (Englewood Cliffs, N.J.: Prentice-Hall, Inc., 1965).
12. Moonitz, Maurice. "The Basic Postulates of Accounting," *Accounting Research Study No. 1*. (New York: AICPA, 1961).
13. Newman, Benjamin and Mellman, Martin. *Accounting Theory: A CPA Review*. (New York: John Wiley & Sons, Inc., 1967).
14. Paton, W. A. "Accounting Procedures and Private Enterprise," in Taggart, Herbert F. (ed.) *Paton on Accounting*. (Ann Arbor: The University of Michigan Press, 1964).
15. Reiling, Henry B. and Taussig, Russell A. "Recent Liability Cases—Implications for Accountants." *The Journal of Accountancy*, 130, no. 3 (September, 1970).
16. Ross, Howard. *The Elusive Art of Accounting*. (New York: The Ronald Press Co., 1966).
17. Sanders, Thomas Henry, Hatfield, Henry Rand, and Moore, Underhill. *A Statement of Accounting Principles*. (Haskins & Sells Foundation, Inc., 1938).
18. Schrader, William J., Malcom, Robert E., and Willingham, John J. *Financial Accounting*. (Homewood, Ill.: Richard D. Irwin, Inc., 1970).
19. Sorter, George H., Becker, Selwyn W., Archibald, T. Ross, and Beaver, William H. "Accounting and Financial Measures as Indicators of Corporate Personality—Some Empirical Findings," in Jaedicke, R. K., Ijiri, Y., and Nielsen, O. (eds.) *Research in Accounting Measurement*. American Accounting Association, 1966.
20. Sprouse, Robert T. and Moonitz, Maurice. "A Tentative Set of Broad Accounting Principles for Business Enterprise," *Accounting Research Study No. 3*. (New York: AICPA, 1962).
21. Sterling, Robert R. "Conservatism: The Fundamental Principle of Valuation," *Abacus*, 3, no. 2 (December, 1967).
22. Study Group at the University of Illinois. *A Statement of Basic Accounting Postulates and Principles*. (University

of Illinois: Center for International Education and Research in Accounting, 1964).

23. *Webster's Third New International Dictionary*. (Springfield, Mass.: G & C Merriam Co., 1966).
24. Whiting, E. A. "What to Write Off?" *Accountancy* (Eng.), 77 (November, 1966).
25. Wilcox, E. G. and Hassler, R. H. "A Foundation for Accounting Principles," reprinted in Moonitz, Maurice and Littleton, A. C. (eds.) *Significant Accounting Essays*. (Englewood Cliffs, N.J.: Prentice-Hall, Inc., 1965).
26. "The Year of the Big Bath," *Forbes*, (March 1, 1971).

QUESTIONS

1. How would you define conservatism?
2. How does conservatism relate to the following accounting concepts: consistency, disclosure, objectivity, and going concern?
3. Why do you think accountants tend to be conservative?
4. Would conservatism be consistent with your objectives if you were a: corporation officer? banker? stockholder? auditor?
5. If a balance sheet is conservative, can subsequent income statements also be conservative?

87 WHAT'S WRONG WITH TODAY'S HUMAN
RESOURCE ACCOUNTING

Robert Comerford

(Reprinted by permission from *Massachusetts CPA Review*, vol. 47, no. 2 (March–April, 1973): 24–27.)

INTRODUCTION

Conventional accounting says nothing about the value of a firm's most important investment: human resources. It is ludicrous that annual reports' presidents' letters include statements to the effect that "our most valuable asset is our employees," but that an interested reader is unable to find this "most valuable asset" on the firm's financial statements. Further, managers register concern over the inaccessability of information on the conditions of their companies' human resources. Similarly, measurement of the changes in composition of human resources is not facilitated by traditional accounting systems. (1)

In response to these needs, "human resource accounting" has emerged in the form of an experimental model at R. G. Barry Corporation under the direction of Professors R. Lee Brummet, Eric G. Flamholtz, and William C. Pyle in conjunction with the firm's management.

This paper examines why human resource accounting systems have not been more widely adopted when such a clear need for them exists along with a working model from which to abstract one's own model.

First, the human resource accounting model implemented at R. G. Barry is briefly described. Second, evidence of the attractiveness of this model is presented. Third, the probable arguments against adoption of a human resource accounting system are categorized and examined individually along with their corresponding rebuttals. Finally, those problem areas not adequately rebutted are highlighted.

ACCOUNTING FOR HUMAN RESOURCES AT R. G. BARRY CORPORATION

The purpose of the human resource accounting system at R. G. Barry Corporation was "to develop an operational information system that will measure changes occurring in the human resources of the business that conventional accounting does not currently consider." (2)

Measurements of the value of human resources can be estimated on these bases: Acquisition costs, replacement costs, or economic value to the organization. At Barry these were combined into multiple measurements of human resources. (3) *Acquisition costs* are derived by summarizing historical data concerning the magnitude of the firm's investment in human resources. *Replacement cost* is an estimate of what it would cost to recruit, hire, train, and develop people to their present level of organizational proficiency and familiarity. And *Economic Value* is an approximation of the present value of that part of the corporation's future earnings attributable to a particular employee. Essentially, these three methods respectively attempt to measure

1. original cost of the resource
2. what it would cost at present
3. its value based on its earning power

Each approach has advantages for measuring different types of managerial decisions; each, also, presents some special problems. (4) These center around the subjective nature of such "functional asset accounts" in Diagram 1 as "Familiarization," "Experience," and "Development."

Several authors admit that any basis to account for human resources poses special problems which must be ameliorated. They conclude that the benefits of human resource accounting outweigh the attendant theoretical shortcomings and lack of precision. (5)

There are many lists of benefits of human resource accounting throughout the literature but nearly all of them paraphrase Brummet's statements. He cites the following benefits of human resource accounting:

1. It assists in recognizing and defining problems with the use of human asset investment turnover ratios.
2. It provides measurement of personnel turnover.

3. Net income which accounts for human resources reflects
    changes in their attributes, and managerial effectiveness.
4. It enhances awareness of the critical nature of human
    resources and thus facilitates searching for alternative
    "solutions" to organizational problems.
5. It makes available quantification of human resource oppor-
    tunity costs which aids in evaluations of alternatives in
    capital budgeting decisions.
6. It provides more accurate evaluations of investments in
    human resources themselves.
7. It changes the nature of the human factor in decisions
    from qualitative and quantitative.
8. It provides a cost control mechanism for standard costs of
    recruiting, hiring, training, and developing individuals
    to "bring them up to their present level of technical com-
    petence and familiarity required for a given position." (6)

IS HUMAN RESOURCE ACCOUNTING
ATTRACTIVE TO INDUSTRY?

The reason that few firms have implemented human resource accounting systems is not lack of interest. *Management Accounting* reports far-
reaching interest in the R. G. Barry model. (7) Mr. Robert Woodruff,
Barry's vice president of human resources reported "approximately six
hundred different companies have made inquiries about the effort . . ."
(8) Further, the Montreal office of Touche Ross and Company, and
Nomura Securities, Tokyo, Japan have implemented experimental human resource accounting systems based upon the Barry concept. (9) Interest
has developed because of the relative success reported of the Barry
experiment.

Barry developed a pro-forma balance sheet for 1969 which included
net investments in human resources of $986,094. Under liabilities,
$493,047 was labeled Deferred Federal Income Taxes as a result of Appro-
priation for Human Resources in the same amount. Finally, the pro-forma
statement showed a positive adjustment of $87,000 which reflected the
fact that investments in human resources outpaced write-downs. (10)

In 1970, cutbacks in management personnel due to "economic uncertainty" were reflected by a decline of $21,950 in after-tax income. The
contention is that Barry's profit figures more closely approximate reality with the results of the human resource accounting system included
in computation of net income. (11)

The Barry model is available for scrutiny and the benefits of the
human resource accounting seem to adequately fill specific corporate
needs. Why, then, have few if any other companies implemented human
resource accounting systems?

The literature contains many descriptions of problems with human
resource accounting. In order to better understand them and to put them
in perspective, the following section is a presentation of human resource accounting problems probably anticipated by most firms. They
have been organized according to these categories: traditional, theoretical, measurement, and practical problem areas.

TRADITIONAL PROBLEMS

Traditional problems are those which have caused the "late emergence of efforts to quantify human resources. The culprits are:

1. cultural lag between accountants and behaviorists
2. communication gaps between accountants and behaviorists

Human resource accounting requires that behavioral scientists and accountants work together in the measurement of appropriate variables. (12) Until recently such cooperation did not exist and the emergence of human resource accounting was impeded.

Sophisticated measurement and accounting procedures are being developed by accountant-behaviorist cooperation because this problem has been solved. Beyond these, though, there are theoretical problems which reflect philosophical objections to human resource accounting.

THEORETICAL PROBLEMS

The first of these states that: *"Human capital (excluding a slave society) cannot be purchased or owned by the firm and therefore would not be recognized as an asset in accounting."* (13) Lev and Schwartz maintain that although this is true with respect to individual employees who can usually resign at will, it is less obvious with respect to groups of the firms' labor force as a whole. For purposes of this discussion the turnover rate of the labor force is unimportant as long as vacancies can be filled. The ownership concept is valid by virtue of the stable association between the firm and its labor force and subgroups. (14)

Second, some objectors contend that: *Labor is not an asset because it has no "service potential" exceeding the current period*. Stated differently, no asset is formed by payment of salaries or wages because employees are paid for rendering *current services*. Lev and Schwartz argue that "if this were true, then no firm would invest in (as opposed to maintain) human capital." (15) Expenditures for orientation programs, management development programs, training programs, etc., are made with the expectation of future returns. Such programs create assets because they enhance the future value and service potential of human capital. (16)

The last theoretical problem is offered by the behavioral scientists who argue that accounting for man as a capital asset will result in: *the dehumanization of employees*. To the contrary, the potential in human resource accounting is to restore the individuality of employees. As a result, the possibility is increased for more humanistic relationships between the firm and its employees. (17) Programs such as individual selection, development, placement, advancement, incentive, and redevelopment will receive greater attention. Enabled to act as "economic man," managers reacting to financial facts will be increasingly motivated to avoid overextending employees, underutilizing their talents and overlooking managerial obsolescence. (18) By emphasizing employees' value to the firm, management and the organization will pay closer attention to them.

Of the three theoretical problem areas, the first is least power-fully defended. Lev and Schwartz, in arguing that the whole labor force can be regarded as being owned by the firm, have merely attempted to de-personalize the owner relationship. At R. G. Barry, however, the owner-ship of employees by the firm is stressed by the human resource account-ing system's structure. In that system each participating executive has his own asset account.

MEASUREMENT PROBLEMS

Intuition tells us that employees cannot be completely valued with-out subjective estimates. This fact has generated much of the criticism of human resource accounting. It is precisely this characteristic of human resources that human resource accounting attempts to overcome. The first of the three measurement problems is that *any evaluation of the human element will be affected by subjectivity.*

Eggers admits that this is clearly a problem but he claims that it is no more serious than it is for such everyday business activities as valuation of fixed property, the valuation of goodwill, and the fore-casting of turnover, profits and capital investment alternatives. (19) This observation ignores the fact that there are many problems with hu-man resource accounting of which the actual valuation process is but one. To illustrate, dehumanization problems, traditional problems, own-ership philosophy problems, etc., are not even possible in his examples. All the problems with human resource accounting cumulatively "push" it out of the fixed property-, goodwill-, and turnover-ball park. Stated differently, if subjectivity were the *only* problem with human resource accounting, it indeed would be no more serious than it is for the exam-ples cited.

The overriding implication is that human resource accounting was developed to fill the need for quantification of historically unquanti-fiable human resources. The first process in the system at R. G. Barry involves *subjectively* determining values of development costs, famili-arization costs, experience costs, etc. These subjective estimates must then be added in various categories, some expensed, others capitalized, and eventually the quantification of human resources is deduced. This sum of subjective evaluations is no more quantitatively "correct" than one subjective evaluation of the final figure. Considering the time and development costs involved with implementing the human resource account-ing system, then, is not the sum of subjective evaluations far less ef-ficient than one subjective evaluation of the human resources' value?

If the pioneers in human resource accounting wish to defend it as the "quantification of human resources," they must do more than break down the human resource into its parts, judgmentally determine their values, and add them up again.

Another aspect of the subjectivity issue is the potential for line-staff conflict that may exist in human resource accounting systems. Line-staff conflict is common in industry today over such processes as

1.   staff cost accountants evaluating the performance of line employees
2.   staff quality control systems evaluating the output of line units

> 3. staff personnel systems appraising the readiness of line
>   employees for promotion

Imagine the line-staff conflict that would erupt in the post-experimen-
tal stages of the development of human resource accounting when staff
accountants judgmentally assess the *value* of line managers! It may be
necessary to re-define "line-staff conflict" to accommodate increased
intensity.

In summary, the managers of firms seek quantification of human resources. It is possible that many of them are reluctant to adopt human
resource accounting systems because they see it as no more than a formal
method of adding up their judgments of the values of various employee
characteristics.

The second measurement problem is: *the lack of suitable yardsticks
for measurement of human resources*. Accountants are trained to make
evaluations of assets with price tags and market values, and with no
human characteristics. Are they equipped (via their training) to make
the subjective evaluations necessary in human resource accounting?
There simply is no experience upon which to base this accounting system
and its parts. As Eggers pointed out, yardsticks have to be created.
We already have them for job evaluation and salary increments, but the
essential point is that there are no yardsticks for human resource accounting. (20) Until we devise them, human resource accounting cannot
progress into its implemental stage of development.

Clearly the weight of measurement problems is critically delaying
the adoption of human resource accounting.

Of the four problem categories, the next one—practical problems—
has the most intuitive appeal, and represents the greatest detraction
from human resource accounting acceptance.

PRACTICAL PROBLEMS

The first of these is that *implementation of a human resource accounting system would require an appreciable increase in total accounting costs*. It is logical that by increasing the expected output of the
accounting department, the cost of its maintenance will increase. Beyond this, though, is the cost of accumulating the detailed information
called for by human resource accounting. Likert suggested that the latter could be reduced significantly by incorporating statistical sampling
techniques for all accounting. (21) Professor Likert's suggestion will
indeed lower costs. But the use of sampling techniques can only detract
from the saleability of the accuracy of human resource accounting. His
estimates will be "acceptably accurate" in that they will be only
slightly more *inaccurate* than they were initially.

It is suspected that sampling will merely move human resource accounting system costs from "very prohibitive" to "less prohibitive" at
this early stage.

The obvious drawback with adoption of operational human resource
accounting systems is that *new systems will necessitate several years of
development of procedures*.

Professor Brummet explained that the R. G. Barry system will progress in these three stages:

1. the development of the human resource accounting system
2. the formulation of a body of generalizations about the ways in which information provided by the system should be used in planning and controlling
3. the development of a set of generalizations about the behavioral impact of a human resource accounting system (22)

The Barry system was implemented in 1968 and is today still in the *first* phase of its development. From this we may safely conclude that even today it will take a great deal of time to develop procedures for a human resource accounting system in any firm.

Mr. Egger contended that the magnitude of the human resource accounting task is no more formidable than a traditional inventory taking process. (23) Suppose, though, that the inventory taking process were not already standardized; how difficult would the process be under this supposition? It is in this non-standardized stage that human resource accounting finds itself today, and operationalizing a system would take years.

Finally, considering the sorts of problems associated with human resource accounting, and the additional fact that *valuation of human resources is not as immediate a problem as is traditional asset valuation*, one wonders, "why try it?" Especially with today's national economic dilemma, human resource accounting is a needed luxury that few firms can afford. At this stage in its development the needs that human resource accounting may fill are far above (in a Maslow sense) the needs of the corporation. As a result, human resource accounting is outside of the "need-concern" of most firms.

EVALUATION OF UNSETTLED PROBLEMS

The adoption of operational human resource accounting systems is blocked by the following problems:

1. Any evaluation of the human element will be affected by subjectivity.
2. There are no suitable yardsticks for measurement of human resources.
3. Implementation of a human resource accounting system would require an appreciable increase in total accounting costs.
4. New human resource accounting systems will necessitate several years of development of procedures.
5. Valuation of human resources is not as immediate a need as traditional asset valuation.

Beyond the individual impacts of these problems, there is an aggregate implication of why human resource accounting systems have not been operationalized. At the risk of oversimplification, this implication is that human resource accounting has not been adequately researched and tested. Valuation of human resources is a problem because not enough research and testing has been conducted to either solve it or to explain its unimportance. No universally acceptable yardsticks for human resource measurement have been provided; the Barry system does not seem to be comprehensive enough to appeal to a broad range of managers. The cost of implementing a system at this time is prohibitive simply because of the great amount of research and development necessary. Managers are waiting to see what happens at Barry before spending anything on human research accounting. Finally, there simply is no pressing need to subject one's firm to the problems outlined herein.

CONCLUSION

The reason that few if any firms have incorporated human resource accounting systems, is simply that there is not yet a system to incorporate. The Barry system is in the developmental stages and beyond that, accounting for human resources cannot be used for outside reporting. Perhaps a nod of recognition of the presence of human resource accounting by the Accounting Principles Board, its successor group or the American Institute of Certified Public Accountants would spur increased activity in the development of the concept.

The issue, then, becomes why has development proceeded so slowly that in five years no attractive system has been developed? The evidence suggests that the answer lies in the subjectivity of the measurement bases. Human resource accounting is touted as quantitative in derivation; closer scrutiny, however, reveals that it is judgmental in derivation. Managers can judgmentally determine the value of human resources without going to the expense of setting up a new system.

Possibly, human resource accounting systems as currently understood are not what is needed at all. One concludes that no less accuracy would result from simply estimating the total value of employees. In this case, the needed structure is regulated by modified maturity tables, or some other simple device, during the audit. If the asset valuation is "too small," let it pass; if it is "too large" reduce it! Then all that are needed are a few account titles to which individual accounts may be closed on financial statements. The result is a human resource accounting system which admits to subjectivity, but which is inexpensive and uncomplicated.

FOOTNOTES

1. Robert Wright, "Managing Man as a Capital Asset," *Personnel Journal* (April, 1970), p. 290.
2. "People are Capital Investments at R. G. Barry Corp.," *Management Accounting* (November, 1971), p. 53.
3. R. Lee Brummet, Eric G. Flamholtz, and William C. Pyle, "Human Resource Measurement—A Challenge for Accountants," *The Accounting Review*, vol. 153 (April, 1968), p. 217.
4. Wright, op. cit., p. 291.
5. Ibid.
6. Brummet, Flamholtz, and Pyle, op. cit., p. 222.
7. Bummet, op. cit., pp. 218-220.
8. "People are Capital," p. 55.
9. Ibid.

10. Ibid.
11. Ibid., p. 54.
12. Ibid.
13. Rensis Likert, *The Human Organization: Its Management and Value* (New York: McGraw-Hill, 1967), p. 146.
14. Baruch Lev and Aba Schwartz, "On the Use of the Economic Concept of Human Capital in Financial Statements," *The Accounting Review* (January, 1971), p. 109.
15. Ibid.
16. Ibid.
17. Ibid.
18. Wright, "Managing Man," p. 298.
19. H. C. Eggers, "The Evaluation of Human Assets," *Management Accounting* (November, 1971), p. 29.
20. Ibid.
21. Ibid.
22. Likert, "The Human Organization," p. 152.
23. Brummet, "Human Resource Measurement," p. 221.

QUESTIONS

1. Of what value would human resource accounting be?
2. What has the R. G. Barry Corporation done in the area of human resource accounting?
3. Why do you think human resource accounting is not widespread?

88   SHOULD ACCOUNTS REFLECT THE CHANGING VALUE OF THE DOLLAR?

Livingston Middleditch, Jr.

(Reprinted by permission from *The Journal of Accountancy*, vol. 25, no. 2 (February, 1918): 114–140. Copyright 1918 by the American Institute of Certified Public Accountants, Inc.)

Practical accounting offers no exception to the firmly established principle that complications and maladjustments are sure to result from the use of an uncertain or variable unit of measure. In view of conditions in recent years the fixity of the unit with which accountants deal most may well be questioned. Is the dollar a definite and invariable unit of measure?

We need not seek far for an answer. The statistician with charts and tables and the economist with his theories cannot tell us half so well as the average man of limited means and a relatively fixed salary.

His knowledge that the dollar is at present rapidly shrinking is based on first-hand contact and cannot safely be disputed. The economist and statistician merely confirm in more precise terms what the average man has already realized in a rough and practical way.

The dollar is standardized by act of congress as equivalent to 23.22 grains of fine gold, but it is not standardized in regard to its use as a medium of exchange—the primary purpose which it serves. It has not a standard and unvarying purchasing power. If our dealings were solely to exchange gold for dollars and dollars for gold—if money were an end rather than a means—the dollar would be perfectly stable. The true value of the dollar is measured not by what it is, but by what it will get. "Money is what money does." If one year prices are at a certain level the purchasing power of the dollar is thereby determined. If a few years later prices have increased, the value of the dollar has declined.

To be more concrete: if you had bought a 20-year, five percent bond at par in 1897, it would have just matured and returned a purchasing power less than the purchasing power you parted with by an amount greater than all the interest you would have received, so that you would have actually and practically lost by the whole transaction. Each dollar invested in 1897 was worth more than the 1917 dollar and twenty years' interest at five percent. Today's dollar is, then, a totally different unit from the dollar of 1897. As the general price level fluctuates, the dollar is bound to become a unit of different magnitude. To mix these units is like mixing inches and centimeters or measuring a field with a rubber tape-line.

Would it not be more reasonable in accounts to treat of the various dollars as distinct units of measure rather than to combine them without distinction? The answer of the accountant depends on the practical effect the exact treatment of the fluctuating dollar would have on the conduct of his client's business and whether the greater precision would be worth the greater effort. Under conditions such as those of the present, the cumulatively changing dollar may attain to such importance over a few years' time as to make it worth consideration. Altogether to disregard the changing dollar in accounts does not permit the true condition of affairs to be set forth. When the inaccuracy attains to a considerable magnitude it is surely worthy of correction.

Suppose that it is decided to treat the dollar as a varying unit. We have then two problems to consider. The first is: How shall we evaluate the dollar at one time in terms of that at another time? The second: How should adjustment be made in the accounts to reflect the changing value of the dollar?

The purchasing power of the dollar at different times has been the subject of considerable study by economists and statisticians and results have been very carefully worked out. They have computed index numbers of prices which are trustworthy measures of the purchasing power of the dollar at various times. These numbers are measures in the inverse sense, however, for the higher prices go and the higher the price-index, the lower the purchasing power of money.

The problem of obtaining an index of the general level of prices, as has been aptly pointed out, (1) is analogous to tracing the movement of a swarm of bees. The relative movements of the individual bees in the swarm are very irregular; nevertheless the movement of the swarm as a whole is well defined. So it is with prices: although the prices of individual commodities may fluctuate without any apparent relation to each other, there is a very definite general level of prices. The index number serves to indicate this general level and variations in the price level are accompanied by corresponding changes in the index.

The several index numbers that have been obtained have been computed by taking wholesale prices of various representative commodities, weighting them according to their relative importance and striking some sort of a statistical average. Each step in computing an index number is subject to considerable variation of method and it is gratifying to notice that the results obtained by different methods are in substantial agreement.

Of the index numbers regularly published for the United States, Bradstreet's seems to make much the best showing as a "business barometer." (2) It is not an index number in the strict meaning of the word but rather a composite price. It agrees surprisingly, however, with the elaborately computed index number of the United States bureau of labor statistics and it has the advantage that it is not computed to a base year, so comparisons may safely be made directly between any two years rather than indirectly by comparison of each of the years and the base period. This index appears monthly and an average of the monthly values appears each year. These yearly averages of the monthly values are given in the table following: (3)

TABLE 16

1892	7.7769	1905	8.0987
1893	7.5324	1906	8.4176
1894	6.6846	1907	8.9045
1895	6.4346	1908	8.0094
1896	5.9124	1909	8.5153
1897	6.1159	1910	8.9881
1898	6.5713	1911	8.7132
1899	7.2100	1912	9.1867
1900	7.8839	1913	9.2076
1901	7.5746	1914	8.9034
1902	7.8759	1915	9.8530
1903	7.9364	1916	11.8251
1904	7.9187	1917	15.6565

The changes of the price index in the United States for the past twenty-five years is shown graphically in the figure. The declining dollar of recent years is clearly evident.

We now have the working basis for a satisfactory quantitative comparison between the dollar at different times. There remains to be considered how this varying unit might be handled in the books of account.

The central problem is to make such adjustments as will express all the open accounts in terms of the same monetary unit and yet not impair the usefulness of any of the information already contained in the

accounts.   In order to minimize the work of adjustment and to give results of greatest use in the conduct of a business, all accounts should
be stated in terms of the current dollar.

FIGURE 7

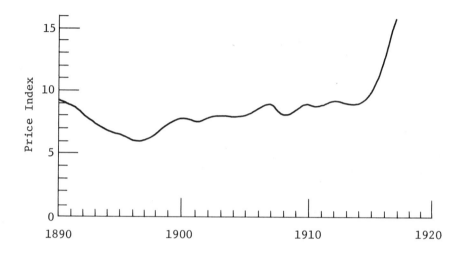

Adjustments would be made at balance-sheet dates with a view to expressing all the items of the balance-sheet in terms of the same unit
and to apportioning whatever advantage or burden there might be to the
period in which it belongs.   Individual yearly variations may be relatively unimportant, but the cumulative effect may be great.   To be specific, let us consider the adjustment of some balance-sheet items and
note also the influence this would have on operating profit and loss accounts.   We will consider assets, liabilities and capital in the order
named.
    Accounts receivable, bills receivable, and inventories will be
supposed to work themselves out frequently enough to reflect the new
price levels without additional adjustment.   They can be considered as
expressed at any time in terms of the current dollar and instances would
probably be rare in which circumstances would call for a different
treatment of these items.   With these items would be grouped cash, temporary investment securities and any others that go to make up the current assets of the business.   Strictly current assets, which will be
converted into cash in reasonable time, will need no adjustment for
balance purposes, as they are already measured in terms of the dollar at
the balance-sheet date.   The customary allowance should, of course, be
made for bad debts, depreciation, obsolescence, etc.
    Adjustment should be made in the profit and loss statement properly
to restate current accounts on the books at the beginning of the fiscal
period in terms of the dollar at the end.   This adjustment will be in
one direction if the general level of prices is rising, and opposite if
the level is falling.   In the case of a rising price index the dollar is

depreciating and current assets (representing money rather than goods) would decline in true value and be therefore an element of expense to the business. This is, of course, not an expense due to operations. Adjustment could be made by debit to some such account title as "monetary fluctuation" and credit to a corresponding reserve or directly into the net worth accounts. In case of a falling price index money would be becoming more valuable in relation to goods, and accounts directly or indirectly representing cash would be appreciating. There would, as already stated, be no balance-sheet adjustment since that is carried out automatically by the change in the dollar, but there would be made a credit to monetary fluctuations with the corresponding debit made to the corresponding reserve or as a deduction from net worth.

Fixed assets, such as land and building, machinery and equipment, long time investment securities, etc., do not circulate rapidly enough to keep pace with the change in money value and should therefore be adjusted for balance-sheet purposes to statement in terms of the current dollar. In a time of rising prices the numerical value must be increased and in a time of falling prices it must be decreased if the true value of these items is to be expressed by the figures. With a rising index a debit would be made to an account such as "monetary fluctuation of fixed assets" or a subdivision of the account and the credit to a reserve or directly to net worth. For example, a building erected 15 years ago should appear on the balance-sheet at cost less adequate depreciation plus an adjustment due to non-equivalence of the dollar at the two times. With a falling index the adjustment would be a deduction, a credit to monetary fluctuation of fixed assets or its subaccounts, and the debit would be to net worth or the reserve. Of course, neither of these adjustments would show any effect on surplus earnings available for dividends. Nor should they apply in full to fixed assets acquired during the fiscal period, but only to those carried over from the one before. The partial adjustment of items acquired during the period might in certain extreme cases be advisable, but good judgment would be necessary in doing it.

Deferred charges would not be affected, except those charges already deferred for longer than one fiscal period. These would be rather infrequent, and, in general, deferred charges could be considered as somewhat similar to current assets.

Accounts, notes and dividends payable, accruals and other current liabilities would be handled in a fashion very similar to current assets, except that they would be opposite in effect. With rising prices debit reserve for monetary fluctuation or debit directly net worth, credit monetary fluctuation, an income not due to business operations. With falling prices, debit monetary fluctuation (an expense unrelated to operations) and credit the reserve or net worth.

Fixed liabilities would be handled in an analogous way, but opposite in effect, to fixed assets.

Proprietorship or net worth accounts would obviously reflect the changes in all the other classes of accounts. If a business has assets consisting chiefly of money items it will naturally suffer from a rising price index unless there is some special force to offset the general influence. If its assets consist chiefly of goods it will be benefited by a rising price index, unless by some special reason the price changes of its goods are exceptions to the general tendency. A falling price index will of course act in the opposite direction, and liabilities to be

ultimately paid with money will be affected oppositely to assets. The
entries indicated in the previous four or five paragraphs will serve to
keep proprietorship or net worth accounts stated in terms of the current
dollar and to show in them the net effect of the fluctuating unit.

We have, then, in the index number a means of comparing the value
of the dollar at one time with its value at another time, and by the
addition of a few adjusting accounts a means of incorporating these values in the books without detracting from the information they already
contain. This would enable the true state of affairs to be set forth,
all accounts being stated in terms of the same unit. It would also be
of value where the accounts are used for comparative purposes, as between houses in the same business, one old and one newly established,
and as between ratio of inventory to total assets, or similar comparison
ratios, for the same house at different times in its business career.
Obviously this last comparison is not a valid one if the fixed assets
have not been reconciled to the current monetary unit, for with the inventories this has happened automatically.

To make a brief summary of the principle underlying all these
adjustments:

1. All accounts should be expressed in terms of the current
    dollar.
2. The value of goods varies directly as the price index.
3. The value of the dollar varies inversely as the price
    index.

Let me state my conclusions in a question:

Would it not be scientific, sound accounting practice, in those
instances in which it makes any essential difference, to make the books
of account reflect the changes in the value of the monetary unit?

FOOTNOTES

1. Irving Fisher, *The Purchasing Power of Money* (New York:
    Macmillan, 1911), p. 194.
2. U.S. Bureau of Labor Statistics, *Index Numbers of Whole-
    sale Prices in the United States and Foreign Countries*,
    Bulletin 173 (Government Printing Office, 1915), p. 11.
3. Bradstreets, December 15, 1917, p. 802.

QUESTIONS

1. Why is the dollar not an unchanging yardstick?
2. Do you believe that the system described by Mr. Middle-
    ditch to adjust all accounting data to current dollars
    would be practical? Why or why not?
3. Why has the accounting profession not put Mr. Middleditch's
    suggestions into practice?
4. This article was written in 1918. Since then, what have
    accountants done to reflect the changing value of the

dollar?   Should something be done to reflect the changing value
of the dollar?   How would you do it?

---

89   CONSUMER PRICES
                                    FIGURE 8

(Reprinted by permission from the *Wall Street Journal* (June 22,
1973).   © Dow Jones & Company, Inc., 1973.)

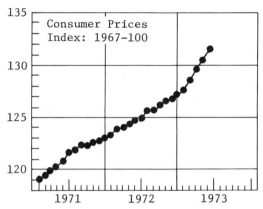

Consumer prices in May rose to
131.5% of the 1967 average from
130.7% in April, the Labor Department reports.

---

90   INFLATION AND CURRENT ACCOUNTING
                          PRACTICE: AN ECONOMIST'S VIEW

                            Solomon Fabricant

(Reprinted by permission from *The Journal of Accountancy*, vol. 132
(December, 1971): 39-44.   Copyright © 1971 by the American Institute of
Certified Public Accountants, Inc.)

(Solomon Fabricant is a faculty member at New York University.)

"The effects of inflation in the United States are not considered
sufficiently important at this time to require recognition in financial
accounting measurements."   So reports the Accounting Principles Board

of the American Institute in its statement on current accounting practice. (1)

I beg to differ. In my opinion—and the opinion of many other
economists, I believe—the effects of inflation are indeed "sufficiently
important." As is clearly recognized in the Board's report, inflation
affects the basic unit of measurement in terms of which financial statements are made and thus distorts the information on which users of financial reports rely. But, as accounting practitioners fail ro recognize, the distortions caused by general price-level changes are considerable "at this time" and have been considerable for years now. Further, it would be flying in the face of all that is known about the
politics and economics of this age to presume that general price-level
changes will be negligible in the future—if that is what the accounting
profession is counting on.

At the very least, it seems to me, the reports of independent
certified public accountants should do two things. First, they should
mention the change in the general price level over the period covered
by the financial statements that are being certified. Second, they
should draw the significance of this price change to the attention of
those who rely on these financial statements. I would hope, however,
that public accountants could decide to go further than this. To assist
the share owners and the public at large, who must make far-reaching decisions on the basis of accounting reports, public accountants should
ask management to provide supplements disclosing the effects of changes
in the general price level or insist on doing so themselves.

The Accounting Principles Board has already recommended such supplementary disclosure. (2) Were the leaders of the profession to set
the example of following this recommendation, the profession at large
would find it easier to move ahead. These supplementary statements
would be valuable even if they were not as detailed as the "basic historical cost statements," and even if they were labeled "approximate"—
as they should be.

Perhaps, ultimately, accountants will see the need to go whole hog,
and introduce a price-level adjustment in the basic financial statements. But this will never happen if the initial steps I have mentioned are not taken first.

I have been brief (I hope not to the point of curtness) in order
to put sharply and quickly before the readers of *The Journal* my main
reaction to the accounting practices described in the Board's Statement
No. 4. With this done, let me now try to be rather less brusk.

RECENT TRENDS IN INFLATION

Inflation continues to be a serious problem of the day. After the
12 months of recession that began in November, 1969, during which unemployment was pushed up to around six percent and the percentage of capacity utilized in manufacturing was pressed below 75 percent, the general price level was still rising, and rising at the exceptionally rapid
rate (for a recession) of five percent per year. Now that business is
recovering, past experience with business-cycle expansions offers little
promise of a stop to the rising general price level.

It is possible that the "worst inflation is behind us," as the
President said in April, 1971. The rate of advance in the general price

level seems indeed to have stopped accelerating. But this is not to say that inflation will soon be over. To judge from the private talk of its officials, the Administration does not look forward with confidence to anything that may fairly be called a stable price level. As the *New York Times* reported in May, a "high and knowledgeable" source in the Administration agreed then that "anyone who thinks the [wage] settlement in steel will be less than the can settlement is out of his mind." As we all now know, the steel settlement did match the high increases given in the can settlement. And the steel wage settlement was promptly followed by a substantial steel price increase. It is not surprising that in recent testimony before a Congressional committee, the chairman of the Federal Reserve Board said that "neither the behavior of prices nor the pattern of wage increases as yet provides evidence of any significant moderation in the advance of costs and prices."

Also revealing is the Executive Order on wage-price stabilization in the construction industry. The Order does not even pretend to be the first step in a rollback of the large wage and price increases that have already been made in that industry. Nor, if the wage settlements already approved under the Order provide a sign of what is to come, will an attempt be made to hold future wage increases in the industry to just the normal rate of increase in national productivity. (3) This means that construction costs will continue to mount.

A "significant moderation" in the rate of inflation may yet come. Most of the economic projections made outside the federal government (as well as those made inside), available at midyear 1971, do indicate a decline in the rate of inflation after the first half of 1971. But none of the nongovernmental projections puts the rate of inflation (measured by the GNP implicit price deflator) even a year and a half later as low as 2.5 percent per annum. The projections for the second half of 1972 range from 2.7 percent to as much as 4.7 percent per annum, with the average equal to 3.6.

Nor would it be reasonable for anyone, inside or outside the Administration, to see an early end to large wage increases or to an appreciable degree of price inflation. The pressures in Washington to reduce the fiscal deficit and the rate of increase in money supply appear no stronger than the pressures to raise them. Further, when some of the current unemployment is sopped up (as the Administration has avowed is one of its prime objectives) and higher output begins to strain available capacity in a widening range of firms, industries, and regions, the general price level may again tend to accelerate even if government policy remains as anti-inflationary as it now is.

As for the longer term, the "secular," trend—looking beyond the present cyclical expansion—perhaps it is sufficient to say that the immediate costs, in terms of unemployment and otherwise, of a strong anti-inflationary policy seem to many people to have turned out to be greater than expected, and greater than they feel to be tolerable. As a result, it is becoming harder for them, and even for those who minimize the costs and maximize the benefits of anti-inflation policy, to be even faintly optimistic about a horizontal trend in the price level. More and more wage contracts, price contracts, and financial dealings are including escalator clauses, built-in wage or price increases, high interest rates, and conversion and other equity privileges. The public is adjusting itself not only to past inflation but also to the likelihood of future secular inflation. It is noteworthy that the majority on the Joint Economic Committee of the Congress, after a close examination of the problem, including listening to much testimony from all sides, found itself willing to settle on a "long-term objective" for the nation that allows for an annual increase in the GNP deflator of "no more than two percent." (4)

Also reflecting general thinking on the prospects ahead is the public demand for improved understanding of the process of inflation. Where there is a demand, a supply comes forth, as we economists say, so television programs are being offered to explain inflation to the layman. And more economists are turning their attention to the scientific study of inflation. There will soon be held, for example, a conference of research economists on "the economics of secular inflation"; and the Life Insurance Association of America recently provided financial support for an intensive study by the National Bureau of Economic Research of "the effects of secular inflation on financial markets."

The wage-price freeze and other actions taken, and proposals made, by the President on August 15, 1971, can (in my opinion) lead to no more than a slowing down somewhat of the rate of advance of the general price level. I seriously doubt that a significant degree of inflation is now only a thing of the past.

It should be noted further that even if and when the price level does stop rising, many years will elapse before the effects on the accounts of the inflation of earlier years become negligible.

THE APB'S FUNDAMENTALS STATEMENT

It is natural, therefore, that when an economist picks up the "Fundamentals Statement" of the Accounting Principles Board—its Statement No. 4—he should turn first to what the Board reports on the current treatment of rising price levels. Of course, this is not the only item of interest to economists. Of all those outside the accounting profession, economists are the most keenly aware of the host of problems that confront accountants when they try to determine the flow of income and the stock of capital in a dynamic economy. Economists know how technological and other changes—in population, tastes, natural resources, economic institutions, and international trade—complicate the task of accountants. But a discussion of what the APB has to report on all these perennial problems would hardly fit into my limited space. I concentrate on the question of inflation, because the distinctive feature of our era, from the accounting viewpoint, is its tendency toward secular inflation.

The fundamental question to be put to a fundamentals statement, then, concerns the unit in which financial statements are to be expressed. On this, we read what is implied by current accounting practice in the Board's Statement quoted at the outset. What is offered to justify this answer? Very little, if anything, I am afraid. Nor could much be offered by anyone. The view of the accounting profession that is reflected in its current practice cannot be reconciled with the objectives and the criteria of good financial reporting that are set forth elsewhere in the Board Statement. Nor can the view of the profession be reconciled with the facts on price-level changes and their effects on financial statements.

In an inflationary era, it seems to me, the public is entitled to
expect something better than this. It is not unreasonable to expect
that accountants will recognize inflation's serious effects on the business accounts they certify, and will help the users of these accounts to
assess these effects. We can hardly be satisifed with what may too
easily be regarded as pussyfooting.

Consider, first, the criteria for adequate financial information
set forth in Statement No. 4, criteria that are presumably widely accepted by the accounting profession.

The function of accounting, according to the Statement, is "to provide quantitative information, primarily financial in nature, about economic entities that is intended to be useful in making economic decisions" (p. 17). This information "is needed to form judgments about the
ability of the enterprise to survive, to adapt, to grow, and to prosper
amid changing economic conditions" (p. 33). Financial statements must
be comparable between periods, and these comparisons will be more informative if "changes in circumstances . . . are disclosed" (p. 39).
Since economic decisions "involve the process of choosing among
alternative courses of action, including choosing among enterprises, an
effort must also be made to achieve greater comparability among the financial statements of different enterprises (pp. 35, 39).

Now, "the effects of economic activities are measured in terms of
money in a monetary economy." However, "fluctuations in the general
purchasing power of money cause problems in using money as a unit of
measure" (p. 29). Even "moderate inflation or deflation," if it per-
sists for several years, may cause "the general purchasing power of the
dollars in which expenses are measured" to "differ significantly from
the general purchasing power of the dollars in which revenue is measured" (p. 65). Presumably—though this is not spelled out in so many
words—even moderate inflation or deflation, if persistent, may cause
the general purchasing power of the dollars in which a company's net
income or net worth is measured at one time to differ significantly from
the value of the dollars in which its income or worth is measured at another time. And it may be said, in addition, that the dollars in which
the accounts of different companies are measured may differ significantly and, to that extent, be incomparable.

The Board's Statement makes clear the understanding by accountants
that accounting principles "change in response to changes in economic
and social conditions, to new knowledge and technology, and to demands
by users for more serviceable financial information" (p. 12). To meet
the need for "adequate disclosure" to facilitate understanding and avoid
erroneous implications (p. 41), therefore, we may expect the Statement
to go on to report the use by most, or at least by many, or at any rate
by some, firms of at least supplementary disclosure of general price-
level information. Yet, after the presentation of what amounts to a
case for doing at least that much—even when inflation is only "moderate"—the Statement offers no comment on the fact that information on
general price levels (supplementary or otherwise) is not provided in
current accounting reports in the United States.

The Statement does mention, first, that Lifo and accelerated depreciation of plant and equipment, "which tend to minimize" the incomparability of revenue and costs caused by change in the general price
level, have become generally accepted and widely used in this country.
However, general acceptance and wide use are not *universal* acceptance

and use. Nor, as I shall indicate, would their universal acceptance and use be sufficient.

Second, the Board does state that "methods of restating financial statements for general price-level changes . . . are not now used in the basic financial statements in the United States" (p. 65). To this a footnote is appended mentioning that Accounting Principles Board Statement No. 3 recommends supplementary disclosure of general price-level information. But Statement No. 3 states only that "general price-level information *may be* presented in addition to the historical-dollar financial statements . . ." (emphasis supplied). This seems to place the emphasis on the statement immediately following, that "general price-level financial statements *should not* be presented as the basic statements" (emphasis supplied). It is hard to read these sentences as "recommending" supplementary disclosure of general price-level information, which is how the footnote in Statement No. 4 refers to them. Rather, I read the recommendation as focused on avoiding the use of general price-level information in the construction of the basic financial statements. (5) But even by the more favorable interpretation, the Board is only recommending a supplement, not requiring one. In any case, as I have already said, few (if any) such supplements are in fact being provided in the United States.

LESS THAN "MODERATE" INFLATION?

After reading the main body of Statement No. 4 and the immediately preceding Statement No. 3, I find it difficult, as an economist, to understand this hesitation of practitioners to follow through. And, I ask, what reason might be given for it?

Can it be that recognition of changes in the general price level would provide only insignificant information—since "financial reporting is only concerned with significant information?" (p. 11 of statement No. 4). I have already quoted the Board's statement that even moderate inflation can mean significant incomparability of revenue and costs, and presumably, therefore, significant misstatement of income; and I shall present some figures in a moment to support the view that the inflation we have experienced not only can mean, but has meant, significant misstatement of income.

Can it be that estimates of change in the general price level, and statements using them, would be too imprecise and subjective for accounting purposes? But every accountant knows that "financial accounting involves approximation and judgment" (p. 41). And while there is no absolutely precise or even unqiue index of the general price level, the difference between the changes revealed by the indexes generally used— the GNP deflator and the consumer price index—is at most the difference between four and five percent per annum. Either estimate is surely better than the assumption of zero change in the general price level. Also important is the general agreement, among the companies participating in the field test authorized by the Board some years ago, that "with proper preparation, practical problems should not present a significant barrier to preparation of general price-level financial statements." (6)

Would a shift to purchasing power units, either in the basic financial statements, or in the supplements, violate the criterion of consistency between financial statements at different times and thus reduce

comparability? But comparability requires, among other things, that
"changes in circumstances" (p. 39) be disclosed. Surely changes in the
purchasing power of money—the fundamental unit of measurement—constitute such changes in circumstances. To stick to an unadjusted dollar is
analogous to refusing to make corrections for changes in temperature
when using metal rules, or in elevation when calculating boiling points.

Would the correction for changes in the general price level during
a period of inflation violate the convention of conservatism? On the
contrary. The level of change in profits is, as a rule, overstated, not
understated, when the general price level is rising. And rates of
change in profits also are overstated.

Implicit in the thinking of the accounting profession, it seems, is
the assumption that inflation in the United States has been (and promises to be) less than "moderate." So we come to the crucial question:
What are the facts?

THE ACTUAL PRICE RISE

During the year preceding the publication of the Board's Statement
No. 3, in 1969, the price level rose by four percent, according to the
GNP implicit price index. Between June, 1969, when Statement No. 3 was
published, and October, 1970, the date of publication of Statement No.
4, the price level moved up by more than six percent. Over a two-year
period, then, the general price level had risen by ten percent, measured by the GNP implicit price deflator, and about the same when measured by the consumer price index. Is this negligible? Looking a bit
further back, to 1963, when the American Institute published its Accounting Research Study No. 6, (7) the general price level has risen
by 30 percent. Since 1948, when the Institute set up its Study Group
on Business Income, (8) which had a good deal to say about general
price-level changes, the price rise has been 75 percent.

The effect of inflation on the unit of measurement in financial accounts cannot be shrugged off by anyone who ponders these quantities.
And these price-level changes can hardly be news to accountants. Statement No. 3 contains the GNP deflator series for 1929-1968; and every
month or quarter the new figures on these and on the consumer price indexes are reported in the daily newspapers. It is surely in recognition
of these changes that the Board (in Statement No. 3, p. 12) expressed
the opinion that "general price-level financial statements or pertinent
information extracted from them present useful information not available
from basic historical-dollar financial statements." It is puzzling to
find accounting practitioners, as reported in the Board's subsequent
Statement No. 4, considering the effects of inflation in the United
States to be not "sufficiently important."

Perhaps accountants believe that Lifo and accelerated depreciation,
to which the Board referred, can meet the problem of changing general
price levels. If so, they are mistaken. First, not all enterprises do
in fact use Lifo and accelerated depreciation, as I have already pointed
out. Second, and more important, even at best these practices can only
partially meet the problem of inflation. Viewed as variants of replacement-cost accounting, Lifo and accelerated depreciation attempt only to
lessen the incomparability between the revenues and costs ascribed to a
particular fiscal period—that is, to take care of the problem of

"heterotemporality." But this step fails to be followed by the second step necessary to put the revenues, costs and incomes of different periods into the comparable terms of a general price level *constant over time*. (9) Third, Lifo and accelerated depreciation are inefficient and erratic as a means of meeting even the problem of heterotemporality. In the case of Lifo, this can be seen if one considers the effect of fluctuations in the physical volume of inventories. In the case of accelerated depreciation, it is obvious that steps in the liberalization of depreciation practices would not—and could not—be geared to the rate or to changes in the rate of inflation. Fourth, the effectiveness of Lifo and depreciation liberalization in redressing the bias caused by inflation must vary among industries and firms, making interfirm and interindustry comparisons difficult. (10)

INADEQUATE MEASURES

We can estimate the extent to which the ameliorative effects of replacement-cost accounting, and accelerated depreciation, if these were universally accepted and applied, would fall short of adjusting aggregate net income for the full effects of inflation. (11) In 1970, the "inventory valuation adjustment" of the Department of Commerce, which in effect assumes a Lifo or equivalent adjustment for those corporations that do not use Lifo, equaled almost $5 billion. A corresponding "depreciation valuation adjustment," which no corporation makes, would be of the order of $8 or $10 billion. (12) Together, these total $13 to $15 billion, or almost 30 to 35 percent of the reported after-tax profits of 1970. The corresponding percentages for 1960 are only about 16 to 23 percent. As for changes between 1960 and 1970, reported profits in 1970 were 73 percent higher than reported profits in 1960. After the adjustment for heterotemporality just mentioned, the rise is about 45 percent. Adjustment for the change in the general price level further reduces the rise in profits between 1960 and 1970 to only about 12 percent. (13)

These figures relate to aggregates, and, therefore, provide a notion only of the average effect of the incomparabilities over time caused by inflation. The degree of incomparability could be a good deal more for many individual corporations. In any case, because companies differ in balance sheet structure, in the rate of turnover of assets and in the timing of new acquisitions of assets, there must be wide differences in the extent of the effects of inflation. (14)

CONCLUSION

To some people, these effects of changes in the general price level in the recent past may seem negligible. To me, and to many other people, they do not appear negligible. Nor, to repeat, does it seem to be reasonable to expect them to become negligible in the future. I believe, therefore, that general price-level information is required at this time for a fair presentation of the financial position of business enterprises—if not in the basic statements, then at least in supplementary statements.

When it is said—or at least implied—that ignoring this information is in conformity with generally accepted accounting principles in the United States, I cannot help but raise my eyebrows. When it is said further that conformity with these principles is sufficient for a fair presentation of the financial position of business enterprises, I must rise to disagree, and say that it is high time that these principles were revised. "Substantial authoritative support" should be given to recognizing the importance of general price level information.

A major objective of financial accounting is to provide information useful in making economic decisions. For accountants to avow this, and then in effect to stop short of doing what needs to be done to reach the objective, is to expose themselves to the charge of nonfeasance. If I were an accountant, I would not want to be subject to this charge.

Statement No. 3 provides a useful guide to the preparation and presentation of "general price-level financial statements." Accountants should begin to use this guide to prepare and present this information. The foreword to the Statement emphasizes that "presentation of such information is not mandatory." But I can see no good reasons for not presenting such information; I can see many good reasons for doing so.

FOOTNOTES

1. Statement of the Accounting Principles Board No. 4, "Basic Concepts and Accounting Principles Underlying Financial Statements of Business Enterprises," October, 1970, p. 64.
2. Statement of the Accounting Principles Board, No. 3, "Financial Statements Restated for General Price-Level Changes," June, 1969, p. 12.
3. Most of the approvals have clustered in the six to nine percent range—far in excess of the normal rise in national productivity, which is around three percent per annum.
4. The statement in full is as follows: "The President and the Congress should adopt as a long-term objective the twin goals of an unemployment rate no higher than three percent and an annual increase in the GNP deflator of no more than two percent." Report of the Joint Economic Committee of the Congress of the United States on the February, 1971 Economic Report of the President, 1971 (92nd Congress, 1st Session, Senate Report No. 92-49, p. 35).
5. In this connection, mention should be made of some of the "Proposals for Change," reported toward the end of Statement No. 4. These are suggestions to use current replacement prices, for example, as the basis of measurement in the basic financial statements; and in these statements to recognize changes in the general level of price (p. 104). The proposals are followed by the caution that "brief mention of . . . these proposals . . . does not, of course, imply a degree of present acceptance nor constitute a forecast of future acceptance. Reference to them in this Statement does not give them substantial authoritative support" (p. 103).

6. Paul Rosenfield, "Accounting for Inflation—A Field Test," *Journal of Accountancy*, June, 1969, p. 50.

7. Staff of the Accounting Research Division, American Institute of Certified Public Accountants, *Reporting the Financial Effects of Price-Level Changes*, Accounting Research Study No. 6, 1963.

8. Study Group on Business Income, American Institute of Accountants, *Changing Concepts of Business Income* (New York: Macmillan, 1952).

9. I pass over the question of whether changes in relative prices should be introduced into accounts, as they are handled by the usual replacement-cost procedures. On these, see my paper on "Inflation and the Lag in Accounting Practice," in R. R. Sterling and W. F. Bentz (editors), *Accounting in Perspective: Contributions to Accounting Thought by Other Disciplines*, Accounting Colloquium I, cosponsored by the University of Kansas School of Business and the Arthur Young Foundation (Cincinnati, Ohio: South-Western Publishing, 1971), pp. 121-126; also Accounting Research Study No. 6, pp. 29-31, and Statement No. 3, Appendix D.

10. A more adequate discussion of these various points appears in my Kansas paper.

11. Estimates for each year, 1929-68, are given in my Kansas paper. I am indebted to the Office of Business Economics, Department of Commerce, for the additional data for 1969-70, as well as for a good part of the earlier estimates.

12. The higher figure assumes that depreciation is generally calculated on a staight-line basis, using Bulletin F service lives. The lower figure assumes that depreciation is generally calculated according to the double-declining balance method, using 75 percent of Bulletin F service lives.

13. The rise in reported profits is about the same, 45 percent, after the adjustment for heterotemporality, whether the adjustment is based on the straight-line Bulletin F assumption or on the double-declining balance 75 percent of Bulletin F assumption. If it is assumed (to allow for the trend toward liberalization) that the former assumption applied to 1960 and the latter to 1970, the rise after adjustment for heterotemporality becomes 57 percent, and, after further adjustment for changes in the general price level, about 20 percent.

   The new rules on depreciation put into effect by the Treasury in June, 1971 would reduce reported after-tax profits for 1971, and thus cut the rise between 1970 and 1971 in reported after-tax profits by an amount estimated to be in excess of the amount needed to correct for the inflation between 1970 and 1971. But the liberalization would do little to make up for the inflation in prior years. Further, because its effect on reported profits in 1972 and immediately following years would be roughly

constant, the rules change could not correct for any inflation during subsequent years. The Treasury's new regulation exemplifies the inefficient and erratic character
of depreciation liberalization as a solution for the
problem of inflation.

14. An idea of the average difference among industrial
groups, drawing on estimates made by George J. Stigler,
was given in my Kansas paper. Individual companies may
differ still more, as Rosenfield's sample study, commissioned by the Accounting Principles Board, has indicated.

QUESTIONS

1. Do you think inflation is significant enough to need to be
disclosed in financial statements? Explain?
2. What are Mr. Fabricant's suggestions for the reports of
independent certified public accountants?
3. What are the arguments for and against reflecting price
changes in financial statements?

91   FIGURE 9

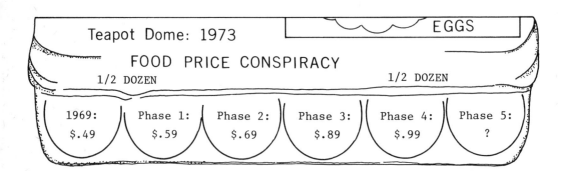

SHOW AND TELL

(compare moderate prices for prime buys in a depression year with 1973 prices)

1933 (Depression) Weekly Salary $30.00		1973 (Phase IV) Weekly Salary $300.00
Weiners	10c/lb. ———————————	.85c/lb.
Prime Ground Beef	7½c/lb. ———————————	1.30/lb.
Picnic Hams	12c/lb. ———————————	1.79/lb.
Rolled Roast.	14c/lb. ———————————	1.59/lb.
Sirloin Steak	11c/lb. ———————————	1.98
Veal Roast.	9c/lb. ———————————	1.65
Bacon	10c/lb. ———————————	1.00
Eggs.	25c a-dozen———————————	.99 a-dozen

QUESTIONS

1. Do you think that price changes averaged over the period 1933 to 1973 were material enough to have been specifically reflected in price level adjusted financial statements? Why or why not?
2. Would your answer to 1 above be the same if the price rise from 1969 through Phase 4 were to continue?

7

Managerial Accounting
for Internal Users

Chapter 7 begins with two articles on overall planning as carried out by the use of budgets or financial planning models. A comparison of the Robert H. Anderson article (p. 349) with Harvey B. Quitel's article (page 360) discloses that financial planning models have as their essence the preparation of budgets under differing assumptions or expectations about future events. Through the use of the computer, results can be simulated quickly and efficiently for a wide range of budgeted expectations. The simple, noncomputerized budget is a powerful management tool. The financial planning simulation models bring this tool to new heights of usefulness.

Once the budget and other standards of performance are set, they are used in the control function to gauge the performance of the organization and individuals in the organization. Joaquin Gomez Morfin (page 366) describes the ways in which this is done. His discussion also includes the concept of internal control as used specifically by accountants. Park E. Leathers and Howard P. Sanders (page 380) present a very specific case, church accounting, of how internal control can be achieved by accounting records and procedures.

Douglas A. Volk (page 388) describes cost accounting as ". . . a refinement of general financial accounting procedures which enables a business concern to determine the unit costs of manufacturing various products or rendering services." He explains the advantages of cost accounting systems and describes briefly how a cost accounting system can be implemented and used.

The breaking up of the business into responsibility centers for control and cost accounting purposes is an important and useful organizational device. Shu S. Liao (page 395) discusses the reasons for this and the ways in which responsibility accounting can contribute to profitable operations.

Accountants are frequently called upon to provide information for special type decisions in addition to the day-to-day planning and control decisions. The M. G. Wright article (page 401) and the Frederick G. Harris article (page 406) provide examples of special type decisions for which accounting data is essential. Wright explains the factors which must be considered in pricing a new product for the market and in pricing that same product at maturity. Changing unit costs as sales increase have a great impact on this decision. He combines the contribution margin with break even analysis to help analyze this pricing problem. Harris analyzes the merits of three methods of preparing projections on proposed capital expenditures: the payback method, the return on investment method, and the discounted cash flow.

The final article (page 409) is a progress report by David H. Li on the Cost Accounting Standards Board (CASB). He reviews the objectives of the board; the authority and origin of the board; the statements issued; research in progress; and relations with the Financial Accounting Standards Board and over governmental units. Since its inception primarily for cost control over defense contracts the influence of the CASB has been spreading. Other than defense agencies have chosen to adopt its standards. Private corporations have voluntarily decided to follow the standards where they were applicable to nondefense business. The future of cost accounting methods and practices, it would appear, will be greatly affected by this board.

---

92   FINANCIAL PLANNING—A MODEL APPROACH

Robert H. Anderson

(Reprinted with permission from *Canadian Chartered Accountant* (May, 1973): 54-59.)

(Robert H. Anderson is a faculty member at the University of Saskatchewan, Regina Campus.)

INTRODUCTION

Planning can be described briefly as setting the objectives of an organization and then specifying the means for achieving these objectives. The planning process is inherent in all activity; all individuals and organizations plan in formal and informal ways. The basic process is carried out in a cyclical and continuing fashion: establish objectives, plan, organize, execute, evaluate, and then replan, entering the cycle again at the stage of organizing. Several stages in the cycle may occur simultaneously; as it is artificial to separate "planning" from the total process, the words plan or planning will be used here to refer to this continuous cycle.

Firms have many objectives, but the financial one is central to business enterprises. Without profits, none of the "higher" level social objectives—such as job training and the support of various community efforts—would be attainable. Therefore, all business decisions are made with profit in mind, and all business planning is ultimately financial planning. Although finance is only one of a number of resources to be planned, the financial plan is particularly important because it provides the only way of assessing the returns to be expected from investments and it tests whether the company's financial resources are adequate for desired programs. In preparing to take action leading to a long-term maximization of profitability, questions concerning

technology, market analysis, and manpower planning will all have an essential part to play. Finally, however, alternative courses of action
emerge, which must be tested in dollar and cent form, relative to the
required costs or investment.

Many companies mistakenly equate financial planning with corporate
planning. Financial planning is only a small part of the total system
of business planning, but it must be treated as an integral part of the
planning process, not as a separate function. Although the financial
planning process is treated as a separate model here, rather than as
one of several aspects of business planning, the reader must be aware
that the separation is for functional understanding and is no more real
than the separation of a motor from a car in understanding the car's
operation.

Planning is an integral part of the financial manager's job. Although management initiates the planning process by first establishing
goals or objectives, the financial manager converts these major policy
decisions into a coordinated financial plan providing action guides
among the interrelated departments, groups and individuals. The plan
provides not only the directive for action, but also the base against
which to measure accomplishment.

Even though the planning and control processes are, or should be,
inseparable, the subject of control will not be considered in this paper. Nor will optimization be the aim of the planning models discussed.
Moreover, this paper is not a primer on budgeting, as present literature
is adequate in that area. The objective is to provide a planning process permitting the examination of alternatives and their effect on the
financial expectations of the business enterprise. The emphasis and examples will be drawn from profit-making enterprises, although the process can be adapted to other organizations.

THE NATURE OF FINANCIAL PLANNING

Financial planning has two objectives:

1. assuring that the goals and objectives of the organization
    are met
2. providing for the attainment of desired levels of profit
    so that enough cash is available for meeting current ob-
    ligations as they become due, and for financing future
    expansion projects

Financial planning should answer such questions as:

1. Can profit objectives be realized with planned activities?
2. Is the projected return on the investments reasonable when
    compared with the industry, the competition, the risk in-
    volved or the other opportunities available?
3. How much financing will be required and when?
4. What form is most appropriate for the financing with re-
    gard for the risk and returns on the project?
5. When is repayment possible?
6. What is the expected effect of differing alternatives on
    the return to investors?

In answering these questions, financial planning must always express the plans of management, not the controller's idea of what the plan should be.

The attitude that financial planning is for large-scale enterprises only is fast disappearing from the business scene due to bankruptcies caused by inadequate planning and because of the availability of and participation in education programs for business management.

Advantages of Financial Planning

The most important benefit of a good financial planning system is that it defines objectives clearly and provides a means to communicate those objectives to all organization levels. Top management must establish goals and priorities as the base for the plan. The subsequent steps of the planning process assure that these goals and priorities are understood and accepted throughout the organization and used as bases for planning at all organization levels.

The second benefit of a good financial planning system is that it coordinates and motivates activities in all facets of the organization. Almost every policy decision affects more than one function; good planning brings an awareness of the impact that decisions will have on other parts of the company. A financial plan provides the opportunity to define the contributions required from the various organization segments. It can also serve to draw attention to potential areas for improvement, as well as providing for a rational allocation of resources to the most effective use.

The third benefit of a good financial planning system is that it encourages forward thinking, and permits the anticipation of problems. Even when problems are not anticipated, a comprehensive planning effort speeds up the reaction time of management, providing a pattern for testing problem solutions. Using a financial planning model makes it possible to consider more alternatives, to determine the full financial effect of these alternatives and to do so with reasonable speed.

A fourth benefit is that the financial plans are targets for performance measurement. With a financial plan, results and accomplishments can be measured and deviations isolated. Constant comparison of the plans with the results of operation not only measure variations from the plan but also aid in the identification of the reasons for the variations. This provides a control over operations. A financial plan establishes norms—standards against which to measure management performance and which help define problems requiring management attention.

Sound forward planning can also be beneficial to groups outside the organization, but involved in its affairs. Product suppliers can plan their commitments in advance and thus make better use of their own resources. Funds suppliers also can arrange their affairs more effectively if approximate requirements are known in advance. Improved resource utilization by suppliers means better service for the user, as well as possible price savings.

Negative Aspects of Financial Planning

It is possible for an organization to weigh itself down with detail that contributes nothing to the objectives of the organization. The planning process is time consuming, both in the executive and clerical effort involved, and is prone to clerical error. These two constraints discourage analysis. The ability to analyze is a strength of the planning model described later and, when linked with a computer, time and error problems disappear.

One of the potential disadvantages of financial planning can be a lack of flexibility—fixed objectives may no longer be appropriate for changed conditions. This inflexibility is magnified by the historical approach that has frequently been the nucleus of the plan. Minimizing the time required to pre-test changes with a model can reduce the inflexibility, and the ability to test changes in historical relationships can sharpen the ability to project.

Too much flexibility may also occur. The plan may be changed so frequently by management that it no longer has any meaning. It is not necessary to change a plan each time a change occurs in the bases for the plan. Instead, isolate the effect of the changes so that performance is measured, based on what the plan should have been if the facts had been known beforehand. With a model it is a simple matter to isolate these uncontrollable factors.

BASIC COMPONENTS OF A FINANCIAL PLANNING SYSTEM

Financial planning is sometimes called "balance sheet planning" because the purpose of the planning system is to specify what the balance sheet position will be at selected points in the future. It is also important to plan how these levels will be attained over time and thus income statements and cash flow statements are an important link between specific balance sheets. Financial planning is largely a matter of estimating the earning assets needed by the business, the form in which these assets will be held (cash, fixed assets, inventories, etc.), how these assets will be financed and the nature and timing of changes in the balance sheet structure.

All planning has two major bases: the objectives of the firm and the data base in the firm from which comprehensive plans may be developed. The necessary data base comprises details of past operations. However, it is incomplete without consideration of what is expected to happen in the future. Consideration must be given to such areas as the sales plan and the implications of a production plan, including personnel requirements and inventory levels. Thus, both historical and forecast information are basic inputs to a financial plan.

The financial planning process starts with top management and involves four basic forecasts: the economic forecast, the sales forecast, the production forecast and the financial forecast.

The Economic Forecast

The starting point for the planning process is some basic consideration of expectations during the planning period. With the present rate of change it may no longer by appropriate for most businesses to assume the status quo, or proportionate growth, or a basic share of the market. If the specific organization is to survive, and certainly survival is the organizational goal (although only implicitly), then it is necessary to adapt to and initiate change, rather than simply to follow.

The first step in the economic forecast is to specify the relationships between general economic conditions (Gross National Product, Personal Disposable Income, etc.) and specific variables in the organization, such as sales or accounts receivable. This step will be described later in more detail under sales and financial forecasts.

Since few organizations have their own economists, an economic consultant, a trade publication, bank forecasts or financial journals would be possible sources for this particular forecast. Once the forecast economic indicators are known, the next step is to develop detailed plans.

The Sales Forecast

Sales forecasting can be carried out through two different approaches: technical and fundamental.

The technical approach relies upon the stability of past patterns of behavior. In many cases it relies entirely on a trend. If sales have increased on the average ten percent per year, this trend is forecast to continue. It assumes that a certain dollar volume will be obtained in the future although it will not necessarily be based on the same products. Exactly what the products are is less important than how much of them are expected to sell. There is no attempt to understand underlying causes; the forecast is on a very mechanistic basis only. This approach is simple to apply, but contains numerous questionable assumptions.

The fundamental approach involves an examination of basic variables including economic factors, total market, market share, advertising, price levels, etc. For example, the total market for a product might be partially dependent on two different economic variables, such as GNP and disposable income. In addition, the price levels for the product for all sellers and the total amount of advertising by the industry would also be expected to affect the total amount sold. The use of past data for all these factors would produce a single equation, or multiple correlation, which explains changes in the total market for a product. Similarly, the market share would depend on the organization's price level and advertising compared to the total industry. Once the basic relationships are established, it is possible to vary the price level and/or the advertising expenditure to see the effect on the sales volume before deciding on the appropriate price level and/or advertising expenditure. It is also possible to see changing relations over time among the variables involved and plan accordingly. This is a more useful method, but also more difficult to apply.

Since the two methods of forecasting are not mutually exclusive, an application of some combination may be effective—one acting as a check on the other. The sales forecast in total dollars, however attained, will be supported by schedules of quantities of products in reasonably large homogeneous groups. This level of detail then provides support for the totals and is also an input to the production and financial forecast.

The Production Forecast

Up to this point the forecast has been largely in dollar terms; the production forecast will primarily be in physical terms. The expected annual sales are adjusted up or down according to desired levels of inventory and the adjusted volume becomes normal volume. After normal volume has been determined, it is used as a guide in estimating the resources necessary to carry out the production plan. An engineering analysis, using a combination of technical know-how and judgment, will be used to project resource requirements.

The production forecast will be made in detail so that manpower, material and fixed asset needs can be forecast from the same information. Supporting schedules for inventories (raw material, work in process, finished goods), changes in plant and equipment, etc., will be necessary for other parts of the planning process. Resource planning, based mainly on the production forecast, will include: requirements, whether resources can be generated or must be acquired, and allocations to producing units. Some replanning may be required before the production forecast is finalized because of limited resources available. For example, it may be discovered that advertising is being increased to increase sales, while at the same time there is insufficient capacity for increased production.

The Financial Forecast

The business enterprise's projected dollar volume of sales is the most important causal variable in determining financial requirements. Financial forecasting, as sales forecasting, can be carried out in two basic ways: technical and fundamental.

The percent of sales method. This is a more exact name for the technical method, but the general assumptions of continuing relationships and unknown causes still are used. The forecaster computes past relationships between balance sheet items and sales, assumes these relationships will continue and applies the relationships to the new sales forecasts to get an estimate of financial requirements. This method is simple, but is unlikely to hold for more than a short time. It is not possible to test for the effect of any changes except in the volume of sales.

The regression method. This is an example of a fundamental method of forecasting. A mathematical relationship between causal variables such as sales, credit conditions, etc., and financial items is established. For example, accounts receivable may be dependent on credit sales for the previous month, general credit conditions, and cash discount terms. Because these latter items "cause" accounts receivable, they are said to be causal variables. Similarly, inventory levels are "caused" by expected sales levels, by cost levels and by savings possible through large orders or long production runs. An equation is

developed, relating the financial item (accounts receivable, inventories) to the causal variables. The forecast values for the causal variables are inserted into the equation and the estimated financial items
emerge. This includes both balance sheet and income statement items.
One figure (usually cash) becomes the balancing amount. This amount is
compared with an ideal, a cash shortage or excess is revealed and
sources or uses planned. This method is more complex than the percent
of sales method, but preferable because it allows for changing relationships and considers more factors than simply sales. The regression
method also allows modification of the relationships as the policies of
the firm change, as the industry or market changes or as the financing
mix changes.

Many supporting schedules are necessary for the financial forecast:
cash flow, ratios and performance indicators, capital expenditures, accounts receivable and payable, etc. A cash flow forecast, for example,
would show the working capital for day-to-day requirements, availability
of liquid funds for dividends or stock or bond retirements, funds necessary for expansion or acquisition of plant facilities and the amounts
and durations of additional funds needs. Cash flow needs will ultimately be detailed on a daily basis. Even weekend money is a salable commodity these days. Based on available cash flows, the optimal timing
for major disbursements can be planned.

Once the amounts and timing of required funds are determined, then
the financial manager must select the most suitable form of financing
from among the following: demand loans, term loans, revolving credit,
bonds, long term leasing, preferred stock, common stock.

As a final test of the financial plan, some performance measures
will be examined. No investment earning less than the best alternative
opportunity available should be made. The earnings on the present investment (after tax earnings per share divided by market value per
share) are usually used as a surrogate for other opportunities. As
finance literature will bear out, the appropriate measure of financial
performance is the subject of much controversy.

If the performance tests prove the results inadequate, the normal
process is to work backwards into the model. For example, if return on
investment is too low, then either the return must be increased or the
investment decreased. It is possible to test individual components of
the model to see the effect of any changes contemplated. The process
may have to be repeated several times until the performance measures
meet the desired levels.

PREPARING THE FINANCIAL PLAN

Planning is optimal when people are fully informed as to objectives, purposes and intentions of the planning process. A clear and
precise definition of responsibility and authority within the management
pyramid is necessary to assure that subsidiary objectives are set within
the appropriate framework of accountability. Information must be disseminated to all subordinates, so that each can identify his individual
targets.

Before planning can begin, objectives must be specified in the following areas: profitability, market position, innovation, productivity,

physical and financial resources, manager performance and development, worker performance and attitude, public responsibility.

Modeling

A financial planning model is a representation of a company based on a set of assumptions. Because of the complexity of the interactions within a firm it is difficult, if not impossible, for a human to think through all of the ramifications of a decision in the systematic form demanded for proper planning. Use of a model facilitates answering "what if" type questions for the decision maker.

Models come in many forms. A set of financial statements is a model. The main difficulty with this type of model is that to test the effect of a change in one of the basic assumptions requires time consuming recalculating of the working papers and supporting schedules. The accounting equation, Assets = Liabilities + Owners Equity is a model, but of limited use for financial planning in its simplified form.

Models have already been discussed in the previous section. A model is simply some representation of the real thing which allows us to abstract and consider a part of the system in isolation and then test the effect on the whole system.

Based on a simple model, it is easy to build more complex algebraic models. For example, accounts receivable are dependent on sales, payment terms, credit conditions, and other variables. It is possible by multiple regression techniques to establish a relationship between accounts receivable and these variables. Once the values of the independent variables are known, the value of accounts receivable is obtained automatically. It is possible to test the effect of a change in credit terms on the necssary amount of accounts receivable by the regression equation previously developed, to explain the level of accounts receivable. These changes are then inserted into the rest of the model to see the effect on sales, cash needs, and so on. On the basis of the changes observed, a logical decision on credit terms may be made.

A modeling approach to planning brings some important benefits:

1. Developing a model of the company requires every planner to take a top management, overall viewpoint.
2. The main aim of modeling is to discover and use relationships between key factors. This brings a better understanding of the whole business enterprise.
3. A model projects over several time periods and forces consideration of leading or lagging relationships which are not apparent in a single period. It also forces consideration of trends—whether sectors of the business are growing or declining.

The financial model must be dynamic in nature and reworked periodically in order to improve the precision with which functional relationships are stated. When an initial model has been developed, it should be tested with actual data to improve the precision of the functional relationships within the model. Building a financial planning model is a difficult and sensitive task—the model builder must be very familiar with the behavior of the organization before he can produce workable and meaningful models.

Once mathematical representations of the relationships in a business enterprise have been shaped into a complete and self-contained
system, a model exists. When "what if" type questions changing the
individual items in the model are asked, the technique is called simulation.

Simulation

Simulation is the manipulation of a mathematical representation of
a system in order to see how a change in one of the elements in the system will affect the others. A financial planning model allows the decision maker to simulate the financial impacts of changing assumptions
regarding many variables such as sales, debt/equity ratios or operating
ratios. The point is not to optimize anything, simply to provide valid
information for the decision maker. By simulating the effect of changes
on the financial model, the decision maker can see the expected effect
of changes before the changes are made.

A balance between oversimplification and complexity must be maintained. The Brookings Institute model of the United States economy contains more than 150 equations. The basic accounting model is one equation. Somewhere, in the middle, are models adequate to describe most
business enterprises.

A set of fifteen to twenty-five simultaneous equations will usually be sufficient to adequately represent a business. A simple model
might be:

1. Sales change at the same rate as GNP.
2. Cost of sales = 50 percent of sales less 1/10 of 1 percent
    for each 1 percent increase in sales.
3. Administrative expenses = 5 percent of sales less 1/2 of
    1 percent for each 1 percent increase in sales.
4. Accounts receivable = 33 days credit sales.
5. Inventories = next 3 months forecast sales.
6. Gross fixed assets = sales.
7. Accounts payable = 31 days purchases.
8. Ownership changes by net income.
9. Balancing figure appears as cash or bank loan.

In this model, a forecast of GNP makes the whole model active, determining a forecast income statement and balance sheet.

A model can provide the financial manager with a means of understanding why the enterprise needs funds, when it needs them and what the
possible risks and rewards are for those supplying the funds. The model
allows management to quantify the effects of alternative policies and
decisions. Solving the model from period to period provides the decision maker with a dynamic model of the firm.

The development and application of simulation is closely tied to
the development and application of computer technology. A small system
of simultaneous equations may be solved with a calculator, but as the
system becomes more complex a more efficient system is necessary. A
fast, comprehensive response to proposed changes is required to aid the
decision maker answer "what if" questions. The use of a computer to
solve the system of equations permits many simulations to be performed
in a short period of time, allowing many changes to be tested.

Simulation techniques allow the businessman to examine the probable consequences of his decision without the risks of real life experimentation. The effect of the decision on the whole enterprise can be tested in a short period on the computer before the decisions are implemented. Simulation provides flexibility by making it possible to formulate several plans quickly, easily, and cheaply. Simulation is particularly useful because it can be applied to problems that are too complex and have too many variables to be reduced to optimization formula.

If the financial simulation model is to be an effective planning tool it must explicitly reflect cause and effect in the internal relationships of the firm and in the external relationships with the markets —both goods and financial markets—in which the firm participates. The model must also be logically consistent with the financial practices of the firm and be an accurate model of the goals and objectives of management. As C. J. Christie points out (*C A magazine*, February, 1973, p. 51), the planning and development of the model must not be delegated "to anyone below the level of the people who are to use it." He also suggests:

> *Do not look to the data processing department for assistance in the design of the model. In general, these people do not have the mathematical or modeling systems background required.*

Construction of a financial planning model is an expensive, time-consuming process, requiring inputs from all levels of management and supported by skills of operations research staff and financial analysts. If simulation techniques are to be used effectively, the business must be thoroughly understood by the model builders. They must be able to quantify the essential cause-effect relationships, as well as provide a realistic representation of management policies. Complex functional relationships must be highlighted throughout the system. The particular variables to which performance is sensitive must be separately identified with a minimum of aggregation.

The financial simulation model is a formal statement of the relationship among the elements of a company's financial structure. The capital position determines the limits for the marketing and production activities. With simulation the manager can determine the effects of altering the financing patterns, and computational restrictions are no longer the limiting factor.

Implications of Risk and Uncertainty

If a simulation model is accepted for financial planning, then risk analysis can be performed easily. It is possible to simulate at various values for key variables, or perform sensitivity analysis of key items or even to use probabilistic forecasts of the variables in the model. With the capability of a computer, single point estimates are no longer necessary for computational reasons. Stochastic processes may be used to simulate the real world and its uncertainty, and ranges of results may be obtained for a given set of financial variables. Thus profit estimates may be stated as a series of ranges and the probabilities of being in any range specified. In this way a closer relationship can be maintained between risk and rate of return.

SUMMARY

Management has increasingly sophisticated but practical tools to use as aids in decision making. The sophistication is more often in the results attainable, rather than in the difficulty of understanding the techniques. Company size should be no barrier to the use of these techniques.

Although the accountant's role in financial planning for business enterprises is not specified, a wide variety exists—on the one hand, he may be solely a supplier of historical costs, on the other, he may be at the forefront, using the many analytical tools available to aid the decision maker. The accountant is the most appropriate person to assist management in specifying the relationships to be represented in a financial planning simulation model.

The major characteristics of an effective financial plan are:

1. It coordinates enterprise goals and objectives and communicates them to all levels of management.
2. It permits management problems to be specified within the framework of individual responsibility.
3. It makes all management levels responsible for achieving the objectives of the financial plan.
4. It provides a framework for the constant communication of objectives and results and the comparison of results with objectives.
5. It provides the decision maker with an opportunity to test alternatives in order to select the best one.
6. It guides the enterprise towards optimization, according to the individual enterprise's definition.

A financial planning simulation model has these characteristics.

BIBLIOGRAPHY

1. Ackoff, Russell L. *A Concept of Corporate Planning.* New York: Wiley-Interscience, 1970.
2. Christie, C. J. "How to Use Corporate Financial Planning Models Successfully." *C A magazine* (February, 1973).
3. Ferchat, Robert A. "Effective Financial Planning," *C A magazine* (October, 1967).
4. Herson, J. L. "A Simplified Approach to Financial Planning." *The Journal of Accountancy* (February, 1966).
5. Irwin, Patrick H. *Business Planning: Key to Profit Growth.* Toronto: The Ryerson Press, 1969.
6. Khowry, E. N. and H. Wayne Nelson. "Simulation in Financial Planning." *Management Services* (March–April, 1965).
7. Krueger, Donald A. and John M. Kohlmeier. "Financial Modeling and 'What If' Budgeting." *Management Accounting* (May, 1972).
8. LoCascio, Vincent R. "Financial Planning Models." *Management Controls* (August, 1972).
9. Reddin, Patrick J., and James C. Cohrs. "Financial Management and Control." *The Journal of Accountancy* (September, 1969).

10.   Warren, James M., and John P. Shelton. "A Simultaneous
      Equation Approach to Financial Planning." *The Journal
      of Finance* (December, 1971).

QUESTIONS

1. What is a financial planning model? What is it used for?
2. How can simulation be used advantageously for financial
    planning?
3. What are the benefits of a financial planning simulation
    model?

---

93   BUDGETING AND FORECASTING

Harvey B. Quitel

(Reprinted by permission from *Pennsylvania CPA Spokesman*, vol. 43,
no. 2 (October, 1972): 12-14.)

(Harvey B. Quitel is vice president-finance and controller of DCA
Educational Products, Inc.)

INTRODUCTION—THE NEED FOR DIRECTION

A *Time* magazine article in 1966 reported: "Today, the President
does not consider the budget just a report on spending or an accounting
of his stewardship, as it once was, but a powerful tool for controlling
the whole government and a potent instrument for manipulating the economy."
    Whether we speak of organizations the size of the U.S. Government,
giant corporations, medium size companies, or the so-called small business; one thing is prevalent—the need for direction. The toll taken on
small businesses since the late sixties indicates that planning and control are just as critical to small concerns as to larger organizations
and institutions.
    During the "good times," from World War II until the late sixties,
running a successful and profitable small business seemed to be a cinch,
almost automatic. Management of many small businesses made money in
spite of themselves. But along came the days of reckoning, and the
rough and unpredictable economy separated the men from the boys. Many
small companies had no direction, no plan of action, no coordination of
activities, no means of controlling operations. As a result, many were
forced out of business.
    There is probably no need to further stress the importance, neces-
sity, and benefits of an efficient system of budgets and forecasts in

small businesses to the financially-oriented readers of this periodical. What should be stressed, however, is the tremendous gap between the theoretical and practical approach to the problem of budget installation and operation.

The incorporation and operation of a budgetary system for purposes of planning and control is probably made more difficult in smaller companies than in larger ones because of two very important factors:

1. availability of necessary funds and trained personnel in smaller businesses is usually less than in larger ones
2. a lesser degree of sophisticated financial thinking among top and middle management of smaller businesses than in larger ones

SELLING THE CONCEPT—THE CRITICAL TASK

The most critical and difficult task of a chief financial officer of a small organization is that of selling the budgeting and forecasting concept. The chief financial officer must convince top and middle management of the need for direction; the need to plan and control the future of the business in order to maximize profits, achieve growth-oriented goals, and in some cases merely to survive.

Long-term profit maximizing is the primary goal of successful management. Other objectives, such as growth, and responsibilities, such as to employees and customers, often are emphasized, but long-run profits are essential for survival. Budgeting and forecasting help plot the future profit course. Budgets are formal expressions of managerial plans. They are targets that encompass all phases of operations—sales, production, engineering, distribution, and financing.

Budgeting is too often considered to be a mechanical exercise; however, the budgetary system relies more on the human elements than accounting techniques. The success of the system depends upon its acceptance by the personnel who are affected by the budgets. Attitudes ideally should be sympathetic, cooperative, and cost conscious.

Budgets focus attention on departmental responsibility. The natural reaction to restriction, control, and criticism is resistance and self-defense. The job of education and selling is extremely important. Many managers feel budgets represent a penny-pinching, negative pressure. They do not accept the idea that, properly utilized, the budgetary system is a tool for establishing standards of performance, for providing motivation, for gauging results, and for aiding management to advance towards its objectives. The budget technique in itself is free of emotion; its administration, however, is often packed with trouble. A major function of the budget is to communicate the various motivations that already exist among management so that everyone can see, understand, and coordinate the goals and drives of the company.

The importance of the human aspects cannot be overemphasized. Without a thoroughly educated and cooperative management group at all levels of responsibility, budgets are a drain on the funds of the business and are a hindrance instead of a help to efficient operations. A budgetary program per se is not a remedy for weak managerial talent, faulty organization, or a poor information system.

A system of budgets and forecasts for small businesses need not be as elaborate as those used by some larger corporations or as outlined in certain financial textbooks, but some planning and control is useful to any size business. Many managers claim their businesses or particular responsibilities make budgets impractical for them. Yet one can nearly always find at least some companies in the same industry that use budgets. Such companies are usually among the industry leaders and they regard budgets as indispensable aids. The point is that managers and businessmen must grapple with uncertainties with or without budgets and forecasts. Budgeting makes the grappling more effective, and the benefits from budgeting nearly always exceed the costs. This picture is very difficult to present to certain businessmen who still believe that only selling and production people contribute to profits.

BUDGETARY SYSTEMS—AN OVERVIEW

Budgets are basically forecasted financial statements which may span a period of one year or less, and in cases of capital budgeting for plant and product changes up to ten years or more. To assure communication and agreement of corporate goals, an organization should ideally have a master budget which would consist of two major units;

1. an operating budget
2. a financial budget

The operating budget should include the sales forecast or budget, the production budget, and various operating expense budgets. The financial budget should consist of the cash budget, budgeted balance sheet, and budgeted statement of sources and disposition of funds.

Long-term budgets, often called capital or facilities budgets, are not directly part of the operational and financial budgets but should always be considered as part of the master plan.

The most important aspect of making a budgetary system work is the analysis—the comparisons of planned performance with actual performance. Too many times this after-the-fact analysis is not given the attention it should receive.

The investigation of budget variances and deviations should be the line manager's responsibility. The controller or some other high ranking financial manager should also be directly involved, but the actual preparation of the various cost center budgets and review of variances should be the ultimate responsibility of the individual responsible for the cost center.

Ineffective budgetary systems are characterized by the failure of management to develop and use budgets to the fullest potential. Specifically, budgets are many times used only for planning purposes. The real benefits from budgeting lie in the quick investigation of deviations and the subsequent corrective action. Budgets should not be prepared if they are to be ignored or improperly applied.

Accounting formalizes plans by expressing them in the language of figures as budgets. It formalizes control by performance reports, which compare results with plans and spotlight exceptions. These reports spur investigation of exceptions and then operations are brought into conformity with the plans or the plans are revised. This is an example of management by exception, which means that the executive's attention and effort are concentrated on the important deviations from expected results. Such a system reflects the needs of management who want their attention directed to unusual situations and who do not want to be bothered about the smoothly running phases of operations.

Well-conceived plans incorporate enough flexibility or discretion so that the manager may feel free to seize any unforeseen opportunities to improve efficiency or effectiveness. It is very important to realize that the definition of control as conformity to plans does not mean that management should rigidly and blindly adhere to a preexisting plan when unfolding events indicate the desirability of actions which were not specifically thought of in the original plan.

SALES FORECASTS—THE STARTING POINT

The sales forecast is the starting point for the preparation of budgets. Just as accounting and financial people have the reputation of being negative, conservative, and pessimistic personalities; sales and marketing people have the reputation of being positive thinking, optimistic types. Management should beware of unreasonably high sales forecasts and projections. It seems that the closer in time projections get to becoming actual results, the smaller become the sales forecasts. Incurrence of cost naturally correlates with production activity. Activity, in turn, depends on expected sales. The sales forecast is the foundation for putting in writing the entire business plan.

The term "sales forecast" is sometimes distinguished from "sales budget" in that the forecast is considered to be an estimate or prediction which may or may not become the budget depending on whether management accepts the figures as being realistic and objective. Preparation of a sales budget or forecast which is attainable and realistic is a critical point in the budgetary process.

There are many variables which must be considered in establishing accurate forecasts. Some of the more important considerations are past sales statistics; general economic and industry conditions; market research studies; pricing policies; competition; advertising and sales promotion; quantity and quality of sales force; production capacity; seasonal variations; and relative productive profitability.

An effective aid to accurate forecasting is to approach the same goal by several methods; each acting as a check on the others. For example, a company may have the entire sales force, as a group, come up with a prediction for a particular period. At the same time, sales management may prepare a forecast independently using a more or less statistical approach involving trend, cycle projection, and correlation analysis. Finally, all top officers including production and financial officers may use their experience and knowledge to project sales on the basis of group opinion. This type of joint involvement by a large group of responsible and pertinent people should help zero in on a set of realistic figures which are so very important to the system. An accurate and meaningful end result is very much worth the effort.

PROBLEMS OF BUDGETING—DEBATABLE QUESTIONS

The key point of this article is that budgeting, which should theoretically be considered as an important and necessary management tool
for small businesses as well as large, is crammed with practical problems. The reason for most of the practical problems is that budgeting
rests on principles which have more in common with concepts of human
relationships than with rules of accounting. The financial executive
probably faces his greatest challenge in his attempts at educating and
selling budgeting theory and concepts to his management associates.

Many pertinent questions and problems, most of which have no
definite clear-cut answers, must be dealt with using all of the executive's prior training, experience, education, and resources. For
example:

1. Should two sets of budgets be employed—a "liberal" one for
   lower level use and a "conservative" one for use by higher
   level management? Perhaps the justification for using a
   conservative or "safe" budget is that it provides a more
   secure basis for corporate planning, especially with respect to cash availability. On the other hand, advocates
   of a more liberal approach to the subject prefer a "reach"
   or "stretch" budget which is designed to induce incentive
   and possibly to apply pressure to the responsible people.
   However, somewhere between the two extremes of liberal and
   conservative is a desirable type of budget which could be
   labeled "most likely to happen."

2. Should the budget be considered a guarantee of performance;
   does meeting the budget automatically indicate that a good
   job has been done and does missing it indicate poor performance? It must be realized that because of many un-
   foreseeable and unpredictable variables which are beyond
   the control of the responsible persons, actual results
   which are better, equal to, or worse than the budget cannot
   be conclusive evidence of the quality of the managerial job
   performed. Appraisal of performance against budget requires sound judgment and good common sense.

3. Should the budget be revised during the year? Pros and
   cons on this question most likely would depend on which
   level of management is answering. Generally, top level
   management would prefer more rigidity in the system once
   all the pains have been taken to prepare a realistic budget. Lower level management tends to prefer more flexibility during the period depending on changing circumstances.

4. Should incentives be in the form of cash or other tangible
   compensation? Proponents of a cash incentive program for
   meeting or bettering the budget use the analogy of piece-
   work as an effective incentive for workers. They claim
   that nothing works like money. The fallacies and problems of this reasoning are numerous. For example, the
   task of setting a completely fair and acceptable budget
   for this purpose is almost impossible considering the un-
   foreseeable changes in operating conditions. Also, the

tendency of a foreman, supervisor, or manager emphasizing budget performance to the detriment of necessary action becomes a distinct possibility.

Arguments supporting both yes and no answers to these questions and others could well be the subjects of many lengthy debates.

CONCLUSION

Perhaps a summary of thoughts for consideration by management of small businesses for purposes of establishing a budgetary system on a sound foundation could be reduced to the following:

1. Establish the system as a means of setting standards of performance, gauging actual results of operations, and guiding management to proper decisions and achievement of goals.
2. Make it well known that the system is not a pressure device to coerce personnel into greater efforts and performance.
3. Integrate the budget system with the overall corporate philosophy and plan. The budget is not the plan; it is the statement of the plan in the language of numbers.
4. Establish the meaning of control; then be sure it is exercised. The budget should not be considered untouchable but neither should it be taken lightly. Managers should be made to understand that budgets will help them control their particular responsibilities.
5. The system must operate within a clear-cut organizational structure. The budget mechanics should be simple and based on common sense accounting which is more oriented to business than bookkeeping.
6. A relentless and continuous selling and educating campaign must be carried out by the top financial people. Active participation in the program by top management must be insured in order to succeed.

QUESTIONS

1. Why should a small business establish a budget?
2. Of what parts does a master budget consist? Why is each part needed?

94   THE FUNCTION OF CONTROL AND INTERNAL CONTROL

Joaquin Gomez Morfin

(Reprinted by permission from *The Internal Auditor*, vol. 30, no. 1 (January/February, 1973): 42-55.)

(Joaquin Gomez Morfin is principal partner for Gomez Morfin and Associates, CPAs.)

THE CONCEPT OF CONTROL

The function of control, as part of administration, became known at the end of the last century. Henry Fayol in his book *General and Industrial Management*, (1) was one of the first to indicate its nature:

> In an enterprise, control consists of checking to see if every-
> thing is going according to the program adopted, the orders
> given and the accepted principles. Its object is to indicate
> shortcomings and mistakes so that they can be corrected and
> not repeated. It applies to everything, things, persons,
> actions.

Despite Fayol's undoubted merit for establishing for the first time a concept of control, his ideas—probably correct in his time—give control a negative character directed principally toward preventing things from happening (for example: preventing the theft of articles, not spending funds which aren't included in the budget, restricting the use of company vehicles, etc.). Nowadays, the opposite viewpoint is precisely what is true. The real purpose of control is *to make things happen* (for example: increase the usefulness of a product, attain an objective at the previously estimated cost, open new markets satisfactorily, etc.).

A company which has negative-type controls, definitely does not possess an understanding of where it is heading. Moreover, and this is from a psychological point of view, controls which are not positive in character, controls which are repressive and do not advance the objectives of the enterprise, invite evasion by employees.

Another erroneous procedure consists in creating controls apart from the fundamental necessities of a firm. This leads to unnecessary expenses and can cause problems with the personnel. Controls cannot exist in isolation; they should always be united with the planning, organizing and managing functions so that they can contribute to the efficiency of the enterprise.

Controls for the most part depend on information which comes from the activities that are going to be controlled. However, it is worthwhile to make a distinction between what is data or adequate figures and what is properly "information." Data or figures are known or accessible facts. Information signifies data which has been processed, which is up to date; that is, useful, correct and presented in such a manner that it can be used in the best way possible to size up a given situation and proceed to make a decision. Also it is worth noting that the controls and the information on which one relies are not an end in themselves, but elements in an integrated system that contribute towards the achievement of objectives previously established by the administration.

Moreover, the idea of control as a police-type coersion, where it is used exclusively to watch the production of subordinates, tends to disappear. Nowadays, modern management philosophy is based on the integration of individual objectives with those of the company, which gives as a result auto-control. If the officials and employees themselves take part in the creation of objectives to be pursued and are interested in them, the procedures of control which are set up will be useful to the extent that people make use of them to measure their performance, trying always to better it.

Such procedures of control then will not be measures for punishing or rewarding, but valuable helps to determine if the results of the operations are contributing towards the realization of the overall objectives, or in other words, if the individual efforts seem to be moving towards the proposed goals, which will result in the progress and development both of the company as a whole and each one of its components.

To sum up, we can affirm that control as a function and part of the administrative process consists in assuring that the operations that take place fulfill the previously determined plans and objectives.

The answers to three simple questions: Where are we going, where are we now, and how well are we progressing are fundamental for achieving up-to-date control, and, therefore, an efficient administration.

DESIGN FOR A CONTROL SYSTEM

No one can master each one of the phases in the operation of a company or of any type of institution of normal size and be aware of the developments which lead to the realization of the final objectives. Nor can they intervene in the detailed procedures by means of which such objectives can be realized. The delegating of responsibilities is a proof of managerial ability. Nevertheless, delegating should be accompanied also by an effective method for establishing contact with the activities that have been delegated.

Next, we will describe the four principal aspects which comprise the function of control and which should be taken into account in designing an efficient system. Such aspects include:

1. establishment of norms and standards
2. adoption of information systems
3. comparison of the norms with the real results
4. correction of discrepancies

However, before treating such aspects in detail it is convenient to enumerate the indispensable prerequisites so that later the setting up of control procedures will be possible.

Prerequisites

A control system can only be set up and maintained if the other functions of the administrative process—planning, organization and management—are operating correctly.

The basis of efficient administration is, without doubt, *correct planning*. Without plans, a company or any type of institution will be at the mercy of circumstances and will act, or rather, will only react with regard to immediate problems.

Planning presupposes the establishment of objectives and goals. Control will be notably facilitated when all company personnel know the principal objectives to be achieved and when they are familiar with the immediate goals of the departments and sections. Moreover the policies which are necessary in planning require, from the point of view of control, some requisites for their efficient functioning. For example, the necessity that they be put in writing along with the operating procedures and programs. In this way, both the established policies and the proceedings and programs will serve the function of control in a more effective way, since they will not allow for confusion or erroneous interpretations.

Policies should be realistic in the sense that they are practical and can be duly coordinated in the distinct areas of the company. Moreover, they should be sufficiently specific to serve as an effective guide, but not to such an extent that they become rigid and difficult to apply. They should be adaptable to changing conditions without losing sight of the previously determined objectives.

An *appropriate organizational structure* is a first indispensable step toward establishing methods of control. Taking for granted that the most adequate type of formal organization will vary according to the conditions of the company, still—in whatever situation—there should be a clear delegation of authority with its consequent fixing of responsibilities. In a diversified company with a large volume of operations, it is necessary to delegate a large part of the authority in such a way as to give to division heads, and they, in turn, to their subordinates, the power to act independently and rapidly without having to constantly consult with the principal managers. One should not forget that although control varies with managers in relation to the amount of authority and responsibility they possess, the managing function of control is an integrating part of all the levels of an organization.

The use of organization charts, both general type and exclusive for each division and department, as well as diagrams of the process of activities, instruction books and operating manuals, will be indispensable for setting up and preserving control procedures. It is worth emphasizing that all these elements should be presented in a clear and simple form, indicating only the fundamental points without trying to include each and every one of the parts which form the organization. Trying to do so would only give rise to confusion and, consequently, to deficiencies in the exercise of the control function.

Another basic condition for making feasible the establishment and preservation of control systems is the *effective management* of the groups that comprise the company. The coordination of activities and the adequate handling of human relations by the managers will permit the setting up of controls that tend to harmonize the individual activities towards the attainment of the predetermined objectives.

In relation to the function of management, an adequate system of communications is indispensable to attain effective control. Information can take various forms depending on conditions and necessities, but in any case it should project a clear image of what is taking place in the company. Finally, we will repeat what we have already said:

Integrating individual goals with the objectives of the company, as the principal task of management, is not only basic for establishing control systems that orient activities, but also for achieving success for the institution in all its aspects.

Establishment of Norms or Standards

Norms or standards of operation should be projected in such a way that they will serve the particular needs of a company and, keeping in mind that with their adoption, those activities which are vital for its functioning can be measured. At the same time, each one of the elements which are considered as a standard measure should include two basic conditions:

1. that they can help the management formulate decisions
2. that they provide sufficient data for comparison so as to establish an opinion

Details which are incidental or foreign to the case should be avoided since they only lead to delay or distortion in the evaluation.

Control cannot possibly exist if it has not been planned beforehand. Therefore, it is necessary to establish norms or standards during the planning stage and, naturally, the more complete and clearer the plans, the easier it will be to set up better control procedures.

The objectives contained in the plans, as also the standards established to measure their accomplishment, should be understood by all the members of the organization. Both the supervisor of a workshop and a seller should understand the importance, meaning and use of the norms that effect the costs and selling procedures. The establishment of controls, as in the case of objectives, should be a joint effort of management and subordinates, applying the principles already outlined for integration and auto control. (2)

Just as the plans and objectives are subject to a periodic revision, so the measurements derived from the controls should be adjusted periodically and have the flexibility necessary to be adopted to changing conditions.

It is not an easy operation to establish adequate standards. Often the desire to control each and every detail of an activity leads to a bureaucracy whose cost does not justify the hoped-for benefits. A sound criterion would be, first of all, to determine the essential points where it is necessary to measure the activity and the results. Next, a simple and easily interpreted measure that can be used for comparison should be established.

In general, the points subject to measurement can be classified in two groups: those which concern the general progress of the business and pertain to the general management and immediate levels, and those which refer to productivity in smaller areas under the responsibility of department and section heads.

It is logical to assume that each company or any type of institution, in accord with its characteristics and needs, will fix its own norms. In the case of general management and referring to industry, the measurements should cover the aspects of marketing techniques, production, finance, industrial relations and public relations.

Adoption of Information Systems

The adoption of information systems belongs properly to the function of organization. Specifying activities with their consequent responsibilities should include procedures for adequate information that succeeds in indicating the key points which provide indications of what is happening and what might be open to comparison with the previously established standards.

An information system in a company implies a careful study of a whole series of elements which include: accounting system, budgets, statistics, and other sources of necessary information, according to the characteristics and needs of the institution. This is in addition to the aid of mechanical and electronic instruments which help to see that the information provided is correct, up-to-date and easy to understand.

Comparison of the Norms with the Real Results

This comparison implies determining the more important differences which arise when the standards are compared with the real results and evaluating the causes or motives which gave rise to such differences. This task should take place periodically at all levels of the organization and in each one of its principal activities. For example, in some companies the administrative council meets monthly to examine the results of the month, comparing them with the budget.

Probably each week or two, some executive committee of the general management has examined the corresponding reports making the respective comparisons. In these cases, the data studies will be referred to the general aspects of the business such as sales, costs, operating expenses, inventories, accounts payable and, in general, the financial aspects and the results of the operation. In other divisions or departments, the comparison of the norms with the real results will be limited to their own activities and will include the most outstanding data that deserves examination.

An adequate communications system which includes up-to-date and truthful information, besides providing duly-studied bases for comparison, will facilitate enormously the evaluation of the causes of the differences encountered. Sometimes, the duly analyzed reports will provide the necessary explanation; nevertheless, in many cases it will be necessary to amplify such explanations by having recourse to additional information from those responsible. One should remember, however, that to judge any situation of importance, informative data, despite its importance, does not substitute completely for the experience and the good judgment of the manager.

Correction of Discrepancies

Just as it is the responsibility of the management in its various levels to determine the reasons which gave rise to the differences between the determined norms and the real results, so too corrective action pertains to it.

In some cases a change or a simple clarification of instructions is sufficient. Other situations merit important changes in the organiza-

tion and even a careful evaluation of the activities realized by a head
of a department or division, above all in the case of persistent discrepancies. Problems of very different sorts can arise, including emotional situations which provoke failures in personal performance. In
each case one should insist on understanding and acceptance of the established goals, which—as has been said—should be identified with
individual responsibility. At the same time, one should take into account that eliminating the cause of a deficiency is better than correcting the effect. Gaining help and favorable attitudes towards control,
seeing it not as a coercive measure but on the contrary, as a valuable
help towards reaching objectives—both personal and of the company—is
a job for management to convince their subordinates, with the aim of
reaching a high degree of administrative efficiency.

CHARACTERISTICS OF A GOOD CONTROL SYSTEM

Wrong Attitudes and Ideas

Before turning to the requirements needed in a control system, we
consider it worthwhile to mention some attitudes and ideas which are
inconsistent and give rise to false interpretations.

There are various viewpoints towards the problem of control stemming principally from the different attitudes and personalities of managers. In every human activity—and administration is one of them—one's
way of life, character, emotional attitude, intelligence, in short, the
structure of one's personality, is reflected definitely in one's manner
of working and doing business. The function of control cannot be an
exception. There are executives who demand minute and detailed controls
for their operations, often unnecessary. Their distrustful nature leads
them to try to control—almost always in appearance only—to the last
detail. The opposite of this type is the self-sufficient man, very sure
of himself, who does not like control and considers it unnecessary to
establish any system. This is an extreme view of freedom of action and
permits subordinates to act without restrictions, with just an apparent
sense of order and direction.

There is also the mistaken idea of considering the control system
as a part independent of the planning and organization of the company.
Control should not only provide adequate measurements for planning and
evaluating execution, but should also stimulate initiative on the part
of officials and employees.

The function of control should not be confined to one person or one
department, nor should it be treated in a way separated from the organization. Actually, control and organization are inseparable when there
is an efficient administration. In this sense, control refers to defining responsibilities at each level of authority, thus constituting an
integral element in each function of the organization.

This leads us to consider a mistaken, yet commonly accepted concept. Frequently it is said that "The controller is the person who controls." The word "control" supposes the mistaken idea that in a company
the function of controlling is centralized in the office of the controller, and that the data, figures, statistics and, in general, all the
information, not only is compiled by the controller but is only for his

exclusive use. Moreover, some people think, in the same fashion, that the controller has authority to take action without assuming the corresponding responsibility.

Although the company controller should be a top executive, a member of the managerial body and at the same level as others who are in charge of divisions or departments, it should be noted that apart from the usual functions of recording operations, watching credits and billings, supervising office routines, etc., such an official does not possess responsibilities of an operational type. As a matter of fact, the most important tasks of the controller are informing the principal manager and other executives, coordinating plans and budgets and setting up and maintaining systems and procedures. It is worth noting the informative character of these obligations.

One can infer the need to understand that the functions of planning and evaluating the performance are part of the organization as a whole, and therefore, should be spread out at each level of authority instead of being concentrated in a centralized office which is commonly called "the controller." On this ground, control is a dynamic function, a function of governing, and should be conceived not as an obstacle but as an important incentive for developing initiative of the executives.

For their part, controllers should recognize that real control is achieved through actions taken by other executives. In this sense, the role of controllers is to advise managers about the best way to fulfill their functions by providing them with useful, correctly presented information.

Requirements for a Control System

Without a doubt, it should be clear that the best control is *auto control*, that is, efforts should tend towards the integration of duties, in such a way that executives adopt their own particular objectives, supervised and advised by the general management. Following this procedure, they will be in a better position to achieve their objectives and, consequently, it will also be possible to establish means of control that aid their attainment. Every manager or department head should have the necessary information to measure his own efforts. He should receive it in sufficient time to make the necessary changes and thus obtain the desired results. In this way, auto control—not a control "from above"—is established.

Controls should have a *positive meaning*, that is, not be based on things which should not happen. On the contrary, the accomplishment of positive results should be the principal purpose of control, in such a way that they contribute to the previously determined goals.

At the same time, an adequate control system should *be adjusted to the needs of the company* in question, establishing the basic instruments of control according to the characteristics of the departments. Although there are techniques that have a general application in the various activities, as for example, the budgets or comparisons of income and expenses, the basic instruments of one department will be different from those of another. The controls that are adopted in a sales department must be different from the controls of the production department. Moreover, a company with many operations will require different controls than another with fewer operations.

An ideal control system would be one which would discover discrepancies between the norms and the real results before they took place. Granted that this will occur on rare occasions, at least the control system should *bring the discrepancies to light as soon as possible.* Otherwise, the information will hardly help the manager. If the accounting registers are not up to date and, consequently, the financial statements and other reports are not presented on time, accounting will not serve as a means of information necessary for control.

Controls should be *flexible* so that they can be adapted to alternate plans that have been proposed for various probable situations. A rigid sales budget, for example, which does not foresee possible variations in sales, as well as other changes that could take place in the plans, will not be of much use when conditions change.

Reports must be simple so that they can be used conveniently. Complicated charts or very elaborate statistical summaries, instead of serving their purpose, produce confusing situations and problems for obtaining useful information. Of course, when designing instruments of control one should take into account the technical capacity and the training of the persons who are going to use them.

No one spends a dollar to save ten cents. This means that control systems should *justify their cost* and be proportionate to the volume of operations. It is for this reason controls should be adopted only after a detailed study to show the need for establishing them at a reasonable cost.

INTERNAL CONTROL

We have treated the subject of control from an administrative point of view; now we turn to internal control from the angle in which it is seen by the accountants. For this purpose, we will make a critique of concepts expressed both by some authors personally and by the associations of accountants of Mexico and the United States in order to arrive, finally, at some conclusions.

The Origin of the Term

While the expression "internal control" is used with great frequency within the profession of public accounting, there does not exist even now—nor can there exist, as we shall see later—agreement as to what it really means.

Among other things, there seems to be confusion about the meaning of "information" and "control." Many persons consider these two terms synonyms, and others use indiscriminantly "internal control" and "information" to refer to the same thing. It is also interesting to note that in few books that treat themes of administration is there mention of "internal control." On the contrary, in every book of auditing this concept, considered by public accountants an essential element in the examination of financial statements, is given treatment.

What is the origin of the term "internal control"?

It seems that one of the oldest references to the term, also called by some authors "internal check," was made in 1905 by L. R. Dicksee. (3) He indicates that a suitable system of internal check frequently

eliminates the need for a detailed audit. Dicksee's concept of internal
control includes three elements: division of labor, use of accounting
records, and rotation of personnel.

In 1930 George E. Bennett (4) defines internal control in the following way:

> *A system of internal check may be defined as the coordination
> of a system of accounts and related office procedure in such
> a manner that the work of one employee independently perform-
> ing his own prescribed duties checks continually the work of
> another as to certain elements involving the possibility of
> fraud.*

As can be seen, these authors' concept of internal control refers
principally to the division of labor, accounting records and some aspects of personnel. In these definitions, as also in others that we
will cite later on, the reference to certain administrative concepts is
evident. Moreover, both Dicksee and Bennett put emphasis on internal
control for its effects of simplifying the work of auditing and of preventing fraud—ideas which have prevailed until the present.

Montgomery's Concept

In Montgomery's Auditing (5) the authors classify internal control
in three areas. The first of these is "internal administrative control!" . . . "which is that which includes the plan of organization and
all of the coordinate methods and measures adopted within a business to
promote operational efficiency and encourage adherence to prescribed
managerial policies." They distinguish this type of control from "internal accounting control" and from "internal check," since, as the
authors say ". . . administrative controls originate in and are usually
conducted by operating departments other than financial or accounting."

Internal accounting control, continues Montgomery's Auditing,
"check the accuracy and reliability of accounting data." This type of
control is of prime interest for the independent auditor who reports on
the fairness of the financial statements drawn from the records these
controls are designed to protect.

Lastly, the same book continues: ". . . internal check may be described as those accounting procedures or statistical, physical, or
other controls which safeguard assets against defalcations or other similar irregularities."

The authors of this book also say that: "It seems clear that in
making an examination of financial statements leading to an opinion the
auditor is not expected to investigate and evaluate internal administrative control as such . . . It is a generally accepted auditing standard that the auditor's examination should include investigation and
evaluation of internal accounting control on which to base his judgment
whether and to what extent his audit procedures may be restricted . . .
Nevertheless, suggestions for improvement in accounting controls will
often result from such a review, and the auditor has a responsibility to
report to his client wherein, in his opinion, the accounting controls
are inadequate, in the circumstances, reasonably to assure the accurate
and suitable recording and summarization of authorized financial transactions."

Various criticisms can be made of the concepts expressed in Montgomery's Auditing:

1. The definition of internal administrative control, which as a matter of fact corresponds to the concept expressed by the American Institute of Public Accountants, is simply a partial statement of what administration is.

2. The classification which is made of internal administrative control, internal accounting control, and internal check is arbitrary and confuses rather than clarifies the concepts enunciated. It is impossible, from any point of view, to separate in such a drastic manner aspects which are stated about control when in reality they are organizational procedures.

3. To say that internal accounting control verifies the correctness and the reliability of the figures of accounting is really to speak of a duly planned and organized information system. Here is where the confusion arises between the terms "information" and "control." Accounting does not control, it simply informs. Control, as we have explained before, is an administrative function that requires for its execution standards, information, comparisons, and determination of discrepancies, as well as corrective procedures.

4. Finally, the term "internal check," applied to preventing fraud, tends to debilitate this task. In accord with modern ideas of administration, the simple fact of establishing determined procedures does not eliminate the perpetration of irregularities. It is imperative that an efficient administration exists at all levels; that is, that the functions of planning, organizing, managing, and control be accomplished in a coordinated manner and, above all, that the human relations in the company be given consideration and importance.

*Concept of the American Institute
of Public Accountants*

The American Institute of Public Accountants (6) defines internal control as:

Internal control comprises the plan of the organization and all the coordinate methods and measures adopted within a business to safeguard its assets, check the accuracy and reliability of its accounting data, promote operational efficiency, and encourage adherence to prescribed managerial policies. This definition possibly is broader than the meaning sometimes attributed to the term . . .

The report referring to internal control in which this definition appears continues to explain ". . . that an internal control system extends beyond those matters which relate directly to the functions of the accounting and financial departments."

This report also indicates,

> . . . *that the characteristics of a satisfactory internal control system are the following:*
>
> 1. *a plan of organization which provides appropriate segregation of functional responsibilities*
> 2. *a system of authorization and record procedures adequate to provide reasonable accounting control over assets, liabilities, revenues, and expenses*
> 3. *sound practices to be followed in performance of duties and functions of each of the organizational departments*
> 4. *a degree of quality of personnel commensurate with responsibilities*

Both with regard to the definition of internal control and the accompanying concepts expressed by the Committee on Auditing Procedures of the American Institute of Accountants, one can make observations similar to those made in the case of the concept by Montgomery.

In reality, they express—also in an inadequate way—administrative ideas related to the organization and handling of personnel. They insist, at the same time, in "the protection of assets" and in "the checking of the correctness and truthfulness of the accounting data."

In our judgment, it would have been preferable to formulate a clear concept with regard to administration, since, as we have stated previously, the function of control can only be exercised if adequate planning and organization exists, as well as managing which includes human relations in its widest sense. In this way assets are protected, operations are efficient and prescribed policies are followed. Moreover, reliability on accounting data is obtained—as we have already said—through an adequate organization of information systems.

Concept of the Mexican Institute of Public Accountants

The Bulletin of the Committee of Auditing Procedures of the Mexican Institute of Public Accountants, referring to internal control (7) states the following:

> *In its widest sense, internal control is the system by which one brings about the administration of an economic entity. In this sense, the term "administration" is used to designate the entirety of activities necessary to achieve the object of the economic entity. It includes, therefore, the activities of management, financing, promotion, production, distribution, and consumption of a company, its public and private relations and general watchfulness for its possessions and for those things on which its preservation and growth depend.*

This same Bulletin goes on to say that:

> *All of the plans which are elaborated and all of the procedures which are realized in each one of the phases of the*

business constitute the general "systems" or "methods" of its administration, by which, still in its widest sense, one designates a "system" of internal control the sum of all the "systems" or "methods" which the administration uses to attain its various objectives.

This Bulletin further states that: "in mercantile associations internal control constitutes the manifestation of the way in which the administrative council and its delegates, such as directors or managers, fulfill their tasks . . ."

According to the Committee on Auditing Procedures of the Mexican Institute, one can group the elements of internal control in four classifications, namely:

1. organization
2. procedure
3. personnel
4. supervision

Just as with the other concepts discussed, the idea which the Bulletin expresses is a mixture of administrative notions with the novelty that internal control is: "the system by which the administration is brought about . . ." It is indeed a very unique concept which only gives rise to confusion, above all when it overemphasizes the fact that internal control is: ". . . the sum of all the 'systems' or 'methods' which the administration utilizes . . ."

Moreover, the fact of affirming that: "internal control constitutes the manifestation of the way in which the administrative council and its delegates fulfill their tasks . . ." gives rise to an increase of confusion about what, all things considered, internal control is.

Other Opinions

Many accountants outside of the United States have continued to busy themselves with the theme of internal control. Although varying explanations are given, in reality, the central idea is that "internal control" as used by accountants is similar to the concept of "control" expressed by administrators.

Eugenio Sisto Velasco (8) expresses it this way:

. . . To my way of thinking, when accountants give the concept "internal control" the amplitude noted in the definitions of both the North American and the Mexican Institutes of Public Accountants, they are giving to this term a meaning similar to that which, in the field of administration, the word "control" by itself has, and which we accountants call "administrative control." The only difference is in the emphasis which is given to the concept in the definition. From the administrative point of view it is the human aspect that stands out, and when the accountant speaks of "internal control" he gives more importance to the structural aspect . . .

Finally, the author of this study in a previous book, (9) established a concept also similar to the ideas which have and still prevail in the area of public accounting. Later, in an article (10) which treats the theme of internal control, when trying to mesh the ideas of accountants with those of administrators concerning this concept, the author affirmed that internal control constitutes the mechanism which helps the administrator to exercise his function of control.

CONCLUSIONS

We have tried to present a general panorama of the theme "internal control" about which enormous quantities of ink have already been spent. Before stating some conclusions, it seems expedient to reaffirm our ideas about the connection existing between administration and the public accountant. We should recognize, first of all, that accounting, the principle discipline in the formation of the public accountant, is only a means towards an end, and that is to provide a historical record of the transactions so that, through their interpretation, the management of a business or any type of institution can make the most suitable decisions. Moreover, it should be emphasized that the public accountant in his typical function of examining financial statements for purposes of expressing an opinion *is informing*. The present tendency of the profession is to intervene not only in information of a financial type but in all those aspects which are of interest for administrators and which help them to exercise control. In this sense, the public accountant will need ample preparation in the area of information systems.

Once again we insist it will do our accounting colleagues a lot of good to review administrative concepts, in such a way that what control signifies from the administrative viewpoint can be expressed in understandable language. For, in the end, this is the only viewpoint that matters since the accounting profession is related to, and really constitutes a specialization of administration in the field of information services.

Based on what has been said, it is possible to make the following conclusions:

1. The public accountant should depend on the information systems of the company. Such systems, of course, include the accounting system as the principal source of financial information.
2. In these conditions, the auditor will need to determine the efficiency of the administration in relation to the correct information the respective systems offer him.
3. A clear and precise distinction should be made that information of any sort, in itself, does not provide control. Accounting figures and other data that the information systems supply are only elements for judging, and they, along with the standards, comparisons made, discrepancies and corrective measures determined (which are derived from administrative action) provide control of activities.
4. In an isolated form, systems of internal check or measures to protect the assets against fraud do not prevent the perpetration of these offenses. In order to prevent de-

ceitful manipulations, administration must be efficient and among other things, give importance and full consideration to all aspects of human relations.

5. In order to avoid confusion and to proceed towards a profitable unification in expressions, it is suggested that the public accounting profession suppress the term "internal control." Moreover, the same profession should spread the concept of "control," in conformity with the administration criterion.

REFERENCES

1. Henry Fayol. *Administración Industrial y General* (México: Herrero Hermanos, 1964).
2. Douglas McGregor. *The Human Side of Enterprise*. (New York: McGraw-Hill, 1960.)
3. Robert H. Montgomery. *Dicksee's Auditing*, quoted in *C. P. A. Handbook*, American Institute of Accountants, 1956.
4. George E. Bennett. *Fraud—Its Control through Accounts* (New York: Appleton-Century, 1930).
5. Norman J. Lenhart and Philip L. Defliese. *Montgomery's Auditing*, 8th edition (New York: The Ronald Press, 1957).
6. *Internal Control*. A special Report made by the Committee on Auditing Procedure of the American Institute of Accountants, 1949.
7. *Examen del Control Interno*. Bulletins of the Committee on Auditing Procedures of the Mexican Institute of Public Accountants, 1957.
8. C. P. A. and Lic. in Administration Eugenio Sisto Velasco. *Control Interno y Control Administrativo—Finanzas y Contabilidad*—México, 1968.
9. C. P. A. Joaquin Gómez Morfin. *El Control Interno en los Negocios*, sixth edition, Fondo de Cultura Económica, México, 1968.
10. C. P. A. Joaquin Gómez Morfin. *The Need for a General Knowledge of Administration on the part of Public Accountants—Modern Techniques of Administration*, Mexican Institute of Public Accountants, México, 1970.

QUESTIONS

1. Define control as it applies to an enterprise.
2. Describe the four major aspects of the function of control.
3. How does the accounting system help establish control?
4. Does the term "internal control" as used in accounting literature mean the same thing as the term control used in administrative literature? Explain.
5. Why is control needed?

95   INTERNAL CONTROL IN CHURCHES

Park E. Leathers
Howard P. Sanders

(Reprinted by permission from *The Internal Auditor*, vol. 29, no. 3
(May/June, 1972): 21-25.)

(Park E. Leathers is a former member of the firm of Arthur Andersen & Co. He is a doctoral candidate at the University of Pennsylvania.
Howard P. Sanders is a faculty member at the University of South Carolina.)

Churches differ in faith and ideology, but one thing they have in
common is that over a year's time they receive and spend a large portion
of their members' disposable incomes. Some churches have annual receipts and expenditures exceeding a million dollars, and even a fairly
small congregation routinely collects and dispenses a thousand dollars
a week. These sums compare favorably with those accounted for by many
of the nation's small- and medium-sized business firms.
All too often these large sums of money are handled in a very
casual way. In this article we discuss common internal control weaknesses in churches and suggest procedural improvements.

ORGANIZATION

Responsibility for church operation generally is vested in a board
of trustees or similar body with delegation of the finance function to
the church treasurer and finance committee. In most of the larger
churches, actual stewardship of church funds is entrusted to a salaried
employee, the financial secretary (or bookkeeper), with nominal supervision by the treasurer. (1) Besides keeping church records, the financial secretary often deposits cash collections, approves disbursements, signs checks, reconciles the bank account, prepares the financial statements, and constitutes the unquestioned authority on church
finances.
Auditors will note the similarity between the financial secretary's
position and the classic business situation of the trusted bookkeeper
who can do no wrong. The financial secretary fits this stereotype well;
he (or she) often has held his job for a long period and is underpaid.
An added dimension is that an aura of virtue is associated with work in
a church. Few members are willing to admit even a possibility of wrong-
doing or mismanagement by those they have entrusted with their contributions.
There are cases on record of misappropriation of church funds, of
course. Underpaid church employees are subject to financial problems
and temptation, and the embezzler usually succeeds in justifying his
malfeasance to himself. There are other reasons, however, for institut-
ing better controls—safeguarding of assets from deterioration and

theft, improvement of the reliability of accounting records, economical management of church finances, and avoidance of questions regarding dishonesty or mismanagement. The advocate of a better system should emphasize the positive benefits of improvements rather than impugning the honesty of long-term employees.

What changes typically are needed in the church organization? First, the finance function should be exercised by the individual or group to which it is nominally assigned, the church treasurer or the finance committee. Second, the financial secretary's activities should be confined to record-keeping and preparation of support for disbursements. He should not handle cash contributions and should not be a check signer. These functions should be exercised by the treasurer or a finance committee representative. Third, it is desirable that an audit committee be appointed. This committee may perform internal audit work or engage an independent auditor.

CONTROL OVER WEEKLY CONTRIBUTIONS

The majority of the church's receipts consists of collections made at weekly services. In a typical situation these collections are made during the service by a voluntary team of ushers, left unattended during the remainder of the service, gathered up by the treasurer or chief usher following the service, and then hidden in a "safe place" or locked in the church safe for counting and deposit by the financial secretary on Monday morning. In other cases the treasurer may count the collection but keep no record. In both situations church funds are vulnerable to misappropriation or error by church officers and employees, other church members, or outsiders.

Collections never should be completely controlled by one person, and they should be deposited as soon as possible. The financial secretary, as previously noted, should not participate in the collection and banking process. He should receive only the report prepared by the money-counters (two or more), and they should retain a copy of this report and furnish one to the audit committee. Money should be counted as soon as possible in a safe protected place and then placed in the bank's night depository. These funds are extremely vulnerable to theft during the period of the count and any time prior to deposit, even though they may be in the church safe.

ENVELOPE SYSTEMS

Many churches use pledge cards and/or envelope systems. The reason for adoption of these systems apparently has been the higher collections they lead to, not the better control they provide. Control aspects often are ignored.

Because so many members do not return all of their envelopes, it generally is impracticable to attempt to account for all the prenumbered envelopes. However, it is practicable to count and record the amounts included in each envelope and maintain a members' contribution record based upon them and the pledge cards. If the church is to furnish proper support for the tax deductibility of members' contributions, this type of record is essential.

Members should receive periodic advices as to the amounts they have pledged and actually contributed. Preparation and circulation of these advices should be properly performed by the audit committee as a confirmation procedure at least once during the year. Besides providing a check on accounting for contributions, the use of contribution advices often will have the beneficial effect of stimulating members to fulfill their pledges.

OTHER RECEIPTS

Weekly worship service collections account for the majority of receipts at most churches, but receipts from other sources also may be substantial. The degree of control, of course, must be varied by the amounts involved. The negative effects of excessive controls upon member and employee morale should not be ignored.

Offerings from the education (or Sunday school) hour are generally made in individual classes. Here the control effort again should be to avoid the handling of cash by unobserved individuals. Rather than permitting the class secretary to take the collection to the money-counting team, it is better to have two members of the team visit each class. A bag locked by the secretary in the presence of the class for opening only by the money-counters is an acceptable alternative, but one which usually will be considered onerous to the individuals involved. A sealed envelope fulfills the same objective to some extent.

Contributions sometimes are mailed to the church office. It is preferable that someone (two people, if possible) other than the financial secretary open incoming mail. A record of mail receipts should be maintained for use by the audit committee, and a report of receipts should be furnished to the financial secretary. Fortunately, most mail contributions are checks, which reduces risks.

The variety of other church receipts precludes comment on each. Where possible, these rules should be followed:

1. The financial secretary should not handle cash.
2. Unrecorded cash should not be within the control of one person and an independent record should be maintained.
3. Record of receipts should be established as soon as it is possible.
4. Receipts for cash should be given.
5. The use of checks by donors should be encouraged, and checks should be restrictively endorsed upon their receipt.
6. Funds should be kept in a safe place and deposited as soon as practicable.

DISBURSEMENTS

Internal control weaknesses in procedures are similar in churches to those encountered in small businesses. The financial secretary typically receives all bills, prepares checks for payment, and reconciles the bank account. He also may be the sole check signer. Many

churches require two signatures, the financial secretary's and the
treasurer's. For the sake of convenience the treasurer often signs
checks in blank.

A better system features the following:

1. Assembly and review of support for disbursements and
    preparation of the check by the financial secretary.
    Invoices should be approved by the person who ordered
    and received the materials or service.
2. Signature and mailing of the check by one or more members
    of the finance committee. The signer should examine sup-
    porting documents and cancel them in some way to prevent
    their use in support of other disbursements.
3. Receipt and reconciliation of the bank statement by the
    audit committee.

Expenditures generally should be made by check. As a practical
matter, it may be necessary to provide the financial secretary with a
petty cash fund. This fund should be imprest, and the financial secretary should be required to provide support for reimbursements of the
fund.

OTHER AREAS FOR IMPROVEMENT

Many churches have budgets, but the budget often is not used as the
effective planning and control device it can be. The budget should not
be ignored in making expenditures, but it also should not be a strait
jacket. Variations from the budget should be explained and approved but
no effort should be made to juggle the bookkeeping to make the budget
and expenditure for each item equal.

Many of the people involved in handling cash and financial records
are untrained for such work. They serve on voluntary and temporary
bases. To provide continuity, it is desirable that written instructions
be prepared.

No accounting system is perfect. Therefore, even though the church
may adopt all of the above procedural recommendations, it is also desirable that members and employees having access to cash or financial records be bonded.

CONCLUSION

The accountant has an opportunity to contribute more than suste-
nance and goodwill to the effectiveness of church operations. His efforts to improve internal control and financial planning often will not
be properly appreciated by all members of the congregation, and certainly he must be tactful in making suggestions. There is important
work to be done, however, and by virtue of his training, he is properly qualified to undertake it.

FOOTNOTE

1. In smaller churches, the duties performed by the paid
    financial secretary are assigned to an unpaid church
    officer, the secretary or treasurer. Inasmuch as there
    is no internal check on this person's activities, this
    discussion also applies to the small church.

BIBLIOGRAPHY

1. Frederickson, "Simplified Cash Receipts System for a Non-
    profit Organization," *The Journal of Accountancy* (January,
    1961), pp. 81–82.
2. Ingalls, *Practical Accounting and Auditing Problems*
    (1966), pp. 111–112.
3. Larson, "Church Accounting," *The Journal of Accountancy*
    (May, 1957), pp. 28–35.
4. Meigs and Larsen, *Principles of Auditing* (1969), pp.
    94–124.

QUESTIONS

1. List the control features which the authors suggest for
    proper accountability.
2. Should an accountant or CPA look at a church any differ-
    ently than he does an industrial enterprise? Is internal
    control as important in a church as it is for General
    Motors?
3. Why would any accountant be interested in the internal
    control problems of a church?

96   "FLASH REPORT" GROSS INCOME
                       TO IDENTIFY BUDGET VARIANCES

                            Arthur P. Nash

(Reprinted from *Hospital Financial Management* (March, 1973): 15–16.
Copyright 1973, Hospital Financial Management Assn.)

So you have a budget. Fine.

You produce a monthly report of budget versus actual. Very good.

Significant variances are analyzed and follow-up action taken where
necessary. Excellent.

But suppose a problem exists from the beginning to the end of
March. In most cases, this situation would not be exposed until the
middle or end of April when the March report is completed.

Since timeliness is a key factor in reducing losses, why not be alerted to the problem's existence in its early stages by using flash reporting?

Flash reporting can be applied to all budget components, but let us restrict it here to gross income.

FLASH REPORTING OF GROSS INCOME

A weekly summary could fill this need for timeliness. The fiscal director could then learn early that a problem is developing, investigate and take corrective action. Such a report would also localize situations to be analyzed in more detail in the monthly budget report. At the very least, the fiscal director will be kept current on the performance of each ancillary service department.

WHY CLOSE SCRUTINY IS IMPORTANT

Five reasons are listed below for close scrutiny of gross income.

1. Rendering ancillary services and producing charges are the first steps of a process which assures cash flow and thereby the hospital's operation. Any delay in producing charges can adversely affect billing and the hospital's cash position.
2. Gross income is the fiscal barometer of ancillary service department activity. Correlated with other statistics it can give the fiscal officer a good picture of what is happening in that area. In other words, it is a measure of activity which can be used for many purposes (e.g., for reference when a department head requests overtime or creation of a new position).
3. Income figures are employed as bases of allocation for ancillary service departments in the annual Medicare report.
4. Even though third party reimbursement is based on per diem cost, charges are still important for self-pay and commercial insurance patients. While these categories have been declining in recent years, they still represent approximately ten percent of total patient days.
5. Third party reimbursement is based on costs, and costs are closely related to income. Anything that significantly affects income will eventually affect costs. Income variances from the budget, therefore, must be analyzed with concern.

HOW SHOULD THIS REPORT LOOK?

The budget should show income by patient classification: inpatient, clinic, emergency room, etc. Further breakdown of inpatient into medical and surgical, maternity, pediatrics, nursery, etc., is desirable.

These classifications could either be listed consecutively or on separate pages. Table 17 shows a sample page.

TABLE 17

XYZ HOSPITAL
REPORT OF GROSS INCOME—MEDICAL AND SURGICAL
FOR THE WEEKLY PERIOD MARCH 1-7, 197_

Type of Income	WEEK				MONTH-TO-DATE			
	Actual	Budget	Over (Under) Budget	Percent of Variance	Actual	Budget	Over (Under) Budget	Percent of Variance
Room & Board								
Ancillary Services:								
Oper. Room								
Deliv. Room								
Radiology								
Laboratory								
Etc.								

Because correlation with departmental statistics is advisable, such figures should be included, perhaps listed directly after the income amounts.

It is only fair to point out that while this report is referred to as a "flash" report it calls for much detail and would most likely work well only if computerized. Manual preparation would be time-consuming and is probably not feasible. One benefit of computerization is that the computer can be programmed to identify significant variations.

HOW TO ALLOCATE BUDGET FIGURES

The budget is usually divided into monthly periods but for this flash report it could be divided into 52 weekly periods based on previous experience or budget estimates of patient day statistics, taking into account budgeted rate increases.

Some argue that the budget should be divided into daily periods as is done in some industrial firms. But a day is probably too short a period to work with because it would be a tedious project to develop daily budget figures based on past experience. And while weekly comparisons would not necessarily disclose poor work scheduling, a day could reflect unrepresentative occurrences. It is not worth the effort to analyze occurrences which are rare and immaterial to the whole picture.

PINPOINTING WHAT IS WRONG

Before discussing the causes, let us review the effects on the hospital of late or missed charges. It will cause a lag in billing, decrease cash flow and lower advances from third party payers. Late charges also confuse patients who receive a second bill. Miscoding of income could also hurt the hospital on the Medicare report.

1. A slowdown may be caused by poor work scheduling, sloppy, unchecked work or even a department head on vacation. A fiscal director who is on his toes should spot this when reviewing his weekly report.
2. It may be that clerical employees are on vacation with no backup staff. All department heads must be made responsible for scheduling vacation relief to insure a steady flow of charges.
3. It may even be that the charges have reached the business office but are not being processed quickly enough.
4. Income may be posted in the wrong period. Friday's charges may not be posted until Monday, thus throwing off two periods.
5. Budgeted rate increases may not have gone into effect as scheduled.

CONCLUSION

Flash reporting can disclose a multitude of sins or show the fiscal director that operations are running smoothly. The flash report can become another administration tool and should be seriously considered for analysis and control of gross income.

QUESTIONS

1. Why is gross income so important to hospital operations? Does this have anything to do with a hospital's mix of fixed and variable costs? Explain.
2. What are the benefits to be gained from timely reporting?

---

97   IMPLEMENTATION AND MAINTENANCE OF
                           A COST ACCOUNTING SYSTEM

Douglas A. Volk

(Reprinted by permission from *Pennsylvania CPA Spokesman*, vol. 43,
no. 2 (October, 1972): 8-11.)

(Douglas A. Volk is a member of the firm of Arthur Young & Co.)

The principles of good business management apply not only to the
giant corporations such as those listed in "Fortune's 500," but extend
to any business enterprise, including the smallest entrepreneur. Profit
can be said to be the prime motivating factor in business, notwithstanding such factors as fulfillment of social responsibilities and development of the individual as a person. In any event, under the free enterprise system, a company that does not operate at a profit will not long
be able to fulfill any of its responsibilities. Profits should not be
treated as a consequence of fate or luck, but should be planned for.
One of the tools that businessmen, both large and small, should have to
enhance the successful pursuit of profit is an adequately implemented
and maintained cost accounting system, one that will enable management
to determine costs useful for profit measurement, to develop costs appropriate for management decisions and to aid in control of operations.
    Cost accounting is a refinement of general financial accounting
procedures which enables a business concern to determine the unit costs
of manufacturing various products or rendering services. This refinement makes it possible to determine these costs not only at the end of
a fiscal period, but at the time an article is manufactured or a service
is rendered. If a business manufactures a relatively small number of
products which require only a few elementary procedures to complete over
a short period of time, satisfactory unit costs could probably be obtained from an analysis of operating statements prepared on a monthly
basis or at other appropriate intervals. As the number of products increases and the manufacturing procedures become more complex, then a
more sophisticated cost accounting system would be required. In the
case of a service industry, such as a janitorial service, adequate unit
costs may be developed through analysis of the various operating expenses. An industry involved in manufacturing will need a more detailed
breakdown of its various costs to enable proper identification of unit
costs. The development and identification of these unit costs enable
management to measure production efficiencies, compute break-even analyses and marginal-income analyses, and establish pricing policies.
Cost accounting thus facilitates the decision-making process by providing management with the data necessary to assist in the control of both
current and future costs, ultimately resulting in the attainment of
profits for the business.

COST ACCOUNTING—IS THERE REALLY A NEED?

As small businesses are organized and operations commenced, initial
emphasis in most instances is directed towards establishment of procedures necessary to produce a product or service and to determine and

penetrate the available market. However, initial successes should not
be allowed to distort the thinking of management to the extent that control of costs are ignored. In the early stages of development, perhaps,
management does have an adequate knowledge of costs sufficient to enable
proper control of the business. However, as the business prospers, the
entrepreneur will be hard pressed to stay on top of the many variable
factors affecting costs which will now drift further away from his
knowledge and control of the cost structures by reason of the dilution
of his efforts over a wider area and the delegation of responsibilities
to subordinates. If, however, he devotes the time necessary to be directly involved in all of the detail areas, he will probably suffer in
other areas. For example, he may lose or reduce the focus of the "big
picture" and personnel problems may develop if subordinates feel they
are not being properly utilized. A relatively simple cost system can
provide the information needed to control the business and free him from
his involvement with detail. In addition to being able to more effectively control the business, an effective cost system can complement the
general financial accounting system and facilitate the preparation of
financial statements and analyses which measure the periodic results of
operations. A company, which does not accumulate and utilize cost data
effectively, may be severely handicapped.

Typical management objections to a cost system are "it's too
costly," "the company is not large enough" or "my good business sense
will tell me when costs are out of control." There are many reasons why
management may be shortsighted in maintaining such an attitude. Although the overall results of operation of a business may be favorable,
a proper analysis of costs may indicate areas where efficiencies may be
effected. Additional benefits are obtained from the ability to identify
responsibility for variations. Favorable variations may be rewarded and
corrective action can be taken to eliminate unfavorable variations. Additionally, adequate knowledge of unit costs will enable management to
avoid the pitfalls of improper product pricing and making market strategy decisions which may adversely affect the business. For example, a
company may have three products, one of which is profitable, one break-
even and one is sold below cost. If management does not have the ability to make this determination, a variance in sales mix could result in
a significant detrimental variation in earnings. For example, a business with products which are profitably priced, but which has a low
marginal income ratio, may attempt a market penetration with a large
sales and advertising effort. In this instance, the increased revenues
may simply not be worth the effort, and could result in a loss situation. However, if management is aware of product line profitability,
sales efforts can be increased in the profitable product lines and cut
back or eliminated in the loss product lines.

The usefulness of the information produced by a cost accounting
system is dependent upon the accuracy of the system. Cost data may be
accumulated in basically two forms. In the first, statistical data may
be gleaned from records such as production orders, material requisitions, job time tickets, production reports, and manufacturing overhead analysis, with no attempt made to integrate or identify with the
general financial accounting system. Under this system, extensive
reconciliations may be necessary to "tie into" the information summarized in the general financial accounting system in order to ensure
that all costs have been accounted for. Perpetual inventories are

normally not maintained under this system; thus periodic and time-consuming physical inventories must be taken. Such a system has certain disadvantages, especially for a manufacturing business, but may be useful to a service business. The second method provides for the accumulation of cost data in accounting records which are integrated with the general financial accounting system, that is, controlled by and subsidiary to the records of that system. The primary advantage of such a system is that it enables the existing internal controls to be extended to the cost areas.

A cost accounting system consists of a series of forms, journals, ledgers, accounting entries and management reports, sufficiently organized so that unit costs can be determined on a timely basis and used by management in the decision-making process. There are two major types of cost accounting systems generally in use, the job order cost system which is used to accumulate costs by specific jobs or lots, and the continuous process, or departmental cost system, which accumulates costs by department for a definite period of time.

JOB ORDER COST SYSTEM

The job order cost system is used when a specific item is manufactured, requiring a complete record of cost for the job. This system collects separately each element of cost for each job or order worked on by the plant. Production may be performed to maintain inventory levels or to manufacture goods made to order for a specific customer. A master summary sheet commonly known as a job order cost sheet is prepared for each job or order, upon which all costs relative to the order are recorded, including direct materials used, direct labor incurred, and manufacturing overhead, which is usually applied based on a predetermined rate. Job order cost sheets may be utilized to compare actual costs of production to estimated costs, and to form a basis for comparison of the relative profitability of different types of goods produced.

Direct materials used are posted to the job order cost sheet from the store's requisition, which may be priced and extended at the time the requisitions are posted to the store's records. The job time tickets, which contain a breakdown of direct and indirect labor, provide the posting source for direct labor by jobs, while indirect labor is recorded on the ticket by department. Manufacturing overhead is usually applied according to a predetermined rate, which may be developed according to two methods, absorption costing and direct costing. Under the former, an estimate is made of all manufacturing costs of a period expected to be incurred which cannot be identified with specific jobs after considering the production expected for that period. The predetermined rate is developed by dividing the total of these manufacturing overhead costs by the production expected in terms of units, labor costs, material costs, labor hours, or other basis. At the end of a period, the total manufacturing overhead costs charged to jobs through use of the predetermined rate may be compared to the actual manufacturing overhead costs incurred and any variations analyzed and explained. Under direct costing, the predetermined manufacturing rate is developed by utilizing only variable manufacturing overhead costs in the calculation of the rate. All other overhead costs are considered period costs and charged to profit and loss. Absorption costing is

almost universally used for purposes of reporting financial information
to persons other than management; however, direct costing provides a
number of advantages over absorption costing when cost data is being
evaluated. Profit contribution calculations may be made by deducting
direct costs from sales. This profit or marginal contribution can
easily be compared with the period costs to show the impact of the
volume of sales. The amount of profit must be great enough to cover all
period costs to achieve a break-even level. Also, because of the difference in method of treating period costs, profits under absorption
costing fluctuate with changes in production. Under direct costing,
profits fluctuate with sales, rather than with production.

Job order cost systems have the advantages of providing management
with the ability to determine individual job profitability, to provide
a basis for estimating costs of a similar job in the future, and to
provide a basis for controlling efficiency of operations. Offsetting
these advantages is the additional cost of operating a job order cost
system, due primarily to the large amount of detail that must be maintained.

Job order cost systems are used in many industries, such as job
printing, manufacture of special types of machinery, and by producers
of goods which are dissimilar. They may also be used in addition to
some other system of cost accounting. For example, a continuous process
plant utilizing a process cost system may use a job order cost system to
determine the cost of special plant repair projects.

CONTINUOUS PROCESS COST SYSTEM

Continuous process cost accounting is used by a business which manufactures products in a more or less continuous flow, without reference
to specific orders or lots. Businesses which utilize continuous process
cost system include textiles, sugar refineries, bakeries, petroleum
products, plastics, chemicals, etc. Costs, including materials, labor
and manufacturing overhead, are accumulated by areas or departments and
divided by equivalent units produced to obtain average unit costs of
processing. Unit costs of each area are combined to obtain a total cost
per unit of product. Overhead manufacturing rates such as those utilized in job order cost systems are not ordinarily required, since in a
continuous process situation there is greater uniformity both in products processed and operations accomplished within one department.

Direct costing may also be utilized with a continuous process system; however, care must be exercised when identifying the variable vs.
fixed costs of each department.

Continuous process cost systems have the advantages of costs being
computed frequently, average costs being easier to compute provided the
product is homogeneous, and a minimum of clerical effort and expense being required. Some disadvantages include varying unit costs for the
same item of inventory when the volume of production fluctuates between
cost periods, and since costs such as material or labor are averaged
over units of production, variations are hidden. For example, reduced
efficiency in the use of materials or manpower may be offset by a decrease in the price of materials or labor rates.

BUDGETING AND STANDARDS

Production and performance assumptions must also be made in terms of normal operating conditions. It would seem unreasonable in most cases to attempt to measure production efficiency against a standard based upon maximum total plant capacity. A more reasonable measure perhaps would be yearly estimated volume based upon sales forecasts.

Budgets are critical to the establishment and usefulness of any cost accounting system. The budget is an estimate or forecast of items such as sales revenues, manufacturing costs, operating expenses, and other items including net income, covering a specific period or periods of time. Budgets would be utilized in the determination of the predetermined manufacturing rate as previously described, and also in the proper formulation and analysis of predetermined or standard costs as noted below.

Cost data may be divided into two additional categories, historical costs and standard costs. The former are computed when the manufacturing process has been completed or at some later date. These costs have value for future use to improve correct practices followed in the past; however, costs may be controlled as they are incurred through the use of standard costs, which are based upon past results and future projections. Standard costs may be compared with historical costs and the extent of variation noted and followed up by management with corrective action. Standard costs do not represent a system separate from other cost systems such as the job order cost and continuous process cost systems noted above, but rather provide an additional means for management to analyze and control costs. Standard costs also reduce clerical expense, since all data related to an item or unit may be stated in consistent terms. Any significant variation from standard to actual may be analyzed and if necessary the standards may be revised to more closely reflect actual conditions. In order to be effective, standards should be formulated utilizing those personnel who will be held responsible for variations from standard. Once standards are met, they should be compared to actual results on a monthly basis or at other appropriate intervals, and any variations (including those which are favorable) should be explained by personnel who have been assigned responsibility for production performance and cost control. This should take the form of a report highlighting variations by cost category, with reasons for variations documented in writing in the report.

COST ACCOUNTING—OTHER USES

The discussion above has demonstrated that an adequate cost accounting system will provide management with reports to help in effectively managing the business. Other areas of usefulness will now be discussed briefly.

The importance of segregating manufacturing costs into fixed and variable elements has been previously mentioned. When direct costing is used, the accounts will already be segregated into fixed and variable categories. Costs incurred by a business which utilizes the absorption method may also be segregated into fixed and variable categories providing that cost data is adequately identified in the accounts. The preceding discussions of costs and cost systems have placed emphasis on costs of manufacturing. However, fixed and variable costs, when segregated and identified, and utilized with other data, can provide management with several additional useful tools. One of these is the break-even analysis, which may by prepared for a single product or a group of products, for example. The starting point in the break-even analysis is the estimation of costs in various levels of output. An illustration of a break-even analysis presented in chart form appears on this page.

From the break-even chart we can determine that all of the fixed costs will have been covered at the break-even point of $1,216,000 in sales volume. Since the break-even chart shows only volumes of production and sales as variable factors, the assumption is made that other factors such as price per unit and fixed costs will remain constant. New charts must be drawn when a change in the underlying assumptions occurs. The break-even chart is also useful in analyzing the effect of price increases or reductions.

Another useful tool for utilizing cost data is the marginal income ratio, representing the difference between the sales revenue and the total of variable costs and expenses. Using the information presented for the break-even chart, we have:

TABLE 18

Sales	$3,000,000	100%
Variable costs and expenses	1,900,000	63%
Marginal income	1,100,000	37%
Fixed costs and expenses	450,000	15%
Net income	$ 650,000	22%

The marginal income is $1,100,000. The marginal income ratio is 37 percent. This ratio enables management to determine the change in profit that will develop from a given change in volume, again assuming that other factors will remain constant. In this case, an additional sales volume of $50,000 will increase the existing profit of the business by $18,500 ($50,000 × 37 percent). A business with a high marginal income ratio would do well to develop a program to increase its sales, since a large percentage of every additional sales dollar would be profit. On the other hand, an increase in sales would not do much, relatively, for the business with a low marginal income ratio, since little profit benefit would be obtained. In this case, it would appear prudent for management to attempt to cut costs, especially those that are variable in nature.

In this brief discussion I have attempted to describe a cost accounting system, as well as various systems in use, and identify advantages and disadvantages of each, and discuss the benefits which can be obtained by management through the proper utilization of a cost accounting system. Although it is recognized that a sophisticated cost accounting system may not be appropriate for all small enterprises, it is

incumbent upon management to provide in some way for the proper accounting and timely evaluation of cost data—profits await those who do.

FIGURE 10

ASSUMPTIONS:

Budgeted Sales 200,000
    Units @ $15. . . . . $3,000,000

Budgeted Costs and
    Expenses:

    Direct Material. . . . . $ 500,000

    Direct Labor . . . . $ 800,000

    Manufacturing
        Overhead . . . . . $200,000 $ 300,000

    Administrative
        Expenses . . . . . $100,000 $ 150,000

    Selling
        Expenses . . . . . $150,000 $ 150,000

    Totals $450,000 $1,900,000 $2,350,000

    Budgeted Net Income. . . . . $ 650,000

BREAK-EVEN CHART: (expressed in $000)

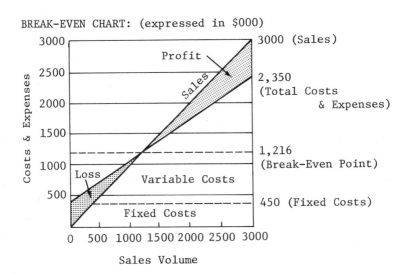

QUESTIONS

1. What does Mr. Volk believe is the prime motivating force of business? Do you agree? Why or why not?
2. Give the reasons why cost accounting is essential to profitable business operations, both small and large.
3. Define cost accounting. How might cost accounting differ between a small and a large company?
4. What are the two major types of cost accounting systems? Briefly describe each.
5. Distinguish between absorption costing and direct costing? What are the advantages and disadvantages of each?
6. Define variable cost and fixed cost. What types of costs are variable in nature? What types fixed in nature?
7. Would you prefer to have a business with mostly variable costs or mostly fixed costs? Why?
8. Define historical costs and standard costs. What is the purpose of each?
9. Of what use is break-even analysis?
10. What, if any, is the difference between a break-even chart as explained in your economics course versus a break-even chart as explained in your accounting course?

---

98   RESPONSIBILITY CENTERS

Shu S. Liao

(Reprinted by permission from *Management Accounting*, vol. 54, no. 1 (July, 1973): 46-48.)

(Shu S. Liao is a faculty member at the University of North Carolina.)

In the past 30 years, the rapid expansion of the size of business firms has resulted in a reappraisal of the roles of the top level and lower levels of management. Top management now realizes that it can direct and motivate lower levels of management more effectively by means of decentralization and delegation. During this period, responsibility accounting has evolved as the accounting correlate of motivation theory. The essence of responsibility accounting is the accumulation of costs and revenues according to areas of responsibility. These areas of responsibility are then defined by the creation of profit centers, a set of semiautonomous subunits whose performances are measured by their contributions to the earnings of the company. Since the manager of each profit center is held responsible for the effect that his decisions will have on profits, it is presumed that he is motivated to make the decisions that will create the maximum profit.

The profit center system as a concept sounds reasonable, and it appears to be an ideal solution to the problems created by growth and

complexity. The implementation of the system, however, is not without
obstacles. For example, a business firm is something different from the
sum of its individual subunits. The subtle relationships between these
subunits preclude such addition. There are certain conditions, then, to
be met before one can divide the business firm into independent profit
centers.

DIVISIBILITY OF OVERALL GOALS

The overall objective(s) of the business firm must be such as to be
easily broken down into subobjectives. Assigning the goals to subunits
is a necessary condition for successful decentralization. (1) This assigning process requires that the overall goal be separable to a certain
degree. If the overall goal cannot be broken down into subgoals, then
it may be that the operations of some subunits are dependent upon those
of other subunits. Accordingly, if there is any difficulty in breaking
the profit goal successfully into many profit subgoals, it tells us that
cost centers (a set of subunits created for the purpose of cost control
decentralization) rather than profit centers should be created as far as
divisional performance evaluation is concerned. (2)

INDEPENDENCE OF DIVISIONAL OPERATIONS

If we want to realize any benefit from the profit center system,
substantial independence of divisional operations is necessary. However, independence or decentralization, to a certain extent, means specialization. And, if the benefits of specialization are less than the
cost of independent planning, then it would be more efficient not to de-
centralize at all. Let us assume for the moment that the organizational
goal is to maximize profits. Then it is necessary that the sum of the
individual profits produced by these independent profit centers must be
greater than the value that would be generated by a centralized operation. The independence is, of course, in relative terms. The profit
centers are still integral parts of the business entity. If independence is carried to an extreme, it would destroy the very idea of the
business firm as a totality. However, if the savings resulting from
shorter channels of information transmission, and the benefits from decisions made at lower levels based on "on-the-spot" knowledge, can offset the additional costs, then the establishment of profit centers is
justified.

PROFIT AS AN INDEX OF PROFIT CENTER PERFORMANCE

The name "profit center" itself implies that the performance of
these independent units is to be measured principally, if not solely,
by their profit contributions. Under a profit center system, a divisional manager is delegated profit responsibility and given operational
independence in the hope that he will be motiviated to optimize profits.
Naturally, he is supposed to be evaluated on his ability to earn a maximum profit for the company. Given two managers running fairly similar
businesses, the manager judged more successful will be the one who makes
the larger profit.

To many accountants, this requirement probably comes as no surprise. Making a profit, however, is a rather vague objective. The term
"profit" means different things to different people. Prudent readers
might ask: "What profit should be used for performance evaluation?"

MARK-OFF OF PROFIT CENTER BOUNDARIES

The profit center is organized so that its profit contribution can
be the main guide to the evaluation of divisional performance and the
main guide by which the division manager makes his critical decisions.
Hence, a profit center is set up only when it has independent access to
outside sources and markets. To make a profit center system achieve its
desired results of motivating and measuring performance, service activities must be segregated from profit centers. These activities which
cannot be organized on a profit responsibility basis are called service
centers to distinguish them from profit centers.
The boundary between profit centers should be marked off in such a
way as to minimize the necessity for corporate allocation of costs and
revenues, since intracompany pricing is necessarily arbitrary and often
controversial. The ideal situation is one in which the profit centers
are self-contained, i.e., a center's operations come closest in scope
and depth to those of separate independent companies. Unfortunately,
these ideal conditions are often unattainable, and intracompany transfer
pricing is inevitable.

SOUND INTRACOMPANY TRANSFER PRICES

Competitive transfer prices negotiated in arm's length bargaining
by profit center managers is an underlying requisite for effectively motivating them. So long as divisional profit is to be used as a basis
for appraisal of profit center management, it is of paramount importance
that factors affecting divisional costs and revenues should be well
within the profit center manager's control.
Since profit centers must have substantial independence in operations, transfer price negotiation presumably will not suboptimize the
interests of the company as a whole. When the independence requirement
is not satisfied, however, transfer price arbitration by the central
staff is necessary in some cases in order to preserve the interests of
the company. Under these circumstances, the profit center system is not
desirable unless all parties involved are satisfied with the arbitration. The more central control, the less reliable divisional profits
will be as a means of evaluating profit center performance. The real
essence of the decentralized profit center system is motivation. It
would be difficult to reap the benefit of motivating divisional managers
if they are not allowed substantial control over revenues and costs.

VIEWS OF CORPORATE CHIEF EXECUTIVE OFFICERS

How successful a profit center is, of course, depends on the degree
to which the division achieves what the central management expects of
it. Hence, the views of corporate chief executive officers on goals and

decision criteria actually determine how the profit centers are evaluated. A recent survey indicates that influence on the company's profits
occupies the undisputed top position as the most important factor in
major policy decisions. (3) The size of a business firm does not appear to have a significant bearing on the position. Large-company executives as well as small-company executives are in substantial agreement that profit making. is the most important goal of their companies.
    Profit making, however, is a rather vague goal. What profits
should be used to measure managerial success? Is a manager judged more
successful because he is the one who makes the largest profit in absolute dollars? In that case, it is open to the criticism that it fails
to take into account the efficiency in capital utilization.

RATE OF RETURN AS A MEASURE OF PERFORMANCE

    Another method that is generally used to measure managerial success
is the rate of return. But, when it comes to the calculation of the
rate of return, another controversy arises. The immediate question is:
Return on what? Previous NAA studies revealed that return on stockholders' equity, return on total assets, and return on total sales were
the bases found in current practice. (4) The most important of these,
as indicated by the survey, was return on stockholders' equity. However, the size of the business firm does play a significant role in
affecting managerial judgment of the importance of these three yardsticks. The larger the firm, the more important is return on stockholders' equity whereas small firms tend to emphasize return on total
sales. The importance of return on total assets, however, seems to
remain fairly stable despite the size of the firm. (5) Another finding
was that smaller firms are more likely to set a sales goal first in
profit budget planning. For the large firms, the trend seems to be the
reverse. An unstable rate of return could explain why the budgets of
smaller firms have to be more dependent on sales goals than do the budgets of larger firms. Thus, the obvious stress on sales in profit planning might account for the finding that the rate of return on sales is
generally emphasized by the small firms in evaluating company performance.
    Once a profit budget is adopted, it becomes a basis for evaluating
profit center performance. Naturally, divisional managers tend to be
conservative in budgeting so that their performance would look better
against their budgets. If profit center managers have their say, however, suboptimization might be the result. If, on the other hand, central management insists on a predetermined rate of return, there would
be no motivational benefit.

HANDS-OFF POLICY

    Once a profit center's budget is accepted, it becomes the basis
for performance evaluation. Central management would not interfere
with profit center operations until divisional performance is found
to be far off the pace. However, this hands-off policy creates another
type of problem. Earnings can be kept up for some periods while the
business is being "milked" by cutting down on some key expenditures or

by manipulating accounts. Even if audits are conducted periodically, central management may get the true facts too late to take remedial action.

Profit center managers in many cases do not want to be embarrassed by the interference of top management. A natural tendency is to try to keep top management out of the division until, hopefully, the divisional manager can straighten out any adverse situations. For this reason, the seriousness of profit variances is frequently understated.

LONG-TERM PROFIT

The true goal of the large business firm is, of course, long-term profit optimization. The survey indicates that large firms tend to emphasize the return on stockholders' equity which represents the long-term commitment of capital. If the executives in large firms can plan their profit budget by setting a profit goal first and then determine necessary sales volumes, as indicated by the survey, it is obvious that the profit they have in mind is a stable return on a long-term basis. (6)

Long-term profits, however, seem difficult to define and measure. It was pointed out earlier that profits can be kept up or down for some periods at the expense of future earnings. Therefore, it is highly questionable whether a company can break down its long-term profit goal into subgoals and properly measure divisional performance if the profit figure can be manipulated.

MULTIPLE YARDSTICKS FOR PERFORMANCE MEASUREMENT

The need to measure managerial performance on a long-run basis is aggravated by the fact that some managers might undercut long-run profits to cover poor performance which would then permanently affect long-run profits. Since the primary function of accounting is to reflect the facts as they exist, the urgent need is to develop a measurement system that would prevent divisional managers from hiding poor performance so that central management can control and coordinate profit center operations on a timely basis.

An alternative method of measuring managerial performance on a long-run basis is to use multiple yardsticks for evaluation. Market position, research and development, productivity and employee morale are the probable areas that will reveal the early signs of long-run profitability. The accounting reports using key economic yardsticks as well as profit figures to measure performance of the profit center managers should give a better picture of managerial performance on a long-run basis.

It would probably be more appropriate to call the decentralized system a "responsibility center system" rather than a "profit center system," since the dollar profit figure is no longer the sole criterion for evaluation. The responsibility center system would also have the added advantage of being applicable to service centers as well.

CONCLUSION

Long-term profits seems to be the main goal of most chief executives, yet there is no single measure that can reflect managerial success in optimizing long-run profit. Profit information transmitted to top management is likely to be somewhat distorted and delayed. The urgent need is to report to top management the facts as they exist in responsibility centers so that divisional performance can be properly measured. The items to be reported and evaluated might vary from company to company, depending on the nature and goal of a firm. Each item may be weighted according to central management's goal structure. The budgeted standards for each item to be measured must be accepted by each division, and once accepted, these standards become the criteria for divisional performance evaluation.

FOOTNOTES

1. See Zenon S. Zannetos, "On the Theory of Divisional Structures: Some Aspects of Centralization and Decentralization of Control and Decision Making," *Management Science* (December, 1965).
2. For the distinction between a profit center and a cost center, see William L. Ferrara, "Responsibility Accounting and the Contribution Approach," *NAA Bulletin* (December, 1963).
3. The survey was based on 191 questionnaires completed by corporation chief executive officers randomly selected from *Poor's Register of Corporations, Directors and Executives*.
4. See *NAA Bulletin*, February, 1962, Accounting Practice Report No. 14, *Experience with Return on Capital to Appraise Management Performance*. Also see NAA Research Report No. 35, *Return on Capital as a Guide to Managerial Decisions* (December, 1969).
5. A study sponsored by Financial Executives Research Foundation suggested that the rate of return on total assets should be used for performance evaluation. This recommendation, however, was theoretical rather than empirical. See David Solomons, *Divisional Performance: Measurement and Control* (Homewood, Ill.: Richard D. Irwin), Chapter V.
6. An earlier empirical study confirms this observation. See A.D.H. Kaplan, J. D. Dirlam, and R. F. Lanziollotti, *Pricing in Big Business, A Case Approach* (Washington, D.C.: The Brookings Institute, 1958).

QUESTIONS

1. What has caused the increasing use of responsibility accounting? Is this in line with economic theory?

2. Describe the essential features of responsibility accounting.
3. Outline the problems which may be encountered when establishing or using profit centers.
4. Why is the transfer price a difficult and important concept? How should the transfer price be established?
5. Should firms emphasize return on stockholders' equity rather than on total assets? Why or why not?
6. Why do you think multiple yardsticks for performance measurement are needed?

---

99   NEW PRODUCT PRICING STRATEGIES

M. G. Wright

(Reprinted by permission from *Certified Accountant* (February, 1973): 91-93.)

The pricing of products, and in particular new, unproven, products, presents serious decision-making problems. Yet making the right decisions can be critical for the financial well-being of a company. While costs and cost behavior will be considered in the decision-making process as well as market and competitor behavior, it is price which effectively determines profitability. Once that has been fixed all that can be controlled is costs.

PRODUCT LIFE CYCLE

New products pass through a life cycle that has a number of stages. These include the early development of ideas; proving the product feasibility from the points of view of technical ability and commercial viability; market launch; product maturity; and final decline as it is overtaken by newer ideas and products and consumer tastes change. The early stages of this cycle are frequently characterized by patent and know-how protection from competitive encroachment, but as sales expand and market acceptance is gained new competitors enter the field and the product begins to lose its uniqueness.

In the early stages the company can control to some degree the extent of competitive encroachment through adopting the right pricing strategy and by other, nonpricing, actions such as patent extension, and product development. As product maturity is reached the seller starts to lose pricing freedom as his product begins to merge into a commodity group made up of products barely distinguishable from each other.

At the same time as the volume of sales rises the unit costs of production and distribution will change. This in itself provides a greater freedom for the price-fixing decision. It follows, therefore, that as the competitiveness and costs of the product vary considerably

over its life the pricing policy may require adjustment at different
stages in the life cycle. Two in particular can be distinguished:

1. pricing in the early development stage
2. pricing at maturity

While these might be considered as independent decision points, the
pricing strategy adopted in the early development stages can have a
significant effect upon the freedom of pricing choice at later stages.
Management should therefore adopt a strategy that is likely to maximize
product profitability over the whole life cycle rather than just the
stages immediately at issue.

COMPETITIVE BEHAVIOR

The likely competitive behavior forms a large element in the initial pricing decision. Difficulties that potential entrants would face
form a barrier insulating the firm to a greater or lesser extent from
competitive forces. Such barriers may be inherent in the technological
problems of production. For example the economies of scale may prohibit
entry without a very substantial investment. Where little capital is
required for entry and there is no effective patent or know-how protection, competitive entry will be almost immediate.

The innovator will therefore be seeking pricing and promotion
strategies designed to discourage potential competitors. One of the
problems in pricing for high profitability in the early stages of the
product life is that high profitability in itself will become a high
inducement to other firms to try to find a way around the barriers to
their entry.

The policies that can be adopted to limit potential competition
during this period include:

1. product improvement and differentiation
2. extension of patent protection
3. pricing in such a way as to discourage new entrants
4. manufacturing know-how

PRICING ALTERNATIVE IN THE
INITIAL LIFE CYCLE STAGES

Management can follow one of two broad policies in the initial
stages. They can adopt a policy of *skimming off the cream* until forced
to reduce prices by competitive pressure, or they can adopt a *saturation
pricing* policy designed to effect swift market penetration in depth thus
achieving the economies of large scale production quickly and at the
same time making the market less inviting for a newcomer.

While it can be seen that the innovator has a wide range of pricing
alternatives at this stage, the effects of the choice made will stretch
out into the remaining stages of the life cycle. The choice of pricing
strategy should therefore only be made after a careful appraisal of all
factors affecting that product. These should include:

Estimate of Demand. Demand for new products is the most difficult
to estimate. Through a process of exploring the preferences and edu-
cability of consumers and the range of competitive prices it should be
possible to arrive at conclusions as to whether the product will sell at
all and the price that will make it attractive to buyers; sales volumes
at prices below this point; and the reaction of firms whose products
might be displaced.

Setting Market Targets. What ultimate market share is wanted for
the product, taking into account the present range of products, the
likely production methods, and the way that costs are likely to vary.

Devising a Promotional Strategy. Creating a market for the product
is a burden which falls on the innovator, not his successors. How he
decides to recover this cost will have a considerable bearing upon the
pricing policy adopted.

Competitor Reaction. In relation to the barriers to new entry
which exist, how quickly will competitors begin to penetrate the market
in some way.

The Effect of Volume on Product Costs. Where the cost of entry is
high firms are likely to have a high level of fixed costs and therefore
unit costs will fall rapidly as volume builds up. In other cases the
level of unit costs falls more slowly and there is less urgency to build
up volume quickly.
    The final element in the choice is an assessment of the likely
level of product profitability over the whole of the product's life
cycle, and not just the initial stages. The pricing policy may be
changed at different stages and what is required now is a policy that
gives the higher profitability in the initial stages combined with the
carry-through of maximum advantages for later pricing decisions, e.g.,
the saturation pricing policy by discouraging new entrants may leave a
wider discretionary element in pricing decisions at product maturity.
The final decision may, of course, be a trade-off between the immediate
and the long term requirements.

FINANCIAL ANALYSIS

One method that can be adopted to analyze the financial outcomes of
the pricing choices is based upon an adaptation of the break-even analysis. The latter analyzes the way in which profit is affected by
changes in total costs and revenue as volume changes, each chart usually
being based upon a single selling price. What is required is a similar
analysis using a range of possible selling prices and which takes into

account the previously determined likely sales volumes at each selling
price.

Let us assume that the possible selling prices and the volume of
sales at each price are as set out below. If the unit variable cost is
£8 then the unit contribution (SP-VC) and the maximum potential contribution can be computed as shown below:

TABLE 19

Selling Price (SP) £	Sales Volume (units)	Unit Contribution £	Maximum Potential Contribution £
10	20,000	2	40,000
12	18,000	4	72,000
14	14,000	6	84,000
16	10,000	8	80,000
18	5,000	10	50,000
20	2,000	12	24,000

The chart in Figure 11 shows on the left hand scale the product
profit or loss, i.e., before taking into account any corporate fixed
costs. On the left hand scale is shown the contribution, the first
£30,000 of which covers the £30,000 estimated product fixed costs and
any contribution above this figure adding directly to profit.

Each of the curves shows the way that the product would add to
contribution for each of the pricing choices. None of the curves is
projected beyond the estimated maximum sales volume for the relevant
selling price. If the ends of each of the curves are now connected with
a dotted line this shows the way that maximum potential contribution
would vary given the selling prices and volumes outlined.

A policy of creaming-off the market would indicate a selling price
of approximately £14 per unit since at this price the initial contribution is maximized. If, however, it is desired to price for quick market
penetration and saturation, then a price more towards the £10 per unit
range would be indicated. This would reduce the initial contribution
but if successful may enable relatively higher prices to be charged at
the maturity stage than would otherwise be possible. Which policy is
most desirable depends upon assessments of the effectiveness of the
saturation policy in keeping out new entrants. It may also take into
account possible effects of scale upon costs if volume is quickly pushed
up to a high level.

FIGURE 11

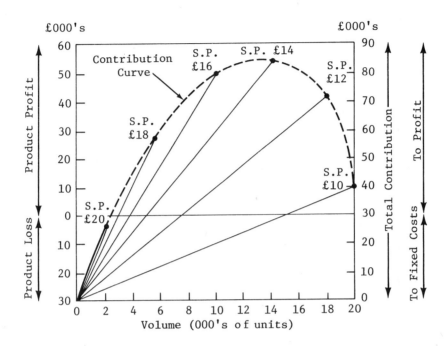

PRICING AT MATURITY

When the new product becomes merely one of a group of competing products, having lost the differentiation which has hitherto character-ized it, a new pricing policy will be called for. This change must be carried out promptly if the entry of private label competitors is to be prevented. Indications of when the maturity stage is being reached are:

1. the innovator's brand preference is eroded
2. products become standardized in the commodity group
3. entry of private label competitors
4. ratio of new to replacement sales indicates market saturation

At this stage of the life cycle, however, che innovator has less freedom in pricing than previously. Price cutting can trigger-off counter action by competitors which reduces industry profitability to dangerous levels. The marketing strategy may instead move towards prod-uct improvement to retain some of the previous uniqueness of the product and to segment the market in some way.

CONCLUSIONS

Pricing decisions in the initial stages of the product life cycle require some projections of potential demand at each price level. While it is feasible to assess the price that will maximize short term profitability at this stage, consideration must be given to the consequences of that decision for later stages in the life cycle. In particular the effect that it will have in attracting or repelling new entrants may considerably influence the product profitability over the total life cycle.

QUESTIONS

1. Assume we have the responsibility to price a new product. What facts would we look at within the company? Outside the company?
2. How would formal training in economics help us price the product?
3. Would formal training in accounting or marketing also help us? Why or why not?

---

100   RETURN ON INVESTMENT

Frederick G. Harris

(Reprinted by permission from *Newspaper Controller*, vol. 26, no. 3 (December, 1972): 6.)

(Frederick G. Harris is comptroller, assistant secretary, *The Wall Street Journal*.)

A year or so ago, Dow Jones was involved in a study to determine the feasibility of a new product to be produced and marketed in conjunction with another company. The other party to the potential joint venture prepared an evaluation of the Return on Investment for the project, based on a discounted cash flow technique, and presented it to the study group. After the meeting, the other Dow Jones' members of the group—all nonfinancial people—said that they thought the presentation was interesting but confusing and suggested that I put the figures into the traditional Dow Jones' format.

This format is simply a projection to determine the time required to recover the investment—(PAY BACK)—and to show at some reasonable point in time the percentage of net income to revenue—(RETURN ON SALES). It is based on the rather simple premise that if the Pay Back is relatively short and the Return on Sales relatively high, then the Return On Investment over the life of the project will be good enough.

REACTION SPURRED RESEARCH

We prepared the projections they suggested and from that point on
ROI presentations to the group complied essentially with the Dow Jones'
format. I discovered that the other company, at least in evaluating
this particular project, was not all that sold on the value of discounted cash flow. This experience aroused my interest and curiosity
about the frequency with which companies use Discounted Cash Flow as a
tool for making investment decisions.

Accounting literature for years has dealt extensively with this
subject, and yet I know that in the past five years Dow Jones has spent
more than $40 million on capital expenditures, all of it justified with-
out the benefit of the knowledge derived from the use of the Discounted
Cash Flow technique.

Many capital expenditures, of course, are justified by factors
other than financial. INCFO's manual on *Profit Planning for Newspapers*
lists four distinct types of capital expenditures:

1. essential replacements
2. strategic investments made for purposes of safety, public
   relations
3. investments resulting in improved efficiency and lower
   costs
4. expansion investments

Replacement of worn-out equipment, furniture, fixtures, etc., is
obviously necessary if the business is to continue. Money spent for
purposes of safety and public relations is justified on the basis of the
intangible benefits that management hopes will be derived.

Most of the $40 million that Dow Jones spent in the last five years
went for essential replacements or strategic investments. I guess capital expenditures of most newspapers would fall under these two classifications.

It is in the latter two—investments resulting in improved efficiency and lower costs, and expansion investments—that financial factors play a part in the evaluation and justification of capital expenditures. But even in these investment decisions, factors other than financial are sometimes equally important, and they frequently predominate.

For example, in the late 1960s, brokerage firms, the principal customers for Dow Jones News Services, were interested in obtaining a large
device to display Dow Jones News in their board rooms. Hardware manufacturers were not responding to this demand, so Dow Jones designed,
produced and in 1969 introduced NEWSBOARD to the brokerage community.

The most important consideration in this expansion investment was
to provide a service to our customers. Financial factors were secondary, concerned primarily with risk. The question posed was "When can
we expect to get our money back?" and a pay-back computation—based on a
reasonable estimate of the market, the price the customers would be
willing to pay, and all costs involved—was sufficient to answer that
question.

Critics of the pay-back method concede that it provides management
with some insight into the risk and liquidity of an investment. But
they point out, quite correctly, that it fails to consider cash flows

after the pay-back period and therefore cannot be regarded as a measure
of profitability. They say, too, that pay-back can be deceiving, because it does not take into consideration the size or timing of cash
flows during the life of the project.

Proponents of the Discounted Cash Flow method contend that the size
and time of cash flows over the life of the investment are extremely important in the investment decision. They say the value of this method
is that it takes these two factors into account and, specifically, it
gives consideration to the interest earned on the reinvestment of the
cash flows over the life of the project—and thus is able to select the
most profitable investment.

PRECISE BUT UNCONVINCING

There is no doubt in my mind that the theory of discounting cash
flows is a superior mathematical technique for evaluating capital expenditures. But the problem, it seems to me, is that its results are
not credible to the people who are responsible for capital expenditure
decisions. The results do not reflect the uncertainties inherent in
predictions regarding life of the project and cash flows during each
year of that life. In other words, Discounted Cash Flow produces a
precise (go—no go) answer that is most difficult to accept, considering
it is based on an unpredictable future. Reliance upon such a precise
tool goes against the grain of cautious decision makers who generally
subscribe to the maxim—"Forecasting is most difficult, especially if it
concerns the future."

Now, I'm not claiming there is no place for Discounted Cash Flow in
evaluation and selection of capital expenditures. A company with limited cash and several potentially profitable investment possibilities
would be wise to use it as one of the tools in the selection process.
What I am saying is that Discounted Cash Flow is a precision tool which
cannot be universally applied and which should not be used indiscriminantly. An imperfect analogy would be: a sledge hammer is not used in a
jewelry store, nor do we use jeweler's tools to drive a stake into the
ground.

To make sure I was on reasonably solid ground, I did a little research and discovered that in 1969 the Planning Executives Institute
sent a questionnaire to its member companies to determine what was being done in the area of corporate modeling. Three hundred twenty three
members responded. One of the questions concerned the methods used to
evaluate capital investment proposals. The results showed that "Only
32 percent of the companies used a time value approach, e.g., DCF rate
of return and/or present worth, to evaluate capital proposals. The majority of companies still use simpler approaches, such as a net income
to gross investment and pay-out period."

In conclusion, I am reminded that critics of the Dow Jones Average
refer to it as a simple approach—uncomplicated, unsophisticated. We
don't disagree but reply that it must have some value because it is
still used a lot, otherwise we wouldn't print it. The pay-back method,
too, is called a simple approach—uncomplicated, unsophisticated—but it
must have some value because it is still used a lot, else I would not
have written this.

QUESTIONS

1. Describe the payback/return on investment technique.
2. Describe the discounted cash flow technique.
3. What are the advantages and disadvantages of each technique discussed in 1 and 2 above?
4. Why do you suppose that of the responding companies in the Planning Executives Institute survey only 32 percent used a time value approach to investment analysis?

101
COST ACCOUNTING STANDARDS BOARD:
A PROGRESS REPORT

David H. Li

(Reprinted by permission from *Management Accounting*, vol. 54, no. 12 (June, 1973): 11-14.)

(David H. Li is a faculty member at the University of Washington.)

The objectives of the Cost Accounting Standards Board, (1) an agent of the Congress, are stated in an amendment to the Defense Production Act of 1950, which was signed by President Nixon on August 15, 1970, as Public Law 91-379. (2) With respect to cost accounting standards, the law directs the Board to "promulgate cost-accounting standards designed to achieve uniformity and consistency in the cost-accounting principles followed by defense contractors and subcontractors under Federal contracts." (3)

Because the word "uniformity" has been subjected to diverse interpretations, the Board, in a recent pronouncement, clarified the issue by stating that "Uniformity is achieved when contractors with the same circumstances (with respect to a given subject) follow the practice appropriate for those circumstances," and that "The Board does not seek to establish a single uniform accounting system or chart of accounts for all the complex and diverse businesses engaged in defense contract work." Similarly, with respect to the word "consistency," the Board stated that "Consistency pertains primarily to one accounting entity over periods of time" and that improved consistency will enhance "the usefulness of comparisons between estimates and actuals." (4) Stated differently, the role of consistency relates mainly to improving intra-contractor comparability when circumstances are alike; that of uniformity, to promoting intercontractor comparability when circumstances are alike.

As to other objectives, the law directs the Board to prescribe regulations that "require defense contractors and subcontractors as a condition of contracting to disclose in writing their cost-accounting principles, including methods of distinguishing direct costs from indirect costs and the basis used for allocating indirect costs. . . ."
(5)

WORK COMPLETED

Given these objectives and directions, the Board has so far promulgated the following:

1. Disclosure Statement (4 CFR 351)
2. Consistency in Estimating, Accumulating, and Reporting Costs (4 CFR 401)
3. Consistency in Allocating Cost Incurred for the Same Purpose (4 CFR 402)
4. Allocation of Home Office Expenses to Segments (4 CFR 403)
5. Capitalization of Tangible Assets (4 CFR 404)
6. Definitions (4 CFR 400)
7. Contract Coverage (4 CFR 331)

Disclosure Statement

The Disclosure Statement (4 CFR 351) is a 26-page document concerning cost accounting practices being followed by a reporting unit, which may be either a contractor or one of his divisions. It is divided into eight parts as follows:

1. general information
2. direct costs
3. direct vs. indirect
4. indirect costs
5. depreciation and capitalization practices
6. other costs and credits
7. deferred compensation and insurance costs
8. corporate or group expenses

At the present time, for administrative reasons, only contractors with $30 million in negotiated national defense prime contracts for the Federal fiscal year 1971 are required to file Disclosure Statements. About 800 separate Disclosure Statements from about 90 such contractors are currently on file.

Standard 401

Consistency in Estimating, Accumulating, and Reporting Costs (4 CFR 401) is the first cost accounting standard issued by the Board. Its purpose is "to enhance the likelihood that comparable transactions are treated alike" which will in turn "facilitate the preparation of reliable cost estimates used in pricing a proposal and their comparison with the costs of performance of the resulting contract." Stated differently, this Standard requires that consistency be maintained throughout the life of a contract: from proposal to performance to postperformance review. This Standard is to be followed by contractors with covered contracts of $100,000 or more.

Standard 402

Consistency in Allocating Costs Incurred for the Same Purpose
(4 CFR 402) is another cost accounting standard addressed to the matter
of consistency. Here, the fundamental requirement is that "All costs
incurred for the same purpose, in like circumstances, are either direct
costs only or indirect costs only with respect to final cost objectives." It is designed "to guard against the over-charging of some cost
objectives and to prevent double counting." This Standard is to be
followed by contractors with covered contracts of $100,000 or more.

Standard 403

Allocation of Home Office Expenses to Segments (4 CFR 403) is the
first cost accounting standard addressed mainly to the uniformity objective and illustrates several important cost accounting concepts that the
Board follows in developing standards. In conventional costing, for
inventory-valuation purposes, only costs related to the manufacturing
process are assigned to products as "product costs"; general and administrative costs are considered "period costs." This is not so in contract costing; in contract costing, all costs, be they related to manufacturing or to general and administrative, are generally to be
accounted for and allocated to final cost objectives.

The provisions of the Standard state that, "to the extent practical," home office expenses are to be "allocated directly to segments."
"Expenses not directly allocated, if significant in amount and in relation to total home office expenses," are to "be grouped in logical and
homogeneous expense pools and allocated" according to criteria stated in
the Standard.

With respect to the selection of a base for allocating centralized
service functions, the Standard further describes "a hierarchy of preferable allocation techniques which represent benefit or causal relationships" between performing functions and receiving functions. In de-
scending order of preference, the hierarchy of allocation bases is:

1. activity of performing function
2. output of performing function
3. activity of receiving function

After expenses in logical and homogeneous pools are allocated to
segments, there might remain costs that represent the management of the
organization as a whole. These remaining costs, or "residual expenses,"
are to be allocated in one of two ways depending upon the materiality of
these residual expenses. (6) Where material, the Standard prescribes
the use of a three-factor formula (payroll dollars, operating revenue,
and capital assets) that best reflects management's concern over the
total activity of the segments. Where these residual expenses are not
material, a contractor may use any base that is representative of the
total activities of the segments.

This Standard will be effective July 1, 1973. When effective,
this Standard is to be followed by contractors who are required to file
Disclosure Statements. At the present time, those with $30 million in
negotiated defense prime contracts for the Federal fiscal year 1971 are

therefore covered; they are to follow this Standard as of the beginning of their fiscal years after September 30, 1973.

Standard 404

Capitalization of Tangible Assets (4 CFR 404), another Standard addressed mainly to the uniformity objective, sets forth still another concept. This Standard states that "Normally, cost measurements are based on the concept of enterprise continuity; this concept implies that major asset acquisitions will be capitalized, so that the cost applicable to current and future accounting periods can be allocated to cost objectives of those periods." It further states that "Capitalization shall be based upon a written policy that is reasonable and consistently applied," and that items with service lives of two years or longer and with acquisition costs of $500 or more meet the criteria for capitalization.

The Standard also states that "Tangible capital assets constructed or fabricated by a contractor for its own use shall be capitalized at amounts which include all indirect costs properly allocable to such assets. This requires the capitalization of general and administrative expenses when such expenses are identifiable with the constructed asset and are material in amount."

The Standard is pending before the Congress; its effective date, barring a concurrent resolution by the Congress disapproving the Standard, is expected to be July 1, 1973. When effective, all contractors with covered contracts of $100,000 or more are to follow it as of the beginning of their fiscal year on or after October 1, 1973.

Definitions

Research on Definitions (4 CFR 400) is an ongoing project. As cost accounting standards are promulgated, definitions of terms of special significance are also promulgated to facilitate communication. Currently, about a dozen or so terms have been promulgated. An example is the definition of "cost objective," which was promulgated along with Standard 402. It is: "A function, organizational subdivision, contract, or other work unit for which cost data are desired and for which provision is made to accumulate and measure the cost of processes, products, jobs, capitalized projects, etc."

As in many aspects of the Board's work, a larger number of people from the accounting profession, defense contractors, and academes are participating in this project by providing comments to the Board's draft definitions.

Contract Coverage

This part (4 CFR 331) covers the contractual mechanisms needed to make cost accounting standards operative. It states what a contractor is to do, what happens when there is a contract dispute, what authority the Board or other governmental agencies have in examining a contractor's records, and what is a subcontractor's responsibility to his con-

tractor.   It also provides interpretations as to the proper adjustment
of a contractor's negotiated prices under a variety of situations.

RESEARCH PROCESS

The Board's research activities (Figure 12) are carried out principally by a 23-member professional staff. After a topic for research
has been authorized by the Board, the staff begins the research process
by reviewing authoritative materials on the subject. This step corresponds roughly to "library research" except that, with CASB, the sources
are wider and include much unpublished, even confidential, information
such as:

1. books, monographs, theses
2. government procurement regulations
3. pronouncements of accounting and regulatory groups
4. court and Board of Contract Appeals decisions
5. excerpts from files of governmental agencies
6. disclosure statements

At the time of reviewing these materials, the staff attempts to
identify issues and problems related to the topic under research: Did
they arise due to a lack of recognition of underlying cost concepts,
due to an inadequacy of guidelines, or due to a misunderstanding in interpreting existing regulations?

While "library research" is underway, the staff begins its initial
phase of liaison with various contractors and governmental agencies
through correspondence, telephone conversation, personal interview, or
plant visit. The purpose of this step is to make the staff cognizant of
actual practices in the field, since library materials may be both generalized and dated.

With information gained from both "library research" and field
work, the staff prepares an "Issues" paper and a list of questions to be
answered. At this stage, if not earlier, the staff, begins to contact
appropriate committees of various professional or industry associations,
such as NAA, AICPA, AAA, FEI, CODSIA, and MAPI for their views. When
needed, a questionnaire is developed to further explore the issues. At
all times during this stage, the Board is apprised of progress and provides continual guidance.

With these diverse sources of input (library research, field
visits, committee liaisons, questionnaire responses, and Board
guidance), the staff evaluates alternative solutions to problems and
proposes possible cost accounting standards. These staff drafts are
again discussed with professional accounting associations, contractors,
and governmental agencies. The drafts are also mailed to as many as 350
organizations and individuals who have agreed to participate actively in
the Board's research and development of standards. The purpose of the
wide exposure of staff drafts is to evaluate their feasibility, to
assess their financial impact, and to estimate their likely benefits.

After responses to staff drafts are analyzed, the staff prepares a
proposed standard and submits it to the Board for review and approval.
When approved, it is published in the *Federal Register*; this initial
publication serves as a public solicitation by the Board to submit

comments on the proposed standard and is an integral part of the research process.

FIGURE 12

RESEARCH PROCESS AT THE COST
ACCOUNTING STANDARDS BOARD

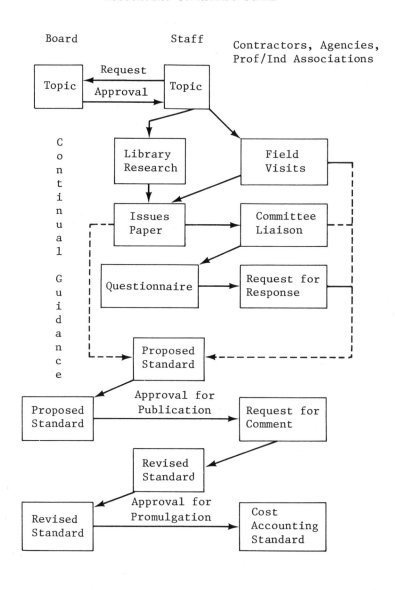

The importance of submitting these comments by members of the public cannot be overemphasized; in many instances, the Board has been persuaded by these comments and made appropriate revisions in the proposed standard. In any event, these comments are summarized and the reasons for revising or not revising various segments of the proposed standard are contained in the second publication in the *Federal Register* as prefatory remarks.

The second publication in the *Federal Register* represents the Board's promulgation of a cost accounting standard which is transmitted to the Congress. Unless the Congress disapproves by passing a concurrent resolution within 60 legislative days, the Board's promulgation "shall have the full force and effect of law" no earlier than 121 days and no later than 219 days after such promulgation.

TOPICS UNDER RESEARCH

In addition to the four Standards already promulgated, many topics have been approved by the Board and are in various stages of staff research. These include:

1. accounting for unallowable costs
2. depreciation of tangible capital assets
3. selection of a cost accounting period
4. appropriate use of standard cost accounting
5. accounting for vacation, holiday, and sick pay costs
6. allocation of segment general and administrative costs
7. accounting for scrap
8. termination accounting
9. inventory pricing
10. accounting for pension costs
11. allocation of segment overheads other than G&A
12. identification of direct versus indirect costs
13. cost of capital
14. accounting for special facilities
15. accounting for deferred incentive compensation
16. accounting for other selected fringe benefit costs
17. gain or loss on the disposition of assets
18. current value accounting

OTHER DEVELOPMENTS

Although the Board's responsibility relates to negotiated defense contracts of $100,000 or more, it must be noted that the General Services Administration, which has jurisdiction over nondefense contracts entered into by governmental agencies, has incorporated cost accounting standards into its Federal Procurement Regulations. This voluntary adoption by nondefense agencies renders cost accounting standards applicable to most government contracts and makes the work of the Board that much more important.

Because many topics relevant to the Board's scope relate to financial accounting, it is conceivable that the Board's work may also involve areas of interest to the Financial Accounting Standards Board as well as to other governmental agencies such as the Securities & Exchange Commission. In this connection, the CASB recently stated that "The Cost Accounting Standards Board seeks to avoid conflict or disagreement with other bodies having similar responsibilities and will through continuous liaison make every reasonable effort to do so. The Board will give careful consideration to the pronouncements affecting financial and tax reporting; and in the formulation of cost accounting standards, it will take those pronouncements into account to the extent it can do so in accomplishing its objectives. The nature of the Board's authority and its mission, however, is such that it must retain and exercise full responsibility for meeting its objectives." (7)

CONCLUDING COMMENT

In addition to publishing articles on the Cost Accounting Standards Board in *Management Accounting* and to appointing a subcommittee of the Management Accounting Practices (MAP) Committee to assist the Board, NAA has contributed significantly in other directions. An outstanding example is the publication of "Concepts for Contract Costing" by the MAP Committee. (8) This statement, as the CASB chairman has noted, "will be considered with other authoritative literature of the accounting profession in the development of Cost Accounting Standards." (9)

In summary, the development of cost accounting standards is a cooperative endeavor involving governmental agencies, the accounting profession, and defense contractors. Every reader of *Management Accounting* is urged to contribute to the Board's various research activities.

FOOTNOTES

1. Readers of *Management Accounting* are probably familiar with developments related to the Cost Accounting Standards Board, as many articles have appeared herein. As a review, one might want to reread: Elmer B. Staats, "Uniform Cost Accounting Standards in Negotiated Defense Contracts," *Management Accounting* (January, 1969); "NAA Testifies on Uniform Cost Accounting Standards," *Management Accounting* (June, 1970); "The Cost Accounting Standards Board," *Management Accounting* (December, 1971).
2. 84 Stat. 796; 50 U.S.C. App. 2168.
3. 84 Stat. 796, 797. It went on to state that only negotiated Federal Contracts "in excess of $100,000" are covered, and that "contracts or subcontracts where the price negotiated is based on (1) established catalog or market prices of commercial items sold in substantial quantities to the general public, or (2) prices set by law or regulations" are not covered.
4. Cost Accounting Standards Board, *Statement of Operating Policies, Procedures, and Objectives*, Washington, D.C., 1973.

5. 84 Stat. 796, 798.
6. Materiality determination is based on the following figures: 3.35 percent of the first $100 million of operating
   revenue; 0.95 percent of the next $200 million of operating
   revenue; 0.30 percent of the next $2.7 billion of operating
   revenue; and 0.20 percent of all amounts over $3 billion of
   operating revenue. Residual expenses are considered material if the percentage figure is higher than that shown
   above.
7. Op Cit., *Statement of Operating Policies, Procedures, and
   Objectives*, pp. 7-8.
8. "Concepts for Contract Costing," *Management Accounting*
   (March, 1972).
9. Ibid., p. 56.

QUESTIONS

1. What is the stated objective of the Cost Accounting
   Standards Board?
2. Do you think that such an authoritative body will have
   influence in nondefense areas of the economy? Explain.
3. What areas of mutual concern will the Cost Accounting
   Standards Board have with the Financial Accounting
   Standards Board?

8

Career Opportunities in Accounting

Students of accounting are generally most interested in the opportunities available in their chosen career area. They are also interested in the qualifications they must have and the tests of ability they must meet to become productive, successful members of the profession. Chapter 8 discusses professional educational requirements and certification programs as well as some of the many opportunities available to budding accountants including members of minorities.

George Gorelik (page 419) addresses the question of what is a profession. He concludes that accounting is, indeed, a profession and makes a number of recommendations for improvements. Through Gorelik's analysis, the reader can better comprehend the nature of the occupational group.

Three professional organizations are now involved with certification programs for accountants: the American Institute of Certified Public Accountants, the National Association of Accountants, and the Institute of Internal Auditors. The articles by Wilton T. Anderson (page 427), James Bulloch (page 435), and William S. Smith (page 439) contain information about each of the certification programs. While the CPA is the best known, the future is promising for the Certified Internal Auditor and the Certificate in Management Accounting.

The man or woman about to enter the field of accounting frequently has such questions as: What are employers looking for in the people they hire? What is the long-term outlook for accounting opportunities? What kinds of training will be available? The William Mitchell (page 448) and Elwood A. Platt (page 451) articles help answer these questions. The picture that emerges is one of a bright, successful future for men and women of "character, intelligence, and motivation." While Mitchell's responses are in terms of the CPA firm, the areas of governmental, nonprofit, and industrial/commercial accounting hold similar opportunities. The Platt article describes training programs available with government agencies. Similar programs of training new accountants and auditors are wide-spread in both the CPA firms and industrial/commercail companies.

The discussion of career opportunities in accounting would be incomplete if the problem of women and minorities was not addressed.

Sybil C. Mobley (page 453) analyzes both the woman's and the black accountant's problems with discrimination. She believes that accounting is a viable career choice for women and for nonwhites. In commenting upon the current status, she writes: "There is a very obvious commitment to integrate the accounting profession 'in fact as well as ideal.'" But this effort has been stymied by the ". . . limited supply of blacks and women available for employment as accountants." The message is clear. For women and ethnic minorities, accounting offers bright prospects for success in a profession which is striving to integrate.

---

102   THE PROFESSIONAL ACCOUNTANT TODAY AND TOMORROW

George Gorelik

(Reprinted by permission from *The Certified General Accountant*, vol. 7, no. 1 (January, 1973): 18-21.)

(George Gorelik is a faculty member at the University of British Columbia.)

Periodic critical review and thoughtful analysis of the present state of the accounting profession are a necessary prelude to any conscious planning of accounting development for the future.

I would like to present to you a viewpoint of an academic on professional accounting, with particular reference to the Canadian accounting scene. More specifically what I would like to do is:

1. To analyze critically the meaning of the term *profession*. I believe, that this term contains some important clues that may be relevant to the present and future development of professional accountants.
2. To highlight some achievements and failures experienced by Canadian accountants in their process of professionalization; and
3. To suggest some opportunities and organizational mechanisms that can still be forged by Canadian accountants in their pursuit of ever rising standards.

THE MEANING OF THE TERM

Generally, the term *profession* is used to specify a vocational group that has achieved a high degree of excellence in certain criteria. Although there is no agreement on the exact nature or number of specific criteria that must be met before an occupational group can be designated as a profession, a group that maintains a strong self-governing association, possesses an elaborate code of ethics, and has attained a high level of accomplishment in some field of learning or science usually fulfills the main requirements for inclusion in the professional ranks.

Thus, the *American Heritage Dictionary* defines a profession as ". . . an occupation or vocation requiring training in the liberal arts or the sciences and advanced study in a specialized field." Closer to home, a *Dictionary for Accountants* defines a profession somewhat differently as

A vocation

1. *generally recognized by universities and colleges as requiring special training leading to a degree distinct from the usual degrees in arts and sciences*
2. *requiring principally mental rather than manual or artistic labor and skill for its successful presentation*
3. *recognizing the duty of public service*
4. *having a code of ethics generally accepted as binding upon its members (1)*

These and similar definitions of the term *profession* have two important shortcomings:

1. they lack universality in application
2. they are static rather than dynamic in nature

These definitions lack universality in that they exclude from professions some individuals who are generally considered to be the true professionals. Some clergymen and judges, for example, who have never been to a university would be denied professional status because a university degree is suggested by the above mentioned definitions as an important characteristic of a professional. This would be done despite the fact that the vocations of theology and law are considered to be two of the three oldest learned professions recognized by man, the third one being medicine.

The above mentioned definitions of the term *profession* are also static in that they imply a finality to certain occupational accomplishments. Passing of an examination at a single point in time for example, would be sufficient to meet an educational requirement for the duration of the professional's life.

In order to avoid these difficulties it may be helpful to think of the term *profession* differently and approach the subject in the spirit of ancient Greeks who conceived of a human as a being who perfects his body, mind, and character by seeking strength, wisdom, and virtue. That is, rather than defining the term *profession* as a vocation in which a fixed level of achievement of certain standards has been attained, it may be better to define it in terms of aims and objectives espoused by leaders of occupational groups, that is, in terms of an ideal state toward which these groups should strive. Since this ideal state cannot ever be achieved in the real world, there cannot be a finish line in the race for professional development.

Therefore, all occupational groups that actively seek the attainment of the recognized vocational goals are engaged in the process of professionalization and the closer they come to the realization of their aims, the greater become their rights to be called professions. Contemporary research reveals that some of the aims that such groups might seek to accomplish include the following: (2)

1. creation, mastery and transmission of complex bodies of knowledge and technique to all recognized practitioners in the field throughout their professional careers
2. evaluation of competence of individual practitioners to perform their functions at an acceptable level of accomplishment and licensing of those who are able to do so
3. maintenance of strong, visible, self-regulating associations and establishment of high standards of ethical practice with penalties for those who fail to act in accordance with those standards

ACCOUNTING TODAY

Canadian accountants certainly deserve the right to be included in the ranks of professionals. Not only do they share the aims and aspirations of other recognized professional groups but they also have a record of significant accomplishments in a number of these aims.

Canadian accountants certainly have a complex body of knowledge that requires years of sustained formal study to assimilate. Further, they do have strong self-regulating professional associations and high standards of ethical practice with all that this implies. Above all, Canadian accountants generally enjoy high public regard and support which comes from the public's realization of the fact that accounting and accountants do meet a deeply felt social need for financial information.

In satisfying this need, accountants greatly facilitate Canadian economic growth. It is hard to imagine the operation of our economy, both in private and public sectors, without the services presently provided by members of the three Canadian professional accounting bodies: the Institute of Chartered Accountants, the Society of Industrial Accountants, and the Certified General Accountants Association.

The rising demand for accounting graduates testifies to the insatiable appetite of Canadian industry, commerce, labor organizations. governments at all levels, and financial institutions for the product of the accountant's work: reliable financial information on various aspects of our complex economy. This information is crucial to economic decision-making of numerous users of accounting data.

In his classic paper *An Historical Defence of Bookkeeping*, read by Henry Rand Hatfield before the American Association of University Instructors in Accounting in 1923, when perhaps the defense of accounting was necessary, he concludes as follows:

> *I have tried to remove the stigma attached to accounting by showing that in its origin it is respectable, nay, even academic: that despite its present disrepute it has from time to time attracted the attention of men of unquestioned intellectual attainment; that it justifies itself in that it has risen to meet a social need. Its functions are to locate responsibility, to prevent fraud, to guide industry, to determine equities, to solve the all-essential condundrum of business: "what are my*

profits?"; to facilitate the government in its fiscal opera-
tions, to guide the business manager in the attempt to secure
efficiency.

Are not these efforts worthy of any man's attention? And
so I close this paper with a quotation from men whom all must
respect: Scott, the romanticist, declared the profession of
accounting "respectable"; Goethe, the Universal Genius speaks
of bookkeeping as "One of the fairest inventions of the human
mind"; and Cayley, scientist beyond question, even more sig-
nificantly declared "Bookkeeping is one of the two perfect
sciences." With these, I rest the defense of my houn' dog. (3)

Today, a half-a-century later, we see accounting taught in most of
the universities of the world and the accounting profession to be a
growing social force. In their efforts to professionalize, however,
Canadian accountants have naturally not been able to achieve all their
aims with equal success. Areas that still need further attention include the following:

1. Creation in the public eye of a sharp and unique concept
    of the accounting profession. The existence of a number
    of professional accounting designations and a potential
    for further proliferation of accounting associations and
    labels weakens the profession as a whole and tends to con-
    fuse rather than enlighten the public on the nature and
    functions of the accounting profession.
2. Absorption by the accounting profession of relevant new
    knowledge emerging from other areas of human activity.
    The unprecedented explosion of knowledge during the last
    two decades, has neither strengthened appreciably our tra-
    ditional accounting curricula with new knowledge emerging
    from such fields as information theory, systems theory,
    cybernetics, economics, management sciences, behavioral
    sciences, and computer sciences nor has it affected much
    the practitioners of accounting.

True we offer in our professional accounting programs courses in
economics, quantitative methods, computers and even in organizational
behavior. We offer these courses however, as separate unintegrated
chunks, little related to the primary concern of accountants: provision
of relevant economic information to various users of that information.
Even less successful is the accounting profession in the area of
providing continuing education for all graduate accountants. Generally,
only the most highly motivated accountants avail themselves of educational opportunities after graduation, with others tending to decelerate
their learning efforts considerably as soon as they have secured admission to the professional ranks. But this is quite contrary to the notion of professionalization as it is used here.

3. Creation of new accounting knowledge and the use of this
    knowledge in conventional and nonconventional ways. This
    involves painstaking research and considerable resources.
    The accounting profession has so far been devoting rela-
    tively a small fraction of its resources to research as

compared with what it currently devotes to the accomplishment of such aims as for example, transmission of knowledge, public relations and with what other professions
such as medicine devote to research.

For the accounting profession to grow, however, it is imperative
that it assimilate from the environment more than it relinquishes to
that environment, that is, it is imperative that accounting continually
renew and enrich itself with new ideas developed internally and ideas
flowing from other specialized fields.

Research can be fruitfully undertaken and disseminated among professional accountants in many areas including the following ones:

    a.   The use of accounting as a tool of public policy in
        regulated and unregulated industries.
    b.   Accounting for "nonprofit" organizations, such as
        hospitals, colleges and universities, and various
        health and welfare organizations. In many cases, their
        basis of financial support has shifted in such a way as
        to make cost analysis a crucial issue.
    c.   Accounting for human resources.

4.   Accounting principles themselves. There are definite
    pressures for improvement in this area. In his 1971 ad-
    dress *"Pressures for Progress,"* Marshall S. Armstrong,
    1970-71 president of the American Society of Certified
    Public Accountants has noted that: "Public feelings run
    high on such matters as inadequate, inaccurate, or mis-
    leading financial reporting practices . . ." and that
    currently heavy ". . . brickbats are being thrown at
    business managers for the scope of their financial dis-
    closures; and at us CPAs, as auditors, for the accounting
    principles established for corporate reporting."

The American Institute of Certified Public Accountants is presently
putting forth a great deal of effort to improve their financial reporting principles. Although this problem has not yet become as acute in
Canada as it is in the U.S.A., reexamination of the objectives of financial statements and reporting standards in the light of their appropriateness to today's Canadian conditions and needs seems to be a highly
desirable undertaking.

OPPORTUNITIES FOR FURTHER DEVELOPMENT

A dynamic concept of professionalization based on discovery,
growth, and innovation challenges accountants continually to undertake
new tasks, to seize upon new opportunities in the never ending race for
professional development. At each point in time, these opportunities
arise basically out of the analysis of the extant problems facing the
accounting profession as a whole.

At the present state of the development of professional accounting
in Canada it may be worthwhile, first of all, to consider seriously the
notion of unification of the profession by creating a single, strong

accounting association. This new organization of accountants could be
possibly patterned after the organization of the medical profession.
   Existence of a single national body of professional accountants
would, in my view, benefit both accountants and users of accounting
information in that:

1. It would remove any confusion that may still exist regard-
    ing the nature and functions of the profession in the eyes
    of the public.
2. It would enable the accounting profession to differentiate
    its services more precisely than is the case at the moment
    by allowing membership to specialize deeply in such complex
    fields as public accounting, managerial accounting, govern-
    ment accounting, general accounting, etc., and thus offer
    more refined skills to the users of various accounting
    services.
3. It would, most probably, result in significant economies
    of scale in all aspects of professional accounting devel-
    opment.

   The second important opportunity for Canadian accountants lies in
the area of both undergraduate and graduate education. Much has been
done in this area by the profession. The knowledge explosion, however,
requires continual upgrading of educational background of an entrant to
the accounting profession and a sustained effort to keep this knowledge
current after his graduation.
   On the first issue, undergraduate accounting education, it may be
worthwhile for all Canadian accounting associations to consider the
wisdom of following in the footsteps of other professions such as law,
medicine, and engineering as far as educational requirements are concerned. The prerequisite to entry into these professions is an appropriate degree from recognized universities: LL.B., for law, M.D. for
medicine, and B.Sc., for engineering.
   The trend toward higher education for professions has already affected some accounting associations. Here at home, one of the present
eligibility requirements for registration as a student with the Institute of Chartered Accountants of B.C. is a university degree.
   Abroad, the American Institute of CPAs adopted in 1969 a series of
recommendations concerned with education and experience requirements
for CPAs. (5) At least five years of college study is recommended by
AICPA as an educational requirement for all CPAs. These recommendations
should be adopted by all states by 1975. In 1971 the state of California acted on these recommendations and other states are expected to
do the same in the near future.
   This trend toward higher educational requirements for entrance into
the accounting profession will undoubtedly continue. The questions that
the profession should ask itself, therefore, are: Given the present circumstances, what is the optimal rate of change in educational standards
that Canadian Accounting profession should adopt? What should be the
common body of knowledge possessed by those who are about to begin their
professional accounting careers?
   What should be the nature of cooperation between the profession and
its academic arm: universities and colleges in upgrading the education
of accountants? Unless these questions are answered satisfactorily from

time to time, it may be difficult to plan for the future development of professional accounting.

It will be hard to find satisfactory answers to the above questions. It will be even harder to find a satisfactory vehicle for the maintenance of skills of those already in the profession.

In an effort to force its members to keep abreast of current developments, the AICPA Council approved in 1971 a resolution urging states to adopt a continuing education requirement for CPAs. This requirement currently exists only for Iowa CPAs. Recent studies indicate, that most CPAs agree that ". . . in the public interest and self-interest of the profession, action must be taken to require continuing education of all CPAs." (6)

This may not be the best road for Canadian accountants to travel on the way to perfection of their skills, but it is one way which ensures at least a minimum level of competence for all persons aspiring to professional accounting status and, therefore, it is worthy of our consideration.

Finally, there is a challenge to the accounting profession in the area of research. Research is a relatively new event in accounting and it is often misunderstood and sometimes it is even considered unnecessary. Yet research is crucial to accounting development. It can be accomplished in a number of ways.

Traditionally, the accounting profession has dealt with the problem of research by setting up research committees and asking them to look into this or that problem. Valuable as this mechanism for producing new ideas is, it fails to recognize the individualistic aspect of research. To quote Chambers on the subject:

> *You have never heard of the committee to discover the law of gravitation, or of the committee to develop the periodic table of elements . . . Only individuals can bring to bear the concentrated attention over long periods, on the facts they observe and on the then accepted ideas of their peers—attention which yields new insights, new knowledge . . . In our time you will hear of committees to finance research of one kind or another; but the individualistic character of research remains. Committees may evaluate; it has never been shown that they can originate." (7)*

I like this idea of organization for research and recommend it to you for further study and discussion.

I have been looking at the past and present so that we may catch a glimpse of the future. In order to achieve its objectives more fully, the accounting profession must continue to search for better ways of organizing itself, its education and its research. In these three areas accountants face excellent opportunities for further progress. I believe that they will be successful in their quest, for many of them, hopefully, share Joseph Conrad's sentiment for perfection of their skills which reads as follows:

> *. . . the attainment of proficiency, the pushing of your skill with attention to the most delicate shades of excellence, is a matter of vital concern. Efficiency of a practically flawless kind may be reached naturally in the struggle for bread, but*

there is something beyond—a higher point, a subtle and unmistakable touch of love and pride beyond mere skill; almost an inspiration which gives to all work that finish which is almost art—which is art.

FOOTNOTES

1. E. L. Kohler, *A Dictionary for Accountants* (Englewood Cliffs, N.J.: Prentice-Hall, 1963), p. 398.
2. C. O. Houle, "The Comparative Study of Continuing Professional Education," *Continuing Education in the Professions,* The Ontario Institute for Studies in Education, November, 1970, pp. 14-15.
3. H. R. Hatfield, "An Historical Defense of Bookkeeping," *The Journal of Accountancy*, vol. 37, no. 4 (April, 1924): 253.
4. M. S. Armstrong, "Pressure for Progress," *The California CPA Quarterly* (September, 1971): 13-14.
5. AICPA, *The Report of the Committee on Education and Experience Requirements for CPAs*, New York, 1969.
6. V. C. Brenner, R. H. Strawser, "Some Observations on Required Continuing Education," *The CPA Journal* (June, 1972): 472.
7. R. J. Chambers, *Accounting Finance and Management*, (Arthur Andersen & Co., 1969), p. 712.

QUESTIONS

1. How would you define the term profession?
2. Why is it important to the public that CPAs and lawyers be professional in the conduct of their business?
3. Is licensing necessary to have a profession?
4. Is continuing education necessary for a profession? Why might it be desirable?

103   CPA REQUIREMENTS OF THE STATES

Wilton T. Anderson

(Reprinted by permission from *Collegiate News and Views*, vol. 25, no. 3 (Spring, 1972): 11-15.)

(Wilton T. Anderson is a faculty member at Oklahoma State University.)

The CPA certificate is awarded to an applicant who meets the statutory and accountancy board requirements of the political jurisdiction to which he applies. These requirements vary considerably, and the principal ones are tabulated and explained on the following pages.

All fifty states, the District of Columbia, Guam, Puerto Rico, and the Virgin Islands, use both the examination and grading service offered by the American Institute of Certified Public Accountants. While most of the jurisdictions have statutes which specify that candidates will be examined in at least theory of accounts, accounting practice, auditing, and business law, the content of the examination is changing within these four broad question groupings. The examination is discussed in the July, 1971, issue of *The Journal of Accountancy* in an article entitled "The Changing Content of the CPA Examination" by H. S. Hendrickson of the AICPA staff.

SOME CHANGES

Education and Experience

In preparing the tabulations of state requirements, several changes in recent years were noticed. One of the changes has been for a number of states to increase the education requirement to the baccalaureate degree. This change provides greater protection to the public by upgrading the professional preparation. It is likely that more and more jurisdictions will enact this educational requirement. Quite often the increase in education is accompanied by a reduction in the required time of work experience under the supervision of a CPA. It is unlikely that the AICPA recommendation of a five-year educational program and no work experience will become law in very many states for several years.

Conditioned Credit

Another significant change has been for state boards of accountancy to accept conditioned credit (passed parts of the examination) from other states. It is quite common for a CPA candidate to take the examination in one state, pass enough parts to receive conditioned credit, then accept employment in another state. In those states having reciprocity of passed parts, the candidate must pass only the previously failed parts in order to receive the CPA certificate.

Minimum Grade in Failed Subjects for Conditioned Credit

Another change has been for more states to require a candidate to earn a minimum grade in failed subjects in order to receive conditioned credit in passed parts of the examination. This requirement is ordinarily a board regulation instead of by means of a statute. It is a good regulation in that it forces candidates to prepare for all parts of the examination. All jurisdictions require candidates to write all parts for which conditioned credit has not been awarded.

Examination Fees

Examination fees have increased in numerous states. The examination and grading service cost to state boards has been increased. Since most state boards must be self-supporting, it was necessary to pass the higher charge on to candidates.

Licensing of All Public Accountants

Most states are licensing all public accountants. Ten years ago only a limited number of states had "permissive" accounting laws which would allow anyone to practice as a public accountant. In a "permissive" state the initials "CPA" can be used only by those people who meet education, experience, examination, and other requirements authorizing the use of those initials. The principal reason for licensing all public accountants has been due to the wording pertaining to auditing grants, agencies, and corporations with which the federal government is involved. The words "licensed or certified public accountant" often appear in regard to who is considered to be an approved auditor. Many noncertified public accountants, therefore, requested their legislatures to enact an accountancy law which would license them so they would be eligible for these audits.

Continuing Education

A few other significant factors pertaining to the statutes or state board regulations affecting CPAs are beginning to emerge. The governing council of the AICPA has taken a position urging the enactment of accountancy statutes which will require continuing education on the part of CPAs. It is in the public interest that the competence of CPAs be maintained by study after they are licensed. Considerable latitude is allowed in the types of programs in which they can study such as collegiate courses, professional development courses and the like so that hardships are minimized.

CORPORATE FORM OF BUSINESS IN
PRACTICE OF PUBLIC ACCOUNTING

Some states have enacted statutes permitting the corporate form of business in the practice of public accounting. Very recently this type of legislation became law in Massachusetts, Nebraska, and South Dakota. Tax regulations pertaining to pension funds had a great deal to do with the change in attitude of the profession about restricting public practice to individuals and to partnerships. Limited liability is rarely permitted in this type of statute.

MEANING OF CPA CERTIFICATE

The meaning of the CPA certificate is being altered. This alteration takes place rather slowly as new accountancy laws are enacted. In all except a few jurisdictions, the certificate has been construed to be a license to practice as a certified public accountant. In practically all states CPAs are considered competent to make opinion audits. The present policy of the AICPA is that the CPA certificate is evidence of basic competence of professional quality in the discipline of accounting. Most interpretations of this new meaning consider experience to be of little significance for licensing. This new meaning of the certificate has been adopted in only a few states; however, as the speciman statutory bill advocated by the AICPA, called the "form" bill, is adopted by the legislative bodies of the states, the meaning of the certificate likely will be altered.

TABLE 20

CPA REQUIREMENTS: RESIDENCE, EDUCATION,
EXPERIENCE, AND EXAMINATION CONDITIONING

State	State Residence Required	Place of Business Fulfills Residence Requirement	Require Post High School Education	Years of Accounting Experience	Public Accounting Experience Required	Other Accounting Experience Substitute	Education Substitutive (whole or part) for Experience	Exp. or Education Mandatory Before Completion of CPA Exam	Exam Fee	Subject Passes Required For Conditioned Credit	Life of Conditioned Credit	Reciprocity of Conditioned Credit
Alabama	NS	Yes	Bach.	3	Yes		(g)	Yes	$65	2 or P	5NE	Yes
Alaska	NS		2 Yr.	4	4	Yes	(g)	Yes	$25	2 or P	5Y(k)	Yes
Arizona	NS		Bach.	(d)	Yes	Yes	(g)	Yes	NS	2 or P	3Y	Yes
Arkansas	NS	(b)	Bach.	1-2	No		(g)	Yes	$40	2	5NE	
California	Yes	Yes	(c)	3-4	3-4	Yes	Yes	(h)	$45	2 or P	3Y	Yes
Colorado	Yes	Yes	(c)	1-3	1-3	Yes	(g)	(h)	$50	2	3NE	Yes
Connecticut	Yes	Yes	Bach.	2	2	Yes	No	(h)	$50	2 or P	3Y	Yes
Delaware	1 Yr.	Yes	(c)	2	Yes		No	NS	$50	2 or P + 50%	5NE	Yes
District of Columbia	1 Yr.	Yes	60 Hrs.	2-4	Yes	1½:1	(d)		$50	2 or P	5NE	
Florida	6 Mo.		Bach.	1	Yes	(f)	(g)	Yes	$75	2	5NE	
Georgia	NS	Yes	Bach.	2	1	2:1	(g)	No	$35	2	5NE	
Hawaii	1 Yr.	No	Bach.	(d)	(d)	(f)	Yes	Yes	$35	2	6NE	
Idaho	NS	Yes	Bach.	(d)	Yes	5	Yes	(h)	$35	2 or P + 50%	5NE	Yes
Illinois	NS	Yes	120 Hrs.	3	Yes	Yes	(g)	Yes	$65	2 or P + 50%	(k)	Yes
Indiana	6 Mo.		(c)	3	3	3-6	(g)	(h)	$50	2	6NE	Yes
Iowa	6 Mo.		(c)	1	1	(f)		No	$25	2 or P + 50%	4NE	
Kansas	NS	Yes	(c)		2		(g)	(h)	$50	2 + 50%	6NE	Yes
Kentucky	NS	Yes	(c)	1-6	1-6	IRS	Yes	Yes	$50	1 + 50%	4NE	Yes
Louisiana	1 Yr.		(c)	1-3	1-3	Yes	(h)	Yes	$35	2 + 45%	(k)	Yes
Maine	NS	(b)	(c)	1-4	Yes	Yes	Yes	Yes	$50	2 or P	3Y	Yes
Maryland	1 Yr.		(c)	2	2	Yes	Yes	Yes	$50	2 or P + 50%	5NE	Yes

State												
Massachusetts	NS		Bach.	3	3	(f)	(g)	No	$ 50	2 or P + 50%	6NE	Yes
Michigan	NS	Yes	(c)	2-4	2-4	Yes	(g)		$ 25	1	6NE	
Minnesota	NS			3	3	Yes	(g)	Yes	$ 50	2 + 50%	5NE	Yes
Mississippi	1 Yr.		(c)	1-2	1-2	1-3	Yes	Yes	$ 60	2 or P + 45%	10NE	
Missouri	NS	Yes	Bach.	1-3	1	5 Yr.	(g)	Yes	$ 50	(j)	2NE	Yes
Montana	1 Yr.	Yes	(c)	1	1	Yes		Yes	$ 25	2 or P	2Y	Yes
Nebraska	NS	Yes	Bach.	4	4	(f)	(g)	Yes	$ 30	2 or P	9NE	
Nevada	NS	Yes	Bach.	2	2	No	No	Yes	$ 50	2 or P + 60%	Unlim.	
New Hampshire	NS	(b)		4	4	Yes		No	$ 75	2		
New Jersey	1 Yr.	Yes	Bach.	3	3	(f)		Yes	$ 35	2	3Y	Yes
New Mexico	NS	Yes	Bach.	1-3	Yes		(g)	Yes	$ 50	2	NS	Yes
New York	NS	Yes	Bach.	2-15	2		(g)	Yes	$ 40	(j)	NS	Yes
North Carolina	1 Yr.	Yes	24 Hrs.	2	2	(f)	(g)	(h)	$ 35	2 or P	5NE	Yes
North Dakota	1 Yr.		Bach.	(d)			(g)		$100	2 or P	5NE	
Ohio	NS	Yes	(c)	2-4	2-4	Yes	Yes	Yes	$ 40	1	8Y	
Oklahoma	1 Yr.		No	(d)	3	Yes	Yes		$ 35	2 or P	(k)	
Oregon	NS		(c)	0-2	0-2	Yes	Yes	Yes	$ 30	2 or P	6NE	Yes
Pennsylvania	NS	Yes	Bach.	2	2	Yes	(g)	Yes	$ 25	2	Unlim.	
Puerto Rico	NS	Yes	(c)	0-6	Yes	Yes	Yes	Yes	$ 25	2	NS	Yes
Rhode Island	NS	Yes	(c)	2-4	2-4	Yes	Yes	Yes	$ 50	2 or P	3NE	Yes
South Carolina	NS		Bach.	(d)	2-3	No	No	No	$ 50	2 or P + 40%		
South Dakota	NS	Yes	Bach.	1	1	No	No	Yes	$ 50		6NE	Yes
Tennessee	1 Yr.	Yes	(c)	2	2		Yes	Yes	$ 35	2 or P	6NE	Yes
Texas	NS	Yes	(c)	1-6	1-6		Yes	Yes	$ 50	2	Unlim.	Yes
Utah	NS	Yes	Bach.	2	2	No	(g)	(h)	$ 40	1	6NE	
Vermont	NS	Yes	0	2	2		(g)	No	$ 50	2	NS	Yes
Virginia	NS	Yes	120 Hrs.	2	2	(f)		Yes	$ 40	1	2NE	Yes
Virgin Islands	NS	Yes	(c)	2-6	2-6	Yes		(h)	$ 25	2	NS	
Washington	NS	Yes	(c)	1-2	1-2	2-4		(h)	$ 40	2 or P	3Y	
West Virginia	NS	Yes	Bach.						$ 40	1	3Y	
Wisconsin	NS	Yes	Bach.	(d)	3		Yes	Yes	$ 30	2 + 50%	(k)	Yes
Wyoming	NS	No	(g)	3	3	(f)	(g)	(g)	$ 75	2 or P	(k)	

NOTES TO TABLE 20

1. *Age and Citizenship*. All jurisdictions require that an
   applicant be 21 years of age except Alaska (19), Kentucky
   (18), Maine (20), Montana (no requirement), and Wisconsin
   (23). Most states further specify that an applicant be a
   citizen of the U.S. or officially declare intent to become
   a citizen. No citizenship is specified in the statutes of
   Indiana, Kansas, and Washington. The following states require U.S. citizenship: Delaware, Georgia, Louisiana, Massachusetts, Mississippi, New Hampshire, New Jersey, and
   Oklahoma. Fifteen states specify the length of residency
   required before an applicant can take the examination.
2. *Place of Business Fulfills Residence Requirement*. Arkansas, Maine, and New Hampshire require that, in addition to
   having a place of residence in the state, an applicant
   must have a place of business or be employed in a place of
   business in the state. Other states marked "Yes" allow a
   person who is not a resident of the state but who has a
   place of business in the state to become a CPA in that
   state. Hawaii specifically states that a place of business will not satisfy the residency requirement. All
   states require at least two character references, most require three, and some require five.
3. *Post High School Education*. In Column three "Bach." means
   bachelor's degree in accounting or the equivalent thereof
   as determined by the respective state boards. *California*:
   College graduate plus three years' experience or junior
   college plus four years' experience or public accountant
   plus four years' experience. *Colorado*: Bachelor's degree
   with one year of experience or high school diploma with
   three years' experience. *Delaware*: Bachelor's degree with
   two years' experience or junior college with four years'
   experience. *Indiana*: No post high school education required until 7/1/72. Between 7/1/72 and 7/1/75, a degree
   will be required. After 7/1/75 a bachelor in accounting
   will be required. *Iowa*: Bachelor in accounting or three
   years' experience. *Kansas*: Bachelor in accounting or
   bachelor with two years' public accounting experience.
   Kentucky: Bachelor in accounting plus two years' experience or master in accounting plus one year's experience or
   bachelor plus three years' experience, or high school plus
   six year's experience. *Louisiana*: Before 9/1/75 a completed course in higher accountancy plus three years' experience. After 9/1/75 a bachelor in accounting plus one
   year of experience. *Maine*: Until 7/1/74, two years'
   college plus four years' experience. After 7/1/74 a bachelor with two years' experience or a master with one year
   experience. *Maryland*: Until 6/30/74, two years or 72 semester hours plus two years' experience. After 7/1/74 a
   bachelor in accounting, no experience. *Michigan*: Prior to
   1/1/75, bachelor plus four years' experience. After 1/1/75
   bachelor in accounting plus two years' experience. *Mississippi*: Bachelor in accounting plus one year experience or

bachelor plus two years' employment with CPA or three
years of government experience or teaching experience.
Montana: Prior to 1/1/75, two years of college required.
After 1/1/75 bachelor's degree required. *Ohio*: Two
years' business college plus four years' experience or
bachelor in accounting plus two years' experience or
master plus one year experience. *Oregon*: Bachelor in
accounting substitutes for all experience. Otherwise two
years' experience required. *Puerto Rico*: Six years' experience required. With degree four years' required.
With bachelor in accounting, no experience required.
Rhode Island: Prior to 6/10/73, two years of college with
four years' experience. Between 6/10/73 and 6/10/76, two
years of college in accounting with four years' experience.
After 6/10/76 bachelor in accounting plus two years' experience. Master's degree substitutes for all but one
year. *Tennessee*: Prior to 3/10/73, two years in accounting. After 3/10/73 bachelor in accounting. Master substitutes for one year of experience. *Texas*: Junior college
in accounting plus six years' experience or bachelor in
accounting plus two years' experience or master in accounting plus one year experience. *Virgin Islands*: High school
plus six years' experience, degree plus three years' experience, or degree in accounting plus two years' experience.
Washington: Business school or degree plus two years' experience or bachelor in accounting plus one year experience.

4. *Experience*. *Arizona*: Two years in a CPA office or four
years in a PA office. *District of Columbia*: Credit given
for one year of experience for each 30 hours of business
education with a maximum of two years credit. *Hawaii*:
three years, two public; or four years, one public; or
five years, zero public. *Idaho*: Three years employed by
CPA, four years employed by self or PA. *New Mexico*: Registered PA must have three years' experience. A bachelor's
degree in accounting will substitute for two years. *New
York*: 15 years' experience required for persons without
degree. *North Dakota*: Four years' experience in public
accounting substitutes for bachelor's degree. *Oklahoma*:
Three years of experience (one of which must have been in
Oklahoma). Bachelor in accounting substitutes for all experience. *South Carolina*: Two years employed by CPA or
three years employed by PA. *Wisconsin*: Three years as
senior accountant required. Degree in accounting substitutes for 1½ years of experience.

5. Some states do not explicitly allow accounting other than
public accounting to fulfill experience requirements. Column six is blank for those states. Other states allow sub-
stitution of experience as an IRS agent, a state audit
agent, etc., for public accounting experience. For these
states Columns five and six should be read together. A
"Yes" in Column five with a "Yes" or numbers in Column six
indicates that public accounting experience is required
but substitutions are specifically mentioned in the

statutes and regulations. A number in Column six indicates the number of years of nonpublic accounting which are required. A ratio indicates the number of years of nonpublic accounting which will substitute for one year of public accounting.

6. Some states allow accounting other than public to satisfy the experience requirement. *Florida*: If under the supervision of a CPA. *Hawaii*: Three years in post audit for federal or state government. *Iowa*: One year of government accounting or three years as an assistant professor. *Massachusetts*: Two years with GS9 level for the U.S. Government substitutes for one year experience in public accounting. *Nebraska*: 3½ years with IRS plus degree substitutes for four years' experience. *New Jersey*: Ten years in self-employment in public accounting or ten years with certain government agencies substitutes for public accounting experience. *North Carolina*: Two years with IRS or state auditor substitutes for experience. *Virginia*: Four years of IRS or state or federal auditing. *Wyoming*: College teachers with master's or IRS grade 11 must have three years experience.

7. *Education Substitutes for Experience*. In the following states the master's degree in accounting substitutes for one year of experience: Alabama, Arkansas, Georgia, Indiana, Massachusetts, Michigan, Missouri, New York, North Carolina, Pennsylvania, and Utah. In Arizona a master's degree substitutes for half of the experience. In Colorado and Kansas a master's degree substitutes for all the experience. In Vermont, Minnesota, and Oklahoma, a bachelor's degree substitutes for all the experience. In Alaska, Illinois, Nebraska, and New Mexico, a bachelor's degree substitutes for two years' experience. In Florida an additional year of accounting courses beyond the bachelor's degree substitutes for all the experience required.

8. In some states a candidate may take the CPA examination before he has completed his experience or educational requirement. An applicant must be within 120 days of graduation in California and Washington; within 90 days in Idaho, Kansas, and North Carolina; within 60 days in Colorado and Indiana; and within 45 days in Louisiana. In Utah the applicant may be in his last semester; and in the Virgin Islands and Connecticut he may not take the practice portion of the exam before he completes the experience requirement.

9. All states use the examination grading service of the AICPA. The following states require an applicant to pass an exam in ethics in addition to the uniform exam of the AICPA: Alabama, Florida, Nebraska, New Mexico, Oklahoma, Utah, Wyoming, and Virginia. Iowa requires an exam in taxation and general commercial knowledge; Michigan requires an exam in finance and economics. The fee noted in the table is the fee for the first application and examination. Reexaminations are usually offered at a reduced fee.

10. Conditioning requirements are listed in the table. The
symbol "2 or P" means that an applicant must pass two
parts of the exam other than practice or practice alone
to receive conditional credit. The symbol "+ 50%" means
that in all subjects not passed an applicant must have a
score of at least 50% for the passed parts to receive conditional credit. In Missouri the experience requirement
is two years for those applicants who pass practice and
auditing on the first try. If only one of these is
passed on the first try, the experience requirement is
three years. In New York auditing must be taken after
the experience requirement has been fulfilled. To condition one must pass theory and law or practice. All states
require a candidate to take all sections of the examination for which he qualifies the first time. Candidates
who are members in good standing of the bar in their
state need not take the law portion of the exam. If a
candidate has conditioned on some parts of the exam, he
must take all other parts each time he sits for the exam
in the future.

11. *Life of Conditional Credit.* "3Y" means three years.
"3NE" means three next examinations. In the following
states the number of the next successive exams which must
be taken to retain conditional credit is noted: Alaska,
one per year; Illinois, three of six; Louisiana, one of
four; Oklahoma, one out of three for ten next exams; Wisconsin, three of six; Wyoming, four of six. In the District of Columbia an applicant must sit for all of the
next five exams. All states extend the life of the condition for time spent in the Armed Services of the United
States.

12. All the states marked "Yes" under Column 12 make some provision for recognizing conditional credit earned in another state if that courtesy is reciprocated by the State
from which the applicant transfers his credits.

---

104   INSTITUTE ACHIEVES SOLID PROGRESS
                    DURING FIRST YEAR

James Bulloch

(Reprinted by permission from *Management Accounting*, vol. 54, no. 1
(July, 1973) : 60-61.)

(James Bulloch is director of the Institute of Management Accounting.)

The Board of Directors of the National Association of Accountants
established, in January, 1972, the Institute of Management Accounting to

implement the Certificate in Management Accounting program. This program was designed to:

1. establish management accounting as a recognized profession
2. identify the role of the management accountant
3. identify the underlying body of knowledge of management accounting and outline a course of study by which such knowledge can be gained
4. foster higher educational standards in the field of management accounting
5. assist employers, educators, and students by establishing an objective measure of an individual's knowledge and competence in the field of management accounting

This is a report on the Institute's activities toward achieving the above objectives. Objective one will be achieved when all the others have been reached and have caused accountants and others to recognize the management accountant. The major activities in this first year have focused on the latter three objectives.

The Board of Regents (the policy board of the IMA) has begun to define the underlying body of knowledge. The five parts of the examination outline this knowledge.

Part 1   Economics and Business Finance
Part 2   Organization and Behavior, Including Ethical Considerations
Part 3   Public Reporting Standards, Auditing and Taxes
Part 4   Periodic Reporting for Internal and External Purposes
Part 5   Decision Analysis, Including Modeling and Information Systems

This outline was further detailed by the preparation of a reading list divided according to examination parts. (The list is available to CMA exam candidates.) The examination also indicates the type of knowledge the Board believes relevant to management accounting. (Questions and unofficial answers to the exam appeared in *Management Accounting* over the past five months.)

The objective of fostering higher educational standards is promoted by the Board's requiring a college degree or evidence of academic ability equivalent to that of a degree holder for a person's admission to the CMA program. The requirement of 90 hours of continuing education in each three-year period to maintain the CMA, once earned, further reinforces the attainment of this objective.

An individual's knowledge and competence in management accounting is measured objectively by the CMA examination and the requirement that a certificate holder must pass a five-part examination and have two years of full-time, continuous experience at a level in which significant judgments employing the principles of management accounting are made regularly.

The first CMA examination is history, but there has been much interest in the examination results. The June issue of *Management Accounting* listed the 61 candidates who passed all five parts of the examination. Fifty-four accountants within that group have satisfied

the experience requirement and have become the first holders of the
Certificate in Management Accounting.

NATURE OF FIRST CMA EXAM CANDIDATES

More than 500 accountants applied to the Institute of Management
Accounting during July, August, and September, 1972. Most satisfied the
program's entrance requirements and were authorized to take the examination. Some candidates, because of work commitments or other reasons,
delayed their examinations until 1973. The final count was 410 taking
two or more examination parts. Most candidates took all five parts.
The candidates came from all segments of the accounting profession:
managerial, teaching, and public accounting. They are profiled in
Table 21.

TABLE 21

SUMMARY PROFILE OF THE DECEMBER, 1972 CMA CANDIDATES

Average age	37
Average number of years since last degree	8
Percent of candidates offering:	
Undergraduate degrees	47
Advanced degrees	48
Foreign degrees	2
Other credentials	3

As mentioned previously, 61 candidates passed all five parts of the
examination. In addition to these 61, many others passed one to four
parts. The description of the candidates who passed one-half or more of
parts they took appears in Table 22.

TABLE 22

SUMMARY PROFILE OF CANDIDATES PASSING
50 PERCENT OR MORE OF THE PARTS ELECTED

Average age	36
Average number of years since last degree	7
Percent of candidates offering:	
Undergraduate degrees	34
Advanced degrees	62
Foreign degrees	1
Other credentials	3

PERFORMANCE ON THE EXAMINATION

The official answers were prepared by professionals in the fields represented on the examination. All possible answers were recognized in developing the official solution. The scoring on each question was determined in accordance with the depth of knowledge expected on each examination part (a reduced level of specialized knowledge on parts 1, 2, and 3 and a high level of specialized knowledge on parts 4 and 5). The scoring keys were tested against a sample of exam papers to ensure the candidates interpreted the questions in the same manner as the answer preparers. The papers were graded by professionals in the several fields in accordance with the official scoring schedules. A random sample of papers was graded by a second grader to make sure they were being graded correctly. In addition to this review, all papers close to the required passing grade of 70 were reviewed carefully to determine if they were passing papers. This quality control review and the careful review of marginal papers assures the candidates their papers were graded fairly and carefully.

The candidates' performances varied on each part, but the average number passing a part was just under 50 percent. The data contained in Table 23 detail the candidates' experience on the first CMA examination.

TABLE 23

SUCCESS RATES ON THE 1972 CMA EXAMINATION

Examination Part	Percent Passing
Part 1 Economics and Business Finance	56
Part 2 Organization and Behavior, Including Ethical Considerations	51
Part 3 Public Reporting Standards, Auditing and Taxes	40
Part 4 Periodic Reporting for Internal and External Purposes	56
Part 5 Decision Analysis, Including Modeling and Information Systems	44
Weighted average for the entire examination	50
All five parts in one sitting	21

The Board of Regents congratulates the first CMA candidates on their performance. Their experience and educational backgrounds correspond to the objectives established for the CMA program. The Board looks forward to an equally good group of candidates and similar results on the 1973 examination to be given in 25 cities December 5, 6, and 7, 1973.

105   CERTIFICATION—A GIANT STEP

William S. Smith

(Reprinted by permission from *The Internal Auditor*, vol. 29, no. 6 (November/December, 1972): 10-19.)

(William S. Smith is controller, distribution services for Agway Inc., Syracuse, New York.)

It was a typical June day at the Los Angeles Hilton. The temperature was in the low 80s. The lobby and corridors were humming with conversations of businessmen. On this particular day, the businessmen were internal auditors attending The Institute's 31st Annual International Conference.

It was a typical day, in many respects, for the Institute. It was the last day of a most successful International Conference. It was the day when International President John Ballard introduced his theme "Better Service to Management." It was the day when former International President Frank Lennon received the Cadmus Memorial Award. It was the day of the Board of Directors meeting.

It also was *not* a typical day for The Institute for one major reason. It was the day when the Board of Directors would need to make a major decision. It was the day when the Board of Directors would need to determine The Institute's future course of action regarding certification of internal auditors. This decision would represent a major turning point in the future of the profession of internal auditing. Before relating what transpired during that Board of Directors meeting, it might be well to trace the events which led to this major decision.

THE PAST

Over the years the question of certification has been discussed time and again by internal auditing practitioners. Although it was generally recognized that the awarding of a certificate might be desirable, it was also recognized that it would be highly difficult, it not impossible, to design an adequate examination to truly test the basic talents required of the internal auditor. My first personal identification with this question arose in the early 1960s when I was chairman of the International Educational Committee of The Institute. Brad Cadmus, who was then director of Research and Education, and I had several conversations involving this matter. The Spring, 1965 issue of *The Internal Auditor* included an article by Cadmus entitled "The Certificated Auditor." In the article he pointed out the basic responsibilities of the Certified Public Accountant compared with the majority of internal auditors. His article includes the following comment:

> *All of this is principally to point up the difficulty of developing an examination that would test for the necessary requirements of business experience and judgment that are the hallmark of the effective internal auditor.*

In 1965, while I was international vice president, I was assigned the specific responsibility of surveying the degree of interest then existent within our membership toward a certification program. A questionnaire was distributed to a broad cross section of internal audit leaders throughout the world. The responses indicated a wide and divergent viewpoint toward this question. Many leaders were strongly opposed to the proposition while others were strongly in favor of moving ahead on a certification program. The responses indicated that about the same number of auditors were opposed as were favorable. Almost without exception, a high emotional level was exhibited in each response. During that year I visited many chapters throughout The Institute. Again, the question of certification arose during many of these visits. The level of member interest was unquestionably high.

Because of this high level of interest, when I became Institute President in 1966, I asked the Board of Directors to authorize creation of the Professional Development Committee, whose primary responsibility was to study the entire question of certification for the internal auditor. Former International President Ken K. Kilgore agreed to chair this committee. I believe the establishment of the Professional Development Committee represents the first official recognition by The Institute of the need for careful and deliberate study involving certification. This provided the organizational structure for future developments.

Attributes of Professionalism

It is not my intention in this article to discuss the various attributes of professionalism nor to debate whether internal auditing is a profession in its fullest form. The Professional Development Committee has carefully researched these questions and is prepared to defend the propriety of internal auditing as a profession in terms of the current definition of professions generally in use throughout the world today. It is important to note, however, that there is general agreement on certain prerequisites for a professional certification program. These are:

1. development of a code of ethics
2. development of standards of experience
3. development of minimum standards of education and supporting training programs
4. development of an examination procedure
5. development of some form of recognition

The Institute has moved forward at a deliberate and carefully planned pace in developing the prerequisites cited.

Code of Ethics

One of the early projects of the Professional Development Committee was the development of a Code of Ethics for The Institute of Internal Auditors. On December 13, 1968, the Board of Directors adopted the Code of Ethics currently in use for the guidance of our members.

Position Papers (1)

The Professional Development Committee then began the development of a series of position papers covering the major aspects of the certification program. A draft of the papers was circulated to officers, directors, and chapter presidents for comments. The chapter presidents were asked to review each paper with their chapter members in the expectation that this would provide the greatest cross section of ideas possible. Responses were included in the later drafts which were then approved by the Board of Directors. In my opinion, these position papers represent a broad cross section of the thinking of our membership. We must recognize that it is practically impossible to obtain 100 percent agreement on every item. I believe, however, that papers do represent the consensus of our membership. They will be discussed at greater length later in this article.

Cadmus Education Foundation

A further key development was the establishment of the Cadmus Education Foundation in 1968. CEF provided the basis for development of training courses both on a seminar as well as home study basis. It also provided the basis for improved working relationships with colleges and universities.

Common Body of Knowledge

A major roadblock to progess in developing a certification program was the lack of a common body of knowledge. This was needed to develop the minimum standards of education and as the basis for examination. The responsibility for the development of a common body of knowledge was assigned to the Educational Committee and specifically to a subcommittee chaired by Robert E. Gobeil. A report of this committee was presented to a joint meeting of the Educational, Research, and Professional Development committees on June 17, 1972. The report is reviewed in depth in an accompanying article in this issue of *The Internal Auditor*. The following is quoted from the minutes of that meeting:

> *On motion made, seconded, and unanimously carried, it was: RESOLVED, That the Educational Committee, Research Committee, and the Professional Development Committee accept and support the content of the "Common Body of Knowledge" study prepared by a subcommittee of the International Educational Committee (R. E. Gobeil, Chairman) as the initial step in the development of the basic educational foundation required of the professional internal auditor and recommend its approval and implementation by the Planning Committee and Board of Directors.*

A large portion of that combined meeting was devoted to discussion of the advantages and disadvantages of certification for the internal auditor. Many of the men present had been strongly opposed to certification over the years. Several of these men spoke at the meeting and without exception indicated that The Institute had completed all necessary preliminary steps and was now ready for a certification program.

Board of Directors Meeting

During the Los Angeles Conference, several meetings and discussions were held involving the subject of certification. All of these led to that eventful moment during the Board of Directors meeting when the question of certification was placed before the Board of Directors. The following resolution was presented by the Professional Development Committee:

BE IT RESOLVED, That:

1. *The Institute of Internal Auditors, Inc., shall develop and implement a certification program, and*

BE IT FURTHER RESOLVED, That:

2. *The Institute of Internal Auditors, Inc., shall assign such resources as are required to accomplish a certification program; and*

BE IT FURTHER RESOLVED, That:

3. *The Executive Vice President of The Institute of Internal Auditors, Inc., is hereby authorized and directed to develop and implement a program of certification within the general guidelines established in the six position papers previously tentatively approved by the Board of Directors and entitled:*

 The Certification Program
 Qualifications of Candidates
 The Examination
 Special Certification
 Waive of Baccalaureate Degree
 Honorary Degree
   and

BE IT FURTHER RESOLVED, That:

4. *The Technical Committees of The Institute of Internal Auditors, Inc., are hereby authorized and directed to provide the supporting technical program required by the certification program, and*

BE IT FURTHER RESOLVED, That:

5. *The designation "Certified Internal Auditor" shall be adopted to identify those candidates who successfully complete the certification program.*

Lengthy discussion followed involving the pros and cons of certification. I have attended meetings of the Board of Directors since 1959, in a voting capacity except for the last two years, and never before has there been the extensive discussion on a subject that was generated by the above resolution. After this lengthy and healthy discussion, the resolution was passed with two dissenting votes. This decision by the Board was made with full recognition of the significance to our profession. The task now is to implement it.

THE FUTURE

In the balance of this article, we will discuss various questions involving the certification program. What is the program? What is its significance to The Institute? What is its significance to the individual member?

The position papers identify some of the specific considerations that have been approved by the Board of Directors on a preliminary basis. S. C. Dew, general manager The Institute of Internal Auditors, has been assigned the responsibility for developing the administrative manuals which will support the certification program. Obviously, before final implementation, many administrative considerations need to be finalized. In addition, some aspects of the position papers will need further clarification. For illustration, the position papers indicate that "A candidate shall be a member of The Institute of Internal Auditors, Inc." The legality of this position has been challenged, and it is being currently studied by legal counsel in the United States and Canada. Additionally, certain aspects may need to be varied in order to fit the particular needs of countries other than the United States and Canada. All such changes will be incorporated into the final plan of action which will be submitted to the Board of Directors in December, 1972.

In order to provide a general understanding of the certification program, I will summarize briefly the contents of the following position papers:

1. the certification program
2. qualification of candidates
3. the examination
4. special certification

These position papers present the basic concepts and a general outline of the program as planned.

The Certification Program

The position paper outlines the objectives of the program which are:

1. to support the professional recognition of members of The Institute of Internal Auditors, Inc., by:

   a. identifying the common body of knowledge and the work
      experience which form the basis for professional quali-
      fication in the field of internal auditing
   b. stimulating and encouraging the self-development of
      those engaged in the practice of internal auditing
   c. defining the qualifications for professional recogni-
      tion of internal audit practitioners
   d. developing a generally accepted examination program
      which will measure the candidate's knowledge and
      ability in respect to the qualifications established
2. to achieve universal acceptance and recognition of the
   designation of Certified Internal Auditor as having
   professional standing

The paper also establishes a Board of Examiners and outlines their
responsibility in regard to the examination program. The Board of Ex-
aminers is elected by the Board of Directors upon recommendation of the
Professional Development Committee through the international president.
Responsibility for the examination program is vested in the Board of
Examiners who shall be responsible for:

1. directing the examination program, including determination
   of scope, timing, testing site selection, fees, selection
   of examiners, scoring, and communications with members of
   The Institute
2. developing the annual examination
3. informing the Professional Development Committee of those
   candidates who have successfully completed the examination

Qualification of Candidates

This position paper sets forth various considerations involving
qualifications of candidates, as follows:

1. work experience: All candidates shall have a minimum of
   three years full-time or equivalent work experience in
   internal auditing.
2. academic requirements: A baccalaureate degree shall be required from an accredited collegel-level institution. The
   Professional Development Committee has recognized the variations in educational programs and standards throughout the
   world. Where the term "baccalaureate" or "accredited" may
   not apply, consideration will be given to educational
   achievement that would be equivalent.
      It is recognized that many of our current practition-
   ers do not possess a baccalaureate degree but are otherwise highly qualified to become Certified Internal Auditors.
   Because of this, it was decided to grant a five-year waiver
   period before enforcing the requirement of a baccalaureate
   degree. However, on a long-range basis, the baccalaureate
   degree is and should be recognized as a basic educational
   standard which should be attained by those wishing to become a Certified Internal Auditor.

3. continuing education: Several societies have included the
    requirement for additional continuing education for mainte-
    nance of a certificate. The Board of Directors has decided
    not to require a program of continuing education at this
    time. However, it is entirely conceivable that in years
    to come this requirement will be added as a means of assur-
    ing that those who have attained their certificates stay
    abreast of developments in the profession.
4. character requirements: References will be required involv-
    ing the moral character of all candidates. Additionally,
    candidates will be expected to support and adhere to The
    Institute's Code of Ethics.

The Examination

This position paper covers some of the major considerations involving the examination program, including objective, scope, conduct of the
examination, applications, and fees.

1. objective: The objective shall be to develop a generally
    accepted examination program which will measure the candi-
    date's knowledge and ability in respect to the qualifica-
    tions established by the Professional Development Committee
    and approved by the Board of Directors.
2. scope: The examination will be developed within the frame-
    work of the common body of knowledge and will be offered in
    four parts. Already many key Institute members have been
    asked to work with S. C. Dew and myself in the development
    of suggested questions for the examination.
3. conducting the examination: The examination will be given
    on the same date in various locations throughout the world.
    It will be given each year in the United States and Canada
    and in other countries in those years when sufficient ap-
    plications are received to cover the cost involved. Ad-
    ministrative rules governing the examination program are
    being developed and will be handled by the administrative
    staff of The Institute. The program will be self-support-
    ing, and a schedule of fees will accompany the program
    announcement.

Special Certification

This position paper outlines The Institute's approach to what is
typically known as the "Grandfather Clause."
The need for such a provision has been discussed at length. Several alternatives are possible. Some societies have automatically
certified all members in good standing at the time a certification program was adopted. Other societies have given no special consideration
to current members. A third course falls somewhere between these two
extremes. This is the course adopted by your Board of Directors. The
position paper identifies the basis for selection of deserving candidates and sets forth the requirements for qualification as a Certified
Internal Auditor.

TITLE

Lengthy debate over the years has ensued as to the proper title to be awarded those successfully achieving the requirements of the program. Titles such as "Registered Internal Auditor," "Fellow of The Institute of Internal Auditors," "Certified Professional Auditor," "Certified Management Auditor," and many others have been considered and discarded. Over the years we have come to the decision that the title which best illustrates the significance of the certification program is "Certified Internal Auditor." No other title seems to adequately identify the significance of the program or our profession. This title has been adopted.

ADVANTAGES FOR THE INSTITUTE

What will The Institute gain by developing and implementing a certification program? It could be argued that this is a costly process which needs to be offset by advantages to the organization. A brief listing of the major advantages are:

1. The certification program is one part of the total professional development program for the internal auditor. As such, it is an integral part of The Institute's programs and needs to be implemented. Without it, our program of professional development will not meet the needs of the internal auditor of the future.
2. It will help to attract members to The Institute. This has been demonstrated in other societies.
3. It will retain the interest of members in The Institute for a longer period of years. A major problem facing The Institute is the 20 percent membership fallout which occurs each year. Certification should demonstrably reduce this rate.
4. It will provide the stimulus for higher-level professional capability and achievement within the internal audit profession. As standards have been raised in other professions, the net result has been a continuing higher level of practice by the practitioners.
5. The Institute itself will receive greater recognition and acceptance by other societies, governmental bodies and the general public.

ADVANTAGES FOR THE MEMBER

What will this mean to you as a member of The Institute of Internal Auditors and a practicing internal auditor? Here are a few thoughts:

1. You will be a participant in a recognized professional group. You will receive the benefits accorded a professional.

2. The program will make available to you a higher level of professional training for your self-development. The existence of a certification program will require that The Institute make available an improved training program. Colleges and universities will also more readily introduce courses in internal auditing and related subjects.

3. The designation "Certified Internal Auditor" will provide a basis for recognition among your peers. Your professional and business associates will recognize the award as representing accomplishment of an established level of competency.

4. It will be useful to you in the job market. This has happened with other groups who have adopted certification programs, e.g., data processing, insurance, and financial analysts.

5. Most important, you will have the personal satisfaction of knowing you have attained a recognized and accepted degree of competency in your chosen profession.

I would like to relate a story—a true story involving my secretary, Mrs. Marjorie Wilson. Some years ago, she visited with me about her interest in preparing to sit for the Certified Professional Secretary's examination. One aspect of her preparation would include an extensive study program suggested by the National Secretaries Association.

With my encouragement she embarked upon the recommended study program. Eighteen months later, she sat for the examination, passed it, met all the other requirements, and was designated a "Certified Professional Secretary" by the National Secretaries Association (International). Mrs. Wilson always was a top-flight secretary. However, since receiving her certification, she is an outstanding secretary, greatly improved over her previous level of performance. She was recently selected as "Secretary of The Year" for the City of Syracuse, which attests to her high professional standing. Certification itself represents a small part of the reason for Mrs. Wilson's success. The real reason lies in the study program and the other professional requirements she has undertaken to qualify as a Certified Professional Secretary. The certificate was merely the "carrot" which induced Mrs. Wilson to become involved in her personal self-development.

The point of this story is that many of our members may very well respond to the same incentive. Certification could well be the goal that will encourage our members to strive for higher levels of proficiency and professionalism.

A decision has been made. A new direction has been charted. To achieve our goal will require full participation and major effort on the part of many, many members. We have come a long way and the goal is in sight. The challenge today and in the future for each Institute member is to devote the time and effort required for the realization of this goal.

FOOTNOTE

1. Editor's Note: Copies of the six position papers may be obtained from The Institute's office at a nominal fee of $1.50 per set to cover printing and handling cost.

106   FIRM AND PROFESSION: THE RECRUITER'S VIEW

William Mitchell

(Reprinted by permission from the *Coopers & Lybrand Journal* (Fall, 1972): 53-55. Published by Coopers & Lybrand.)

(Bill Mitchell is a member of the firm of Coopers & Lybrand.)

The advent of a new Lybrand recruiting brochure earlier this year was significant in that it forced us to look at ourselves, to decide what kind of people we want to attract—to represent us not merely for today but also for five, ten, and 20 years ahead. This means that we had to examine ourselves, against the background of the world in which we now function and will be functioning in through the 1990s. This may sound like a visionary exercise, but, after all, a 22-year-old college graduate joining Lybrand in 1973 will be less than 40 years old in 1990.

In this context, the following question-and-answer session with William Mitchell, Lybrand's National Director of Personnel, may shed some light not only on the type of people Lybrand seeks to recruit but also on why we seek them and where we want them to take us.

Q. Do you see the role and the image of the CPA changing—as against 20 years ago or even five years ago?

A. The status of the accounting profession has undergone a transformation in the last 15 years. During this period, business operations became increasingly sophisticated and businessmen relied more and more on accountants to supply specialized, indispensable skills. It is safe to say that the image of the bookkeeper squinting over ledgers no longer dominates the public's conception of accountants.

Q. What does an accounting firm, in terms of a career, offer to a bright college graduate?

A. First, early recognition and rapid advancement. The average age of partners has fallen steadily over the last 15 years. New technology-oriented disciplines place a premium on talent and training rather than on long experience. This trend has been reflected in industry but not, on the whole, to the same extent in accounting. Second, diversification. Accounting is acquiring new techniques and extending into more areas of business and administration. A young practitioner's choice of specializations is impressive, as are his opportunities for education, travel, social service, and professional development. Third, elbow room. The working atmosphere of a modern accounting firm is frequently characterized by an informality that is by no means the rule in large corporations and law firms. Care is taken to avoid impeding individual initiative, whether by over-centralized authority or procedural rigidity. Fourth, social relevance. Accounting is into social action. Accountants serve as consultants to public and private agencies doing vital work in housing, antipoverty resource allocation, and environmental control projects.

$Q.$ What sort of a role do you feel accounting firms will play in the years ahead?

$A.$ A big role. First, let me put the question in perspective. One aspect of progress is the emergence of a public conscience that won't tolerate a multiple standard of ethics. The activities of the Accounting Principles Board evidenced the profession's recognition that its obligations to the public could no longer be left to individual discretion. Through the APB, the accounting profession not only anticipated the public pressure for full disclosure (and everything that goes with it), but also made itself a prime factor in that pressure.

In the last decade we have had a tremendous expansion of activity in the public sector. But the emphasis has been more on growth than on efficiency. Structural requirements have been neglected, with a predictable increase in waste and top-heaviness. The problem is acute, and the need for auditing and accounting skills on a large scale has been recognized by Congress. The audit arm of Congress, through the U.S. Comptroller General, Elmer B. Staats, has been pressing to broaden the scope of auditing beyond historical concerns for custodial and financial controls. Staats believes auditors can and should develop new criteria to measure the ultimate effectiveness of public programs.

A few months ago, HEW Assistant Secretary James B. Cardwell outlined a major role for auditors in the department's forthcoming drive for greater efficiency. Cardwell announced plans for an audit network to square local auditing practices with those of the agency and a program of management consultation to HEW grantees. His most important suggestion from our point of view was that auditors could play a part in output evaluation—the systematic assessing of the impact and accomplishment of programs. This is a bold concept that will further extend the frontiers of auditing practice.

Every project in the public and private sector for environmental control, urban development and rehabilitation, and allocation of resources uses accounting and its related skills. Today, accountants, often under the aegis of their state societies, are giving their time and resources to programs for the training of ghetto businessmen and for assistance to nonprofit organizations. On the other hand, I admit that we are still not doing enough. The next step is to coordinate these activities into a broader effort in which everyone would participate.

Q.   What sort of qualifications—personal and professional—are accounting firms looking for in their recruiting?

A. Professional.   We lean towards the business school graduates or those students with concentration in business, economics, or in the mathematics-logic area.   But a respectable number of credits in the social sciences or humanities is no disadvantage, nor is a degree in any of these subjects or in law, where the applicant holds a second degree. On the contrary, business and the professions are expanding their intellectual horizons, and the specialist whose education stops with his specialty has gone out of style.

Personal.   The three basic qualities we look for are character, intelligence, and motivation.   By character we mean honesty, the courage to uphold principles, and an exacting standard of self-assessment.   Our concept of intelligence goes beyond the academic.   It involves the capacity to translate knowledge into action—and the reverse—to learn by doing.   Motivation combines ambition with drive, the expectation of reward with the willingness to earn it.   I should also mention that the ability to work with people is essential to the successful practice of accountancy.

Q.   What opportunity do you see for women and minorities in accounting firms?

A.   Opportunities have never been better.   The demand for accountants far exceeds the supply.   In a recent year, the requirements of the public accounting firms equaled 90 percent of the total number of the year's accounting graduates.   That left only ten percent to satisfy the demands of business and industry.   Add to this the breakthrough in public attitudes that has swept away most of the old barriers, and you have a situation that is highly favorable to women and blacks.

I would say we have been with the times if not ahead of them.   When the AICPA pledged the profession to integration in 1969, the major firms were already fully committed.   In 1969–70, the profession hired more black staff members than in the previous 75 years.

The practitioner of accounting and its related disciplines becomes familiar with the most vital aspects of business, finance, and administration.   Thus accountancy provides a springboard into any of these areas.   No other profession can approach us in this respect.

Q.   Do you think that firms like Lybrand have reached their size limits?   Was the boom of the 1960s the last great expansion period for the major accounting firms?

A. No to both questions. Although we quadrupled in size during the 1960s, we continued expanding even during the 1970-71 recession. You might say that over the last decade we've never ceased to grow. With the economy now moving into an upward thrust, I anticipate another period of dynamic expansion.

Q. Can you summarize the importance of accounting in today's business economy?

A. Accounting provides the economic cement that holds the modern economy together. It is an essential planning tool, vital for a systematic approach to problems of goal assessment and resource allocation.

---

107 FEDERAL INTERAGENCY AUDITOR TRAINING CENTER

Elwood A. Platt

(Reprinted by permission from *The Internal Auditor*, vol. 30, no. 1 (January/February, 1973): 74-75.)

(Elwood A. Platt is director of the Interagency Auditor Training Center.)

In the three complete fiscal years since passage of the Intergovernmental Cooperation Act, the Interagency Auditor Training Center has awarded training certificates to 595 auditors from state and local audit departments. Now that the Intergovernmental Personnel Act has become law, and with the emphasis even greater on strengthening state and local personnel resources, the projection for FY 1973 is for up to 400 enrollments from this source.

These enrollments are strongly influenced by the increasing recognition of the value of auditing as a means of improving government operations and by the resulting greater demands on state and local government auditors and their staffs. Governmental auditing at all levels has moved from strictly financial examinations to a broader and deeper inquiry into the method of program performance. This calls for competence in determining compliance with legal and administrative requirements and in highlighting problems that need attention in attaining greater economy, efficiency, and effectiveness.

The Interagency Auditor Training Center was not developed originally to provide intergovernmental training but rather was created to meet the training needs of several smaller federal agencies that did not have their own training unit.

In December, 1967, the audit chiefs of several smaller federal agencies with similar training needs met and agreed that their training needs could best be met by a cooperative pooling of resources to establish a training center.

The Civil Service Commission's Bureau of Training provided the group with technical guidance on establishing the center as an interagency activity. The commission requested that the training be made available to federal agencies other than the sponsors and officially approved the establishment of an interagency training center for auditors in May, 1968.

The center is organizationally located in the Office of the Assistant Secretary for Administration, Department of Commerce. It is managed by a director—Elwood Platt, a professional auditor. Representatives of the sponsor agencies act as a Board of Directors and meet with the center's director to discuss broad policy and major problems as the need arises.

The center is a self-supporting, reimbursable activity with tuition receipts sufficient to maintain a quality program. Approximately 27 different courses are offered—all of them dealing with some aspect of the audit function. The length of the course varies from two to five days depending on subject matter. They run the gamut from written communication for auditors to graphic and computational analysis techniques as an audit tool.

Two years ago when it became possible to include state and local auditors in the program, the director wrote to the chief auditors in all 50 states to obtain some thoughts on the idea of extending the facilities of the program to their staff members.

In addition to inquiries, suggestions, and nominations from the states, there were other developments during the year to indicate that the center should arrange its operations to be even more accommodating to state and local training needs.

The Administration's concept of New Federalism began to take shape —particularly the concept of revenue-sharing—and it became apparent that state and local auditors would play a vital role in the success of such programs. The center made a special effort to coordinate the audit capabilities of state and local government, and as a result special courses were developed for FY 1972 that dealt specifically with the interface between the federal auditor and his counterpart at the state and local level. During FY 1972, 49 states sent nominees to 20 different courses.

With the new broadened charter to admit state and local government employees to federal training programs under the Intergovernmental Personnel Act, even larger contingents of audit trainees from other governmental jurisdictions will be expected in center courses during the next several years.

The mix of federal, state, and local auditors in the classroom has provided a valuable interchange of ideas and better understanding of the nature of each other's areas of responsibility.

As the program continues and grows, it will lead to a more effective working relationship and understanding at the various levels of government. There are many avenues of approach that contribute to improving intergovernmental relations. The Interagency Auditor Training Center's program is one of the most forward-looking and innovative.

108   FOR THE YOUNG ACCOUNTANT

(Reprinted by permission from *The Journal of Accountancy*, vol. 2, no. 2 (June, 1906): 141. Copyright 1906 by the American Institute of Certified Public Accountants, Inc.)

Mr. Thomas P. Ryan, CPA, addressed the New York University School of Commerce, Accounts and Finance the other evening on "Essential Qualifications for the Public Accountant." In the course of his address he said:

My advice to the budding accountant is to keep his theories and methods clearly in mind, but to be prepared to add much to his knowledge from contact with actual conditions as they confront him. If he is fortunate enough to come in touch with men of long practical experience, let him be prepared, while insisting on knowing the reason, to defer to their superior judgment, and with each new piece of work he will add practice to theory, and thus finally be able to reconcile the one with the other. He must not be impatient to be intrusted with the personal care of business, but rather prepared to begin at the foot of the ladder and climb step by step to the top. His education and training should assist him to make the ascent safely and quickly; but if he is not prepared to subject himself to this necessary training, which only experience can give, I fear he is not possessed of the patience necessay to learn how to obey, without which he will never know how to command. There is "always room at the top," but it is safer and surer to climb the stairs than to attempt entrance from the window or through the chimney.

---

109   REFLECTIONS ON INTEGRATION IN THE
                              ACCOUNTING PROFESSION

Sybil C. Mobley

(Reprinted by permission from *The Woman CPA*, vol. 35, no. 1 (January, 1973): 5-8.)

(Sybil C. Mobley is a faculty member at Florida Agricultural and Mechanical University.)

As a black, female accountant, the writer may be assumed to occupy a position which permits a close view of some of the problems of both blacks and females existing in the accounting profession. This paper will report one black woman's reflections on these two phases of discrimination in the accounting profession.

The legislative push for employment of blacks preceded that for women. Not only did it start earlier, but the intensity of the effort has been greater. This has been entirely appropriate, for the barriers to black employment have been formal and supported and rationalized by deeply held emotional arguments. In addition, the problems involved in hiring blacks are much greater than in employing women.

Effective employment of blacks required that an entirely new recruitment program be structured and that many basic, deeply-rooted notions which had been institutionalized and accepted as axiomatic be
abandoned.   In the typical case, firms removed the barriers to the employment of white women feeling that they had removed an unfair and unfounded barrier.   However, upon removal of the barriers to the employment of blacks, firms grieved that they were being forced to lower their
standards; many who habitually take a positive attitude felt that the
act was a charitable one which would enhance the firm's public posture
providing the firm managed to prevent the black accountant from getting
in the way of performance.   Failure to conduct a sincere profession-wide
exposé of the myths held has been the major cause of difficulty in the
integration of blacks in the profession.

GOVERNMENTAL, INDUSTRIAL, AND PUBLIC ACCOUNTING

The accounting profession is frequently referred to as comprising
three groups—governmental, industrial or private, and public.   Penetration for blacks and women has been both earlier and to a greater degree in government, with industry second, and public accounting third.
This order not only reflects the sequence in which legislation has been
imposed, but the degree of objectivity permitted by the structure of
these groups.
Equal opportunity regulations were first imposed on governmental
bodies.   In addition, because their appointments follow civil service
regulations and are therefore made in a highly objective fashion, blacks
and women have fared best with governmental agencies.
In industry, action toward compliance with equal opportunity legislation as well as appointments in general have been an internal matter
reflecting company policy; these tend to be less objective than the criteria which guide governmental appointments and vary from firm to firm.
It is therefore difficult to generalize about the status of blacks and
women in industrial accounting but there is no evidence which indicates
that it has been more satisfactory than for blacks and women in nonaccounting functions of industry.
Policy for appointments in public accounting traditionally com-
pounds the subjective attitudes of the individual firms with those that
are real or imagined of their clients and those which have tended to
crystallize for public accounting firms as a group.   As this body of
accountants has identified itself as a professional group, policies common to members of the group tend to become institutionalized.   Policies
so affirmed attain the status of the profession's code of ethics and
violation is automatically considered as detrimental to the profession.
With time, the fact that cosmetic values prompted some of the group policies is forgotten and the patterns, which may be unrelated to the
service rendered by accountants, are accepted as valid indexes to quality performance.   Some invalid signs which over the years have suggested
capability in accounting have been the white male, the businessman's
attire, a northern accent, slang-free diction, and the ability to discuss the arts.   These distinguishing features created for the profession
an image, a trademark so to speak, which served to increase public reliance while reducing competition, thereby making practice more profitable.   It will not be easy to persuade the profession to abandon these
created illusions especially if the profitableness of their practices
will be diminished.

The problems involved in integrating public accounting are therefore much greater than for government or industry. Nevertheless, equal
opportunity legislation is applied with equal force to public accounting. In addition, to meet the ever increasing demand for accountants,
firms must hire accountants in larger numbers than the white, male population has supplied. Public accounting firms fully realize that equal
employment has become a matter of life and growth. Their great problem
is one of changing their employment practices without changing their
image. There seems to be little effort directed at examining the merits
of maintaining the image or its real value in current times. It should
be obvious that society is now assessing a smaller and smaller value to
cosmetic features. Yet, all efforts are directed toward fitting blacks
and women into a structure designed to exclude them.

CURRENT PROBLEMS

Although the effectiveness of firms in integrating their accounting
staffs may be challenged, there can be little doubt of their sincerity.
The results to date do not fairly reflect the extent of the efforts of
the firms. The results reflect the failure of the approaches applied to
remedy the following problems:

1. Preconceived notions about the innnate ability of blacks
    and women.

Preconceived notions of innate inferiority are casual for women but
deeply rooted for blacks. Firms justified their past failure to hire
women with explanations such as, "they will marry and leave the firm to
raise a family," "they will not agree to travel," "the physical demands
are too great," etc. Even in cases where white female accountants are
intially assumed to know less than white male accountants, competent
performance is believable. In many instances, there is no level of
competence that blacks can display which will influence the preconceived notions of innate inferiority held. Highly professional people
are not quick to admit that their anticipations dictate their perceptions, but they do. Many firms hire blacks hoping that they will eventually earn a first promotion but thoroughly convinced that they will
not be able to advance higher. They boast and feel proud of having
held this "liberal" hope.

2. The "save face" attitudes of professional groups which
    resent charges reflecting on their reputed professionalism.

It is difficult to arrive at solutions to problems without first
admitting their existence. Most firms are unwilling to take a good
look at themselves. They are only willing to make changes that can be
made while "saving the face" of the firm. Big people are often too
little to admit error. This fact precludes any honest approach to the
problems and has proved extremely discouraging to those who search for
real solutions.

3. The lengthy maturation period necessary for advancement
    within the firm.

Entry level positions are not very visible and provide little support to the sincerity of motive of hiring firms.   Charges of striving
for "numbers" result from blacks and women being concentrated at the
entry level.   However, there can be no "instant" managers or partners.
The nature of the professional service offered requires that advancement
be based on meaningful supervised experience.   Even if no other problems
exist, firms are doomed to be criticized during the lengthy period required for advancement of their newly-hired blacks and females.

4.   The limited supply of blacks and women available for em-
     ployment as accountants.

Pursuit of a career for most people is correlated with known or
anticipated employment opportunities.   Because of the very limited opportunities for blacks and women in accounting in the past, few selected
accounting as their careers.   Evidence of existing opportunities must
extend beyond high school career-day presentations and encouragement
from guidance counselors but must include visible examples of successful
blacks and women in accounting.   As already established, success in accounting takes time; it also takes people.   Hence, the profession is
confronted with the problem that success is needed to get the people,
while people are needed to accomplish the success.

5.   The informal organization of the firm which at the profes-
     sional level encompasses a social dimension that perpetu-
     ates the present structure.

At the professional level, there is a social phase of the informal
organization which is an important vehicle for advancement.   However,
legislation for equal employment opportunity has not extended to social
aspects.   As long as the informal organization is contained within the
firm, all employees may hold hopes of eventual access.   However, when a
phase extends to the social life outside of the firm, there is little
reason for some to hope.   White women are a part of the social order,
blacks are not.   White women are able to attack the problem from the inside, blacks are not.

LIMITED SUCCESS

Currently blacks and women are greatly encouraged to pursue accounting careers.   A number of public accounting firms and some industrial firms have launched outreach programs which involve them in active
recruitment.   They not only visit the placement offices of universities
where they see graduating seniors who have selected accounting as a
major, but they visit lower level university classes and high schools
where they contact and influence students who have not yet made a selection.   These firms have also provided the significant financial support
necessary for many talented black youths to pursue accounting majors.
There is a very obvious commitment to integrate the accounting profession "in fact as well as ideal."
      The limited success suggests the enormity of the problem.   Profes-
sional blacks and women currently employed by the Big Eight CPA firms
are:

TABLE 24

PROFESSIONAL BLACKS
AND WOMEN EMPLOYED

	Total Employed	Management Group	Partners
Blacks	697	16	1
Women	1,579	110	5

Whereas the absolute number of women employed is significantly higher, it must be remembered that women are not a minority group. If the total female population is considered, the number, in a relative sense, is lower for women than for blacks. It is also significant that the progress made by women has been over a longer period than for blacks. So in terms of relative numbers, employed within a given period of time, black employment has exceeded that of women. It is not known whether this is due to the greater difficulty in interesting women in accounting or the greater difficulty in interesting accounting firms in women. However, it has been noted that females currently account for only eight percent of accounting graduates.

Comments from firms indicate that there is a higher turnover of women than of other accountants. Turnover during the first two years of employment is similar for all groups. However, turnover is significantly greater for women than for white, male accountants after three or four years. No meaningful comparison can be made of the turnover of women and blacks after three or four years because of the smallness of the number of blacks employed four years ago.

Comments from women employed in accounting firms indicate a promising level of satisfaction, promising because they feel that the problems that do exist seem to be diminishing. However, many blacks feel that this recent effort to employ women will dampen the firms' efforts to employ blacks. They feel that the firms have found "a more palatable way of satisfying equal opportunity compliance requirements." Blacks are much more skeptical about their futures with the firms than are women.

FUTURE HOPE

As a black woman accountant who is frequently asked to compare her two "handicaps" and who has more than a normal share of other personal limitations, it became necessary that the writer identify her primary struggle. This was not a difficult task as society has clearly displayed clues as to which of the two problems is more serious—her blackness. Many responsible accounting positions which have been held for years by white women are only recently being opened to blacks. The writer knows of no important employment situation in America where black males are denied but black women are admitted because white women have won admittance. Her life provides many unpleasant memories of "white only" barriers, while the "male only" restrictions are difficult to recall.

Although the past structures a frame of reference for everybody, it is the current problems to which attention must be devoted. The fact is that tacit, although in many instances unconscious, discrimination in accounting does currently exist for both women and blacks. The effect is a waste that the profession cannot afford. The problems of integrating blacks and women are not unique to accounting. What is unique to accounting is its ability to examine objectively, to analyze, and to arrive at rational solutions. The accounting profession is in a unique position to provide a much needed model for society to follow. It is not only the writer's hope that the profession will achieve this distinction, she bets on it!

9
The Practicing Accountant

Chapter 9 deals with three topics of interest to accountants and auditors: professional issues in public accounting, computers, and clear writing. Independence is essential to the proper performance of public accountants. Surendra Agrawal (page 460) considers auditors' independence and makes recommendations on how to maintain it. Legal liabilities of independent auditors have become an increasingly serious problem. Johnnie L. Clark (page 468) examines the current status of the auditor's legal liability. His discussion centers on *Rusch Factors* and the *1136 Tenants' Corporation* cases. He suggests that court decisions in these cases have established new boundaries of auditors' legal liabilities to which the profession can and should respond. The *Business Week* report (page 474) is a clear example of what audits can cost auditors even though they may have complied with all professional standards. Not all auditors are out of favor. *The Wall Street Journal* item (page 475) indicates that 80 percent of corporate financial executives are happy with their auditors.

The computer has had enormous impact on the world, and it promises to have even greater impact in the future. With the increasing sophistication of computers and their uses, the suggestion is frequently made that the computer will replace accountants. Felix Kaufman (page 476) looks at the specific ways in which the computer influences the CPA's work. He finds that the computer is a powerful tool to aid the CPA in both his audit work and his write-up work. While Kaufman believes that CPAs have been slow to respond to this change in their environment, he thinks that they can keep abreast. He challenges them to do so.

No skill is more important to the accountant than clear writing. The final two articles encourage the preparation of readable, clear, effectively written communications. Lawrence B. Sawyer (page 485) discusses numerous ways in which audit reports can be written so that people will want to read them. William F. Laurie (page 493) found the reading level of General Accounting Office communications at too high a level to be read with ease and with maximum comprehension. He includes a test to keep writing at a proper level of difficulty including length of words and numbers of words.

459

---

110   AUDITOR'S INDEPENDENCE:
                          A BEHAVIORAL PERSPECTIVE

Surendra P. Agrawal

(Reprinted by permission from *The Florida Certified Public Accountant*, vol. 12, no. 2 (July, 1972): 42-48.)

(Surendra P. Agrawal is a graduate teaching assistant in the Department of Accounting of the University of Florida.)

One of the generally accepted auditing standards states that in all
matters relating to the assignment, an independence in mental attitude
is to be maintained by the auditor. As a code of its ethics, the profession has gradually compiled precepts and conditions to guard against
the *presumption* of loss of independence. Presumption is stressed because insofar as intrinsic independence is synonymous with mental integrity, its possession is a matter of personal quality rather than of
rules that formulate certain objective tests. (1) The purpose of this
article is to study and analyze the concept of independence from a behavioral perspective. An attempt is made to identify the principles of
behavioral sciences relevant to this problem. No empirical verification, however, has been made. Examples cited are for illustrative purposes only, and are not based on any empirical study.

PROFESSIONAL CONCEPT OF INDEPENDENCE

From a broad ethical point of view, a man can be held to be independent only when his higher or rational self, or his ideal personality,
determines his actions. Independence may be used in two senses. In the
ordinary sense it is used as a synonym for integrity, and in this sense
all professionals have to maintain independence. This amounts to saying
that a professional should not subordinate his judgment to that of the
client in matters within his professional competence. It is employed in
another—technical—sense in conjunction with the expression of opinions
on financial statements, and in this sense independence may be considered to be a distinguishing attribute of certified public accountants.
Independence of the auditor has been defined as an honest disinter-
estedness in the formulation and expression of his opinion, which means
unbiased judgment and objective consideration of facts as the determinants of that opinion. (2) The CPA should not only refuse to subordinate
his judgment to that of others, but he should be independent of any
self-interest which might warp his judgment even subconsciously in reporting whether or not the financial position and net income are fairly
presented. Independence in this context means objectivity or lack of
bias in forming delicate judgments. (3)

In accounting literature, considerable attention has been given to certain aspects of independence. An auditor should not only be independent in fact, but should also appear to third parties to be independent. There is considerable controversy about the question of whether an accountant can maintain his independence in his attest function while he also renders other services to his client.

ACQUISITION OF THE ATTITUDE OF INDEPENDENCE

From the viewpoint of behavioral sciences, pure independent behavior occurs whenever the individual perceives relevant normative expectations, but gives zero weight to them in formulating his decisions. This does not mean that he does not "weigh" the expectations in the sense of evaluating their importance and appropriateness, but rather that the outcome of this process of evaluation leads him to reject them as guides to his behavior. The independent person is one capable of *resisting* social pressures, rather than one who is unaware of them or who merely ignores them. He "sticks to his guns" so to speak. (4)
Independence has two criteria:

1. seeking nurturence from others relatively infrequently
2. showing initiative and achievement striving

Thus, independence is seen as not only self-reliance, but also self-assertion. This conceptualization makes of independence something much more than lack of dependence. (5)
The attitude of independence is acquired by an accountant as a norm of his professional group. This acquisition may be made by the processes of identification and internalization. Identification occurs when a person adopts behavior derived from the group because this behavior is associated with a satisfying role relationship with the group that forms a part of the person's self-image. Internalization occurs when an individual accepts influence of the group because the induced behavior is congruent with his value system, the most obvious examples being those that involve the evaluation and acceptance of induced behavior on rational grounds. (6) An attitude acquired in this way is likely to remain so long as the relation with the group remains a satisfying one, and so long as the values relevant to its adoption are maintained.
Early independence training also has great significance in the acquisition of such an attitude. (7)

CAUSES OF A CHANGE IN THE ATTITUDE OF INDEPENDENCE

A change in the auditor's attitude of independence with respect to a particular case will normally involve a choice situation. Two alternative courses of action may be open to an auditor: one that is determined by his rational self or ideal personality, and the other that is directed by his self-interest or by subordination to another person's judgment. If he chooses the first course of action, he may be consid-

ered to act independently. In the case of the latter choice, he may be
considered to have lost his independence.

Causes of attitude change which appear to be relevant in the context of the auditor's independence are discussed below:

Conflict of Motives

The choice situation arising between an independent action and an
action directed toward self-interest may be analyzed in terms of a conflict of motives or goals. Such a conflict arises when two or more ends
are presented as desirable, either simultaneously or in immediately succeeding states of consciousness. The conflict is terminated by decision
or choice. Making of the choice, however, is not easy. Since all the
ends are desirable, the person is placed on the horns of a dilemma and
finds it difficult to arrive at a decision.

An example of such a choice situation would be where the accountant thinks that the financial statements do not constitute fair presentation, but maintenance of pleasant and rewarding relations with the
client would require expression of an unqualified opinion. The question
whether the accountant did act independently or not in choosing a particular course of action can be answered only with reference to his motives and dispositions (which may be conscious or subconscious). If his
choice is based on self-interest and not on rationality, he may be considered as having lost his independence. In the case of strong subconscious dispositions, however, he may not even be aware of making such
a choice.

Persuasive Communication

One person may cause a change in the attitude of another person by
means of persuasive communication. The following factors play an important role in the persuading ability of a communication:

Creditibility of the communicator. The bases for credibility are:
communicator's expertness and trustworthiness.

Content of communication. The communication may contain rational
appeals and emotional appeals. One type of emotional appeal is the
fear-appeal, which threatens the individual with unfortunate consequences unless he follows the advice of the communicator. High pressure
tactics of the fear-appeal are, however, offensive and arouse resistance.

Organization of the communication. The communication may be one-
sided or two-sided, may draw conclusions or may not do so, may present
its elements in various orders, and different communications may be presented in different orders.

Another relevant factor is the persuasibility of the individual. Some persons are more susceptible to persuasive communication than others. A person may be highly persuasible on certain topics but not at all persuasible on others. His susceptibility might also vary with different forms of appeal, different communicators, different media or other aspects of the communication situation. (8)

Three factors—attention, comprehension, and anticipation—facilitate persuasibility, while one factor—evaluation—interferes with it. This interference factor refers to the set of abilities that make for careful scrutiny of the truth and cogency of arguments and appeals and of the logic with which the main conclusions are drawn. To be effective, the ability to evaluate has to be accompanied by a high degree of motivation to evaluate. (9)

It is not easy to determine under what circumstances an accountant may be suspected of losing his independence by persuasion. Apparently, he relies on a well-organized communication containing rational appeal and presented to him by a trustworthy person, he may be considered to have acted independently. But the following, for example, may point to a contrary conclusion:

1. if the auditor is persuaded by the fear-arousing or other emotional appeal of a communication
2. if he relies on a communication from a person of high status, knowing that it is not sufficient competent evidential matter

Role Conflict

When a person occupies several postions at any one time, his behavior is subject to a number of sets of expectations, some of which may be in conflict or competition. The severity of role conflict varies with two factors:

1. the relative incompatibility of the expectations involved
2. the rigor with which expectations are defined in a given situation. (10)

In the case of an accountant, role conflict may arise when, for example, he occupies the position of the independent auditor as well as management advisor. In his position as auditor he is expected to act independently, while in his position as management advisor he is expected to work for the welfare of the client. If in a specific situation he feels obliged to give some advice for the welfare of the client to which he would take exception in his role as auditor, a severe strain will result. If he does give such advice, and then knowingly omits to take exception to it as auditor, he may be suspected of losing his independence in the latter role.

RESISTANCE TO CHANGE IN THE ATTITUDE OF INDEPENDENCE

Several forces resist the process of change in attitudes. The important forces in the present context seem to be the following:

Consistency

The concept of consistency (which includes the concepts of balance, congruity and dissonance-avoidance) underscores and presumes human rationality. After the accountant has acquired a general attitude of independence, any action contrary to such an attitude would give rise to inconsistency. Inconsistency is a noxious state setting up pressures to eliminate it or reduce it.

Belief dilemmas faced in a choice situation, may be resolved in several ways:

Denial. A direct attack upon one or both of the cognitive elements or the relation between them. The value felt toward the object is denied, or the sign of the relation between the elements is explained away, or the opposite is asserted. (For example, the accountant may dismiss the possibility of the actual carrying out of the threatened withdrawal of work by the client, if he expresses a qualified opinion.)

Bolstering. One of the two objectives is additionally supported by relating it to other cognitive objects in a balanced way. (For example, the accountant may find that other accountants express qualified opinion in similar situations.)

Differentiation. An element may be split into two parts with a strong disassociative relation between the parts. (For example, the accountant may think that though a particular client might withdraw his work from him because of a qualified opinion, the increase in his reputation as a strong and independent auditor will bring in other clientele.)

Transcedence. Elements are built up and combined into larger units organized on a superordinate level. (For example, the accountant may consider maintenance of professional standards to be more important than financial gain to him.) (11)

Conformity with Group Norms

It has been indicated earlier that the attitude of independence is acquired by identification with the professional group and internalizing its norms. Conformity with such norms provides resistance to a change in the attitude of independence. The effectiveness of such resistance would depend upon the following factors:

1.   rewards and costs of conformity in terms of behavior or attitudes of other members

2.   power structure of the group
3.   intrinsic costs and rewards
4.   surveillance and sanctions by the group

Resolution of Role Strain

A number of features exist in a social system and individual processes that serve to reduce strain resulting from conflicting role expectations.   The following seem to be relevant in the context of the attitude of independence:

Hierarchy of obligations.   The person faced with the role conflict,
or all the participants in a system, may recognize that certain obligations take precedence over others.   For example, the accountant's function as independent auditor may take precedence over his functions as
management advisor, either in his own mind or in tacit agreement between
him and the client.

Merging of roles.   Certain tendencies, operating over time, result
in gradual modification of role structure in the direction of reducing
conflicting expectations.   One such tendency is the development and recognition of a third role which is specifically the pattern viewed as
consistent when both roles might be applicable.   For example, the client
may come to regard the accountant as an expert whose actions are then
considered as a pattern consistent with all his roles.

Modification of expectations.   When many incumbents of the same
role position find themselves subject to similar role strains, mutual
support is present for finding a common means of resolution.   This may
lead to a gradual modification of the conflicting role expectations.   A
guideline by the AICPA is an example of such common action.

Reward-Cost Outcome

A person cannot possibly meet all the expectations involved in the
relations he has with all his role partners because of competition, conflict and related problems.   Hence the optimum allocation of his role
performance is a central problem.   He will try to obtain the best
reward-cost-outcome from his performance.   The extent to which he will
meet the expectations of his role partner will be the resultant of the
interaction of the following three factors:

1.   his desire to carry out the activity because of such fac-
     tors as the intrinsic gratification he receives from it,
     his commitment to it in terms of his internalized values,
     etc.

2.   his perception of how much the role partner will reward
     or punish him for his role performance.
3.   the esteem or disesteem with which others who are signif-
     icant to him will respond to both his performance and the
     attempt of his partner to make him perform adequately. (12)

SUMMARY AND CONCLUSIONS

Independence of mental attitude is a necessary condition for the
accountant to carry out an audit. It requires that he should be guided
in his work by his own rational self or ideal personality (not by the
normative expectations of his client), that he should be self-reliant
and self-assertive. The attitude of independence is acquired by training, by identification with the professional group and by internalizing
its norms.

In many situations an accountant has to make a choice between alternative courses of action. The choice may be very difficult where the
situation has arisen because of a conflict of his own motives, where he
receives persuasive communication from the client to act in a particular
way which may be different from his own best judgment or where he occupies two distinct roles and there is conflict between the expectations
from him in those roles.

Generally, an individual tends to be consistent and conforms with
his group norms. He tries to resolve his role strains and behaves in
the way that will maximize his reward-cost outcome.

In view of the above observations, it seems that the following conditions would be conducive to maintenance of the attitude of independence by accountants in their role as independent auditors:

1.   During the education and training of accountants, emphasis
     should be placed on the development of the attitude of in-
     dependence, with the objective that it becomes part of
     their value system.
2.   The emphasis on independence should be based on rational
     conviction and supported by as many cognitive elements
     as possible.
3.   Accounting societies and institutes should be cohesive
     groups and lay emphasis on the attitude of independence
     as the norm of the group. They should give adequate sup-
     port for conformance with this norm, and watch out for
     nonconformance.
4.   Accountants and their clients should consider the role of
     the former as independent auditors to be more important
     than any other role they might occupy.

FOOTNOTES

1.   American Institute of Accountants, *Generally Accepted Audit-
     ing Standards: Their Significance and Scope*, 1954, p. 13.

2. Ibid, p. 21.
3. John L. Carey, *Professional Ethics of Certified Public Accountants*, AICPA, 1956, p. 21.
4. R. H. Willis, "The Basic Response Modes of Conformity, Independence, and Anticonformity," in *Current Perspectives in Social Psychology*, E. H. Hollander and R. G. Hunt, eds. (New York: Oxford University Press, 1967), p. 434.
5. E. Zigler and I. L. Child, "Socialization," in *Handbook of Social Psychology*, vol. 3, G. Lindzey and E. Aronson, eds. (Reading, Mass.: Addison-Wesley, 1969), pp. 542-543.
6. H. C. Kelman, "Processes of Opinion Change," *Public Opinion Quarterly* (1961) 25, pp. 57-78.
7. D. Marlowe and K. J. Gergen, "Personality and Social Interaction," in *Handbook of Social Psychology*, p. 612.
8. I. L. Janis and G. I. Hovland, eds., "An Overview of Persuasibility Research," in *Personality and Persuasibility* (New Haven, Conn.: Yale University Press, 1959).
9. I. L. Janis and C. I. Hovland, "Postscript: Theoretical Categories for Analyzing Individual Differences," in *Personality and Persuasibility*.
10. J. W. Getzels and E. G. Guba, "Role, Role Conflict, and Effectiveness; An Empirical Study," *American Sociological Review* (1954) 19, pp. 164-175.
11. R. P. Abelson, "Modes of Resolution of Belief Dilemmas," *Journal of Conflict Resolution* (1959) 3, pp. 343-352.
12. W. J. Goode, "A Theory of Role Strain," *American Sociological Review* (1960) 25, pp. 483-496.

QUESTIONS

1. Why must any professional remain independent?
2. "He who pays the piper, calls the tune." In view of this quotation, can an auditor be independent under today's conditions? Why or why not?
3. How might the "conflict of motives" for auditors be reduced?

111   CHANGING CONCEPTS OF THE ACCOUNTANT'S
              LEGAL LIABILITY—A FOCUS ON FORESEEABILITY

Johnnie L. Clark

(Reprinted by permission from *The Georgia CPA*, vol. 14, no. 4
(1972-1973): 15-19.)

(Johnnie L. Clark is a faculty member at Atlanta University.)

Among the unresolved inssues in accounting are those related to the
ambit of legal liability in all areas in which the accountant renders
services to clients.

The disputes resulting from the disparity between professional
standards, together with their implementation, and societal expectations
are often brought before the courts for reconcilement. The legal in-
strumentality, therefore, becomes a means of social control where there
is significant disharmony between professional standards and the requirements of the larger community. This control is manifested in the
establishing, shaping, and modifying of accounting practice standards as
well as in the exacting of extremely harsh penalties at times.

In a dynamic environment, the ethical and performance standards
governing behavior and practice for members of a profession must evolve
to meet the needs and increasing expectations of society. Positive response to these needs and expectations through the progression of generally accepted accounting principles, generally accepted auditing standards, and rules of conduct is fundamental to the future viability of the
accounting profession. The ethical and performance standards of the accounting profession do not exist in a vacuum, but within a socioeconomic, legal framework to which they must be responsive.

Today's challenges confront the profession against the backdrop of
an increased awareness and activism by a significant segment of society,
indicative of changes in individual and group behavior. The manifestations of these changes are the increased awareness of the consumer, the
environmentalists' emphasis on quality of life, the ongoing activity for
minority rights and equal opportunity, the upsurge of concern for corporate social responsibility, the concern for management responsibility
for full disclosure in financial reports, and others as well.

The plethora of lawsuits brought against independent public accountants, particularly in their role as auditors—the concern here being primarily on the attest function, has resulted in a situational
dilemma which must be satisfactorily resolved in the interest of the
profession and in the interest of the beneficiaries of the accountant's
services.

Legal claims can no longer be viewed simply as undue publicity but
must be regarded as an integral part of the changing societal fabric of
the culture, reflecting a greater awareness on the part of individuals
and groups of the litigious possibilities in dealings with renderers of
professional services. In this sense, accountants are but one among
the many professional groups subject to such claims and which must be
meaningfully attuned to societal needs.

Interaction between standards of the accounting profession and
interpretations of those standards by the legal system is seen in the
settlement of disputes, as well as the issues raised by them, in courts

of law. Settlements have reflected acceptance, rejection, redefinition, and modification of accounting standards. The accountant, therefore, finds himself in search of a safe harbor as he contemplates the hazards of present and future litigation.

The public accountant customarily exercises his professional skill in a given undertaking as a result of a contract which may be formal and reduced to writing or informal and oral. The contract states what the accountant has agreed to do. The law, however, exacts from him a standard of reasonable care in his performance in accordance with professional standards. Liability may result from breach of contract or from breach of duty to exercise due care flowing out of the contractual relations. (1)

The certified public accountant in plying his craft does so under the assumption that his adherence to the ethical and performance standards of the profession will amply provide an adequate legal defense. For today's accountant, this may be an inadequate posture from which to cope with the legal problems likely to be encountered.

One quest suggests a guide to action inherent in a foreseeability formulation. That is, a reasonably considered outcome from one's act or one's failure to act would be decisive. Foreseeability, then, becomes a point of departure in the determination of the probable boundaries of the accountant's legal liability in a given situation. Foreseeability is defined as "the ability to see or know in advance, hence, the reasonable anticipation that harm or injury is a likely result of acts or omissions." (2) Basic to this criterion is an anticipatory stance regarding the environment, clients, and indirect users of financial statements. Further, this criterion presupposes a possible amplification and extension of the concept of reasonable care.

Two cases which have received considerable attention in the literature and which have implications for a foreseeability criterion are now explored. These cases are *Rusch Factors* (3) and *1136 Tenants' Corporation*. (4)

Rusch Factors, a New York commercial banking and factoring company, sought to recover damages in a civil action from Leonard M. Levin, a Rhode Island certified public accountant. The allegations of Rusch were:

1. misrepresentation by defendant
2. negligence in the preparation of financial statements

Capsuling the facts of the case, a Rhode Island corporation, during the latter part of 1963, and the early part of 1964, sought financing from Rusch Factors. Rusch, in response to this attempt, asked for certified financial statements to determine the financial status of the company. The statements were provided. They depicted a solvent company. In actuality, the company was insolvent. Rusch had loaned the company more than $337,000, relying on the statements prepared by the defendant. The corporation later went into receivership and Rusch recovered only a portion of the advanced loan funds.

Ultramares established the common law precedent which protected accountants from successful third party claims for mere negligence for more than three decades.

(It) held that an accountant could be liable for negligent misrepresentation only to the person who hired him or to

*a person whom the accountant, at the time he prepared his state-
ment, knew would rely upon it. The only third party to whom
the accountant owed a duty of care was one "in effect, if not
in name, a party to the contract" under which the accountant's
services were performed. The holding was carefully limited to
cases involving only negligence. (5)*

The court's stand in Rusch Factors *represents a significant departure from* Ultramares. *Repeating the principle that
lack of privity of contract provided no defense for fraud, the
court mentioned the doubt expressed by legal authorities as to
the wisdom of the* Ultramares *decision. Expressing its own
doubt, the court stated:*

*. . . Why should an innocent reliant party be forced to
carry the weighty burden of an accountant's professional malpractice? Isn't the risk of loss more easily distributed and
fairly spread by imposing it on the accounting profession,
which can pass the cost of insuring against the risk onto its
customers, who can in turn pass the cost onto the entire consuming public? Finally, wouldn't a rule of foreseeability ele-
vate the cautionary techniques of the accounting profession?
For these reasons it appears to this Court that the decision
in* Ultramares *constitutes an unwarranted inroad upon the principle that "the risk reasonably to be perceived defines the
duty to be obeyed." (6)*

Another view regarding *Rusch Factors* is that:

. . . Rusch's shortcoming was its failure to reject Ultramares *completely. Had* Rusch *gone all the way and permitted
foreseeable as well as actually foreseen plaintiffs a cause of
action, perhaps the court would have filled the gaps left in
its arguments for doing so. (7)*

With respect to the negligence theory, the court held that "an accountant should be liable in negligence for careless financial misrepresentations relied upon by actually foreseen and limited classes of
persons." (8)

The fact that gaps have been left in foreseeability interpretations
as presently set forth by the courts provides an opportunity and a challenge to the accounting profession to articulate guides for action beyond the boundaries previously established.

In *1136 Tenants' Corporation*, action was brought against Max Rothenberg & Company, for alleged

1. breach of retainer to audit Tenants' accounts
2. negligence in the performance of accounting services to
    plaintiff

The plaintiff (forty-four tenant-shareholders) was the owner of a single
cooperative apartment building; the defendant was a firm of certified
public accountants.

The plaintiff averred that the defendant had been engaged to do all
essential accounting and auditing services for it, but had failed to
test and audit the books, records, invoices, check vouchers, and bank

statements. Because of this conduct, defendant failed to find the peculations of the plaintiff's funds by its managing agent. The managing agent was Riker & Company, Incorporated, a realty management concern headed by I. Jerome Riker. The company served as managing agent for Tenants' as well as several other cooperatives.

The defendant contended that it had been engaged to perform write-up work; it had not been engaged to perform an audit. Under such circumstances, there was no liability for an accountant's failure to perform auditing procedures; defendant had not negligently performed the write-up function. Each party, of course, advanced evidence in support of its view of the original oral agreement as to what defendant had been engaged to do.

The decision held for the plaintiff at the trial level and on appeals. The key issues raised in this case were whether Max Rothenberg was retained by 1136 Tenants' Corporation to audit its accounts and whether defendant adhered to generally accepted professional standards in performing its task.

As to an audit, the literature in the field offers guidance to the accountant for engagement as well as retainer contracts.

> . . . *The accountant must fully understand the needs of the client. Merely agreeing to "make an audit" is certain to result in misunderstanding, confusion, and disagreement during the conduct of the engagement. The accountant should know exactly what it is that the client wants and expects, although frequently the accountant may find that what the client actually needs is something entirely different.* (9)

If one views the case from the alternate assumption of a write-up rather than an audit, the following statements provide additional insight:

> . . . *Aside from the resolution of the question as to the nature of the oral retainer, the particular issue presented by this case, which was of such fundamental importance to the accounting profession as to result in the intervention of both the New York State Society of CPAs and the American Institute of CPAs as* amici curiae, *was this: What are the professional obligations of CPAs in preparing unaudited financial statements, particularly write-ups, and what are the fair and reasonable expectations of users of such statements as to work performed by CPAs with respect thereto?* (10)

Answers to these queries are still being sought. Yet, if the results of *1136 Tenants' Corporation* serve as a benchmark, one can foresee the negation of the unaudited financial statements as meaningful tools to statement users.

The following conclusory statements present some general observations and implications drawn from the two cases discussed here:

1. The privity doctrine still appears to be the fundamental guideline as to the negligence of accountants. Case outcomes, however, point to significant inroads in the privity doctrine and many predict its demise.

2. Complex issues may be decided by judges and juries with little or no expertise in such matters. This appears to be the case in *1136 Tenants' Corporation* as to the lay understanding of audited versus unaudited financial statements. Unaudited statements, acceptable to the profession, were indefensible as viewed by the court.

3. The small size of client and/or a meager fee is no deterrent to litigation. What is more, legal defense must be provided against suits with or without merit, requiring considerable expenditure of time, effort, and funds.

4. Some test to determine the adequacy and understandability of disclosures from the viewpoint of the laity might be meaningfully employed.

5. Some practical inquiry as to the character of the prospective client and/or its management might be useful in making a choice to accept or reject an engagement.

6. The acceptance of engagements to prepare unaudited statements is hazardous. The lay understanding of audited statements versus unaudited statements is at best tenuous. Where such engagements are accepted, standard audit procedures may be applicable to unaudited statements and write-up engagements as they are to audited statements.

The conclusory statements related to the two cases explored as well as others suggest to the writer that a foreseeability criterion may be an appropriate guide to action. That is, the accountant's choices would give consideration to the anticipated results of his acts and those of others. Litigious boundaries would be interpreted not only within the context of enunciated professional standards but with a degree of empathy for the requirements of the client and other users of the financials. For example, in *1136 Tenants' Corporation*, had the need for assurance the cooperative owner might require in statements prepared for his use been anticipated, one might have concluded that the client needed an audit. Hence, through foresight the more appropriate client need would have been identified and communicated. Further, it suggests that presently articulated professional standards would not necessarily provide a ceiling as to what ought or ought not be done as to a particular kind of engagement. Though adherence to such standards may provide at least a first line defense in malpractice suits.

At this juncture, inroads on the privity doctrine via court cases suggest a limited rule of foreseeability in dealings with those beyond privity. Dicta, however, point to a broadening of liability in fraud, to a broad rule of foreseeability, to the fall or modification of the privity doctrine, and to an accountant's liability to third parties for mere negligence.

The public tends more and more to expect the CPA to provide protection against managements and boards of directors that fail to discharge properly their stewardships. Demand in the public and private sectors for a rapid narrowing of the diversity in accounting principles and practices for investor protection have resulted in movements which may facilitate the resolution of some of the legal problems facing the profession. To effectively meet the demands of the public and private sectors, the accountant must be able to do so without unreasonable

litigious assaults.   One aid may be the appropriate use of a foreseeability criterion in the decision process.

FOOTNOTES

1. Carl S. Hawkins, "Professional Negligence Liability of
    Public Accountants," in *Professional Negligence*, Thomas
    G. Roady, Jr., and William R. Andersen, eds. (Nashville:
    Vanderbilt University Press, 1960), p. 256.
2. Henry Campbell Black, *Black's Law Dictionary*, rev. 4th
    ed. (St. Paul: West Publishing Company, 1968), p. 777.
3. *Rusch Factors, Inc.* v. *Levin*, 284 F. Supp. 85 (D.R.I.
    1968).
4. *1136 Tenants' Corporation* v. *Rothenberg & Co.*, 27 App.
    Div. 2d 830, 277 N.Y.S. 2d 996 (1st Dept. 1967); aff'd
    21 N.Y. 2d 995, 238 N.E. 2d 322, 290 N.Y.S. 2d 919
    (1968); 36 A.D. 2d 804, 319 N.Y.S. 2d 1007 (1st Dept.
    1971).
5. "Accountants' Liabilities for False and Misleading Finan-
    cial Statements," *Columbia Law Review*, vol. 67 (1967),
    1438-1439.
6. *Rusch Factors, Inc.* v. *Levin*, 284 F. Supp. 85 (D.R.I.
    1968).
7. Leonard Mentzer, "Accountant's Common Law Liability to
    Third Persons for Misrepresentations—*Rusch Factors, Inc.*
    v. *Levin* (D.R.I. 1968)," *California Law Review*, vol. 57
    (1969), p. 282.
8. *Rusch Factors, Inc.* v. *Levin*, 284 F. Supp. 85 (D.R.I.
    1968).
9. Howard F. Stettler, *Systems Based Independent Audits*
    (Englewood Cliffs: Prentice-Hall, 1967), p. 573.
10. Emanuel Saxe, "Unaudited Financial Statements: Rules,
    Risks and Recommendations," *The CPA Journal*, vol. 42
    (June, 1972), p. 458.

QUESTIONS

1. How does the auditor's liability arise?
2. How does the certified public accountant protect himself
    against legal liability?
3. What does foreseeability mean to the auditor's liability?

112   WHAT AN AUDIT CAN COST THE AUDITOR

(Reprinted by permission from *Business Week* (March 31, 1973): 29.)

How much liability does a certified public accounting firm have for its audit of a company's physical inventory? That question surfaced again last week when Los Angeles-based Whittaker Corporation revealed it had received $875,000 from its outside auditors, Arthur Andersen & Company, one of the largest of the U.S.'s big Eight CPA firms. Andersen's payment, made without an admission of liability, represents reimbursement for expenses Whittaker incurred when it uncovered a $6.3 million inventory discrepancy at its subsidiary, Crown Aluminum Industries, Incorporated.

Public disclosure of such payments stemming from accounting and auditing disputes is unusual, but in today's "sue the auditors" atmosphere, such settlements are anything but rare. "There must be 500 claims outstanding against all accountants in the industry," says Harvey Kapnick, Arthur Andersen's feisty chairman. "We once were in a suit over an audit which we hadn't as yet certified."

Crown Aluminum, which had annual sales of about $30 million, smelts scrap aluminum and resells the end product. Last March Whittaker announced an agreement to sell the subsidiary to Chamberlain Manufacturing Corporation, an Elmhurst (Ill.) ordnance and metal fabricating company, pending a physical audit of Crown's inventory. Six months earlier, Andersen had completed such an inventory audit, which has been mandatory for more than 40 years.

NONEXISTENT ROLLS

When Whittaker and Chamberlain accountants ran their own audit, however, they discovered the $6.3 million discrepancy between the price inventory and what appeared on the books, says Harry S. Derbyshire, Whittaker's financial vice-president. And the sale agreement with Chamberlain was rescinded.

What apparently happened, says Derbyshire, was that before the Andersen audit, several Crown employees had made inventory tags for nonexistent rolls of aluminum. These tags were added to the tags that Andersen counted in its audit, but the discrepancy was not discovered until after the sale agreement.

While Whittaker's inside auditors and an investigative firm went over the inventories of all of the company's subsidiaries, Derbyshire and Whittaker's president, Joseph F. Alibrandi, called on Andersen officials at the firm's Chicago headquarters. Kapnick and other high-ranking Andersen executives would not admit to "anything less than a professional" auditing job. Nevertheless, they agreed to make the payment and to continue some work with inventory reporting systems at no additional cost to Whittaker.

Derbyshire says he agrees with the argument that an outside auditor cannot always guarantee an inventory, but he believes that a CPA firm "also has some liability."

REELECTION

At Whittaker's annual meeting last week, the selection of the company's independent accountant was put to a stockholder vote for the first time. Andersen was again selected to make the company's yearly audit.

It was not the first time Andersen has indicated that it feels it owes financial responsibilities to clients. In the fall of 1971, after an audit of Louisiana & Southern Life Insurance Company and after Andersen resigned the account, a question arose as to the company's reserve position.

Kapnick says that because the insurance company's capital had been impaired, his firm agreed to purchase a $3.5 million convertible debenture to infuse enough cash into the company to give it a positive capital position.

"Who had responsibility for those problems could not be clearly identified," Kapnick contends. "But the future of the company was in doubt." He says that the debentures have since been converted to common stock, which has been distributed among Andersen partners.

---

113   CORPORATIONS AND THEIR OUTSIDE AUDITORS

(Reprinted by permission from the *Wall Street Journal* (June 22, 1973). © Dow Jones & Company, Inc., 1973.)

More than 90 percent of the 190 corporations surveyed for this Conference Board study retain one of the "Big Eight" CPA firms to examine company accounts. Just what do corporate financial executives think of their CPAs? More than 80 percent say they are happy with the relationship. Those who are critical cite inexperience and frequent turnover of CPA staffs, poor quality of audit work overseas, and excessive time spent on "unimportant" matters.

---

114   THE COMPUTER, THE ACCOUNTANT, AND THE NEXT DECADE

Felix Kaufman

(Reprinted by permission from *The Journal of Accountancy*, vol. 132 (August, 1971): 33-39. Copyright © 1971 by the American Institute of Certified Public Accountants, Inc.)

(Felix Kaufman is a member of the firm of Coopers & Lybrand.)

Not too many years ago prophets of doom predicted that computers were destined to take over all information processing. If accountants didn't have a deep understanding of what was going on in computer development, they said, they would be preempted by those who did. These predictions proved to be a substantial exaggeration of what was really happening. In fact most CPAs, notably those in small and medium-sized firms, observed little or no impact on their day-to-day affairs. Thus the danger is that they may now be lulled into feeling that the computer, notwithstanding its power and pervasiveness, is not going to have much effect on their lives.

I am convinced that the computer *will* have a significant, basic impact on the CPA, even in serving small clients. It is therefore in his best interest to manage promptly the changes in his education, training, and attitude that are required by this major technological development.

And there is evidence already that the accountant's role in data processing is being preempted by others. Al Zipf, executive vice president of the Bank of America, a person with impressive experience in the computer field, recently observed that "data processing was, thank God, emerging from an obscure niche in the controller's department." This view is shared by a lot of people with similar vantage points.

It's time to reconsider the impact of the computer on certified public accountants and to speculate on what may happen in the next few years. Computer technology moves at a dizzy pace and it seems prudent to look at the cumulative impact.

How might we conduct a reassessment?

First, let's examine current technical developments so as to determine whether their nature bears on the question.

Second, let's ask ourselves again what CPAs do, examine the computer's effects to date on these roles and consider prospective outcomes.

Third, let's conclude by asking whether CPAs are likely to adapt to forecasted changes and what happens if they do not.

RECENT TECHNOLOGICAL DEVELOPMENTS

During the last half of 1970, computer manufacturers announced that a new price performance dimension was available if you had enough work to put through new, more powerful devices. This continued the tendency to provide hardware that can process a transaction at a lower cost than could its predecessor, although frequently at a greater total cost. In any case, the machines continue to be described by specifications that boggle the mind.

For example, we went through a period trying to understand what a microsecond was. (That's a millionth of a second and no mortal can really quite comprehend a second divided into a million parts.) Now our friends who make computers ask us to contemplate what a billionth of a second is, a so-called nanosecond.

The second development of significance is the burgeoning market for small computers. The IBM System 3 is a case in point. A large number of the several thousand customers for the system are companies with no previous computer experience. A related development involves the so-called minicomputer. The minicomputer appeared on the scene about ten years ago as a small-scale, relatively inexpensive computer, surrounded by very primitive peripheral capability. Although the mini increased in popularity through the 1960s, its uses were confined to the scientific and engineering environment. For example, it was frequently used in process control situations. In recent years, there have been improvements in the input-output devices that can be attached to minicomputers. Input-output devices include card readers, paper tape readers, magnetic tape handlers, disk packs and card punches, as well as line printers. These machines behave just like the peripherals we are accustomed to using with conventional business computers, but they tend to have abbreviated capabilities and accordingly are more modest in price.

The important point is this—it is now possible to attach devices to a minicomputer that cause it to behave like a full-fledged machine in the sense that it can perform all of the functions of a business data processor.

In addition, the minis are now appearing in the market place, set up to be operated like accounting machines in the conventional sense. These are operated by a keyboard with arrangements for handling one or more ledger cards and their running speed is a function of the operator's speed. *Probably, all accounting machines in the next few years will really be small computers with appropriate keyboard and forms adaptation.*

In the data entry environment, we are moving rapidly toward a variety of methods for capturing transactions in machine-sensible condition at the point of origin. It follows that our incentive to use automatic data processing methods is increased substantially if we are favored with a variety of inexpensive data capturing devices. If the cost of converting a transaction to computerized processing is substantially reduced, it follows that another large chunk of the data processing environment becomes eligible for automation.

The prospective user is presented with an array of data processing options. He can have his own machine on his premises, he can transport data by conventional means to remote computers or he can communicate directly with remote computers.

Now it may be feasible to get data to remote computers even when it is only economically practical to operate in the batch mode. In one intriguing arrangement, a time-sharing facility provides a billing package which allows for the transmission of charges and credits to customer accounts through the use of conventional teletype terminals. When monthly statements are required, the time-sharing facility provides a magnetic tape of the statements to a collaborating bank. The bank prints and mails the statements, receives the remittances, converts the remittances to magnetic tape on its own system and dispatches that magnetic tape to the time-sharing facility so that its master files may be updated.

Another development of merit involves those technological changes that can cut the cost of programing. Perhaps it will be cheaper to turn out programs for specific applications that do not have to be customized to any significant extent by each user. The minicomputer employed as an accounting machine represents this tendency. In the case of one manufacturer, programs can be written for a conventional machine of substantial power and automatically converted to the language of the minicomputer. Then, the minicomputer manufacturer produces a wired version of the program which literally plugs in whenever it is required.

WHAT THE CHANGES MEAN

What are the implications of these technical tendencies?

1. Equipment costs continue to decrease. This means a wider range of use and, of course, a wider range of users.
2. The number of processing options now available indicates a movement toward being able to select the amount of power appropriate to each job. Too often in the past hardware had to be geared to the most demanding assignment; this meant under-utilization on many tasks.
3. Computer power is now portable. It's as close as the telephone. You can now go from place to place carrying a terminal and when the terminal is plugged into a telephone and the computer is called, you are on the air. *These possibilities in the time-shared environment also mean that the charge for using the computer has become a variable cost.* You pay when you're connected.

Some of these developments should reduce the serious difficulties encountered in designing and operating computer systems. This is because the spread of the small economical machine to thousands of new users rationalizes a greater effort to develop package programs, and the cumulative experience of thousands of man-years of mistakes has to finally turn into an advantage.

We can summarize by saying that the cost of making computer power available has reached levels that could hardly have been anticipated a few years ago; that the raw data processing power of this capability cannot be rivaled, and that we are reaching a condition where large low-volume sectors of data processing may now be economically attractive. To CPAs, the meaning of all this is fairly evident. In due course a great many of your clients will use this capability in one form or another. For some of you this is true now.

IMPACT ON AUDITING

The CPA is first and foremost an auditor. Where he does not choose, or is not called upon, to perform the attest function, he also may be a keeper of records, and thus he may be doing his client's data processing. When he counsels his client, he helps to assemble, present, and interpret information used for decision-making. He also may be a designer of systems, advising his client as to how to organize and how to link methods and procedures so that information processing takes place efficiently.

The computer's impact on auditing has been very gradual and should continue to develop in an undramatic way. It's hard to understand how people can think that the attest function can be automated. Auditing has mechanical features and it has formality, but it is not a cookbook process. It cannot be programed as a set of explicit steps to be followed on successive occasions in the same manner. Auditing cannot be accomplished by the numbers.

The opportunity for computerizing auditing depends to some extent on the auditor's ability to examine the attest function and, in specific situations, to separate activity which is structured, objective, and explicit from that which is unstructured and subjective. The elements in the former segment are receptive to computer programing.

To be more specific, here are some audit activities that can be done by computer:

1. Whenever the client's files are in machine-sensible form, those files can be queried for what we want via the use of our own programs. This capability is the basis for software packages which have been developed by a number of CPA firms.

2. It is now relatively easy to analyze information using powerful statistical techniques. One does not have to be a statistician in order to be able to do this, but a knowledge of where the programs are and how to call on them is required. It now becomes possible to take a stream of information—a series of account balances, for example —and analyze their trends on a sophisticated basis.

3. There are interesting possibilities that relate to a consideration of materiality. It is now easier to analyze account relationships rapidly and to determine the sensitivity of profits, for example, to the behavior of specific accounts. Further investigation and experience in this area might help us do a better job when we write audit programs by ranking the significance of accounts, thereby facilitating the allocation of effort.

4. It follows that to the extent that one can automate the process of examining files, the size of the sample—the number of accounts observed—will be larger than it was likely to have been under other mechanical and manual methods. Given some of the characteristics of file updating, there will be situations where it is practical, using your own programs, to examine every record in a large file.

THE ACCOUNTANT AS A RECORD-KEEPER

The second role that was referred to earlier involved the accountant as a data processor. Perhaps this was the role that engendered the attitude that the computer might make CPAs obsolete. Such reasoning, although probably correct, treats the CPA in the context of a role that is not important to him professionally, notwithstanding its importance to some of the members of the profession. Therefore, I feel that the profession at large has no basis for worrying about this aspect of the accountant's activities, although it is likely that the "worst" will happen. No one who pushes a pencil to keep records can, in the long run, compete with the computer. Therefore the act of picking up data, storing it in the right place and returning it as required is no longer a job that ought to or will be done manually.

Some of the time-sharing arrangements mentioned earlier and the new type of accounting machines witness the accelerating displacement of manual activity. We should not be concerned that this role is being usurped from those accountants who do this sort of thing. They can preserve their relationship with clients and maintain responsibility for data processing by learning how to use the new tools.

TAX PREPARATION

Another data processing role worth mentioning is tax return preparation. Readers are aware of the extent to which computerized tax return packages have become available in the last few years. We can expect tax return packages to improve from year to year in terms of the scope of the tasks they are able to handle at the federal level, and the number of state returns that they are gradually able to comprehend. Also, time-sharing packages are being developed to facilitate financial counseling on a range of matters involving cash management, investments, tax planning, tax return preparation, estate planning, and other matters. The CPA will have interesting possibilities for expanding his purview through the use of such programs.

HELPING CLIENTS USE INFORMATION

With the premise that the CPA is involved in helping his client to use information more effectively, let's examine the potential of the computer for improving and expanding the performance of this role. The computer probably enlarges the CPA's role as a presenter and interpreter of information which is really part of the process of facilitating the making of business decisions. Then, the decision-making process becomes a way of assembling information, a method of interpretation once it has been assembled and the loop in which the process is repeated. Because of new capabilities that can be implemented by the computer, it is likely that CPAs must know a lot more about ways in which information can be developed than they have heretofore. This idea has to be elaborated carefully.

THE BUDGET AS A FINANCIAL MODEL

The accountant has always understood that he could provide interpretive assistance by examining the figures presented in a conventional set of accounts by relating one account to another in order to produce meaningful ratios, by comparing an account to a standard in order to detect a variance and by comparing an account to comparable values in the past in order to detect a trend.

The accountant also knows that he can synthesize a set of transactions by making assumptions as to what will happen in the future. By "processing" these transactions so as to come up with pro forma financial statements he creates a budget. Since all of these activities could only be effected at occasional intervals, the accountant could not be aware of the latent power inherent in the fact that the accounting system—particularly the manifestation we call the budget—is in fact a model of the business. The model is a representation, other than reality itself, that can be employed to study the effect of certain assumptions as if these things had really happened. This can be accomplished without having to complete these events in a normal time framework.

To repeat, a model is a representation of reality. Models which are effective for planning purposes compress time and space and dramatically decrease the cost of testing various propositions. The budgeting process has two aspects. First, we process certain assumptions as to what will happen by "passing" the transactions representing these assumptions through the budget system. This allows us to perceive what the financial effects will be. Then we determine whether the effects are tolerable. For example, do we have the capacity to do what the budget implies we will do? Have we violated some condition or constraint, such as exceeding available working capital? If so, we must redo the budget so that it predicts financial effects based upon activities that we really think can take place. As a rule, once this has been done, let's say once a year, it is not repeated simply because the clerical process is too ponderous. This then is an official budget and, until the same process occurs a year later, we use it primarily to control costs.

This must be regarded as a disturbing state of affairs. Is there some underlying condition that says it suffices to plan once a year? Clearly, the answer is no. Financial planning should be done as often as the dynamics of the situation dictate—whenever something significant happens to clearly alter conditions.

Now, what does this all have to do with the computer? Simply this. Early in the EDP era it became clear that models could be used in a much more powerful way if their logic could be implemented by a computer. It would no longer be necessary to conclude that rebudgeting was too ponderous even though an important condition had changed significantly. The computer is the device that permits us to change in a very dramatic way the time frame with which we associate a modeling process. *It opens up the possibility of continuous budgeting*. In addition, the enormous increase in experience in financial modeling probably is leading to a profound improvement in the design of the model itself. CPAs can and should employ this planning capability in behalf of their clients.

The CPA has access to a series of financial statements expressing the financial history of a particular client. Allowing for the fact that the account structure may change to some extent from year to year, it is an easy matter for the CPA to array a series of balances for the same account over a period of years—the sort of thing a statistician would call a time series. It is now possible to take the data to a computer and treat the information with a variety of statistical programs. It is not necessary for the user to understand the underlying mathematics in order to employ these programs. The act of using these programs reveals much more about the way the values in a particular account have been changing than the primitive processes employed in the past.

A meaningful example would involve a series of values describing sales for a particular product month by month over a period of years. Statistical treatment of this series would produce a forecast of future sales with a higher degree of accuracy and with appropriate adjustments for seasonal trends and random conditions. This statistical treatment can also determine whether one account predicts the behavior of another or is dependent upon another and in what way. This leads to a series

of observations about the character of the data and it is now possible
to construct the model (define relationships) that I referred to earlier.

Consider this illustration. Statistical analysis reveals how
sales are behaving and future sales can now be expressed as an equation
in which factors which appear to affect sales are properly related.
Also, assuming that a statistical relationship between sales and several
significant expense accounts has been ascertained, an equation can be
written to "take" us to net income. Once the profit and loss environment has been modeled, this can be put to work by making assumptions
about what is going to happen—forecasting sales. The model has now
taken the form of a program which is inserted into the computer. We
can run the program frequently, which means that as we try assumptions
and examine results we are probably disposed to alter our assumptions
and examine new facts. Computer people call this "iteration" and it is
a powerful dimension. By trial and error, or what is now fashionably
called "what if," we can examine assumptions continuously. This is
likely to lead to the consideration of a better model.

PROBABILITY AND SENSITIVITY

There is also some icing on this cake in the form of additional
capabilities. Whenever you do financial planning, or any kind of planning for that matter, you must acknowledge that your forecasts are estimates. Sales may increase ten percent next year, but then again they
may not. Labor costs may go up six percent next year, but maybe they
will go up ten percent. You think you may be able to increase certain
prices but you are not sure how the market will react. In fact anyone
who forecasts says: *"I am guessing and I would really be more comfortable if I only had to tell you waht range my forecast would fall in."*

The only thing that is certain about a forecast is that the specified value is not the actual one. The critical issue is not, "Will we
be off the mark?" but "How far?" In the computer world the values we
assign to the variables in our equations are values which can only be
expressed over some range, but within that range we have some confidence. In short, it is now possible to comprehend probability and to do
financial planning which recognizes that the planner himself is saying
"Look, what I am doing is educated guessing."

Probability is one leg of sophistication in financial planning.
Sensitivity is the other. Sensitivity is the capability built into our
model to recognize that in complicated processes involving many variables each has a different degree of influence on the final result and
the degree of influence is not necessarily visible to the naked eye. If
a company makes a product composed of seven parts of direct labor and
three parts of material, it might assert that profits are far more sensitive to fluctuation in the price of labor than the price of material.
This would seem to be obvious. Sensitivity calculations, however, would
recognize the degree of confidence that we have in predicting the future
cost of labor and materials. They would reflect the effect, the sensitivity, on profits of stable labor costs and unstable or uncertain material costs for example. Sensitivity measures materiality.

The structure of a new world in financial planning has been outlined; it may sound sophisticated. It does require new know-how. It
does not, however, require depth or credentials as a mathematician, an

extensive understanding of statistical techniques, an understanding of how a particular computer works or even the manner in which it is programed.

A good deal of what is involved here is the process of knitting together programs that already exist and of being able to interpret data after the model has been run and tentative conclusions have been reached.

Thus far we have concentrated on a model that produces future financial statements. We know, however, that specific values on the financial statements depend upon what happens over some period of time as we operate various segments of the business activity. For example, the future value of a parts inventory depends upon the way in which we manage that inventory. The future value of accounts receivable is more than the function of a low level of sales. It also depends on credit-granting policy and the management of accounts. There are a wide variety of situations for which models can be designed. Accordingly, lack of imagination, ingenuity and energy are the only important constraints preventing one from using the computer to forecast the level of a specific account by building and operating a model of the subsystem that affects the value of that account.

I would add that there is practically no such thing as a business model that does not have a financial ramification. Can the accountant say that he is not interested in a model that represents the way in which orders are scheduled in a factory when such a model predicts the back order condition and inventory levels as well as the speed with which orders turn into sales?

It all boils down to this. A business is a set of coordinated activities. The accounting system measures and reports the financial effect of all of these activities. One can program a representation of these financial relationships and also can program representations of many of the underlying processes that have an effect on the financial statements. In theory one can construct a model that is representative of the entire firm. However, this is no mean task.

There are some collateral values in all of this model building. The kind of account analysis that I advocated in the earlier discussion of statistical evaluation is, perhaps, a tool of some value to the planning of an audit engagement. Once the auditor can determine account sensitivity with a precision that he could never achieve before, he can organize his engagement plan and the related allocation of effort by himself and his staff by ranking the accounts based on their influence. It is also possible that the emerging forecasting art foreshadows the possibility that the value of significant accounts can be predicted in advance and an important effect will bear on an audit when the accountant observes significant differences between the actual value of an account and its predicted value.

A very significant increase in the power of the budgeting process can be obtained if one does nothing more than program the procedures already in place.

WILL CPAs RESPOND?

I have tried to provide an understanding of the forces currently operating to widen and deepen the impact of the computer on CPAs. The subject cannot be left without examining the question of our concern over this changing environment and whether or not we are disposed to

adapt to it. I could have concluded innocuously by saying "Here are
my observations; draw your own conclusions," but that would seem coward-
ly, particularly in the context of my feeling that a significant response is imperative.

The accountant has a serious problem. The evidence seems to indicate that he is unconcerned. He is behaving as if the computer is having no effect on him. This attitude is not surprising since it is impossible to discern day-to-day developments involving the computer that
have bread and butter significance to the CPA; nothing strikes him as a
threat, nothing is compelling him to join or to fight. No doubt this is
because the forces in motion are asserting themselves gradually and fur-
tively.

Why are accountants so unconcerned? First, because the effects are
not conspicuous. Second, professional groups—perhaps any group with a
vested interest—makes slow adjustment to profound structural changes.
Third, the field of information science as we know it has attracted a
lot of people who five years ago might have found it difficult to locate
a niche in business. These mathematicians and scientists have so far
played a greater role in shaping information science than have accountants. In the aggregate they are a powerful group intellectually. Are
they better fitted to the requirements of the computer game than accountants? Perhaps there is some support for this view arising from the
comments made recently by academicians that there isn't a sufficient
flow of top-flight students into accounting programs.

The principal reason for thinking that accountants may be occupying
a changing position is the growing awareness that although accounting
systems were the first formal information systems and are probably the
most highly developed, they have now become subsets of a larger information process. In a report rendered by the Committee on Information Systems of the American Accounting Association, it was observed that a
major development in the information function is "the formalization of
information processes in many parts of the organization" and that now
"the accounting information system is that operation of the formal information system concerned with the measurement of production, income,
wealth, and other economic events." The same report also observes,
"It is clear that the accountant has ceased to be the information broker
standing between the source of information and the user."

What can we do to obtain greater interest and a desire on the part
of CPAs to play a more important role? I've reached some rather fatal-
istic conclusions. If accountants decline to some lessor role than they
now play, would it pose a problem in our society? If the decline is the
consequence of being displaced by others who do certain things better,
such a shift is not prejudicial to the total business community. This
might be a distinct possibility. Accordingly, the whole question of the
accountant's adaptation to radical change in the information environment
precipitated by the use of computers, and now by the management sciences
as well, is something that CPAs have to work out themselves. They will
have to consider the consequences and then conclude whether it is preferable to let the situation unfold, unmolested by any action on their
part, or whether the profession should come together, reach a conclusion
and, if they find it necessary, develop a program.

115   HOW DO YOU WRITE AN AUDIT REPORT, GRANDFATHER?

Lawrence B. Sawyer

(Reprinted by permission from *The Internal Auditor*, vol. 30, no. 1 (January/February, 1973): 56-61.)

(Lawrence B. Sawyer is supervising internal auditor for Lockheed Aircraft Corporation.)

"How do you write an audit report, Grandfather?"

"In such a way that somebody will want to read it."

"They *have* to read it don't they?"

"Sure. But I've seen lots of reports nobody *wants* to read."

"Why?"

"They look forbidding. They're hard to read. They ramble. They're poorly expressed. They're just a plain, boring drag."

"You mean that after these smart internal auditors—and you told me they're smart—finish a great piece of auditing, nobody wants to read their reports?"

"I speak true."

"How could that be?"

"I really think that sometimes the auditor doesn't understand his own—OK, Randy, what word am I about to use?"

"*Objective*. That seems to be the thing you always get back to, Grandfather."

"Can you think of a better starting place?"

"No. So what is the objective?"

"To serve management. That means to provide the very best service possible. And it's really a shame."

"What's a shame?"

"Very often, the one time that the man upstairs knows the auditor is alive is when he gets an audit report. Here is the lifeline between the auditor and the big boss. Here is the chance to really parade the auditor's wares. And what happens?"

"I don't know."

"He very often blows it."

"How does he do that?"

"Lack of salesmanship. He has a great product; yet he packages it in brown wrapping paper."

"Don't keep me in suspense. Exactly what is he doing wrong."

"Okay. The things he's doing wrong involve:

1. "The format of the report
2. "The size of the report
3. "The way it's written."

"What's the format?"

"That's the way it's put together."

"What's so important about that?"

"It should be inviting. It should ask to be read. It should explain what the project is all about. It should tell the reader what he's going to read. It should summarize important points for the busy reader, and it should give detail for the reader who's interested in detail."

"That's a tall order."

"So's building a boat. But if you don't want it to leak you'd better build it right."

"How do you write the report so that it asks to be read?"

"Give it an attractive cover. Leave a lot of white space. Use short paragraphs. Write crisp, active sentences. Start with a paragraph that's clear, simple, and attractive. Devise headings that tell you what's coming; and a text that fulfills the promise."

"Wow. What else?"

"Prepare a summary report for top management to read, followed by detailed information for operating management."

"Would the two be set up differently?"

"Yes."

"How?"

"Some auditors have the summary double-spaced and the detail single-spaced. They feel that the extra bit of white space in the summary makes it more inviting and easier on the eyes of higher management."

"What if you send a copy to the president? Maybe even the summaries of a whole lot of reports might be too much to read."

"Good thinking. In that case, a half-page transmittal memo should go along with the report—just enough to tell him the gist of the report—the highest of highlights."

"What would you put in the summary report?"

"What I think management ought to see."

"For instance."

"First, a little background to put the audit in its proper place in the company's activities. For a procurement audit, I'd show the value of total purchases for the year. For an accounts payable audit, I'd show the total payments and transactions for the year—and so forth."

"What else?"

"Then I like to show the purpose and scope of the audit—what we set out to do and what we decided not to do."

"And then?"

"An overall opinion. I know a lot of auditors don't agree with that. But it seems to me that when the top men in the company know the auditor has done a particular audit, the first question that comes to mind is: 'What's the overall situation?' It's a natural question and it deserves an answer."

"Then?"

"Some comments on the main things brought out by the audit: the things that should be fixed; the things that were fixed; and the steps taken to fix the rest."

"How about the detail?"

"I'd reserve that for an in-depth discussion of the problems."

"How would you write those up?"

"Remember the talk we had about deficiencies?"

"Sure do."

"I'd set up the discussions in pretty much the same way. First a punch line, telling what the problem is all about. Then a statement of criteria or standards: how things should be done. What the facts are. The cause. The effect. The recommendation. And, finally, what was done about it."

"Suppose they didn't agree with you and told you to go fly a kite."

"I'd put down exactly what they said about the situation. But I'd leave out the kite."

"Is that it?"

"Just about."

"How about the size of the report?"

"I think that if there weren't any deficiencies, then just a one- or two-page report should do the job. If there were deficiencies, then the detailed section would be as long as it takes to cover them."

"Would you write a report even though nobody had to take any action?"

"You bet. People shouldn't think the auditor is one-sided. If he's got something good to say about an operation, he should have the courage to say it."

"Why courage?"

"You'd be surprised how some departments take the auditor to task when he praises another department."

"Really?"

"You bet. So the auditor has to be as sure of his facts when he gives praise as he is when he is critical. Remember what I said about an audit opinion?"

"Yes. It's a professional opinion."

"And every professional opinion must be based on facts—whether the opinion is good or bad. When the doctor examines you and says you're all right you want to be satisfied that he hasn't overlooked some malignant disease."

"What's the last thing you said about the audit report?

"The way it's written."

"What's so hard about that?"

"A good deal. Simple, clear, concise writing just isn't that easy. It takes study and practice."

"I don't understand. If you have something to say, you just say it. And that's that."

"No, that's not that. Usually, the auditor has spent much less time in learning how to write than in learning how to audit."

"What's his problem?"

"Making his writing readable."

"Can't he learn?"

"Of course he can. But it takes work, and it takes an understanding of just why his writing is unreadable."

"Do you have any suggestions?"

"Plenty."

"Let's go."

"There are dozens of good books on writing, with all sorts of ideas on how to write better. We don't have the time to cover the broad subject, so I'll just concentrate on some of the ideas for keeping writing simple. For example, many auditors get very formal. They make believe that they don't exist and that some disembodied spirit made the audit."

"What do you mean?"

"They have an aversion for the first person. They'll say 'It was determined that periodic inventories were not being taken.'"

"How should they say it?"

"Use the first person. It's direct and simple. 'We found that periodic inventories were not being taken.'"

"That's simpler."

"And easier to understand. Another problem is the long sentence. It's like a meandering trail. By the time you reach the end you've forgotten what the beginning was all about."

"For instance."

"Here goes: 'Of the 250 transactions we examined, using statistical sampling to select them from a population of 10,000, we found that 45 were not properly approved in accordance with the governing regulations which require the manager's approval in such cases.'"

"I've got a headache."

"I sympathize. Listen to this: 'Governing procedures call for the manager to approve these transactions. We checked for approvals on a statistical sample of 250 out of the 10,000 transactions in the population. We found that 45 of the transactions were not properly approved. Is that better?"

"Much."

"Why?"

"You get one thought at a time. You don't have to sort things out in your head."

"What else was wrong with the first sentence, besides being too long?"

"It sounds as if not being properly approved was in accordance with the regulations. That doesn't make sense."

"Right. Yet I've seen many sentences like that in audit reports. It's one result of jamming a lot of things into one sentence."

"How do you keep from writing long sentences."

"One way is not to fall into the trap of starting a sentence with 'although,' 'while,' 'since,' and words like that. You're almost sure to wind up with a long and tangled sentence."

"For instance."

"I've seen something like this often: 'Although instructions require three bids for every purchase over $500, we found that 20 out of the 100 procurements we examined were supported by fewer than three bids.'"

"What should it be?"

"This is better: 'Instructions required three bids for every purchase over $500. Yet we found that 20 out of the 100 procurements we examined were supported by fewer than three bids.'"

"Don't short sentences tend to get choppy?"

"Not if you use connecting thoughts or words. In the correction of the first example I gave you, the word 'transactions' knitted the three sentences together. In the correction of the second one the word 'yet' helped the transition and removed the choppiness."

"Should you always avoid long sentences?"

"Oh no. You should mix up short ones with some long ones. Otherwise the reader might start getting breathless. But a good long sentence is hard to write. So try to keep them short. Remember, though, to use connecting words to knit the sentences together."

"I see. For instance, the sentences you just used have connecting words like 'otherwise,' 'but,' 'so,' and 'though.' That kept the sentences from getting too choppy, and they carried the thoughts out more clearly."

"You've got it."

"What else?"

"Use the active voice."

"Why?"

"Again, simplicity."

"Prove it."

"Okay. Which do you like better; 'The active voice should be used' or 'Use the active voice'?"

"The second one."

"Why?"

"It's shorter."

"Right. Brevity is the soul of wit."

"Are audit reports supposed to be witty?"

"Sorry. I turned pontifical."

"What's that?"

"Never mind. What else?"

"The active is more direct. It has punch."

"Splendid. Using the active voice helps you to write more clearly. And it makes your writing easier to read."

"What else?"

"Be careful of making a verb into a noun."

"Why?"

"That's another way to get tangled up."

"Show me."

"Here's something I see all the time: Taking a perfectly good verb, making a noun out of it, and then cluttering up a sentence with it."

"Like what?"

"Here's one: 'Reconciliation of the accounts was effected.'"

"What should it be?"

"How much simpler it is to say, 'We reconciled the accounts.'"

"Any more like that?"

"Yes. A lot of the 'the's' and 'of's' are used unnecessarily to
clutter up sentences. Eliminate them and the sentences get shorter and
clearer."

"Such as?"

"'Preliminary surveys in the planning of audits' becomes simpler
when you say 'preliminary surveys in planning audits.'"

"How else can you make writing simple?"

"Parallel construction."

"What's that?"

"It's a form of consistency. Inconsistent writing puzzles the
reader. It slows him up and makes him backtrack. The writing is therefore harder to read—less simple."

"Give me some examples."

"Okay. 'The Receiving Department is responsible for recording receipts, counting parts, and the delivery of the parts to stores.'"

"That bothered me, but I didn't know why."

"The words 'the delivery of' were not parallel with the other action words. It's much simpler when you say 'for recording receipts,
counting parts, and delivery of the parts to stores.'"

"I get it."

"You also get our of parallel when you mix the active and the pas-
sive voice. Like, 'The manager considered our suggestions but no action
was taken.'"

"I see. It should read, 'The manager considered our suggestions
but took no action.'"

"Precisely. Now here's a constant violation of the parallelism
rule. When thoughts in audit reports are listed, they often do not
agree with the introduction. For instance:

"'The operation is controlled through:

"1. 'Management approvals.
"2. 'Monthly reports.
"3. 'Supervisors made weekly checks.'"

"What's wrong with it, Grandfather?"

"Item 3 is out of parallel and is annoying. It should read 'Weekly
Supervisory checks.'"

"Any more?"

"Loads. But let's just wind up with my pet peeve."

"What's that?"

"Using a fancy word when a simpler and clearer one is at hand."

"What words?"

"Why use 'however' when you can use 'but'?

"Why not 'made' instead of 'conducted' or 'effected'?

"Or 'done' instead of 'accomplished' or 'performed.'

"Or 'use' instead of 'utilize.'

"Or 'told' instead of 'informed' or 'indicated.'

"Or 'carry out' instead of 'implement.'

"or 'show' instead of 'reflect.'"

"Wow. You've given me a lot to think about, Grandfather."

"Keep those things in mind when you write your own reports. Then maybe people will *want* to read them and not just *have* to read them, Randy."

"Write on, Grandfather."

---

116   SESQUIPEDALIAN VERBOSITY

William F. Laurie

(Reprinted by permission from *The GAO Review* (Winter, 1973): 72-76.)

(William F. Laurie is supervisory auditor with the GAO.)

Stilted
Ponderous.
Pompous
Complicated

These words all too often describe GAO reports. The Comptroller General in his February 24, 1970, memorandum asked all staff members to improve the language of GAO reports. Why? So that people can easily *read* and effectively *use* them.

The readers' interest is influenced by two elements, long words and number of words. If there are too many long words and too many words, reading becomes difficult. The result: the reader stops reading.

Let's look at the reading level of our reports. A reading level is the number of years of formal schooling needed to read a document easily, quickly, and with maximum comprehension. The reading level was computed for the Comptroller General's memorandum on writing—considered a standard—and for ten congressional reports issued in February, 1971 and for ten issued in April, 1972. The comparison was dramatic.

The graph on reading level shows that a person with 13 years of education could read the Comptroller General's memorandum *easily, quickly,* and with *maximum comprehension.* For a person to read our congressional

FIGURE 13

READING LEVEL

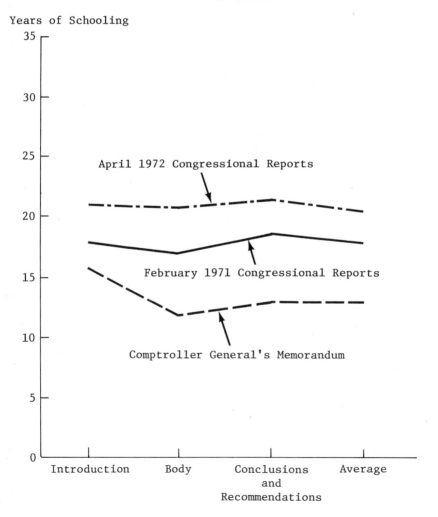

reports in the same way would require a master's degree (1971 reports—reading level 18) or a Ph.D. degree (1972 reports—reading level 21).   We must face up to it: many of our reports are extremely difficult to read.

The graph shows also that the conclusions and recommendations are more difficult to read than the rest of the report (1971 reports—reading level 19; 1972 reports—reading level 22).   A *paradox*: We want to motivate the reader to do something, but we write so that the reader will not easily understand.

The solution: Write our reports like the Comptroller General's memorandum—with a reading level of 13 or less.   How can a writer do this?   By varying sentence length and choice of words.

SENTENCE LENGTH

Grammar textbooks suggest an *average* sentence length of 22 words. This average requires that a variety of sentences be used—both long *and* short sentences.

The Comptroller General's memorandum met this criteria (19 words); our congressional reports did not (1971 reports—30 words; 1972 reports —31 words), as shown on the graph on sentence length.

FIGURE 14

SENTENCE LENGTH

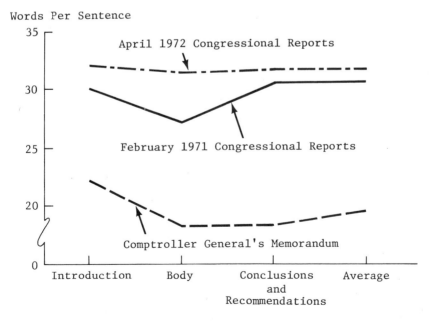

The graph shows also that the introductions to our reports, where we are trying to encourage our readers to read on, have the longest sentences. Will the reader read on? No!

WORD CHOICE

To maintain a reading level of 12, assuming an average sentence length of 20 words, the number of polysyllable words (three or more syllables a word) should be limited to an average of ten for each 100 words. This is not easy. "Governmentese," gobbledygook, technical words, and jargon of the trade creep into our writing; all are polysyllable words. In the following graph, note the extensive use of polysyllable words (1971 reports—17 polysyllables per 100 words; 1972 reports—24 polysyllables per 100 words).

Again, the greatest number of long words are used in the conclusions and recommendations. Usually these are concept words. Concept words do not form immediate mental images when read. Instead, they require mental effort to understand. *Example*: the word "tree" forms an immediate mental image; the word "instrumentation" (a concept word) does not. Will readers take the time to think out polysyllable words? Definitely not!

THE SOLUTION

Step back from your written product and perform the following simple test—here lies the first step toward readable writing. (1)

1. Sample 100 words from the introduction, body, and conclusions and recommendations (or closing) of a report or memorandum.
2. Determine the average number of words per sentence. Independent clauses are counted as separate sentences.
3. Count the number of polysyllable words per 100 words. Do not count polysyllable words which are capitalized or verbs made into three syllables by adding "es" or "ed."
4. Add the average number of words per sentence to the number of polysyllable words per 100 words and multiply by .4. Eliminate digits after the decimal point. The answer is the reading level.

If the reading level exceeds 12, look deeper into what you have written. Try the following.

Sentence Length

1. Is there variety in sentence length?
2. If sentences contain 40 or 50 words, why are they so long? Can they be shortened and thereby give more impact?
3. Are qualifiers, hedgers, and redundant expressions at work in the longer sentences? Eliminate them.

FIGURE 15

POLYSYLLABLE WORDS

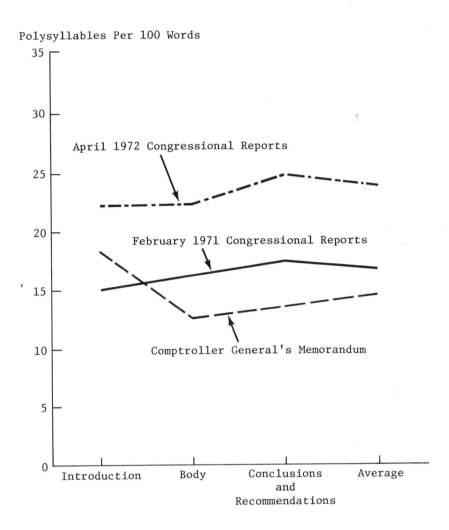

Polysyllable Words

1. Look for words ending in "ation, tion, ion, ment, ence, and ency." Usually, a good verb has been changed to a noun by adding these endings. The result: Governmentese, a poly-syllable word, and the loss of a good action word. Recon-struct the sentence and eliminate them—turn them back into verbs.
2. Look for technical terms. Usually they are polysyllable words and mean little to a layman. Eliminate them.

3. Look for concept words. They are also polysyllable words.
    Simplify them by using words that readily form mental
    images.

Finally, writing must become a labor of love. Tremendous amounts
of mental energy have to be expended if a written product is to motivate
the reader. Adequate planning at the outset will save energy throughout
the assignment, especially in writing. The result will be a written
product with a reading level of 12 and devoid of sesquipedalian verbosity!

FOOTNOTE

1. This technique is suggested by Mr. Robert Gunning in his
    booklet, "How to Take the Fog Out of Writing," an excel-
    lent source of helpful hints for readable and interesting
    writing.